FIGHTING WORDS

FIGHTING WORDS

COMPETING VOICES FROM NATIVE AMERICA

Dewi Ioan Ball and Joy Porter

GREENWOOD PRESS
An Imprint of ABC-CLIO, LLC

A B C 🟤 C L I O

Santa Barbara, California • Denver, Colorado • Oxford, England

First published in 2009 by Greenwood Press

1 2 3 4 5 6 7 8 9 10

Introduction and Compilation © Dewi Ball and Joy Porter 2009

ABC-CLIO, LLC
130 Cremona Drive, P.O. Box 1911
Santa Barbara, California 93116-1911

British Library Cataloguing-in-Publication Data: a catalogue record for this book
is available from the British Library

Library of Congress Cataloging-in-Publication Data

Competing voices from native America : fighting words / edited by Dewi Ioan Ball and
Joy Porter.
    p. cm.—(Fighting words)
    Includes bibliographical references and index.
    ISBN 978-1-84645-016-7
    1. Indians of North America--History. I. Ball, Dewi Ioan. II. Porter, Joy, 1967-.

E77.C743 2009
970.004 – dc22

9781846450167

ISBN 978-1-84645-016-7 (hardback)

Designed by Fraser Muggeridge studio
Pictures researched by Zooid
Typeset by TexTech International

This book is dedicated to Dewi's wonderful and loving wife, Helen Elizabeth Ball, and their son, Joshua Edward Ioan Ball, who was born while his dad was writing this volume and editing all of the primary documents. Diolch yn fawr iawn i'r ddau ohonych chi am rhoi'r egni a'r ysbrydoliaeth i ysgrifennu'r llyfr hwn i gyd, or cychwyn hyd at y diwedd, ac diolch Helen am rhoi genedigaeth i Joshua, sy'n plentyn mor hapus a hardd, ac am fod yn wraig a mam prydferth a perffaith. (DB)

With respect for the bright line (JP).

CONTENTS

SERIES FOREWORD

Fighting Words is a unique new series aimed at a broad audience, from college-level professors and undergraduates, to high-school teachers, students and the general reader. Each volume in this series focuses on a unique historical controversy, told through firsthand accounts from the diverse perspectives of both the victors and the vanquished. The series is designed to introduce readers to a broad range of competing narratives about the past, giving voices to those often left silent in the secondary literature.

Each volume offers competing perspectives through relatively short primary documents, such as newspaper articles, contemporary chronicles, excerpts from participants' letters or memoirs, as well as other carefully selected sources; brief introductions provide the necessary background information and context to help guide readers through the disparate accounts. Where necessary, key documents are reproduced in their entirety. However, most of the documents are brief in nature, and sharp in content, which will help to promote general classroom discussion and debate. The inclusion of vivid and colourful accounts from the participants themselves, combined with other primary sources from all sides, give the series an exciting and engaging flavour. The *Fighting Words* series is designed to promote meaningful discussion and debate about the past. Furthermore, the volumes in this series encourage readers to think critically about the evidence that historians use, or ignore, to reconstruct an understanding of that past. Each volume will challenge accepted assumptions about the topics covered, and readers will question the nature of primary sources, the motivations, agendas, and perspectives of the authors, and the silences inherent in all of the sources. Ultimately, readers will be left to ponder the question, whose history is this?

J. Michael Francis

ABOUT THE SERIES EDITOR

Dr. J. Michael Francis received his PhD in 1998 from the University of Cambridge, where he specialised in colonial Latin American history. Since then, he has taught at the University of North Florida, where he is an associate professor of history. He has written numerous articles on the history of early-colonial New Granada (Colombia). In 2006, he edited a three-volume reference work called *Iberia and the Americas: Culture, Politics, and History* (ABC-CLIO). His most recent book, *Invading Colombia: Spanish Accounts of the Gonzalo Jiménez de Quesada Expedition of Conquest*, was published in 2007 by Penn State University Press.

Dr. Francis serves as book review editor for the journal *Ethnohistory*, and series co-editor for *Latin American Originals* (Penn State University Press). He also sits on the advisory board of the University Press of Florida. In 2007, Dr. Francis was appointed as a research associate at the American Museum of Natural History in New York. At present, he is completing a new manuscript, entitled *Politics, Murder, and Martyrdom in Spanish Florida: Don Juan and the Guale Uprising of 1597*, which will be published in 2009 by the American Museum of Natural History Press.

ABOUT THE AUTHORS

Dr. Dewi Ioan Ball, independent scholar, specialist in Native American history, and authority on Federal Indian Law, is a former pupil of Ysgol Gynradd Lon Las and Ysgol Gyfun Gwyr, Swansea, Wales, U.K., who gained his PhD, entitled, 'The Silent Revolution: How the Key Attributes of Tribal Power have been Fundamentally Eroded by the United States Supreme Court from 1973', from the University of Wales, Swansea, U.K., in May 2007. His PhD was funded by the Thomas and Elizabeth Williams Scholarship, City and County of Swansea, Wales, U.K. He gained his B.A. (Hons.) in Law and Politics from Staffordshire University, U.K., in 1997 and M.A. in United States History and Politics from Keele University, U.K., in 1999. He contributed a number of entries to *Treaties with American Indians: An Encyclopedia of Rights, Conflicts, and Sovereignty*, edited by Donald L. Fixico (ABC-CLIO, Inc., 2007) and has written many book reviews for *H-Net Reviews: Humanities and Social Sciences Online*, *The Southern Historian* and *American Studies International*. His next publication will be a monograph of his PhD for the University of Nebraska Press, followed by another monograph looking in-depth at the everyday effects of Supreme Court case law on a number of Native American reservations from 1959 to the present day.

Dr. Joy Porter's research specialism is Native American Indian history and literature. She is Associate Dean of the Faculty of Arts and Humanities and lectures in the Department of American Studies at the

University of Wales, Swansea, U.K. She gained her M.A. and PhD in American Studies from the University of Nottingham, U.K., in 1990 and 1993 respectively. She is the author of *To Be Indian: The Life of Seneca-Iroquois Arthur Caswell Parker, 1881–1955* (University of Oklahoma Press, 2002), co-editor with Professor Kenneth Roemer of *The Cambridge Companion to Native American Literature* (University of Cambridge Press, 2005) and editor of *Place and Indian History, Literature & Culture* for Peter Lang (2007). Her work on Indian themes can be found in a variety of books such as the *Cambridge Companion to Native American Literature* (2005), *America's Americans: The Populations of the United States* (Brookings Institution Press, 2007), *First Nations of North America: Politics & Representation* (VU University Press, 2005), *The State of U.S. History* (Berg, 2002) and in journals such as *American Studies* (MAAMS & Univ. Kansas), *New York History* and *Irish Studies Review*. Her next books are three monographs, *Native American Freemasonry* (University of Nebraska Press, 2010), *Land & Spirit in Native America* (Praeger Publishers, 2011) and *The American Indian Poet of World War One: Modernism and the Indian Identity of Frank 'Toronto' Prewett, 1893–1962* (The University of Toronto Press, 2012).

INTRODUCTION

American Indian history is diverse and the competing voices that echo across it equally so. It encompasses a multitude of sometimes discrete histories, cultures and identities that have developed over the course of tens of thousands of years. As an area of study, Native American Indian history links directly to Native American studies, to American studies as well as to the study of the American social, legal, political, economic and cultural past. It is a subject, whether it is read with a passing interest or studied at an in-depth level, that inevitably shows us that Native Americans are an integral part of Western and non-Western thought both in the present and the future. This book has been unable to deal in depth with regional differences between Indian peoples over time, with the specifics of deep-seated conflicts over traditional versus assimilative ways of living in Indian country or with important debates surrounding nuclear power and the best use of existing Indian land. However, it is hoped that the further reading and notes provided will prompt the reader to explore these issues further elsewhere.

What this volume does do is to bring together a broad range of material including a number of previously unheard voices, underdiscussed issues, rarely seen archival sources and court records, in an attempt to make the conflicted nature of Indian history better understood. This is not to suggest that all, or even the bulk, of Indian history has been characterized by conflict but it is hoped that the excerpts included here will stimulate reading and re-reading of the major contested themes that continue to reverberate within Indian country. Even though the selections should not be read as a proscriptive labelling of the only things that matter in American Indian history, in general it is hoped that they will upset the notion that Indian displacement within the boundaries of the United States was smooth and even from either the Indian or non-Indian perspective. The focus in this volume, for example, on Leonard Peltier, the activist of the American Indian Movement (AIM) who was sentenced to life for the murder of two FBI agents in 1977, and on controversial contemporary issues surrounding Indian law, jurisdiction and Indian gaming, should not be considered as exclusive issues of concern for all Indians. They have been highlighted here because they have been underrepresented elsewhere and because they remain of importance to a number of ongoing struggles for justice that are of concern to both Indians and non-Indians alike.

Thankfully, since the late 1960s academics have begun to supplant the idea of a unitary 'discovery' of the Americas by Christopher Columbus in 1492. The idea of history on the American continent somehow beginning only at the point when Europeans appeared has also been resoundingly ridiculed by Native American writers. Although history in the limited sense of written records in a European language was not in existence prior to 1492, history in the sense of events of tangible significance to multiple communities clearly did. Thus American history began far earlier than 1492. There is an ongoing disagreement between anthropologists and historians over the precise origins of Indian peoples in the Americas but approximate estimates range from 12,000 BC to 70,000 BC, with some dating the first Indian peoples in the Americas at 200,000 BC.[1] What is important is that we recognize that American Indian history includes divergent peoples, identities, cultures and environments that long pre-date European arrival. The Indian heritage on American soil has an inherent primacy since it stems from the repeated birth and rebirth of Indian communities over centuries.

What was taught about American history up until the late 1960s and early 1970s was largely based on a master narrative that in the main condemned Native Americans and American Indian history to a tiny footnote.[2] Many American history courses put forward a simple, progressive narrative where the continent of the Americas in 1492 was 'virgin land' upon which Christians settled and developed an American nation based upon the principles of liberty and equality. One could say that the story of the 'conqueror' dominated and obscured the stories of the 'conquered' (terms that in themselves are problematic given that many Indian nations were never in fact militarily conquered and made treaties with the United States as sovereign nations in their own right). Until relatively recently non-Indians have taken centre stage in the story of the United States even though that story took place and continues to unfold on Indian land and amid great numbers of Indian peoples. It is hoped that this volume will help to redress this imbalance and that it will bring a broader sense of the complexity and diversity that is an essential part of the American story.

A further complexity comes from the fact that the role of conflict within Indian life has changed over the centuries. For thousands of years before 1492, numbers of Indian peoples and groups interacted in large conglomerations, while others had a more separate and autonomous existence. While it is difficult to detail the precise relationships between the peoples in the Americas before 1492, what is certain is that environments and circumstances often changed. An ongoing state of change and rebirth, war and peace, and trade and isolation defined Indian life just as these same processes defined life in other continents. This may seem an obvious point but it is one that needs to be made since too often pre-1492 America has been presented as culturally static, with Indian peoples described as living as if trapped in a somehow changeless state of primitivism. After 1492 conflict with the colonial powers including Spain, England and France became increasingly important but it is essential that we remember that conflict between Indian nations over lands and resources also continued into the colonial period and beyond. Often, this conflict was defined by long-held rivalries between certain groups and nations. There were also periods of co-operation and coexistence between the Indian nations and the colonial powers, as well as between the Indian nations themselves in response to colonial encroachment and discreet from it. After the formation of the United States, conflict began to move gradually from the amphitheatres of war to the battlegrounds of the courtrooms, political institutions and public newspapers. Centuries old conflicts over resources, cultural autonomy and national sovereignty continue today, played out between Indian nations and the US Supreme Court and within the US Congress. Conflict over resources and self-determination are as vital and impactful for Indian peoples today as they were in the seventeenth, eighteenth, nineteenth and twentieth centuries.

This book will detail conflict between Indian nations and the US government, but equally important is the long history of sustained periods of interaction and co-operation both between differing tribal groups and between Indians and non-Indians. Of special significance is the often downplayed record of Indian involvement in major US conflicts overseas and the histories of Indian warriors of both genders serving to protect and serve the larger American nation. During the First and Second World Wars, thousands of men and women of Indian extraction proudly served as they did in successive American military conflicts in Korea, Vietnam and in the Gulf Wars of the 1990s and the twenty-first century. One could argue that this relationship of military assistance has in many ways defined American-Indian relationships over centuries.

This volume is both chronological and thematic. It traces key events, policy changes and moments of cultural conflict over time in fourteen chapters using both Indian and non-Indian primary sources to isolate key points of debate and co-operation. It highlights common important cultural and ideological differences between Indians and non-Indians. Readers may be surprised to notice that the primary source accounts sometimes invert usual expectations and show Indians supporting non-Indians and non-Indians supporting Indians. The reader will be able to access competing voices from the period of 'discovery', through the colonial era, with its long record of wars and specific moments of atrocity and massacre, to American governmental policy developments in the twentieth century. The book ends by touching upon some of the most contentious issues of our time as they are played out in Indian country. These include debates surrounding Leonard Peltier, arguments over issues of Indian law and jurisdiction over non-Indians on and away from Indian land, discussions over Indian gaming and the battles for cultural respect for Indian peoples in terms of their representation in modern-day America. This book will also examine interlinked themes such as spirituality and faith, the abiding significance of land and the environment and Indian assimilation versus Indian traditionalism. The reader is asked to bear in mind with the extracts provided that they are composite documents and products of their times. The Indian voices revealed here are sometimes from records that in all likelihood have undergone multiple translation (often in early records from a specific Indian language to Spanish and then to English) and as such should be considered with care. The act of translation within a wider context of war or conflict has always been open to influence and the reader should consider carefully the wider provenance of each excerpt. It is worth remembering that the war of words concerning Indian interests and values is as old as the conflict over Indian land and resources.

The terms 'Indian' and 'non-Indian' have been used throughout because 'Indian' is the pan-tribal term most used by indigenous American peoples themselves.[3] The specific names of Indian nations have also been used at every opportunity. We acknowledge that to some, 'Indian' or 'American Indian' are disliked because they are loaded with incorrect meaning and historical inaccuracy; since 'Indian' is in one sense a non-Indian term stemming from Columbus' faulty geography. Others view the term 'Native American' equally negatively, seeing it as a politically correct term that further patronises the divergent numbers of indigenous peoples in modern America. The choice of the term 'Indian nation(s)', rather than 'tribe(s)', to define a distinct group of Indian peoples is used where possible in this volume so as to reflect the inherent sovereignty and the everyday authority and power Indian nations continue to have today over their lands and their futures.

The reader is asked to bear in mind that the conflicts surrounding Native American Indians within the United States are destined to fundamentally change in the near future as America changes. The most obvious reason for this concerns population numbers. Indian communities today persist and in many cases thrive in spite of a legacy of displacement, disease, loss of land, resources and cultural sovereignty. This legacy of disadvantage coupled with ongoing discrimination has resulted in acutely disproportionate levels of mortality, suicide, diabetes, tuberculosis, alcoholism amongst other indicators within Indian communities. Whether they live on reservations or, like the bulk of Indian peoples, in urban contexts, Indians are more likely to suffer disadvantage, ill-health and all the stresses and difficulties that accompany poverty. However, since the all-time low in 1900 at approximately 237,000, the

Indian population has been rising significantly. Today there are upwards of 4.9 million American Indians and Alaskan Natives and by 2050 the US Census predicts that that number is expected to reach 8.6 million or two percent of the overall American population. So there will be many more Indians in what will be by mid-century, an even more diverse nation. Minorities, now roughly a third of the US population, are expected to become the majority by 2042. In this new American world, Indian voices are likely to have greater cultural and political power and the conflict and consensus that may surround them will have a completely new context.

CHAPTER ONE
ORIGINS OF THE WORLD
AND 'DISCOVERY'

To many non-Indians in the United States today, the 'discovery' of unknown lands by Christian Europeans in 1492 represents the beginning of history in what has been termed the 'New World'.[1] European voyages of discovery, such as the Norse voyages of the eleventh century and the journey of Welsh Prince Madoc to the Americas during the twelfth century, long pre-date 1492, but the voyage of Christopher Columbus in 1492 is often held as the starting point of the political, social and cultural collision between two worlds of Europe and Native America. However, in contrast to what has been a dominant non-Indian perspective, the lands of what is known today as the United States of America were occupied by a culturally and linguistically diverse range of peoples with differing traditions and a multitude of histories. The history of the American continent is as long and culturally varied as that of any other continent, and it is a history that did not begin with the arrival of the Europeans. The history of the Indians in North America is much deeper and more profound than the stories and written histories that unfolded from the European and American perspectives following the arrival of the Europeans. Moreover, there was and remains a contrast between the spiritual approaches of many indigenous peoples and that of the settler communities who came to what is now the United States. The former had a deep-rooted connection to the land and a vast repository of stories about how they came to live and develop upon it; the latter lacked this wealth of cultural connection.

Long before the European 'discovery' of the Americas in 1492, Indian North America was inhabited by millions of people and many hundreds of separate groups with different languages, cultures and social systems.[2] Scholars argue over whether the number of Indian languages in pre-contact North America was a few hundred or a few thousand, but there is a degree of consensus that there were between 600 and 2,000 separate Indian societies. Evidence exists of vast Indian trading routes and of the operation of complex systems of exchange, with Indians trading goods such as minerals and foods often over long distances. Interdependency led to the passing of ideas and social and religious customs between many different societies.[3] The existence of the famous pre-1492 Indian cities of Cahokia and Chaco Canyon are examples of the complexity of Indian life before European contact and of the interaction that existed between thousands of Indians.[4] However, in contrast to the territorial size and vast populations of the major Indian cities, there were also small, mobile and autonomous Indian societies, with some Indians, for example in what is known today as California, living within groups of 100–1,000 people who protected their autonomy.[5]

For thousands of years before 1492, diverse groups of Indians had found, settled and lived on the lands that were 'discovered' by the Europeans. Social scientists have debated on how the ancestors of the people that Europeans found in 1492 had arrived in the Americas. The precise dates and origin of Indian settlement in what today is termed North America are not agreed, but estimates range from 12,000 BC to 70,000 BC, with some scholars dating Indian genesis in North America at 200,000 BC. [6] One respected theory discusses the idea that a glacier formed and connected Asia and North America, called the 'Bering Strait', in the last ice age, c.75,000–8,000 BC and that this allowed the passage of the ancestors of the Indians Columbus encountered in 1492. Another theory suggests that groups of people migrated along the archipelagos of Australia and the Pacific coast. Some Indian scholars feel that the whole debate is futile and political, while others argue that Indians had been living on the continent from the beginning of time and did not actually migrate or travel at all.[7] Some Europeans in the eighteenth and nineteenth centuries believed that the Indians were descendents of the lost tribes of Israel and, therefore, part of the Christian tradition and history.[8] However we conceive of the origins of Native America over those thousands of years since their settlement in North America, the environment and Indian bonds to their lands have not been static. The people and environment of North America have always changed, existing in a spiritual and cultural state of birth and rebirth. Indian cultures, cities, languages and societies have developed and evolved, formed and disappeared just as cultures, languages and settlements have done elsewhere on the planet.[9] New strategies for survival came and went, political relationships were formed and broken, and times of peace and war developed and receded. This point seems obvious, but it contradicts a long-held non-Indian supposition that somehow Indian societies were static and unchanging, that somehow as 'primitive' cultures, they lacked any developmental dynamic and existed as if set in stone, devoid of the patterns of change that have characterized all human societies across time.

Estimates for pre-1492 Indian population numbers range from a conservative 500,000 to 18 million.[10] After 1492, the Indian population fell significantly because many millions of Indians died from a number of infectious diseases brought over by Europeans to the Americas and because of sustained conflict including repeated massacres as non-Indians fought to gain access to Indian land and resources. As non-Indians encroached upon Indian lands, they brought military conflict, enforced displacement of communities and encouraged the erosion of Indian cultural, political, spiritual and social norms. All of this contributed to what has been perhaps the largest deliberate sustained period of aggression towards a set of peoples in human history. Estimates of how many died have risen sharply since the late 1960s, but whichever figure is chosen, it is clear that the myth that America was a virgin land ripe for conquest had no basis in fact.

Just as surviving Indian communities do today, the diverse Indian cultures of the pre-1492 American continent held dear creation stories that were shaped by a fundamental spiritual connection between the development of each society and the lands upon which they lived. Often but not exclusively, these stories were passed orally from one generation to another. They had an essential coherence but were responsive to their context and to the specifics of how they were retold among different communities.[11] Many creation stories were first recorded and written down in the nineteenth and twentieth centuries and are not easily understood outside of their cultural context and the specifics of their genesis. Ancient origin stories still have a tangible significance within contemporary Indian society. They often express a fundamental connection between Indian communities and the environment, tying specific groups of Indian peoples together in a fundamental kinship with the animate and inanimate world in a specific location.[12]

The European 'discovery' of the Americas by Christopher Columbus (1451–1506) in 1492 began in one sense with the imposition of the European word and definition 'Indian'. The word was used by Columbus to denote the Taino people he first encountered. He believed he had reached the Indies and used the word *indios* for peoples encountered east of the river Indus. His faulty geography served to reduce multiple, heterogeneous groups of people living in the Americas to, in the European viewpoint, one single race of people.[13] As a result of Columbus' determination to view all the peoples of the Americas as one, the entire continent from the Abenaki to the Yakima became known as 'Indians'. Today the term 'Indian' is often retained by groups within indigenous America, peoples who have long since reinscribed its meaning and in many ways transcended its colonial context. It is sometimes deemed to be useful as a term that unites all indigenous Americans, even though in many cases, their primary affiliation may be with their specific homelands and their specific tribes.

European discovery of the Americas was in theory supposed to have been regulated by European principles formulated under a set of political and legal concepts known collectively as the doctrine of discovery. This doctrine had two important elements. First, Europeans could only acquire land that was deemed unoccupied, termed '*terra nullius*'. Thus to occupy land, European powers had to deny the title, rights and connections to the land of its indigenous populations. Second, the doctrine was supposed to regulate the way that European nations claimed 'discovered' new lands, with the first nation to come across land having the right to claim the lands and trade with the indigenous population.[14] However, despite these existing doctrinal and political rules, European nations did not adhere to them, fought each other in territorial wars, and generally ignored the natural land rights of the Indian inhabitants.[15]

The 'discovery' of the Americas was held to have opened up what was termed a 'New World' full of fertile, unoccupied lands with an abundance of natural riches and resources to be exploited and taken back to Europe.

Religion was used to justify the invasion and conquest of the Americas. A rhetoric developed that claimed to be redeeming indigenous populations for their own good by encouraging or enforcing their conversion to the Christian faith. The Spanish forced the Indian peoples they encountered to decide between accepting their terms of engagement or facing slavery and death. Generally, the Spanish believed they were superior to other people, including the Indians that they found, because they believed that the Pope had ordained their right to expand the Spanish empire through the will of God. European powers set about a process of acquiring Indian lands through coercion, displacement or war with scant regard for indigenous claims of occupancy and title. Successive Indian national and pan-tribal efforts to stem this process were at points successful for a time, but the ever-increasing numbers of Europeans demanding access to Indian land and carrying with them lethal disease ensured that the odds remained in the European settlers' favour.[16]

SOURCES

Origin Myth of Acoma

The following extract describes the Acoma origin myth. It was obtained from a group of Pueblo Indians from Acoma and Santa Ana visiting Washington in 1928.

In the beginning two female human beings were born. These two children were born underground at a place called Shipapu. As they grew up, they began to be aware of each other. There was no light and they could only feel each other. Being in the dark they grew slowly.

After they had grown considerably, a Spirit whom they afterward called Tsichtinako spoke to them, and they found that it would give them nourishment. After they had grown large enough to think for themselves, they spoke to the Spirit when it had come to them one day and asked it to make itself known to them and to say whether it was male or female, but it replied only that it was not allowed to meet with them. They then asked why they were living in the dark without knowing each other by name, but the Spirit answered that they were nuk'timi (under the earth); but they were to be patient in waiting until everything was ready for them to go up into the light. So they waited a long time, and as they grew they learned their language from Tsichtinako.

When all was ready, they found a present from Tsichtinako, two baskets of seeds and little images of all the different animals (there were to be) in the world. The Spirit said they were sent by their father. They asked who was meant by their father, and Tsichtinako replied that his name was Ūch'tsiti and that he wished them to take their baskets out into the light, when the time came. Tsichtinako instructed them, "You will find the seeds of four kinds of pine trees, lā'khok, gēi'etsu (dyai'its), wanūka, and lǎ'nye, in your baskets. You are to plant these seeds and will use the trees to get up into the light." They could not see the things in their baskets but feeling each object in turn they asked, "Is this it?" until the seeds were found. They then planted the seeds as Tsichtinako instructed. All of the four seeds sprouted, but in the darkness the trees grew very slowly and the two sisters became very anxious to reach the light as they waited this long time. They slept for many years as they had no use for eyes. Each time they awoke they would feel the trees to see how they were growing. The tree lanye grew faster than the others and after a very long time pushed a hole through the earth for them and let in a very little light. The others stopped growing, at various heights, when this happened.

The hole that the tree lanye made was not large enough for them to pass through, so Tsichtinako advised them to look again in their baskets where they would find the image of an animal called dyu·p[i] (badger) and tell it to become alive. They told it to live, and it did so as they spoke, exclaiming, "A'uha! Why have you given me life?" They told it not to be afraid nor to worry about coming to life. "We have brought you to life because you are to be useful." Tsichtinako spoke to them again, instructing them to tell Badger to climb the pine tree, to bore a hole large enough for them to crawl up, cautioning him not to go out into the light, but to return, when the hole was finished. Badger climbed the tree and after he had dug a hole large enough, returned saying that he had done his work. They thanked him and said, "As a reward you will come up with us to the light and thereafter you will live happily. You will always know how to dig and your home will be in the ground where you will be neither too hot nor too cold."

Tsichtinako now spoke again, telling them to look in the basket for Tāwāi'nū (locust), giving it life and asking it to smooth the hole by plastering. It, too was to be cautioned to return. This they did and Locust smoothed the hole but, having finished, went out into the light. When it returned reporting that it had done its work, they asked it if it had gone out. Locust said no, and every time he was asked he replied no, until the fourth time when he admitted that he had gone out. They asked Locust what it was like outside. Locust replied that it was just tsī'ītī (laid out flat). They said, "From now on you will be known as Tsi·k'ă. You will also come up with us, but you will be punished for disobedience by being allowed out only a short time. Your home will be in the ground and you will have to return when the weather is bad. You will soon die but you will be reborn each season."

The hole now let light into the place where the two sisters were, and Tsichtinako spoke to them, "Now is the time you are to go out. You are able to take your baskets with you. In them you will find pollen and sacred corn meal. When you reach the top, you will wait for the sun to come up and that direction will be called ha'nami (east). With the pollen and the sacred corn meal you will pray to the Sun. You will thank the Sun for bringing you to light, ask for a long life and happiness, and for success in the purpose for which you were created." Tsichtinako then taught them the prayers and the creation song, which they were to sing. This took a long while, but finally the sisters followed by Badger and Locust, went out into the light, climbing the pine tree. Badger was very strong and skillful and helped them. On reaching the earth, they set down their baskets and saw for the first time what they had. The earth was soft and spongy under their feet as they walked, and they said, "This is not ripe." They stood waiting for the sun, not knowing where it would appear. Gradually it grew lighter and finally the sun came up. Before they began to pray, Tsichtinako told them they were facing east and that their right side, the side their best aim was on, would be known as kū'ā'mē (South) and the left ti dyami (north) while behind at their backs was the direction pūna'me (west) where the sun would go down. They had already learned while underground the direction nŭk'ŭmi (down) and later, when they asked where their father was, they were told tyunami (four skies above.)

And as they waited to pray to the Sun, the girl on the right moved her best hand and was named Iatiku which meant "bringing to life." Tsichtinako then told her to name her sister, but it took a long time. Finally Tsichtinako noticed that the other had more in her basket, so Tsichtinako told Iatiku to name her thus, and Iatiku called her Nautsiti which meant "more of everything in the basket."

They now prayed to the Sun as they had been taught by Tsichtinako, and sang the creation song. Their eyes hurt for they were not accustomed to the strong light. For the first time they asked Tsichtinako why they were on earth and why they were created. Tsichtinako replied, "I did not make you. Your father, Uchtsiti made you, and it is he who has made the world, the sun which you have seen, the sky, and many other things which you will see. But Uchtsiti says the world is not yet completed, not yet satisfactory, as he wants it. This is the reason he has made you. You will rule and bring to life the rest of the things he has given you in the baskets." The sisters then asked how they themselves had come into being. Tsichtinako answered saying, "Uchtsiti first made the world. He threw a clot of his own blood into space and by his power it grew and grew until it became the earth. Then Uchtsiti planted you in this and by it you were nourished as you developed. Now that you have emerged from within the earth, you will have to provide nourishment for yourselves. I will instruct you in this." They then asked where their father lived and Tsichtinako replied, "You will never see your father, he lives four skies above, and has made you to live in this world. He has made you in the image of himself." So they asked why Tsichtinako did not become visible to them, but Tsichtinako replied, "I don't know how to live like a human being. I have been asked by Uchtsiti to look after you and to teach you. I will always guide you." And they asked again how they were to live, whether they could go down once more under the ground, for they were afraid of the winds and rains and their eyes were hurt by the light. Tsichtinako replied that Uchtsiti would take care of that and would furnish them means to keep warm and change the atmosphere so that they would get used to it...

When they had completed their prayers to the sun, Tsichtinako said, "You have done everything well and now you are both to take up your baskets and you must look to the north, west, south, and east, for you are now to pray to the Earth to accept the things in the basket and to give them life. First you must pray to the north, at the same time lift up your baskets in that direction. You will then do the same to the west, then to the south and east." They did as they were told and did it well. And Tsichtinako, said to them, "From now on you will rule in every direction, north, west, south, and east."

They now questioned Tsichtinako again so that they would understand more clearly why they were given the baskets and their contents, and Tsichtinako, replied, "Everything in the baskets is to be created by your word, for you are made in the image of Uchtsiti and your word will be as powerful as his word. He has created you to help him complete the world. You are to plant the seeds of the different plants to be used when anything is needed. I shall always be ready to point out to you the various plants and animals."...

...They were then told to place the tobacco with the pollen and the corn meal and to remember that these three were always to be together, and to be used in making prayers.

Now they were told that they were to give life to an animal whose flesh they were going to use for food. Tsichtinako named this animal as Ba'shya (kangaroo mouse) and also taught them the first song to be sung to animals. She told them to sing this song in order to make the images alive, and pointed out the images to them in the basket.

They did everything as they were taught. They sang the song to the image and with the word, "Come to life, Bashya," it came to life. As it did so it asked, "Why have I come to life?" Tsichtinako told it not to ask any questions because, "It is you that is going to give life to other life." After this was done, Nautsiti and Iatiku, told this animal that it was going to live on the ground and said to it, "Go now and increase." After the animal increased, Tsichtinako told the sisters to kill one of the animals. "Now eat the two together, the corn and the field mouse, and also the salt to see how it tastes." ... They roasted their corn and roasted the flesh of the field mouse with some salt on it. After it was cooked, Tsichtinako told them to pray with the food, not with all of it, but with little pieces from each--corn, flesh, and salt. Each sister did this and prayed to Uchtsiti, the creator of the world, who lives up in the fourth sky. Tsichtinako told them they were to do this always before eating ... They liked the flesh so well that they asked Tsichtinako if they might have something larger that would yield more flesh. Tsichtinako answered that they would find other things in their baskets. They went back to them, and Tsichtinako said they would find Tsū'na (rat) and another animal Katsa (mole) and also Nīte. (prairie dog). "Go, make these images alive," said Tsichtinako, pointing them out according to their names. They were to do this in the same way as with Bashya. Tsichtinako also told them that these animals were to be used as food and that they must tell each of these animals to live in the ground because as yet there was no shade on earth to live in. "But before you give life to them," said Tsichtinako, "it is necessary that you plant seeds of grass which will be the food for them." Tsichtinako pointed out the seeds they were to plant, and they took the seeds of the grasses and scattered them first to the North, next to the West, then some to the South, and then to the East. And immediately grass covered the ground. They then took the images and prayed to the cardinal points, and, according to the instructions of Tsichtinako, gave life to all of these animals, giving them names as they came to life. Each one as it came to life asked why it had come to life but Tsichtinako told them not to ask questions, that they would give life to other life ... The two sisters were now very happy, they had plenty and some to spare. "It is not time for the larger animals to be given life," said Tsichtinako, "first the world must have sufficient plants and small animals to feed them."

After a long time, Tsichtinako spoke to them, "What we are going to do now concerns the earth. We are going to make the mountains." She told them to remember the words she was going to say. They were to say, "Kaweshtima kōtⁱ (North Mountain), appear in the north, and we will always know you to be in that direction." Tsichtinako also pointed out an article in the basket that she named ya'ōni (stone) and instructed them to throw the stone to the North direction as they spoke the words. When they did so, a big mountain appeared in the North. After they had done this, Tsichtinako instructed them to do the same thing in the West, but to name this mountain Tsipīna kotⁱ, and in the South, naming it Da'ōtyuma kotⁱ, and in the East, naming it G'ūchana kotⁱ.

After all this was done, Tsichtinako spoke again and told them, "Now that you have all the mountains around you with plains, mesas, and canyons, you must make the growing things of these places." Tsichtinako told them to go back to the trees which they had planted underground, lakhok, geietsu, wanuka, and lanye. She told them to take the seeds from these trees, and they did so. Following her instructions they spread some to each of the four directions, naming the mountains in each direction ... Tsichtinako said to them, "These are going to be tall trees; from them you will get logs. Later you will build houses and will use these." They asked if that was all that was going to grow on the mountains, and Tsichtinako said, "No, there are many other seeds left in your baskets. You have seeds of trees which are going to yield food. You will find dyai'its (piñon tree), sē'isha (kind of cedar), hapani (oak, acorn) and maka'yawi (walnut)." ... When everything had been done well, Tsichtinako told (them) that there were many smaller seeds left in the baskets and she gave a name to each, telling them to fill the rest of the land. These seeds were planted on every one of the four mountains and in the rest of the world. Tsichtinako spoke to the sisters again and told them, "You still have seeds in your baskets which you will know as scuts'ōⁱbewi (wild fruits). These trees you will grow around you and care for." But they mistook the instructions and instead of instructing them to grow nearby, they named the mountains, and that is where they grew...

They saw that there were still seeds and images in their baskets, and asked Tsichtinako how many more kinds there were. Tsichtinako, said there were yet many other seeds which would also be important food. They would grow quickly and easily and she named them squash and beans. They were instructed to act with them as with the other seeds, and these also grew into plants. After a time, when they were ripe, Tsichtinako pointed out the parts of the plants which they, were to use as food.

Iatiku later asked Tsichtinako, "What remains in my basket?" and she was answered, "You have still many animals; these will be multiplied to populate the mountains." And as the two grew larger, they required more food. Tsichtinako saw this and told them that they were now to bring to life larger animals. She said they would find in their baskets cottontails, jack rabbits, antelope, and water deer ... As they again asked Tsichtinako what remained in their baskets, Tsichtinako said, "You have images of the still bigger game. You will find deer, elk, mountain sheep, and bison."...

The sisters again asked what was in their baskets, and they were told, "You will find birds which will fly in the air. These birds win also use small game for their food. You will find in the basket the eagles and the hawks (shpi·ya, ga·wa, i·tsa)." Tsichtinako pointed these out to them and they brought them to life. The birds flew up into the high mountains and over the plains. The sisters told the birds to use small game for food, and again latiku asked what was in the basket. Tsichtinako pointed out smaller birds which would populate the country, each living in a different kind of region. They were then given life, as the animals before them ... Again latiku asked what remained in the baskets, because she found things there that were thorny. Tsichtinako told them their names. They were the various cacti and were said to be very good for food. But Tsichtinako explained that most were intended for animals to eat. All these were planted as before and tried for food, and they found that some tasted good, stī'ăne, īcht, ya'tăp, iteō'on. After they asked again what was left, Tsichtinako pointed out to them that there were still fish, water snakes, and turtles, of which there were many kinds of each. They gave life to them as before and told them all to live in the water as instructed. Tsichtinako pointed out several that were to be used for food. They tried them all for food, and they found that some were good, and others poor, but offered prayers to all and gave thanks to Uchtsiti. So it happened that many animals came alive in the world and they all increased.

Iroquois Creation Myth

The following document presents one version of a creation myth taken from the Iroquois of New York State. It was one of the earliest to be documented in writing and was recorded by Major John Norton, son of Scottish and Cherokee parents, around 1816.

The tradition of the Nottowegui or Five Nations says, "that in the beginning before the formation of the earth; the country above the sky was inhabited by Superior Beings, over whom the Great Spirit presided. His daughter having become pregnant by an illicit connection, he pulled up a great tree by the roots, and threw her through the cavity thereby formed; but, to prevent her utter destruction, he previously ordered the Great Turtle, to get from the bottom of the waters, some slime on its back, and to wait on the surface of the water to receive her on it. When she had fallen on the back of the Turtle, with the mud she found there, she began to form the earth, and by the time of her delivery had increased it to the extent of a little island. Her child was a daughter, and as she grew up the earth extended under their hands. When the young woman had arrived at the age of discretion, the Spirits who roved about, in human forms, made proposals of marriage for the young woman: the mother always rejected their offers, until a middle aged man, of a dignified appearance, his bow in his hand, and his quiver on his back, paid his addresses.

On being accepted, he entered the house, and seated himself on the birth of his intended spouse; the mother was in a birth on the other side of the fire. She observed that her son-in-law did not lie down all night; but taking two arrows out of his quiver, he put them by the side of his bride: at the dawn of day he took them up, and having replaced them in his quiver, he went out.

"After some time, the old woman perceived her daughter to be pregnant, but could not discover where the father had gone, or who he was. At the time of delivery, the twins disputed which way they should go out of the womb; the wicked one said, let us go out of the side; but the other said, not so, lest we kill our mother; then the wicked one pretending to acquiesce, desired his brother to go out first: but as soon as he was delivered, the wicked one, in attempting to go out at her side, caused the death of his mother.

"The twin brothers were nurtured and raised by their Grandmother; the eldest was named Teharonghyawago, or the Holder of Heaven; the youngest was called Tawiskaron, or Flinty rock, from his body being entirely covered with such a substance. They grew up, and with their bows and arrows, amused themselves throughout the island, which encreased in extent, and they were favoured with various animals of Chace. Tawiskaron was the most fortunate hunter, and enjoyed the favour of his Grandmother. Teharonghyawago was not so successful in the Chace, and suffered from their unkindness. When he was a youth, and roaming alone, in melancholy mood, through the island, a human figure, of noble aspect, appearing to him, addressed him thus; 'My son, I have seen your distress, and heard your solitary lamentations; you are unhappy in the loss of a mother, in the unkindness of your Grandmother and brother. I now come to comfort you, I am your father, and will be you Protector; therefore take courage, and suffer not your spirit to sink. Take this [giving him an ear of *maize*] plant it, and attend it in the manner, I shall direct; it will yield you a certain support, independent of the Chace, at the same time that it will render more palatable the viands, which you may thereby obtain. I am the Great Turtle which supports the earth, on which you move. Your brother's ill treatment will increase with his years; bear it with patience till the time appointed, before which you shall hear further.'

"After saying this, and directing him how to plant the corn, he disappeared. Teharonghyawago planted the corn, and returned home. When its verdant sprouts began to flourish above the ground, he spent his time in clearing from all growth of grass and weeds, which might smother it or retard its advancement while yet in its tender state, before it had acquired sufficient grandeur to shade the ground. He now discovered that his wicked brother caught the timid deer, the stately elk with branching horns, and all the harmless inhabitants of the Forest; and imprisoned them in an extensive cave, for his own particular; use, depriving mortals from having the benefit of them that was original intended by the Great Spirit. Teharonghyawago discovered the direction the brother took in conducting these animals captive to the Cave; but never could trace him quite to the spot, as he eluded his sight with more than common dexterity!

"Teharonghyawago endeavoured to conceal himself on the path that led to the cave, so that he might follow him imperceptibly; but he found impossible to hide himself from the penetrating Tawiskaron. At length it observed, that altho' his brother saw, with extraordinary acuteness, every surrounding object, yet he never raised his eyes to look above: Teharonghyawago then climbed a lofty tree, which grew near to where he thought the place of confinement was situated: in the meantime, his brother passed, searching with his eyes the thickest recesses of the Forest, but never casting a glance above. He then saw his brother take a straight course, and when he was out of sight, Teharonghyawago descended, and came to the Cave, a short time after he had deposited his charge; and finding there an innumerable number of animals confined, he set them free, and returned home.

"It was not long before Tawiskaron, visiting the Cave, discovered that all his captives, which he had taken so much pains to deprive of their liberty, had been liberated: he knew this to be an act of his brother, but dissembling his anger, he meditated revenge, at some future period.

"Teharonghyawago laboured to people the earth with inhabitants, and to found Villages in happy situations, extending the comforts of men. Tawiskaron was equally active in destroying the works his brother had done; and in accumulating every evil in his power on the heads of ill fated mortals. Teharonghyawago saw, with regret, his brother persevere in every wickedness; but waited with patience the result of what his father had told him.

"At one time, being in conversation with his brother, Tawiskaron said 'Brother, what do you think there is on earth, with which you might be killed?' Teharonghyawago replied, 'I know of nothing that could affect my life, unless it be the foam of the billows of the Lake or the downy topped reed.' 'What do you think would take your life?' Tawiskaron answered, 'Nothing except horn or flint.' Here their discourse ended.

"Teharonghyawago returning from hunting, heard a voice singing a plaintive air: he listened and heard it name his Mother, who was killed by Tawiskaron; he immediately hastened towards the spot from whence the voice proceeded, crying, 'Who is that, who dares to name my deceased mother in my hearing?' When he came there, he saw the track of a fawn, which he pursued, without overtaking it, till the autumn, when it dropped its first horns; these he took up, and fixed upon the forked branches of a tree.

"He continued the pursuit seven years; and every autumn, when its horns fell, he picked them up, and placed them as he had done the first. At last, he overtook the deer, now grown to be a stately buck: it begged its life, and said, 'Spare me, and I will give you information that may be great service to you.' When he had promised it its life, it spoke as follows, 'It was to give you the necessary information that I have been subjected to your pursuit, and that which I shall now tell you was the intended reward of your perseverance and clemency. Your brother, in coming into the world, caused the death of your Mother; if he was then wicked in his infancy, his malice has grown with his stature; he now premeditates evil against you; be therefore on your guard: as soon as he assaults you, exert yourself, and you will overcome him.'

"He returned home; and not long after this adventure, was attacked by his brother. They fought; the one made use of the horn and flint stone which he had provided: the other sought for froth and the reed, which made little impression on the body of Teharonghyawago. They fought a long time, over the whole of the island, until at last Tawiskaron fell under the conquering hand of his brother. According to the varied tones of their voices in the different places through which they passed during the contest, the people, who afterwards sprung up there, spoke different languages."

Extracts from the Journal of Christopher Columbus, 1492

Provided here are extracts from the diary of Christopher Columbus (1451–1506) on his first voyage to the Indies in 1492. He tells of his duty to claim discovered lands in the name of Spain and Christianity and to convert the people to his faith. In addition, Columbus describes the people that he meets and refers to them as 'Indians'.

IN THE NAME OF OUR LORD JESUS CHRIST

Most Christian and most exalted and most excellent and most powerful Princes, King and Queen of the Spains and of the islands of the sea, Our Sovereigns ... Your Highnesses, as Catholic Christians and princes devoted to the holy Christian faith and the furtherance of its cause, and enemies of the sect of Mohammed and of all idolatry and heresy, resolved to send me, Christopher Columbus, to the said regions of India to see the said princes and the peoples and lands and determine the nature of them and of all other things, and the measures to be taken to convert them to our holy faith; and you ordered that I should not go by land to the East, which is the customary route, but by way of the West, a route which to this day we cannot be certain has been taken by anyone else: So then, after having expelled all the Jews from all your kingdoms and domains, in the same month of January, Your Highnesses commanded me to take sufficient ships and sail to the said regions of India. And in consideration you granted me great favours and honoured me thenceforth with the title 'Don' and the rank of Admiral of the Ocean Sea and Viceroy and Governor in perpetuity of all the islands and mainland that I should discover and take possession of and which should hereafter be discovered and occupied in the Ocean Sea, and that my eldest son should succeed in turn, and so on from generation to generation for ever...

Thursday 11 October

...Two hours after midnight land appeared at a distance of about two leagues ... Then they saw some naked people and the Admiral went ashore in the armed boat ... The Admiral brought out the royal standard ... The Admiral called the two captains and the others who landed ... and made them bear witness and testimony that he, in their presence, took possession, as in fact he did take possession, of the said island in the names of the King and Queen, His Sovereigns, making the requisite declarations ... Then, many islanders gathered round. What follows are the Admiral's own words from the journal of his first voyage and discovery of these Indies. In order to win their good will, he says, because I could see that they were a people who could more easily be won over and converted to our holy faith by kindness than by force, I gave some of them red hats and glass beads that they put round their necks, and many other things of little value, with which they were very pleased and became so friendly that it was a wonder to see ... In fact they took and gave everything they had with good will, but it seemed to me that they were a people who were very poor in everything. They go as naked as their mothers bore them, even the women, though I only saw one girl, and she was very young. All those I did see were young men, none of them more than thirty years old. They were well built, with handsome bodies and fine features. Their hair is thick, almost like a horse's tail, but short; they wear it down over their eyebrows except for a few strands behind which they wear long and never cut. Some of them paint themselves black, though they are naturally the colour of Canary Islanders, neither black nor white; and some paint themselves white, some red and some whatever colour they can find; some paint their faces, some their whole bodies, some only the eyes and some only the nose. They do not carry arms and do not know of them because I showed them some swords and they grasped them by the blade and cut themselves out of ignorance. They have no iron: their spears are just shafts without a metal tip, and some have a fish tooth at the end, and some have other things. They are all fairly tall, good looking and well proportioned. I saw some who had signs of wounds on their bodies and in sign language I asked them what they were, and they indicated that other people came from other islands nearby and tried to capture them, and they defended themselves. I believed then and still believe that they come here from the mainland to take them as slaves. They ought to make good slaves for they are of quick intelligence since I notice that they are quick to repeat what is said to them, and I believe that they could very easily become Christians, for it seemed to me that they had no religion of their own...

Monday 15 October

...And being midway between these two islands, that is, between Santa Marnd this large island to which I have given the name Fernandina, I found a man alone in a canoe who was crossing from Santa María to Fernandina and he had with him a piece of their bread about the size of a fist and a gourd of water and a piece of brown earth powdered and kneaded into a mass and some dried leaves, which must be something they value highly because I was brought some on San Salvador as a present … He came alongside the flagship; I brought him aboard at his request and told him to bring his canoe aboard also and ordered that everything he was carrying should be kept safely, and that he should be given bread and honey to eat and something to drink. And so I shall take him across to Fernandina and give him back all his belongings, so that he will spread good news about us, and when, God willing, Your Highnesses send others here, those who come will be received with honour and the Indians will give us everything there is.

The Bull *Inter Caetera* (Alexander VI), 4 May 1493

The following document is an English translation of the Papal Bull of Pope Alexander VI (Inter Caetera), which outlines the superiority of Christians over Indians and justifies the claims of the Spanish to Indian land.

Alexander, bishop, servant of the servants of God, to the illustrious sovereigns, our very dear son in Christ, Ferdinand, king, and our very dear daughter in Christ, Isabella, queen of Castile, Leon, Aragon, Sicily, and Granada, health and apostolic benediction. Among other works well pleasing to the Divine Majesty and cherished of our heart, this assuredly ranks highest, that in our times especially the Catholic faith and the Christian religion be exalted and be everywhere increased and spread, that the health of souls be cared for and that barbarous nations be overthrown and brought to the faith itself. Wherefore inasmuch as by the favor of divine clemency, we, though of insufficient merits, have been called to this Holy See of Peter, recognizing that as true Catholic kings and princes, such as we have known you always to be, and as your illustrious deeds already known to almost the whole world declare, you not only eagerly desire but with every effort, zeal, and diligence, without regard to hardships, expenses, dangers, with the shedding even of your blood, are laboring to that end … we therefore are rightly led, and hold it as our duty, to grant you even of our own accord and in your favor those things whereby with effort each day more hearty you may be enabled for the honor of God himself and the spread of the Christian rule to carry forward your holy and praiseworthy purpose so pleasing to immortal God. We have indeed learned that you, who for a long time had intended to seek out and discover certain islands and mainlands remote and unknown and not hitherto discovered by others, to the end that you might bring to the worship of our Redeemer and the profession of the Catholic faith their residents and inhabitants, having been up to the present time greatly engaged in the siege and recovery of the kingdom itself of Granada were unable to accomplish this holy and praiseworthy purpose; but the said kingdom having at length been regained, as was pleasing to the Lord, you, with the wish to fulfill your desire, chose our beloved son, Christopher Columbus, a man assuredly worthy and of the highest recommendations and fitted for so great an undertaking, whom you furnished with ships and men equipped for like designs, not without the greatest hardships, dangers, and expenses, to make diligent quest for these remote and unknown mainlands and islands through the sea, where hitherto no one had sailed; and they at length, with divine aid and with the utmost diligence sailing in the ocean sea, discovered certain very remote islands and even mainlands that hitherto had not been discovered by others; wherein dwell very many peoples living in peace, and, as reported, going unclothed, and not eating flesh. Moreover, as your aforesaid envoys are of opinion, these very peoples living in the said islands and countries believe in one God, the Creator in heaven, and seem sufficiently disposed to embrace the Catholic faith and be trained in good morals. And it is hoped that, were they instructed, the name of the Savior, our Lord Jesus Christ, would easily be introduced into the said countries and islands. Also, on one of the chief of these aforesaid islands the said Christopher has already caused to be put together and built a fortress fairly equipped, wherein he has stationed as garrison certain Christians, companions of his, who are to make search for other remote and unknown islands and mainlands. In the islands and countries already discovered are found gold, spices, and very many other precious things of diverse kinds and qualities. Wherefore, as becomes Catholic kings and princes, after earnest consideration of all matters, especially of the rise and spread of the Catholic faith, as was the fashion of your ancestors, kings of renowned memory, you have purposed with the favor of divine clemency to bring under your sway the said mainlands and islands with their residents and inhabitants and to bring them to the Catholic faith. Hence, heartily commending in the Lord this your holy and praiseworthy purpose, and desirous that it be duly accomplished, and that the name of our Savior be carried into those regions, we exhort you very earnestly in the Lord and by your reception of holy baptism, whereby you are bound to our apostolic commands, and by the bowels of the mercy of our Lord Jesus Christ, enjoin strictly, that inasmuch as with eager zeal for the true faith you design to equip and despatch this expedition, you purpose also, as is your duty, to lead the peoples dwelling in those islands and countries to embrace the Christian religion; nor at any time let dangers or hardships deter you therefrom, with the stout hope and trust in your hearts that Almighty God will further your undertakings. And, in order that you may enter upon so great an undertaking with greater readiness and heartiness endowed with the benefit of our apostolic favor, we, of our own accord, not at your instance nor the request of anyone else in your regard, but of our own sole largess and certain knowledge and out of the fullness of our apostolic power, by the authority of Almighty God conferred upon us in blessed Peter and of the vicarship of Jesus Christ, which we hold on earth, do by tenor of these presents, should any of said islands have been found by your envoys and captains, give, grant, and assign to you and your heirs and successors, kings of Castile and Leon, forever, together with all their dominions, cities, camps, places, and villages, and all rights, jurisdictions, and appurtenances, all islands and mainlands found and to be found, discovered and to be discovered towards the west and south, by drawing and establishing a line from the Arctic pole, namely the north, to the Antarctic pole, namely the south, no matter whether the said mainlands and islands are found and to be found in the direction of India or towards any other quarter, the said line to be distant one hundred leagues towards the west and south from any of the islands commonly known as the Azores and Cape Verde. With this proviso however that none of the islands and mainlands, found and to be found, discovered and to be discovered, beyond that said line towards the west and south, be in the actual possession of any Christian king or prince up to the birthday of our Lord Jesus Christ just past from which the present year one thousand four hundred and ninety-three begins. And we make, appoint, and depute you and your said heirs and successors lords of them with full and free power, authority, and jurisdiction of every kind; with this proviso however, that by this our gift, grant, and assignment no right acquired by any Christian prince, who may be in actual possession of said islands and mainlands prior to the said birthday of our Lord Jesus Christ, is hereby to be understood to be withdrawn or taken away. Moreover we command you in virtue of holy obedience that, employing all due diligence in the premises, as you also promise -- nor do we doubt your compliance therein in accordance with your loyalty and royal greatness of spirit -- you should appoint to the aforesaid mainlands and islands worthy, God-fearing, learned, skilled, and experienced men, in order to instruct the aforesaid inhabitants and residents in the Catholic faith and train them in good morals. Furthermore, under penalty of excommunication *late sententie* to be incurred *ipso facto*, should anyone thus contravene, we strictly forbid all persons of whatsoever rank, even imperial and royal, or of whatsoever estate, degree, order, or condition, to dare, without your special permit or that of your aforesaid heirs and successors, to go for the purpose of trade or any other reason to the islands or mainlands, found and to be found, discovered and to be discovered, towards the west and south, by drawing and establishing a line from the Arctic pole to the Antarctic pole, no matter whether the mainlands and islands, found and to be found, lie in the direction of India or toward any other quarter whatsoever, the said line to be distant one hundred leagues towards the west and south, as is aforesaid, from any of the islands commonly known as the Azores and Cape Verde; apostolic constitutions and ordinances and other decrees whatsoever to the contrary notwithstanding. We trust in Him from whom empires and governments and all good things proceed, that, should you, with the Lord's guidance, pursue this holy and praiseworthy undertaking, in a short while your hardships and endeavors will attain the most felicitous result, to the happiness and glory of all Christendom. But inasmuch as it would be difficult to have these present letters sent to all places where desirable, we wish, and with similar accord and knowledge do decree, that to copies of them, signed by the hand of a public notary commissioned therefor, and sealed with the seal of any ecclesiastical officer or ecclesiastical court, the same respect is to be shown in court and outside as well as anywhere else as would be given to these presents should they thus be exhibited or shown. Let no one, therefore, infringe, or with rash boldness contravene, this our recommendation, exhortation, requisition, gift, grant, assignment, constitution, deputation, decree, mandate, prohibition, and will. Should anyone presume to attempt this, be it known to him that he will incur the wrath of Almighty God and of the blessed apostles Peter and Paul. Given at Rome, at St. Peter's, in the year of the incarnation of our Lord one thousand four hundred and ninety-three, the fourth of May, and the first year of our pontificate.

Gratis by order of our most holy lord, the pope.

CHAPTER TWO
SPIRITUALITY AND FAITH, 1550–1805

Debates characterized Christian faiths (Francis of Assisi) but overall an attitude of spiritual superiority prevailed. One of the key points of conflict between Indians and non-Indians has concerned each set of cultures' approach to religion and spirituality and their appropriate relationships to nature. It is impossible to compare the practices and beliefs of hundreds, if not thousands, of Indian nations; however, it is possible to isolate aspects of the complexity of Indian beliefs and spiritual traditions. Generally, many Indian communities across time have registered a kinship with all things living, including animals, people, plants and foods, and connections with the spirits of dead ancestors and the spirits of each living thing. In comparison to the complexities of the spiritual relationships of many groups of Indians to what we think of as nature including animate and inanimate entities, the general religious beliefs of the people of England, France, Holland and Spain involved the worship of one singular god and did not involve overt spiritual connections to animals and foods or other peoples, unless they worshipped the same god. European Christians believed in the superiority of the Christian religion over all others, and as a result, many non-Indians perceived Indians to be 'ungodly', 'inferior' and 'savage heathens'. To many Europeans, Indian spiritual life smacked of the paganism of their own relatively recent past which had successfully and often violently been supplanted by Christianity. European colonialism went hand in hand with a desire to spread the message of Christianity in the Americas and convert the Indians away from their traditional beliefs and cultures. This was done both for the benefit of Europeans (since evangelism was part of most Christian traditions) and for the supposed benefit of indigenous Americans whom Europeans thought of as being in spiritual peril.

In contrast to the European practice of worshipping one superior god, many Indian groups including, for example, the Iroquois, Fox, Crow, Chippewa, Navajo, Cahuilla and Acoma Pueblo had developed different and complex spiritual traditions and rituals over many centuries. The Iroquois at the time were warriors and farmers who believed that the world was occupied by invisible spirits. These spirits included the Great Spirit, who created all people, plants, animals and forces of good in nature, the Thunderer, who brought rain and to whom the Iroquois prayed for the successful production of crops, Spirit of the Winds, who controlled the winds, and the Three Sisters, the spirits of maize, beans and squash. Specific spiritual associations existed between the Iroquois and nature, particularly things that helped them like plants, fire and water.[1] These traditions were built on the belief in a complex and intricate ecosystem and network within the environment and the universe. The Mesquakie or Fox, warriors and farmers of the east-central United States, believed (and some still believe) in the importance of a personal relationship with the supernatural forces of nature. The relationship was defined by a concept called Manitou and the use of group ceremonies. Manitou was a feature of nature which included animals and humans and was used to give power to a person when called upon. Religious traditions often involved rituals conducted in specific places of importance and demonstrated a close spiritual relationship to the environment.[2] The Crow of the Plains used hunting rituals to ensure success when they hunted bison, deer, elk and antelope; whereas the Chipewayan of Canada attached charms to fishing nets because they feared the fish would not be taken without them.[3] Navajo daily life was surrounded by rituals. Corn pollen offerings were made in the morning as well as prayer and song and parts of chants were used when herding sheep or conducting other tasks. Navajo spirituality involved a close connection to Navajo ancestors and the practical expression of kinship to both nature and animals. Post-contact evidence suggests that the Navajo believed that bears, coyotes and snakes could never be killed as otherwise it would lead to illness or injury.[4] The Cahuilla of the south-west believed in the supernatural powers of the eagle to provide life after death and continuity of lineage among their people. The Acoma Pueblo believed in a reciprocal relationship between human culture and the natural environment.[5] Many Indians today show the same respect for the spirit world and their place within it as their ancestors. The spiritual traditions that Europeans encountered following 1492 are by no means dead or moribund; to the contrary the spiritual traditions of specific Indian communities continue to develop and thrive in the present day even though rituals and practices have been heavily and violently curtailed by non-Indians at various points.[6]

Not all Spaniards supported the imposition of Christianity on Indian cultures. In 1550, there was a great debate in Valladolid, Spain, between Bartolomé de Las Casas (1484–1558) and Juan Ginés de Sepúlveda (1494–1573) about the correct way for the Spanish to treat the Indians and acquire Indian lands. The ideological conflict between the two men was stark. Las Casas was a Dominican priest who defended the rights of the Indians and had first-hand knowledge of the Indians after his first visit in 1502 and his subsequent travels to the Americas. In contrast, Juan Ginés de Sepúlveda was the official historian of the Spanish Crown and was a philosopher and theologian who believed in the Spanish conquest and colonisation of the Indians.[7] The only agreement between the two men was over the issues of war against the Indians, which could be justified in certain circumstances, and the work of the missionaries to convert the Indians to Christianity and to worship a Christian god.

The dominant European views about Indians in the sixteenth and seventeenth centuries followed those of Sepúlveda, with many Spanish and French settlers believing that the religious practices of the Indians were inferior to those of the Christian religion.[8] Spanish and French commentators of the time described the cultural and religious customs of the Indians they came across as evil and comparable to the work of the devil although some did describe the complexity of the Indian practices and portrayed Indian peoples in a positive way.[9] Such contrasting viewpoints can be found between accounts written by the Spaniard Juan de Oñate (c.1550–1626), who sometimes describes the complex cultural and spiritual lives of the Indians of the south-west United States, and those of Louis Hennepin (c.1626–1701), a French Recollect Missionary, who believed that the Indians should convert to Christianity.[10]

For centuries after the 'discovery' of the Americas, many European missionaries attempted to convert the Indians to Christianity, away from their traditional belief systems, and while some Indians converted, many more resented the process and rebelled to protect their cultures. In the eighteenth century, an English missionary named David Brainerd (1718–1747) was one among many who preached the gospel to Indians and attempted to turn them against their religious and cultural traditions.[11] However, the successes of the missionaries at turning the Indians towards the Christian faith were mixed. Samson Occom (1723–1792), a Mohegan born at Mohegan, Connecticut, was an Indian in the eighteenth century who was influenced by a Christian educator.[12] In stark contrast, during the nineteenth century, Sagoyewatha (Shay-go-ye-watha) or Red Jacket (c.1756–1830), a Seneca chief, never gave in to the ideas of the missionaries and, indeed, vociferously defended his culture and his people.[13]

SOURCES

Samson Occom: A Short Narrative of My Life, 1768

Provided here are extracts taken from the diary of Samson Occom (1723–1792), a Mohegan born at Mohegan, Connecticut. Occom describes his traditional Indian upbringing and explains his belief in the new Christian religion and his desire to impart it to other Indians.

From my Birth till I received the Christian Religion

I was Born a Heathen and Brought up in Heathenism, till I was between 16 & 17 years of age, at a Place Calld Mohegan, in New London, Connecticut, in New England. My parents Livd a wandering life, for did all the Indians at Mohegan, they Chiefly Depended upon Hunting, Fishing, & Fowling for their Living and had no Connection with the English, excepting to Traffic with them in their small Trifles; and they Strictly maintained and followed their Heathenish Ways, Customs & Religion, though there was Some Preaching among them. Once a Fortnight, in ye Summer Season, a Minister from New London used to come up, and the Indians to attend; not that they regarded the Christian Religion, but they had Blankets given to them every Fall of the Year and for these things they would attend and there was a Sort of School kept, when I was quite young, but I believe there never was one that ever Learnt to read any thing, - and when I was about 10 Years of age there was a man who went about among the Indian Wigwams, and wherever he Could find the Indian Children, would make them read; but the Children Used to take Care to keep out of his way; - and he used to Catch me Some times and make me Say over my Letters; and I believe I learnt Some of them. But this was Soon over too; an all this Time there was not one amongst us, that made a Profession of Christianity -- Neither did we Cultivate our Land, nor kept any Sort of Creatures except Dogs, which we used in Hunting; and we Dwelt in Wigwams. These are a Sort of Tents, Covered with Matts, made of Flags. And to this Time we were unaquainted with the English Tongue in general though there were a few, who understood a little of it.

From the Time of our Reformation till I left Mr. Wheelocks

When I was 16 years of age, we heard a Strange Rumour among the English, that there were Extraordinary Ministers Preaching from Place to Place and a Strange Concern among the White People. This was in the Spring of the Year. But we Saw nothing of these things, till Some Time in the Summer, when Some Ministers began to visit us and Preach the Word of God; and the Common People all Came frequently and exhorted us to the things of God, which it pleased the Lord, as I humbly hope, to Bless and accompany with Divine Influence to the Conviction and Saving Conversion of a Number of us; amongst whom I was one that was Imprest with the things we had heard. These Preachers did not only come to us, but we frequently went to their meetings and Churches. After I was awakened & converted, I went to all the meetings, I could come at; & Continued under Trouble of Mind about 6 months; at which time I began to Learn the English Letters; got me a Primer, and used to go to my English Neighbours frequently for Assistance in Reading, but went to no School. And when I was 17 years of age, I had, as I trust, a Discovery of the way of Salvation through Jesus Christ, and was enabl'd to put my trust in him alone for Life & Salvation. From this Time the Distress and Burden of my mind was removed, and I found Serenity and Pleasure of Soul, in Serving God. By this time I just began to Read in the New Testament without Spelling, - and I had a Stronger Desire Still to Learn to read the Word of God, and at the Same Time had an uncommon Pity and Compassion to my Poor Brethren According to the Flesh. I used to wish I was capable of Instructing my poor Kindred … At this Time my Poor Mother was going to Lebanon, and having had Some Knowledge of Mr. Wheelock and hearing he had a Number of English youth under his Tuition, I had a great Inclination to go to him and be with him a week or a Fortnight, and Desired my Mother to Ask Mr. Wheelock whether he would take me a little while to Instruct me in Reading. Mother did so; and when She Came Back, She Said Mr. Wheelock wanted to See me as Soon as possible … I Spent 4 Years with him…

From the Time I left Mr. Wheelock till I went to Europe

As soon as I left Mr. Wheelock, I endeavoured to find Some Employ among the Indians … and heard a number of our Indians were going to Montauk, on Long Island, and I went with them, and the Indians there were very desirous to have me keep a School amongst them, and I Consented … they had a Minister, one Mr. Horton, the Scotch Society's Missionary … We met together 3 times for Divine Worship every Sabbath and once on every Wednesday evening. I (used) to read the Scriptures to them and used to expound upon Some particular Passages in my own Tongue…

Red Jacket: Speech to a Missionary, 1805

In stark contrast to the conversion of Samson Occom, the extract taken from a conversation between Red Jacket (c.1756–1830), a Seneca chief, diplomat and representative of the Six Nations who negotiated with many US presidents from George Washington to Andrew Jackson, and a missionary reveals the feelings of Red Jacket towards the missionaries and highlights the cultural conflict between the defence of the Seneca way of life and religious conversion. Indeed, Red Jacket explicitly cautions a Christian missionary against the religious conversion of his people.

Friend and Brother! It was the will of the Great Spirit that we should meet together this day. He orders all things and has given us a fine day for our council. He has taken his garment from before the sun, and caused it to shine with brightness upon us…

Brother! Listen to what we say. There was a time when our forefathers owned this great island. Their seats extended from the rising to the setting sun. The Great Spirit had made it for the use of the Indians ... But an evil day came upon us. Your forefathers crossed the great waters, and landed on this island. Their numbers were small. They found friends and not enemies. They told us they had fled their own country for fear of wicked men, and had come here to enjoy their religion. They asked for a small seat. We took pity on them, granted their request, and they sat down amongst us ... The white people had now found our country ... Yet we did not fear them. We took them to be friends. They called us brothers. We believed them, and gave them a large seat. At length their numbers had greatly increased. They wanted more land. They wanted our country ... Wars took place. Indians were hired to fight against Indians, and many of our people were destroyed...

Brother! Our seats were once large, and yours very small. You have now become a great people, and we have scarcely a place left to spread our blankets. You have got our country, but you are not satisfied. You want to force your religion upon us.

Brother! Continue to listen. You say that you are sent to instruct us how to worship the Great Spirit agreeably to his mind; and if we do not take hold of the religion which you white people teach, we shall be unhappy hereafter. You say that you are right, and we are lost. How do you know this to be true? We understand that your religion is written in a book. If it was intended for us as well as for you, why has not the Great Spirit given it to us; and not only to us, but why did he not give to our forefathers knowledge of that book, with the means of understanding it rightly? We only know what you tell us about it. How shall we know when to believe, being so often deceived by the white people?

Brother! You say there is but one way to worship and serve the Great Spirit. If there is but one religion, why do you white people differ so much about it? Why not all agree, as you can all read the book?

Brother! We do not understand these things. We are told that your religion was given to your forefathers and has been handed down from father to son. We also have a religion which was given to our forefathers, and has been handed down to us their children. We worship that way. It teaches us to be thankful for all the favours we receive, to love each other, and to be united. We never quarrel about religion.

Brother! The Great Spirit has made us all. But he has made a great difference between his white and red children. He has given us a different complexion and different customs. To you he has given the arts; to these he has not opened our eyes. We know these things to be true. Since he has made so great a difference between us in other things, why may we not conclude that he has given us a different religion, according to our understanding? The Great Spirit does right. He knows what is best for his children. We are satisfied.

Brother! We do not wish to destroy your religion, or to take it from you. We only want to enjoy our own.

Brother! You say you have not come to get our land or our money, but to enlighten our minds. I will now tell you that I have been at your meetings and saw you collecting money from the meeting. I cannot tell what this money was intended for, but suppose it was for your minister; and if we should conform to your way of thinking, perhaps you may want some from us.

Brother! We are told that you have been preaching to the white people in this place. These people are our neighbours. We are acquainted with them. We will wait a little while, and see what effect your preaching has upon them. If we find it does them good and makes them honest and less disposed to cheat Indians, we will then consider again what you have said.

Brother! You have now heard our answer to your talk, and this is all we have to say at present. As we are going to part, we will come and take you by the hand, and hope the Great Spirit will protect you on your journey, and return you safe to your friends.

Bartolomé de Las Casas: Lobbied for Peace and Indian Freedom, 1550

The following extracts are taken from the debate that took place between Bartolomé de Las Casas (1484–1558) and Juan Ginés de Sepúlveda (1494–1573) in Valladolid, 1550. Las Casas believed Indians were kind, peaceful, and clever, skilled in the arts, had organised religions and beliefs, and that some lived in large and prosperous cities like those of Europe with laws and commerce.

God created these simple people without evil and without guile. They are most obedient and faithful to their natural lords and to the Christians whom they serve. They are most submissive, patient, peaceful and virtuous. Nor are they quarrelsome rancorous, querulous, or vengeful. Moreover they are more delicate than princes and die easily from work or illness. They neither possess nor desire to possess worldly wealth. Surely these people would be the most blessed in the world if only they worshipped the true God.

—Bartolomé de Las Casas, an example of the noble savage

Furthermore, they are so skilled in every mechanical art that with every right they should be set ahead of all the nations of the known world on this score, so very beautiful in their skill and artistry are the things this people produces in the grace of its architecture, its painting, and its needle-work. But Sepulveda despises these mechanical arts, as if these things do not reflect inventiveness, ingenuity, industry, and right reason. For a mechanical art is an operative habit or the intellect … So these men are not stupid … Their skilfully fashioned works of superior refinement awaken the admiration of all nations, because works proclaim a man's talent, for, as the poet says, the work commends the craftsman.

—Bartolomé de Las Casas, defending the Indians

[They have] important kingdoms, large numbers of people who live settled lives in a society, great cities, kings, judges and laws, persons who engage in commerce, buying, selling, lending, and the other contracts of the law of nations, will it not stand proved that the Reverend Doctor Sepulveda has spoken wrongly and viciously against peoples like these, either out of malice or ignorance of Aristotle's teaching, and, therefore, has falsely and perhaps irreparably slandered them before the entire world? From the fact that the Indians are barbarians it does not necessarily follow that they are incapable of government and have to be ruled by others, except to be taught about the Catholic faith and to be admitted to the holy sacraments. They are not ignorant, inhuman, or bestial. Rather, long before they had heard the word Spaniard, they had properly organised states, wisely ordered by excellent laws, religion, and custom. *They cultivated friendship and, bound together in common fellowship, lived in populous cities in which they wisely administered the affairs of both peace and war justly and equitably, truly governed by laws which at very many points surpass ours, and could have won the admiration of the sages of Athens..."*

—Bartolomé de Las Casas, defending the Indians

The Indians are our brothers, and Christ has given his life for them. Why, then, do we persecute them with such inhuman savagery when they do not deserve such treatment? ... [They] will embrace the teaching of the gospel, as I well know, for they are not stupid or barbarous but have a native sincerity and are simple, moderate, and meek, and, finally, such that I do not know whether there is any people readier to receive the gospel. Once they have embraced it, it is marvellous with what piety, eagerness, faith, and charity they obey Christ's precepts and venerate the sacraments. For they are docile and clever, and in their diligence and gifts of nature, they excel most peoples of the known world.

—Bartolomé de Las Casas, imposition of Christianity

Juan Ginés de Sepúlveda: Justified Spanish Conquest and Indian Enslavement, 1550

In these series of extracts taken from the debate between Juan Ginés de Sepúlveda (1494–1573) and Bartolomé de Las Casas (1484–1558) in Valladolid, 1550, Sepúlveda argues that the Indians were cruel and unintelligent and lacked humanity, practised a religion that was wicked, evil and barbarous, lived in constant warfare and ate the flesh of their enemies. Generally, Sepúlveda believed Indians were inferior to the Spanish in every possible way, and because of this, he argued that the Spanish had the inherent right to wage war and acquire Indian lands.

In prudence, talent, virtue, and humanity they are as inferior to the Spaniards as children to adults, women to men, as the wild and cruel to the most meek, as the prodigiously intemperate to the continent and temperate, that I have almost said, as monkeys to men.

—Juan Ginés de Sepúlveda, inferiority of Indians

Now compare their gifts of prudence, talent, magnanimity, temperance, humanity, and religion with those little men (*homunculos*) in whom you will scarcely find traces of humanity; who not only lack culture but do not even know how to write, who keep no records of their history except certain obscure and vague reminiscences of some things put down in certain pictures, and who do not have written laws but only barbarous institutions and customs. But if you deal with the virtues, if you look for temperance or meekness, what can you expect from men who were involved in every kind of intemperance and wicked lust and who used to eat human flesh? And don't think that before the arrival of the Christians they were living in quiet and the Saturnian peace of the poets. On the contrary they were making war continuously and ferociously against each other with such rage that they considered their victory worthless if they did not satisfy their monstrous hunger with the flesh of their enemies, an inhumanity which in them is so much more monstrous since they are so distant from the unconquered and wild Scythians, who also fed on human flesh, for these Indians are so cowardly and timid, that they scarcely withstand the appearance of our soldiers and often many thousands of them have given ground, fleeing like women before a very few Spaniards, who did not even number a hundred.

—Juan Ginés de Sepúlveda, inferiority of Indians

Nothing shows more of the crudity, barbarism, and native slavery of these men than making known their institutions. For homes, some manner of community living, and commerce--which natural necessity demands--what do these prove except that they are not bears or monkeys and that they are not completely devoid of reason? … Shall we doubt that those peoples, so uncivilised, so barbarous, so wicked, contaminated with so many evils and wicked religious practices, have been justly subjugated by an excellent, pious, and most just king, such as was Ferdinand and the Caesar Charles is now, and by a most civilised nation that is outstanding in every kind of virtue?

—Juan Ginés de Sepúlveda, the superiority of the Spanish

The greatest philosophers declare that such wars may be undertaken by a very civilised nation against uncivilised people who are more barbarous than can be imagined, for they are absolutely lacking in any knowledge of letters, do not know the use of money, generally go about naked, even the women, and carry burdens on their shoulders and backs just like beasts for great distances.

The proof of their savage life, similar to that of beasts, may be seen in the execrable and prodigious sacrifices of human victims to their devils; it may also be seen in their eating of human flesh, their burial alive of the living widows of important persons, and in the other crimes condemned by natural law, whose description offends the ears and horrifies the spirit of civilised people. They on the contrary do these terrible things in public and consider them pious acts. The protection of innocent persons from such injurious acts may alone give us the right, already granted by God and nature, to wage war against these barbarians to submit them to Spanish rule.

—Juan Ginés de Sepúlveda, the justification of war

Juan de Oñate: 'Their Religion Consists in Worshipping of Idols', 1599

The following text shows the opinion of Juan de Oñate (c.1550–1626), a Mexican of Spanish ancestry who led an expedition from Mexico into the south-west of the United States and established a Spanish colony in New Mexico, discussing his idea on Indian religious practices. Oñate describes the complexity of the Indian cultural and the spiritual traditions from a compassionate Spanish viewpoint.

The people are as a rule of good disposition, generally of the color of those of New Spain, and almost the same in customs, dress, grinding of meal, food, dances, songs, and in many other respects. This is not true of their languages, which here are numerous and different from those in Mexico. Their religion consists in worshipping of idols, of which they have many; in their temples they worship them in their own way with fire, painted reeds, feathers, and general offerings of almost everything: little animals, birds, vegetables, etc. Their government is one of complete freedom, for although they have some chieftains they obey them badly and in very few matters.

We have seen other nations, such as Querechos or Vaqueros, who live among the Cibola in tents of tanned hides. The Apaches, some of whom we also saw, are extremely numerous. Although I was told that they lived in rancherias, in recent days I have learned that they live in pueblos the same as the people here … They are a people that has not yet publicly rendered obedience to his majesty. … Because of failure to exercise as much caution as was necessary, my maese de campo and twelve companions were killed at a fortress pueblo named Acoma, which must have contained three thousand Indians more or less. In punishment of their wickedness and treason to his majesty … and as a warning to others, I razed and burned their pueblo…

Louis Hennepin: Origins of the Indians from Description of Louisiana

The following extract is taken from the writings of Louis Hennepin (c.1626–1701), a French missionary sent to Canada in 1675 who returned to France in 1681. He discusses the origin and the spiritual connection of the Indians to their environment and describes it as a 'curious story', which he felt proved that they were cursed by his Christian god.

I am no longer surprised at the avowal of our historians, that they cannot tell how the Indian country has been populated, since the inhabitants, who ought to be the best informed, know nothing about it themselves. Besides which, if in Europe, we were like them deprived of writing, and if we had not the use of that ingenious art, which brings the dead back to life, and recalls past times and which preserves for us an eternal memory of all things, we should not be less ignorant then they. It is true that they recount some things about their origin; but when you ask whether what they say about it is true, they answer that they know nothing about it, that they would not assure us of it, and that they believe them to be stories of their old men, to which they do not give much credit. If all North America had been discovered, we might perhaps learn the spot where these persons came over to it, which would contribute not a little to throw light on some points of ancient history.

A rather curious story is related among them. They say that a woman descended from heaven and remained sometime fluttering in the air, unable to find a spot to rest her foot. The fish of the sea, having taken compassion oh her, held a council to deliberate which of them should receive her; the Tortoise presented himself and offered his back above the water. This woman came there to rest and made her abode there. The unclean matter of the sea being gathered around this tortoise, a great extent of land had formed in time, which now constitutes America. But as solitude did not at all please this woman, who grew weary of having no one to converse with, in order to spend her days a little more agreeably than she was doing, a spirit descended from on high, who found her asleep from sorrow. He approached her imperceptibly, and begot by her two sons, who came out of her side. These two children could never, as time went on, agree, because one was a better hunter than the other, every day they had some quarrel with each other, and they came to such a pitch that they could not at all bear one another; especially one who was of an extremely fierce temper, conceived a deadly envy of his brother, whose disposition was completely mild. This one, unable to endure the ill treatment which he continually received, was at last obliged to depart from him and retire to heaven, whence as a mark of his just resentment, he from time to time makes the thunder roar over the head of his unhappy brother. Sometime after the spirit descended again to this woman and had by her a daughter, from whom have come the mighty nation which now occupies one of the biggest parts of the world. There are some other circumstances, which I do not remember, but fabulous as this story is, you can not fail to discern in it some truths. The women's sleep has some analogy with that of Adam; the estrangement of the two brothers bears some resemblance to the irreconcilable hatred which Cain had for Abel, and the thunder pealing from heaven, shows us very clearly the curse which God pronounced upon that merciless fratricide. One might even doubt whether they are not of Jewish origin, because they have many tings in common with them. They make their cabins in the form of a tent like the Jews. They anoint themselves with oil, they are superstitiously attached to dreams, they bewail the dead with lamentations and horrible howlings, women wear mourning for their near relatives for over a year, abstain from dances and feasts, and wear a kind of hood on their head. Usually the father of the deceased takes care of the widow. It seems too that the curse of God has fallen on them, as on the Jews, for they are brutal and extremely stubborn...

David Brainerd: The Life and Diary
of the Rev. David Brainerd, 1744–1746

Here is partial text from the journal of David Brainerd (1718–1747), a missionary who began his work with Indians in New York and worked with Indians in New Jersey and Eastern Pennsylvania until his death in 1747. Brainerd describes his views of the 'inferior' and 'heathen' spiritual existence of the Indians and his limited but at points partially successful attempts at converting some Indians to Christianity.

Lord's day, May 20. [1744] Preached twice to the poor Indians, and enjoyed some freedom in speaking, while I attempted to remove their prejudices against Christianity. My soul longed for assistance from above, all the while; for I saw I had no strength sufficient for that work...

Lord's day, May 27. Visited my Indians in the morning, and attended upon a *funeral* among them; was affected to see their *heathenish practices.* O that they might be 'turned from darkness to light!' Afterwards got a considerable number of them together, and preached to them; and observed them very attentive...

Monday, June 25 ... Had more freedom and fervency in prayer than usual of late; especially longed for the presence of God in my work, and that the poor heathen might be converted. And in evening prayer my faith and hope in God were much raised. *To an eye of reason every thing that respects the conversion of the heathen is as dark as midnight;* and yet I cannot but hope in God for the accomplishment of something glorious among them. My soul longed much for the advancement of the Redeemer's kingdom on earth...

Tuesday, June 26 ... Was busy most of the day in translating prayers into the language of the Delaware Indians ... In prayer my soul was enlarged, and my faith drawn into sensible exercise; was enabled to cry to God for my poor Indians; and though the work of their conversion appeared *impossible with man,* yet *with* God I saw *all things were possible* ... I was much assisted in prayer for dear Christian friends, and for others that I apprehended to be Christless; but was more especially concerned for the poor heathen, and those of my own charge: was enabled to be instant in prayer for them; and hoped that God would bow the heavens and come down for their salvation...

Wednesday, June 27 ... In the afternoon rode several miles to see if I could procure any lands for the poor Indians, that they might live together, and be under better advantages for instruction. While I was riding had a deep sense of the greatness and difficulty of my work; and my soul seemed to rely wholly upon God for success, in the diligent and faithful use of means. Saw, with greatest certainty, that *the arm of the Lord* must be *revealed*, for the help of these poor heathen, if ever they were delivered from the bondage of the powers of darkness ...

Saturday, July 21 ... Towards night in my burden respecting my work among the Indians began to increase much; and was aggravated by hearing sundry things that looked very discouraging; in particular, that they intended to meet together the next day for an idolatrous feast and dance. Then I began to be in anguish: I thought I must in conscience go, and endeavour to break them up; and knew not how to attempt such a thing. However, I withdrew for prayer, hoping for strength from above. And in prayer I was exceedingly enlarged, and my soul was as much drawn out as ever I remember it to have been in my life, or near ... So far as I could judge, I was wholly free from selfish ends in my fervent supplications for the poor Indians. I knew they were met together to worship devils, and not God; and this made me cry earnestly, that God would now appear, and help me in my attempts to break up this idolatrous meeting ... And thus I spent the evening praying incessantly for divine assistance, and that I might not be self-dependent, but still have my whole dependence upon God. What I passed through was remarkable, and indeed inexpressible. All things here below vanished; and there appeared to be nothing of any considerable importance to me, but holiness of heart and life, and the conversion of the heathen to God. All my cares, fears, and desires, which might be said to be of a worldly nature, disappeared; and were, in my esteem, of little more importance than a puff of wind. I exceedingly longed, that God would get to himself a name among the heathen ... While I was asleep, I dreamed of these things; and when I waked, (as I frequently did,) the first thing I thought of was this great work of pleading for God against Satan.

Lord's day, Sept. 2. Was enabled to speak to my poor Indians with much concern and fervency; and I am persuaded God enabled me to exercise faith in him, while I was speaking to them. I perceived that some of them were afraid to hearken to and embrace *Christianity*, lest they should be enchanted and poisoned by some of the *powows*: but I was enabled to plead with them not to fear these; and confiding in God for safety and deliverance, I bid a challenge to all these *powers of darkness*, to do their worst upon *me* first. I told my people I was a *Christian*, and asked them why the *powows* did not bewitch and poison me. I scarcely ever felt more sensible of my own unworthiness, than in this action: I saw, that the honour of God was concerned in the affair...

Saturday, Sept. 14 [1745] ... I could not but hope, that God would bring in these miserable, wicked Indians; though there appeared little human probability of it; for they were then *dancing* and *revelling*, as if possessd by the *devil*. But yet I *hoped*, though *against hope*, that God would be glorified, and that his name would be glorified by these poor Indians...

Monday, Feb. 3. [1746] My spirits were still much sunk with what I heard the day before, of my being suspected to be engaged in the *Pretender's* interest: it grieved me, that after there had been so much evidence of a glorious *work of grace* among these poor Indians, as that the most carnal men could not but take notice of the great *change* made among them ... This put me upon searching whether I had ever dropped any thing inadvertently, that might give *occasion* to any to suspect that I was stirring up the Indians against the English: and could think of nothing, unless it was my attempting sometimes to vindicate the rights of the Indians, and complaining of the horrid practice of making the Indians drunk, and then cheating them out of their lands and other properties: and once, I remembered, I had done this with too much warmth of spirit, which much distressed me; thinking that it might possibly prejudice them against this work of grace, to their everlasting destruction...

Saturday, April 5. [1746] After public worship a number of my dear Christian Indians came to my house; with whom I felt a sweet union of soul. My heart was knit to them; and I cannot say I have felt such a sweet and fervent *love to the brethren* for some time past; and I saw in them appearances of the same love...

CHAPTER THREE
LAND AND THE ENVIRONMENT, 1500s–1810

One of the largest aspects of conflict between Indians and non-Indians revolved around the approaches taken to land and its use and relationship to community. Soon after the landing of Columbus, stark ideological and cultural differences between the European nations, which included England, France and Spain, and the various Indian nations that occupied North America began to appear over the issue of lands. In general, the European ideas about land and the use of lands differed significantly from those of the Indian nations. Whereas many Indian groups had lived on specific lands for generations and developed agricultural, fishing, and hunting and gathering techniques to provide sustenance for their communities without over-exploitation, many of the English, French and Spanish believed that the Indians underused the potential of land or simply were not using it at all. What looked to European eyes as unused land was often land being used differently than how Europeans might use it. For example land left fallow to regenerate or land carefully managed so as to encourage the proliferation of game often looked empty or underutilised. The diversity of Indian use of land was also misunderstood by Europeans. For example, the Eastern Cherokee, who were farmers who planted and harvested different crops, were also hunters and fishermen. Other Indians, such as the Crow, were primarily hunters of game such as bison, deer and elk, whereas the Chipewyan were hunters who sometimes also fished.[1] Moreover, Indian lands were generally held in different ways, from lands in common for the benefit of a community to Indian personal property or certain kin groups having more claims to particular pieces of land.[2] To many Indians, land was not a commodity to be bought, sold, owned or fixed with territorial boundaries. However, many Europeans believed that land was there to be owned and divided into separate pieces for personal use and traded for profit to create public and private wealth. A fundamental cultural incomprehension played an important part in the volatile relationship between European nations and most of the Indian nations in North America.

In the south-east and south-west of North America, the Spanish were deliberate and quite often brutal in securing land from indigenous peoples. During the sixteenth century, they used the Requerimiento, a written document that claimed the 'discovered' lands in the name of Spanish royalty. It was read aloud to all of the Indians present before land was seized.[3] However, the Requerimiento did not have anything to do with winning the consent of Indian peoples to Spanish acquisition of their land. Instead, it was a document read in a language that they did not understand based primarily on ideas of conquest and subjugation.[4]

During the sixteenth and seventeenth centuries, England and France used the concept of 'discovery' to justify the legal acquisition of Indian lands and to disregard the ancient rights and claims of indigenous peoples to their homelands.[5] Englishmen such as George Peckham (sixteenth century) offered advice on the correct practices for the English to take with the natives.[6] An early Indian response to English colonisation, and in particular the way that the English used the principle of discovery to establish settlements, was articulated by William Apes (c.1798–1836), a Pequot, in his autobiography of 1836.[7] After the first English settlement was established at Jamestown, Virginia, in 1607, the way in which the English acquisitioned Indian lands concerned Powhatan (c.1550–1618), leader of the Powhatan Indians of Virginia and ruler of most of the tribes in the Chesapeake Bay area. Powhatan's relationship with the English was ambivalent; on occasions, Powhatan ordered attacks on the English and at other times he traded food for English goods. Finally, as tensions grew between the English settlers and Powhatan, war broke out in 1609.[8] Like the English, the French used the principles of discovery to acquire Indian lands in the north-east of North America. From the sixteenth century, French explorers, traders and priests set out to establish an empire within North America built on alliances with the Indians, such as the Algonquins and Hurons. They traded with groups such as the Iroquois from the seventeenth century for furs.[9] Missionaries such as Louis Hennepin (c.1626–1701), sent to Canada in 1675, used Christianity and the principles of discovery to justify the occupation of Indian lands in the name of the French king.[10]

Indian communities had a diverse and varying approach to land use.[11] In many instances, Indian lands were held in common and therefore, even though Indian peoples fought at points over territory and resources, land was not always owned or divided up along specific and absolute boundaries. The general ideological differences between the two worlds of the Europeans and the Indians is symbolised by the contrast between the experiences of Chrestien LeClerq (c.1630–1695), a Recollect missionary from France, and the Micmac of eastern Canada. The differences between the French and the Micmac revolved around the transient nature of the Micmac culture, which relied on hunting and gathering and fishing, in accordance with the spirits of their ancestors and the French, who lived in homes on lands with fixed boundaries.[12]

Many Europeans viewed Indian lands as ripe and fertile and an ideal economic tool for exploitation, profit and a source of revenue and wealth for their nations. The French were one such nation that saw vast economic opportunity in the fertility of the Indians lands in the eastern parts of North America. Samuel de Champlain (c.1570–1635) was one French explorer who first travelled to North America at the beginning of the seventeenth century and advocated further French exploration and expansion within North America in order to benefit and bring added wealth to France.[13] This desire for lands and profit also led to colonial wars between the European powers themselves. In contrast to the position of many Indians who took foods in keeping with the balance of the environment, many non-Indian traders and land speculators took an abundance of materials, extracting resources from North America in a mercantilist fashion so as to bring wealth directly back to their home nation. The actions of the English during the seventeenth century were sometimes based around greed and the over-exploitation of the environment. The relationship between various Indian nations, such as the Pequot, and the English during the early seventeenth century became hostile after large numbers of English settlers began to arrive on and occupy Pequot lands, stripped the Pequot lands of game and foods and were dishonest in their trade dealings with the Pequot.[14] Tensions between the Pequot and the English led to war in 1637 and soon after, the Pequot were annihilated by a pugnacious English force. Following the Pequot War, the Narragansett, who had sided with the English in their war with the Pequot, soon began to view the English with disdain and attempted to build a united Indian force to contend with the military strength of the English. Miantonomo (c.1565–1643), chief of the Narragansett, recognised the problems inflicted on the Narragansett and other Indians by the English and, in 1642, attempted to build an alliance between the Indians of the north-east to stop the destruction of the Indian environment by the English colonists.[15]

The encroachment of diverse European settlements on Indian lands and the rate of Indian land loss increased throughout the eighteenth century and early nineteenth century and in response, many Indians fought and died to end the flow of European advancement. By the end of the eighteenth century, many Indian nations had lost millions of acres of homelands and the patterns of land use for food and support, upon which many Indians relied, had dramatically changed. The loss of Indian lands was rarely equitable. Many non-Indian speculators, traders and settlers employed methods of intimidation, bribery and chicanery as well as the political tool of the treaty, to precipitate the loss of Indian lands. This seismic shift had caused many Indian lives and cultures to move away from their traditions and history and as a direct result, a movement grew that called on Indian peoples to return to traditional ways of life. During the eighteenth century, the English and French had dramatically affected the practices of the Delaware of the north-east and the Indians of the Ohio Valley, and in response in 1762, Neolin, an eighteenth-century prophet of the Delaware Indians, called for the end of Indian reliance on English and French goods and a return to past Indian practices.[16] The message preached by Neolin resurfaced nearly fifty years later with groups of Indians in the Ohio Valley, led by Tecumseh (1768–1813), a Shawnee chief, calling for the end of non-Indian encroachment on Indian lands. Tensions over Indian land cessations had been building between the Indians of the Ohio Valley and the United States, and the actions of William Henry Harrison, governor of the Indiana Territory, who negotiated treaties with the Delaware, Miami, Kaskaskia, and Potawatomi, led to millions of acres of Indian lands being illegally ceded to non-Indians.[17] These actions infuriated Tecumseh and during the early nineteenth century, he called for the formation of a confederacy of Indians west of the Appalachian Mountains to form a stronger military threat against the Americans. However, this confederation could not prevent the continuation of non-Indian settlements and the spread of the American nation.

Progressive increases in the population and settlements of non-Indians as they gradually spread west dramatically affected most Indian cultures and environments and in response, groups of Indians joined forces and attempted to repel non-Indian influence. These spiritual and political instances of resistance were the precursor of other pan-tribal organizations striving for Indian autonomy in the late nineteenth and twentieth centuries.

SOURCES

Powhatan to John Smith, 1609

Provided here is a speech made by Powhatan (c.1550–1618), leader of the Powhatan Indians of Virginia and ruler of most of the tribes in the Chesapeake Bay area, to Captain John Smith. The speech was taken from the recollections of John Smith published in 1612. Here Powhatan outlines his concerns about the prospects of war and the invasion of his and the Powhatan Indians' spiritual homelands by the English.

Captaine Smith, you may understand that I having seene the death of all my people thrice, and not any one living of these three generations but my selfe; I know the difference of Peace and Warre better than any in my Country. But now I am old and ere long must die, my brethren, namely Opitchapam, Opechancanough, and Kekataugh, my two sisters, and their two daughters, are distinctly each others successors. I wish their experience no lesse then mine, and your love to them no lesse then mine to you. But this bruit from Nandsamund, that you are come to destroy my Country, so much affrighteth all my people as they dare not visit you. What will it availe you to take that by force you may quickly have by love, or to destroy them that provide you food. What can you get by warre, when we can hide our provisions and fly to the woods? whereby you must famish by wronging us your friends. And why are you thus jealous of our loves seeing us unarmed, and both doe, and are willing still to feede you, with that you cannot get but by our labours? Thinke you I am so simple, not to know it is better to eate good meate, lye well, and sleepe quietly with my women and children, laugh and be merry with you, have copper, hatchets, or what I want being your friend: then be forced to flie from all, to lie cold in the woods, feede upon Acornes, rootes, and such trash, and be so hunted by you, that I can neither rest, eate, nor sleepe; but my tyred men must watch, and if a twig but breake, every one cryeth there commeth Captaine Smith: then must I fly I know not whether: and thus with miserable feare, end my miserable life, leaving my pleasures to such youths as you, which through your rash unadvisednesse may quickly as miserably end, for want of that, you never know where to finde. Let this therefore assure you of our loves, and every yeare our friendly trade shall furnish you with Corne; and now also, if you would come in friendly manner to see us, and not thus with your guns and swords as to invade your foes.

William Apes: Relations with the English, 1836

The following document is taken from the autobiography of William Apes (c.1798–1836), a Pequot and Methodist Preacher from Connecticut who was believed to be the great-great-great grandson of King Philip, written in 1836.

It speaks of the uneasy relationship between the Indians and the English settlers and describes the way the English occupied and settled Indian lands.

December, 1620, the Pilgrims landed at Plymouth, and without asking liberty from anyone, they possessed themselves of a portion of the country, and built themselves houses, and then made a treaty and commanded them to accede to it ... And yet for their kindness and resignation towards the whites, they were called savages, and made by God on purpose for them to destroy...

The next we present before you are things very appalling. We turn our attention to dates, 1623, January and March, when Mr. Weston Colony, came very near to starving to death; some of them were obliged to hire themselves to the Indians, to become their servants in order that they might live. Their principal work was to bring wood and water; but not being contented with this, many of the white sought to steal the Indians' corn; and because the Indians complained of it, and through their complaint, some one of their number being punished, as they say, to appease the savages. Now let us see who the greatest savages were; the person that stole the corn was a stout athletic man, and because of this, they wished to spare him, and take an old man who was lame and sickly ... and because they thought he would not be of so much use to them, he was, although innocent of any crime, hung in his stead ... Another act of humanity for Christians, as they call themselves, that one Capt. Standish, gathering some fruit and provisions, goes forward with a black and hypocritical heart, and pretends to prepare a feast for the Indians; and when they sit down to eat, they seize the Indians' knives hanging around their necks, and stab them in the heart...

The Pilgrims promised to deliver up every transgressor of the Indian treaty, to them, to be punished according to their laws, and the Indians were to do likewise. Now it appears that an Indian had committed treason, by conspiring against the king's life, which is punishable with death ... and the Pilgrims refused to give him, although by their oath of alliance they had promised to do so...

In this history of Massasoit [king] we find that his own head men were not satisfied with the Pilgrims; that they looked upon them to be intruders, and had a wish to expel those intruders out of their coast. A false report was made respecting one Tisquantum, that he was murdered by an Indian ... Upon this news, one Standish, a vile and malicious fellow, took fourteen of his lewd Pilgrims with him ... at midnight ... At that late hour of the night, meeting at house in the wilderness, whose inmates heard--Move not, upon the peril of your life. At the same time some of the females were so frightened, that some of them undertook to make their escape, upon which they were fired upon ... These Indians had not done one single wrong act to the whites, but were as innocent of any crime, as any beings in the world. But if the real suffers say one word, they are denounced, as being wild and savage beasts...

We might suppose that meek Christians had better gods and weapons than cannon. But let us again review their weapons to civilize the nations of this soil. What were they: rum and powder, and ball, together with all the diseases, such as the small pox, and every other disease imaginable; and in this way sweep of thousands and tens of thousands.

Miantonomo's Call for Indian Unity, 1642

Miantonomo (c.1565–1643), chief of the Narragansett who fought against the Pequot in favour of the English colonies in the Pequot War of 1637, highlights the differences between the lives of the Narragansett before and after the arrival of the English.

Brothers, we must be as one as the English are, or we shall all be destroyed. You know our fathers had plenty of deer and skins and our plains were full of game and turkeys, and our coves and rivers were full of fish.

But, brothers, since these Englishmen have seized our country, they have cut down the grass with scythes, and the trees with axes. Their cows and horses eat up the grass, and their hogs spoil our bed of clams; and finally we shall all starve to death; therefore, stand not in your own light, I ask you, but resolve to act like men. All the sachems both to the east and the west have joined with us, and we are resolved to fall upon them at a day appointed, and therefore I come secretly to you, cause you can persuade your Indians to do what you will.

Chrestien Le Clerq: Micmac Response to the French People, c.1676–1677

The contrast between the lives of the Micmac Indians and the French is brought to life by Chrestien Le Clerq (c.1630–1695), a Recollect missionary to the Micmac of the Gaspe Peninsula in south-eastern Canada, who translated and recorded a message given by a Micmac elder to a group of French settlers. The Micmac elder defends the transient nature of Micmac life, as hunters and gatherers and fishermen, and the belief that the environment and lands as a whole were there to accommodate the Micmac people. Indeed, he describes the happiness and contentedness of the Micmac people who lived in accordance with the spirits of their ancestors and then contrasts this lifestyle with that of the French. He criticises them for their reliance on fixed land boundaries and for their fixation upon the pleasures of over-consumption.

I am greatly astonished that the French have so little cleverness, as they seem to exhibit in the matter of which thou hast just told me on their behalf, in the effort to persuade us to convert our poles, our barks, and our wigwams into those houses of stone and of wood which are tall and lofty, according to their account, as these trees. Very well! But why now, do men of five to six feet in height need houses which are sixty to eighty? For, in fact, as thou knowest very well thyself. Patriarch – do we not find in our own all the conveniences and the advantages that you have with yours, such as reposing, drinking, sleeping, eating, and amusing ourselves with our friends when we wish? This is not all, my brother, hast thou as much ingenuity and cleverness as the Indians, who carry their houses and their wigwams with them so they may lodge wheresoever they please, independently of any seignior whatsoever? Thou are not as bold nor as stout as we, because when thou goest on a voyage thou canst not carry upon thy shoulders thy buildings and thy edifices. Therefore it is necessary that thou preparest as many lodgings as thou makest changes of residence, or else thou lodgest in a hired house which does not belong to thee. As for us, we find ourselves secure from all these inconveniences, and we can always say, more truly than thou, that we are at home everywhere, because we set up our wigwams with ease wheresoever we go, and without asking permission of anybody. Thou reproachest us, very inappropriately, that our country is a little hell in contrast with France, which thou comparest to a terrestrial paradise, inasmuch as it yields thee, so thou sayest, every kind of provision in abundance. Thou sayest of us also that we are the most miserable and unhappy of all men, living without religion, without manners, without honour, without social order, and, in a word, without any rules, like the beasts in our woods and our forests, lacking bread, wine, and a thousand other comforts which thou hast in superfluity in Europe. Well, my brother, if thou dost not yet know the real feelings which our Indians have towards thy country and towards all thy nation, it is proper that I inform thee at once. I beg thee now to believe that, all miserable as we seem in thine eyes, we consider ourselves nevertheless much happier than thou in this, that we are very content with the little that we have; and believe also once for all, I pray, that thou deceivest thyself greatly if thou thinkest to persuade us that thy country is better than ours. For if France, as thou sayest, is a little terrestrial paradise, art thou sensible to leave it? And why abandon wives, children, relatives, and friends? Why risk thy life and thy property every year, and why venture thyself with such risk, in any season whatsoever, to the storms and tempests of the sea in order to come to a strange and barbarous country which thou considerest the poorest and least fortunate of the world? Besides, since we are wholly convinced of the contrary, we scarcely take the trouble to go to France, because we fear, with good reason, lest we find little satisfaction there, seeing, in our own experience, that those who are natives thereof leave it every year in order to enrich themselves on our shores. We believe, further, that you are also incomparably poorer than we, and that you are only simple journeymen, valets, servants, and slaves, all masters and grand captains though you may appear, seeing that you glory in our old rags and in our miserable suits of beaver which can no longer be of use to us, and that you find among us, in the fishery for cod which you make in these parts, the wherewithal to comfort your misery and the poverty which oppresses you. As to us, we find all our riches and all our conveniences among ourselves, without trouble and without exposing our lives to the dangers in which you find yourselves constantly through your long voyages. And, whilst feeling compassion for you in the sweetness of our repose, we wonder at the anxieties and cares which you give yourselves night and day in order to load your ship. We see also that all your people live, as a rule, only upon cod which you catch among us. It is everlastingly nothing but cod—cod in the morning, cod at midday, cod at evening, and always cod, until things come to such a pass that if you wish some good morsels, it is at our expense; and you are obliged to have recourse to the Indians, whom you despise so much, and to beg them to go a-hunting that you may be regaled. Now tell me this one little thing, if thou hast any sense: Which of these two is the wisest and happiest—he who labours without ceasing and only obtains, and that with great trouble, enough to live on, or he who rests in comfort and finds all that he needs in the pleasure of hunting and fishing? It is true, that we have not always had the use of bread and of wine which your France produces; but, in fact, before the arrival of the French in these parts, did not the Gaspesians live much longer than now? And if we have not any longer among us any of those old men of a hundred and thirty to forty years, it is only because we are gradually adopting your manner of living, for experience is making it very plain that those of us live longest who, despising your bread, your wine, and your brandy, are content with their natural food of beaver, of moose, of waterfowl, and fish, in accord with the custom of our ancestors and of all the Gaspesian nation. Learn now, my brother, once for all, because I must open to thee my heart: there is no Indian who does not consider himself infinitely more happy and more powerful than the French.

Pontiac's Prophet Neolin Speaks Out, 1762

In the following text, Neolin contrasts the lives of the Indians before and after the settlement of the English. He calls on all Indians to fight and drive the English away.

I am the maker of Heaven and Earth, the trees, lakes, rivers, men, and all that thou seest ... and because I love you, you must do my will; you must avoid also that which I hate; I hate you to drink as you do, until you lose your reason; I wish you not to fight one another...

The land on which you are, I have made for you, not for others: wherefore do you suffer the whites to dwell upon your lands? Can you not do without them? ... Before those whom you call your [white] brothers had arrived, did not your bow and arrow maintain you? You needed neither gun, powder, nor any other object. The flesh of animals was your food, their skins your raiment. But when I saw you inclined to evil, I removed the animals into the depths of the forests...

Drive from your lands those dogs in red clothing [the British]; they are only an injury to you. When you want anything, apply to me ... Do not sell to your brothers that which I have placed on earth as food ... Become good and you shall want for nothing.

Tecumseh Speaks Out against Land Cessations, 1810

In a reaction to the build-up of conflict between the United States and the Indians of the Ohio Valley, in this document, Tecumseh (1768–1813), a Shawnee chief, calls for the end of non-Indian encroachment on Indian lands and for the unification of all Indians to fight non-Indian settlement. In addition, Tecumseh outlines his thoughts about Indian claims to land.

…It is true I am a Shawnee. My forefathers were warriors. Their son is a warrior. From them I only take my existence; from my tribe I take nothing. I am the maker of my own fortune; and oh! that I could make that of my red people, and of my country, as great as the conceptions of my mind, when I think of the Spirit that rules the universe. I would not then come to Governor Harrison, to ask him to tear the treaty, and to obliterate the landmark; but I would say to him, Sir, you have liberty to return to your own country. The being within, communing with the past ages, tells me, that once, nor until lately, there was no white man on this continent. That it then all belonged to red men, children of the same parents, placed on it by the Great Spirit that made them, to keep it, to traverse it, to enjoy its production, and to fill it with the same race. Once a happy race. Since made miserable by the white people, who are never contented, but always encroaching. The way, and the only way to check and stop this evil, is, for all the red men to unite in claiming a common and equal right in the land, as it was at first, and should be yet; for it never was divided, but belongs to all, for the use of each. That no part has a right to sell, even to each other, much less to strangers; those who want all, and will not do with less. The white people have no right to take the land from the Indians, because they had it first; it is theirs. They may sell, but all must join. Any sale not made by all is not valid. The late sale is bad. It was made by a part only. Part do not know how to sell. It requires all to make a bargain for all. All red men have equal rights to the unoccupied land. The right of occupancy is as good in one place as in another. There cannot be two occupations in the same place. The first excludes all others. It is not so in hunting or travelling; for there the same ground will serve many, as they may follow each other all day; but the camp is stationary, and that is occupancy. It belongs to the first who sits down on his blanket or skins, which he has thrown upon the ground, and till he leaves it no other has a right.

Spain: Requerimiento Written by the Jurist Palacios Rubio of the Council of Castile, 1510

The Requerimiento, which appears in the following text, was a legal document formulated by legal scholar Juan López Palacios Rubio. It offered a choice to the Indians to consent to the Spanish belief that the lands of the Americas were donated to the Pope and the King of Spain by God or face the punishment of invasion and slavery. The document justified the acquisition of the Americas because of the inherent supremacy of the Christian religion over all others.

On the part of the King, Don Fernando, and of Doña Juana, his daughter, Queen of Castile and León, subduers of the barbarous nations, we their servants notify and make known to you, as best we can, that the Lord our God, Living and Eternal, created the Heaven and the Earth, and one man and one woman, of whom you and we, all the men of the world, were and are descendants, and all those who came after us. But, on account of the multitude which has sprung from this man and woman in the five thousand years since the world was created, it was necessary that some men should go one way and some another, and that they should be divided into many kingdoms and provinces, for in one alone they could not be sustained.

Of all these nations God our Lord gave charge to one man, called St. Peter, that he should be Lord and Superior of all the men in the world, that all should obey him, and that he should be the head of the whole human race, wherever men should live, and under whatever law, sect, or belief they should be; and he gave him the world for his kingdom and jurisdiction.

And he commanded him to place his seat in Rome, as the spot most fitting to rule the world from; but also he permitted him to have his seat in any other part of the world, and to judge and govern all Christians, Moors, Jews, Gentiles, and all other sects. This man was called Pope, as if to say, Admirable Great Father and Governor of men…

One of these Pontiffs, who succeeded that St. Peter as Lord of the world, in the dignity and seat which I have before mentioned, made donation of these isles and Tierra-firme to the aforesaid King and Queen and to their successors, our lords, with all that there are in these territories, as is contained in certain writings which passed upon the subject as aforesaid, which you can see if you wish.

So their Highnesses are kings and lords of these islands and land of Tierra-firme by virtue of this donation: and some islands, and indeed almost all those to whom this has been notified, have received and served their Highnesses, as lords and kings, in the way that subjects ought to do, with good will, without any resistance, immediately, without delay, when they were informed of the aforesaid facts. And also they received and obeyed the priests whom their Highnesses sent to preach to them and to teach them our Holy Faith; and all these, of their own free will, without any reward or condition, have become Christians, and are so, and their Highnesses have joyfully and benignantly received them, and also have commanded them to be treated as their subjects and vassals; and you too are held and obliged to do the same. Wherefore, as best we can, we ask and require you that you consider what we have said to you, and that you take the time that shall be necessary to understand and deliberate upon it, and that you acknowledge the Church as the Ruler and Superior of the whole world, and the high priest called Pope, and in his name the King and Queen Doña Juana our lords, in his place, as superiors and lords and kings of these islands and this Tierra-firme by virtue of the said donation, and that you consent and give place that these religious fathers should declare and preach to you the aforesaid.

If you do so, you will do well, and that which you are obliged to do to their Highnesses, and we in their name shall receive you in all love and charity, and shall leave you, your wives, and your children, and your lands, free without servitude, that you may do with them and with yourselves freely that which you like and think best, and they shall not compel you to turn Christians, unless you yourselves, when informed of the truth, should wish to be converted to our Holy Catholic Faith, as almost all the inhabitants of the rest of the islands have done. And, besides this, their Highnesses award you many privileges and exemptions and will grant you many benefits.

But, if you do not do this, and maliciously make delay in it, I certify to you that, with the help of God, we shall powerfully enter into your country, and shall make war against you in all ways and manners that we can, and shall subject you to the yoke and obedience of the Church and of their Highnesses; we shall take you and your wives and your children, and shall make slaves of them, and as such shall sell and dispose of them as their Highnesses may command; and we shall take away your goods, and shall do you all the mischief and damage that we can, as to vassals who do not obey, and refuse to receive their lord, and resist and contradict him; and we protest that the deaths and losses which shall accrue from this are your fault, and not that of their Highnesses, or ours, nor of these cavaliers who come with us. And that we have said this to you and made this Requisition, we request the notary here present to give us his testimony in writing, and we ask the rest who are present that they should be witnesses of this Requisition.

England: George Peckham, a True Report of the Late Discoveries, 1584

In the text that follows, George Peckham, a prominent Catholic nobleman, offers advice to English colonists about the correct practices to pursue with the natives after the discovery of their lands.

The Second chapter showeth that it is lawful and necessary to trade and traffic with the savages, and to plant in their countries…

They should first well and strongly fortify themselves, which being done, then by all fair speeches, and every other good means of persuasion, to seek to take away all occasions of offense. As letting them to understand, how they came not to their hurt, but for their good, and to no other end, but to dwell peaceably among them, and to trade with them for their own commodity, without molesting or grieving them any way, which must not be done by words only, but also by deeds…

For albeit as yet the Christians are not so thoroughly furnished with the perfectness of their language, either to express their minds to them, or again to conceive the savages intent; yet for the present opportunity, such policy may be used by friendly signs, and courteous tokens towards them, as the savages may easily perceive were their senses never so gross an assured friendship to be offered them, and that they are encountered with such a nation, as brings them benefit, commodity, peace, tranquility, and safety. To further this, and to accomplish it in deeds, there must be presented unto them gratis, some kinds of our petty merchandises and trifles: as looking glasses, bells, beads, bracelets, chains, or collars of bugle, crystal, amber, jet, or glass, etc. For such be the things, though to us of small value, yet accounted by them of high price and estimation, and soonest will induce their barbarous natures to a liking and mutual society with us.

...For it appeareth ... that the savages generally for the most part are at continual wars with their next adjoining neighbors, and especially the cannibals, being a cruel kind of people, whose food is man's flesh, and have teeth like dogs, and do pursue them with ravenous minds, to eat their flesh, and devour them. And it is not to be doubted, but that the Christians may in this case justly and lawfully aid the savages against the cannibals...

But if after these good and fair means used, the savages nevertheless will not be herewithal satisfied, but barbarously will go about to practice violence either in repelling the Christians from their ports and safe landings, or in withstanding them afterwards to enjoy the rights for which both painfully and lawfully they have adventured themselves thither: then in such a case I hold it no breach of equity for the Christians to defend themselves, to pursue revenge with force, and to do whatsoever is necessary for the attaining of their safety ... Wherein if also they shall not be suffered in reasonable quietness to continue, there is no bar (as I judge) but that in stout assemblies the Christians may issue out, and by strong hand pursue their enemies, subdue them, take possession of their towns, cities, or villages, and (in avoiding murderous tyranny) to use the law of arms, as in like case among all nations at this day is used. And most especially to the end they may with security hold their lawful possession...

France: Samuel de Champlain, 'The Voyages of 1604–1607'

In this extract, Samuel de Champlain (c.1570–1635), a French explorer who first travelled to North America in 1603 and led an expedition to establish a trading post in Port Royal, Nova Scotia in 1604, outlines the problems encountered by the first French settlers in North America. He justifies French exploration on the basis of the vast amount of profit available from Indian lands.

...So many voyages and discoveries without result, and attended with so much hardship and expense, have caused us French in late years to attempt a permanent settlement in those lands which we call New France ... These considerations had induced the Marquis de la Roche, in 1598, to take a commission from the king for making a settlement in the above region. With this object, he landed men and supplies on Sable Island; but, as the conditions which had been accorded to him by his Majesty were not fulfilled, he was obliged to abandon his undertaking, and leave his men there…

…notwithstanding all these accidents and disappointments, Sieur de Monts desired to attempt what had been given up in despair, and requested a commission for this purpose of his Majesty … He proposed to his Majesty a means for covering these expenses, without drawing any thing from the royal revenues; viz., by granting to him the monopoly of the fur-trade in this land. This having been granted to him, he made great and excessive outlays, and carried out with him a large number of men of various vocations. Upon his arrival, he caused the necessary number of habitations for his followers to be constructed…

But since a report had been made to the king on the fertility of the soil by him … his Majesty directed Sieur de Monts to make a new outfit, and send men to continue what he had commenced. This he did. And, in view of the uncertainty of his commission, he chose a new spot for his settlement, in order to deprive jealous persons of any such distrust as they had previously conceived. He was also influenced by the hope of greater advantages in case of settling in the interior, where the people are civilised, and where it is easier to plant the Christian faith and establish such order as is necessary for the protection of a country, than along the seashore, where the savages generally dwell. From this course, he believed the king would derive an inestimable profit; for it is easy to suppose that Europeans will seek out this advantage rather than those of a jealous and intractable disposition to be found on the shores, and the barbarous tribes…

F. Louis Hennepin: Letter to King Louis XIV, from Description to Louisiana

The following text is a letter written by Louis Hennepin (c.1626–1701), a recollect missionary sent to Canada in 1675 and author of 'Description of Louisiana' (1683), to the King of France, in which he discusses the discovery and occupation of Indian lands, named Louisiana after King Louis XIV, and the way Christianity was used to overcome the hostility of the Indians.

Sire:

I never should have ventured to take the liberty of offering to your Majesty the Relation of a new Discovery which the Sieur de la Salle, Governor of Fort Frontenac, my companions and myself, have just made south-west of New France, had it not been undertaken by your orders, and had not the glory of obeying so glorious a Monarch, in an employment having in view the conversion of the heathen, led me into this enterprise.

It is in this thought, Sire, that I undertook so long and so painful a voyage, without fearing the greatest dangers. I even venture to assure your Majesty, that the bloody death of one of my Recollect companions, massacred by those savages, a captivity of eight months in which I have seen my life cruelly exposed, could not weaken my courage, having always made it a consolation amid my hardships, to labour for a God, whom I wished to see known and adored by these nations, and for a King whose glory and whose virtues are unbounded.

It is clear, Sire, that as soon as we have been able to tame them and win their friendship, the partial account we have given them of your Most Christian Majesty's heroic virtues, your surprising actions in your conquests, the happiness and love of your subjects, has inclined them to receive more readily the principles of Gospel truths and to reverence the cross which we have carved on trees above your Arms, as a mark of the continual protection which you give the Christian religion, and to make them remember the principles which we have happily taught them.

We have given the name of Louisiana to this great Discovery, being persuaded that your Majesty would not disapprove that a part of the earth watered by a river more than eight hundred leagues in length, and much greater than Europe, which we may call the Delight of America and which is capable of forming a great Empire, should henceforth be known under the august name of Louis, that it may thereby have some show of right to aspire to the honour of your protection, and hope for the advantage of belonging to you.

It seems, Sire, that God has destined you to be its Master, by the happy correspondence that there is between your glorious name and the Sun, which they call Louis in their language, and to which in token of their respect and adoration, they extend their pipe before smoking, with these words: Tchendiouba Louis, that is to say "Smoke O Sun." Thus your Majesty's name is every moment on their lips...

After that, Sire, no one will doubt that it is a secret mystery of Providence which has reserved to your care and your piety, the glory of causing the Light of Faith to be borne to these blind ones, and of drawing them from the darkness in which they would always have lived, had not your Majesty, more devoted to the service of God and religion than to the government of your States, honoured us with this pious task, while you labour successfully for the destruction of heresy.

I implore of heaven, Sire, that the happiness which attends the justice of your actions, may crown such noble, grand and holy undertakings...

CHAPTER FOUR
WAR AND REVOLUTION, 1675–1800s

The period between 1675 and the 1800s was defined by both episodes of conflict and episodes of co-operation between groups of Indians and between competing non-Indian powers (including England, France, Holland, Spain and the newly formed United States). Generally, European nations had geographic strongholds that were situated in places with an abundance of water, such as alongside rivers or on the coasts. By the early eighteenth century, Spain controlled modern-day Florida, the south-west and parts of the west coast, England held the eastern seaboard and France had authority over the Mississippi Valley and Canada.[1] However, the European competition for land and resources in a continent occupied by numerous Indian nations led to a number of bloody battles and wars. Indians fought strategically to protect their interests relative to competing non-Indians and for a time held the balance of power on American land, but towards the early 1800s, the conflicts they were involved in increasingly became battles of survival for the Indian nations to the east of the Mississippi River. Conflict was not exclusively between Indians and non-Indians; conflict between Indian nations themselves resulted from the competition for resources and territory caused by progressive non-Indian encroachment upon Indian lands.

During the late seventeenth and early eighteenth century, the relationships of Spain and France with various groups of Indians in North America contrasted significantly. Relations between the Spaniards and the Indians were generally defined by sustained periods of conflict and occasional co-operation.[2] One of the most famous episodes of conflict took place between the Spanish and the Pueblo in the south-west of modern-day America. For decades, the Spanish had appropriated Pueblo lands, persecuted the religious practices of the Pueblo, forced them to adopt Christianity and brought diseases that ravaged the population. Then in 1680, numerous Pueblo villages successfully united to overthrow the Spanish and ousted them from the lands of the Pueblo for a number of years.[3] In contrast, the French generally co-operated and relied on mutual agreements with the Indians of north-eastern modern-day America, mainly because relations revolved around the fur-trade for which the French needed Indian expertise and knowledge. Furthermore, French alliances with various groups of Indians were the most important military assets they possessed in North America. The French ensured the support of some Indian groups by living in Indian communities, using diplomacy and learning Indian ways.[4] These practices strengthened the French against attacks by other Indian groups. However, relations were not always smooth. During the late seventeenth century, the French invaded Iroquois lands on numerous occasions and during the early eighteenth century, the French waged war against the Chickasaws, the Natchez and the Fox.[5]

In 1620, the English established a permanent settlement in Cape Cod and over two centuries, relations with the Indians of the eastern seaboard gradually moved from co-operation and trust to suspicion and conflict. There were many wars fought between the English and the Indians, and one of the most famous was King Philip's War between 1675 and 1676. English settlers had encroached on Indian lands, such as those of the Wampanoag, for a number of years and claimed authority over them. However, the Indians took exception to this practice and their resentment of the English increased. In 1675, Metacomet, called King Philip by the English, formed a military alliance between the Wampanoag and other Indian groups of the north-east, and war began.[6] During the war, the English government set about finding the causes and the problems that had led them into conflict with the Indians and despatched Edmund Randolph (1632–1703), an Englishman, to find some answers.[7] Despite the successes of the Indians in some battles, in 1676, this destructive war ended with Indian defeat.

Nearly a century later, the British once again clashed with groups of Indians in Pontiac's War, also known as Pontiac's Rebellion of 1763. After the end of the Seven Years War (1756–1763), also termed the French and Indian War, France ceded Canada and much of Ohio and the Mississippi Valley to the British in the Peace of Paris of 1763. However, from the European peace, conflict soon erupted between the British and the Indians from the Ohio Valley and the Great Lakes region. The Indians were suspicious of the British, and because the British treatment of them contrasted significantly with the practices of diplomacy and trade of their predecessors, the Indians feared the loss of more lands and the erosion of their cultures.[8] Pontiac (1720–1769), an Ottawa war chief, feared that the Indians were being influenced by European culture and were far too dependent on European goods, and in order to counteract the British influence, during the months of May and June in 1763, he led a confederation of Indians and carried out attacks on British military posts throughout the Great Lakes region and the Ohio Valley.[9] In late May of 1763, the Indian groups besieged Fort Pitt in western Pennsylvania. In response to the Indian attacks, the British used traditional military methods and notoriously other more sinister tools of war, such as smallpox-infested blankets. One person situated and in command of the militia at Fort Pitt was Captain William Trent (1715–1787), a soldier who had served in both King George's War and the French and Indian War. He used smallpox blankets as a weapon of war against the Indians that he considered to be friendly to the British.[10] As well as Trent, other British military men including Henry Bouquet (1719–1765), a colonel of the British Army who played a prominent role in Pontiac's War, and Sir Jeffery Amherst (1717–1797), commander of the British forces that defeated the French to acquire Canada during the French and Indian

War, both openly reviled the Indians and had no problems using smallpox blankets against Pontiac and the Indians in 1763.[11]

Only a short time after Pontiac's War, the British were defeated in the American Revolution. The formation of the United States began a volatile relationship between the Americans and Indian communities. For many years, relations between the United States and Indian groups were perceived in terms of the workings of one sovereign nation in relation to another and treaties were often used between the negotiating parties. The first ever treaty negotiated between the United States and an Indian nation was the Treaty with the Delaware of 1778, which brought peace between the two nations.[12] Indeed, the strength of the Delaware Nation in terms of their jurisdiction over their lands and all of the people within those lands was symbolised by the grant of permission, written into the treaty, to allow US military personnel to cross their lands to pursue military battles with the British. Furthermore, the Americans promised not to take Delaware lands and to actively protect Delaware territorial rights, but as time passed, these turned out to be hollow platitudes. Over the course of the next centuries, the Americans reneged time and time again on their legally and morally binding treaty commitments.

Relations between the United States and other Indians on the east coast were just as fraught. Between the late 1780s and the early 1800s, a number of separate conflicts took place between a number of Indian groups and the United States. The source of conflict revolved around Indian lands and the intent of the United States to expand west beyond the Appalachian Mountains into lands known as the Northwest Territory, then occupied by numerous Indian nations. Indeed, the United States' plan was to turn the Northwest Territory, modern-day Ohio, Illinois, Indiana, Michigan and Wisconsin, into separate States of the Union. In 1787, the US government adopted the Northwest Ordinance, which created a mechanism that allowed the expansion of the United States into the Northwest Territory.[13] Despite American plans for unilateral expansion into the north-west, the ordinance stated that the American government would show the 'utmost good faith' towards the Indians and their lands.[14] However, these conflicting objectives were not reconcilable, especially when it involved forming new political entities on lands owned by Indians.

In 1791, conflict erupted between an alliance of Indians, including the Miami, Delaware, Shawnee, Chippewa, Potawatomi and Ottawa, and General Arthur St. Clair, governor of the Northwest Territory. Little Turtle (1752–1812), a Miami war chief, and Blue Jacket, a Shawnee, led the north-western Indian confederacy and defeated an army of the United States under the control of St. Clair.[15] In response, the United States sent representatives to negotiate a settlement. In 1793, negotiations were held in north-western Ohio between American commissioners and representatives from over fifteen Indian nations, termed the north-western Indian confederacy. The demands of the confederacy were simple, to allow the Ohio River to act as a natural border between the United States and their Indian neighbours.[16] In the end, these talks failed and a year later, the Indians were defeated in the Battle of Fallen Timbers (1794) in north-western Ohio. Indians were forced to cede most of Ohio in the Treaty of Grenville of 1795. Despite the protests of Little Turtle at the Treaty of Grenville negotiations about keeping their homelands, the defeat of Little Turtle in war required that he and other Indian groups cede their lands.[17] In little over two years, the shift in bargaining power between the groups of Indians and the United States had altered dramatically.

The military resistance of the Indians on the eastern seaboard of the United States was slowly faltering, but during the early nineteenth century, an Indian by the name of Tecumseh (1768–1813), a Shawnee chief, attempted to unite Indian peoples against the might of the United States. The formation of a pan-Indian religious and political movement was born from the loss of Indian lands, defeat in battle and the continued assault on Indian cultures. The illicit treaty dealings of many non-Indians, such as William Henry Harrison, which led to the loss of Indian lands in modern-day states like Illinois, Indiana and parts of Michigan and Wisconsin, provided Tecumseh with the force to unite the Indians against the Americans in order to protect their cultures from further encroachment.[18] Tecumseh recognised the threat of the increasing non-Indian population and settlements in the Ohio Valley and called for resistance to these settlements and the formation of a military confederacy of Indians west of the Appalachian Mountains. Tecumseh believed that all Indians owned the land in common and that land cessation by treaty or agreement was illegal if it was not agreed to by all Indians concerned.[19] However, in stark contrast to the opinions of Tecumseh, Pushmataha (1764–1824), a Choctaw chief who fought with the British in the Battle of New Orleans, declared that the Indians would destroy themselves if they fought the Americans.[20] Conflict between Tecumseh and his followers and the United States followed and eventually these battles merged into the War of 1812 between England and the United States. In 1813, the death of Tecumseh in the Battle of the Thames ended the last hope of Indian unity against the Americans to the east of the Mississippi River and as a result, Americans took control of the Northwest Territory.[21]

The period between 1675 and the early nineteenth century saw profound conflict between numerous Indian nations and a number of European nations, including England, France and Spain and the United States around issues of land, trade and competing colonial interests. Geopolitical struggles between all of these parties made for a continent that was forever in a state of change. As well as conflict, on other occasions, there was co-operation between the competing colonial powers and the Indian nations, such as when particular parties needed goods or required a strategic advantage over their enemies. In the late eighteenth century, the formation of the United States led to increased conflict with all Indian peoples in general, as the desire of the United States to expand territorially conflicted with existing treaty obligations already established. In the end, the Indians to the east of the Appalachian Mountains were forced to sign further treaties and to cede lands to the United States in order to live in peace.

SOURCES

Pontiac: 'Drive Them Out, Make War on Them', 1763

To repel the advances of the British military, Pontiac (1720–1769), an Ottawa war chief, formed an alliance between the Indians of the Ohio Valley and the Great Lakes region. In the following text, Pontiac outlines his reasons for the Indians to amalgamate into one force, and speaks of how Indian peoples must return to their traditional ways of life.

I am the Master of Life, whom thou desirest to know and to whom thou wouldst speak. Listen well to what I am going to say to thee and all thy red brethren. I am he who made heaven and earth, the trees, lakes, rivers, all men, and all that thou seest, and all that thou hast seen on earth. Because [I have done this and because] I love you, you must do what I say and [not do] what I hate. I do not like that you drink until you lose your reason, as you do; or that you fight with each other; or that you take two wives, or run after the wives of others; you do not well; I hate that. You must have but one wife, and keep her until death. When you are going to war, you juggle, join the medicine dance, and believe that I am speaking. You are mistaken, it is to Manitou to whom you speak; he is a bad spirit who whispers to you nothing but evil, and to whom you listen because you do not know me well. This land, where you live, I have made for you and not for others. How comes it that you suffer the whites on your lands? Can you not do without them? I know that those whom you call the children of your Great Father supply your wants, but if you were not bad, as you are, you would well do without them. You might live wholly as you did before you knew them. Before those whom you call your brothers come on your lands, did you not live by bow and arrow? You had no need of gun nor powder, nor the rest of their things, and nevertheless you caught animals to live and clothe yourselves with their skins, but when I saw that you inclined to the evil, I called back the animals into the depths of the woods, so that you had need of your brothers to have your wants supplied and I shall send back to you the animals to live on. I do not forbid you, for all that, to suffer amongst you the children of your father. I love them, they know me and pray to me, and I give them their necessities and all that they bring to you, but as regards those who have come to trouble your country, drive them out, make war on them. I love them not, they know me not, they are my enemies and the enemies of your brothers. Send them back to the country which I made for them. There let them remain.

General Council between Indians and American Commissioners, 1793

The following short extract is taken from the 1793 council between the United States and the north-western Indian confederacy. It underlines the powerful position of the confederacy after their victory over one of the armies of the United States. Here Indian peoples demand an end to all hostilities with the United States so that they may live in peace, with the Ohio River forming a natural border between the confederacy and the United States.

Brothers;—

Money, to us, is of no value, & to most of us unknown, and as no consideration whatever can induce us to sell the lands on which we get sustenance for our women and children; we hope we may be allowed to point out a mode by which your settlers may be easily removed, and peace thereby obtained.

Brothers;—

We know that these settlers are poor, or they would never have ventured to live in a country which have been in continual trouble ever since they crossed the Ohio; divide therefore this large sum of money which you have offered to us, among these people, give to each also a portion of what you say you would give us annually over and above this very large sum of money, and we are persuaded they would most readily accept of it in lieu of the lands you sold to them, if you add also the great sums you must expend in raising and paying Armies, with a view to force us to yield you our Country, you will certainly have more than sufficient for the purposes of repaying these settlers for all their labour and improvements.

Brothers; —

You have talked to us about concessions. It appears strange that you should expect any from us, who have only been defending our just Rights against your invasion; We want Peace; Restore to us our Country and we shall be Enemies no longer.

Brothers; —

You make one concession to us, by offering us your money, and another by having agreed to do us justice, after having long and injuriously withheld it. We mean in the acknowledgement you have now made, that the King of England never did, nor never had a right, to give you our Country, by the Treaty of peace, and you want to make this act of Common Justice, a great part of your concessions, and seem to expect that because you have at last acknowledged our independence, we should for such a favour surrender to you our Country.

Brothers; —

You have talked also a great deal about pre-emption and your exclusive right to purchase Indian lands, as ceded to you by the King at the Treaty of peace.

Brothers; —

We never made any agreement with the King, nor with any Nation that we would give to either the exclusive right of purchasing our lands. And we declare to you that we consider ourselves free to make any bargain or cession of lands, whenever & to whomsoever we please, if the white people as you say, made a treaty that none of them but the King should purchase of us, and that he has given that right to the U. States, it is an affair which concerns you & him & not us. We have never parted with such power.

Brothers; —

At our general Council held at the Glaize last Fall, we agreed to meet Commissioners from the U. States, for the purpose of restoring Peace, provided they consented to acknowledge and confirm our boundary line to be the Ohio; and we determined not to meet you until you gave us satisfaction on that point; that is the reason we have never met.

We desire you to consider Brothers, that our only demand, is the peaceable possession of a small part of our once great Country. Look back and view the lands from whence we have been driven to this spot, we can retreat no further, because the country behind hardly affords food for its present inhabitants. And we have therefore resolved, to leave our bones in this small space, to which we are now confined.

Brothers; —

We shall be persuaded that you mean to do us justice if you agree, that the Ohio, shall remain the boundary line between us, if you will not consent thereto, our meeting will be altogether unnecessary.

Little Turtle on the Treaty of Greenville, 1795

After Little Turtle (1752–1812), a Miami war chief, and many of the north-western Indian nations were defeated by an American army led by General Anthony Wayne, they were forced to sit down and negotiate a treaty. In the following document, Little Turtle speaks at the Treaty of Grenville negotiations expressing his hopes that the treaty will form a continuing relationship of peace and security. He hopes that despite defeat in war, the United States will keep its word and allow the peoples he represents to hold on to their lands.

Elder Brother, and all you present: I am going to say a few words, in the name of Pottawatamies, Weas and Kickapoos. It is well known to you all, that people are appointed on those occasions, to speak the sentiments of others; therefore am I appointed for those three nations.

Elder Brother: You told your younger brothers, when we first assembled, that peace was your object; you swore your interpreters before us, to the faithful discharge of their duty, and told them the Great Spirit would punish them, did they not perform it. You told us, that it was not you, but the President of the Fifteen Fires [states] of the United States, who spoke to us; that, whatever he should say, should be firm and lasting; that it was impossible he should say what was not true. Rest assured, that your younger brothers, the Miamis, Ottawas, Chippewas, Pottawatamies, Shawnees, Weas, Kickapoos, Piankeshaws, and Kaskaskias, are well pleased with your words, and are persuaded of their sincerity. You have told us to consider of the boundaries you showed us; your younger brothers have done so, and now proceed to give you their answer.

Elder Brother: Your younger brothers do not wish to hide their sentiments from you. I wish to be the same with those of the Wyandottes and Delawares; you have told us that most of the reservations you proposed to us belonged to our fathers, the French and the British. Permit your younger brothers to make a few observations on this subject.

Elder Brother: We wish you to listen with attention to our words. You have told your younger brothers that the British imposed falsehoods on us when they said the United States wished to take our lands from us, and that the United States had no such designs. You pointed out to us the boundary line, which crossed a little below Loromie's Store and struck Fort Recovery and runs from thence to the Ohio, opposite the mouth of the Kentucky River.

Elder Brother: You have told us to speak our minds freely, and we now do it. This line takes in the greater and best part of your brothers' hunting ground. Therefore, your younger brothers are of the opinion you take too much of their lands away and confine the hunting of our young men within the limits too contracted. Your brothers, the Miamis, the proprietors of those lands, and all your younger brothers present, wish you to run the lines as you mentioned to Fort Recovery and to continue it along the road; from thence to Fort Hamilton, on the great Miami River. This is what your brothers request you to do, and you may rest assured of the free navigation of that river, from thence to its mouth, forever.

Brother: Here is the road we wish to be the boundary between us. What lies to the east we wish to be yours; that to the west, we would desire to be ours.

Elder Brother: In speaking of the reservations, you say they are designed for the same purpose as those for which our fathers, the French and English, occupied them. Your younger brothers now wish to make some observations on them.

Elder Brother: Listen to me with attention. You told us you discovered on the Great Miami traces of an old fort. It was not a French fort, brother; it was a fort built by me. You perceived another at Loromies. 'Tis true a Frenchman once lived there for a year or two. The Miami villages were occupied as you remarked, but it was unknown to your younger brothers until you told them that we had sold the land there to the French or English. I was much surprised to hear you say that is was my forefathers had set the example to other Indians in selling their lands. I will inform you in what manner the French and English occupied those places.

Elder Brother: These people were seen by our forefathers first at Detroit. Afterwards we saw them at the Miami village – that glorious gate, which your younger brothers had the happiness to own, and through which all the good words of our chiefs had to pass, from the north to the south, and from the east to the west. Brothers, these people never told us they wished to purchase our lands from us.

Elder Brother: I now give you the true sentiment of your younger brothers the Miamis, with respect to the reservation at the Miami villages. We thank you for kindly contracting the limits you at first proposed. We wish you to take this six miles square on the side of the river where your fort now stands, as your younger brothers wish to inhabit that beloved spot again. You shall cut hay for your cattle wherever you please, and you shall never require in vain the assistance of your younger brothers at that place.

Elder Brother: The next place you pointed to was the Little River, and said you wanted two miles square at that place. This is a request that our fathers, the French or British, never made us. It was always ours. This carrying place has heretofore proved in a great degree the subsistence of your younger brothers. That place has brought us in the course of one day the amount of one hundred dollars. Let us both own this place and enjoy in common the advantages it affords. You told us at Chicago the French possessed a fort. We have never heard of it. We thank you for the trade you promised to open in our country, and permit us to remark that we wish our former traders may be continued and mixed with yours.

Elder Brother: On the subject of hostages, I have only to observe that I trust all my brothers present are of my opinion with regard to peace and our future happiness. I expect to be with you every day when you settle on your reservations, and it will be impossible for me or my people to withhold from you a single prisoner. Therefore, we don't know why any of us should remain here. These are the sentiments of your younger brothers present, on these particulars.

Tecumseh: 'When Jesus Christ Came Upon the Earth You Killed Him and Nailed Him to the Cross', 1810

In the following text, the Shawnee chief Tecumseh (1768–1813) attempts to stir up support for the formation of a military confederacy to fight the American military and a growing non-Indian population. Tecumseh explains that the selling of Indian lands was destroying Indian communities and that in order to rectify the situation, Indians should unite to fight for their common survival and refuse to sell any more land.

You wish to prevent the Indians from doing as we wish them, to unite and let them consider their lands as the common property of the whole. You take the tribes aside and advise them not to come into this measure. … You want by your distinctions of Indian tribes, in allotting to each a particular, to make them war with each other. You never see an Indian endeavor to make the white people do this. You are continually driving the red people, when at last you will drive them onto the great lake, where they can neither stand nor work.

Since my residence at Tippecanoe, we have endeavored to leave all distinctions, to destroy village chiefs, by whom all mischiefs are done. It is they who sell the land to the Americans. Brother, this land that was sold, and the goods that was given for it, was only done by a few. … In the future we are prepared to punish those who propose to sell land to the Americans. If you continue to purchase them, it will make war among the different tribes, and at last I do not know what will be the consequences among the white people. Brother, I wish you would take pity on the red people and do as I have requested. If you will not give up the land and do cross the boundary of our present settlement, it will be very hard, and produce great trouble between us.

The way, the only way to stop this evil is for the red men to unite in claiming a common and equal right in the land, as it was at first, and should be now--for it was never divided, but belongs to all. No tribe has the right to sell, even to each other, much less to strangers. … Sell a country! Why not sell the air, the great sea, as well as the earth? Did not the Great Spirit make them for all the use of his children?

How can we have confidence in the white people?

When Jesus Christ came upon the earth you killed Him and nailed Him to the cross. You thought He was dead and you were mistaken. …

Tecumseh: 'Where Today Are the Pequot?' 1811

Provided here is an extract where Tecumseh (1768–1813) pleads to other Indians, including the Choctaws and Chickasaws, to stand firm against the United States and prevent the destruction of other Indian people, like the Pequot and Mohican, had already experienced.

Where today are the Pequot? Where are the Narragansett, the Mohican, the Pocanet, and other powerful tribes of our people? They have vanished before the avarice and oppression of the white man, as snow before the summer sun. … Will we let ourselves be destroyed in our turn, without making an effort worthy of our race? Shall we, without a struggle, give up our homes, our lands, bequeathed to us by the Great Spirit? The graves of our dead and everything that is dear and sacred to us? … I know you will say with me, Never! Never!

Sleep not longer, O Choctaws and Chickasaws, in false security and delusive hopes. … Will not the bones of our dead be plowed up, and their graves turned into plowed fields?

Pushmataha: 'You Now Have No Just Cause to Declare War against the American People', 1811

The viewpoints of Pushmataha (1764–1824), a Choctaw chief who fought with the British in the Battle of New Orleans, differed from those of Tecumseh.

He told fellow Indians that the waging of war against the Americans was foolish since it would result in the destruction of all Indians.

The question before us now is not what wrongs have been inflicted upon our race, but what measures are best for us to adopt in regard to them; and though our race may have been unjustly treated and shamefully wronged by them [the whites], yet I shall not for that reason alone advise you to destroy them unless it was just and wise for you so to do; nor would I advise you to forgive them, though worthy of your commiseration, unless I believe it would be to the interest of our common good…

My friends and fellow countrymen! You now have no just cause to declare war against the American people, or wreak your vengeance upon them as enemies, since they have ever manifested feelings of friendship towards you. It is … a disgrace to the memory of your forefathers, to wage war against the American people merely to gratify the malice of the English.

The war, which you are now contemplating against the Americans … forbodes nothing but destruction to our entire race. It is a war against a people whose territories are now far greater than our own, and who are far better provided with all the necessary implements of war, with men, guns, horses, wealth, far beyond that of all our race combined, and where is the necessity or wisdom to make war upon such a people?

Edmund Randolph, King Philip's War, c.1676

In the following document, Edmund Randolph (1632–1703), an Englishman sent by the king to assess the damage and causes of King Philip's War in New England, reports that the ungodly nature of the Indians and the zealous practices of the English to Christianise them contributed to the causes of war.

Various are the reports and conjectures of the causes of the present Indian warre. Some impute it to an imprudent zeal in the magistrates of Boston to christianize those heathen before they were civilized and enjoining them the strict observation of their laws, which, to a people so rude and licentious, hath proved even intolerable, and that the more, for that while the magistrates, for their profit, put the laws severely in execution against the Indians, the people, on the other side, for lucre and gain, entice and provoke the Indians to the breach thereof, especially to drunkenness, to which those people are so generally addicted that they will strip themselves to their skin to have their fill of rum and brandy…

Some believe there have been vagrant and jesuitical priests, who have made it their business, for some years past, to go from Sachem to Sachem, to exasperate the Indians against the English and to bring them into a confederacy, and that they were promised supplies from France and other parts to extirpate the English nation out of the continent of America. Others impute the cause to some injuries offered to the Sachem Philip; for he being possessed of a tract of land called Mount Hope ... some English had a mind to dispossess him thereof, who never wanting one pretence or other to attain their end, complained of injuries done by Philip and his Indians to their stock and cattle, whereupon Philip was often summoned before the magistrate, sometimes imprisoned, and never released but upon parting with a considerable part of his land.

But the government of the Massachusetts ... do declare these are the great evils for which God hath given the heathen commission to rise against them ... For men wearing long hair and perewigs made of womens hair; for women ... cutting, curling and laying out the hair ... For profaneness in the people not frequenting their meetings...

With many such reasons ... the English have contributed much to their misfortunes, for they first taught the Indians the use of arms, and admitted them to be present at all their musters and trainings, and shewed them how to handle, mend and fix their muskets and have been furnished with all sorts of arms by permission of the government...

The loss to the English in the several colonies, in their habitations and stock, is reckoned to amount to 150,000 l. [pounds sterling] there having been about 1200 houses burned, 8000 head of cattle, great and small, killed, and many thousand bushels of wheat, pease and other grain burned ... and upward of 3000 Indians men women and children destroyed.

Treaty with the Delaware, 1778

The first ever treaty between an Indian nation and the United States in 1778, proclaimed peace between two nations. Both parties were to forgive one another for previous offences, and assist one another in times of war. The treaty testifies to the strength of the Delaware Nation and their dominion over their lands since it contains their dispensation allowing free passage of United States troops through their homelands to fight the troops of the King of England. In return, the United States promised to avoid the violent war practices of their enemies and if called upon, to protect the territorial rights of the Delaware both in the present and in the future.

Articles of agreement and confederation, made and entered into by Andrew and Thomas Lewis, Esquires, Commissioners for, and in Behalf of the United States of North-America of the one Part, and Capt. White Eyes, Capt. John Kill Buck, Junior, and Capt. Pipe, Deputies and Chief Men of the Delaware Nation of the other Part.

ARTICLE I.

That all offences or acts of hostilities by one, or either of the contracting parties against the other, be mutually forgiven, and buried in the depth of oblivion, never more to be had in remembrance.

ARTICLE 2.

That a perpetual peace and friendship shall from henceforth take place, and subsist between the contracting parties aforesaid, through all succeeding generations: and if either of the parties are engaged in a just and necessary war with any other nation or nations, that then each shall assist the other in due proportion to their abilities, till their enemies are brought to reasonable terms of accommodation: and that if either of them shall discover any hostile designs forming against the other, they shall give the earliest notice thereof, that timeous measures may be taken to prevent their ill effect.

ARTICLE 3.

And whereas the United States are engaged in a just and necessary war, in defence and support of life, liberty and independence, against the King of England and his adherents, and as said King is yet possessed of several posts and forts on the lakes and other places, the reduction of which is of great importance to the peace and security of the contracting parties, and as the most practicable way for the troops of the United States to some of the posts and forts is by passing through the country of the Delaware nation, the aforesaid deputies, on behalf of themselves and their nation, do hereby stipulate and agree to give a free passage through their country to the troops aforesaid, and the same to conduct by the nearest and best ways to the posts, forts or towns of the enemies of the United States, affording to said troops such supplies of corn, meat, horses, or whatever may be in their power for the accommodation of such troops, on the commanding officer's, &c. paying, or engageing to pay, the full value of whatever they can supply them with. And the said deputies, on the behalf of their nation, engage to join the troops of the United States aforesaid, with such a number of their best and most expert warriors as they can spare, consistent with their own safety, and act in concert with them; and for the better security of the old men, women and children of the aforesaid nation, whilst their warriors are engaged against the common enemy, it is agreed on the part of the United States, that a fort of sufficient strength and capacity be built at the expense of the said States, with such assistance as it may be in the power of the said Delaware Nation to give, in the most convenient place, and advantageous situation, as shall be agreed on by the commanding officer of the troops aforesaid, with the advice and concurrence of the deputies of the aforesaid Delaware Nation, which fort shall be garrisoned by such a number of the troops of the United States, as the commanding officer can spare for the present, and hereafter by such numbers, as the wise men of the United States in council, shall think most conducive to the common good.

ARTICLE 4.

For the better security of the peace and friendship now entered into by the contracting parties, against all infractions of the same by the citizens of either party, to the prejudice of the other, neither party shall proceed to the infliction of punishments on the citizens of the other, otherwise than by securing the offender or offenders by imprisonment, or any other competent means, till a fair and impartial trial can be had by judges or juries of both parties, as near as can be to the laws, customs and usages of the contracting parties and natural justice: The mode of such trials to be hereafter fixed by the wise men of the United States in Congress assembled, with the assistance of such deputies of the Delaware nation, as may be appointed to act in concert with them in adjusting this matter to their mutual liking. And it is further agreed between the parties aforesaid, that neither shall entertain or give countenance to the enemies of the other, or protect in their respective states, criminal fugitives, servants or slaves, but the same to apprehend, and secure and deliver to the State or States, to which such enemies, criminals, servants or slaves respectively belong.

ARTICLE 5.

Whereas the confederation entered into by the Delaware nation and the United States, renders the first dependent on the latter for all the articles of clothing, utensils and implements of war, and it is judged not only reasonable, but indispensably necessary, that the aforesaid Nation be supplied with such articles from time to time, as far as the United States may have it in their power, by a well-regulated trade, under the conduct of an intelligent, candid agent, with an adequate salary, one more influenced by the love of his country, and a constant attention to the duties of his department by promoting the common interest, than the sinister purposes of converting and binding all the duties of his office to his private emolument: Convinced of the necessity of such measures, the Commissioners of the United States, at the earnest solicitation of the deputies aforesaid, have engaged in behalf of the United States, that such a trade shall be afforded said nation, conducted on such principles of mutual interest as the wisdom of the United States in Congress assembled shall think most conducive to adopt for their mutual convenience.

ARTICLE 6.

Whereas the enemies of the United States have endeavored, by every artifice in their power, to possess the Indians in general with an opinion, that it is the design of the States aforesaid, to extirpate the Indians and take possession of their country: to obviate such false suggestion, the United States do engage to guarantee to the aforesaid nation of Delawares, and their heirs, all their territorial rights in the fullest and most ample manner, as it hath been bounded by former treaties, as long as they the said Delaware nation shall abide by, and hold fast the chain of friendship now entered into. And it is further agreed on between the contracting parties should it for the future be found conducive for the mutual interest of both parties to invite any other tribes who have been friends to the interest of the United States, to join the present confederation, and to form a state whereof the Delaware nation shall be the head, and have a representation in Congress: Provided, nothing contained in this article to be considered as conclusive until it meets with the approbation of Congress. And it is also the intent and meaning of this article, that no protection or countenance shall be afforded to any who are at present our enemies, by which they might escape the punishment they deserve.

In witness whereof, the parties have hereunto interchangeably set their hands and seals, at Fort Pitt, September seventeenth, anno Domini one thousand seven hundred and seventy-eight.

Andrew Lewis, [L. S.]
Thomas Lewis, [L. S.]
White Eyes, his x mark, [L. S.]
The Pipe, his x mark, [L. S.]
John Kill Buck, his x mark, [L. S.]

In presence of—

Lach'n McIntosh, brigadier-general, commander the Western Department.
Daniel Brodhead, colonel Eighth Pennsylvania Regiment,
W. Crawford, colonel,
John Campbell,
John Stephenson,
John Gibson, colonel Thirteenth Virginia Regiment,
A. Graham, brigade major,
Lach. McIntosh, jr., major brigade,
Benjamin Mills,
Joseph L. Finley, captain Eighth Pennsylvania Regiment,
John Finley, captain Eighth Pennsylvania Regiment.

Northwest Ordinance, 1787

The following excerpts from the Northwest Ordinance reveal the contradictory objectives of the US government towards establishing States of the Union in the Northwest Territory. It speaks of showing the 'utmost good faith' towards the Indian occupants and their lands.

An Ordinance for the government of the Territory of the United States north-west of the River Ohio...

Sec. 14. It is hereby ordained and declared by the authority aforesaid, That the following articles shall be considered as articles of compact between the original States and the people and States in the said territory and forever remain unalterable, unless by common consent, to wit:...

Art. 3. Religion, morality, and knowledge, being necessary to good government and the happiness of mankind, schools and the means of education shall forever be encouraged. The utmost good faith shall always be observed towards the Indians; their lands and property shall never be taken from them without their consent; and, in their property, rights, and liberty, they shall never be invaded or disturbed, unless in just and lawful wars authorized by Congress; but laws founded in justice and humanity, shall from time to time be made for preventing wrongs being done to them, and for preserving peace and friendship with them...

Art. 5. There shall be formed in the said territory, not less than three nor more than five States; and the boundaries of the States, as soon as Virginia shall alter her act of cession, and consent to the same, shall become fixed and established as follows, to wit: The western State in the said territory, shall be bounded by the Mississippi, the Ohio, and Wabash Rivers; a direct line drawn from the Wabash and Post Vincents, due North, to the territorial line between the United States and Canada; and, by the said territorial line, to the Lake of the Woods and Mississippi. The middle State shall be bounded by the said direct line, the Wabash from Post Vincents to the Ohio, by the Ohio, by a direct line, drawn due north from the mouth of the Great Miami, to the said territorial line, and by the said territorial line. The eastern State shall be bounded by the last mentioned direct line, the Ohio, Pennsylvania, and the said territorial line: *Provided, however,* and it is further understood and declared, that the boundaries of these three States shall be subject so far to be altered, that, if Congress shall hereafter find it expedient, they shall have authority to form one or two States in that part of the said territory which lies north of an east and west line drawn through the southerly bend or extreme of Lake Michigan. And, whenever any of the said States shall have sixty thousand free inhabitants therein, such State shall be admitted, by its delegates, into the Congress of the United States, on an equal footing with the original States in all respects whatever, and shall be at liberty to form a permanent constitution and State government: *Provided,* the constitution and government so to be formed, shall be republican, and in conformity to the principles contained in these articles; and, so far as it can be consistent with the general interest of the confederacy, such admission shall be allowed at an earlier period, and when there may be a less number of free inhabitants in the State than sixty thousand.

The Generals Discuss Tactics during the French and Indian War (1754–1763): (a) Journal of William Trent, 24 May 1763

In an extract taken from the journal of Captain William Trent (1715–1787) during the siege at Fort Pitt, Pittsburgh, Trent explains that Indians friendly to the British had alerted the military post of impending Indian attacks. In response, he handed out smallpox-infested blankets.

The Turtles Heart a principal Warrior of the Delawares and Mamaltee a Chief came within a small distance of the Fort Mr. McKee went out to them and they made a Speech letting us know that all our [posts] as Ligonier was destroyed, that great numbers of Indians [were coming and] that out of regard to us, they had prevailed on 6 Nations [not to] attack us but give us time to go down the Country and they desired we would set of immediately. The Commanding Officer thanked them, let them know that we had everything we wanted, that we could defend it against all the Indians in the Woods, that we had three large Armys marching to Chastise those Indians that had struck us, told them to take care of their Women and Children, but not to tell any other Natives, they said they would go and speak to their Chiefs and come and tell us what they said, they returned and said they would hold fast of the Chain of friendship. Out of our regard to them we gave them two Blankets and an Handkerchief out of the Small Pox Hospital. I hope it will have the desired effect. They then told us that Ligonier had been attacked, but that the Enemy were beat…

(b) Colonel Henry Bouquet to Jeffery Amherst: '…That Vermine … Have Forfeited All Claim to the Rights of Humanity', 25 June 1763

The following extract is taken from a letter written by Henry Bouquet (1719–1765), a colonel of the British Army who played a prominent role in Pontiac's War, to Sir Jeffery Amherst (1717–1797) in which he explains his visceral hatred of Indians.

The reinforcement you have ordered this way, so considerable by the additional number of officers, will fully enable me to crush the little opposition they may dare to offer along the Road, and Secure that Part of the Country against all their future attempts, till you think proper to order us to act in conjunction with the rest of your Forces to extirpate that Vermine from a Country they have forfeited, and with it all claim to the rights of humanity.

(c) Bouquet to Amherst: Suggestion to 'Inocculate the Indians', 13 July 1763

In another letter written by Henry Bouquet (1719–1765) to Sir Jeffery Amherst (1717–1797), he explains that his deep-seated hatred of the Indians justified the use of smallpox-infested blankets. This was one of the earliest examples of germ warfare.

P.S. I will try to inocculate the Indians by means of Blankets that may fall in their hands, taking care however not to get the disease myself. As it is pity to oppose good men against them, I wish we could make use of the Spaniard's Method, and hunt them with English Dogs. Supported by Rangers, and some Light Horse, who would I think effectively extirpate or remove that Vermine. H.B.

(d) Amherst to Bouquet:
'…To Try Every Method That Can Serve to Extirpate
This Execrable Race', 16 July 1763

In response to the writings of Bouquet, Jeffery Amherst (1717–1797), commander of the British forces that defeated the French to acquire Canada during the French and Indian War, highlights his appreciation of the illicit tactics used to defeat an enemy that he reviled and considered less than human.

P.S. You will Do well to try to Innoculate the Indians by means of Blankets, as well as to try Every other method that can serve to Extirpate this Execrable Race. I should be very glad your Scheme for Hunting them Down by Dogs could take Effect, but England is at too great a Distance to think of that at present.

CHAPTER FIVE
REMOVAL ERA, 1800s–1840s

Conflict in the removal era was deep-seated and revolved around the voluntary and forceful relocation of many Indian groups from east of the Mississippi River to the west. Rapid growth in the American population and the industrialisation of the United States resulted in a large demand for lands and resources. Many Indian groups negotiated treaties with the United States during the beginning of the nineteenth century and transferred large amounts of land to the United States. Only small pockets of land were retained east of the Mississippi River, but the US government still felt the need to legislate the Indian Removal Act of 1830. Indian resistance to removal took the form of media protest, a proactive stance within the legal system of the United States and protests to Congress and the president. By the early 1800s, conflict between the Indians and the United States was fought out as much in the US courts as within the battlefields of war. Military resistance gave way to political protest and to arguments about Indian sovereignty and authority over land. Indian removal was also a contentious issue for the American people and American politicians, with many non-Indians either in vociferous support or in opposition to the policy. Conflict over Indian land resulted in thousands of Indian deaths, displaced many thousands more and instilled a resentment within Indian communities that has reverberated across generations.

Indian removal as a concept was debated and examined by the American government during the early part of the nineteenth century. In 1803, Thomas Jefferson (1743–1826), the third president of the United States from 1801 to 1809, began the territorial expansion of the United States and brought the idea of the removal of the Indians to the west of the Mississippi River in his secret message to Congress on 18 January 1803.[1] In the end, Congress agreed to Jefferson's demands and funded an expedition led by Meriwether Lewis and William Clark. The primary objective of Jefferson and the US government was to survey Indian lands with a view to extending US commerce and to ultimately present Indian peoples with two options: to integrate into American society or move west beyond the Mississippi River.[2]

The objectives of removal were designed to free up Indian lands and to prevent confrontation between groups of Indians and non-Indians. Demand for Indian lands was particularly strong in the states of Alabama, Florida, Georgia and Tennessee and it directly affected many groups of Indians including the Cherokee, Choctaw, Chickasaw, Muscogee and Seminole nations.[3] During the early 1800s, the process of removal was generally based on the voluntary acceptance of removal by the Indians themselves. However, the pressure on Indian groups to move west intensified, and in 1823, the process of freeing up Indian lands in the east was made a lot easier by the US Supreme Court when Chief Justice John Marshall handed down the judgement on *Johnson v. McIntosh* (1823) and forever changed the relationship between Indian nations and the United States.[4] The decision held that Indians were only occupants of their homelands and real title to the lands belonged to the United States as the 'superior' Christian nation, a position justified through the questionable doctrine of discovery. Although the *Johnson v. McIntosh* decision made the American acquisition of Indian lands easier, it led to further court battles and further opposition to Indian removal.

The election of President Andrew Jackson (1767–1845) in 1828, as the seventh American president, facilitated the onset of Indian removal and the introduction of the Indian Removal Act. In his second annual message to Congress, Jackson portrayed removal as a benevolent policy that was going to protect the Indians from settlers and allow them to live in peace to the west of the Mississippi River.[5] Indeed, Jackson successfully oversaw the passage of the Indian Removal Act by Congress in 1830 and made it legal under American law for the United States to force Indian peoples west. Although some Indian nations had voluntarily relocated before 1830, the Removal Act was the starting point for a number of forced Indian removals conducted by the US government. The Act was hated by many Indians including Speckled Snake, the nineteenth-century Cherokee warrior. He derided the actions of Andrew Jackson, the specifics of the removal policy and particularly the broken promises of the US government.[6]

The policy pursued by Andrew Jackson led the Cherokee to establish a national newspaper called the *Cherokee Phoenix* (1828–1834) in order to counter and respond to the growing pressures and threats of removal. The newspaper addressed the views of both Indians and non-Indians and the ongoing problems removal brought. It openly argued against the policy of the American government and its politicians, including Secretary of War Thomas Loraine McKenney (1785–1859). In addition, the newspaper gave a voice and a platform for a number of Indian nations, such as the Creek, to openly question the policy and actions of non-Indians and it provided support for those who were in direct conflict with the federal government and various state governments.[7]

During the period of the Indian removal, conflict existed between groups of Indians and non-Indians and between groups of non-Indians themselves. Although many New England politicians condemned the removal of Indian groups from the south, many non-Indians considered removal a necessary process to save Indian communities from non-Indian settlers and anti-Indian policies within many states of the American Union.[8] Debates within Congress allowed elected officials to present their cases and personal reasons for supporting or opposing removal. Edward Everett (1794–1865), a congressman and senator, opposed removal; however, his efforts to thwart the policy of Andrew Jackson were unsuccessful.[9]

The removal policy of the US government brought it into direct conflict with the Cherokee Nation and these battles were primarily played out in court. During the 1820s, the State of Georgia encroached on Cherokee lands, and when gold was discovered on these lands in the late 1820s, Georgia passed a resolution which held that Georgia had authority over all Cherokee lands within the boundaries of the state.[10] Georgian laws were designed to harass the Cherokee and to destroy their economy and political and social cultures. Legal proceedings brought by the Cherokee to end the encroachment of Georgia law over the Cherokee resulted in the first of the two seminal Cherokee cases. In *Cherokee Nation v. Georgia* (1831), Marshall declared that the Supreme Court did not have authority to hear the case because the Cherokee were not foreign nations under the US Constitution but were instead, 'domestic dependent nations'.[11] Although the Cherokee lost in 1831, they had another chance in 1832. The second Cherokee case of *Worcester v. Georgia* (1832) involved the sovereignty of the Cherokee versus the sovereignty of the State of Georgia over non-Indians on Indian lands.[12] In his seminal opinion, Chief Justice Marshall declared that the sovereignty of the State of Georgia ended at the boundary of Indian lands, and therefore, the Cherokee had sovereignty over their own lands, with the caveat that they were answerable only to the US government. However, despite the historic victory for the Cherokee and the support of the highest court in the land, it did not protect the Cherokee or any other Indians from removal since the State of Georgia and the US government ignored the ruling of the Supreme Court. As a result prominent Americans, such as William Wirt (1772–1834), openly questioned the morality of Indian removal and criticised the illegality of the process embarked upon by the United States.[13]

Despite the protests of the Cherokee and the US Supreme Court *Worcester* opinion of 1832, Indian removal continued and included groups such as the Choctaw and the Seneca. Initially, the Choctaw were able to resist the intense pressure to move put on them by both the State of Mississippi and the United States. However, in 1830 they were forced to sign the Treaty of Dancing Rabbit Creek and agree to move west. Throughout the 1830s, the Choctaw were encouraged to leave their homelands and by the mid-1840s, the last Choctaw migrations had taken place.[14] However, despite the removal of many Choctaw, including Choctaw leader George W. Harkins, many thousands of Choctaw refused to be removed and remained on their homelands in Mississippi.[15] The Seneca were in a similar predicament to the Choctaw, divided between selling their lands and removing to the west or staying on their homelands in the east. In 1838 pressure mounted on them to sell their lands and negotiations took place between the Ogden Land Company and the Seneca chiefs to discuss the terms of a treaty. The Seneca signed the

Treaty of Buffalo Creek in 1838. Soon after the signing of the treaty, Maris Bryant Pierce (1811–1874), a Seneca born on the Allegany Reservation in western New York State, vented his anger towards the Ogden Land Company and attempted to influence the US Senate to reject the treaty's ratification.[16]

The process of removal unilaterally abrogated treaties already negotiated between many groups of Indians and the United States. Existing treaties had been designed to allow the Indians to live in peace and to be protected on their homelands from non-Indian encroachment and settlement. Inevitably, conflict surrounding this issue arose both between groups of Indians and non-Indians and between non-Indians themselves. Thomas Loraine McKenney (1785–1859), Commissioner of Indian Affairs between 1824 and 1830 until he was dismissed by President Andrew Jackson, was a non-Indian opposed to removal because it ignored the legal terms of treaties signed between Indian nations and the United States.[17] John Ross (1790–1866), principal chief of the Cherokee, was vehemently opposed to removal and viewed the removal policy as an illegal process that directly contradicted the US treaty promises.[18] In the end, the Cherokee were forced into removal by the American government and by a minority of their own people. In 1835, a small number of Cherokee, termed the 'Treaty Party', signed the Treaty of New Echota, including Elias Boudinot and John Ridge, ceding Cherokee homelands in the east for lands in the west. Although the 'Treaty Party' felt there was no alternative to the American demands, Chief John Ross and the majority of Cherokee opposed the signing of the 1835 treaty.[19] Despite the opposition to Cherokee removal and the refusal of the Cherokee themselves to move west, in 1838, President Andrew Jackson began military action to remove them from their homelands.

The forced removal of the Cherokee by the US government resulted in incalculable suffering and many thousands of deaths. One of the most infamous events of the removal period involved the Cherokee and what has become known as the Trail of Tears. In 1838, President Andrew Jackson ordered General Winfield Scott to round up the Cherokee and forcibly migrate them away from their treaty-protected lands. The Cherokee marched over hundreds of miles and suffered from malnutrition and disease and thousands perished.[20] The removal of Indian nations, such as the Seminole and Cherokee, were documented by non-Indian newspapers, including the Arkansas Gazette and the Batesville News. However, these newspapers did not portray the true extent of the misery and suffering inflicted on the Indians nor did they report that the thousands of deaths that occurred were a direct result of a misconceived federal government policy. Instead, the newspapers generally reported the movements of the Indians and the reactions of army personnel and local state residents.[21]

The period of removal thus involved conflict over lands and a conflict fought out in the courtrooms of the United States. Indian voices exposed the hypocrisy at the heart of American moral concern for Indian welfare, a concern that masked a desire for Indians to shift further and further west so that non-Indians could have access to their land and resources. Indian removal involved many eastern tribes including the Choctaw, Chickasaw, Creeks, Cherokee and the Seminoles—often referred to as the 'Five Civilized Tribes' because of the way in which they had adopted so many Euro-American ways from settled agriculture, to written communication to slave-holding—and northern tribes including the Potawatomi, Shawnee, Seneca, Ottawa, Chippewa, Miami, Wyandot, Menominee and the Winnebago. Between 1832 and 1842 the federal government removed nineteen tribes and more than 50,000 native Americans.[22] The overall cost of Indian removal for the federal government was around $68 million, but it brought about the acquisition of 100 million acres of land in the east and 32 million acres of land in the west.[23] Although many Indian nations were forced to the west and suffered on the forced migrations, other Indian groups defied the pressures of removal and remained in the east. These included the Iroquois in New York and Pennsylvania, remnant groups of Seminole, Choctaw, Cherokee in the east and the Menominee and Ottawa in the Great Lakes region.[24] The removal period was defined by conflict between groups of Indians and non-Indians, conflict amongst non-Indians themselves over what was clearly a reprehensible policy violently carried out and inevitable conflict between groups of Indians over the best response to aggressive requests that they give up their homelands to make way for Euro-American settlements. Even though some Indian communities took on non-Indian ways and fulfilled the requirement to assimilate in the way that the United States demanded of them in this era, this did not prevent them from losing their land. Although the public rhetoric of the time was about individual Indian assimilation, what really got assimilated during the removal era was Indian land and Indian material resources.

SOURCES

Speckled Snake's Reply to President Andrew Jackson, 1830

In a direct response to the removal policy implemented by Andrew Jackson, Speckled Snake derides the seemingly solicitous nature of Andrew Jackson concerning the need for Indian removal. Speckled Snake describes a history of hollow American promises made to all Indians and of the desire underlying American policy to force the Indians away from their ancestral lands.

Brothers! We have heard the talk of our great father; it is very kind. He says he loves his red children. *Brothers!* When the white man first came to these shores, the Muscogees gave him land, and kindled him a fire to make him comfortable; and when the pale faces of the south made war on him, their young men drew the tomahawk, and protected his head from the scalping knife. But when the white man had warmed himself before the Indian's fire, and filled himself with the Indian's hominy, he became very large; he stopped not for the mountain tops, and his feet covered the plains and the valleys. His hands grasped the eastern and the western sea. Then he became our great father. He loved his red children; but said, "You must move a little farther, lest I should, by accident, tread on you. With one foot he pushed the red man over the Oconee, and with the other he trampled down the graves of his fathers. But our great father still loved his red children, and he soon made them another talk. He said much; but it all meant nothing, but "move a little farther; you are too near me." I heard a great many talks from our great father, and they all begun and ended the same, *Brothers!* When he made us a talk on a former occasion, he said, "Get a little farther; go beyond the Oconee and the Oakmulgee; there is a pleasant country." He also said, "It shall be yours forever." Now he says, "The land you live on is not yours; go beyond the Mississippi; there is game; there you may remain while the grass grows or the water runs." *Brothers!* Will not our great father come there also? He loves his red children, and his tongue is not forked.

Chief John Ross:
Cherokee Letter Protesting the Treaty of New Echota, 1836

In the following extract, John Ross (1790–1866), principal chief of the Cherokee, describes in a letter written to Congress the disappointment felt by himself and a number of the Cherokee over the ratification of the Treaty of New Echota (1835) by the United States, when it was clear that the Cherokee who signed the treaty had no prior Cherokee consent or authority.

It is well known that for a number of years past we have been harassed by a series of vexations, which it is deemed unnecessary to recite in detail, but the evidence of which our delegation will be prepared to furnish. With a view to bringing our troubles to a close, a delegation was appointed on the 23rd of October, 1835, by the General Council of the nation, clothed with full powers to enter into arrangements with the Government of the United States, for the final adjustment of all our existing difficulties. The delegation failing to effect an arrangement with the United States commissioner, then in the nation, proceeded, agreeably to their instructions in that case, to Washington City, for the purpose of negotiating a treaty with the authorities of the United States.

After the departure of the Delegation, a contract was made by the Rev. John F. Schermerhorn, and certain individual Cherokees, purporting to be a "treaty, concluded at New Echota, in the State of Georgia, on the 29th day of December, 1835, by General William Carroll and John F. Schermerhorn, commissioners on the part of the United States, and the chiefs, headmen, and people of the Cherokee tribes of Indians." A spurious Delegation, in violation of a special injunction of the general council of the nation, proceeded to Washington City with this pretended treaty, and by false and fraudulent representations supplanted in the favor of the Government the legal and accredited Delegation of the Cherokee people, and obtained for this instrument, after making important alterations in its provisions, the recognition of the United States Government. And now it is presented to us as a treaty, ratified by the Senate, and approved by the President [Andrew Jackson], and our acquiescence in its requirements demanded, under the sanction of the displeasure of the United States, and the threat of summary compulsion, in case of refusal. It comes to us, not through our legitimate authorities, the known and usual medium of communication between the Government of the United States and our nation, but through the agency of a complication of powers, civil and military.

By the stipulations of this instrument, we are despoiled of our private possessions, the indefeasible property of individuals. We are stripped of every attribute of freedom and eligibility for legal self-defence. Our property may be plundered before our eyes; violence may be committed on our persons; even our lives may be taken away, and there is none to regard our complaints. We are denationalized; we are disfranchised. We are deprived of membership in the human family! We have neither land nor home, nor resting place that can be called our own. And this is effected by the provisions of a compact which assumes the venerated, the sacred appellation of treaty.

We are overwhelmed! Our hearts are sickened, our utterance is paralized, when we reflect on the condition in which we are placed, by the audacious ftices of unprincipled men, who have managed their stratagems with so much dexterity as to impose on the Government of the United States, in the face of our earnest, solemn, and reiterated protestations.

The instrument in question is not the act of our Nation; we are not parties to its covenants; it has not received the sanction of our people. The makers of it sustain no office nor appointment in our Nation, under the designation of Chiefs, Head men, or any other title, by which they hold, or could acquire, authority to assume the reins of Government, and to make bargain and sale of our rights, our possessions, and our common country. And we are constrained solemnly to declare, that we cannot but contemplate the enforcement of the stipulations of this instrument on us, against our consent, as an act of injustice and oppression, which, we are well persuaded, can never knowingly be countenanced by the Government and people of the United States; nor can we believe it to be the design of these honorable and highminded individuals, who stand at the head of the Govt., to bind a whole Nation, by the acts of a few unauthorized individuals. And, therefore, we, the parties to be affected by the result, appeal with confidence to the justice, the magnanimity, the compassion, of your honorable bodies, against the enforcement, on us, of the provisions of a compact, in the formation of which we have had no agency.

Protest of George W. Harkins over Removal:
'We Must Go Forth as Wanderers in a Strange Land!' 1831

In a letter to the American people, George W. Harkins, a nineteenth-century Choctaw leader who denounced the American policy of removal, describes his reasons and those of the Choctaw for leaving their homelands in favour of lands west of the Mississippi River.

It is with considerable diffidence that I attempt to address the American people, knowing and feeling sensibly my incompetency; and believing that your highly and well improved minds would not be well entertained by the address of a Choctaw. But having determined to emigrate west of the Mississippi river this fall, I have thought proper in budding you farewell to make a few remarks expressive of my views, and the feelings that actuate me on the subject of our removal. Believing that our all is at stake and knowing that you readily sympathize with the distressed of every country, I confidently throw myself upon your indulgence and ask you to listen patiently. I do not arrogate to myself the prerogative of deciding upon the expediency of the late treaty, yet I feel bound as a Choctaw, to give a distinct expression of my feelings on that interesting, (and to the Choctaws), all important subject. We were hedged in by two evils, and we chose that which we thought the least. Yet we could not recognize the right that the state of Mississippi had assumed, to legislate for us.—Although the legislature of the state were qualified to make laws for their own citizens, that did not qualify the to become law makers to a people that were so dissimilar in manners and customs as the Choctaws are to the Mississippians. Admitting that they understood the people, could they remove that mountain of prejudice that has ever obstructed the streams of justice, and prevent their salutary influence from reaching my devoted countrymen. We as Choctaws rather shoes to suffer and be free, than live under the degrading influence of laws, which our voice could be heard in their formation.

Much as the state of Mississippi has wronged us, I cannot find in my heart any other sentiment than an ardent wish for her prosperity and happiness.

I could cheerfully hope, that those of another age and generation may not feel the effects of those oppressive measures that have been so illiberally dealt out to us; and that peace and happiness may be their reward. Amid the gloom and horrors of the present separation, we are cheered with a hope that ere long we shall reach our destined land, and that nothing short of the basest acts of treachery will ever be able to wrest it from us, and that we may live free. Although your ancestors won freedom on the field of danger and glory, our ancestors owned it as their birthright, and we have had to purchase it from you as the vilest slaves buy their freedom.

Yet it is said that our present movements are our own voluntary acts—such is not the case. We found ourselves like a benighted stranger, following false guides, until he was surrounded on every side, with fire and water. The fire was certain destruction, and a feeble hope was left him of escaping by water. A distant view of the opposite shore encourages the hope; to remain would be inevitable annihilation. Who would hesitate, or who would say that his plunging into the water was his own voluntary act? Painful in the extreme is the mandate of our expulsion. We regret that it should proceed from the mouth of our professed friend, for whom our blood was co-mingled with that of his bravest warriors, on the field of danger and death.

But such is the instability of professions. The man who said that he would plant a stake and draw a line around us, that never should be passed, was the first to say he could not guard the lines, and drew up the stake and wiped out all traces of the line. I will not conceal from you my fears, that the present grounds may be removed. I have my foreboding; who of us can tell after witnessing what has already been done, what the next force may be. I ask you in the name of justice, for repose for myself and for my injured people. Let us alone—we will not harm you, we want rest. We hope, in the name of justice, that another outrage may never be committed against us, and that we may for the future be cared for as children, and not driven about as beasts, which are benefited by a change of pasture.

Taking an example from the American government, and knowing the happiness which its citizens enjoy under the influence of mild republican institutions, it is the intention of our countrymen to form a government assimilated to that of our white brethren in the United States, as nearly as their condition will permit. We know that in order to protect the rights and secure the liberties of the people, no government approximates so nearly to perfection as the one to which we have alluded. As east of the Mississippi we have been friends, so west we will cherish the same feelings with additional fervour; and although we may be removed to the desert, still we shall look with fond regard, upon those who have promised us their protection. Let that feeling be reciprocated.

Friends, my attachment to my native land was strong—that cord is now broken; and we must go forth as wanderers in a strange land! I must go—Let me entreat you to regard us with feelings of kindness, and when the hand of oppression is stretched against us, let me hope that a warning voice may be hard from every part of the U. States, filling the mountains and valleys will echo, and say stop, you have no power, we are the sovereign people, and our friends shall no more be disturbed. We ask you for nothing, that is incompatible with your other duties.

We go forth sorrowful, knowing that wrong has been done. Will you extend to us your sympathizing regards until all traces of disagreeable oppositions are obliterated, and we again shall have confidence in the professions of our white brethren. Here is the land of our progenitors, and here are their bones; they left them as a sacred deposit, and we have been compelled to venerate its trust; it dear to us, yet we cannot stay, my people is dear to me, with them I must go. Could I stay and forget them and leave them to struggle alone, unaided, unfriended, and forgotten, by our great father? I should then be unworthy the name of a Choctaw, and be a disgrace to my blood. I must go with them; my destiny is cast among the Choctaw people. If they suffer, so will I; if they prosper, then will I rejoice. Let me again ask you to regard us with feelings of kindness. Yours , with respect, GEORGE W. HARKINS.

Cherokee Phoenix (1828–1834):
(a) Creek Removal, 'Cherokee Phoenix', 21 and 28 February 1828

Provided here are two articles from the Cherokee Phoenix that outline the reasons of the Secretary of War for pursuing Creek removal and confirm the end of Creek resistance against the actions of the State of Georgia.

INDIAN EMIGRATION. [Creeks]

Excerpt of a letter from Thomas L.M'Kenney to the Secretary of War, dated. Nov. 29, 1827.

I have come to the conclusion, (I refer now mainly to the Creeks) and from close and personal observation that no treaty can be concluded with these people as such, and that whatever may be attempted, in this way will be with persons not of the Creek nation…

From this may be inferred the ignorance and weakness of the Creeks, and the inference is just. Conscious of their own inefficiency to manage for themselves their concerns, they have yielded to this State of dependence on others. But this is not all. They are a wretched people. Poverty and distress are visible everywhere; and these have become entailed upon them by habitual drunkenness. No man who has the feelings of a man can go through their country and see their total abandonment in this vice, without emotions of the most painful kind. I hold their recovery from it, and from its long train of miseries, while they retain their present relations to the State to be hopeless. No human agency can reform them as a people. It is vain to try. They are a devoted people and destruction just before them. Humanity and justice unite in calling loudly upon the government as a parent promptly to interfere and save them.

They feel the miseries of their condition; and many of them look most imploringly for help. I believe they would submit cheerfully to be guided by the government in regard to any new relation which it might be that proper to establish for them...

...the measures which may be adopted for bettering their condition shall be ... First- In the preparation of a suitable (and none other would be offered to them) and last home, for these unfortunate people, and Second- In providing suitable means and support for their transportation, and taking them kindly but firmly by the hand and telling they must go and enjoy it; and Lastly- In letting those persons who interfere in such matter know, that the object of the government being kind to the Indians, and intended wholly to better their condition, its determination is final, and that no persons will be permitted with impunity to interfere in it. To sustain this last position the presence of a few troops only would be required.

I would have it distinctly understood that a reasonable number of reservations should be granted and that they should be given in fee simple to those who might prefer to remain...

'*Cherokee Phoenix*', 28 February 1828

Creek Indians. – The controversy between Georgia and the Creek Indians is at length amicably and finally terminated. The Georgia Telagraph [sic] informs us that a full Council of the Creek Nation of Indians assembled at their Council Ground on Monday, the 31st ult. and continued for several days. At this council, the Treaty made by Col. McKenney, with the Chiefs, for the purchase of their remaining strip of lands in the boundaries of Georgia was laid before them by the Agent, and received their full assent. The Government is to pay them $47,491 – being $5,000 more than mentioned by Colonel McKenney, in his letter to the Secretary of War...

(b) Choctaw Removal:
'*Cherokee Phoenix*', 28 February 1828

The following excerpt details the Choctaw determination to remain on their homelands and to oppose the process of removal.

CHOCTAWS.

From a letter lately addressed to us by Col. David Folsom one of the Principal Chiefs of our Choctaw brethren, we make the following extract.

"The Choctaw people are determined to hold on to their land. They have no disposition whatever to sell their Country and make off to the west of the

Mississippi. Civilization is rapidly taken place among them, and they are visibly improving in their habits. Much industry is displayed among them, and considerable exertions are used to educate their sons and daughters. Some of the leading men feel much interested in the education of their people. But notwithstanding all this, there is a great deal of opposition among us."

(c) Cherokee Removal:
'Cherokee Phoenix', 21 February 1828

The following newspaper article examines the conflict of words and ideas between Secretary of War Thomas Loraine McKenney (1785–1859), who did not want the Cherokee to exist outside of United States law, and the newspaper itself, which opposed the idea of removal.

INDIAN EMIGRATION. [Cherokee]

Excerpt of a letter from Thomas L.M'Kenney to the Secretary of War, dated. Nov. 29, 1827.

Of the Cherokees it is due, that I should speak from my knowledge, obtained, however, otherwise than by personal observations, in terms of high commendation. They have done much for themselves. It has been their food fortune to have had born among them some great men; of these the late Charles Hicks stood pre-eminent. Under his wisdom, which was guided by virtues of a rare quality, these people have been elevated in privileges of every local description, high above their neighbors. They seek to be a people, and to maintain by law and good government, those principles which maintain the security of persons, defend the rights of property, &c.- They deserve to be respected, and to be helped. But with the kindest regards to them, and with a firm conviction the propriety and truth of the remark, they ought not to be encouraged in forming a constitution and government within a State of the Republic, to exist and operate independently of our laws. The sooner they have the assurance given them, that this cannot be permitted, the better it will be for them. If they will agree to come at once under our laws, and be merged as citizens in our privileges would it be objected against? But if they will not, then no people, of all the Indians within our limits, are better qualified to go into a territory, such as it is proposed to provide for our Indians, and by their superior lights, confer, under the suitable form of government, benefits upon the Indian race…

We cannot but express our regret that Col. McKinney should believe that the greater portion of the Cherokees would follow the Creeks, Chickasaws, and Choctaws, in their emigration to, we know not where, when we are confident that this belief is founded upon no evidence whatever. He did not pay us a visit, and of course could not obtain the views of our people in regard to the present policy of the General Government, in its intercourse with the Indians; and we presume that those with when he might have had an interview, never assured him anything of this nature. We have formed our opinion on the subject from personal observation, and would not hesitate to express our belief, that the Cherokee (I think unanimously) are adverse to remove. The public are already aware that we have frequently made known our reluctance to part with our Country, & betake ourselves to the west of Mississippi. And let it here be stated that this reluctance, on our part, not a thing of late origin, as it has been insinuated. At a conference held in Philadelphia 1792 between Gen. Knox, Secretary of War, & deputation of the Cherokees, Al-neshe-loo-yah (or Bloody Fellow) delivered a speech of which the following is an extract, which will show the disposition of the Cherokees on this matter at that early period. The speeches of the Deputation, and the answers of the President and the Secretary of War will be given in future numbers of our paper...

We are very fearful that the policy and measurers of the General Government, in civilizing the Indians, is about to take a new turn...they are gravely told that their case is hopeless, whilst they retain their present relation to the States. We have always thought that we were related to the General Government, and not to the states; and let it be remembered that our relation with the United States has been one of the most efficient causes in bringing to pass the improvement amongst us...

(d) United States Senate:
Arguments for and against Removal,
'Cherokee Phoenix', 6 May 1828

Conflict took place between elected officials in Congress. The following excerpt explores the type of conflict that occurred and the reasons for some senators either justifying or opposing removal. In addition, the text deals with the prospect of sending delegations of Choctaw and Chickasaw nations to explore and choose new homelands to the west of the Mississippi River.

CONGRESS
SENATE
REMOVAL OF INDIANS.

The Senate proceeded to the consideration of a bill making appropriations to enable the President of the United States to defray the expenses of a delegation of the Choctaw and Chickasaw nations of Indians to explore the country west of the Mississippi.

MR. BENTON explained the object, and supported the policy of the measure. The States of Mississippi, Alabama, and others had, he said a numerous Indian population who, in all wars, whether foreign, civil, or servile, were ready to rise against those States. It was desirable that these Indians should be sent away. The measure was for the benefit of the Indians no less than of the States in which they now dwelt…

Mr. ELLIS opposed the motion. It did not appear that the Creeks and Cherokees were desirous of removing. They had not asked to be removed. He hoped the amendment would not be pressed. Mr. Johnson of Kentucky said, the proposition authorizes the President to send agents, with three or four chief men of the Indian tribes, to explore the country west of the Mississippi, with a view of removal hereafter. No coercion was proposed. If they liked the lands which they saw, they might remove to them. The change of residence would greatly contribute to the happiness and independence of the Indians. He hoped the amendment would be adopted.

Mr COBB said he could not consent to withdraw the amendment. The government was bound by the obligations of a solemn compact, to remove the Indians from the State of Georgia. They had frequent opportunities, of removing them if they choose, but they had refused to do it. He could show four different occasions on which the Indians might have been removed, but on each occasion, the government, from policy, interest or other motive, neglected to do it. Justice to Georgia required the United States an immense consideration for it, which made her poor. If the government does refuse to comply with the compact, it will show that the government is not very closely pinched by the obligations which it takes upon itself. He would place at the disposal of the President of the United States a large sum of money to enable him to hold treaties, send out exploring parties, and adopt all other proper means to induce the Indians to remove. If this could be done, he would include all the Indians. But he would not give a vote to remove a single Indian until the removal of those in Georgia had been provided for. In Ohio, there were not more than 500 Indians. From Indiana, Illinois, and Missouri, nearly all the Indians had been removed. These States came into the Union after the compact was entered into with Georgia; and still, the Georgia Indians were not removed. He knew not what impression these things made on the Senate, but he would assure gentlemen that they made deep impression on the people of Georgia. If he could get the consent of those who had the management of the bill, he would move it so as to authorize and enable the President to take measures to induce the Indians to remove…

Mr. KING said he would not enter into an examination of the rights of Georgia as connected with the subject. He agreed that less had been done than might have been done towards the removal of the Georgia Indians. But this was not the proper time to discuss that matter. His object was to make a small appropriation to enable the chiefs to explore the country, and if they liked it, and determined to remove to it, it may be proper for the government to prepare for their removal.

In reply to the Senator from North Carolina he stated that an exploring party, under Col. Brearly, had gone out, and some of the Creeks had been removed. But they were of the M'Intosh party. The hostile party, who now wish to explore, will examine for themselves, rather than take the place chosen by their enemies. With respect to the Cherokees, he doubted whether they were willing to go. It was not his wish to coerce any of them. He was sorry they had not been before removed. They might now have been placed in a comfortable situation. At present, they were almost in a state of starvation. They were compelled to subsist on roots. It was said that, in the woods they might lose their civilization and become wild. Mr. K. said that they had only contracted the vices of civilization. The wild man of the woods, he thought, had much more character than the drunken and thievish half-civilized Indians.

The above remarks of Mr. King, discover notorious ignorance of the Cherokees.- We should like to know where this honorable Senator obtained his knowledge of our wretched condition. The advocates of the removal of the Indians seem to possess means of information inaccessible to others. We are the more opposed to this system when it is sustained by such palpable ignorance, we mean, of the condition of the Indians generally. Will it not be best for such men as Mr. King, to learn who these Indians are, & what is their real condition, before they begin to legislate on their removal?

Chief John Ross: Memorial and Protest of the Cherokee Nation, 1836

Provided here is part of the memorial and protest presented by John Ross (1790–1866), principal chief of the Cherokee who led the movement against removal, to Congress in which he declares that the treaties that supposedly justified Cherokee removal had been obtained by fraud.

…The United States solemnly guaranteed to such nation all their land not ceded, and pledged the faith of the government, that "all white people who have intruded, or may hereafter intrude on the lands reserved for the Cherokees, shall be removed by the United States. …" The Cherokees were happy and prosperous under a scrupulous observance of treaty stipulations by the government of the United States, and from the fostering hand extended over them, they made rapid advances in civilization, morals, and in the arts and sciences. Little did they anticipate, that when taught to think and feel as the American citizen, and to have with him a common interest, they were to be despoiled by their guardian, to become strangers and wanderers in the land of their fathers, forced to return to the savage life, and to seek a new home in the wilds of the far west, and that without their consent. An instrument purporting to be a treaty with the Cherokee people, has recently been made public by the President of the United States, that will have such an operation if carried into effect. This instrument, the delegation aver before the civilized world, and in the presence of Almighty God, is fraudulent, false upon its face, made by unauthorized individuals, without the sanction, and against the wishes of the great body of the Cherokee people. Upwards of fifteen thousand of those people have protested against it, solemnly declaring they will never acquiesce.

Speech by M.B. Pierce, Chief of the Seneca Nation, at Buffalo, New York, 1839

Provided here is a written version of an address made by Maris Bryant Pierce (1811–1874), a Seneca born on the Allegany Reservation in western New York State, given to influence the United States Senate to reject the Treaty of Buffalo Creek (1838) and to raise awareness about the general plight of Indians forced into removal.

The condition and circumstances of the race of people of whom I am by blood one, and in the well being of whom I am, by the ties of kindred and the common feelings of humanity, deeply interested, sufficiently apologize, and tell the reason for my seeking this occasion of appearing before this audience, in this city. Not only the eyes and attention of *you*, our neighbors--but also of the councils of this great nation, are turned upon us. We are expected to do, or to refuse to do, what the councils of this nation, and many private men, are now asking of us--what many favour and advocate--yet also what many discountenance and condemn...

The only question which I shall now consider, included in the subject I am treating, is, *how* can this undertaking be carried into operation most advantageously for securing its ultimate object?

Can it be by remaining where we now are located, or by selling our lands and removing to the afore-mentioned "terra incognita?" The right and possession of our lands is undisputed--so with us it a question appealing directly *to our interest;* and how stands the matter in relation *to that?* Our lands are as fertile and as well situated for agricultural pursuits as any we shall get by a removal. The graves of our fathers and mothers and kin are here, and about them still cling our affections and memories. Here is the theatre on which our tribe has thus far acted its part in the drama of its existence, and about it are wreathed the associations which ever bind the human affections to the soil, whereon one's nation, and kindred, and self, have arisen and acted. We are here situated in the midst of facilities for physical, intellectual and moral improvement; we are in the midst of the enlightened; we see their ways and their works, and can thus profit by their example. We can avail ourselves of their implements, and wares and merchandise, and once having learned the convenience of using them, we shall be led to deem them indispensable. We here are more in the way of instruction from teachers, having greater facilities for getting up and sustaining schools; and as we, in the progress of our improvement, may come to feel the want and the usefulness of books and prints, so we shall be able readily and cheaply to get whatever we may choose. In this view of facts, surely there is no inducement for removing.

But let us look at the other side of the question. In the first place the white man wants our land; in the next place it is said that the offer for it is liberal; in the next place that we shall be better off to remove from the vicinity of the whites, and settle in the neighborhood of our fellow red men, where the woods flock with game, and the streams abound with fishes. These are the reasons offered and urged in favour of our removal.

Let us consider each of these reasons a little in detail. The fact that the whites want our land imposes no obligation on us to sell it; nor does it hold forth an inducement to do so, unless it leads them to offer a price equal to its value. We neither know nor feel any debt of gratitude which we owe to them, in consequence of their "loving kindness or tender mercies" towards us, that should cause us to make a sacrifice of our property or our interest, to their wonted avarice, and which, like the mother of the horse leech, cries, Give, give, and is never sated.

And is the offer liberal? Of that who but ourselves are to be the final judges? If we do not deem one or two dollars an acre liberal for the land, which will to the white man's pocket bring fifteen to fifty, I don't know that we can be held heinously criminal for our opinion. It is well known that those who are anxious to purchase our Reservations, calculate safely on fifteen dollars the acre for the poorest, and by gradation up to fifty and more, for the other qualities. By what mode of calculation or rules of judgment, is one or two dollars a liberal offer to us, when many times that sum would be only fair to the avarice of the land speculator? Since in us is vested a perfect title to the land, I know not why we may not, when we wish, dispose of it at such prices as we may see fit to agree upon.

"But the land company have the right of purchase," it is said--granted; but they have not the right, nor, we trust in God, the power to force us to accept of their offers. And when that company finds that a whistle or a rattle, or one dollar or two, per acre, will not induce us to part with our lands, is it not in the nature of things that they should offer better and more attractive terms? If they could not make forty-nine dollars on an acre of land, I know no reason why they would fail of trying to make forty-five, or thirty, or ten. So I see no obstacle to our selling when and at such reasonable prices as we may wish, in the *fact* that the land company have the right of purchase: nor do I see any thing extortionate in us, in an unwillingness to part with our soil on the terms offered,--nor even in the *desire*, if our lands are sold, of putting into our *own* pockets a due portion of their value.

But the point of chief importance is, shall we be better off? If our object was to return to the manners and pursuits of life which characterized our ancestors, and we could be put in a *safe, unmolested* and *durable* possession of a wilderness of game, whose streams abound in fish, we might be better off; but though that were our object, I deny that we could possess *such a territory* this side of the shores of the Pacific, with *safety, free of molestation,* and in *perpetuity.*

…[whenever] Empire is held by the white man, nothing is safe or unmolested or enduring against his avidity for gain. Population is with rapid strides going beyond the Mississippi, and even casting its eye with longing gaze for the woody peaks of the Rocky Mountains--nay even for the surf-beaten shore of the Western Ocean.--And in process of time, will not our territory there be as subject to the wants of the whites, as that which we now occupy is? Shall we not then be as strongly solicited, and by the same arguments, to remove still farther west? But there is one condition of a removal which must certainly render it hazardous in the extreme to us. The proximity of our then situation to that of other and more warlike tribes, will expose us to constant harassing by them; and not only this, but the character of those worse than Indians, those *white borderers* who infest, yes *infest* the western border of the white population, will annoy us more fatally than even the Indians themselves. Surrounded thus by the natives of the soil, and hunted by such a class of whites ... how shall we be better off there than where we are now?

Having said thus much as to our condition after a removal, under the supposition that we wish to return to and continue in the habits of life which prevailed when the country was first taken possession of by the Europeans, I proceed now to say, that we do not wish so to do, and to repeat, that so far from it, we desire to renounce those habits of mind and body, and adopt in their stead those habits and feelings--those modes of living, and acting and thinking, which result from the cultivation and enlightening of the moral and intellectual faculties of man. And on this point, I need not insult your common sense by endeavoring to show that it is *stupid folly* to suppose that a removal from our present location to the western wilds would improve our condition. What! leave a fertile and somewhat improved soil--a home in the midst of civilization and christianity, where the very breezes are redolent of improvement and exaltation,--where, by induction as it were, we must be pervaded by the spirit of the enterprise,--where books, and preaching, and conversation, and business and conduct, whose influence we need, are all around us, so that we have but to stretch forth our hands, and open our ears, and turn our eyes, to experience in full their improving and enlightening effects,--leave these! and for what? and echo answers *for what?* But methinks I hear the echo followed by the anxious guileful whisper of some government land company agent--for one or two dollars the acre, and a western wilderness beyond the white man's reach, where an Eden lies in all its freshness of beauty for you to possess and enjoy. But ours, I reply, is sufficiently an Eden now, if but the emissaries of the arch fiend, not so much in the form of a serpent as of man, can be kept from its borders.

But I will relieve your patience by closing my remarks ... And now I ask, what feature of our condition is there which should induce us to leave our present location and seek another in the western wilds? Does justice, does humanity, does religion, in their relations to us demand it? Does the interest and the well being of the whites require it? The plainest dictates of common sense and common honesty, answer *No!* I ask then, in behalf of the New York Indians and myself, that our white brethren will not urge us to do that which justice or humanity not only do not require, but condemn. I ask then to let us live on, where our fathers have lived; let us enjoy the advantages which our location affords us; that thus we, who have been converted heathen, may be made meet for that inheritance which the *Father* hath promised to give his *Son*, our Saviour; so that the deserts and waste places may be made to blossom like the rose, and the inhabitants thereof utter forth the high praises of our God.

Thomas Jefferson:
Transcript of His Secret Message to Congress about the Lewis and Clark Expedition, 1803

The text that follows is taken from a speech made by President Thomas Jefferson (1743–1826) to the Houses of Congress about the intent of the US government to expand beyond the Mississippi River into lands that did not belong to them. Jefferson planned to turn Indian peoples away from hunting towards an agricultural 'civilised' lifestyle and to establish trading posts to further destabilise Indian cultures. In addition, Jefferson saw westward expansion as an unprecedented economic opportunity for the creation of wealth.

Confidential Gentlemen of the Senate, and of the House of Representatives:

As the continuance of the act for establishing trading houses with the Indian tribes will be under the consideration of the Legislature at its present session, I think it my duty to communicate the views which have guided me in the execution of that act, in order that you may decide on the policy of continuing it, in the present or any other form, or discontinue it altogether, if that shall, on the whole, seem most for the public good.

The Indian tribes residing within the limits of the United States, have, for a considerable time, been growing more and more uneasy at the constant diminution of the territory they occupy, although effected by their own voluntary sales: and the policy has long been gaining strength with them, of refusing absolutely all further sale, on any conditions; insomuch that, at this time, it hazards their friendship, and excites dangerous jealousies and perturbations in their minds to make any overture for the purchase of the smallest portions of their land. A very few tribes only are not yet obstinately in these dispositions. In order peaceably to counteract this policy of theirs, and to provide an extension of territory which the rapid increase of our numbers will call for, two measures are deemed expedient. First: to encourage them to abandon hunting, to apply to the raising stock, to agriculture and domestic manufacture, and thereby prove to themselves that less land and labor will maintain them in this, better than in their former mode of living. The extensive forests necessary in the hunting life, will then become useless, and they will see advantage in exchanging them for the means of improving their farms, and of increasing their domestic comforts. Secondly: to multiply trading houses among them, and place within their reach those things which will contribute more to their domestic comfort, than the possession of extensive, but uncultivated wilds. Experience and reflection will develop to them the wisdom of exchanging what they can spare and we want, for what we can spare and they want. In leading them to agriculture, to manufactures, and civilization; in bringing together their and our settlements, and in preparing them ultimately to participate in the benefits of our governments, I trust and believe we are acting for their greatest good. At these trading houses we have pursued the principles of the act of Congress, which directs that the commerce shall be carried on liberally, and requires only that the capital stock shall not be diminished. We consequently undersell private traders, foreign and domestic, drive them from the competition; and thus, with the good will of the Indians, rid ourselves of a description of men who are constantly endeavoring to excite in the Indian mind suspicions, fears, and irritations towards us. A letter now enclosed, shows the effect of our competition on the operations of the traders, while the Indians, perceiving the advantage of purchasing from us, are soliciting generally, our establishment of trading houses among them. In one quarter this is particularly interesting. The Legislature, reflecting on the late occurrences on the Mississippi, must be sensible how desirable it is to possess a respectable breadth of country on that river, from our Southern limit to the Illinois at least; so that we may present as firm a front on that as on our Eastern border. We possess what is below the Yazoo, and can probably acquire a certain breadth from the Illinois and Wabash to the Ohio; but between the Ohio and Yazoo, the country all belongs to the Chickasaws, the most friendly tribe within our limits, but the most decided against the alienation of lands. The portion of their country most important for us is exactly that which they do not inhabit. Their settlements are not on the Mississippi, but in the interior country. They have lately shown a desire to become agricultural; and this leads to the desire of buying implements and comforts. In the strengthening and gratifying of these wants, I see the only prospect of planting on the Mississippi itself, the means of its own safety. Duty has required me to submit these views to the judgment of the Legislature; but as their disclosure might embarrass and defeat their effect, they are committed to the special confidence of the two Houses.

   While the extension of the public commerce among the Indian tribes, may deprive of that source of profit such of our citizens as are engaged in it, it might be worthy the attention of Congress, in their care of individual as well as of the general interest, to point, in another direction, the enterprise of these citizens, as profitably for themselves, and more usefully for the public. The river Missouri, and the Indians inhabiting it, are not as well known as is rendered desirable by their connexion with the Mississippi, and consequently with us. It is, however, understood, that the country on that river is inhabited by numerous tribes, who furnish great supplies of furs and peltry to the trade of another nation, carried on in a high latitude, through an infinite number of portages and lakes, shut up by ice through a long season. The commerce on that line could bear no competition with that of the Missouri, traversing a moderate climate, offering according to the best accounts, a continued navigation from its source, and possibly with a single portage, from the Western Ocean, and finding to the Atlantic a choice of channels through the Illinois or Wabash, the lakes and Hudson, through the Ohio and Susquehanna, or Potomac or James rivers, and through the Tennessee and Savannah, rivers. An intelligent officer, with ten or twelve chosen men, fit for the enterprise, and willing to undertake it, taken from our posts, where they may be spared without inconvenience, might explore the whole line, even to the Western Ocean, have conferences with the natives on the subject of commercial intercourse, get admission among them for our traders, as others are admitted, agree on convenient deposits for an interchange of articles, and return with the information acquired, in the course of two summers. Their arms and accoutrements, some instruments of observation, and light and cheap presents for the Indians, would be all the apparatus they could carry, and with an expectation of a soldier's portion of land on their return, would constitute the whole expense. Their pay would be going on, whether here or there. While other civilized nations have encountered great expense to enlarge the boundaries of knowledge by undertaking voyages of discovery, and for other literary purposes, in various parts and directions, our nation seems to owe to the same object, as well as to its own interests, to explore this, the only line of easy communication across the continent, and so directly traversing our own part of it. The interests of commerce place the principal object within the constitutional powers and care of Congress, and that it should incidentally advance the geographical knowledge of our own continent, cannot be but an additional gratification. The nation claiming the territory, regarding this as a literary pursuit, which is in the habit of permitting within its dominions, would not be disposed to view it with jealousy, even if the expiring state of its interests there did not render it a matter of indifference. The appropriation of two thousand five hundred dollars, "for the purpose of extending the external commerce of the United States," while understood and considered by the Executive as giving the legislative sanction, would cover the undertaking from notice, and prevent the obstructions which interested individuals might otherwise previously prepare in its way.

TH. Jefferson

Thomas Loraine McKenney:
Protest over Removal, 'In Vain Did the Indians Implore the Government to Protect Them', 1830

In the following extract, Thomas Loraine McKenney (1785–1859), Commissioner of Indian Affairs between 1824 and 1830 until he was dismissed by President Andrew Jackson, highlights the failure of the American government to protect the Cherokee and to honour their treaty obligations.

The fifth article of the treaty [between the Cherokee Nation and the United States] … contains this provision: "--And all white people who have intruded, or may hereafter intrude, on the lands of the Cherokees, shall be removed by the United States". …

But this law was destined, at last, though unrepealed, to become a dead letter! The solemn compacts with the Indians, guaranteeing to them "protection," were treated as things obsolete, or regarded as mockeries. In the face, and in violations of the provisions … surveyors were permitted to penetrate the Indian territory, roam over it, lay it off into counties, and to proceed, in all things, for its settlement, as though no Indians occupied it, and no laws existed, demanding the interference of the government to prevent it! In vain did the Indians implore the government to protect them; in vain did they call the attention of the Executive to the provisions of treaties, and to the pledges of the law.

Andrew Jackson Outlines His Indian Removal Policy: Second Annual Message to Congress, 6 December 1830

The following text is taken from the second annual message of President Andrew Jackson (1767–1845), who became a national hero after his defeat of the British in the War of 1812 and the seventh American president from 1828 to 1837, to Congress in 1830. It highlights the objectives and key reasons behind the policy of Indian removal.

It gives me pleasure to announce to Congress that the benevolent policy of the government, steadily pursued for nearly thirty years, in relation to the removal of the Indians beyond the white settlements is approaching to a happy consummation. Two important tribes have accepted the provision made for their removal … and it is believed that their example will induce the remaining tribes also to seek the same obvious advantages.

The consequences of a speedy removal will be important to the United States, to individual States, and to the Indians themselves. … It puts an end to all possible danger of collision between the authorities of the General and State governments on account of the Indians. It will place a dense and civilized population in large parts of country now occupied by a few savage hunters. By opening the whole territory between Tennessee on the north and Louisiana on the south to the settlement of the whites it will incalculably strengthen the southwestern frontier and render the adjacent States strong enough to repel future invasions without remote aid. It will relieve the whole State of Mississippi and the western part of Alabama of Indian occupancy, and enable those States to advance rapidly in population, wealth and power. It will separate the Indians from immediate contact with settlements of whites; free them from the power of the States; enable them to pursue happiness in their own way and under their own rude institutions; will retard the progress of

decay, which is lessening their numbers, and perhaps cause them gradually …
to cast off their savage habits and become an interesting, civilized, and
Christian community. …

Toward the aborigines of the country no one can indulge a more friendly
feeling than myself, or would go further in attempting to reclaim them from
their wandering habits and make them a happy, prosperous people. …

Humanity has often wept over the fate of the aborigines of this country. …
To follow to the tomb the last of his race and to tread on the graves of
extinct nations excite melancholy reflections. But true philanthropy
reconciles the mind to these vicissitudes as it does to the extinction of one
generation to make room for another. In the monuments and fortresses of
an unknown people, spread over the extensive regions of the West, we
behold the memorials of a once powerful race, which was exterminated or
has disappeared to make room for the existing savage tribes. … What good
man would prefer a country covered with forests and ranged by a few
thousand savages to our extensive Republic, studded with cities, towns, and
prosperous farms … and filled with all the blessings of liberty, civilization,
and religion? …

Doubtless it will be painful to leave the graves of their fathers; but what do
they more than our ancestors did or than our children are now doing. To
better their condition in an unknown land our forefathers left all that was
dear in earthly objects. … Can it be cruel in this Government when, by events
which it can not control, the Indian is made discontented in his ancient home,
to purchase his lands, to give him a new and extensive territory, to pay the
expense of his removal, and support him a year in his new abode? How many
thousands of our own people would gladly embrace the opportunity of
removing to the West on such conditions!

Edward Everett:
Criticises Removal, 'Nations of Dependent Indians …
Are Driven from Their Homes into the Wilderness', 1830

*In the following extract, Edward Everett (1794–1865), a congressman and
senator who was one of the staunchest opponents of removal policy, highlights
the unjust nature of the forced migration of independent Indian nations from
their homelands.*

The evil, Sir, is enormous; the inevitable suffering incalculable. Do not stain the
fair fame of the country. … Nations of dependent Indians, against their will,
under color of law, are driven from their homes into the wilderness. You
cannot explain it; you cannot reason it away. … Our friends will view this
measure with sorrow, and our enemies alone with joy. And we ourselves, Sir,
when the interests and passions of the day are past, shall look back upon it,
I fear, with self-reproach, and a regret as bitter as unavailing.

Andrew Jackson Defends Indian Removal:
Seventh Annual Message to Congress on 7 December 1835

Provided here are excerpts taken from a message delivered by President Andrew Jackson to Congress in 1835 in which he explains the supposed moral reasons for the pursuit of Indian removal and the need to separate 'civilised' non-Indians from Indian groups.

...The plan of removing the aboriginal people who yet remain within the settled portions of the United States to the country west of the Mississippi River approaches its consummation. It was adopted on the most mature consideration of the condition of this race, and ought to be persisted in till the object is accomplished, and prosecuted with as much vigor as a just regard to their circumstances will permit, and as fast as their consent can be obtained. All preceding experiments for the improvement of the Indians have failed. It seems now to be an established fact that they can not live in contact with a civilized community and prosper. Ages of fruitless endeavors have at length brought us to a knowledge of this principle of intercommunication with them. The past we can not recall, but the future we can provide for.

Independently of the treaty stipulations into which we have entered with the various tribes for the usufructuary rights they have ceded to us, no one can doubt the moral duty of the Government of the United States to protect and if possible to preserve and perpetuate the scattered remnants of this race which are left within our borders. In the discharge of this duty an extensive region in the West has been assigned for their permanent residence. It has been divided into districts and allotted among them. Many have already removed and others are preparing to go, and with the exception of two small bands living in Ohio and Indiana, not exceeding 1,500 persons, and of the Cherokees, all the tribes on the east side of the Mississippi, and extending from Lake Michigan to Florida, have entered into engagements which will lead to their transplantation.

The plan for their removal and reestablishment is founded upon the knowledge we have gained of their character and habits, and has been dictated by a spirit of enlarged liberality. A territory exceeding in extent that relinquished has been granted to each tribe. Of its climate, fertility, and capacity to support an Indian population the representations are highly favorable. To these districts the Indians are removed at the expense of the United States, and with certain supplies of clothing, arms, ammunition, and other indispensable articles; they are also furnished gratuitously with provisions for the period of a year after their arrival at their new homes. In that time, from the nature of the country and of the products raised by them, they can subsist themselves by agricultural labor, if they choose to resort to that mode of life; if they do not they are upon the skirts of the great prairies, where countless herds of buffalo roam, and a short time suffices to adapt their own habits to the changes which a change of the animals destined for their food may require.

Ample arrangements have also been made for the support of schools; in some instances council houses and churches are to be erected, dwellings constructed for the chiefs, and mills for common use. Funds have been set apart for the maintenance of the poor; the most necessary mechanical arts have been introduced, and blacksmiths, gunsmiths, wheelwrights, millwrights, etc., are supported among them. Steel and iron, and sometimes salt, are purchased for them, and plows and other farming utensils, domestic animals, looms, spinning wheels, cards, etc., are presented to them. And besides these beneficial arrangements, annuities are in all cases paid, amounting in some instances to more than $30 for each individual of the tribe, and in all cases sufficiently great, if justly divided and prudently expended, to enable them, in addition to their own exertions, to live comfortably. And as a stimulus for exertion, it is now provided by law that "in all cases of the appointment of interpreters or other persons employed for the benefit of the Indians a preference shall be given to persons of Indian descent, if such can be found who are properly qualified for the discharge of the duties."

Such are the arrangements for the physical comfort and for the moral improvement of the Indians. The necessary measures for their political advancement and for their separation from our citizens have not been neglected. The pledge of the United States has been given by Congress that the country destined for the residence of this people shall be forever "secured and guaranteed to them." A country west of Missouri and Arkansas has been assigned to them, into which the white settlements are not to be pushed. No political communities can be formed in that extensive region, except those which are established by the Indians themselves or by the United States for them and with their concurrence. A barrier has thus been raised for their protection against the encroachment of our citizens, and guarding the Indians as far as possible from those evils which have brought them to their present condition. Summary authority has been given by law to destroy all ardent spirits found in their country, without waiting the doubtful result and slow process of a legal seizure. I consider the absolute and unconditional interdiction of this article among these people as the first and great step in their melioration. Halfway measures will answer no purpose. These can not successfully contend against the cupidity of the seller and the overpowering appetite of the buyer. And the destructive effects of the traffic are marked in every page of the history of our Indian intercourse.

Some general legislation seems necessary for the regulation of the relations which will exist in this new state of things between the Government and people of the United States and these transplanted Indian tribes, and for the establishment among the latter, and with their own consent, of some principles of intercommunication which their juxtaposition will call for; that moral may be substituted for physical force, the authority of a few and simple laws for the tomahawk, and that an end may be put to those bloody wars whose prosecution seems to have made part of their social system.

After the further details of this arrangement are completed, with a very general supervision over them, they ought to be left to the progress of events. These, I indulge the hope, will secure their prosperity and improvement, and a large portion of the moral debt we owe them will then be paid…

Testimony of John G. Burnett over the Removal of the Cherokee in 1838

Provided here are the memories of John G. Burnett (nineteenth century), a private in the US army and an interpreter during the forced removal of the Cherokee from 1838 to 1839. Fifty years after the Trail of Tears he vividly portrays the horrific experiences and destruction forced on the Cherokee by the US military.

…The removal of Cherokee Indians from their life long homes in the year of 1838 found me a young man in the prime of life and a Private soldier in the American Army. Being acquainted with many of the Indians and able to fluently speak their language, I was sent as interpreter into the Smoky Mountain Country in May, 1838, and witnessed the execution of the most brutal order in the History of American Warfare. I saw the helpless Cherokees arrested and dragged from their homes, and driven at the bayonet point into the stockades. And in the chill of a drizzling rain on an October morning I saw them loaded like cattle or sheep into six hundred and forty-five wagons and started toward the west.

One can never forget the sadness and solemnity of that morning. Chief John Ross led in prayer and when the bugle sounded and the wagons started rolling many of the children rose to their feet and waved their little hands good-by to their mountain homes, knowing they were leaving them forever. Many of these helpless people did not have blankets and many of them had been driven from home barefooted.

On the morning of November the 17th we encountered a terrific sleet and snow storm with freezing temperatures and from that day until we reached the end of the fateful journey on March the 26th 1839, the sufferings of the Cherokees were awful. The trail of the exiles was a trail of death. They had to sleep in the wagons and on the ground without fire. And I have known as many as twenty-two of them to die in one night of pneumonia due to ill treatment, cold, and exposure. Among this number was the beautiful Christian wife of Chief John Ross. This noble hearted woman died a martyr to childhood, giving her only blanket for the protection of a sick child. She rode thinly clad through a blinding sleet and snow storm, developed pneumonia and died in the still hours of a bleak winter night…

I made the long journey to the west with the Cherokees and did all that a Private soldier could do to alleviate their sufferings. When on guard duty at night I have many times walked my beat in my blouse in order that some sick child might have the warmth of my overcoat.

I was on guard duty the night Mrs. Ross died. When relieved at midnight I did not retire, but remained around the wagon out of sympathy for Chief

Ross, and at daylight was detailed by Captain McClellan to assist in the burial like the other unfortunates who died on the way. Her unconfined body was buried in a shallow grave by the roadside far from her native home, and the sorrowing Cavalcade moved on...

The only trouble that I had with anybody on the entire journey to the west was a brutal teamster by the name of Ben McDonal, who was using his whip on an old feeble Cherokee to hasten him into the wagon. The sight of that old and nearly blind creature quivering under the lashes of a bull whip was too much for me. I attempted to stop McDonal and it ended in a personal encounter. He lashed me across the face, the wire tip on his whip cutting a bad gash in my cheek. The little hatchet that I had carried in my hunting days was in my belt and McDonal was carried unconscious from the scene.

I was placed under guard but, Ensign Henry Bullock and Private Elkanah Millard had both witnessed the encounter. They gave Captain McClellan the facts and I was never brought to trial. Years later I met 2nd Lieutenant Riley and Ensign Bullock at Bristol at John Roberson's show, and Bullock jokingly reminded me that there was a case still pending against me before a court martial and wanted to know how much longer I was going to have the trial put off?...

The long painful journey to the west ended March 26th, 1839, with four-thousand silent graves reaching from the foothills of the Smoky Mountains to what is known as Indian territory in the West. And covetousness on the part of the white race was the cause of all that the Cherokees had to suffer...

At this time, 1890, we are too near the removal of the Cherokees for our young people to fully understand the enormity of the crime that was committed against a helpless race. Truth is, the facts are being concealed from the young people of today. School children of today do not know that we are living on lands that were taken from a helpless race at the bayonet point to satisfy the white man's greed...Murder is murder, and somebody must answer. Somebody must explain the streams of blood that flowed in the Indian country in the summer of 1838. Somebody must explain the 4000 silent graves that mark the trail of the Cherokees to their exile. I wish I could forget it all, but the picture of 645 wagons lumbering over the frozen ground with their cargo of suffering humanity still lingers in my memory.

Let the historian of a future day tell the sad story with its sighs, its tears and dying groans. Let the great Judge of all the earth weigh our actions and reward us according to our work...

Newspaper Reports about Cherokee and Seminole Removal: (a) Seminole Removal, '*Arkansas Gazette*', 1838–1843

Provided here are six articles from the Arkansas Gazette that describe the removal of the Seminole from their homelands in the east to their new homelands west of the Mississippi River.

Arkansas Gazette, May 30, 1838

The Seminoles are coming - The s.b. Renown, Capt. McGuire, arrived from N. Orleans, on Saturday evening last, and passed up, same night, with 455 Seminole Indians, from Florida, in charge of Lieut. Reynolds, U.S.A. They belong to Micanopy's band, and another detachment of the same tribe, together with the old Chief, may be looked for daily, on board the s.b South Alabama. Among those who have passed up, are about 150 Spanish Indians, or Spaniards who have intermarried with the Seminoles. Take the whole as a body, it is the most dirty, naked, and squalid one that we have seen. Armed sentries of U.S. soldiers were stationed in the different parts of the boat, and not an Indian was permitted to step ashore during the few hours the boat laid at our landing.

Arkansas Gazette, June 13, 1838

More Seminoles - The steam-boat Mount Pleasant brought up 117 Seminoles, from Florida. They were brought up from New Orleans on the steam-boat Ozark, and after the sinking of that boat, were transferred to the Mount Pleasant, and arrived here on Monday evening. We understand they were very serviceable in saving the cargo of the Ozark. Much of it would have been lost but for the aid afforded by them. The Indians were transferred to the steamboat Fox, on yesterday morning, and have proceeded up river. [June 13, 1838]

Arkansas Gazette, November 21, 1838

More Indians -- The steam-boat Rodney is now in the river, with 300 or 400 Seminoles, from Florida, on board, destined for the west, and may be expected here to-day.

Arkansas Gazette, April 3, 1839

Emigrating Seminoles -- About 260 Seminoles arrived here yesterday, from New Orleans, on the s.b. Buckeye, under the charge of Capt. Morrison, of the U. S. Army, on their way to the country assigned them in the west. They are a portion of the band who have been bothering our troops in the hammocks of Florida, headed by the negro Abram, who is with the party. They are all fat and good humored, and look as if they had been living a life of indolent ease, instead of being hunted like wild beasts from fastness to fastness. A good portion of the party is composed of women and children. The Buckeye remains here with the Indians on board, waiting for water to convey them to Fort Gibson.

Arkansas Gazette, April 14, 1841

The Seminoles -- The steamer President arrived at our landing on Saturday last, having on board, in charge of Maj. Belknap, 3d infantry, accompanied by Lieut.

Sprague, and Dr. Barnes, U.S.A., two hundred and twenty Seminole Indians. They are a part of the Talahassee band. Among them were sixty fierce looking warriors. As the boat left the landing the Indians gave a fair specimen of their skill in vocal music, by yelling most vociferously. We learned on board the President that upward of three hundred more of the same band are ready to embark for Arkansas. It does not afford us any pleasure to record the arrival of treacherous enemies on our border; neither is it a pleasing task to be continually, but justly, calling on the Government to send us a force adequate to the protection of the frontier; upon which she is concentrating an immense number of the sworn enemies of the white man. As to the promises of uncivilized Indians, they are made only to be broken. We have no faith in them. Of one thing they may be certain, should they attempt a warlike movement in their new home, that they have not the swamps and hammocks of Florida to hide in; and that the frontiersmen of Arkansas know every nook and hiding place so well, that the utter extermination of the Indians would follow any depredations committed by them on our citizens. We would prefer, however, that a force sufficiently large to awe them should be sent, which would deter the Indians from even attempting hostilities, and remove the alluring bait now shown to them on our unprotected frontier.

Arkansas Gazette, March 15, 1843

There has been a slight rise in the river, and the steamers Arkansas, and Lucy Walker have both passed up, the latter having on board upward of two hundred Seminole Indians, on their way to the west. We learned by her that the distinguished Chief Tiger Tail, died in New Orleans, while accompanying the band, of an affection of the lungs, it is said. We have seldom looked upon men of finer mould or muscular power than these sons of the forest seem to display.

(b) Cherokee Removal, '*Arkansas Gazette*', 1831–1839, and '*Batesville News*', 1838

Contained here are four articles from the Arkansas Gazette and one article from the Batesville News that describe the removal of the Cherokee to their new homelands west of the Mississippi River.

Arkansas Gazette, October 19, 1831

Removal of Indians - We understand that Capt. J.B. CLARK, superintendent for the subsistence and removal of the emigrating Indians, who is located at this place, received advices by the last mail, that the Choctaws are collecting for the purpose of removing to their lands west of Arkansas, and that they will shortly be ready to cross the Mississippi at the following points, viz: Vicksburg, Point Chicot, Mouth of White river, and Memphis, under the direction and control of such Agents as have been appointed to superintend their subsistence and removal.-We also learn, that, in addition to the parties about crossing at the above named places, under the direction of Agents of the Government, a party consisting of about 200 souls, is collecting, for the purpose of emigrating in their own way, and accepting the commutation of $10 per head offered by the Government, in lieu of rations, &c. The last named party will cross the Mississippi at Memphis, and will pass to their new homes at Kiamicha, via this place, and Washington, in Hempstead country.

We are also informed, that Lieut. Ryan has received a letter from Maj. Hook, of the Commissary Department, advising him that the Cherokees within the State of Georgia are about to emigrate to Arkansas, and that the appointment of Superintendent of their removal had been offered to an officer of the Army.

Arkansas Gazette, May 2, 1832

EMIGRATING CHEROKEES

The steam-boat Thomas Yeatman, Capt. Irwin, arrived opposite this place, on Sunday morning last, in eight days from Waterloo, Alabama, with about 400 Cherokee Indians, emigrating to the west from the Old Nation within the limits of Georgia, and passed up the river on the same evening. The party, we learn, were all in good health and fine spirits.

This party is under the charge of Maj. Benj. F. Currey, Superintendent of the Removal and Subsistence of the Cherokees east of the Mississippi, and is the last party of any considerable extent that will emigrate this spring.

It gives us pleasure to learn from Maj. Currey, that the rumor recently afloat here, that the President had proposed to cede Washington and Crawford counties to the Cherokees, on condition that they would cede to the U. States all their lands east of the Mississippi, and remove *en masse* to the west, is destitute of foundation. No such proposition has ever been made to them, nor any other giving any reasonable grounds for such a rumor, or for the alarm which it has excited in some of our western counties. The situation held by Maj. Currey, with respect to this matter, leaves no doubt of the correctness of his information on the subject.

Arkansas Gazette, April 22, 1834

The Cherokee emigrants, who passed up the river, about two weeks since, on board the steam-boat Thomas Yeatman, in charge of Lieut. HARRIS, U.S.A., we understand, are encamped near the mouth of the Cadron, about 35 miles above this place, in consequence of the water being too low for the boat to proceed farther up. Lieut. Harris came down to this place on Friday last, for the purpose of procuring wagons and teams to transport the emigrants to their destination by land, and, having made the necessary arrangements to employ the number require, returned on Saturday evening.

We are sorry to learn, that, in addition to the measles, which was prevailing among the emigrants, when they passed here, and which had caused a number of deaths, principally children, the Cholera has made its appearance among them, and carried off a good many victims. About 30 had died since they landed, previous to Lieut. Harris' leaving, but the mortality had considerably abated within the preceding 24 hours-and subsequent information brings the pleasing news that the disease had nearly subsided, only one death having occurred during the previous 24 hours.

Arkansas Gazette, January 2, 1839

The Cherokees -- A correspondent of the Batesville News, says, under date of Smithville, Lawrence Co., Dec. 13, 1838.

"About twelve hundred Indians passed through this place yesterday, many of whom appeared very respectable. The whole company appear to be well clothed, and comfortably fixed for travelling. I am informed that they are very peaceable, and commit no depredations upon any property in the country through which they pass. They have upwards of one hundred wagons employed in transporting them; their horses are the finest I have ever seen in such a collection. The company consumes about one hundred and fifty bushels of corn per day.

It is stated that they have the measles and whooping-cough among them, and there is an average of four deaths per day."

Batesville News, **December 20, 1838**

CHEROKEE INDIANS

On the 15th inst., a detachment of the Cherokee Indians passed near Batesville, Independence co., Ark., on their way to their new home in the "far west." Many of them came through the town to get their carriages repaired, horses shod, &c. &c...

They left Gunter's Landing, on Tennessee River, about 25 miles above Huntsville, Ala., the 10th of Oct.; since which time, owing to their exposure to the inclemency of the weather, and many of them being destitute of shoes, and other necessary articles of clothing, about 50 of them have died...

Many large and flourishing societies, and schools were gotten up among them. They had a Printing Press of their own, from which a weekly paper, called "The Cherokee Pheonix," was issued for some years, and edited by a native Cherokee. They also had the great part, if not the whole, of the New Testament translated into their own language. Indeed, no aboriginal tribe of Indians in North America, were tending faster toward civilization, and Christianity, than the Cherokee.

But in the difficulties between them and the Georgians, and the General Government, the Georgians, I am credibly informed, destroyed their press; and the turbulence of the times had the unhappy tendency to break up their schools, dissolve their societies, and produce a state of general confusion and distress; so that many who had professed faith in Christ, measured back their steps to earth again … May the Great Disposer of events overrule every thing for their good, and may they be prosperous and happy…

William Wirt:
'The Faith of Our Nation is Fatally Linked with the Existence of the Cherokees …', (c.1830)

In the following text, William Wirt (1772–1834), a prominent lawyer, Attorney General and statesman who represented the Cherokee Nation before the US Supreme Court in both 1831 and 1832, describes what he considered to be the shame and illegality of Cherokee removal and of Indian removal in general.

The faith or our nation is fatally linked with the existence of the Cherokees, and the blow which destroys them quashes forever our glory: for what glory can there be of which a patriot can be proud, after the good name of his country shall have departed? We may gather laurels on the field of battle, and trophies on the ocean, but they will never hide this foul blot on our escutcheon. 'Remember the Cherokee Nation', will be answer enough for the proudest boasts that we can ever make. I cannot believe that this honorable court, possessing the power of preservation, will stand by and see these people stripped of their property and extirpated from the earth while they are holding up to us their treaties and claiming fulfillment of our engagements. If truth and faith and honor and justice have fled from every part of the country, we shall find them here. If not, our sun has gone down in treachery, blood and crime in the face of the world; and instead of being proud of our country, we may well call upon the rocks and mountains to hide our shame from earth and heaven.

Key Extracts from the Marshall Trilogy Cases:
(a) *Johnson v. McIntosh* (1823)

Provided here are the key parts of Chief Justice Marshall's decision that explore the way in which the Supreme Court undermined the Indian ownership of land. Indeed, the court viewed Indian peoples' as merely occupants. Indeed, the court viewed Indian peoples' as merely occupants and declared that the rights of America to acquire land through the process of discovery supplanted those of the Indians.

The plaintiffs in this cause claim the land, in their declaration mentioned, under two grants, purporting to be made, the first in 1773, and the last in 1775, by the chiefs of certain Indian tribes, constituting the Illinois and the Piankeshaw nations; and the question is, whether this title can be recognised in the Courts of the United States?

…The inquiry, therefore, is, in a great measure, confined to the power of Indians to give, and of private individuals to receive, a title which can be sustained in the Courts of this country.

...On the discovery of this immense continent, the great nations of Europe were eager to appropriate to themselves so much of it as they could respectively acquire. Its vast extent offered an ample field to the ambition and enterprise of all; and the character and religion of its inhabitants afforded an apology for considering them as a people over whom the superior genius of Europe might claim an ascendency. The potentates of the old world found no difficulty in convincing themselves that they made ample compensation to the inhabitants of the new, by bestowing on them civilization and Christianity, in exchange for unlimited independence ... This [discovery] principle was, that discovery gave title to the government by whose subjects, or by whose authority, it was made, against all other European governments, which title might be consummated by possession.

...In the establishment of these relations, the rights of the original inhabitants were, in no instance, entirely disregarded; but were necessarily, to a considerable extent, impaired. They were admitted to be the rightful occupants of the soil, with a legal as well as just claim to retain possession of it, and to use it according to their own discretion; but their rights to complete sovereignty, as independent nations, were necessarily diminished, and their power to dispose of the soil at their own will, to whomsoever they pleased, was denied by the original fundamental principle, that discovery gave exclusive title to those who made it.

While the different nations of Europe respected the right of the natives, as occupants, they asserted the ultimate dominion to be in themselves; and claimed and exercised, as a consequence of this ultimate dominion, a power to grant the soil, while yet in possession of the natives. These grants have been understood by all, to convey a title to the grantees, subject only to the Indian right of occupancy.

...It has never been doubted, that either the United States, or the several States, had a clear title to all the lands within the boundary lines described in the treaty, subject only to the Indian right of occupancy, and that the exclusive power to extinguish that right, was vested in that government which might constitutionally exercise it.

...discovery gave an exclusive right to extinguish the Indian title of occupancy, either by purchase or by conquest; and gave also a right to such a degree of sovereignty, as the circumstances of the people would allow them to exercise.

...We will not enter into the controversy, whether agriculturists, merchants, and manufacturers, have a right, on abstract principles, to expel hunters from the territory they possess, or to contract their limits. Conquest gives a title which the Courts of the conqueror cannot deny ... These claims have been maintained and established as far west as the river Mississippi, by the sword. The title to a vast portion of the lands we now hold, originates in them. It is not for the Courts of this country to question the validity of this title, or to sustain one which is incompatible with it.

The title by conquest is acquired and maintained by force. The conqueror prescribes its limits … the conquered shall not be wantonly oppressed, and that their condition shall remain as eligible as is compatible with the objects of the conquest. Most usually, they are incorporated with the victorious nation, and become subjects or citizens of the government with which they are connected. The new and old members of the society mingle with each other; the distinction between them is gradually lost, and they make one people…

…But the tribes of Indians inhabiting this country were fierce savages, whose occupation was war, and whose subsistence was drawn chiefly from the forest. To leave them in possession of their country, was to leave the country a wilderness; to govern them as a distinct people, was impossible, because they were as brave and as high spirited as they were fierce, and were ready to repel by arms every attempt on their independence.

…However extravagant the pretension of converting the discovery of an inhabited country into conquest may appear; if the principle has been asserted in the first instance, and afterwards sustained; if a country has been acquired and held under it; if the property of the great mass of the community originates in it, it becomes the law of the land, and cannot be questioned. So, too, with respect to the concomitant principle, that the Indian inhabitants are to be considered merely as occupants, to be protected, indeed, while in peace, in the possession of their lands, but to be deemed incapable of transferring the absolute title to others…

…It is supposed to be a principle of universal law, that, if an uninhabited country be discovered by a number of individuals, who acknowledge no connexion with, and owe no allegiance to, any government whatever, the country becomes the property of the discoverers, so far at least as they can use it. They acquire a title in common…

…the Court is decidedly of opinion, that the plaintiffs do not exhibit a title which can be sustained in the Courts of the United States; and that there is no error in the judgment which was rendered against them in the District Court of Illinois.

(b) *Cherokee Nation v. Georgia* (1831)

Provided here are key excerpts taken from the opinion of Chief Justice John Marshall. Here he dramatically limits the sovereignty of all Indian nations to act with other international nations, such as France or the United Kingdom, and famously, terms them 'domestic dependent nations'. Therefore, Indian nations under American law were now within the internal authority and boundaries of the United States of America.

…This bill is brought by the Cherokee nation, praying an injunction to restrain the state of Georgia from the execution of certain laws of that state, which, as is alleged, go directly to annihilate the Cherokees as a political society, and to seize, for the use of Georgia, the lands of the nation which have been assured to them by the United States in solemn treaties repeatedly made and still in force.

If courts were permitted to indulge their sympathies, a case better calculated to excite them can scarcely be imagined. A people once numerous, powerful, and truly independent, found by our ancestors in the quiet and uncontrolled possession of an ample domain, gradually sinking beneath our superior policy, our arts and our arms, have yielded their lands by successive treaties, each of which contains a solemn guarantee of the residue, until they retain no more of their formerly extensive territory than is deemed necessary to their comfortable subsistence. To preserve this remnant, the present application is made.

…Is the Cherokee nation a foreign state in the sense in which that term is used in the constitution?

The counsel for the plaintiffs have maintained the affirmative of this proposition with great earnestness and ability. So much of the argument as was intended to prove the character of the Cherokees as a state, as a distinct political society, separated from others, capable of managing its own affairs and governing itself, has, in the opinion of a majority of the judges, been completely successful. They have been uniformly treated as a state from the settlement of our country. The numerous treaties made with them by the United States recognize them as a people capable of maintaining the relations of peace and war, of being responsible in their political character for any violation of their engagements, or for any aggression committed on the citizens of the United States by any individual of their community. Laws have been enacted in the spirit of these treaties. The acts of our government plainly recognize the Cherokee nation as a state, and the courts are bound by those acts.

A question of much more difficulty remains. Do the Cherokees constitute a foreign state in the sense of the constitution?

…This argument is imposing, but we must examine it more closely before we yield to it. The condition of the Indians in relation to the United States is perhaps unlike that of any other two people in existence. In the general, nations not owing a common allegiance are foreign to each other. The term foreign nation is, with strict propriety, applicable by either to the other. But the relation of the Indians to the United States is marked by peculiar and cardinal distinctions which exist no where else. The Indian territory is admitted to compose a part of the United States. In all our maps, geographical treatises, histories, and laws, it is so considered. In all our intercourse with foreign nations, in our commercial regulations, in any attempt at intercourse between Indians and foreign nations, they are considered as within the jurisdictional limits of the United States, subject to many of those restraints which are imposed upon our own citizens. They acknowledge themselves in their treaties to be under the protection of the United States; they admit that the United States shall have the sole and exclusive right of regulating the trade with them, and managing all their affairs as they think proper...

Though the Indians are acknowledged to have an unquestionable, and, heretofore, unquestioned right to the lands they occupy, until that right shall be extinguished by a voluntary cession to our government; yet it may well be doubted whether those tribes which reside within the acknowledged boundaries of the United States can, with strict accuracy, be denominated foreign nations. They may, more correctly, perhaps, be denominated domestic dependent nations. They occupy a territory to which we assert a title independent of their will, which must take effect in point of possession when their right of possession ceases. Meanwhile they are in a state of pupilage. Their relation to the United States resembles that of a ward to his guardian.

They look to our government for protection; rely upon its kindness and its power; appeal to it for relief to their wants; and address the president as their great father. They and their country are considered by foreign nations, as well as by ourselves, as being so completely under the sovereignty and dominion of the United States, that any attempt to acquire their lands, or to form a political connexion with them, would be considered by all as an invasion of our territory, and an act of hostility.

...The court has bestowed its best attention on this question, and, after mature deliberation, the majority is of opinion that an Indian tribe or nation within the United States is not a foreign state in the sense of the constitution, and cannot maintain an action in the courts of the United States.

...If it be true that the Cherokee nation have rights, this is not the tribunal in which those rights are to be asserted. If it be true that wrongs have been inflicted, and that still greater are to be apprehended, this is not the tribunal which can redress the past or prevent the future...

(c) *Worcester v. Georgia* (1832)

Provided here are key excerpts and principles of the seminal 1832 decision delivered by Chief Justice John Marshall and the Supreme Court. In this ruling, Chief Justice John Marshall held that the expression of sovereignty of the State of Georgia within Cherokee lands was repugnant to Cherokee sovereignty and to the laws, treaties and the Constitution of the United States. Therefore, Cherokee sovereignty had precedence and it ousted Georgia law from Cherokee lands.

This cause, in every point of view in which it can be placed, is of the deepest interest.

The defendant is a state, a member of the union, which has exercised the powers of government over a people who deny its jurisdiction, and are under the protection of the United States.

The plaintiff is a citizen of the state of Vermont, condemned to hard labour for four years in the penitentiary of Georgia; under colour of an act which he alleges to be repugnant to the constitution, laws, and treaties of the United States.

…The first step, then, in the inquiry, which the constitution and laws impose on this court, is an examination of the right-fulness of this claim.

America, separated from Europe by a wide ocean, was inhabited by a distinct people, divided into separate nations, independent of each other and of the rest of the world, having institutions of their own, and governing themselves by their own laws. It is difficult to comprehend the proposition, that the inhabitants of either quarter of the globe could have rightful original claims of dominion over the inhabitants of the other, or over the lands they occupied; or that the discovery of either by the other should give the discoverer rights in the country discovered, which annulled the pre- existing rights of its ancient possessors.

After lying concealed for a series of ages, the enterprise of Europe, guided by nautical science, conducted some of her adventurous sons into this western world. They found it in possession of a people who had made small progress in agriculture or manufactures, and whose general employment was war, hunting, and fishing.

Did these adventurers, by sailing along the coast, and occasionally landing on it, acquire for the several governments to whom they belonged, or by whom they were commissioned, a rightful property in the soil, from the Atlantic to the Pacific; or rightful dominion over the numerous people who occupied it?

…[Discovery] … regulated the right given by discovery among the European discoverers; but could not affect the rights of those already in possession, either as aboriginal occupants, or as occupants by virtue of a discovery made before the memory of man. It gave the exclusive right to purchase, but did not found that right on a denial of the right of the possessor to sell.

…The treaties and laws of the United States contemplate the Indian territory as completely separated from that of the states; and provide that all intercourse with them shall be carried on exclusively by the government of the union…

…The Indian nations had always been considered as distinct, independent political communities, retaining their original natural rights, as the undisputed possessors of the soil, from time immemorial … The very term 'nation,' so generally applied to them, means 'a people distinct from others.' The constitution, by declaring treaties already made, as well as those to be made, to be the supreme law of the land, has adopted and sanctioned the previous treaties with the Indian nations, and consequently admits their rank among those powers who are capable of making treaties. The words 'treaty' and 'nation' are words of our own language, selected in our diplomatic and legislative proceedings, by ourselves, having each a definite and well understood meaning. We have applied them to Indians, as we have applied them to the other nations of the earth. They are applied to all in the same sense.

…The very fact of repeated treaties with them recognizes it; and the settled doctrine of the law of nations is, that a weaker power does not surrender its independence-its right to self government, by associating with a stronger, and taking its protection. A weak state, in order to provide for its safety, may place itself under the protection of one more powerful, without stripping itself of the right of government, and ceasing to be a state…

The Cherokee nation, then, is a distinct community occupying its own territory, with boundaries accurately described, in which the laws of Georgia can have no force, and which the citizens of Georgia have no right to enter, but with the assent of the Cherokees themselves, or in conformity with treaties, and with the acts of congress. The whole intercourse between the United States and this nation, is, by our constitution and laws, vested in the government of the United States.

The act of the state of Georgia, under which the plaintiff in error was prosecuted, is consequently void, and the judgment a nullity…

…If the review which has been taken be correct, and we think it is, the acts of Georgia are repugnant to the constitution, laws, and treaties of the United States.

They interfere forcibly with the relations established between the United States and the Cherokee nation, the regulation of which, according to the settled principles of our constitution, are committed exclusively to the government of the union.

They are in direct hostility with treaties, repeated in a succession of years, which mark out the boundary that separates the Cherokee country from Georgia; guaranty to them all the land within their boundary; solemnly pledge the faith of the United States to restrain their citizens from trespassing on it; and recognize the pre-existing power of the nation to govern itself.

…The forcible seizure and abduction of the plaintiff in error, who was residing in the nation with its permission, any by authority of the president of the United States, is also a violation of the acts which authorise the chief magistrate to exercise this authority.

…It is the opinion of this court that the judgment of the superior court for the county of Gwinnett, in the state of Georgia, condemning Samuel A. Worcester to hard labour, in the penitentiary of the state of Georgia, for four years, was pronounced by that court under colour of a law which is void, as being repugnant to the constitution, treaties, and laws of the United States, and ought, therefore, to be reversed and annulled.

CHAPTER SIX

THREE KEY EVENTS IN WESTERN EXPANSION: SAND CREEK (1864), LITTLE BIG HORN (1876) AND WOUNDED KNEE (1890)

The period of Indian removal was soon followed by increased western expansion by the United States into Indian lands west of the Mississippi River. American expansionism was built on the doctrine of Manifest Destiny, which declared that America was sanctioned by God to claim, occupy and use all lands from the Mississippi to the Pacific Ocean. This doctrine brought the United States into direct conflict with Indian groups which included the Apache, Blackfeet, Cheyenne, Hidatsa and Sioux and it fundamentally changed the complexion of Indian country and Indian land title to the west of the Mississippi. American land acquisition, the creation of new states within the American Union, the opening of the Oregon Trail and the discovery of gold in California during 1848, all allowed miners, settlers and land speculators to encroach on Indian lands. The overall impact of the land acquisition policy by the United States and piecemeal non-Indian encroachment on Indian territory resulted in increased tension between many non-Indian settlers and groups of Indians, and it led directly to massacres and military conflicts between groups of Indians and the US army. This chapter examines the varied responses by both Indians and non-Indians to three pivotal events: Sand Creek (1864), Little Big Horn (1876) and Wounded Knee (1890).

One of the worst massacres perpetrated by the US army in the West was against the Cheyenne in Sand Creek during 1864. The discovery of gold on Indian lands in 1858, on land called Colorado by the United States, resulted in thousands of non-Indian settlers encroaching on Cheyenne territory. Settlers disrupted Cheyenne culture and upset the established Cheyenne reliance on hunting buffalo.[1] During 1864 the Cheyenne (led by Black Kettle) and Southern Arapaho were camped at Sand Creek, lands under the protection of the United States government and army. On the morning of 29 November 1864, Colonel J. M. Chivington (1821–1894) and the Colorado Cavalry attacked the camp as the Cheyenne and Arapaho slept. During the attack, Chief Black Kettle raised an American and white flag but it did not stop the massacre and murder of 270 men, women and children. However, there were survivors from the events that unfolded at Sand Creek, and many Cheyenne, such as George Bent (1843–1917), and United States army personnel witnessed the horrendous atrocities. Only a few months after the massacre, the US Congress heard testimony from personnel who were at Sand Creek in 1864.[2] In contrast to the evidence presented by Chivington to the Joint Committee on the Conduct of War in Denver, Territory of Colorado, on 26 April 1865, in which he defended and praised his efforts at Sand Creek, the evidence of John S. Smith (c.1810–1871), a United States–Indian interpreter and special Indian agent based at Fort Lyon, Colorado, to Congress on 14 March 1865, openly questioned the tactics and brutality used by Chivington and his men against defenceless Indians and their families.[3] However some other opinions offered by non-Indians, such as those of the *Rocky Mountain News*, a Colorado newspaper, depicted the actions of Chivington and his men as 'heroic' and spoke of the importance of defeating the 'Indians'.[4]

One of the most famous military events in the wars of the West took place at Little Big Horn in 1876, with the defeat of George Custer by Sitting Bull and the Sioux and Cheyenne nations. The pretext to this event revolved around Sioux lands, in particular the Black Hills. These are sacred to the Sioux, were recognised as such by the United States and other Indian nations and protected by the Treaty of Fort Laramie of 1868. In 1874, Custer led an expedition to confirm the existence of gold in the Black Hills region whereupon the US government offered to purchase the lands. However, Sitting Bull refused to sell. Then in 1876, in direct contravention to treaties, the United States launched attacks on the Sioux and Cheyenne to acquire the Black Hills and remove them to reservations. On 25 June 1876, George Custer and the Seventh Cavalry, assisted by Major Marcus Reno and Captain Frederick Benteen, attacked what was thought to be a small Indian village of Lakota and Cheyenne at the Little Big Horn. However, Custer chose to divide his forces and send Reno and his men to the south and Benteen and his men to the southwest.[5] In the events that unfolded, Reno lost nearly half of his men and because Custer miscalculated his tactics and the surrounding terrain, he eventually was surrounded by superior opponents. In less than an hour, the Lakota and Cheyenne were victorious and Custer and his hundreds of men had been killed.[6] Soon after the events at Little Big Horn, many non-Indians, including George Herendon (nineteenth/ twentieth century), a scout for the Seventh Cavalry who was under the command of Marcus Reno, as well as American newspapers told their vivid accounts of the events that took place on 25 June 1876.[7] In contrast, many years after the events that took place at Little Big Horn, a number of Indians, which included Chief Red Horse of the Lakota (nineteenth century) and Two Moons (c.1842–1917), a famous Northern Cheyenne warrior, told their sides of the story. They described one of the most famous Indian victories over a US army in American history.[8]

Wounded Knee in 1890 is often put forward as symbolizing the end of nearly a century of Indian military resistance against American encroachment into Indian lands west of the Mississippi River. In truth, however, sporadic Indian armed resistance to non-Indian encroachment onto Indian lands has continued over time up into the present day. During the 1870s–1890 period, the intent of the US government and army was to destroy Indian resistance to American demands for land and to ensure that non-assimilated Indians were confined to reservations. Facing sustained American military aggression, many Indian nations adopted new rituals and ways of expressing their spiritual beliefs in this period. Indian prophets suggested that the performance of the Ghost Dance ritual would see the return of the buffalo, the return of the great number of Indians lost in previous generations and result in the disappearance of the Americans.[9] The Paiute prophet Wovoka (c.1856–1932), born in Nevada and known also as Jack Wilson, was one man who practised and spread the Ghost Dance faith to many Indian nations in the American West. He promised a general return of traditional Indian life-ways if the Indians themselves gave up alcohol, lived in peace and danced. The Ghost Dance originated in Nevada and during the 1880s, it quickly spread among the Plains Indians, including the Lakota. It was a potent spiritual weapon in the quest to defeat the non-Indian encroachment.[10] However, the Ghost Dance led many non-Indians, including General Nelson A. Miles (1839–1925), a decorated member of the US army who took a lead role in most of the campaigns against the Indian nations of the Great Plains, to question and fear the strange new rituals practised by the Lakota.[11] The Ghost Dance was said by non-Indians to have precipitated the Wounded Knee Massacre on 29 December 1890.

The events that led to the massacre began when American troops, suspicious of a Sioux uprising, ordered Indian police to arrest Chief Sitting Bull and in the fracas, Sitting Bull resisted arrest and was killed. The Sioux fled. A number of Sioux were tracked down by the US army and held at a camp at Wounded Knee Creek. On the morning of 29 December 1890, the American army was sent to disarm some Mineconjou men and in the process a gun shot went off. What followed was one of the most brutal and dishonourable events in American history. The Seventh Cavalry attacked Big Foot and his band of Mineconjou Sioux and murdered over 200 men, women and children with indiscriminate firing of machine guns through the Indian encampment.[12] Although the Wounded Knee Massacre is often held to symbolise the culmination of conflict between American culture and diverse Indian cultures, it did not result in the end of the Lakota or the end of hundreds of separate Indian nations. Indeed in 1973, nearly a century after the 1890 massacre, Wounded Knee became the crucible of yet another conflict between a number of Indian nations and the United States. Indian actions in 1973 surrounding Wounded Knee symbolised a new cultural and political renaissance of Native America.

The events that took place at Sand Creek, Little Big Horn and Wounded Knee were precipitated by decades of conflict and suspicion between numerous Indian nations and the United States. The victory of the Cheyenne and the Sioux over the US army in 1876 represented one of the finest Indian military achievements and, for a brief moment, halted the campaign of the US army to end Indian resistance and slowed the territorial expansion of the United States from the east to the west coast. However, the bloody and inhumane massacres carried out by the US army against the Cheyenne in 1864 and the Sioux in 1890 were a gruesome part of the military campaign exercised by the United States in the West. These massacres devastated the lives of many Indians and their families for generations and increased the suspicions and acrimony between Indians and the United States. As a result, many Indians turned to different spiritual paths including the Ghost Dance, in order to find ways of ending the climate of hopelessness. Although overt large-scale Indian military resistance to America ended in 1890 and Indian population numbers were reduced to an all-time low, these events did not result in the complete destruction of Indian nations and their cultures. After 1890 the strength and resilience of Indian cultures and their ways of life against the policies of the American government allowed them to survive against unprecedented odds as proud Indian nations.

SOURCES

George Bent: Firsthand Account of the Sand Creek Massacre, 1864

The following extract presents a Cheyenne viewpoint on the fateful morning at Sand Creek in 1864. The extract below is the evidence of George Bent (1843–1917), a Cheyenne living at Sand Creek who witnessed the atrocities. Bent describes the bloodshed and devastation caused by the unprovoked attack of the US army on the Indian camp and how those who survived the onslaught fled.

When I looked toward the chief's lodge, I saw that Black Kettle had a large American flag up on a long lodgepole as a signal to the troop that the camp was friendly. Part of the warriors were running out toward the pony herds and the rest of the people were rushing about the camp in great fear. All the time Black Kettle kept calling out not to be frightened; that the camp was under protection and there was no danger. Then suddenly the troops opened fire on this mass of men, women, and children, and all began to scatter and run.

The main body of Indians rushed up the bed of the creek, which was dry, level sand with only a few little pools of water here and there. On each side of this wide bed stood banks from two to ten feet high. While the main body of the people fled up this dry bed, a part of the young men were trying to save the herd from the soldiers, and small parties were running in all directions toward the sand hills. One of these parties, made up of perhaps ten middle-aged Cheyenne men, started for the sand hills west of the creek, and I joined them. Before we had gone far, the troops saw us and opened a heavy fire on us, forcing us to run back and take shelter in the bed of the creek. We now started up the stream bed, following the main body of Indians and with a whole company of cavalry close on our heels shooting at us every foot of the way. As we went along we passed many Indians, men, women, and children, some wounded, others dead, lying on the sand and in the pools of water. Presently we came to a place where the main party had stopped, and were now hiding in pits that they had dug in the high bank of the stream. Just as we reached this place, I was struck by a ball [bullet] in the hip and badly wounded, but I managed to get into one of the pits. About these pits nearly all Chivington's men had gathered and more were continually coming up, for they had given up the pursuit of the small bodies of Indians who had fled to the sand hills.

The soldiers concentrated their fire on the people in the pits, and we fought back as well as we could with guns and bows, but we had only a few guns. The troops did not rush in and fight hand to hand, but once or twice after they had killed many of the men in a certain pit, they rushed in and finished up the work, killing the wounded and the women and children that had not been hurt. The fight here was kept up until nearly sundown, when at last the commanding officer called off his men and all started back down the creek toward the camp that they had driven us from. As they went back, the soldiers scalped the dead lying in the bed of the stream and cut up the bodies in a manner that no Indian could equal. Little Bear told me recently that after the fight he saw the soldiers scalping the dead and saw an old woman who had been scalped by the soldiers walk about, but unable to see where to go. Her whole scalp had been taken and the skin of her forehead fell down over her eyes…

Black Kettle and his wife followed the Indians in their flight up the dry bed of the creek. The soldiers pursued them, firing at them constantly, and before the two had gone far, the woman was shot down. Black Kettle supposed she was dead and, the soldiers being close behind him, continued his flight. The troops followed him all the way to the rifle pits, but he reached them unhurt. After the fight he returned down the stream looking for his wife's body. Presently he found her alive and not dangerously wounded. She told him that after she had fallen wounded, the soldiers had ridden up and again shot her several times as she lay there on the sand. Black Kettle put her on his back and carried her up the stream until he met a mounted man, and the two put her on the horse…

Soon after the troops left us, we came out of the pits and began to move slowly up the stream. More than half of us were wounded and all were on foot. When we had gone up the stream a few miles, we began to meet some of our men who had left camp at the beginning of the attack and tried to save the horses … I was so badly wounded that I could hardly walk.

When our party had gone about ten miles above the captured camp, we went into a ravine and stopped there for the night. It was very dark and bitterly cold. Very few of us had warm clothing, for we had been driven out of our beds and had had no time to dress. The wounded suffered greatly. There was no wood to be had, but the unwounded men and women collected grass and made fires. The wounded were placed near the fires and covered with grass to keep them from freezing. All night long the people kept up a constant hallooing to attract the attention of any Indians who might be wandering about in the sand hills. Our people had been scattered all over the country by the troops, and no one knows how many of them may have been frozen to death in the open country that night.

Battle of the Little Bighorn: An Eyewitness Account by Lakota Chief Red Horse, 1881

The following text is taken from the eyewitness account of Chief Red Horse, a Lakota, recorded at the Cheyenne River Reservation in 1881. It offers a detailed perspective on the actions of the US army and the successful tactics used by the Indians to defeat Custer.

Five springs ago I, with many Sioux Indians, took down and packed up our tipis and moved from Cheyenne river to the Rosebud river, where we camped a few days; then took down and packed up our lodges and moved to the Little Bighorn river and pitched our lodges with the large camp of Sioux.

The Sioux were camped on the Little Bighorn river as follows: The lodges of the Uncpapas were pitched highest up the river under a bluff. The Santee lodges were pitched next. The Oglala's lodges were pitched next. The Brule lodges were pitched next. The Minneconjou lodges were pitched next. The Sans Arcs' lodges were pitched next. The Blackfeet lodges were pitched next. The Cheyenne lodges were pitched next. A few Arikara Indians were among the Sioux (being without lodges of their own). Two-Kettles, among the other Sioux (without lodges).

I was a Sioux chief in the council lodge. My lodge was pitched in the center of the camp. The day of the attack I and four women were a short distance from the camp digging wild turnips. Suddenly one of the women attracted my attention to a cloud of dust rising a short distance from camp. I soon saw that the soldiers were charging the camp. To the camp I and the women ran. When I arrived a person told me to hurry to the council lodge. The soldiers charged so quickly we could not talk (council). We came out of the council lodge and talked in all directions. The Sioux mount horses, take guns, and go fight the soldiers. Women and children mount horses and go, meaning to get out of the way.

Among the soldiers was an officer who rode a horse with four white feet. The Sioux have for a long time fought many brave men of different people, but the Sioux say this officer was the bravest man they had ever fought. I don't know whether this was Gen. Custer or not. Many of the Sioux men that I hear talking tell me it was. I saw this officer in the fight many times, but did not see his body. It has been told me that he was killed by a Santee Indian, who took his horse. This officer wore a large-brimmed hat and a deerskin coat. This officer saved the lives of many soldiers by turning his horse and covering the retreat. Sioux say this officer was the bravest man they ever fought. I saw two officers looking alike, both having long yellowish hair.

Before the attack the Sioux were camped on the Rosebud river. Sioux moved down a river running into the Little Bighorn river, crossed the Little Bighorn river, and camped on its west bank.

This day [day of attack] a Sioux man started to go to Red Cloud agency, but when he had gone a short distance from camp he saw a cloud of dust rising and turned back and said he thought a herd of buffalo was coming near the village.

The day was hot. In a short time the soldiers charged the camp. [This was Maj. Reno's battalion of the Seventh Cavalry.] The soldiers came on the trail made by the Sioux camp in moving, and crossed the Little Bighorn river above where the Sioux crossed, and attacked the lodges of the Uncpapas, farthest up the river. The women and children ran down the Little Bighorn river a short distance into a ravine. The soldiers set fire to the lodges. All the Sioux now charged the soldiers and drove them in confusion across the Little Bighorn river, which was very rapid, and several soldiers were drowned in it. On a hill the soldiers stopped and the Sioux surrounded them. A Sioux man came and said that a different party of Soldiers had all the women and children prisoners. Like a whirlwind the word went around, and the Sioux all heard it and left the soldiers on the hill and went quickly to save the women and children.

From the hill that the soldiers were on to the place where the different soldiers [by this term Red-Horse always means the battalion immediately commanded by General Custer, his mode of distinction being that they were a different body from that first encountered] were seen was level ground with the exception of a creek. Sioux thought the soldiers on the hill [i.e., Reno's battalion] would charge them in rear, but when they did not the Sioux thought the soldiers on the hill were out of cartridges. As soon as we had killed all the different soldiers the Sioux all went back to kill the soldiers on the hill. All the Sioux watched around the hill on which were the soldiers until a Sioux man came and said many walking soldiers were coming near. The coming of the walking soldiers was the saving of the soldiers on the hill. Sioux can not fight the walking soldiers [infantry], being afraid of them, so the Sioux hurriedly left.

The soldiers charged the Sioux camp about noon. The soldiers were divided, one party charging right into the camp. After driving these soldiers across the river, the Sioux charged the different soldiers [i.e., Custer's] below, and drive them in confusion; these soldiers became foolish, many throwing away their guns and raising their hands, saying, "Sioux, pity us; take us prisoners." The Sioux did not take a single soldier prisoner, but killed all of them; none were left alive for even a few minutes. These different soldiers discharged their guns but little. I took a gun and two belts off two dead soldiers; out of one belt two cartridges were gone, out of the other five.

The Sioux took the guns and cartridges off the dead soldiers and went to the hill on which the soldiers were, surrounded and fought them with the guns and cartridges of the dead soldiers. Had the soldiers not divided I think they would have killed many Sioux. The different soldiers [i.e., Custer's battalion] that the Sioux killed made five brave stands. Once the Sioux charged right in the midst of the different soldiers and scattered them all, fighting among the soldiers hand to hand.

One band of soldiers was in rear of the Sioux. When this band of soldiers charged, the Sioux fell back, and the Sioux and the soldiers stood facing each other. Then all the Sioux became brave and charged the soldiers. The Sioux went but a short distance before they separated and surrounded the soldiers. I could see the officers riding in front of the soldiers and hear them shooting. Now the Sioux had many killed. The soldiers killed 136 and wounded 160 Sioux. The Sioux killed all these different soldiers in the ravine.

The soldiers charged the Sioux camp farthest up the river. A short time after the different soldiers charged the village below. While the different soldiers and Sioux were fighting together the Sioux chief said, "Sioux men, go watch soldiers on the hill and prevent their joining the different soldiers." The Sioux men took the clothing off the dead and dressed themselves in it. Among the soldiers were white men who were not soldiers. The Sioux dressed in the soldiers' and white men's clothing fought the soldiers on the hill.

The banks of the Little Bighorn river were high, and the Sioux killed many of the soldiers while crossing. The soldiers on the hill dug up the ground [i.e., made earth-works], and the soldiers and Sioux fought at long range, sometimes the Sioux charging close up. The fight continued at long range until a Sioux man saw the walking soldiers coming. When the walking soldiers came near the Sioux became afraid and ran away.

Two Moons: 'All the Soldiers Were Now Killed', 1876

Provided here is a Cheyenne account of the Battle of Little Big Horn by Two Moons (c.1842–1917), a famous Northern Cheyenne warrior, in an interview with Hamlin Garland for McClure's Magazine in 1898. Two Moons describes the Cheyenne success at the Little Big Horn and the death of the American soldiers involved in the battle.

We traveled far, and one day we met a big camp of Sioux at Charcoal Butte. We camped with the Sioux, and had a good time, plenty grass, plenty game, good water. Crazy Horse was head chief of the camp. Sitting Bull was camped a little ways below, on the Little Missouri River.

Crazy Horse said to me, "I'm glad you are come. We are going to fight the white man again."

The camp was already full of wounded men, women, and children.

I said to Crazy Horse, "All right. I am ready to fight. I have fought already. My people have been killed, my horses stolen; I am satisfied to fight".…

About May, when the grass was tall and the horses strong, we broke camp, and started across the country to the mouth of the Tongue River. Then Sitting Bull and Crazy Horse and all went up the Rosebud. There we had a big fight with General Crook, and whipped him. Many soldiers were killed--few Indians. It was a great fight, much smoke and dust.

From there we all went over the divide, and camped in the valley of Little Horn. Everybody thought, "Now we are out of the white man's country. He can live there, we will live here." After a few days, one morning when I was in camp north of Sitting Bull, a Sioux messenger rode up and said, "Let everybody paint up, cook, and great ready for a big dance."

Cheyennes then went to work to cook, cut up tobacco, and get ready. We all thought to dance all day. We were very glad to think we were far away from the white man.

I went to water my horses at the creek, and washed them off with cool water, then took a swim myself. I came back to the camp afoot. When I got near my lodge, I looked up the Little Horn towards Sitting Bull's camp. I saw a great dust rising. It looked like a whirlwind. Soon Sioux horsemen came rushing into camp shouting, "Soldiers come! Plenty white soldiers"....

I got on my horse, and rode out into my camp. I called out to the people all running about: "I am Two Moons, your chief. Don't run away. Stay here and fight. You must stay and fight the white soldiers. I shall stay even if I am to be killed"....

While I was sitting on my horse I saw flags come up over the hill to the east. Then the soldiers rose all at once, all on horses. ... They formed into three bunches with a little ways between. Then a bugle sounded, and they all got off horses, and some soldiers led the horses back over the hill.

Then the Sioux rode up the ridge on all sides, riding very fast. The Cheyennes went up the left way. Then the shooting was quick, quick. Pop-pop-pop very fast. Some of the soldiers were down on their knees, some standing. Officers all in front. The smoke was like a great cloud, and everywhere the Sioux went the dust rose like smoke. We circled all round him--swirling like water round a stone. We shoot, we ride fast, we shoot again. Soldiers drop, and horses fall on them. Soldiers in line drop, but one man rides up and down the line--all the time shouting. He rode a sorrel horse with white face and white fore-legs. I don't know who he was. He was a brave man.

Indians kept swirling round and round, and the soldiers killed only a few. Many soldiers fell. At last all horses killed but five. Once in a while some man would break out and run toward the river, but he would fall. At last about a hundred men and five horsemen stood on the hill all bunched together. All along the bugler kept blowing his commands. He was very brave too. Then a chief was killed. I hear it was Long Hair [George Armstrong Custer], I don't know; and then the five horsemen and the bunch of men, maybe so forty, started toward the river. The man on the sorrel horse led them, shouting all the time. He wore a buckskin shirt, and had long black hair and mustache. He fought hard with a big knife. His men were all covered with white dust. I couldn't tell whether they were officers or not. One man all alone ran far down toward the river, then round up over the hill. I thought he was going to escape, but a Sioux fired and hit him in the head....

All the soldiers were now killed, and the bodies were stripped. After that no one could tell which were officers. The bodies were left where they fell. We had no dance that night. We were sorrowful.

Next day four Sioux chiefs and two Cheyennes and I, Two Moons, went upon the battlefield to count the dead. One man carried a little bundle of sticks. When we came to dead men, we took a little stick and gave it to another man, so we counted the dead. There were 388. There were thirty-nine Sioux and seven Cheyennes killed, and about a hundred wounded.

Some white soldiers were cut with knives, to make sure they were dead; and the war women had mangled some. Most were left just where they fell.

Lakota Accounts of the Massacre at Wounded Knee, 1891

Provided here are three Lakota accounts of the massacre in 1890, which were recorded by stenograph during a council between delegations of the Sioux and the Commissioner of Indian Affairs in Washington, D.C. in 1891.

TURNING HAWK, Pine Ridge (Mr. Cook, interpreter)…

In the course of time we heard that the soldiers were moving toward the scene of trouble. After awhile some of the soldiers finally reached our place and we heard that a number of them also reached our friends at Rosebud. Of course, when a large body of soldiers is moving toward a certain direction they inspire a more or less amount of awe, and it is natural that the women and children who see this large moving mass are made afraid of it and be put in a condition to make them run away. At first we thought the Pine Ridge and Rosebud were the only two agencies where soldiers were sent, but finally we heard that the other agencies fared likewise. We heard and saw that about half our friends at Rosebud agency, from fear at seeing the soldiers, began the move of running away from their agency toward ours (Pine Ridge), and when they had gotten inside of our reservation they there learned that right ahead of them at our agency was another large crowd of soldiers, and while the soldiers were there, there was constantly a great deal of false rumour flying back and forth. The special rumour I have in mind is the threat that the soldiers had come there to disarm the Indians entirely and to take away all their horses from them. That was the oft-repeated story.

…TURNING HAWK. When we heard that these people were coming toward our agency we also heard this. These people were coming toward Pine Ridge agency, and when they were almost on the agency they were met by the soldiers and surrounded and finally taken to the Wounded Knee creek, and there at a given time their guns were demanded. When they had delivered them up, the men were separated from their families, from the tipis, and taken to a certain spot. When the guns were thus taken and the men thus separated, there was a crazy man, a young man of very bad influence and in fact a nobody, among that bunch of Indians fired his gun, and of course the firing of a gun must have been the breaking of a military rule of some sort, because immediately the soldiers returned fire and indiscriminate killing followed.

SPOTTED HORSE. This man shot an officer in the army; the first shot killed this officer. I was a voluntary scout at that encounter and I saw exactly what was done, and that was what I noticed; that the first shot killed an officer. As soon as this shot was fired the Indians immediately began drawing their knives, and they were exhorted from all sides to desist, but this was not obeyed. Consequently the firing began immediately on the part of the soldiers.

TURNING HAWK. All the men who were in a bunch were killed right there, and those who escaped that first fire got into the ravine, and as they went along up the ravine for a long distance they were pursued on both sides by the soldiers and shot down, as the dead bodies showed afterwards. The women were standing off at a different place form where the men were stationed, and when the firing began, those of the men who escaped the first onslaught went in one direction up the ravine, and then the women, who were bunched together at another place, went entirely in a different direction through an open field, and the women fared the same fate as the men who went up the deep ravine.

AMERICAN HORSE. The men were separated, as has already been said, from the women, and they were surrounded by the soldiers. Then came next the village of the Indians and that was entirely surrounded by the soldiers also. When the firing began, of course the people who were standing immediately around the young man who fired the first shot were killed right together, and then they turned their guns, Hotchkill guns, etc., upon the women who were in the lodges standing there under a flag of truce, and of course as soon as they were fired upon they fled, the men fleeing in one direction and the women running in two different directions. So that there were three general directions in which they took flight.

There was a woman with an infant in her arms who was killed as she almost touched the flag of truce, and the women and children of course were strewn all along the circular village until they were dispatched. Right near the flag of truce a mother was shot down with her infant; the child not knowing that its mother was dead was still nursing, and that especially was a very sad sight. The women as they were fleeing with their babes were killed together, shot right through, and the women who were very heavy with child were also killed. All the Indians fled in these three directions, and after most all of them had been killed a cry was made that all those who were not killed wounded should come forth and they would be safe. Little boys who were not wounded came out of their places of refuge, and as soon as they came in sight a number of soldiers surrounded them and butchered them there.

Of course we all feel very sad about this affair. I stood very loyal to the government all through those troublesome days, and believing so much in the government and being so loyal to it, my disappointment was very strong, and I have come to Washington with a very great blame on my heart. Of course it would have been all right if only the men were killed; we would feel almost grateful for it. But the fact of the killing of the women, and more especially the killing of the young boys and girls who are to go to make up the future strength of the Indian people, is the saddest part of the whole affair and we feel it very sorely.

I was not there at the time before the burial of the bodies, but I did go there with some of the police and the Indian doctor and a great many of the people, men from the agency, and we went through the battlefield and saw where the bodies were from the track of the blood.

TURNING HAWK. I had just reached the point where I said that the women were killed. We heard, besides the killing of the men, of the onslaught also made upon the women and children, and they were treated as roughly and indiscriminately as the men and boys were…

Wovoka's Message: The Promise of the Ghost Dance

The following document presents Wovoka's Message, a set of guidelines outlined by Wovoka, or Jack Wilson (c.1856–1932), for all Indians to follow in order to defeat non-Indian incursion. This message was recorded by James Mooney, an ethnologist with the Bureau of American Ethnology after he obtained Wovoka's message from Black Short Nose, a Cheyenne.

THE MESSIAH LETTER

When you get home you must make a dance to continue five days. Dance four successive nights, and the last night keep us the dance until the morning of the fifth day, when all must bathe in the river and then disperse to their homes. You must all do in the same way.

I, Jack Wilson, love you all, and my heart is full of gladness for the gifts you have brought me. When you get home I shall give you a good cloud which will make you feel good. I give you a good spirit and give you all good paint. I want you to come again in three months, some from each tribe there [the Indian Territory]. There will be a good deal of snow this year and some rain. In the fall there will be such a rain as I have never given you before.

Grandfather [a universal title of reverence among Indians and here meaning the messiah] says, when your friends die you must not cry. You must not hurt anybody or do harm to anyone. You must not fight. Do right always. It will give you satisfaction in life. This young man has a good father and mother. [Possibly this refers to Casper Edson, the young Arapaho who wrote down this message of Wovoka for the delegation].

Do not tell the white people about this. Jesus is now upon the earth. He appears like a cloud. The dead are still alive again. I do not know when they will be here; maybe this fall or in the spring. When the time comes there will be no more sickness and everyone will be young again.

Do not refuse to work for the whites and do not make any trouble with them until you leave them. When the earth shakes [at the coming of the new world] do not be afraid. It will not hurt you.

I want you to dance every six weeks. Make a feast at the dance and have food that everybody may eat. Then bathe in the water. That is all. You will receive good words again from me some time. Do not tell lies.

Congressional Testimony of Mr. John S. Smith, 1865

Provided here is an account of the Sand Creek Massacre given by John S. Smith (c.1810–1871), a US–Indian interpreter and special Indian agent based at Fort Lyon, Colorado, to Congress on 14 March 1865. Smith describes the brutal actions of the Colorado Cavalry and the way in which the situation was manipulated so that the army attacked the Cheyenne and Arapaho.

Question. Will you state to the committee all that you know in relation to the attack of Colonel Chivington upon the Cheyenne and Arapahoe Indians in November last?

Answer. Major Anthony was in command at Fort Lyon at the time. Those Indians had been induced to remain in the vicinity of Fort Lyon, and were promised protection by the commanding officer at Fort Lyon. The commanding officer saw proper to keep them some thirty or forty miles distant from the fort, for fear of some conflict between them and the soldiers or the traveling population, for Fort Lyon is on a great thoroughfare. He advised them to go out on what is called Sand creek, about forty miles, a little east of north from Fort Lyon...

Question. What was the necessity for obtaining that information?

Answer. Because there were different bands which were supposed to be at war; in fact, we knew at the time that they were at war with the white population in that country; but this band had been in and left the post perfectly satisfied ... On the morning of the 29th, between daylight and sunrise - nearer sunrise than daybreak - a large number of troops were discovered from three-quarters of a mile to a mile below the village. The Indians, who discovered them, ran to my camp, called me out, and wanted to me to go and see what troops they were, and what they wanted. The head chief of the nation, Black Kettle, and head chief of the Cheyennes, was encamped there with us. Some years previous he had been presented with a fine American flag by Colonel Greenwood, a commissioner, who had been sent out there. Black Kettle ran this American flag up to the top of his lodge, with a small white flag tied right under it, as he had been advised to do in case he should meet with any troops out on the prairies...

...By this time the Indians had fled; had scattered in every direction. The troops were some on one side of the river and some on the other, following up the Indians. We had been encamped on the north side of the river; I followed along, holding on the caisson, sometimes running, sometimes walking. Finally, about a mile above the village, the troops had got a parcel of the Indians hemmed in under the bank of the river; as soon as the troops overtook them, they commenced firing on them; some troops had got above them, so that they were completely surrounded. There were probably a hundred Indians hemmed in there, men, women, and children; the most of the men in the village escaped.

By the time I got up with the battery to the place where these Indians were surrounded there had been some considerable firing. Four or five soldiers had been killed, some with arrows and some with bullets. The soldiers continued firing on these Indians, who numbered about a hundred, until they had almost completely destroyed them. I think I saw altogether some seventy dead bodies lying there; the greater portion women and children. There may have been thirty warriors, old and young; the rest were women and small children of different ages and sizes.

The troops at that time were very much scattered. There were not over two hundred troops in the main fight, engaged in killing this body of Indians under the bank. The balance of the troops were scattered in different directions, running after small parties of Indians who were trying to make their escape. I did not go to see how many they might have killed outside of this party under the bank of the river. Being still quite weak from my last sickness, I returned with the first body of troops that went back to the camp.

The Indians had left their lodges and property; everything they owned. I do not think more than one-half of the Indians left their lodges with their arms. I think there were between 800 and 1,000 men in this command of United States troops. There was a part of three companies of the 1st Colorado, and the balance were what were called 100 days men of the 3rd regiment. I am not able to say which party did the most execution on the Indians, because it was very much mixed up at the time...

Question. How many Indians were there?

Answer. There were 100 families of Cheyennes, and some six or eight lodges of Arapahoes...

Question. 500 men, women and children?

Answer. Yes, sir.

Question. Do you know the reason for that attack on the Indians?

Answer. I do not know any exact reason. I have heard a great many reasons given. I have heard that that whole Indian war had been brought on for selfish purposes. Colonel Chivington was running for Congress in Colorado, and there were other things of that kind; and last spring a year ago he was looking for an order to go to the front, and I understand he had this Indian war in view to retain himself and his troops in that country, to carry out his electioneering purposes.

Question. In what way did this attack on the Indians further the purpose of Colonel Chivington?

Answer. It was said - I did not hear him say it myself, but it was said that he would do something; he had this regiment of three-months men, and did not want them to go out without doing some service. Now he had been told repeatedly by different persons - by myself, as well as others - where he could find the hostile bands.

The same chiefs who were killed in this village of Cheyennes had been up to see Colonel Chivington in Denver but a short time previous to this attack...

Question. Had there been, to your knowledge, any hostile act or demonstration on the part of these Indians or any of them?

Answer. Not in this band. But the northern band, the band known by the name of Dog soldiers of Cheyennes, had committed many depredations on the Platte.

Question. Do you know whether or not Colonel Chivington knew the friendly character of these Indians before he made the attack upon them?

Answer. It is my opinion that he did...

Question. When did you talk with him?

Answer. On the day of the attack. He asked me many questions about the chiefs who were there, and if I could recognize them if I saw them ... They were terribly mutilated, lying there in the water and sand; most of them in the bed of the creek, dead and dying, making many struggles. They were so badly mutilated and covered with sand and water that it was very hard for me to tell one from another. However, I recognized some of them - among them the chief One Eye, who was employed by our government at $125 a month and rations to remain in the village as a spy ... I supposed Black Kettle was among them, but it was not Black Kettle. There was one there of his size and dimensions in every way, but so tremendously mutilated that I was mistaken in him...

Question: Did you tell Colonel Chivington the character and disposition of these Indians at any time during your interviews on this day?

Answer. Yes, sir.

Question. What did he say in reply?

Answer. He said he could not help it; that his orders were positive to attack the Indians...

Question. Were the women and children slaughtered indiscriminately, or only so far as they were with the warriors?

Answer. Indiscriminately.

Question. Were there any acts of barbarity perpetrated there that came under your own observation?

Answer. Yes, sir; I saw the bodies of those lying there cut all to pieces, worse mutilated than any I ever saw before; the women cut all to pieces...

Question. How cut?

Answer. With knives; scalped; their brains knocked out; children two or three months old; all ages lying there, from sucking infants up to warriors...

Question. Did you see it done?

Answer. Yes, sir; I saw them fall...

Question. Did you see them when they were mutilated?

Answer. Yes, sir.

Question. By whom were they mutilated?

Answer. By the United States troops...

Question. Can you state how many Indians were killed - how many women and how many children?

Answer. Perhaps one-half were men, and the balance were women and children. I do not think that I saw more than 70 lying dead then, as far as I went. But I saw parties of men scattered in every direction, pursuing little bands of Indians.

Question. What time of day or night was this attack made?

Answer. The attack commenced about sunrise, and lasted until between 10 and 11 o'clock.

Question. How large a body of troops?

Answer. I think that probably there may have been about 60 or 70 warriors who were armed and stood their ground and fought. Those that were unarmed got out of the way as they best could.

Question. How many of our troops were killed and how many wounded?

Answer. There were ten killed on the ground, and thirty-eight wounded; four of the wounded died at Fort Lyon before I came on east...

Question. Were the women and children that were killed, killed during the fight with the Indians?

Answer. During the fight, or during the time of the attack...

Question. Were the warriors and women and children all huddled together when they were attacked?

Answer. They started and left the village altogether, in a body, trying to escape...

Question. How many warriors were estimated in Colonel Chivington's report as having been in this Indian camp?

Answer. About nine hundred.

Question. How many were there?

Answer. About two hundred warriors; they average about two warriors to a lodge, and there were about one hundred lodges.

Two Editorials from the *Rocky Mountain News*, 1864

In the following document are two editorials from the Rocky Mountain News that glorify the actions of the Colorado Cavalry and portray Chivington and his men as heroes for the indiscriminate killing of innocent Indian men, women and children.

The Battle of Sand Creek

Among the brilliant feats of arms in Indian warfare, the recent campaign of our Colorado volunteers will stand in history with few rivals, and none to exceed it in final results. We are not prepared to write its history, which can only be done by some one who accompanied the expedition, but we have gathered from those who participated in it and from others who were in that part of the country, some facts which will doubtless interest many of our readers.

...At Fort Lyon the force was strengthened by about two hundred and fifty men of the first regiment, and at nine o'clock in the evening the command set out for the Indian village ... As daylight dawned they came in sight of the Indian camp, after a forced midnight march of forty-two miles, in eight hours, across the rough, unbroken plain ... The forces had been divided and arranged for battle on the march, and just as the sun rose they dashed upon the enemy with yells that would put a Comanche army to blush. Although utterly surprised, the savages were not unprepared, and for a time their defence told terribly against our ranks. Their main force rallied and formed in line of battle on the bluffs beyond the creek, where they were protected by rudely constructed rifle-pits, from which they maintained a steady fire until the shells from company C's (third regiment) howitzers began dropping among them, when they scattered and fought each for himself in genuine Indian fashion. As the battle progressed the field of carriage widened until it extended over not less than twelve miles of territory. The Indians who could escaped or secreted themselves, and by three o'clock in the afternoon the carnage had ceased. It was estimated that between three and four hundred of the savages got away with their lives. Of the balance there were neither wounded nor prisoners. Their strength at the beginning of the action was estimated at nine hundred.

Their village consisted of one hundred and thirty Cheyenne and with Arapahoe lodges. These, with their contents, were totally destroyed. Among their effects were large supplies of flour, sugar, coffee, tea, &c. Women's and children's clothing were found; also books and many other articles which must have been taken from captured trains or houses. One white man's scalp was found which had evidently been taken but a few days before. The Chiefs fought with unparalleled bravery, falling in front of their men. One of them charged alone against a force of two or three hundred, and fell pierced with balls far in advance of his braves.

Our attack was made by five battalions. The first regiment, Colonel Chivington, part of companies C,D,E,G, H and K, numbering altogether about two hundred and fifty men, was divided into two battalions; the first under command of Major Anthony, and the second under Lieutenant Wilson ... The action was begun by the battalion of Lieutenant Wilson, who occupied the right, and by a quick and bold movement cut off the enemy from their herd of stock. From this circumstance we gained our great advantage. A few Indians secured horses, but the great majority of them had to fight or fly on foot...

Among the killed were all the Cheyenne chiefs, Black Kettle, White Antelope, Little Robe, Left Hand, Knock Knee, One Eye, and another, name unknown. Not a single prominent man of the tribe remains, and the tribe itself is almost annihilated. The Arapahoes probably suffered but little. It has been reported that the chief Left Hand, of that tribe, was killed, but Colonel Chivington is of the opinion that he was not. Among the stock captured were a number of government horses and mules, including the twenty or thirty stolen from the command of Lieutenant Chase at Jimmy's camp last summer.

The Indian camp was well supplied with defensive works. For half a mile along the creek there was an almost continuous chain of rifle-pits, and another similar line of works crowned the adjacent bluff. Pits had been dug at all the salient points for miles. After the battle twenty-tree dead Indians were taken from one of these pits and twenty-seven from another.

Whether viewed as a march or as a battle, the exploit has few, if any, parallels. A march of 260 miles in but a fraction more than five days, with deep snow, scanty forage, and no road, is a remarkable feat, whilst the utter surprise of a large Indian village is unprecedented. In no single battle in North America, we believe, have so many Indians been slain.

It is said that a short time before the command reached the scene of battle of [sic] an old squaw partially alarmed the village by reporting that a great herd of buffalo were coming. She heard the rumbling of the artillery and tramp of the moving squadrons, but her people doubted. In a little time the doubt was dispelled, but not by buffaloes.

A thousand incidents of individual daring and the passing events of the day might be told, but space forbids. We leave the task for eye-witnesses to chronicle. All acquitted themselves well, and Colorado soldiers have again covered themselves with glory.

The Fort Lyon Affair

The issue of yesterday's News, containing the following despatch, created considerable of a sensation in this city, particularly among the Thirdsters and others who participated in the recent campaign and the battle on Sand creek.

Washington, December 20, 1864
"The affair at Fort Lyon, Colorado, in which Colonel Chivington destroyed a large Indian village, and all its inhabitants, is to be made the subject of congressional investigation. Letters received from high officials [sic] in Colorado say that the Indians were killed after surrendering, and that a large proportion of them were women and children."

Indignation was loudly and unequivocally expressed, and some less considerate of the boys were very persistent in their inquiries as to who those "high officials" were, with a mild intimation that they had half a mind to "go for them." This talk about "friendly Indians" and a "surrendered" village will do to "tell to marines," but to us out here it is all bosh.

The confessed murderers of the Hungate family - a man and wife and their two little babes, whose scalped and mutilated remains were seen by all our citizens -- were "friendly Indians," we suppose, in the eyes of these "high officials." They fell in the Sand creek battle.

The confessed participants in a score of other murders of peaceful settlers and inoffensive travellers upon our borders and along our roads in the past six months must have been friendly, or else the "high officials" wouldn't say so.

The band of marauders in whose possession were found scores of horses and mules stolen from government and from individuals; wagon loads of flour, coffee, sugar and tea, and rolls of broad cloth, calico, books, &c, robbed from freighters and emigrants on the plains; underclothes of white women and children, stripped from their murdered victims, were probably peaceably disposed toward some of those "high officials," but the mass of our people "can't see it."

Probably those scalps of white men, women and children, one of them fresh, not three days taken, found drying in their lodges, were taken in a friendly, playful manner; or possibly those Indian saddle-blankets trimmed with the scalp's of white women, and with braids and fringes of their hair, were kept simply as mementos of their owners' high affection for the pale face. At any rate, these delicate and tasteful ornaments could not have been taken from the heads of the wives, sisters or daughters of these "high officials."

...the savages fought like devils to the end, and one of our pickets was killed and scalped by them the next day after the battle, and a number of others were fired upon. In one instance a party of the vidette pickets were compelled to beat a hasty retreat to save their lives, full twenty-four hours after the battle closed. This does not look much like the Indians had surrendered.

But we are not sure that an investigation may not be a good thing ... It is unquestioned and undenied that the site of the Sand creek battle was the rendezvous of the thieving and marauding bands of savages who roamed over this country last summer and fall, and it is shrewdly suspected that somebody was all the time making a very good thing out of it. By all means let there be an investigation, but we advise the honourable congressional committee, who may be appointed to conduct it, to get their scalps insured before they pass Plum creek on their way out.

Deposition of John M. Chivington, 1865

Provided here are key excerpts from the testimony given by Colonel J. M. Chivington (1821–1894), Colonel of the 1st Colorado Cavalry, to the Joint

Committee on the Conduct of War in Denver, Territory of Colorado, about why he decided to attack the Cheyenne at Sand Creek. Chivington defended his actions by arguing that the Indians were hostile and incapable of peace with the United States.

...3d question. Did you, as colonel in command of Colorado troops, about the 29th of November, 1864, make an attack on an Indian village or camp at a place known as Sand creek? If so, state particularly the number of men under your command; how armed and equipped; whether mounted or not; and if you had any artillery, state the number of guns, and the batteries to which they belonged.

Answer. On the 29th day of November, 1864, the troops under my command attacked a camp of Cheyenne and Arapaho Indians at a place known as Big Bend of Sandy, about forty miles north of Fort Lyon, Colorado Territory. There were in my command at that time about (500) five hundred men of the 3d regiment Colorado cavalry, under the immediate command of Colonel George L. Shoup, of said 3d regiment, and about (250) two hundred and fifty men of the 1st Colorado cavalry...

4th question. State as nearly as you can the number of Indians that were in the village or camp at the time the attack was made; how many of them were warriors; how many of them were old men, how many of them were women, and how many of them were children?

Answer. From the best and most reliable information I could obtain, there were in the Indian camp, at the time of the attack, about eleven (11) or twelve (12) hundred Indians: of these about seven hundred were warriors, and the remainder were women and children. I am not aware that there were any old men among them. There was an unusual number of males among them, for the reason that the war chiefs of both nations were assembled there evidently for some special purpose.

5th question. At what time of the day or night was the attack made? Was it a surprise to the Indians? What preparation, if any, had they made for defence or offence?

Answer. The attack was made about sunrise. In my opinion the Indians were surprised; they began, as soon as the attack was made, to oppose my troops, however, and were soon fighting desperately. Many of the Indians were armed with rifles and many with revolvers; I think all had bows and arrows. They had excavated trenches under the bank of Sand creek, which in the vicinity of the Indian camp is high, and in many places precipitous. These trenches were two to three feet deep, and, in connexion with the banks, were evidently designed to protect the occupants from the fire of an enemy ... The Indians took shelter in these trenches as soon as the attack was made, and from thence resisted the advance of my troops.

6th question. What number did you lose in killed, what number in wounded, and what number in missing?

Answer. There were seven men killed, forty-seven wounded, and one was missing.

7th question. What number of Indians were killed; and what number of the killed were women, and what number were children?

Answer. From the best information I could obtain, I judge there were five hundred or six hundred Indians killed; I cannot state positively the number killed, nor can I state positively the number of women and children killed. Officers who passed over the field, by my orders, after the battle, for the purpose of ascertaining the number of Indians killed, report that they saw but few women or children dead, no more than would certainly fall in an attack upon a camp in which they were. I myself passed over some portions of the field after the fight, and I saw but one woman who had been killed, and one who had hanged herself; I saw no dead children. From all I could learn, I arrived at the conclusion that but few women or children had been slain. I am of the opinion that when the attack was made on the Indian camp the greater number of squaws and children made their escape, while the warriors remained to fight my troops.

8th question. State, as nearly as you can, the number of Indians that were wounded, giving the number of women and the number of children among the wounded.

Answer ... Indians usually fight as long as they have strength to resist. Eight Indians fell into the hands of the troops alive, to my knowledge; these, with one exception, were sent to Fort Lyon and properly cared for.

...There was a large quantity of Indian trinkets taken at the Indian camp which were of no value. The soldiers retained a few of these as trophies; the remainder with the Indian lodges were destroyed.

10th question. What reason had you for making the attack? What reasons, if any, had you to believe that Black Kettle or any other Indian or Indians in the camp entertained feelings of hostility towards the whites? Give in detail the names of all Indians so believed to be hostile, with the dates and places of their hostile acts, so far as you may be able to do so.

Answer. My reason for making the attack on the Indian camp was, that I believed the Indians in the camp were hostile to the whites. That they were of the same tribes with those who had murdered many persons and destroyed much valuable property on the Platte and Arkansas rivers during the previous spring, summer and fall was beyond a doubt. When a tribe of Indians is at war with the whites it is impossible to determine what party or band of the tribe or the name of the Indian or Indians belonging to the tribe so at war are guilty of the acts of hostility ... During the spring, summer and fall of the year 1864, the Arapaho and Cheyenne Indians, in some instances assisted or led on by Sioux, Kiowas, Comanches and Apaches, had committed many acts of hostility ... They had murdered many of the whites and taken others prisoners, and had destroyed valuable property, probably amounting to $200,000 or $300,000 ... I had every reason to believe that these Indians were either directly or indirectly concerned in the outrages which had been committed upon the whites. I had no means of ascertaining what were the names of the Indians who had committed these outrages other than the declarations of the Indians themselves ... We found in the camp the scalps of nineteen (19) white persons. One of the surgeons informed me that one of these scalps had been taken from the victim's head not more than four days previously. I can furnish a child captured at the camp ornamented with six white women's scalps; these scalps must have been taken by these Indians or furnished to them for their gratification and amusement by some of their brethren...

11th question. Had you any, and if so, what reason, to believe that Black Kettle and the Indians with him, at the time of your attack, were at peace with the whites, and desired to remain at peace with them?

Answer. I had no reason to believe that Black Kettle and the Indians with him were in good faith at peace with the whites. The day before the attack Major Scott J. Anthony, 1st Colorado cavalry, then in command at Fort Lyon, told me that these Indians were hostile; that he had ordered his sentinels to fire on them if they attempted to come into the post, and that the sentinels had fired on them; that he was apprehensive of an attack from these Indians, and had taken every precaution to prevent a surprise. Major Samuel G. Colby, United States Indian agent for these Indians, told me on the same day that he had done everything in his power to make them behave themselves, and that for the last six months he could do nothing with them; that nothing but a sound whipping would bring a lasting peace with them...

17th question. What measures were taken by you, at any time, to render the attack on those Indians a surprise?

Answer. I took every precaution to render the attack upon the Indians a surprise, for the reason that we had been able to catch them, and it appeared to me that the only way to deal with them was to surprise them in their place of rendezvous...

19th question. Make such further statement as you may desire, or which may be necessary to a full understanding of all matters relating to the attack upon the Indians at Sand creek.

Answer. Since August, 1863, I had been in possession of the most conclusive evidence of the alliance, for the purposes of hostility against the whites, of the Sioux, Cheyennes, Arapahoes, Camanche River, and Apache Indians. Their plan was to interrupt, or, if possible, entirely prevent all travel on the routes along the Arkansas and Platte rivers from the States to the Rocky mountains, and thereby depopulate this country. Rebel emissaries were long since sent among the Indians to incite them against the whites, and afford a medium of communication between the rebels and the Indians; among whom was Gerry Bent, a half-breed Cheyenne Indian, but educated, and to all appearances a white man, who, having served under Price in Missouri, and afterwards becoming a bushwacker, being taken prisoner, took the oath of allegiance, and was paroled, after which he immediately joined the Indians, and has ever since been one of their most prominent leaders in all depredations upon the whites...

...the Indians had determined to make war upon the whites as soon as the grass was green, and that they were making preparations for such an event by the large number of arrows they were making and the quantity of arms and ammunition they were collecting; that the settlers along the Platte and Arkansas rivers should be warned of the approaching danger; that the Indians had declared their intention to prosecute the war vigorously when they commenced...

Last April, 1864, the Indians, Cheyennes, Arapahoes, and others, commenced their depredations upon the whites by entering their isolated habitations in the distant parts of this territory, taking therefrom everything they desired, and destroying the balance; driving off their stock, horses, mules and cattle...

...But we think we have related enough to satisfy the most incredulous of the determined hostility of these Indians; suffice it to say that during the spring, summer, and fall such atrocious acts were of almost daily occurrence along the Platte and Arkansas routes ... After seeing which, any person who could for a moment believe that these Indians were friendly, to say the least, must have strange ideas of their habits. We could not see it in that light.

...besides the sparsely settled and distant settlements of this Territory, to protect, I could not do anything till the 3d regiment was organized and equipped, when I determined to strike a blow against this savage and determined foe. When I reached Fort Lyon, after passing over from three to five feet of snow, and greatly suffering from the intensity of the cold, the thermometer ranging from 28 to 30 degrees below zero, I questioned Major Anthony in regard to the whereabouts of hostile Indians. He said there was a camp of Cheyennes and Arapahoes about fifty miles distant; that he would have attacked before, but did not consider his force sufficient; that these Indians had threatened to attack the post, &c., and ought to be whipped ... and resulted in the battle of Sand Creek, which has created such a sensation in Congress through the lying reports of interested and malicious parties.

On my arrival at Fort Lyon, in all my conversations with Major Anthony, commanding the post, and Major Colley, Indian agent, I heard nothing of this recent statement that the Indians were under the protection of the government, &c.,; but Major Anthony repeatedly stated to me that he had at different times fired upon these Indians, and that they were hostile, and, during my stay at Fort Lyon, urged the necessity of any immediately attacking the Indians before they could learn of the number of troops at Fort Lyon … I have learned recently that these men, Anthony and Colly, are the most bitter in their denunciations of the attack upon the Indians at Sand creek. Therefore, I would, in conclusion, most respectfully demand, as an act of justice to myself and the brave men whom I have had the honour to command in one of the hardest campaigns ever made in this country, whether against white men or red, that we be allowed that right guaranteed to every American citizen, of introducing evidence in our behalf to sustain us in what we believe to have been an act of duty to ourselves and to civilization…

J.M. CHIVINGTON,
Lieu't Col. 1st Cavalry of Colerado, [sic] Com'd'g Dist. of Colerado. [sic]

George Herendon: Recounts His Story to *The New York Herald*, 1876

The following document is an account given by George Herendon (nineteenth/ twentieth century), Scout for the Seventh Cavalry of the US army and attached to the command of Major Reno, to a reporter from the New York Herald Tribune in 1876.

Reno took a steady gallop down the creek bottom three miles where it emptied into the Little Horn, and found a natural ford across the Little Horn River. He started to cross, when the scouts came back and called out to him to hold on, that the Sioux were coming in large numbers to meet him. He crossed over, however, formed his companies on the prairie in line of battle, and moved forward at a trot but soon took a gallop.

The Valley was about three fourth of a mile wide, on the left a line of low, round hills, and on the right the river bottom covered with a growth of cottonwood trees and bushes. After scattering shots were fired from the hills and a few from the river bottom and Reno's skirmishers returned the shots.

He advanced about a mile from the ford to a line of timber on the right and dismounted his men to fight on foot. The horses were sent into the timber, and the men forward on the prairie and advanced toward the Indians. The Indians, mounted on ponies, came across the prairie and opened a heavy fire on the soldiers. After skirmishing for a few minutes Reno fell back to his horses in the timber. The Indians moved to his left and rear, evidently with the intention of cutting him off from the ford.

Reno ordered his men to mount and move through the timber, but as his men got into the saddle the Sioux, who had advanced in the timber, fired at close range and killed one soldier. Colonel Reno then commanded the men to dismount, and they did so, but he soon ordered them to mount again, and moved out on to the open prairie.

The command headed for the ford, pressed closely by Indians in large numbers, and at every moment the rate of speed was increased, until it became a dead run for the ford. The Sioux, mounted on their swift ponies, dashed up by the side of the soldiers and fired at them, killing both men and horses. Little resistance was offered, and it was complete rout to the ford. I did not see the men at the ford, and do not know what took place further than a good many were killed when the command left the timber.

Just as I got out, my horse stumbled and fell and I was dismounted, the horse running away after Reno's command. I saw several soldiers who were dismounted, their horses having been killed or run away. There were also some soldiers mounted who had remained behind, I should think in all as many as thirteen soldiers, and seeing no chance of getting away, I called on them to come into the timber and we would stand off the Indians.

Three of the soldiers were wounded, and two of them so badly they could not use their arms. The soldiers wanted to go out, but I said no, we can't get to the ford, and besides, we have wounded men and must stand by them. The soldiers still wanted to go, but I told them I was an old frontiersman, understood the Indians, and if they would do as I said I would get them out of the scrape which was no worse than scrapes I had been in before. About half of the men were mounted, and they wanted to keep their horses with them, but I told them to let the horses go and fight on foot.

We stayed in the bush about three hours, and I could hear heavy firing below in the river, apparently about two miles distant. I did not know who it was, but knew the Indians were fighting some of our men, and learned afterward it was Custer's command. Nearly all the Indians in the upper part of the valley drew off down the river, and the fight with Custer lasted about one hour, when the heavy firing ceased. When the shooting below began to die away I said to the boys 'come, now is the time to get out'. Most of them did not go, but waited for night. I told them the Indians would come back and we had better be off at once. Eleven of the thirteen said they would go, but two stayed behind.

I deployed the men as skirmishers and we moved forward on foot toward the river. When we had got nearly to the river we met five Indians on ponies, and they fired on us. I returned the fire and the Indians broke and we then forded the river, the water being heart deep. We finally got over, wounded men and all, and headed for Reno's command which I could see drawn up on the bluffs along the river about a mile off. We reached Reno in safety.

We had not been with Reno more than fifteen minutes when I saw the Indians coming up the valley from Custer's fight. Reno was then moving his whole command down the ridge toward Custer. The Indians crossed the river below Reno and swarmed up the bluff on all sides. After skirmishing with them Reno went back to his old position which was on one of the highest fronts along the bluffs. It was now about five o'clock, and the fight lasted until it was too dark to see to shoot.

As soon as it was dark Reno took the packs and saddles off the mules and horses and made breast works of them. He also dragged the dead horses and mules on the line and sheltered the men behind them. Some of the men dug rifle pits with their butcher knives and all slept on their arms.

At the peep of day the Indians opened a heavy fire and a desperate fight ensued, lasting until 10 o'clock. The Indians charged our position three or four times, coming up close enough to hit our men with stones, which they threw by hand. Captain Benteen saw a large mass of Indians gathered on his front to charge, and ordered his men to charge on foot and scatter them.

Benteen led the charge and was upon the Indians before they knew what they were about and killed a great many. They were evidently much surprised at this offensive movement, and I think in desperate fighting Benteen is one of the bravest men I ever saw in a fight. All the time he was going about through the bullets, encouraging the soldiers to stand up to their work and not let the Indians whip them; he went among the horses and pack mules and drove out the men who were skulking there, compelling them to go into the line and do their duty. He never sheltered his own person once during the battle, and I do not see how he escaped being killed. The desperate charging and fighting was over at about one o'clock, but firing was kept up on both sides until late in the afternoon.

Chicago Tribune Account of the Little Bighorn, 1876

The following text is a newspaper article printed by the Chicago Tribune in July 1876 about Custer, his 'reckless' military actions during the Battle of the Little Big Horn and the courage of 'the Indians'.

Since the murder of General Canby by the Modocs the country has not been more startled than it was by the announcement that General Custer and five companies of his regiment, the Seventh Cavalry, had been massacred by the Sioux Indians in a ravine ... the Indians outnumbering our troops ten to one. General Custer had personal and soldierly traits which commended him to the people. He was an officer who did not know the word fear, and, as is often the case with soldiers of this stamp, he was reckless, hasty, and impulsive, preferring to make a daredevil rush and take risks rather than to move slower and with more certainty. He was a brave, brilliant soldier, handsome and dashing, with all the attributes to make him beloved of women and admired of men; but these qualities, however admirable they may be, should not blind our eyes to the fact that it was his own madcap haste, rashness, and love of fame that cost him his own life, and cost the service the loss of many brave officers and gallant men. They drew him into an ambuscade ravine. ... In this instance, three hundred troops were instantly surrounded by 3,000 Indians, and the fatal ravine became a slaughter-pen from which but a few escaped. ... No account seems to have been taken of numbers, of the leadership of the Sioux, of their record of courage and military skill.

General Nelson A. Miles on the 'Sioux Outbreak' of 1890

The following text highlights the thoughts of General Nelson A. Miles (1839–1925), a leading military figure in the campaign and wars of the US army against the Nations of the Great Plains, about the practice of the Ghost Dance by the Lakota.

Cause of Indian dissatisfaction -- The causes that led to the serious disturbance of the peace in the northwest last autumn and winter were so remarkable that an explanation of them is necessary in order to comprehend the seriousness of the situation. The Indians assuming the most threatening attitude of hostility were the Cheyennes and Sioux. Their condition may be stated as follows: For several years following their subjugation in 1877, 1878, and 1879 the most dangerous element of the Cheyennes and the Sioux were under military control. Many of them were disarmed and dismounted; their war ponies were sold and the proceeds returned to them in domestic stock, farming utensils, wagons, etc. Many of the Cheyennes, under the charge of military officers, were located on land in accordance with the laws of Congress, but after they were turned over to civil agents and the vase herds of buffalo and large game had been destroyed their supplies were insufficient, and they were forced to kill cattle belonging to white people to sustain life.

The fact that they had not received sufficient food is admitted by the agents and the officers of the government who have had opportunities of knowing. The majority of the Sioux were under the charge of civil agents, frequently changed and often inexperienced. Many of the tribes became rearmed and remounted. They claimed that the government had not fulfilled its treaties and had failed to make large enough appropriations for their support; that they had suffered for want of food, and the evidence of this is beyond question and sufficient to satisfy any unprejudiced intelligent mind. The statements of officers, inspectors, both of the military and the Interior departments, of agents, of missionaries, ad civilians familiar with their condition, leave no room for reasonable doubt that this was one of the principal causes. While statements may be made as to the amount of money that has been expended by the government to feed the different tribes, the manner of distributing those appropriations will furnish one reason for the deficit.

The unfortunate failure of the crops in the plains country during the years of 1889 and 1890 added to the distress and suffering of the Indians, and it was possible for them to raise but very little from the ground for self-support; in fact, white settlers have been most unfortunate, and their losses have been serious and universal throughout a large section of that country. They have struggled on from year to year; occasionally they would raise good crops, which they were compelled to sell at low prices, while in the season of drought their labor was almost entirely lost. So serious have been their misfortunes that thousands have left that country within the last few years, passing over the mountains to the Pacific slope or returning to the east of the Missouri or the Mississippi.

The Indians, however, could not migrate from one part of the United States to another; neither could they obtain employment as readily as white people, either upon or beyond the Indian reservations. They must remain in comparative idleness and accept the results of the drought-an insufficient supply of food. This created a feeling of discontent even among the loyal and well disposed and added to the feeling of hostility of the element opposed to every process of civilization.

CHAPTER SEVEN
ERA OF ASSIMILATION AND ALLOTMENT, 1887–1934

As Indian military resistance in the West slowly came to an end, native America still found itself under attack from the American government. Rather than being pursued by the military in real or contrived conflicts, Indians were subjected to a relentless drive towards cultural assimilation, a policy that tried to undermine tribal culture and turn Indians into a homogenous version of American citizens in one generation. Indian communities were pressured to turn their hands to farming and live a sedentary life on individually owned parcels of land, and to give up hunting and traditional methods of living on tribal and communally owned lands. Once again, this period of Native American history saw the American government take many thousands of acres of Indian reservation lands away from many Indian nations. The General Allotment Act of 1887, often referred to as the Dawes Act, allowed tribal reservations to be broken up and land to be purchased by non-Indians. In addition, the American government sanctioned the relocation, and in certain circumstances, the forced relocation, of Indian children to boarding schools where they were to be educated as 'Americans', often in environments hundreds of miles away from their homes and the influence of their cultures on or off reservations. Although there is evidence that Indian schools allowed for the growth of a pan-Indian consciousness in native America, in the main, they were deeply resented by Indian peoples and served to create further rifts between generations. The impact of congressional power over Indian affairs during this period was very strong. The Major Crimes Act of 1885, which overruled a Supreme Court decision that ruled in favour of inherent tribal sovereignty, was an example of this new wave of congressional authority exercised over Indians. Whereas the previous period of removal generally concentrated on shifting Indians away from non-Indians, this period focused on assimilating all Indians into the dominant version of American culture. This policy shift of the American government and Congress left deep scars within Indian communities, and the negative impact of the period continues to affect generations today.

One of the first times that the idea of Indian assimilation and allotment was discussed as a federal policy by an incumbent president was in the early 1880s. In his first annual message to Congress in 1881, President Chester A. Arthur (1829–1886), the twenty-first president of the United States who served from 1881 to 1885, proposed to break up the tribal reservations in order to assimilate all Indians into mainstream American culture and force them to adopt an agricultural lifestyle.[1] In addition, discussions about Indian allotment among American politicians served to support the American contention that the Indians still owned too much land in the West, and were thus slowing down the process of western settlement.[2]

Only six years after the speech of President Arthur, the American government passed the General Allotment Act of 1887. The act authorised the division of tribal lands into individually owned tracts where the head of the family was allotted 80 acres of agricultural land or 160 acres of grazing land. Single people over eighteen or orphans were allotted half that amount. The lands were to be held in trust by the American government for twenty-five years and after the expiration of the trust period, tribal members were to become subject to the laws of the States of the Union.[3] The central idea of the 1887 Act was to ensure that communally owned tribal reservation lands were broken up and transferred to individual ownership. The effect of the 1887 Act on many Indians, including the Cherokee, was disastrous, with prominent Cherokee, such as William Eubanks (c.1841–1906), an intellectual, translator and writer, vehement in their hatred of allotment and angry with the devastation forced upon their cultures by the US government.[4] Although the US government supported allotment, not all non-Indians thought that the 1887 Act was the correct measure to assimilate the Indians into American society. President Theodore Roosevelt (1858–1919), twenty-sixth president of the United States who served from 1901–1909, was vociferous in his support for the process of allotment and believed that it was an essential tool to weaken tribal culture and their association with their lands.[5] In stark contrast, Richard H. Pratt (1840–1924), a captain who had guarded the imprisoned Plains Indians in Florida after the Red River War of 1874 and founded the Carlisle Indian School in Pennsylvania in 1879, believed that allotment did not allow enough Indian families to be mixed within high volumes of non-Indian families in order to assimilate and 'civilise' them.[6] The protections afforded to many Indians by the 1887 Act were inevitably weakened by an American Congress that thought that allotment and assimilation was happening too slowly. In 1906, the Burke Act allowed the Secretary of the Interior to waive the twenty-five year protection offered to Indians, which meant that individual Indians could then sell or be pressurized into selling their allotted lands. Much Indian land fell into Euro-American hands because Indian peoples were forced into debt. Overall, the impact of allotment reduced the Indian land base in 1887 of 138 million acres to approximately 48 million acres by 1934.[7]

During the 1880s, the pressure on Indian tribes to assimilate was intense. Even a decision by the US Supreme Court in favour of the Indians was not enough to prevent Congress from nullifying the decision. In the court case of *Ex Parte Crow Dog* (1883), the Supreme Court reversed the conviction of Crow Dog (Kan-gi-shun-ca) by the First District Court of Dakota and ruled that the US government did not have the right to arrest and criminally prosecute an Indian for an offence against another Indian within the boundaries of a reservation.[8]

Therefore, the inherent sovereignty and authority of the Indian nation was superior to the right of American law to prosecute tribal members within the reservation. Despite this positive opinion in favour of tribal governmental sovereignty, in 1885, Congress passed the Major Crimes Act and removed the inherent sovereignty of the tribes to punish tribal crimes inside their own reservations. This act of Congress was designed to further assimilate the Indian peoples into American culture and, even though it contradicted other aspects of legislation, for them on paper to enjoy the same privileges as other Americans under the laws of the United States.

Another highly contentious issue in this period was the conflict between the US government and numerous Indian tribes over the removal of Indian children from the reservations. The policy was designed by the American government specifically to erode tribal cultures and to 'civilise' future Indian generations. The underlying principles of the American government in this regard were explained in 1889 by Thomas J. Morgan (c.1840–1902), Commissioner of Indian Affairs from 1889 to 1893.[9] Indian children reacted in their own ways to being forced to learn non-Indian ways of life. Some, such as Don C. Talayesva (c.1890–1976), a Hopi who grew up on a reservation in Oraibi, Arizona, embraced the process of learning alien ways while others, such as Zitkala-Ša or Gertrude Bonin (1876–1938), a Yankton Sioux writer, found it disturbing and hated the entire process. Many Indian children were burdened by schooling, with a permanent emotional scar for their entire lives.[10]

However, the resilience of the Indian children to the practices of the American government and the boarding schools was based on a web of strong cultural connections, often taught through oral customs, between the children and their respective nations. The use of oral traditions conflicted with the practices of the written word used by the American model of education. The experiences of Luther Standing Bear (1868–1939), a Lakota Sioux, and Charles Alexander Eastman (1858–1939), a Santee Sioux who became a well-respected doctor, writer and reformer, are examples that show how traditional upbringings in their respective cultures gave Indian children of the period the strength to survive the schooling process.[11]

The period of assimilation and allotment brought conflict between Indian nations and the American government over land, culture and identity. Indian peoples saw their land taken by dubious means especially after the introduction of the General Allotment Act of 1887, and saw that their future cultural survival was fundamentally threatened. The forced removal of Indian children was a highly contentious policy employed by the American government during the late nineteenth century and the early-to-mid part of the twentieth century with supposedly benign intent, to 'civilise' future Indian generations and turn them into the ideal American citizen of the time. The education of Indian children at boarding schools did not end during the 1930s or 1940s but continued beyond the 1980s. The ideological underpinnings of American governmental policy had dramatically shifted from the previous era when the desire was for Indians to live away from American citizens towards a policy intent upon Indian assimilation and the destruction of traditional Indian ways of life. The US government's desire to control Indian peoples and to culturally obliterate them through assimilation even caused the American Congress to overrule a Supreme Court decision so as to devalue tribal sovereignty.

SOURCES

Charles Alexander Eastman: 'An Indian Boy's Training' from *Indian Boyhood*, 1902

The following extracts are taken from a book written by Charles Alexander Eastman (1858–1939), a Santee Sioux who became a well-respected doctor, writer and reformer. Here he describes how he was taught at an early age within the oral tradition about the culture and the history of his people. Although Eastman became a staunch advocate of educating the Sioux in American ways and supported the 1887 Act, it was the traditional teachings of his nation that gave him lasting respect for his people and eventually led him to write in support of Indian rights and about the hypocrisy of the American government.

It is commonly supposed that there is no systematic education of their children among the aborigines of this country. Nothing could be farther from the truth. All the customs of this primitive people were held to be divinely instituted, and those in connection with the training of children were scrupulously adhered to and transmitted from one generation to another.

The expectant parents conjointly bent all their efforts to the task of giving the newcomer the best they could gather from a long line of ancestors. A pregnant Indian woman would often choose one of the greatest characters of her family and tribe as a model for her child. This hero was daily called to mind. She would gather from tradition all of his noted deeds and daring exploits, rehearsing them to herself when alone…

Scarcely was the embryo warrior ushered into the world, when he was met by lullabies that speak of wonderful exploits in hunting and war. Those ideas which so fully occupied his mother's mind before his birth are now put into words by all about the child, who is as yet quite unresponsive to their appeals to his honour and ambition…

In hunting songs, the leading animals are introduced; they come to the boy to offer their bodies for the sustenance of his tribe. The animals are regarded as his friends, and spoken of almost as tribes of people, or as his cousins, grandfathers and grandmothers. The songs of wooing, adapted as lullabies, were equally imaginative, and the suitors were often animals personified, while pretty maidens were represented by the mink and the doe.

Very early, the Indian boy assumed the task of preserving and transmitting the legends of his ancestors and his race. Almost every evening a myth, or a true story of some deed done in the past, was narrated by one of the parents or grandparents, while the boy listened with parted lips and glistening eyes. On the following evening, he was usually required to repeat it. If he was not an apt scholar, he struggled long with his task; but, as a rule, the Indian boy is a good listener and has a good memory, so that the stories were tolerably well mastered. The household became his audience, by which he was alternately criticized and applauded.

This sort of teaching at once enlightens the boy's mind and stimulates his ambition. His conception of his own future career becomes a vivid and irresistible force. Whatever there is for him to learn must be learned; whatever qualifications are necessary to a truly great man he must seek at any expense of danger and hardship. Such was the feeling of the imaginative and brave young Indian. It became apparent to him in early life that he must accustom himself to rove alone and not to fear or dislike the impression of solitude.

It seems to be a popular idea that all the characteristic skill of the Indian is instinctive and hereditary. This is a mistake. All the stoicism and patience of the Indian are acquired traits, and continual practice alone makes him master of the art of wood-craft...

My uncle, who educated me up to the age of fifteen years, was a strict disciplinarian and a good teacher. When I left the teepee in the morning, he would say: "Hakadah, look closely to everything you see;" and at evening, on my return, he used often to catechize me for an hour or so...

Sometimes my uncle would waken me very early in the morning and challenge me to fast with him all day. I had to accept the challenge. We blackened our faces with charcoal, so that every boy in the village would know that I was fasting for the day. Then the little tempters would make my life a misery until the merciful sun hid behind the western hills...

Yet I never objected, for that would show cowardice. I picked my way through the woods, dipped my pail in the water and hurried back, always careful to make as little noise as a cat. Being only a boy, my heart would leap at every crackling of a dry twig or distant hooting of an owl, until, at last, I reached our teepee. Then my uncle would perhaps say: "Ah, Hakadah, you are a thorough warrior," empty out the precious contents of the pail, and order me to go a second time.

Imagine how I felt! But I wished to be a brave man as much as a white boy desires to be a great lawyer or even President of the United States. Silently I would take the pail and endeavour to retrace my footsteps in the dark.

With all this, our manners and morals were not neglected. I was made to respect the adults and especially the aged. I was not allowed to join in their discussions, nor even to speak in their presence, unless requested to do so. Indian etiquette was very strict, and among the requirements was that of avoiding the direct address. A term of relationship or some title of courtesy was commonly used instead of the personal name by those who wished to show respect. We were taught generosity to the poor and reverence for the "Great Mystery." Religion was the basis of all Indian training...

Zitkala-Ša: *The School Days of an Indian Girl*, 1900

The following extracts are taken from the writings of Zitkala-Ša or Gertrude Bonin (1876–1938), a Yankton Sioux writer, in which she remembers her relocation from South Dakota to a Quaker-sponsored school in Indiana in 1876.

She describes the fear and pain of a young Indian girl travelling across country away from her home and family and the bitterness that she felt over being stripped of her heritage and educated in ways that were alien to her. She explains how the process was so harrowing that over forty years later, she still bore the raw emotional scars of those 'black days'.

THE SCHOOL DAYS OF AN INDIAN GIRL

The Land of Red Apples

There were eight in our party of bronzed children who were going East with the missionaries. Among us were three young braves, two tall girls, and we three little ones, Judéwin, Thowin, and I.

We had been very impatient to start on our journey to the Red Apple Country, which, we were told, lay a little beyond the great circular horizon of the Western prairie. Under a sky of rosy apples we dreamt of roaming as freely and happily as we had chased the cloud shadows on the Dakota plains. We had anticipated much pleasure from a ride on the iron horse, but the throngs of staring palefaces disturbed and troubled us.

On the train, fair women, with tottering babies on each arm, stopped their haste and scrutinized the children of absent mothers. Large men, with heavy bundles in their hands, halted near by, and riveted their glassy blue eyes upon us.

I sank deep into the corner of my seat, for I resented being watched. Directly in front of me, children who were no larger than I hung themselves upon the backs of their seats, with their bold white faces toward me. Sometimes they took their forefingers out of their mouths and pointed at my moccasined feet. Their mothers, instead of reproving such rude curiosity, looked closely at me, and attracted their children's further notice to my blanket. This embarrassed me, and kept me constantly on the verge of tears.

I sat perfectly still, with my eyes downcast, daring only now and then to shoot long glances around me...

[After several days] It was night when we reached the school grounds. The lights from the windows of the large buildings fell upon some of the icicled trees that stood beneath them. We were led toward an open door, where the brightness of the lights within flooded out over the heads of the excited palefaces who blocked our way. My body trembled more from fear than from the snow I trod upon.

Entering the house, I stood close against the wall ... As I was wondering in which direction to escape from all this confusion, two warm hands grasped me firmly, and in the same moment I was tossed high in midair. A rosy-cheeked paleface woman caught me in her arms. I was both frightened and insulted by such trifling. I stared into her eyes, wishing her to let me stand on my own feet, but she jumped me up and down with increasing enthusiasm. My mother had never made a plaything of her wee daughter. Remembering this I began to cry aloud.

They misunderstood the cause of my tears, and placed me at a white table loaded with food. There our party were united again. As I did not hush my crying, one of the older ones whispered to me, "Wait until you are alone in the night."

It was very little I could swallow besides my sobs, that evening.

"Oh, I want my mother and my brother Dawée! I want to go to my aunt!" I pleaded; but the ears of the palefaces could not hear me.

From the table we were taken along an upward incline of wooden boxes, which I learned afterward to call a stairway. At the top was a quiet hall, dimly lighted. Many narrow beds were in one straight line down the entire length of the wall. In them lay sleeping brown faces, which peeped just out of the coverings. I was tucked into bed with one of the tall girls, because she talked to me in my mother tongue and seemed to soothe me.

I had arrived in the wonderful land of rosy skies, but I was not happy, as I had thought I should be. My long travel and the bewildering sights had exhausted me. I fell asleep, heaving deep, tired sobs. My tears were left to dry themselves in streaks, because neither my aunt nor my mother was near to wipe them away.

The Cutting of My Long Hair

The first day in the land of a.pples was a bitter-cold one; for the snow still covered the ground, and the trees were bare. A large bell rang for breakfast, its loud metallic voice crashing through the belfry overhead and into our sensitive ears. The annoying clatter of shoes on bare floors gave us no peace. The constant clash of harsh noises, with an undercurrent of many voices murmuring an unknown tongue, made a bedlam within which I was securely tied. And though my spirit tore itself in struggling for its lost freedom, all was useless

Late in the morning, my friend Judéwin gave me a terrible warning. Judéwin knew a few words of English, and she had overheard the paleface woman talk about cutting our long, heavy hair. Our mothers had taught us that only unskilled warriors who were captured had their hair shingled by the enemy. Among our people, short hair was worn by mourners, and shingled hair by cowards!

We discussed our fate some moments, and when Judéwin said, "We have to submit, because they are strong," I rebelled.

"No, I will not submit! I will struggle first!" I answered.

I watched my chance, and when no one noticed I disappeared ... On my hands and knees I crawled under the bed, and cuddled myself in the dark corner.

From my hiding place I peered out, shuddering with fear whenever I heard footsteps near by ... Some one threw up the curtains, and the room was filled with sudden light. What caused them to stoop and look under the bed I do not know. I remember being dragged out, though I resisted by kicking and scratching wildly. In spite of myself, I was carried downstairs and tied fast in a chair.

I cried aloud, shaking my head all the while until I felt the cold blades of the scissors against my neck, and heard them gnaw off one of my thick braids. Then I lost my spirit. Since the day I was taken from my mother I had suffered extreme indignities. People had stared at me. I had been tossed about in the air like a wooden puppet. And now my long hair was shingled like a coward's! In my anguish I moaned for my mother, but no one came to comfort me. Not a soul reasoned quietly with me, as my own mother used to do; for now I was only one of many little animals driven by a herder...

Iron Routine

A loud-clamoring bell awakened us at half-past six in the cold winter mornings. From happy dreams of Western rolling lands and unlassoed freedom we tumbled out upon chilly bare floors back again into a paleface day. We had short time to jump into our shoes and clothes, and wet our eyes with icy water, before a small hand bell was vigorously rung for roll call.

There were too many drowsy children and too numerous orders for the day to waste a moment in any apology to nature for giving her children such a shock in the early morning. We rushed downstairs, bounding over two high steps at a time, to land in the assembly room.

A paleface woman, with a yellow-covered roll book open on her arm and a gnawed pencil in her hand, appeared at the door. Her small, tired face was coldly lighted with a pair of large gray eyes.

She stood still in a halo of authority, while over the rim of her spectacles her eyes pried nervously about the room. Having glanced at her long list of names and called out the first one, she tossed up her chin and peered through the crystals of her spectacles to make sure of the answer "Here."

Relentlessly her pencil black-marked our daily records if we were not present to respond to our names, and no chum of ours had done it successfully for us. No matter if a dull headache or the painful cough of slow consumption had delayed the absentee, there was only time enough to mark the tardiness. It was next to impossible to leave the iron routine after the civilizing machine had once begun its day's buzzing; and as it was inbred in me to suffer in silence rather than to appeal to the ears of one whose open eyes could not see my pain, I have many times trudged in the day's harness heavy-footed, like a dumb sick brute.

Once I lost a dear classmate. I remember well how she used to mope along at my side, until one morning she could not raise her head from her pillow. At her deathbed I stood weeping, as the paleface woman sat near her moistening the dry lips. Among the folds of the bedclothes I saw the open pages of the white man's Bible. The dying Indian girl talked disconnectedly of Jesus the Christ and the paleface who was cooling her swollen hands and feet.

I grew bitter, and censured the woman for cruel neglect of our physical ills. I despised the pencils that moved automatically, and the one teaspoon which dealt out, from a large bottle, healing to a row of variously ailing Indian children. I blamed the hard-working, well-meaning, ignorant woman who was inculcating in our hearts her superstitious ideas. Though I was sullen in all my little troubles, as soon as I felt better I was ready again to smile upon the cruel woman. Within a week I was again actively testing the chains which tightly bound my individuality like a mummy for burial.

The melancholy of those black days has left so long a shadow that it darkens the path of years that have since gone by. These sad memories rise above those of smoothly grinding school days. Perhaps my Indian nature is the moaning wind which stirs them now for their present record. But, however tempestuous this is within me, it comes out as the low voice of a curiously coloured seashell, which is only for those ears that are bent with compassion to hear it…

Luther Standing Bear Recalls His Time at Carlisle Indian Industrial School, 1933

In the following text, Luther Standing Bear (1868–1939) describes growing up as a boy in the traditional ways of the Lakota Sioux and then how his people were forced to send him to Carlisle Boarding School in Pennsylvania. He explains the procedures and practices used by the school to indoctrinate him, and how, because of his strong cultural upbringing, he managed to overcome an imperial education system and retain his identity and sense of himself as Lakota Sioux.

I grew up leading the traditional life of my people, learning the crafts of hunter, scout, and warrior from my father, kindness to the old and feeble from mother, respect for wisdom and council from our wise men, and was trained by grandfather and older boys in the devotional rites of the Great Mystery. This was the scheme of existence as followed by my forefathers for many centuries, and more centuries might have come and gone in much the same way had it not been for a strange people who came from a far land to change and reshape our world.

At the age of eleven years, ancestral life for me and my people was most abruptly ended without regard for our wishes, comforts, or rights in the matter. At once I was thrust into an alien world, into an environment as different from the one into which I had been born as it is possible to imagine, to remake myself, if I could, into the likeness of the invader.

By 1879, my people were no longer free, but were subjects confined on reservations under the rule of agents. One day there came to the agency a party of white people from the East. Their presence aroused considerable excitement when it became known that these people were school teachers who wanted some Indian boys and girls to take away with them to train as were white boys and girls.

Now, father was a 'blanket Indian,' but he was wise. He listened to the white strangers, their offers and promises that if they took his son they would care well for him, teach him how to read and write, and how to wear white man's clothes. But to father all this was just 'sweet talk,' and I know that it was with great misgivings that he left the decision to me and asked if I cared to go with these people. I, of course, shared with the rest of my tribe a distrust of the white people, so I know that for all my dear father's anxiety he was proud to hear me say 'Yes.' That meant that I was brave.

I could not think of no reason why white people wanted Indian boys and girls except to kill them, and not having the remotest idea of what a school was, I thought we were going East to die. But so well had courage and bravery been trained into us that it became a part of our unconscious thinking and acting, and personal life was nothing when it came time to do something for the tribe … In my decision to go, I gave up many things dear to the heart of a little Indian boy, and one of the things over which my child mind grieved was the thought of saying good-bye to my pony. I rode him as far as I could on the journey, which was to the Missouri River, where we took the boat. There we parted from our parents, and it was a heart-breaking scene, women and children weeping. Some of the children changed their minds but were and were unable to go on the boat, but for many who did go it was a final parting.

On our way to school we saw many white people … Whenever our train stopped at the railway stations, it was met by great numbers of white people who came to gaze upon the little Indian 'savages.' The shy little ones sat quietly at the car windows looking at the people who swarmed on the platform. Some of the children wrapped themselves in their blankets, covering all but their eyes. At one place we were taken off the train and marched a distance down the street to a restaurant. We walked down the street between two rows of uniformed men whom we called soldiers, though I suppose they were policeman … Back of the rows of uniformed men stood the white people craning their necks, talking, laughing, and making a great noise. They yelled and tried to mimic us by giving what they thought were war-whoops … In my mind I often recall that scene – eighty-odd blanketed boys and girls marching down the street surrounded by a jeering, unsympathetic people whose only emotions were those of hate and fear; the conquerors looking upon the conquered. And no more understanding us than if we had suddenly been dropped from the moon.

At last at Carlisle the transforming, the 'civilizing' process began. It began with clothes. Never, no matter what our philosophy or spiritual quality, could we be civilized while wearing the moccasin and blanket. The task before us was not only that of accepting new ideas and adopting new manners, but actual physical changes and discomfort has to be borne uncomplainingly until the body adjusted itself to new tastes and habits. Our accustomed dress was taken and replaced with clothing that felt cumbersome and awkward. Against trousers and handkerchiefs we had a distinct feeling – they were unsanitary and the trousers kept us from breathing well. High collars, stiff-bosomed shirts, and suspenders fully three inches in width were uncomfortable, while leather boots caused actual suffering. We longed to go barefoot, but were told that the dew in the grass would give us colds. That was a new warning for us, for our mothers had never told us to beware of colds, and I remember as a child coming into the tipi with moccasins full of snow. Unconcernedly I would take them off my feet, pour out the snow, and put them on my feet again without any thought of sickness, for in that time colds, catarrh, bronchitis, and *la grippe* were unknown. But we were soon to know them. Then, red flannel undergarments were given us for winter wear, and for me, at least, discomfort grew into actual torture. I used to endure it as long as possible, then run upstairs and quickly taken them off the flannel garments and hide them. When inspection time came, I ran and put them on again, for I knew that if I were found disobeying the orders of the school I should be punished. My niece once asked me what it was that I disliked the most during those first bewildering days, and I said, 'red flannel.' Not knowing what I meant, she laughed, but I still remember those horrid, sticky garments which we had to wear next to the skin, and I still squirm and itch when I think of them. Of course, our hair was cut, and then there was much disapproval. But that was part of the transformation process and in some mysterious way long hair stood in the path of our development. For all the grumbling among the bigger boys, we soon had our heads shaven. How strange I felt! Involuntarily, time and time again, my hands went to my head, and that night it was a long time before I went to sleep. If we did not learn much at first, it will not be wondered at, I think. Everything was queer, and it took a few months to get adjusted to the new surroundings.

Almost immediately our names were changed to those in common use in the English language. Instead of translating our names into English and calling Zinkcaziwin, Yellow Bird, and Wanbli K'leska, Spotted Eagle, which in itself would have been educational, we were just John, Henry, or Maggie, as the case might be. I was told to take a pointer and select a name for myself from the list written on the blackboard. I did, and since one was just as good as another, and as I could not distinguish any differences in them, I placed the pointer on the name Luther. I then learned to call myself by that name and got used to hearing others call me by it, too. By that time we had been forbidden to speak our mother tongue, which is the rule in all boarding-schools. This rule is uncalled for, and today is not only robbing the Indian, but America of a rich heritage. The language of a people is part of their history. Today we should be perpetuating history instead of destroying it, and this can only be effectively done by allowing and encouraging young to keep it alive. A language, unused, embalmed, and reposing only in a book, is a dead language. Only the people themselves, and never the scholars, can nourish it into life.

Of all the changes we were forced to make, that of diet was doubtless the most injurious, for it was immediate and drastic. White bread we had for out first meal and thereafter, as well as coffee and sugar. Had we been allowed our own simple diet of meat, either boiled with soup or dried, and fruit, with perhaps a few vegetables, we should have thrived. But the change in clothing, housing, food, and confinement combined with lonesomeness was too much, and in three years nearly one half of the children from the Plains were dead and through with all earthly schools. In the graveyard at Carlisle most of the graves are those of little ones.

…I returned from the East at about the age of sixteen, after five years' contact with the white people, to resume life upon the reservation. But I returned, to spend some thirty years before again leaving, just as I had gone – a Lakota.

Outwardly I lived the life of a white man, yet all the while I kept in direct contact with tribal life. While I had learned all that I could of the white man's culture, I never forgot that of my people. I kept the language, tribal manners and usages, sang the songs and danced the dances. I still listened to and respected the advice of the older people of the tribe. I did not come home so 'progressive' that I could not speak the language of my father and mother. I did not learn the vices of chewing tobacco, smoking, drinking, and swearing, and for all this I am grateful. I have never, in fact, 'progressed' that far.

But I soon began to see the sad sight, so common today, of returned students who could not speak their native tongue, or, worse yet, some who pretended they could no longer converse in the mother tongue…

…When I came back to the reservation to resume life there, it was too late to go on the warpath to prove, as I had always hoped to prove to my people, that I was a real brave. However, there came the battle of my life – the battle with agents to retain my individuality and my life as a Lakota. I wanted to take part in the tribal dances, sing the songs I had heard since I was born, and repeat and cherish the tales that had been the delight of my boyhood. It was in these things and through these things that my people lived and could continue to live, so it was up to me to keep them alive in my mind.

Now and then the Lakotas were holding their tribal dances in the old way, and I attended. Though my hair had been cut and I wore civilian clothes, I never forsook the blanket. For convenience, no coat I have ever worn can take the place of the blanket robe; and the same with the moccasins, which are sensible, comfortable, and beautiful. Besides, they were devised by people who danced – not for pastime, excitement, or fashion – but because it was an innate urge. Even when studying under the missionary, I went to the dances of my tribe.

Don C. Talayesva: A Perspective on Assimilation, 1942

In the following document, Don C. Talayesva (1890–c.1976), a Hopi who grew up on a reservation in Oraibi, Arizona, describes the experience of attending a reservation and an off-reservation boarding school. Although he was reluctant, at first, to attend school, he quickly found that he enjoyed being a 'schoolboy' and, despite having a strong tribal cultural understanding and connection, he felt comfortable attending non-Indian run boarding schools.

I grew up believing that Whites are wicked, deceitful people. It seemed that most of them were soldiers, government agents, or missionaries, and that quite a few were Two-Hearts...

Our chief had to show respect to them and pretend to obey their orders, but we knew that he did it half-heartedly and that he put his trust in our Hopi gods. Our ancestors had predicted the coming of these Whites and said that they would cause as much trouble. But it was understood that we had to put up with them until our gods saw fit to recall out Great White Brother from the East to deliver us...

A few years before my birth the United States Government had built a boarding school at the Keams Canyon Agency. At first our chief, Lolulomai, had not wanted to send Oraibi children, but chiefs from other villages came and persuaded him to accept clothes, tools, and other supplies, and to let them go. Most of the people disliked this and refused to cooperate. Troops came to Oraibi several times to take the children by force and carry them off in wagons. The people said that it was a terrible sight to see Negro soldiers come and tear children from their parents. Some boys later escaped from Keams Canyon and returned home on foot, a distance of forty miles.

Some years later a day school was opened at the foot of the mesa in New Oraibi, where there were a trading post, a post office, and a few government buildings. Some parents were permitted to send their children to this school. When my sister started, the teacher cut her hair, burned all her clothes, and gave her a new outfit and a new name, Nellie...

In 1899 it was decided that I should go to school. I was willing to try it but I did not want a policeman to come for me and I did not want my shirt taken from my back and burned. So one morning in September I left it off, wrapped myself in my Navaho blanket, the one my grandfather had given me, and went down the mesa barefoot and bareheaded...

...Just before Christmas we heard that a disease, smallpox, was coming west from First Mesa. Within a few weeks news came to us that on Second Mesa the people were dying so fast that the Hopi did not have time to bury them, but just pitched their bodies over the cliff. The government employees and some of the schoolteachers fled from Oraibi, leaving only the principal and missionaries, who said that they would stay...

One day when I was playing with the boys in the plaza in Oraibi, the school principal and the missionary came to vaccine us. My mother brought me in to the principal who was holding a knife in his hand. Trembling, I took hold of his arm which caused him to laugh. They had a small bottle of soap like liquid which they opened, and placed a little on my arm. After it had dried, they rubbed my arm with a cloth and the missionary took a sharp instrument and stuck it into my skin three times. I proved myself brave enough to take it and set a good example for the rest of the family who were vaccinated in their turn. It was spring when the disease disappeared. We were lucky. The old people said that the vaccinations were all nonsense but probably harmless,

and that by our prayers we had persuaded the spirits to banish the disease -
that it was Masau'u, who guards the village with his fire-brand, who had
protected us...

That autumn some of the people took their children to Keams Canyon to
attend the boarding school ... My mother and father took three burros and
accompanied me to Keams Canyon...

There were a great many of us and we had to stand in line. The agent shook
hands with us and patted us on the head, telling us through an interpreter that
we had come to be educated...

Then we went to camp, where my father saddled a burro and told my
mother to mount. "Well, son," they advised me, "don't ever try to run away
from here. You are not a good runner, and you might get lost and starve to
death. We would not know where to find you, and the coyotes would eat
you." I promised. My father climbed on a burro and they started off. I kept my
eyes upon them until finally they disappeared in the direction of Oraibi. I
moaned and began to cry, fearing that I should never see them again. A Hopi
boy named Nash, whom I did not know, spoke to me and told me to stop
crying. My parents would come back again, he reassured me, and they might
bring me some good Hopi food...

On June the fourteenth my father came for me and we returned home ...
It was a joy to get home again, to see all my folks, and to tell about my
experiences at school. I had learned many English words and could recite part
of the Ten Commandments. I knew how to sleep on a bed, pray to Jesus, comb
my hair, eat with a knife and fork, and use a toilet. I had learned that the world
is round instead of flat, that it is indecent to go naked in the presence of girls,
and to eat the testes of sheep or goats. I had also learned that a person thinks
with his head instead of his heart...

By the end of summer I had had enough of hoeing weeds and tending
sheep. Helping my father was hard work and I thought it was better to be
educated. My grandfather agreed that it was useful to know something of the
white man's ways, but said that he feared I might neglect the Hopi rules which
were more important. He cautioned me that if I had bad dreams while at
school, I should spit four times in order to drive them from my mind and
counteract their evil influences.

Before sunrise on the tenth of September the police came to Oraibi and
surrounded the village, with the intention of capturing the children of the
Hostile families and taking them to school by force. They herded us all
together at the east edge of the mesa. Although I had planned to go later, they
put me with the others. The people were excited, the children and the
mothers were crying, and the men wanted to fight. I was not much afraid
because I had learned a little about education and knew that the police had
not come without orders...

The children already at the school were eating their supper when we
arrived. Rex and I went to the kitchen and asked for food. We each got a loaf

of bread and ate it with some syrup ... We ate our food at the door and told the people in the kitchen that the children were coming in wagons. Then we went to the dormitory and rested. The next morning we took a bath, had our hair clipped, put on new clothes, and were schoolboys again.

William Eubanks: 'Destruction of the Cherokee People' from the *Cherokee Advocate*, 20 April 1901

In the following text, William Eubanks (c.1841–c.1906), a Cherokee intellectual, translator and writer, explains how the policy of allotment was forced upon the Cherokee after their removal from the eastern United States.

One of the most damnable schemes to destroy the Cherokee Nation and rob its people of all that is valuable and worth living for is to be found in the provisions of the so called agreement, entered into by the United States Congress and the Dawes Commission, instigated by that enormously wealthy railroad corporation whose pathway and play ground is between its two headquarters - St. Louis and Galveston - through the Cherokee Nation.

In a few days the citizens of the Cherokee Nation will be at the polls for the purpose of voting as to whether to ratify or reject this outrage. This enormous outrage in the form of an agreement made, as we say, and as claimed by the purported Cherokee delegation, was entered into, amended sanctioned and ratified by the Congress of the United States and the Dawes Commission, over the signatures of said delegation affixed to an agreement of which this the amended agreement upon which we are to vote has no relation or resemblance. It appears now that a foul game has been played upon said delegation by confidence men of the Congress of the United States and the Dawes Commission, with the approval of the railroad corporation. Now if this is a fact we see no reason why the Principal Chief would not have the right to revoke the proclamation issued by him setting forth a day upon which to vote for the ratification of this spurious and illegitimate agreement.

Now before we vote upon this death warrant that seals the fate of the Cherokee people, I wish to point out a few of the objectionable features, to be found in nearly every clause.

I think I have a right to do this. I think I have a right to defend the interests of my people...

After the Cherokees were driven to the Indian Territory, and settled down in their homes on land for which the government of the United States had given a patent, or deed, the United States, as though regretting that she had unwittingly given the Cherokees a patent to their lands, offered a prize to a great railroad corporation to destroy the Cherokee Nation by annulling this deed to their lands. The prize was 800,000 acres of Cherokee lands to be deeded to this railroad corporation when the Cherokee Nation should become extinct and their title to the lands extinguished.

This railroad went to work years ago to win this prize offered by the United States, and this agreement is one of their plans. If we ratify this agreement, the lands this corporation will get will be worth $50,000,000; money enough to feed and clothe the Cherokee people fifty years ... What does the railroad corporation care for a title from the Indian? This railroad corporation will simply wait until after 1906, when the Cherokee Nation will be dead, and then the Cherokee lands having reverted to the United States, they, the United States, will then give the railroad a title for this land. Then the railroad company will have won the prize, and come into possession of $50,000,000 worth of property...

Nearly the whole agreement is in relation to town lots and town sites, and made so complicated that it is difficult to understand just what is meant in some of these clauses. This is done on purpose, so that after the Nation is destroyed, the ordinarily intelligent owner of these lots will be beat out of them. I heard a lawyer from the states remark a few days ago: "When this agreement is ratified, all we will have to do then will be to kill and eat." This lawyer spoke the truth, for when this agreement is ratified, the only thing the lawyers will have to do will be to take the provision of this agreement and the Arkansas law and by law, suits to kill out the unsuspecting owner of allotments and town lot holders and eat up his property in the courts...

Now, after giving away to the U. S., about 2,000,000 acres of land for which you relinquish your right and title - and to the railroad company about 800,000 acres for which you relinquish all your right and title - to the towns about 600,000 acres to which you will have no right and title - and 157,600 acres segregated in the Delaware suit for which you will never live long enough to get a title - and giving to the U. S., all your invested funds of which you will never see a dollar - and after you have destroyed your Cherokee government and given up all your schools and other institutions to the U. S., of which you will never receive a dollar's worth of benefit after 1906 - Yes, after you have destroyed your manhood and liberty and sacrificed thousand of your poor people to this infernal god of greed, to be dragged around in the courts of the U. S., until the last vestige of their property is eat up by this Christian demon who proposes to have nothing to do after the agreement is ratified but to kill and eat. I say after fully knowing all these things are you Cherokees going to vote for the ratification of this agreement? I ask you adopted white citizens of the Cherokee Nation, if you are going to cast your vote for the ratification of this agreement when you know well and good that the ratification of this damnable railroad scheme will open the doors for this country to be flooded by that proud arrogant class from the States who will look upon your half Indian children as a mongrel cross between the whites from the states and the Cherokee Indian woman, you have already been reproached, by this class, with the opprobrious name of squaw men. Do you propose to give this class the opportunity to add more of these insults to your Cherokee wives and Cherokee children, they will continue to call you squaw men and your wives as squaw-women and your children as squaw children.

What are you darkies of the Cherokee Nation going to do? Whatever you do I want you to remember what the Cherokees have done for you, in the way of giving you homes, a portion of our funds and schools in which to educate your children.

Now, before the die is cast and a vote is taken on this agreement - the outgrowth of an unrighteous proposition, made by an unrighteous government, to an unrighteous corporation for an unrighteous purpose.

I wish to say that, whatever their fate may be, the Cherokee has kept the law and preserved a living tradition coinciding with the ancient Hebrew command:- "The stranger that comes to you shall be among you as the native, and thou shalt love him as thyself." This we have done and kept our souls clean, and in order to keep clean and pure our higher spirits, we have also preserved that law of the higher gods in words like these: "If thou findest a hungry serpent creeping into thy house, seeking for food, and, out of fear it should bite thee, instead of offering it milk thou turnest it out to suffer and starve, thou turnest away from the Path of Compassion."

Chester A. Arthur on Indian Policy Reform: First Annual Message to Congress, 6 December 1881

In the following excerpts taken from a speech to Congress made by President Chester A. Arthur (1829–1886), the twenty-first president of the United States who served from 1881 to 1885, he reveals his full support for breaking up the tribal reservations and introducing allotments to individual Indians. The purpose of allotment, Arthur claimed, was to 'help' Indian communities give up hunting, force them to adopt agriculturalism and thus assimilate them away from what were perceived to be their 'savage' ways of life.

...Prominent among the matters which challenge the attention of Congress at its present session is the management of our Indian affairs. While this question has been a cause of trouble and embarrassment from the infancy of the Government, it is but recently that any effort has been made for its solution at once serious, determined, consistent, and promising success.

It has been easier to resort to convenient makeshifts for tiding over temporary difficulties than to grapple with the great permanent problem, and accordingly the easier course has almost invariably been pursued.

It was natural, at a time when the national territory seemed almost illimitable and contained many millions of acres far outside the bounds of civilized settlements, that a policy should have been initiated which more than aught else has been the fruitful source of our Indian complications.

I refer, of course, to the policy of dealing with the various Indian tribes as separate nationalities, of relegating them by treaty stipulations to the occupancy of immense reservations in the West, and of encouraging them to live a savage life, undisturbed by any earnest and well-directed efforts to bring them under the influences of civilization.

The unsatisfactory results which have sprung from this policy are becoming apparent to all.

As the white settlements have crowded the borders of the reservations, the Indians, sometimes contentedly and sometimes against their will, have been transferred to other hunting grounds, from which they have again been dislodged whenever their new-found homes have been desired by the adventurous settlers.

These removals and the frontier collisions by which they have often been preceded have led to frequent and disastrous conflicts between the races.

It is profitless to discuss here which of them has been chiefly responsible for the disturbances whose recital occupies so large a space upon the pages of our history.

We have to deal with the appalling fact that though thousands of lives have been sacrificed and hundreds of millions of dollars expended in the attempt to solve the Indian problem, it has until within the past few years seemed scarcely nearer a solution than it was half a century ago. But the Government has of late been cautiously but steadily feeling its way to the adoption of a policy which has already produced gratifying results, and which, in my judgment, is likely, if Congress and the Executive accord in its support, to relieve us ere long from the difficulties which have hitherto beset us.

For the success of the efforts now making to introduce among the Indians the customs and pursuits of civilized life and gradually to absorb them into the mass of our citizens, sharing their rights and holden to their responsibilities, there is imperative need for legislative action.

My suggestions in that regard will be chiefly such as have been already called to the attention of Congress and have received to some extent its consideration.

First. I recommend the passage of an act making the laws of the various States and Territories applicable to the Indian reservations within their borders and extending the laws of the State of Arkansas to the portion of the Indian Territory not occupied by the Five Civilized Tribes.

The Indian should receive the protection of the law. He should be allowed to maintain in court his rights of person and property. He has repeatedly begged for this privilege. Its exercise would be very valuable to him in his progress toward civilization.

Second. Of even greater importance is a measure which has been frequently recommended by my predecessors in office, and in furtherance of which several bills have been from time to time introduced in both Houses of Congress. The enactment of a general law permitting the allotment in severalty, to such Indians, at least, as desire it, of a reasonable quantity of land secured to them by patent, and for their own protection made inalienable for twenty or twenty-five years, is demanded for their present welfare and their permanent advancement.

In return for such considerate action on the part of the Government, there is reason to believe that the Indians in large numbers would be persuaded to sever their tribal relations and to engage at once in agricultural pursuits. Many of them realize the fact that their hunting days are over and that it is now for their best interests to conform their manner of life to the new order of things. By no greater inducement than the assurance of permanent title to the soil can they be led to engage in the occupation of tilling it.

The well-attested reports of the their increasing interest in husbandry justify the hope and belief that the enactment of such a statute as I recommend would be at once attended with gratifying results. A resort to the allotment system would have a direct and powerful influence in dissolving the tribal bond, which is so prominent a feature of savage life, and which tends so strongly to perpetuate it...

General Allotment Act (Dawes Act), 1887

Provided here are key excerpts from the General Allotment Act showing the details, terms and conditions the 1887 Act imposed upon a number of Indian groups and their tribal reservations.

An act to provide for the allotment of lands in severalty to Indians on the various reservations, and to extend the protection of the laws of the United States and the Territories over the Indians, and for other purposes.

Be it enacted by the Senate and House of Representatives of the United States of America in Congress assembled, That in all cases where any tribe or band of Indians has been, or shall hereafter be, located upon any reservation created for their use, either by treaty stipulation or by virtue of an act of Congress or executive order setting apart the same for their use, the President of the United States be, and he hereby is, authorized, whenever in his opinion any reservation or any part thereof of such Indians is advantageous for agricultural and grazing purposes, to cause said reservation, or any part thereof, to be surveyed, or resurveyed if necessary, and to allot the lands in said reservation in severalty to any Indian located thereon in quantities as follows:

To each head of a family, one-quarter of a section;

To each single person over eighteen years of age, one-eighth of a section;

To each orphan child under eighteen years of age, one eighth of a section; and

To each other single person under eighteen years now living, or who may be born prior to the date of the order of the President directing an allotment of the lands embraced in any reservation, one-sixteenth of a section: *Provided*, That in case there is not sufficient land in any of said reservations to allot lands to each individual of the classes above named in quantities as above provided, the lands embraced in such reservation or reservations shall be allotted to each individual of each of said classes pro rata in accordance with the provisions of this act: *And provided further,* That where the treaty or act of Congress setting apart such reservation provides the allotment of lands in severalty in quantities in excess of those herein provided, the President, in making allotments upon such reservation, shall allot the lands to each individual Indian belonging thereon in quantity as specified in such treaty or act: *And provided further,* That when the lands allotted are only valuable for grazing purposes, an additional allotment of such grazing lands, in quantities as above provided, shall be made to each individual.

SEC. 2. That all allotments set apart under the provisions of this act shall be selected by the Indians, heads of families selecting for their minor children, and the agents shall select for each orphan child, and in such manner as to embrace the improvements of the Indians making the selection...

SEC. 4. That where any Indian not residing upon a reservation, or for whose tribe no reservation has been provided by treaty, act of Congress, or executive order, shall make settlement upon any surveyed or unsurveyed lands of the United States not otherwise appropriated, he or she shall be entitled, upon application to the local land-office for the district in which the lands are located, to have the same allotted to him or her, and to his or her children, in quantities and manner as provided in this act for Indians residing upon reservations; and when such settlement is made upon unsurveyed lands, the grant to such Indians shall be adjusted upon the survey of the lands so as to conform thereto; and patents shall be issued to them for such lands in the manner and with the restrictions as herein provided.

SEC. 5. That upon the approval of the allotments provided for in this act by the Secretary of the Interior, he shall cause patents to issue therefore in the name of the allottees, which patents shall be of the legal effect, and declare that the United States does and will hold the land thus allotted, for the period of twenty-five years, in trust for the sole use and benefit of the Indian to whom such allotment shall have been made, or, in case of his decease, of his heirs according to the laws of the State or Territory where such land is located, and that at the expiration of said period the United States will convey the same by patent to said Indian, or his heirs as aforesaid, in fee, discharged of said trust and free of all charge or incumbrance whatsoever...

SEC. 6. That upon the completion of said allotments and the patenting of the lands to said allottees, each and every member of the respective bands or tribes of Indians to whom allotments have been made shall have the benefit of and be subject to the laws, both civil and criminal, of the State or Territory in which they may reside; and no Territory shall pass or enforce any law denying any such Indian within its jurisdiction the equal protection of the law. And every Indian born within the territorial limits of the United States to whom allotments shall have been made under the provisions of this act, or under any law or treaty, and every Indian born within the territorial limits of the United States who has voluntarily taken up, within said limits, his residence separate and apart from any tribe of Indians therein, and has adopted the habits of civilized life, is hereby declared to be a citizen of the United States...

SEC. 8. That the provisions of this act shall not extend to the territory occupied by the Cherokees, Creeks, Choctaws, Chickasaws, Seminoles, and Osage, Miamies and Peorias, and Sacs and Foxes, in the Indian Territory, nor to any of the reservations of the Seneca Nation of New York Indians in the State of New York, nor to that strip of territory in the State of Nebraska adjoining the Sioux Nation on the south added by executive order...

Ex Parte Crow Dog, 1883

The following extract highlights the main parts of the Supreme Court opinion and its reasons for supporting the release of Crow Dog from prison.

The petitioner is in the custody of the marshal of the United States for the territory of Dakota, imprisoned in the jail of Lawrence county, in the first judicial district of that territory, under sentence of death, adjudged against him by the district court for that district, to be carried into execution January 14, 1884. That judgment was rendered upon a conviction for the murder of an Indian of the Brule Sioux band of the Sioux nation of Indians, by the name of Sin-ta-ge-le-Scka, or in English, Spotted Tail, the prisoner also being an Indian of the same band and nation, and the homicide having occurred, as alleged in the indictment, in the Indian country, within a place and district of country under the exclusive jurisdiction of the United States and within the said judicial district. The judgment was affirmed on a writ of error, by the supreme court of the territory. It is claimed on behalf of the prisoner that the crime charged against him, and of which he stands convicted, is not an offence under the laws of the United States; that the district court had no jurisdiction to try him, and that its judgment and sentence are void. It therefore prays for a writ of habeas corpus, that he may be delivered from an imprisonment which he asserts to be illegal...

The reservation of the Sioux Indians, lying within the exterior boundaries of the territory of Dakota, was defined by article 2 of the treaty concluded April 29, 1868, and by section 1839 Rev. St., it is excepted out of and constitutes no part of that territory. The object of this exception is stated to be to exclude the jurisdiction of any state or territorial government over Indians within its exterior lines, without their consent, where their rights have been reserved and remain unextinguished by treaty...

The pledge to secure to these people, with whom the United States was contracting as a distinct political body, an orderly government, by appropriate legislation thereafter to be framed and enacted, necessarily implies, having regard to all the circumstances attending the transaction, that among the arts of civilized life, which it was the very purpose of all these arrangements to introduce and naturalize among them, was the highest and best of all, - that of self-government, the regulation by themselves of their own domestic affairs, the maintenance of order and peace among their own members by the administration of their own laws and customs. They were nevertheless to be subject to the laws of the United States, not in the sense of citizens, but, as they had always been, as wards, subject to a guardian; not as individuals, constituted members of the political community of the United States, with a voice in the selection of representatives and the framing of the laws, but as a dependent community who were in a state of pupilage, advancing from the condition of a savage tribe to that of a people who, through the discipline of labour, and by education, it was hoped might become a self-supporting and self-governed society. The laws to which they were declared to be subject were the laws then existing, and which applied to them as Indians, and, of course, included the very statute under consideration, which excepted from the operation of the general laws of the United States, otherwise applicable, the very case of the prisoner. Declaring them subject to the laws made them so, if it effected any change in their situation, only in respect to laws in force and as existing, and did not effect any change in the laws themselves...

It is a case involving the judgment of a court of special and limited jurisdiction, not to be assumed without clear warrant of law. It is a case of life and death. It is a case where, against an express exception in the law itself, that law, by argument and inference only, is sought to be extended over aliens and strangers; over the members of a community, separated by race, by tradition, by the instincts of a free though savage life, from the authority and power which seeks to impose upon them the restraints of an external and unknown code, and to subject them to the responsibilities of civil conduct, according to rules and penalties of which they could have no previous warning; which judges them by a standard made by others, and not for them, which takes no account of the conditions which should except them from its exactions, and makes no allowance for their inability to understand it. It tries them not by their peers, nor by the customs of their people, nor the law of their land, but by superiors of a different race, according to the law of a social state of which they have an imperfect conception, and which is opposed to the traditions of their history, to the habits of their lives, to the strongest prejudices of their savage nature; one which measures the red man's revenge by the maxims of the white man's morality. It is a case, too, of first impression, so far as we are advised; for, if the question has been mooted heretofore in any courts of the United States, the jurisdiction has never before been practically asserted as in the present instance...

It results that the first district court of Dakota was without jurisdiction to find or try the indictment against the prisoner; that the conviction and sentence are void, and that his imprisonment is illegal.

Thomas J. Morgan: 'Inculcation of Patriotism in Indian Schools', 1889

In the following document, Thomas J. Morgan (c.1840–1902), Commissioner of Indian Affairs from 1889 to 1893, argues that formally educating young Indian children will prepare them for an American life and enable them to become Americans, particularly if the correct educational criteria are followed.

To Indian Agents and Superintendents of Indian Schools:

The great purpose which the Government has in view in providing an ample system of common school education for all Indian youth of school age, is the preparation of them for American citizenship. The Indians are destined to become absorbed into the national life, not as Indians, but as Americans. They are to share with their fellow-citizens in all the rights and privileges and are likewise to be called upon to bear fully their share of all the duties and responsibilities involved in American citizenship.

It is the highest degree important, therefore, that special attention should be paid, particularly in the higher grades of the schools, to the instruction of Indian youth in the elements of American history, acquainting them especially with the leading facts in the lives of the most notable and worthy historical characters. While in such study the wrongs of their ancestors can not be ignored, the injustice which their race has suffered can be contrasted with the larger future open to them, and their duties and opportunities rather than their wrongs will most profitably engage their attention.

Pupils should also be made acquainted with the elementary principles of the Government under which they live, and with their duties and privileges as citizens. To this end, regular instructions should be given them in the form of familiar talks, or by means of the use of some elementary text-book in civics. Debating societies should be organised in which may be learned the practical rules of procedure which govern public assemblies. Some simple manual of rules of order should be put into the hands of the more advanced students, and they should be carefully instructed in its use.

On the campus of all the more important schools there should be erected a flagstaff, from which should float constantly, in suitable weather, the American flag. In all schools of whatever size and character, supported wholly or in part by the Government, the "Stars and Stripes" should be a familiar object, and students should be taught to reverence the flag as a symbol of their nation's power and protection.

Patriotic songs should be taught to the pupils, and they should sing them frequently until they acquire complete familiarity with them. Patriotic selections should be committed and recited publicly, and should constitute a portion of the reading exercises.

National holidays – Washington's birthday, Decoration Day, Fourth of July, Thanksgiving, and Christmas - should be observed with appropriate exercises in all the Indian schools. It will also be well to observe the anniversary of the day upon which the "Dawes bill" for giving to Indians allotments of land in severalty became a law, viz, February 8, 1887, and to use that occasion to impress upon Indian youth the enlarged scope and opportunity given them by this law and the new obligations which it imposes.

In all proper way, teachers in the Indian schools should endeavour to appeal to the highest elements of manhood and womanhood in their pupils, exciting in them an ambition after excellence in character and dignity of surroundings, and they should carefully avoid any unnecessary references to the fact that they are Indians.

They should point out to their pupils the provisions which the Government has made for their education, and the opportunities which it affords them for earning a livelihood, and for achieving for themselves honourable places in life, and should endeavour to awaken reverence for the nation's power, gratitude for its beneficence, pride in its history, and a laudable ambition to contribute to its prosperity.

Agents and school superintendents are specially charged with the duty of putting these suggestions into practical operation.

Richard H. Pratt: 'Kill the Indian, Save the Man', 1892

The following extract explores the position taken by Richard H. Pratt (1840–1924), a captain who had guarded the imprisoned Plains Indians in Florida after the Red River War of 1874 and founded the Carlisle Indian School in Pennsylvania in 1879. He believed that the allotment policy was an inappropriate tool because it did not allow for the complete absorption of Indians into American society or to disperse Indian individuals among groups of 'civilised' non-Indians.

A great general has said that the only good Indian is a dead one, and that high sanction of his destruction has been an enormous factor in promoting Indian massacres. In a sense, I agree with the sentiment, but only in this: that all the Indian there is in the race should be dead. Kill the Indian in him, and save the man…

The Indians under our care remained savage, because forced back upon themselves and away from association with English-speaking and civilized people, and because of our savage example and treatment of them.…

We have never made any attempt to civilize them with the idea of taking them into the nation, and all of our policies have been against citizenizing and absorbing them. Although some of the policies now prominent are advertised to carry them into citizenship and consequent association and competition with other masses of the nation, they are not, in reality, calculated to do this.

We are after the facts. Let us take the Land in Severalty Bill. Land in severalty, as administered, is in the way of the individualizing and civilization of the Indians, and is a means of holding the tribes together. Land in severalty is given to individuals adjoining each other on their present reservations. And experience shows that in some cases, after the allotments have been made, the Indians have entered into a compact among themselves to continue to hold their lands in common as a reservation. The inducement of the bill is in this direction. The Indians are not only invited to remain separate tribes and communities, but are practically compelled to remain so. The Indian must either cling to his tribe and its locality, or take great chances of losing his rights and property.

The day on which the Land in Severalty Bill was signed was announced to be the emancipation day for the Indians. The fallacy of that idea is so entirely demonstrated that the emancipation assumption is now withdrawn...

We make our greatest mistake in feeding our civilization to the Indians instead of feeding the Indians to our civilization. America has different customs and civilizations from Germany. What would be the result of an attempt to plant American customs and civilization among the Germans in Germany, demanding that they shall become thoroughly American before we admit them to the country? Now, what we have all along attempted to do for and with the Indians is just exactly that, and nothing else. We invite the Germans to come into our country and communities, and share our customs, our civilization, to be of it; and the result is immediate success. Why not try it on the Indians? Why not invite them into experiences in our communities? Why always invite and compel them to remain a people unto themselves?

It is a great mistake to think that the Indian is born an inevitable savage. He is born a blank, like all the rest of us. Left in the surroundings of savagery, he grows to possess a savage language, superstition, and life. We, left in the surroundings of civilization, grow to possess a civilized language, life, and purpose. Transfer the infant white to the savage surroundings, he will grow to possess a savage language, superstition, and habit. Transfer the savage-born infant to the surroundings of civilization, and he will grow to possess a civilized language and habit. These results have been established over and over again beyond all question; and it is also well established that those advanced in life, even to maturity, of either class, lose already acquired qualities belonging to the side of their birth, and gradually take on those of the side to which they have been transferred.

...it would seem that the time may have arrived when we can very properly make at least the attempt to assimilate our two hundred and fifty thousand Indians, using this proven potent line, and see if that will not end this vexed question and remove them from public attention, where they occupy so much more space than they are entitled to either by numbers or worth.

...The Land in Severalty Bill can be made far more useful than it is, but it can be made so only by assigning the land so as to intersperse good, civilized people among them. If, in the distribution, it is so arranged that two or three white families come between two Indian families, then there would necessarily grow up a community of fellowship along all the lines of our American civilization that would help the Indian at once to his feet...

Theorizing citizenship into people is a slow operation ... Neither can the Indians understand or use American citizenship theoretically taught to them on Indian reservations. They must get into the swim of American citizenship. They must feel the touch of it day after day, until they become saturated with the spirit of it, and thus become equal to it.

When we cease to teach the Indian that he is less than a man; when we recognize fully that he is capable in all respects as we are, and that he only needs the opportunities and privileges which we possess to enable him to assert his humanity and manhood; when we act consistently towards him in accordance with that recognition; when we cease to fetter him to conditions which keep him in bondage, surrounded by retrogressive influences; when we allow him the freedom of association and the developing influences of social contact—then the Indian will quickly demonstrate that he can be truly civilized, and he himself will solve the question of what to do with the Indian.

Theodore Roosevelt: First Annual Message to Congress, 'A Mighty Pulverizing Engine to Break Up the Tribal Mass', 3 December 1901

President Theodore Roosevelt (1858–1919), twenty-sixth president of the United States who served from 1901 to 1909, in his first annual message to Congress in 1901 explains how allotment policy was an ideal tool to break up tribal reservations and tribal lifestyles.

In my judgment the time has arrived when we should definitely make up our minds to recognize the Indian as an individual and not as a member of a tribe. The General Allotment Act is a mighty pulverizing engine to break up the tribal mass ... Under its provisions some sixty thousand Indians have already become citizens of the United States. We should now break up the tribal funds, doing for them what allotment does for the tribal lands; that is, they should be divided into individual holdings ... A stop should be put upon the indiscriminate permission to Indians to lease their allotments. The effort should be steadily to make the Indian work like any other man on his own ground...

In the schools the education should be elementary and largely industrial. The need of higher education among the Indians is very, very limited ... The ration system, which is merely the corral and the reservation system, is highly detrimental to the Indians. It promotes beggary, perpetuates pauperism, and stifles industry. It is an effectual barrier to progress ... The Indian should be treated as an individual - like the white man.

CHAPTER EIGHT

INDIAN NEW DEAL ERA, 1928–1941

The period of the Indian New Deal contrasted sharply with the ethos, ideology and practice of assimilation and allotment. For the first time in over a century, the New Deal offered the Indians a chance to reclaim and reassert their cultural heritage and identity in a much-changed United States of America. The beginnings of this change came during and after the First World War when many thousands of Indians fought on behalf of the United States. To some extent in response to this public evidence of ability and loyalty, the American government passed the Indian Citizenship Act of 1924, which granted full American citizenship to all Indians born within its borders.[1] Many Indians, however, saw citizenship as yet another push towards assimilation and as another means whereby the American government could sidestep its responsibility to provide for the Indian peoples it had dispossessed. The First World War, however, had also diverted much-needed American funds away from Indian health, education and welfare provision and forced many Indians into poverty. The loss of federal support, the ongoing failure of the allotment policy and the desperate living conditions on many Indian reservations were exposed when reform movements organised by Indians and non-Indians during the 1920s forced the federal government to begin an investigation into the state of Indian affairs and the conditions in Indian country.[2] In 1928, an investigation led by Lewis Meriam published a final report that shocked America. The impact of the Meriam Report coupled with the appointment of John Collier as the commissioner of the Bureau of Indian Affairs (BIA) led to an Indian reform programme that produced the Indian Reorganisation Act of 1934. It allowed Indian peoples to have more control and authority over decision-making, including cultural, educational and health issues within the reservations. Many Indians and Indian nations supported the 1934 Act and the relaxation of BIA control over Indian affairs. However, despite the change in federal policy away from allotment, not all Indian people thought the 1934 Act was positive. They saw it as yet another policy that controlled and moulded Indians into a non-Indian version of their identity. Once again they were to become American citizens, but this time while retaining certain aspects of 'Indianness' that appealed to Euro-American intellectuals and policy makers who were by then disaffected with the pressures of modern life. Commissioner John Collier found both support and ambivalence within Indian country for his reforms. The Indian New Deal restored land to Indian communities and made a number of improvements to Indian environments before funds were redirected with the onset of the Second World War.

During the 1920s, the devastation the American government policy of allotment had brought to the lives of countless Indians and their traditional ways of life was brought to the attention of America with the Meriam Report of 1928. Criticism at the beginning of the 1920s had compelled the American government to authorise the Institute for Government Research to conduct the economic and social survey. In 1926, Lewis Meriam began this important project. After two years, Meriam published what was officially entitled, The Problem of Indian Administration, calling for a radically new approach to Indian affairs with more federal money to be guided towards the reservations.[3] The 1928 Meriam report was comprehensive and covered issues such as Indian education, health, lands, economic conditions and legal matters. The report exposed many issues including the adverse affects of allotment and the loss of Indian allotted lands as a result of death, bankruptcy and fraud, the devastation wrought by educational programmes that weakened tribal cultures, and the lack of economic opportunities leading to high rates of Indian poverty and illiteracy.[4] The report outlined how the federal government might help Indian communities and recommended that more funds be directed towards Indian programmes. Although the Meriam Report was condemned by some in Congress as biased, it undoubtedly opened the eyes of many Americans to Indian suffering and to the mess that had been created on Indian reservations by the federal government. In 1932, the American people elected Franklin Delano Roosevelt (1882–1945), and under his administration, the BIA began a period of radical reform in Indian affairs, centred upon a flagship piece of legislation, the Indian Reorganisation Act of 1934.

The development of the Indian New Deal programme began when the administration appointed key non-Indian personnel, including John Collier (1884–1968) as Commissioner of Indian Affairs from 1933 to 1945, Harold L. Ickes (1874–1952) as Secretary of the Interior, and Felix S. Cohen (1907–1953) as solicitor in the Solicitor's Office of the Interior Department. Under Collier's guidance, the administration began to appoint Indians, including Henry Roe Cloud (Winnebago) and Wade Crawford (Klamath), to influence policy and make bureaucratic changes to the BIA in order to facilitate pro-Indian programmes.[5] However, not all Indians supported the policies being pursued by Collier and many feared and distrusted the introduction of the Indian Reorganisation bill in Congress.

At the outset, the Indian Reorganisation bill, also known as the Wheeler-Howard Bill, was opposed by many non-Indians and Indians. The Oneida nation, as well as many other Indian groups such as the Navajo, the Flathead of Montana and the Yakima openly questioned why the federal government had to pass legislation to reaffirm tribal authority and sovereignty when it continued to be legally recognised under the auspices of treaties conducted between Indian nations and the American government.[6] In order to placate the concerns of many Indian nations, the federal government organised regional meetings in Oregon, Arizona,

South Dakota, New Mexico, California, Wisconsin and Oklahoma,
to discuss the bill and its future impact. During these meetings, many
Indians voiced their general suspicions about any federal legislation and
raised concerns that the bill would not solve localised problems, such
as those involving fishing rights in the Pacific-Northwest and water in
the Southwest.[7] Moreover, non-Indians, including Congressmen and
Senators, distrusted the level of authority that the new bill gave to tribal
governments over reservation actions. In particular, it was considered a
policy too far removed from the overriding federal policies of assimilation
and allotment.[8] However, despite not gaining any sort of consensus
from a number of non-Indians and Indians, such as the Navajo, Collier
succeeded in passing a severely compromised Indian Reorganisation
Act in 1934, also known as the Wheeler-Howard Act.[9]

The 1934 Act contained many important principles that broke away
from the past and gave many Indians hope for a brighter future. The Act
ended nearly half a century of destructive allotment policy and ensured
that Indian lands were no longer allotted. In addition, the Act granted
special authority and powers to the Secretary of the Interior to ensure
that the New Deal assisted Indian communities. The Secretary had the
authority, among others, to return lands to Indian tribes, to grant federal
loans to support Indian education, Indian businesses and economies, and
to assist Indian tribes in adopting tribal governments and written
constitutions.[10] Arguably, one of the most important elements of the Act
was the reversal of some of the powerful influence that the BIA had over
Indian affairs and daily reservation life. One of the key architects of the
1934 Act, John Collier, strongly supported the principle of undoing the
process of allotment, so as to rebuild tribal morale, and to allow a
renaissance in Indian cultural expression and authority within the
reservations.[11] Tribal culture and tribal ideas were to be integral to the
success of the federal government's Indian policy.

The reactions of some Indians to the content of the Indian
Reorganisation Act (IRA) were multiple. Some Indian groups supported
the policy and welcomed the end of the allotment era but others flatly
rejected the imposition of federal policy on their cultures.[12] Under the
details of the 1934 Act, Indian groups had the opportunity to vote for and
adopt federally approved written constitutions and laws and organise
themselves into political entities. In the end, over a hundred tribes voted
to accept the provisions of the 1934 Act and adopt a written constitution,
including the Blackfeet, most of the Pueblos and the Ottawa of
Oklahoma.[13] Many other Indian groups adopted constitutions and by-
laws including the Confederated Salish and Kootenai Tribes of the
Flathead Reservation Montana in 1935 and the White Mountain
Apache Tribe of the Fort Apache Indian Reservation Arizona in 1938. In
contrast, other Indian tribes refused to vote for the IRA and adopt tribal

constitutions, including the Navajo and the Crow of Montana, because it forced disparate and culturally independent groups into the political unit of the tribe.[14] Occasionally, the act of forcing Indians together created long-term and irreversible problems. This happened, for example, when numerous groups were amalgamated into what became the Washo tribe of California in 1937. Differences between the groups after 1937 limited the success of tribal government.[15] Despite the overall limitations of the Indian Reorganisation Act of 1934 and its paternalism, there can be no question that the efforts and intent of the federal government and John Collier to improve the lives of Indian groups were intended to be enabling and positive for Indian communities.[16]

However, despite the best efforts of the Roosevelt administration, the Indian New Deal never fulfilled its promise. In the end, the scepticism of numerous Indian groups to the IRA and the opposition of many Americans and American politicians to the Indian New Deal and John Collier, including opposition from missionaries, conservatives, Congressmen and the American Indian Federation, allowed the federal government to end the New Deal and adopt the federal policy of termination.[17]

The period of the Indian New Deal was one of the most pro-Indian in many centuries. It is to the nation's credit that the individuals of this era recognised that something had to be done to protect the lives and the diversity of Indian cultures. The end of the First World War brought with it a climate of change and protest that forced America to examine the social and economic conditions of its minorities and immigrants including Indians. The publication of the Meriam Report in 1928 revealed how misguided and devastating the policy of allotment had been to many Indian communities. With the election of Franklin Roosevelt to the White House, the federal government ended allotment and provided something of a cultural, economic, social and political renaissance in Indian country. However, not all Indians agreed with the agenda of the Indian New Deal. The specifics of the Indian Reorganisation Act of 1934 caused many Indian groups to oppose its principles. Even so, under the guidance of John Collier from 1933 to 1945, the Indian New Deal allowed for a new vista of Indian self-government and decision-making. It also protected and repatriated significant amounts of Indian land. Overall the New Deal can be seen as a fundamental shift in the history of US governmental policy. For many Indian communities it offered a sense of hope after centuries of displacement, death and cultural erosion.

SOURCES

Oneida Resolution Presented to IRA Sponsor Wheeler, 1934

In the following document, the Oneida justify their opposition to the implementation of the Indian reorganisation bill arguing that their sovereignty was protected through legally binding treaties and therefore the IRA was an unnecessary piece of legislation.

The Oneida nation firmly adheres to the terms of the Treaty of Canandaigua between our nation, our confederacy, and the U.S. on November 11, 1794. [We insist] that the laws of the U.S., the acts of Congress, and the customs and usages of the Oneida nation are the controlling provisions of Oneida basic law … the exponents of such basic law and the guides for the sachems, chiefs, headmen and warriors [are all bound to comply with the treaty].

Constitution and By-Laws of the Ottawa Tribe of Oklahoma, 1938

The following text outlines key parts of the constitution and by-laws of the Ottawa Tribe of Oklahoma (1938) and offers an insight into the powers and legal rights agreed between the Ottawa Tribe and the Office of Indian Affairs within the United States Department of the Interior.

PREAMBLE

We, the Ottawa Indians of Oklahoma, in order to take advantage of the opportunities of economic independence and social advancement offered by the Thomas-Rogers Oklahoma Indian Welfare Act of June 26, 1936, do hereby amend our present Constitution and By-laws and do adopt the following Constitution and By-laws pursuant to that Act.

ARTICLE I-NAME

The name of this organization shall be the Ottawa Tribe of Oklahoma.

ARTICLE II -OBJECT

The object shall be to promote the general welfare of the Ottawa Tribe of Oklahoma.

ARTICLE III -MEMBERSHIP

SECTION I. The membership of the Ottawa Tribe of Oklahoma shall consist of the following persons:

    (a) All persons of Indian blood whose names appear on the official census roll of the Tribe as of January 1, 1938.

    (b) All children born since the date of the said roll, both of whose parents are members of the Tribe.

(c) Any child born of a marriage between a member of the Ottawa Tribe and a member of any other Indian tribe whose parents choose to enroll said child with the Ottawa Tribe.

(d) Any child born of a marriage between a member of the Ottawa Tribe and any other person, if such child is one-sixteenth or more degree of Indian blood and is enrolled on the official Tribal roll before attaining the age of five years; if less than one-sixteenth said child may be admitted to membership by a majority vote of the Ottawa Council.

SEC. 2. The Council shall have power to prescribe rules and regulations, subject to the approval of the Secretary of the Interior, covering future membership including adoptions and loss of membership.

ARTICLE IV -MEMBERSHIP OF COUNCIL

The supreme governing body of this organization shall be the Ottawa Council. The membership of the Council shall be all the members of the Ottawa Tribe of Oklahoma: males, 21 years of age; and females, 18 years of age, of sound mind.

ARTICLE V -OFFICERS

The officers of the tribe shall be the Chief, Second Chief, Secretary-Treasurer, and two councilmen, who shall be elected at an open Council meeting by a majority vote of the membership present.

ARTICLE VI -BUSINESS COMMITTEE

There shall be a Business Committee which shall consist of the officers and councilmen as provided in Article V.

The Business Committee shall have power to transact business and otherwise speak or act on behalf of the Ottawa Tribe, in all matters on which the Tribe is empowered to act. The powers of the Tribe shall be set forth in detail in the corporate charter which may be requested by the Business Committee...

ARTICLE VIII-ELECTIONS

SECTION 1. Regular elections of officers shall be held by the Council on the first Monday of May, 1939, and on each odd-numbered year thereafter: *Provided*, That the present officers shall hold office until the first regular election. SEC. 2. The term of office shall be for two years or until their successors are elected and installed: *Provided*, That the present officers shall serve until the first regular election...

ARTICLE XI- AMENDMENTS

Amendments to this Constitution and the attached By-laws may be proposed by a majority vote of the Business Committee or by a petition signed by 30 per cent of the adult members of the Tribe, and if approved by the Secretary of the Interior, shall be submitted to a referendum vote of the members of the Tribe, and shall be effective if approved by a majority vote.

BY-LAWS

ARTICLE I-DUTIES OF OFFICERS

SECTION 1. *Chief.-*It shall be the duty of the chief to preside at all meetings and perform all duties appertaining to the office, also to act as Chairman of the Business Committee...

ARTICLE V-ADOPTION

This Constitution and By-Laws shall be effective when approved by the Secretary of the Interior and ratified by a majority vote of the Indians of the Ottawa Tribe voting at an election called by the Secretary of the Interior under regulations which he may prescribe pursuant to Section 13 of the Oklahoma Indian Welfare Act of June 26, 1936, provided that at least 30% of the eligible voters vote in such election. I, E. K. Burlew, the Acting Secretary of the Interior of the United States of America, by virtue of the authority granted me by the Act of June 26, 1936 (49 Stat. 1967), do hereby approve the attached constitution and by-laws of the Ottawa Tribe of Oklahoma, subject to ratification by the Tribe in the manner therein provided. Upon ratification of this constitution all rules and regulations heretofore promulgated by the Interior Department or by the Office of Indian Affairs, so far as they may be incompatible with any of the provisions of the said constitution and by-laws, are declared inapplicable to the Ottawa Tribe of Oklahoma.

All officers and employees of the Interior Department are ordered to abide by the provisions of the said constitution and by-laws.
Approval recommended October 5, 1938.

F.H. DAIKER,
Acting Commissioner of Indian Affairs.

E.K. BURLEW,
Acting Secretary of the Interior.

WASHINGTON, D.C., *October 10, 1938.*

CERTIFICATION OF ADOPTION

Pursuant to an order, approved October 10, 1938 by the Acting Secretary of the Interior, the attached constitution and by-laws was submitted for ratification to the members of the Ottawa Tribe of Indians of Oklahoma and was on November 30, 1938 duly approved by a vote of 93 for, and none against, in an election in which over 30 per cent of those entitled to vote cast their ballots, pursuant to section 3 of the Oklahoma Indian Welfare Act of June 26, 1936 (49 Stat. 1967).

THE OTTAWA BUSINESS COMMITTEE,
By GUY JENNISON, *Chief.*
L.H. DAGENETTE.
FRED S. KING.
DAVE GEBOE, *Second Chief.*
ABE G. WILLIAMS, *Secretary-Treasurer.*
H.A. ANDREWS, *Superintendent, Quapaw Agency.*

Meriam Report, 1928: Chapter I – General Summary of Findings and Recommendations

The following excerpts are taken from the Meriam Report of 1928, officially known as the Problem of Indian Administration. They detail key procedures and recommendations and describe how the federal government had failed Indian communities through the policy of allotment.

The Conditions Among the Indians. An overwhelming majority of the Indians are poor, even extremely poor, and they are not adjusted to the economic and social system of the dominant white civilization.

The poverty of the Indians and their lack of adjustment to the dominant economic and social systems produce the vicious circle ordinarily found among any people under such circumstances. Because of interrelationships, causes cannot be differentiated from effects. The only course is to state briefly the conditions found that are part of this vicious circle of poverty and maladjustment.

Health. The health of the Indians as compared with that of the general population is bad. Although accurate mortality and morbidity statistics are commonly lacking, the existing evidence warrants the statement that both the general death rate and the infant mortality rate are high. Tuberculosis is extremely prevalent. Trachoma, a communicable disease which produces blindness, is a major problem because of its great prevalence and the danger of its spreading among both the Indians and the whites.

Living Conditions. The prevailing living conditions among the great majority of the Indians are conducive to the development and spread of disease. With comparatively few exceptions, the diet of the Indians is bad. It is generally insufficient in quantity, lacking in variety, and poorly prepared. The two great preventive elements in diet, milk, and fruits and green vegetables, are notably absent. Most tribes use fruits and vegetables in season, but even then the supply is ordinarily insufficient. The use of milk is rare, and it is generally not available even for infants. Babies, when weaned, are ordinarily put on substantially the same diet as older children and adults, a diet consisting mainly of meats and starches.

The housing conditions are likewise conducive to bad health. Both in the primitive dwellings and in the majority of more or less permanent homes which in some cases have replaced them, there is great overcrowding, so that all members of the family are exposed to any disease that develops, and it is virtually impossible in any way even partially to isolate a person suffering from a communicable disease...

Sanitary facilities are generally lacking. Except among the relatively few well-to-do Indians, the houses seldom have a private water supply or any toilet facilities whatever. Even privies are exceptional. Water is ordinarily carried considerable distances from natural springs or streams, or occasionally from wells. In many sections the supply is inadequate, although in some jurisdictions, notably in the desert country of the Southwest, the government has materially improved the situation, an activity that is appreciated by the Indians.

Economic Conditions. The income of the typical Indian family is low and the earned income extremely low. From the standpoint of the white man, the typical Indian is not industrious, nor is he an effective worker when he does work. Much of his activity is expended in lines which produce a relatively small return either in goods or money. He generally ekes out an existence through unearned income from leases of his land, the sale of land, per capita payments from tribal funds, or in exceptional cases through rations given him by the government. The number of Indians who are supporting themselves through their own efforts, according to what a white man would regard as the minimum standard of health and decency, is extremely small. What little they secure from their own efforts or from other sources is rarely effectively used.

The main occupations of the men are some outdoor work, mostly of an agricultural nature, but the number of real farmers is comparatively small. A considerable proportion engage more or less casually in unskilled labour. By many Indians several different kinds of activity are followed spasmodically: a little agriculture, a little fishing, hunting, trapping, wood cutting, or gathering of native products, occasional labour and hauling, and a great deal of just idling. Very seldom do the Indians work about their homes as the typical white man does. Although the permanent structures in which they live after giving up primitive dwellings are simple and such as they might easily build and develop for themselves, little evidence of such activity was seen. Even where more advanced Indians occupied structures similar to those occupied by neighbouring whites, it was almost always possible to tell the Indian homes from the white by the fact that the white man did much more than the Indian in keeping his house in condition.

In justice to the Indians, it should be said that many of them are living on lands from which a trained and experienced white man could scarcely wrest a reasonable living. In some instances the land originally set apart for the Indians was of little value for agricultural operations other than grazing. In other instances part of the land was excellent but the Indians did not appreciate its value. Often when individual allotments were made, they chose for themselves the poorer parts, because those parts were near a domestic water supply or a source of firewood, or because they furnished some native product important to the Indians in their primitive life. Frequently the better sections of the land originally set apart for the Indians have fallen into the hands of the whites, and the Indians have retreated to the poorer lands remote from markets.

In many places crops can be raised only by the practice of irrigation. Many Indians in the Southwest are successful in a small way with their own primitive systems of irrigation. When modern, highly developed irrigation systems have been supplied by governmental activities, the Indians have rarely been ready to make effective use of the land and water. If the modern irrigation enterprise has been successful from an economic standpoint, the tendency has been for whites to gain possession of the land either by purchase or by leases. If the enterprise has not been economically a success, the Indians generally retain possession of the land, but they do not know how to use it effectively and get much less out of it than a white man would.

The remoteness of their homes often prevents them from easily securing opportunities for wage earning, nor do they have many contacts with persons dwelling in urban communities where they might find employment. Even the boys and girls graduating from government schools have comparatively little vocational guidance or aid in finding profitable employment.

When all these factors are taken into consideration, it is not surprising to find low incomes, low standards of living, and poor health.

Suffering and Discontent. Some people assert that the Indians prefer to live as they do; that they are happier in their idleness and irresponsibility. The question may be raised whether these persons do not mistake for happiness and content an almost oriental fatalism and resignation. The survey staff found altogether too much evidence of real suffering and discontent to subscribe to the belief that the Indians are reasonably satisfied with their condition. The amount of serious illness and poverty is too great to permit of real contentment. The Indian is like the white man in his affection for his children, and he feels keenly the sickness and the loss of his offspring.

The Causes of Poverty. The economic basis of the primitive culture of the Indians has been largely destroyed by the encroachment of white civilization. The Indians can no longer make a living as they did in the past by hunting, fishing, gathering wild products, and the extremely limited practice of primitive agriculture. The social system that evolved from their past economic life is ill suited to the conditions that now confront them, notably in the matter of the division of labour between the men and the women. They are by no means yet adjusted to the new economic and social conditions that confront them.

Several past policies adopted by the government in dealing with the Indians have been of a type which, if long continued, would tend to pauperize any race. Most notable was the practice of issuing rations to able-bodied Indians. Having moved the Indians from their ancestral lands to restricted reservations as a war measure, the government undertook to feed them and to perform certain services for them which a normal people do for themselves. The Indians at the outset had to accept this aid as a matter of necessity, but promptly they came to regard it as a matter of right, as indeed it was at the time and under the conditions of the inauguration of the ration system. They felt, and many of them still feel, that the government owes them a living, having taken their lands from them, and that they are under no obligation to support themselves. They have thus inevitably developed a pauper point of view.

When the government adopted the policy of individual ownership of the land on the reservations, the expectation was that the Indians would become farmers. Part of the plan was to instruct and aid them in agriculture, but this vital part was not pressed with vigour and intelligence. It almost seems as if the government assumed that some magic in individual ownership of property would in itself prove an educational civilizing factor, but unfortunately this policy has for the most part operated in the opposite direction. Individual ownership has in many instances permitted Indians to sell their allotments and to live for a time on the unearned income resulting from the sale. Individual ownership brought promptly all the details of inheritance, and frequently the sale of the property of the deceased Indians to whites so that the estate could be divided among the heirs. To the heirs the sale brought further unearned income, thereby lessening the necessity for self support. Many Indians were not ready to make effective use of their individual allotments. Some of the allotments were of such a character that they could not be effectively used by anyone in small units. The solution was to permit the Indians through the government to lease their lands to the whites. In some instances government officers encouraged leasing, as the whites were anxious for the use of the land and it was far easier to administer property leased to whites than to educate and stimulate Indians to use their own property. The lease money, though generally small in amount, gave the Indians further unearned income to permit the continuance of a life of idleness.

Surplus land remaining after allotments were made was often sold and the proceeds placed in a tribal fund. Natural resources, such as timber and oil, were sold and the money paid either into tribal funds or to individual Indians if the land had been allotted. From time to time per capita payments were made to the individual Indians from tribal funds. These policies all added to the unearned income of the Indian and postponed the day when it would be necessary for him to go to work to support himself.

Since the Indians were ignorant of money and its use, had little or no sense of values, and fell an easy victim to any white man who wanted to take away their property, the government, through its Indian Service employees, often took the easiest course of managing all the Indians' property for them. The government kept the Indians' money for them at the agency. When the Indians wanted something they would go to the government agent, as a child would go to his parents, and ask for it. The government agent would make all the decisions, and in many instances would either buy the thing requested or give the Indians a store order for it. Although money was sometimes given the Indians, the general belief was that the Indians could not be trusted to spend the money for the purpose agreed upon with the agent, and therefore they must not be given opportunity to misapply it. At some agencies this practice still exists, although it gives the Indians no education in the use of money, is irritating to them, and tends to decrease responsibility and increase the pauper attitude.

The typical Indian, however, has not yet advanced to the point where he has the knowledge of money and values, and of business methods that will permit him to control his own property without aid, advice, and some restrictions; nor is he ready to work consistently and regularly at more or less routine labour...

Indian Reorganisation Act (Wheeler-Howard Act), 1934

Provided here are some of the most important details of the Indian Reorganisation Act of 1934. The Act allowed tribes greater freedom and authority over their own reservations and limited the extraordinary influence of the BIA over Indian affairs.

An Act to conserve and develop Indian lands and resources; to extend to Indians the right to form business and other organizations; to establish a credit system for Indians; to grant certain rights of home rule to Indians; to provide for vocational education for Indians; and for other purposes.

Be it enacted by the Senate and House of Representatives of the United States of America in Congress assembled, That hereafter no land of any Indian reservation, created or set apart by treaty or agreement with the Indians, Act of Congress, Executive order, purchase, or otherwise, shall be allotted in severalty to any Indian.

Sec. 2. The existing periods of trust placed upon any Indian lands and any restriction on alienation thereof are hereby extended and continued until otherwise directed by Congress.

Sec. 3. The Secretary of the Interior, if he shall find it to be in the public interest, is hereby authorized to restore to tribal ownership the remaining surplus lands of any Indian reservation heretofore opened, or authorized to be opened, to sale, or any other form of disposal by Presidential proclamation, or by any of the public land laws of the United States...

Sec. 4. Except as herein provided, no sale, devise, gift, exchange or other transfer of restricted Indian lands or of shares in the assets of any Indian tribe or corporation organized hereunder, shall be made or approved...

Sec. 5. The Secretary of the Interior is hereby authorized, in his discretion, to acquire through purchase, relinquishment, gift, exchange, or assignment, any interest in lands, water rights or surface rights to lands, within or without existing reservations, including trust or otherwise restricted allotments whether the allottee be living or deceased, for the purpose of providing lands for Indians.

For the acquisition of such lands, interests in lands, water rights, and surface rights, and for expenses incident to such acquisition, there is hereby authorized to be appropriated, out of any funds in the Treasury not otherwise appropriated, a sum not to exceed $2,000,000 in any one fiscal year...

Title to any lands or rights acquired pursuant to this Act shall be taken in the name of the United States in trust for the Indian tribe or individual Indian for which the land is acquired, and such lands or rights shall be exempt from State and local taxation.

Sec. 6. The Secretary of the Interior is directed to make rules and regulations for the operation and management of Indian forestry units on the principle of sustained-yield management, to restrict the number of livestock grazed on Indian range units to the estimated carrying capacity of such ranges, and to promulgate such other rules and regulations as may be necessary to protect the range from deterioration, to prevent soil erosion, to assure full utilization of the range, and like purposes.

Sec. 7. The Secretary of the Interior is hereby authorized to proclaim new Indian reservations on lands acquired pursuant to any authority conferred by this Act, or to add such lands to existing reservations...

Sec. 8. Nothing contained in this Act shall be construed to relate to Indian holdings of allotments or homesteads upon the public domain outside of the geographic boundaries of any Indian reservation now existing or established hereafter.

Sec. 9. There is hereby authorized to be appropriated, out of any funds in the Treasury not otherwise appropriated, such sums as may be necessary, but not to exceed $250,000 in any fiscal year, to be expended at the order of the Secretary of the Interior, in defraying the expenses of organizing Indian chartered corporations or other organizations created under this Act.

Sec. 10. There is hereby authorized to be appropriated, out of any funds in the Treasury not otherwise appropriated, the sum of $10,000,000 to be established as a revolving fund from which the Secretary of the Interior, under such rules and regulations as he may prescribe, may make loans to Indian chartered corporations for the purpose of promoting the economic development of such tribes and of their members, and may defray the expenses of administering such loans...

Sec. 11. There is hereby authorized to be appropriated, out of any funds in the United States Treasury not otherwise appropriated, a sum not to exceed $250,000 annually, together with any unexpended balances of previous appropriations made pursuant to this section, for loans to Indians for the payment of tuition and other expenses in recognized vocational and trade schools...

Sec. 12. The Secretary of the Interior is directed to establish standards of health, age, character, experience, knowledge, and ability for Indians who may be appointed, without regard to civil-service laws, to the various positions maintained, now or hereafter, by the Indian office, in the administrations functions or services affecting any Indian tribe. Such qualified Indians shall hereafter have the preference to appointment to vacancies in any such positions.

Sec. 13. [Sections of the Act applicable to Alaska and not applicable to specific tribes]

Sec. 14. [Dealing with Sioux allotments]

Sec. 15. Nothing in this Act shall be construed to impair or prejudice any claim or suit of any Indian tribe against the United States. It is hereby declared to be the intent of Congress that no expenditures for the benefit of Indians made out of appropriations authorized by this Act shall be considered as offsets in any suit brought to recover upon any claim of such Indians against the United States.

Sec. 16. Any Indian tribe, or tribes, residing on the same reservation, shall have the right to organize for its common welfare, and may adopt an appropriate constitution and bylaws, which shall become effective when ratified by a majority vote of the adult members of the tribe, or of the adult Indians residing on such reservation, as the case may be, at a special election authorized and called by the Secretary of the Interior under such rules and regulations as he may prescribe. Such constitution and bylaws when ratified as aforesaid and approved by the Secretary of the Interior shall be revocable by an election open to the same voters and conducted in the same manner as hereinabove provided. Amendments to the constitution and bylaws may be ratified and approved by the Secretary in the same manner as the original constitution and bylaws.

In addition to all powers vested in any Indian tribe or tribal council by existing law, the constitution adopted by said tribe shall also vest in such tribe or its tribal council the following rights and powers: To employ legal counsel, the choice of counsel and fixing of fees to be subject to the approval of the Secretary of the Interior; to prevent the sale, disposition, lease, or encumbrance of tribal lands, interests in lands, or other tribal assets without the consent of the tribe; and to negotiate with the Federal, State, and local Governments. The Secretary of the Interior shall advise such tribe or its tribal council of all appropriation estimates or Federal projects for the benefit of the tribe prior to the submission of such estimates to the Bureau of the Budget and the Congress.

Sec. 17. The Secretary of the Interior may, upon petition by at least one-third of the adult Indians, issue a charter of incorporation to such tribe: *Provided*, That such charter shall not become operative until ratified at a special election by a majority vote of the adult Indians living on the reservation. Such charter may convey to the incorporated tribe the power to purchase, take by gift, or bequest, or otherwise, own, hold, manage, operate, and dispose of property of every description, real and personal, including the power to purchase restricted Indian lands and to issue in exchange therefor interests in corporate property, and such further powers as may be incidental to the conduct of corporate business, not inconsistent with law, but no authority shall be granted to sell, mortgage, or lease for a period exceeding ten years any of the land included in the limits of the reservation. Any charter so issued shall not be revoked or surrendered except by Act of Congress.

Sec. 18. This Act shall not apply to any reservation wherein a majority of the adult Indians, voting at a special election duly called by the Secretary of the Interior, shall vote against its application. It shall be the duty of the Secretary of the Interior, within one year after the passage and approval of this Act, to call such an election, which election shall be held by secret ballot upon thirty days' notice.

Sec. 19. The term "Indian" as used in this Act shall include all persons of Indian descent who are members of any recognized Indian tribe now under Federal jurisdiction, and all persons who are descendants of such members who were, on June 1, 1934, residing within the present boundaries of any Indian reservation and shall further include all other persons of one-half or more Indian blood. For the purposes of this Act, Eskimos and other aboriginal peoples of Alaska shall be considered Indians. The term "tribe" wherever used in this Act shall be construed to refer to any Indian tribe, organized band, pueblo, or the Indians residing on one reservation. The words "adult Indians" wherever used in this Act shall be construed to refer to Indians who have attained the age of twenty-one years.

John Collier: 'End the Long, Painful, Futile Effort to Speed Up the Normal Rate of Indian Assimilation by Individualising Tribal Land', 1934

In the following text, John Collier (1884–1968), who served as Commissioner of Indian Affairs from 1933 to 1945, outlines his personal opinions about the way that the 1934 Act might assist the economies of Indian communities.

The Wheeler-Howard Act, the most important piece of Indian legislation since the eighties, not only ends the long, painful, futile effort to speed up the normal rate of Indian assimilation by individualizing tribal land and other capital assets, but it also endeavours to provide the means, statutory and financial, to repair as far as possible, the incalculable damage done by the allotment policy and its corollaries...

The repair work authorized by Congress ... aims at both the economic and spiritual rehabilitation of the Indian race. Congress and the President recognized that the cumulative loss of land brought about by the allotment system, a loss reaching 90,000,000 acres - two-thirds of the land heritage of the Indian race in 1887 - has robbed the Indians in large part of the necessary basis for self-support. They clearly saw that this loss and the companion effort to break up all Indian tribal relations had condemned large numbers of Indians to become chronic recipients of charity; that the system of leasing individualized holdings had created many thousands of petty landlords unfitted to support themselves when their rental income vanished; that a major proportion of the red race was, therefore, ruined economically and pauperized spiritually...

Through 50 years of "individualization," coupled with an ever-increasing supervision over the affairs of individuals and tribes so long as these individuals and tribes had any assets left, the Indians have been robbed of initiative, their spirit has been broken, their health undermined, and their native pride ground into the dust. The efforts at economic rehabilitation cannot and will not be more than partially successful unless they are accompanied by a determined simultaneous effort to rebuild the shattered morale of a subjugated people that has been taught to believe in its racial inferiority.

The Wheeler-Howard Act provides the means of destroying this inferiority complex, through those features which authorize and legalize tribal organization and incorporation, which give these tribal organizations and corporations limited but real power, and authority over their own affairs, which broaden the educational opportunities for Indians, and which give Indians a better chance to enter the Indian Service.

John Collier Promises to Reform Indian Policy: 'We Took Away Their Best Lands, Broke Treaties', 1938

In this document, John Collier (1884–1968) describes the resolve of the Indians over the centuries and the intention of the federal government to support Indian interests through the development of self-sustainable economies, access to health care, and education, and the reacquisition of lost lands.

In all our colourful American life there is no group around which there so steadfastly persists an aura compounded of glamour, suspicion, and romance as the Indian. For generations the Indian has been, and is today, the centre of an amazing series of wonderings, fears, legends, hopes.

Yet those who have worked with Indians know that they are neither the cruel, warlike, irreligious savages imagined by some, nor are they the "fortunate children of nature's bounty" described by tourists who see them for an hour at some glowing ceremonial. We find the Indians, in all the basic forces and forms of life, human beings like ourselves. The majority of them are very poor people living under severely simple conditions. We know them to be deeply religious. We know them to be possessed of all the powers, intelligence, and genius within the range of human endowment. Just as we yearn to live out our own lives in our own ways, so, too, do the Indians, in their ways.

For nearly 300 years white Americans, in our zeal to carve out a nation made to order, have dealt with the Indians on the erroneous, yet tragic, assumption that the Indians were a dying race - to be liquidated. We took away their best lands; broke treaties, promises; tossed them the most nearly worthless scraps of a continent that had once been wholly theirs. But we did not liquidate their spirit. The vital spark which kept them alive was hardy. So hardy, indeed, that we now face an astounding, heartening fact.

Actually, the Indians, on the evidence of federal census rolls of the past eight years, are increasing at almost twice the rate of the population as a whole.

With this fact before us, our whole attitude toward the Indians has necessarily undergone a profound change. Dead is the centuries-old notion that the sooner we eliminated this doomed race, preferably humanely, the better. No longer can we, with even the most generous intentions, pour millions of dollars and vast reservoirs of energy, sympathy, and effort into any unproductive attempts at some single, artificial permanent solution of the Indian problem. No longer can we naively talk of or think of the "Indian problem." Our task is to help Indians meet the myriad of complex, interrelated, mutually dependent situations which develop among them according to the very best light we can get on those happenings - much as we deal with our own perplexities and opportunities.

We, therefore, define our Indian policy somewhat as follows: So productively to use the moneys appropriated by the Congress for Indians as to enable them, on good, adequate lands of their own, to earn decent livelihoods and lead self-respecting, organized lives in harmony with their own aims and ideals, as an integral part of American life. Under such a policy, the ideal end result will be the ultimate disappearance of any need for government aid or supervision. This will not happen tomorrow; perhaps not in our lifetime; but with the revitalization of Indian hope due to the actions and attitudes of this government during the last few years, that aim is a probability, and a real one...

In looking at the Indian picture as a social whole, we will consider certain broad phases - land use and industrial enterprises, health and education, roads and rehabilitation, political organization - which touch Indian life everywhere, including the 30,000 natives of Alaska for whose health, education, and social and economic advancement the Indian Service is responsible. Lastly, this report will tell wherein the Indian Service, or the government's effort as a whole for the Indians, still falls short.

So intimately is all of Indian life tied up with the land and its utilization that to think of Indians is to think of land. The two are inseparable. Upon the land and its intelligent use depends the main future of the American Indian.

The Indian feels toward his land, not a mere ownership sense but a devotion and veneration befitting what is not only a home but a refuge. At least nine out of ten Indians remain on or near the land. When times are good, a certain number drift away to town or city to work for wages. When times become bad, home to the reservation the Indian comes, and to the comparative security which he knows is waiting for him. The Indian still has much to learn in adjusting himself to the strains of competition amid an acquisitive society; but he long ago learned how to contend with the stresses of nature. Not only does the Indian's major source of livelihood derive from the land but his social and political organizations are rooted in the soil.

A major aim, then, of the Indian Service is to help the Indians to keep and consolidate what lands they now have and to provide more and better lands upon which they may effectively carry on their lives. Just as important is the task of helping the Indian make such use of his land as will conserve the land, insure Indian self-support, and safeguard or build up the Indian's social life...

In 1887, the General Allotment Act was passed, providing that after a certain trust period, fee simple title to parcels of land should be given to individual Indians. Individual proprietorship meant loss - a paradox in view of the Indian's love for the land, yet an inevitable result, when it is understood that the Indian by tradition was not concerned with possession, did not worry about titles or recordings, but regarded the land as a fisherman might regard the sea, as a gift of nature, to be loved and feared, to be fought and revered, and to be drawn on by all as an inexhaustible source of life and strength.

The Indian let the ownership of his allotted lands slip from him. The job of taking the Indian's lands away, begun by the white man through military expeditions and treaty commissions, was completed by cash purchase - always of course, of the best lands which the Indian had left. In 1887, the Indian had remaining 130 million acres. In 1933, the Indian had left only 49 million acres, much of it waste and desert.

Since 1933, the Indian Service has made a concerted effort - an effort which is as yet but a mere beginning - to help the Indian to build back his landholdings to a point where they will provide an adequate basis for a self-sustaining economy, a self-satisfying social organization.

CHAPTER NINE
TERMINATION ERA, 1945–1970

Soon after the end of the Second World War, the American government moved towards a policy known as termination which began to undermine the centuries old federal trust relationship between the United States and Indian nations. The dramatic shift away from the Indian New Deal and its values caused an uproar in Indian country and was to leave scars within Indian communities and between Indian and federal bodies that continue to the present day.[1] The American government intended termination as a means of freeing tribes from the federal bureaucracy of the Bureau of Indian Affairs (BIA) and as a means of stemming the economic reliance of many Indian communities on the American government. However, behind the rhetoric of the times lay a familiar ultimate goal, the structural and to a lesser extent cultural assimilation of Indians into mainstream American society. With strict federal budget limitations in place after the Second World War, the American government was keen to save money by cutting federal budget ties with many Indian tribes using a rhetoric that stressed Indian economic autonomy and freedom. Various acts of Congress were introduced to lessen the perceived differences between the Indians and American society and to resolve the historical problems between Indians and non-Indians. The Indian response to termination was generally one of protest. Even so, between the early 1950s and 1966, Congress passed over a hundred pieces of termination legislation and as a result, many Indian nations lost lands, tribal economies were devastated and tribal cultures suffered. However, Indian resolve ensured that the terminated Indian nations fought back in subsequent decades to regain significant amounts of lost lands and to develop successful reservation economies. The combination of Indian resistance and protest to termination throughout the 1950s and 1960s and the support of non-Indians against Indian termination, including Presidents Lyndon Baines Johnson and Richard Nixon, led to its downfall of termination and the beginning of the federal policy era of tribal self-determination in 1970.

Generally, the termination policy of the US government was implemented through three congressional acts including House Concurrent Resolution 108, Public Law 280 in 1953 and the Relocation Act of 1956. Representative William Henry Harrison of Wyoming introduced House Concurrent Resolution 108 in June 1953. This legislation was designed to end the Indians' status as wards of the US government and to withdraw all federal funding to specific tribes. The resolution declared that the Indian tribes from the four states of California, Florida, New York and Texas were to be freed from the control of the federal government and the policies of the BIA.[2] In only a few months, Congress passed another controversial piece of legislation called Public Law 280, which allowed state governments to exercise civil and criminal authority over specific tribal reservations and over tribal members within those reservations in the states of California, Minnesota,

Nebraska, Oregon, Wisconsin and Alaska.[3] However, the legislation did not allow the states to tax the tribes or take away tribal fishing and hunting rights within reservations. The third piece of federal legislation was the Relocation Act of 1956, which provided federal funding to tribal members who actively sought employment away from the reservations in urban centres. Predictably, withdrawal of federal funding to the tribes reduced economic opportunities within the reservations and forced tribal members to relocate off-reservation.[4]

The 1950s federal policy of termination was designed to end the trust status of Indians, also referred to as ward status or federal trusteeship, and to assimilate them into mainstream society. Many non-Indians supported termination, including liberals who championed civil rights and saw the reservations as bastions of a racist past and conservatives who agreed with the process of assimilation.[5] However, other non-Indians and many Indians raised genuine concerns that the loss of the Indian trust status and the protection of the federal government would lead to the loss of large amounts of Indian land.[6] While Arthur V. Watkins (1886–1973), a prominent Republican Senator from Utah and a strong proponent of termination, believed that the American government should assimilate the tribes into mainstream American culture, E. Morgan Pryse, BIA Area Director from Portland, Oregon, believed that termination would be detrimental to the Indian communities and significantly jeopardise Indian land holdings.[7] Moreover, many Indians believed that ending the ward status of Indian peoples was unfair and contrary to the spirit and ethos of existing federal policy. Ruth Muskrat Bronson (1898–1982), a Cherokee who became Executive Secretary of the National Congress of American Indians, vociferously criticised the American government's policy of termination expressing widely felt fears about the loss of Indian lands and resources.[8]

Indian nations that went through the process of termination included the Seminoles of Florida, the Potawatomi of Kansas and Nebraska, the Klamath of Oregon and the Menominee of Wisconsin, all of whom as a result lost reservation lands and suffered economic distress.[9] The Klamath were targeted for termination because their densely forested reservation of approximately one million acres, covered in rivers, marshlands and wetlands, was valued at approximately $120 million. Lured in part by the prospect of earning $50,000 each from the sale of the reservation, a majority of the Klamath consented to termination. The US government saw the value of the Klamath environment as justifying their termination and the liquidation of Klamath assets.[10] However, Boyd Jackson, secretary of the business committee of the Klamath Tribal Council and official Klamath delegate at the joint House and Senate Indian Committees termination hearings of 1954, opposed termination of the Klamath and expressed concern over the loss of trust status and large amounts of Klamath land.[11] However, despite the prescience of Boyd Jackson, termination became a reality and the Klamath faced state taxes, and eventually poverty and cultural and economic devastation. The Menominee were another nation that suffered the disaster of termination. In 1951, the Menominee successfully brought an action against the BIA for the mismanagement of their reservation timber resources in the US Court of Claims and were awarded $8.5 million in compensation. However, Senator Arthur Watkins refused to adhere to the demands of the court and pay the Menominee until they consented to termination. After Congress began the termination of the Menominee in 1961, the Menominee went from one of the wealthiest Indian nations in the United States to one of the most indigent groups of Indians within the nation.[12] Moreover, the Menominee reservation was incorporated as a county within the State of Wisconsin where the Menominee, under federal law, were subservient to state laws and had to pay state taxes. Unfortunately, by the early 1970s, more than half of the Menominee had left the reservation for cities such as Milwaukee and Chicago to find employment. It was from this off-reservation environment that Ada Deer (1935–), a social worker and spokesperson for an organisation called DRUMS (Determination of Rights and Unity for Menominee Shareholders), campaigned for the restoration of Menominee tribal government.[13]

Despite the strong impetus driving termination, the US Supreme Court on more than one occasion directly contradicted the federal demands to advance termination and protected Indian tribal interests. In 1959, the Supreme Court issued an important decision that reinvigorated the authority and power of the tribes over their own homelands, including non-Indians on reservation lands. This was termed inherent tribal sovereignty and it contrasted heavily with the ethos of termination. In the case of *Williams v. Lee*, a non-Indian shop owner on the Navajo reservation brought an action in the Arizona State Court against a Navajo couple who had not paid their bills and insisted that state law took precedence over Navajo law for the resolution of the dispute.[14] However, the unanimous opinion handed down by Justice Hugo Black relied on the principles of inherent tribal sovereignty and Indian territorial sovereignty to overrule the opinion issued by the lower court. Furthermore, the interpretation of the *Williams* court allowed tribal governments to coexist as a third branch of government alongside state governments and the federal government, in contravention of termination policy. In 1968, the Supreme Court once again directly ruled against aspects of federal termination as it applied to the Menominee. In the case of *Menominee Tribe v. United States* (1968), the Supreme Court had to decide whether the termination of the Menominee in 1954 extinguished their treaty-protected fishing and hunting rights, and therefore whether the

Menominee had to abide by the hunting and fishing regulations of the State of Wisconsin.[15] In contrast with the federal government policy of termination, the opinion issued by Justice William O. Douglas held that the termination of the Menominee had not affected their hunting and fishing rights, and the State of Wisconsin did not have authority over the treaty-protected rights of the Menominee.

After nearly thirty years of federal termination policy, during the late 1960s the federal government discussed its abandonment. Then in 1970 the federal government formally ended termination and moved towards a policy called tribal self-determination. President Richard Nixon (1913–1994), the thirty-seventh president of the United States who served from 1969 to 1974, introduced the federal policy of tribal self-determination, building on the ideas that President Lyndon Johnson had discussed in his Special Message to Congress in March 1968. President Johnson wanted to increase the involvement of Indians and Indian nations in the policy process and to allow more decisions to be made by Indian governments at a local level.[16] In a Special Message on Indian Affairs in 1970, Richard Nixon made clear his intention to end termination and to move towards a federal policy based on tribal self-determination, a policy which supported increased tribal autonomy and the continuation of Indian tribes within the boundaries of the United States.[17]

To recap, following the renaissance of Indian rights during the 1930s and early 1940s, Indian nations in the late 1940s and early 1950s had been faced with the prospect of termination, a federal policy that was a continuation of the assimilation policy enacted at the end of the nineteenth century. However, in contrast to earlier assimilation practices and legislation, this time, many Indian nations were stripped of historic federal protections and their entire reservations and assets sold. In addition, this form of assimilation involved a policy that encouraged Indians to move away from reservations, termed relocation, to find employment and attempt to survive away from their communities within urban American society. Although termination did not affect all Indian nations such as the Navajo and the Apache, the spectre of possible termination had an impact on each and every Indian nation. The process of termination saw Congress pass legislation to end Indian trust status and federal services and programmes to over a hundred Indian nations. The Indian nations that were terminated, including the Klamath and the Menominee, suffered widespread poverty and land loss because without reservation employment or federal services and programmes, tribes were forced to sell reservation lands and businesses to survive. Some terminated Indian nations such as the Menominee had to abide by state laws and regulations as well as pay state taxes. By 1968, 109 tribes and bands had been terminated and 11,466 Native Americans lost 1,362,155 acres of land.[18] The US Supreme Court provided some respite against the tide of termination with its seminal opinion in *Williams v. Lee* (1959) which reinvigorated Indian sovereignty and authority over reservation lands and all Indian and non-Indians on those lands. Indian protest in the late 1960s against termination was rewarded when the US government in 1970 moved away from the assimilationist agenda of the 1950s and 1960s and adopted the federal policy of tribal self-determination.

SOURCES

Ruth Muskrat Bronson Criticises Termination, 1955

In the following extract, Ruth Muskrat Bronson (1898–1982), a Cherokee who became Executive Secretary of the National Congress of American Indians, reveals her fears about the termination of trusteeship relationships between the federal government and specific Indian communities. She speaks out about the possibility of a dramatic loss of Indian land and resources and voices her concern about the threat to Indian nations and their cultures.

If the official policies of the Federal Government, as reflected by the current policies of the Bureau of Indian Affairs and the actions of the 83rd Congress, continue to be pursued the American Indian (like that other living creature associated with him in history, the buffalo) is likely, similarly, to continue to exist only on the American nickel.

The tragedy is that this may come about through misunderstanding of the issues involved in the proposed termination of Federal trusteeship over the Indian. These issues have been almost completely obscured in a miasma of confusion caused by conflicting financial interests, conflicting opinions on proper psychological solutions, and of justice itself. And, most important of all, caused by uninformed sentiment.

The average American is noted for his sympathy with the underdog. He is also apt to have romantic sentiment for the American Indian. Add to these two admirable qualities a vague sense of guilt for the actions of his forbears in ousting the original inhabitants of the rich land they adopted and for the long and shameful history of broken treaties with these dispossessed, and you have a tendency toward impulsive action based on a desire to make amends. If this action is founded on superficial or inaccurate knowledge rather than on thoughtful study or familiarity with fact and reality the result can be exceedingly serious, even disastrous, for the Indian. This is true in the case of the termination bills since these jeopardise the Indian's very existence and unquestionably would lead to his eventual – literal - extinction.

There is even widespread misconception as to what is involved in the Federal trusteeship. The casually informed citizen, dedicated to fair play, feels there is something definitely insulting in labelling an adult a ward of the government, as though he were being branded as too incompetent to function without a guardian…

In addition, he has special privileges, which is what trusteeship boils down to, which he gained by bargaining with his conquerors. In the not so distant past the Indians agreed to end their fighting and cede land to white settlers in exchange for certain defined, inalienable lands and specified services which the Indians could not provide for themselves and which are provided by the States and local communities for non-Indian citizens. It is hard to see how benefits make a "second class" citizen out of an Indian, especially when preferential treatment seems not to jeopardise the status of veterans, farmers, subsidized airlines and steamship companies, manufacturers protected by tariffs, or the businessmen with rapid tax write-offs.

On the contrary, it would seem to be our established political philosophy that the economic well-being of particular groups is a legitimate concern of the Federal government – all this aside from the fact that, in the case of the Indians, it is a matter of solemn treaty…

In the 83rd Congress there was a concerted effort to abrogate this Act [Indian Reorganisation Act of 1934], by means of over 100 bills claiming to "free" Indians. Tens of those bills proposed termination of trusteeship over specific tribes. Five of them were passed and signed by the President. All of the bills follow the same pattern. They were introduced by less than a handful of men, but were designed to cut down the Indian on many fronts: the family, the band, the tribe and at State level. They would destroy the tribal organizations, abolish tribal constitutions and corporations formed under the Act of 1934 and void Federal-Indian treaties. Government supervision of the sale of Indian property and expert guidance on the development of natural resources which has been provided up to now would also be cut off, thus exposing the individual Indian, the weak as well as the strong, to exploitation by the unscrupulous and those more knowledgeable in the commercial ways of a highly complex and competitive society. This would take away from him the protection that was preventing further depletion of his last remaining resources. Such a loss would be the country's as well as the Indian's…

In addition, there would be a cessation of education, health and welfare services now supplied by the Federal Government, guaranteed by treaty and sorely needed, without assurance that these would be provided by the States or local communities…

Actually very few voices are raised against eventual termination of trusteeship over the Indians. The Indian people themselves, the friends of the Indians, and the authorities on Indian affairs who are deeply concerned about the trend toward termination are frightened and deeply disturbed, not only because of the inequities contained in the legislation proposed in the 83rd Congress, but at the haste, without proper safeguards or study in relation to the conditions of individual tribes.

And most of all, we are deeply concerned that termination is being decided upon without the consent, nay, over the protests, of the Indians concerned. Too often when Indian consent is given it has been obtained by unfair pressures amounting to nothing less than administrative blackmail, as in the case of two tribes which accepted termination bills because they were denied their own funds until they consented. This seems to them a shocking violation of faith.

The informed feel that there should be an attack on the major forces that are keeping the Indian from realizing his potentialities: ill health, lack of educational opportunities, widespread poverty. By attacking these problems at the root, they feel the day will be hastened when the Indian people will no longer need the protection of a special relationship with the Federal Government.

...The consent of the Indians, moreover, should not be obtained by pressure amounting to duress such as was used last year in the cases of Menominee and Klamath when it was made clear to these two tribes that they would be permitted to withdraw their own money in the United States Treasury only if that withdrawal was coupled with "termination."

More than one theorist has stated that "the solution to the Indian problem" is the absorption of the Indian into the culture, race and society of the European-oriented American way. Shouldn't the Indian have something to say about this? Should the Indian be forced to give up his beliefs, his way of conducting his affairs, his method of organized living, his kind of life on the land he is a part of, if he chooses not to? Shouldn't the Indians have the same right to self-determination that our government has stated, often and officially, is the inalienable right of peoples in far parts of the world? Do we apply a different set of principles, of ethics, to the people within our own borders?...

Ada Deer Discusses Termination, 1974

In the following text, Ada Deer (1935–), a social worker and spokesperson for an organisation called DRUMS (Determination of Rights and Unity for Menominee Shareholders), speaking in 1974, explains the economic, political and cultural devastation caused by the termination of the Menominee. She voices the personal suffering termination caused and the work the Menominee had to undertake to rebuild their lives and communities.

...Termination occurred in 1954, it became finalised in 1961. Our people have had a strong sense of identity as a group, also a strong adherence to the land. We live in one of the most beautiful areas in this entire country, even if I have to admit it myself ... In 1961, our tribe, which at that time was composed of 3,270 members, had 10 million dollars in the treasury. We were one of the wealthiest tribes in the country and paid for almost all our services that were provided by the Bureau of Indian Affairs. We had a lumber mill and our land was intact. This changed. First of all, our land and assets were taken out of trust. Our areas are approximately 234,000 acres. This became a separate county in the state of Wisconsin. We are now the poorest county in the state and the poorest in the nation. Again, to make the story short, it's been an economic, political, a cultural disaster, and instead of taking away federal supervision and giving tribal supervision, as you would think by looking at the resolution, and at the termination law, this did not occur. The trust was taken away; all the protection and services of the Bureau of Indian Affairs were taken away, and a very oppressive and private trust was thrust upon us. First of all, we became a county. Our people had no experience in county government, did not understand how a county functioned, what the responsibilities, the obligations of county government were. Many people had no experience in business enterprise. A separate tribal corporation called MEI, Menominee Enterprises Incorporated, was established. However, this was not controlled by the Menominees because we had another group called the Menominee Common Stock and Voting Trust which was established ... So from 1961 to 1970, we were controlled by white banking and financial institutions. The only participation that the Menominees were able to have in the tribal affairs was to elect one trustee per year at the annual meeting. It was very frustrating. The hospital was closed, many of the youngsters were consolidated into attending one school, the dropout rate has been phenomenal, we've had many serious problems as a result of termination. It has accentuated the values of competitiveness, selfishness, greed, and it's had a disastrous effect not only on our people as a group, but on many individuals. Many people have gone off to Milwaukee, Chicago and other areas across the country.

However, that thing that galvanised us into action was the fact that our board of directors got into partnership with land developers. Land developers are not only a problem to the Indians but to every single person in this country ... We have an area of over 80 natural lakes; they created an artificial lake. They channelled some of these; it's an ecological disaster. The lakes are continually changing. They're pumping water from one to another. The shoreline trees have been destroyed in many areas. We've got motor boats, snowmobiles, pollution, terrible situations. Two thousand lots were slotted for sale and we started demonstrating. We demonstrated, we marched, we started to use the press, we formed a grass roots group called DRUMS, "Determination of Rights and Unity for Menominee Shareholders." This is a real grass roots group, because there were several of us that got together in 1970 and decided that no matter what we felt, it was important to fight for our land and people...

Restoration has three points: (1) putting our land assets into trust, (2) making us eligible for federal services, such as education and health services, and (3) giving us federal recognition as a tribe. Our bill was introduced last year, but we didn't get through the entire legislative process because of the presidential campaign. It was re-introduced again this year in May...

I especially tell this to Indian people because it's a typical response of bureaucrats and other people that work with you. They say, "You can't do it, it's going to take a lot of work and there's no way you can change the system." This is not really true. We have chosen another path and this is to beat the system. Now it's taken four years, and in a way, I feel like I've been preparing for this all my life, because my background is a social worker, community action person, and in social action every now and then you have to put your money where your mouth is, and I feel that we as Indians have to practise our Indian values, which is concern for your tribe, and be involved when it's of vital importance. Now, this has meant that several of us have had to change our lives around. I was in law school; the people that I was starting with are going to be graduating this year and will be joining the legal profession. My car is falling apart, some of the others' cars are falling apart, but along with this we are about to achieve the most significant victory in all of American Indian history. On Tuesday of this week, the House passed our act, the Menominee Restoration Act, with a vote of 404 to 3; everybody wants to know who the three that voted against it and how did I let them get away…

Boyd Jackson Speaks against Termination, 1954

In the following text taken from the joint House and Senate Indian Committee termination hearings of 1954, Boyd Jackson, Secretary of the Business Committee of the Klamath Tribal Council and official Klamath delegate at the termination hearings of 1954, highlights the similarity between the proposed policy of termination and the federal policy of assimilation and allotment.

MR. JACKSON. It seems to me that the present move is in a sense a repetition of something that happened years ago and something that has been discussed here during the present time.

In 1917, the Secretary of the Interior and Commissioner of Indian Affairs set up a policy whereby they felt that the time had come when the individual members of tribes should be dealt with individually as to their tribal properties. The result of that was that fee patents were issued, sort of on the right and left basis. And it also affected us, the Klamath Indians.

In a relatively short time, as to lands, which in those times were relatively low, we woke up and found that we had received fee patents to some hundred thousand or more acres of land. And those lands represented our best river bottom and marshlands.

These lands went out of our ownership. Just why and how the Secretary decided to change his views, I don't know. But these patents were closed down; that is, the issuing of the patents at the rate at which they were being issued. And, as a result of that, we now have something over 136,000 acres of land, which was discussed here…

SENATOR WATKINS. The thing that is bothering me, Boyd, is this: You have enough judgment and intelligence you think to come here and say "no" to us. In effect, you are saying "No, we don't want this." Haven't you got enough courage to say "No" to the fellow who comes along and wants to buy your land?

MR. JACKSON. The loss of a hundred thousand acres of land shows that we lacked guts at that time when such a thing was thrown open to us.

SENATOR WATKINS. How long has that been?

MR. JACKSON. 1917.

SENATOR WATKINS. That is a long time, and you have made great progress since then.

MR. JACKSON. And since that time it has been said that it would never do to pass anything the size of Klamath over to the Indians because they would lose it overnight. That has been said not too long ago. And quite a bit of that is quite true.

House Concurrent Resolution 108, 1953

The general goal of this piece of legislation was to end Indian communities' status as wards of the US government and therefore to withdraw all federal spending and support. The rationale was that Indian people could then be treated formally as full citizens of American society.

Whereas it is the policy of Congress, as rapidly as possible, to make the Indians within the territorial limits of the United States subject to the same laws and entitled to the same privileges and responsibilities as are applicable to other citizens of the United States, to end their status as wards of the United States, and to grant them all of the rights and prerogatives pertaining to American citizenship; and

Whereas the Indians within the territorial limits of the United States should assume their full responsibilities as American citizens: Now, therefore, be it

Resolved by the House of Representatives (the Senate concurring),

That it is declared to be the sense of Congress that, at the earliest possible time, all of the Indian tribes and the individual members thereof located within the States of California, Florida, New York, and Texas, and all of the following named Indian tribes and individuals members thereof, should be freed from Federal supervision and control and from all disabilities and limitations specifically applicable to Indians: The Flathead Tribe of Montana, the Klamath Tribe of Oregon, the Menominee Tribe of Wisconsin, the Potowatamie Tribe of Kansas and Nebraska, and those members of the Chippewa Tribe who are on the Turtle Mountain Reservation, North Dakota. It is further declared to be the sense of Congress that, upon the release of such tribes and individual members thereof from such disabilities and limitations, all offices of the Bureau of Indian Affairs in the States of California, Florida, New York, and Texas and all other offices of the Bureau of Indian Affairs whose primary purpose was to serve any Indian tribe or individual Indian freed from Federal supervision should be abolished. It is further declared to be the sense of Congress that the Secretary of the Interior should examine all existing legislation dealing with such Indians, and treaties between the Government of the United States and each such tribe, and report to Congress at the earliest practicable date, but not later than January 1, 1954, his recommendations for such legislation as, in his judgement, may be necessary to accomplish the purposes of this resolution.

Public Law 280, 1953

The following extract highlights the main principles and key themes of the controversial piece of legislation termed Public Law 280 which granted certain States of the Union civil and criminal jurisdiction over Indians within their boundaries.

An Act To confer jurisdiction on the States of California, Minnesota, Nebraska, Oregon, and Wisconsin, with respect to criminal offenses and civil causes of action committed or arising on Indian reservations within such States, and for other purposes.

...SEC. 2. Title 18, United States Code, is hereby amended by inserting in chapter 53 thereof immediately after section 1161 a new section, to be designated as section 1162, as follows:

"§ 1162. State Jurisdiction over offenses committed by or against Indians in the Indian country

"(a) Each of the States listed in the following table shall have jurisdiction over offenses committed by or against Indians in the areas of Indian country listed opposite the name of the State to the same extent that such State has jurisdiction over offenses committed elsewhere within the State, and the criminal laws of such State shall have the same force and effect within such Indian country as they have elsewhere within the State:

"State of Indian country affected
California...All Indian country within the State
Minnesota...All Indian country within the State, except the Red Lake Reservation
Nebraska...All Indian country within the State
Oregon...All Indian country within the State, except the Warm Springs Reservation
Wisconsin...All Indian country within the State, except the Menominee Reservation

"(b) Nothing in this section shall authorize the alienation, encumbrance, or taxation of any real or personal property, including water rights, belonging to any Indian or any Indian tribe, band, or community that is held in trust by the United States or is subject to a restriction against alienation imposed by the United States; or shall authorize regulation of the use of such property in a manner inconsistent with any Federal treaty, agreement, or statute or with any regulation made pursuant thereto; or shall deprive any Indian or any Indian tribe, band, or community of any right, privilege, or immunity afforded under Federal treaty, agreement, or statute with respect to hunting, trapping, or fishing or the control, licensing, or regulation thereof...

SEC. 7. The consent of the United States is hereby given to any other State not having jurisdiction with respect to criminal offenses or civil causes of action, or with respect to both, as provided for in this Act, to assume jurisdiction at such time and in such manner as the people of the State shall, by affirmative legislative action, obligate and bind the State to assumption thereof.

Senator Arthur V. Watkins: Proponent of Termination, 1957

In the following extract, Arthur V. Watkins (1886–1973), a Republican senator from Utah and a strong proponent of termination, discusses his views about the need to integrate Indian peoples into American society and free them from the bureaucracy of the BIA.

Virtually since the first decade of our national life the Indian, as tribesman and individual, was accorded a status apart. Now, however, we think constructively and affirmatively of the Indian as a fellow American. We seek to assure that in health, education, and welfare, in social, political, economic, and cultural opportunity, he or she stands as one with us in the enjoyment and responsibilities of our national citizenship...

One facet of this over-all development concerns the freeing of the Indians from special federal restrictions on the property and the person of the tribes and their members. This is not a novel development, but a natural outgrowth of our relationship with the Indians. Congress is fully agreed upon its accomplishment. By unanimous vote in both the Senate and the House of Representatives termination of such federal supervision has been called for as soon as possible...

A little more than two years ago – June 17, 1954 – President Dwight D. Eisenhower signed a bill approved by the Eighty-third Congress that signified a landmark in Indian legislative history. By this measure's terms an Indian tribe and its members, the Menominee of Wisconsin, were assured that after a brief transition period they would at last have full control of their own affairs and would possess all of the attributes of complete American citizenship. This was a most worthy moment in our history. We should all dwell upon its deep meaning. Considering the lengthy span of our Indian relationship, the recency of this event is significant. Obviously, such affirmative action for the great majority of Indians has just begun. Moreover, it should be noted that the foundations laid are solid.

...The basic principle enunciated so clearly and approved unanimously by the Senate and House in House Concurrent Resolution 108 of the Eighty-third Congress continues to be the over-all guiding policy of Congress in Indian affairs. In view of the historic policy of Congress favouring freedom for the Indians, we may well expect future Congresses to continue to indorse the principle that "as rapidly as possible" we should end the status of Indians as wards of the government and grant them all of the rights and prerogatives pertaining to American citizenship.

With the aim of "equality before the law" in mind of course should rightly be no other. Firm and constant consideration for those of Indian ancestry should lead us all to work diligently and carefully for the full realization of their national citizenship with all other Americans. Following in the footsteps of the Emancipation Proclamation of ninety-four years ago, I see the following words emblazoned in letters of fire about the heads of the Indians – THESE PEOPLE SHALL BE FREE!

Williams v. Lee, 1959

Provided here are the key extracts from the unanimous opinion of Justice Hugo Black. In his opinion, Black relied on the principles of inherent tribal sovereignty and Indian territorial sovereignty to strike down the ruling that state law and state courts had precedence over tribal law and tribal courts when issues involving non-Indians arose inside the reservation.

MR. JUSTICE BLACK delivered the opinion of the Court.

Respondent, who is not an Indian, operates a general store in Arizona on the Navajo Indian Reservation under a license required by federal statute. He brought this action in the Superior Court of Arizona against petitioners, a Navajo Indian and his wife who live on the Reservation, to collect for goods sold them there on credit. Over petitioners' motion to dismiss on the ground that jurisdiction lay in the tribal court rather than in the state court, judgment was entered in favor of respondent. The Supreme Court of Arizona affirmed, holding that since no Act of Congress expressly forbids their doing so Arizona courts are free to exercise jurisdiction over civil suits by non-Indians against Indians though the action arises on an Indian reservation. Because this was a doubtful determination of the important question of state power over Indian affairs, we granted certiorari.

…Essentially, absent governing Acts of Congress, the question has always been whether the state action infringed on the right of reservation Indians to make their own laws and be ruled by them…

Congress has also acted consistently upon the assumption that the States have no power to regulate the affairs of Indians on a reservation. To assure adequate government of the Indian tribes it enacted comprehensive statutes in 1834 regulating trade with Indians and organizing a Department of Indian Affairs … it encouraged tribal governments and courts to become stronger and more highly organized … Congress has followed a policy calculated eventually to make all Indians full-fledged participants in American society. This policy contemplates criminal and civil jurisdiction over Indians by any State ready to assume the burdens that go with it as soon as the educational and economic status of the Indians permits the change without disadvantage to them…

No departure from the policies which have been applied to other Indians is apparent in the relationship between the United States and the Navajos. On June 1, 1868, a treaty was signed between General William T. Sherman, for the United States, and numerous chiefs and headmen of the "Navajo nation or tribe of Indians." At the time this document was signed the Navajos were an exiled people, forced by the United States to live crowded together on a small piece of land on the Pecos River in eastern New Mexico, some 300 miles east of the area they had occupied before the coming of the white man. In return for their promises to keep peace, this treaty "set apart" for "their permanent home" a portion of what had been their native country, and provided that no one, except United States Government personnel, was to enter the reserved area. Implicit in these treaty terms, as it was in the treaties with the Cherokees involved in Worcester v. Georgia, was the understanding that the internal affairs of the Indians remained exclusively within the jurisdiction of whatever tribal government existed. Since then, Congress and the Bureau of Indian Affairs have assisted in strengthening the Navajo tribal government and its courts. See the Navajo-Hopi Rehabilitation Act of 1950. The Tribe itself has in recent years greatly improved its legal system through increased expenditures and better-trained personnel. Today the Navajo Courts of Indian Offenses exercise broad criminal and civil jurisdiction which covers suits by outsiders against Indian defendants. No Federal Act has given state courts jurisdiction over such controversies. In a general statute Congress did express its willingness to have any State assume jurisdiction over reservation Indians if the State Legislature or the people vote affirmatively to accept such responsibility. To date, Arizona has not accepted jurisdiction, possibly because the people of the State anticipate that the burdens accompanying such power might be considerable.

There can be no doubt that to allow the exercise of state jurisdiction here would undermine the authority of the tribal courts over Reservation affairs and hence would infringe on the right of the Indians to govern themselves. It is immaterial that respondent is not an Indian. He was on the Reservation and the transaction with an Indian took place there ... The cases in this Court have consistently guarded the authority of Indian governments over their reservations. Congress recognized this authority in the Navajos in the Treaty of 1868, and has done so ever since. If this power is to be taken away from them, it is for Congress to do it...

Menominee v. United States, 1968

Provided here are key excerpts from the opinion of Justice William O. Douglas. Here the Supreme Court ruled that the termination of the Menominee had not extinguished their rights to hunt and fish and in addition, the State of Wisconsin did not have authority over the treaty-protected rights.

MR. JUSTICE DOUGLAS delivered the opinion of the Court.

The Menominee Tribe of Indians was granted a reservation in Wisconsin by the Treaty of Wolf River in 1854. By this treaty the Menominees retroceded certain lands they had acquired under an earlier treaty and the United States confirmed to them the Wolf River Reservation "for a home, to be held as Indian lands are held." Nothing was said in the 1854 treaty about hunting and fishing rights. Yet we agree with the Court of Claims that the language "to be held as Indian lands are held" includes the right to fish and to hunt. The record shows that the lands covered by the Wolf River Treaty of 1854 were selected precisely because they had an abundance of game. The essence of the Treaty of Wolf River was that the Indians were authorized to maintain on the new lands ceded to them as a reservation their way of life which included hunting and fishing.

...the issue tendered by the present decision of the Court of Claims, is whether those rights, whatever their precise extent, have been extinguished.

That issue arose because, beginning in 1962, Wisconsin took the position that the Menominees were subject to her hunting and fishing regulations. Wisconsin prosecuted three Menominees for violating those regulations and the Wisconsin Supreme Court held that the state regulations were valid, as the hunting and fishing rights of the Menominees had been abrogated by Congress in the Menominee Indian Termination Act of 1954.

Thereupon the tribe brought suit in the Court of Claims against the United States to recover just compensation for the loss of those hunting and fishing rights. The Court of Claims by a divided vote held that the tribe possessed hunting and fishing rights under the Wolf River Treaty; but it held, contrary to the Wisconsin Supreme Court, that those rights were not abrogated by the Termination Act of 1954. We granted the petition for a writ of certiorari in order to resolve that conflict between the two courts...

In 1953 Congress by concurrent resolution instructed the Secretary of the Interior to recommend legislation for the withdrawal of federal supervision over certain American Indian tribes, including the Menominees. Several bills were offered, one for the Menominee Tribe that expressly preserved hunting and fishing rights. But the one that became the Termination Act of 1954, did not mention hunting and fishing rights. Moreover, counsel for the Menominees spoke against the bill, arguing that its silence would by implication abolish those hunting and fishing rights. It is therefore argued that they were abolished by the Termination Act.

The purpose of the 1954 Act was by its terms "to provide for orderly termination of Federal supervision over the property and members" of the tribe. Under its provisions, the tribe was to formulate a plan for future control of tribal property and service functions theretofore conducted by the United States. On or before April 30, 1961, the Secretary was to transfer to a tribal corporation or to a trustee chosen by him all property real and personal held in trust for the tribe by the United States.

The Menominees submitted a plan, looking toward the creation of a county in Wisconsin out of the former reservation and the creation by the Indians of a Wisconsin corporation to hold other property of the tribe and its members. The Secretary of the Interior approved the plan with modifications; the Menominee Enterprises, Inc., was incorporated; and numerous ancillary laws were passed by Wisconsin integrating the former reservation into its county system of government. The Termination Act provided that after the transfer by the Secretary of title to the property of the tribe, all federal supervision was to end and "the laws of the several States shall apply to the tribe and its members in the same manner as they apply to other citizens or persons within their jurisdiction."

It is therefore argued with force that the Termination Act of 1954, which became fully effective in 1961, submitted the hunting and fishing rights of the Indians to state regulation and control. We reach, however, the opposite conclusion. The same Congress that passed the Termination Act also passed Public Law 280. The latter came out of the same committees of the Senate and the House as did the Termination Act; and it was amended in a way that is critical here only two months after the Termination Act became law ... Public Law 280 went on to say that "Nothing in this section ... shall deprive any Indian or any Indian tribe, band, or community of any right, privilege, or immunity afforded under Federal treaty, agreement, or statute with respect to hunting, trapping, or fishing or the control, licensing, or regulation thereof." (Emphasis added.) That provision on its face contains no limitation; it protects any hunting, trapping, or fishing right granted by a federal treaty. Public Law 280, as amended, became the law in 1954, nearly seven years before the Termination Act became fully effective in 1961. In 1954, when Public Law 280 became effective, the Menominee Reservation was still "Indian country" within the meaning of Public Law 280.

Public Law 280 must therefore be considered in pari materia with the Termination Act. The two Acts read together mean to us that, although federal supervision of the tribe was to cease and all tribal property was to be transferred to new hands, the hunting and fishing rights granted or preserved by the Wolf River Treaty of 1854 survived the Termination Act of 1954...

We decline to construe the Termination Act as a backhanded way of abrogating the hunting and fishing rights of these Indians...

Our conclusion is buttressed by the remarks of the legislator chiefly responsible for guiding the Termination Act to enactment, Senator Watkins, who stated upon the occasion of the signing of the bill that it "in no way violates any treaty obligation with this tribe."

We find it difficult to believe that Congress, without explicit statement, would subject the United States to a claim for compensation by destroying property rights conferred by treaty, particularly when Congress was purporting by the Termination Act to settle the Government's financial obligations toward the Indians...

President Lyndon Johnson: 'I Propose a New Goal for Our Indian Programs', 1968

In the following text, President Johnson (1908–1973), the thirty-sixth president of the United States who served from 1963 to 1969, articulates his administration's aim of ending termination and moving forward towards an era of self-determination built on the involvement of Indian tribes in policy making, allowing Indian communities to have more authority within their own reservations.

...I propose a new goal for our Indian programs: A goal that ends the old debate about "termination" of Indian programs and stresses self-determination; a goal that erases old attitudes of paternalism and promotes partnership self-help.

Our goal must be:

-A standard of living for the Indians equal to that of the country at a whole.
-Freedom of Choice: An opportunity to remain in their homelands, if they choose, without surrendering their dignity; an opportunity to move to the towns and cities of America, if they choose, equipped with the skills to live in equality and dignity.
-Full participation in the life of modern America, with a full share of economic opportunity and social justice.

I propose, in short, a policy of maximum choice for the American Indian: a policy expressed in programs of self-help, self-development, self-determination.

To start toward our goal in Fiscal 1969, I recommend that the Congress appropriate one-half a billion dollars for programs targeted at the American Indian - about 10 percent more than Fiscal 1968.

STRENGTHENED FEDERAL LEADERSHIP

In the past four years, with the advent of major new programs, several agencies have undertaken independent efforts to help the American Indian. Too often, there has been too little coordination between agencies; and no clear, unified policy which applied to all.

To launch an undivided, Government-wide effort in this area, I am today issuing an Executive Order to establish a National Council on Indian Opportunity.

The Chairman of the Council will be the Vice President who will bring the problems of the Indians to the highest levels of Government. The Council will include a cross section of Indian leaders, and high government officials who have programs in this field:

-The Secretary of the Interior, who has primary responsibility for Indian Affairs.
-The Secretary of Agriculture, whose programs affect thousands of Indians.
-The Secretary of Commerce, who can help promote economic development of Indian lands.

-The Secretary of Labor, whose man-power programs can train more Indians for more useful employment.

-The Secretary of Health, Education and Welfare, who can help Indian communities with two of their most pressing needs - health and education.

-The Secretary of Housing and Urban Development, who can bring better housing to Indian lands.

-The Director of the Office of Economic Opportunity, whose programs are already operating in several Indian community.

The Council will review Federal programs for Indians, make broad policy recommendations, and ensure that programs reflect the needs and desires of the Indian people. Most important, I have asked the Vice President, as Chairman of the Council, to make certain that the American Indian shares fully in all our federal programs.

SELF-HELP AND SELF-DETERMINATION

The greatest hope for Indian progress lies in the emergence of Indian leadership and initiative in solving Indian problems. Indians must have a voice in making the plans and decisions in programs which are important to their daily life

Within the last few months we have seen a new concept of community development - a concept based on self-help - work successfully among Indians. Many tribes have begun to administer activities which Federal agencies had long performed in their behalf...

Passive acceptance of Federal service is giving way to Indian involvement. More than ever before, Indian needs are being identified from the Indian viewpoint - as they should be.

This principle is the key to progress for Indians - just as it has been for other Americans. If we base our programs upon it, the day will come when the relationship between Indians and the Government will be one of full partnership - not dependency...

THE FIRST AMERICANS

The program I propose seeks to promote Indian development by improving health and education, encouraging long-term economic growth, and strengthening community institutions.

Underlying this program is the assumption that the Federal government can best be a responsible partner in Indian progress by treating the Indian himself as a full citizen, responsible for the pace and direction of his development.

But there can be no question that the government and the people of the United States have a responsibility to the Indians.

In our efforts to meet that responsibility, we must pledge to respect fully the dignity and the uniqueness of the Indian citizen.

That means partnership - not paternalism.

We must affirm the right of the first Americans to remain Indians while exercising their rights as Americans.

We must affirm their right to freedom of choice and self-determination.

We must seek new ways to provide Federal assistance to Indians - with new emphasis on Indian self-help and with respect for Indian culture.

And we must assure the Indian people that it is our desire and intention that the special relationship between the Indian and his government grow and flourish.

For, the first among us must not be last.

I urge the Congress to affirm this policy and to enact this program.

President Richard Nixon: 'Special Message on Indian Affairs', 1970

In the following document, President Richard Nixon (1913–1994), the thirty-seventh president of the United States who served from 1969 to 1974, speaks about his goal of tribal self-determination and about a strategy to support tribal autonomy.

To the Congress of the United States:

The first Americans - the Indians - are the most deprived and most isolated minority group in our nation. On virtually every scale of measurement - employment, income, education, health - the condition of the Indian people ranks at the bottom.

This condition is the heritage of centuries of injustice. From the time of their first contact with European settlers, the American Indians have been oppressed and brutalized, deprived of their ancestral lands and denied the opportunity to control their own destiny. Even the Federal programs which are intended to meet their needs have frequently proven to be ineffective and demeaning.

But the story of the Indian in America is something more than the record of the white man's frequent aggression, broken agreements, intermittent remorse and prolonged failure. It is a record also of endurance, of survival, of adaptation and creativity in the face of overwhelming obstacles. It is a record of enormous contributions to this country – to its art and culture, to its strength and spirit, to its sense of history and its sense of purpose.

It is long past time that the Indian policies of the Federal government began to recognize and build upon the capacities and insights of the Indian people. Both as a matter of justice and as a matter of enlightened social policy, we must begin to act on the basis of what the Indians themselves have long been telling us. The time has come to break decisively with the past and to create the conditions for a new era in which the Indian future is determined by Indian acts and Indian decisions.

SELF-DETERMINATION WITHOUT TERMINATION

The first and most basic question that must be answered with respect to Indian policy concerns the history and legal relationship between the Federal government and Indian communities. In the past, this relationship has oscillated between two equally harsh and unacceptable extremes.

On the other hand, it has – at various times during previous Administrations – been the stated policy objective of both the Executive and Legislative branches of the Federal government eventually to terminate the trusteeship relationship between the Federal government and the Indian people. As recently as August of 1953, in House Concurrent Resolution 108, the Congress declared that termination was the long-range goal of its Indian policies. This would mean that Indian tribes would eventually lose any special standing they had under Federal law: the tax exempt status of their lands would be discontinued; Federal responsibility for their economic and social well-being would be repudiated; and the tribes themselves would be effectively dismantled. Tribal property would be divided among individual members who would then be assimilated into the society at large.

This policy of forced termination is wrong, in my judgment, for a number of reasons. First, the premises on which it rests are wrong. Termination implies that the Federal government has taken on a trusteeship responsibility for Indian communities as an act of generosity toward a disadvantaged people and that it can therefore discontinue this responsibility on a unilateral basis whenever it sees fit. But the unique status of Indian tribes does not rest on any premise such as this. The special relationship between Indians and the Federal government is the result instead of solemn obligations which have been entered into by the United States Government. Down through the years, through written treaties and through formal and informal agreements, our government has made specific commitments to the Indian people. For their part, the Indians have often surrendered claims to vast tracts of land and have accepted life on government reservations. In exchange, the government has agreed to provide community services such as health, education and public safety, services which would presumably allow Indian communities to enjoy a standard of living comparable to that of other Americans.

This goal, of course, has never been achieved. But the special relationship between the Indian tribes and the Federal government which arises from these agreements continues to carry immense moral and legal force. To terminate this relationship would be no more appropriate than to terminate the citizenship rights of any other American.

The second reason for rejecting forced termination is that the practical results have been clearly harmful in the few instances in which termination actually has been tried. The removal of Federal trusteeship responsibility has produced considerable disorientation among the affected Indians and has left them unable to relate to a myriad of Federal, State and local assistance efforts.

Their economic and social condition has often been worse after termination than it was before.

The third argument I would make against forced termination concerns the effect it has had upon the overwhelming majority of tribes which still enjoy a special relationship with the Federal government. The very threat that this relationship may someday be ended has created a great deal of apprehension among Indian groups and this apprehension, in turn, has had a blighting effect on tribal progress. Any step that might result in greater social, economic or political autonomy is regarded with suspicion by many Indians who fear that it will only bring them closer to the day when the Federal government will disavow its responsibility and cut them adrift.

In short, the fear of one extreme policy, forced termination, has often worked to produce the opposite extreme: excessive dependence on the Federal government. In many cases this dependence is so great that the Indian community is almost entirely run by outsiders who are responsible and responsive to Federal officials in Washington, D.C., rather than to the communities they are supposed to be serving. This is the second of the two harsh approaches which have long plagued our Indian policies. Of the Department of Interior's programs directly serving Indians, for example, only 1.5 percent are presently under Indian control. Only 2.4 percent of HEW's Indian health programs are run by Indians. The result is a burgeoning Federal bureaucracy, programs which are far less effective than they ought to be, and an erosion of Indian initiative and morale.

I believe that both of these policy extremes are wrong. Federal termination errs in one direction, Federal paternalism errs in the other. Only by clearly rejecting both of these extremes can we achieve a policy which truly serves the best interests of the Indian people. Self-determination among the Indian people can and must be encouraged without the threat of eventual termination. In my view, in fact, that is the only way that self-determination can effectively be fostered.

This, then, must be the goal of any new national policy toward the Indian people: to strengthen the Indian's sense of autonomy without threatening his sense of community. We must assure the Indian that he can assume control of his own life without being separated involuntarily from the tribal group. And we must make it clear that Indians can become independent of Federal control without being cut off from Federal concern and Federal support. My specific recommendations to the Congress are designed to carry out this policy...

The recommendations of this administration represent an historic step forward in Indian policy. We are proposing to break sharply with past approaches to Indian problems. In place of a long series of piecemeal reforms, we suggest a new and coherent strategy. In place of policies which simply call for more spending, we suggest policies which call for wiser spending. In place of policies which oscillate between the deadly extremes of forced termination and constant paternalism, we suggest a policy in which the Federal government and the Indian community play complementary roles.

But most importantly, we have turned from the question of *whether* the Federal government has a responsibility to Indians to the question of *how* that responsibility can best be fulfilled. We have concluded that the Indians will get better programs and that public monies will be more effectively expended if the people who are most affected by these programs are responsible for operating them.

The Indians of America need Federal assistance – this much has long been clear. What has not always been clear, however, is that the Federal government needs Indian energies and Indian leadership if its assistance is to be effective in improving the conditions of Indian life. It is a new and balanced relationship between the United States government and the first Americans that is at the heart of our approach to Indian problems. And that is why we now approach these problems with new confidence that they will successfully be overcome.

E. Morgan Pryse Speaks against Klamath Termination, 1954

In the following text, E. Morgan Pryse, BIA area director from Portland, Oregon, discusses the potential effects of termination of the Klamath with Senator Watkins and Representative Berry. He raises concerns about loss of federal trust status and the possibility of extensive loss of Klamath reservation lands.

REPRESENTATIVE BERRY. I would just like to ask this question. What percentage of this land, in your judgement, would be sold by the individual Indians when they obtain title?

MR. PRYSE. Well, experience has shown that as fast as the Indian obtains a fee simple title, he generally sells it. There has been sold around 88 million acres of Indian land, probably the best land, by the Indians, since the Allotment Act of 1887.

SENATOR WATKINS. You mean in this one reservation?

MR. PRYSE. No; I am talking about the whole United States. There has been quite a lot of forest land pass out of Indian ownership on the Klamath Reservation.

SENATOR WATKINS. That was quite a long time ago when that was done.

MR. PRYSE. That is right.

SENATOR WATKINS. We hope they have made progress in ability to make decisions since that time.

MR. PRYSE. Most of them would like to retain trust status as to their land, because they feel that once a patent is granted, it is just a question of time until it passes out of Indian ownership.

REPRESENTATIVE BERRY. What is your opinion on this? Do you think within a reasonably short time they will have disposed of their properties?

MR. PRYSE. If a bill was passed transferring fee simple title to them?

REPRESENTATIVE BERRY. Yes.

MR. PRYSE. Well, I am afraid it would. I am afraid it would pass out of Indian ownership, a great portion of it, in a matter of a few years. That is just my personal opinion. I am not speaking for anyone else, or the Department, but since you asked me for my own personal opinion, that would be my opinion.

SENATOR WATKINS. Is that because the Indian has not the ability to determine whether he ought to sell or not?

MR. PRYSE. Well, probably because they haven't had the experience of making a living and providing for taxes and also withstanding the pressure of people to buy their property.

CHAPTER TEN

KEY EVENTS OF THE RED POWER ERA: ALCATRAZ (1969), TRAIL OF BROKEN TREATIES AND THE OCCUPATION OF THE BIA HEADQUARTERS (1972) AND WOUNDED KNEE (1973)

The problems forced on Indian communities by the American government's policy of termination led to a groundswell of protest in the 1960s and 1970s and saw the beginnings of another cultural, social and political resurgence in Indian country. Termination had relocated thousands of Indians to the cities and forced many of them into a life of isolation plagued by social and economic problems and detached from their reservation homelands. In addition, the relocation of many Indians detrimentally impacted on the economies and infrastructures of the reservations and further impoverished those communities. During the 1960s, Indian peoples fought back and brought the economic and social problems of their urban and reservation communities into the cultural and political mainstream. Indian protest forced the American government to listen to Indian demands for more autonomy and for decision-making powers for tribal governments. Protests also called for the US government to recognise Indian treaty and land rights and therefore the sovereignty of Indian nations. Indian activism, enabled by a new urban and young constituency and supported by the Civil Rights generation, allowed Indians to better define their own futures. Protests from the late 1960s to the late 1970s are collectively referred to as the Red Power Movement, an umbrella association of urban and reservation Indians agitating for change with common themes but at points, divergent ideas.[1] Alcatraz in 1969, the Trail of Broken Treaties, the occupation of the Bureau of Indian Affairs (BIA) headquarters in 1972 and Wounded Knee in 1973, all helped to place Indian concerns at the forefront of the fervour for reform that characterised the era.

The occupation of Alcatraz Island in 1969 launched nearly a decade of Red Power protest. It began when a group of eighty-nine Indians, calling themselves the Indians of All Tribes and led by a Mohawk called Richard Oakes (1942–1972), occupied Alcatraz Island in San Francisco Bay, California on 20 November 1969.[2] A keen sense of irony was a trademark of protest in this era, especially in contrast to the more earnest forms of protest within the Black Civil Rights movement. The Indians of All Tribes put together an Alcatraz Proclamation and claimed Alcatraz island as Indian land. The proclamation highlighted how the American government over the centuries had done similar work, repeatedly taking away acres of Indian land by simply proclaiming their right to do so.[3] The occupation of Alcatraz lasted for nineteen months and was a watershed event. It attracted ongoing press and media coverage and developed and entrenched a new era of Indian pride and cultural resistance. To many Indians, including prominent women such as Principal Chief Wilma Mankiller (1945–) of the Cherokee nation, the events at Alcatraz galvanised their own self-confidence, reinvigorated Indian culture generally and provided the impetus to rectify the injustices of the past by ensuring Indian voices were heard by America.[4]

The political climate of the early 1970s saw Indian activism increase in volume and intensity. The Trail of Broken Treaties and the occupation of the BIA building symbolised a new radicalism. A strong force informing this new radicalism was the American Indian Movement (AIM), an organisation formed in Minneapolis during the summer of 1968 by Clyde Bellecourt, Dennis Banks and George Mitchell.[5] The Trail of Broken Treaties from October to November 1972 involved AIM and a number of other Indian groups who organised a caravan of nearly a thousand Indians from all over America who travelled from the West Coast of the United States to Washington, D.C. The purpose of the Trail was to bring attention to Indian treaty rights and long-standing Indian social problems, including poor housing and substandard living conditions. The event also saw the creation of the 20-Point position paper, a manifesto drafted to show how the American government could alleviate modern-day Indian problems.[6] It called for the restoration of treaty-making powers and the return of millions of acres of Indian land. A plea was made for the abolition of the BIA and for urgent further investment in Indian education, health, housing and Indian economic development. Events culminated with the takeover and occupation of the BIA headquarters for six days in November of 1972.[7] The takeover allowed the Indians to seize large numbers of BIA files and to bring national attention to a number of issues of specific concern to many in Indian country. The takeover of the BIA sent out a powerful message to mainstream America but many national newspapers including the *Washington Post* focused instead on the damage caused by the Indians within the building.[8] The destruction of the BIA building may have been regrettable but it served its purpose, bringing national attention to Indian treaty and sovereignty rights and to one of the key demands issued in the 20-Point paper; the abolition of the BIA.

Wounded Knee is perhaps the event from the 1970s that is now best remembered. A small village on the Pine Ridge reservation in South Dakota became the focus of protest for seventy-one days from 27 February to 8 May of 1973. Events at Wounded Knee were preceded by differences in opinion between the reservation tribal leaders, who felt that the system of government in place and the services they obtained from the federal government were serving their community in the correct manner, and AIM activists, who openly questioned the motives of tribal leaders, in particular Tribal Chair Richard Wilson. They believed he had misused tribal funds, ignored tribal rules and was a corrupt pawn of the BIA and the American government.[9] The killing of Wesley Bad Heart Bull, a Lakota who lived on the reservation, exposed the differences between the two opposing groups and led to AIM and a number of Lakota clashing with the police. After Tribal Chairman Richard Wilson banned AIM from the reservation, the BIA called for federal troops.

A show of force by the federal government did not prevent over 200 Indians, with the support of Oglala elders, occupying Wounded Knee, the historic site of the massacre of Indians by American troops in 1890, and declaring that the Fort Laramie Treaty of 1868 sanctioned the independence of the Oglala Sioux Nation as a sovereign state.[10]

Actions precipitated by AIM leaders, Dennis Banks and Russell Means ensured that there was a tense stand-off between, on the one side, American troops, FBI agents and federal marshals with heavy artillery and armoured vehicles, and on the other side, AIM members with guns and the support of the traditional Oglala Sioux.[11] Many of the Indians, including Russell Means (1939–), recognised the military superiority of the FBI and in response, fortified defensive positions and prepared for a long and arduous battle within the reservation.[12] For their part the federal authorities were ready to use various types and amounts of military hardware to flush out Indians they considered to be violent criminals.[13] The FBI and other federal agencies were suspicious of AIM, their members and objectives, and at Wounded Knee these fears played out with a show of force by the United States government that presented itself as though it was at war with the Indians.[14] The impasse that resulted between the two sides brought unprecedented levels of national and international media coverage to the Pine Ridge reservation and more importantly, to all Indians throughout the United States. However, within the seventy-one day struggle, two Indians, Frank Clearwater and Lawrence Lamont, were killed and many others were injured with hundreds of thousands of rounds of ammunition fired by the federal authorities at the village of Wounded Knee.[15] The symbolism of AIMs actions in 1973, over ninety years after the events at Wounded Knee of 1890, reminded the American public and elected officials that Indian communities had not vanished with the close of the frontier but were very much alive and leading a radical charge for the recognition of Indian sovereignty and self-determination within American society.

Relations between Indian nations and the US government dramatically changed during the 1960s and 1970s. The federal policy of termination, the relocation of Indians away from reservations to urban centres and the perpetuation of poverty and social problems blighting many Indian lives, provided the impetus for a new generation of young Indian activists to spearhead change in the 1960s and into the 1970s. The activism of Indian organisations such as AIM and Indians of All Tribes brought national and international media attention to Indian concerns and forced the American government to change its policies. Although mainstream America was still most comfortable with a romantic and stereotyped version of Indian identity, Indian activism tended to unsettle such a view, preferring instead to showcase Indian pride and a new sense of hope for an Indian cultural and political resurgence. The occupation of Alcatraz in 1969 was a watershed that began a period of sustained and successful pressure on the American government. The direct action of many Indians during the Trail of Broken Treaties, the occupation of the BIA building and Wounded Knee brought national and international attention to the problems of poverty and exclusion faced by Indian communities and showed that a new generation of Indian activists alongside a wider non-Indian coalition were ready to fight for a better future.

SOURCES

The Indians of All Tribes Alcatraz Proclamation, 1969

The following document presents the words of the proclamation and brings the historical actions of the illegal appropriation of Indian lands by the American government into a contemporary America but significantly, it was the Indians that were undertaking the exact same process against the American government in 1969.

We, the native Americans, re-claim the land known as Alcatraz Island in the name of all American Indians by right of discovery.

We wish to be fair and honorable in our dealings with the Caucasian inhabitants of this land, and hereby offer the following treaty:

We will purchase said Alcatraz Island for twenty-four dollars (24) in glass beads and red cloth, a precedent set by the white man's purchase of a similar island about 300 years ago. We know that $24 in trade goods for these 16 acres is more than was paid when Manhattan Island was sold, but we know that land values have risen over the years. Our offer of $1.24 per acre is greater than the 47 cents per acre the white men are now paying the California Indians for their land.

We will give to the inhabitants of this island a portion of the land for their own to be held in trust by the American Indian Affairs and by the bureau of Caucasian Affairs to hold in perpetuity--for as long as the sun shall rise and the rivers go down to the sea. We will further guide the inhabitants in the proper way of living. We will offer them our religion, our education, our life-ways, in order to help them achieve our level of civilization and thus raise them and all their white brothers up from their savage and unhappy state. We offer this treaty in good faith and wish to be fair and honorable in our dealings with all white men.

We feel that the so-called Alcatraz Island is more than suitable for an Indian reservation, as determined by the white man's own standards. By this we mean that this place resembles most Indian reservations in that:

1. It is isolated from modern facilities, and without adequate means of transportation.
2. It has no fresh running water.
3. It has inadequate sanitation facilities.
4. There are no oil or mineral rights.
5. There is no industry and so unemployment is very great.
6. There are no health care facilities.
7. The soil is rocky and non-productive; and the land does not support game.
8. There are no educational facilities.
9. The population has always exceeded the land base.
10. The population has always been held as prisoners and kept dependent upon others.

Further, it would be fitting and symbolic that ships from all over the world, entering the Golden Gate, would first see Indian land, and thus be reminded of the true history of this nation. This tiny nation would be a symbol of the great lands once ruled by free and noble Indians.

Richard Oakes: Spokesman for the Indians of All Tribes on Alcatraz

The symbolism and spiritual power behind the actions at Alcatraz was clear to Richard Oakes (1942–1972), a Mohawk and significant figure during the Alcatraz occupation. In the following extract he describes the feelings of Indian occupiers of the small island that once housed the infamous prison and the feeling of renaissance felt more generally in Indian circles.

Alcatraz was symbolic to a lot of people, and it meant something real to a lot of people. There are many old prophecies that speak of the younger people rising up and finding a way for the People to live. The Hopi, the spiritual leaders of the Indian people, have a prophecy that is at least 1,200 years old. It says that the People would be pushed off their land from the East to the West, and when they reached the Westernmost tip of America, they would begin to take back the land that was stolen from them…

Alcatraz was a place where thousands of people had been imprisoned, some of them Indians. We sensed the spirits of the prisoners. At times it was spooky, but mostly the spirit of mercy was in the air. The spirits were free. They mingled with the spirits of the Indians that came on the island and hoped for a better future.

Principal Chief Wilma Mankiller on the Meaning of Alcatraz

In the next document, Principal Chief Wilma Mankiller (1945–) of the Cherokee nation speaks about the sense of purpose and cultural reinvigoration that Alcatraz gave to her and the divergent groups of Indian activists fighting for justice against the American government.

Although Alcatraz ultimately would not remain a sovereign Indian nation, the incredible publicity generated by the occupation served all of us well by dramatizing the injustices that the modern Native Americans have endured at the hands of white America. The Alcatraz experience nurtured a sense among us that anything was possible – even, perhaps, justice for native people.

…The occupation of Alcatraz excited me like nothing ever had before. It helped to centre me and caused me to focus on my own rich and valuable Cherokee heritage.

Trail of Broken Treaties 20-Point Plan, 1972

The following excerpts highlight key parts of the 20-Point paper showing how the Indians involved wanted the restoration of their treaty-making powers, which had been nullified in 1871 and the restoration of a land base that had been dramatically eroded after 1887.

"Trail of Broken Treaties": For Renewal of Contracts – Reconstruction of Indian Communities & Securing an Indian Future in America!

1. Restoration of Constitutional Treaty-Making Authority:

The U.S. President should propose by executive message, and the Congress should consider and enact legislation, to repeal the provision in the 1871 Indian Appropriations Act which withdrew federal recognition from Indian Tribes and Nations as political entities, which could be contracted by treaties with the United States, in order that the President may resume the exercise of his full constitutional authority for acting in the matters of Indian Affairs - and in order that Indian Nations may represent their own interests in the manner and method envisioned and provided in the Federal Constitution.

2. Establishment of Treaty Commission to Make New Treaties:

The President should impanel and the Congress establish, with next year, a Treaty
Commission to contract a security and assistance treaty of treaties, with Indian people to negotiate a national commitment to the future of Indian people for the last quarter of the Twentieth Century. Authority should be granted to allow tribes to contract by separate and individual treaty, multi-tribal or regional groupings or national collective, respecting general or limited subject matter and provide that no provisions of existing treaty agreements may be withdrawn or in any manner affected without the explicit consent and agreement of any particularly related Indian Nation.

3. An Address to the American People & Joint Sessions of Congress: [about the commitment of the President and Congress to the Indian future]…

4. Commission to Review Treaty Commitments & Violations:…

5. Resubmission of Unratified Treaties to the Senate:

The President should resubmit to the U.S. Senate of the next Congress those treaties negotiated with Indian nations or their representatives, but never heretofore ratified nor rendered moot by subsequent treaty contract with such Indians not having ratified treaties with the United States. The primary purpose to be served shall be that of restoring the rule of law to the relationships between such Indians and the United States, and resuming a recognition of rights controlled by treaty relations…

6. All Indians to be Governed by Treaty Relations:

The Congress should enact a Joint Resolution declaring that as a matter of public policy and good faith, all Indian people in the United States shall be considered to be in treaty relations with the Federal Government and governed by doctrines of such relationship.

7. Mandatory Relief Against Treaty Rights Violations: [protection of Indian Treaty rights]…

8. Judicial Recognition of Indian Right to Interpret Treaties:…

9. Creation of Congressional Joint Committee on Reconstruction of Indian Relations:

The next Congress of the United States, and its respective houses, should agree at its outset and in its organization to withdraw jurisdiction over Indian Affairs and Indian-related program authorizations from all existing Committees except Appropriations of the House and Senate, and create a Joint House-Senate "Committee on Reconstruction of Indian Relations and Programs" to assume such jurisdiction and responsibilities for recommending new legislation and program authorizations to both houses of Congress - including consideration and action upon all proposals presented herewith by the "Trail of Broken Treaties Caravan," as well as matters from other sources…

10. Land Reform and Restoration of a 110-Million Acre Native Land Base:

The next Congress and Administration should commit themselves and effect a national commitment implemented by statutes or executive and administrative actions, to restore a permanent non-diminishing Native American land base of not less than 110-million acres by July 4, 1976. This land base and its separate parts, should be vested with the recognized rights and conditions of being perpetually non-taxable except by autonomous and sovereign Indian authority, and should never again be permitted to be alienated from Native American or Indian ownership and control.

A. Priorities In Restoration of the Native American Line Base:
    When Congress acted to delimit the President's authority and the Indian Nations' powers for making treaties in 1871, approximately 135,000,000 acres of land and territory had been secured to Indian ownership against cession or relinquishment … in 1887, under the General Allotment Act and other measures of the period … the 135 million acres, collectively held, immediately became subject to loss … The Interior Department efficiently managed the loss of 100-million acres of Indian land … Simple justice would seem to demand that priorities in restorations of land bases be granted to those Indian Nations who are land-less by fault of unratified or unfulfilled treaty provision…

B. Consolidation of Indians' Land, Water, Natural and Economic Resources:

The restoration of an equitable Native American Land Base should be accompanied by enlightened revision in the present character of alleged "trust relationships and by reaffirmation of that creative and positive characters of Indian sovereignty and sovereign rights...

C. Termination of Losses and Condemnation of Non-Indian Land Title:

Most short-term and long term leases of some four million acres of Indians' agricultural and industrial-use lands represent a constant pattern of mismanagement of trust responsibilities with the federal trustees knowingly and willfully administering properties in methods and terms which are adverse or inimical to the interests of the Indian beneficiaries and their tribes. Non-Indians have benefit of the best of Indian agricultural range and dry farm lands, and of some irrigation systems, generally having the lowest investment/highest return ratios, while Indians are relegated to lands requiring high investments/low returns ... Indian Tribes should be authorized to re-secure Indian ownership of alienated lands within reservation boundaries under a system of condemnation for national policy purposes, with the federal government bearing the basic costs of "just compensation"...

D. Repeal of the Menominee, Klamath, and Other Termination Acts:

The Congress should act immediately to repeal the Termination Acts of the 1950s and 1960s and restore ownership of the several million acres of land to the Indian people involved, perpetually non-alienable and tax-exempt. The Indians rights to autonomous self-government and sovereign control of their resources and development should be reinstated ... The impact of termination and its various forms have never been understood fully by the American people, the Congress, and many Indian people. Few wars between nations have ever accomplished as much as the total dispossession of a people of their rights and resources as have the total victories and total surrenders legislated by the Termination Laws...

11. Revision of 25 U.S.C. 163; Restoration of Rights to Indians Terminated by Enrollment and Revocation of Prohibitions against "Dual Benefits":

The Congress should enact measures fully in support of the doctrine that an Indian Nation has complete power to govern and control its own membership - but eradicating the extortive and coercive devices in federal policy and programming which have subverted and denied the natural human relationships and natural development of Indian communities, and committed countless injuries upon Indian families and individuals...

12. Repeal of State Laws Enacted Under Public Law 280 (1953):

State enactment's under the authority conferred by the Congress in Public Law 280 has posed the most serious threat to Indian sovereignty and local self-government of any measure in recent decades. Congress must now nullify those State statutes. Represented as a "law enforcement" measure, PL280 robs Indian communities of the core of their governing authority and operates to convert reservation areas into refuges from responsibilities...

13. Resume Federal Protective Jurisdiction for Offenses Against Indians:...

14. Abolition of the Bureau of Indian Affairs by 1976:

A New Structure: The Congress working through the proposed Senate-House "Joint Committee on Reconstruction of Indian Relations and Programs," in formulation of an Indian Community Reconstruction Act should direct that the Bureau of Indian Affairs shall be abolished as an agency on or before July 4, 1976; to provide for an alternative structure of government for sustaining and revitalizing the Indian-federal relationship between the President and the Congress of the United States, respectively, and the respective Indian Nations and Indian people at last consistent with constitutional criteria, national treaty commitments, and Indian sovereignty, and provide for transformation and transition into the new system as rapidly as possible prior to abolition of the BIA.

15. Creation of an "Office of Federal Indian Relations and Community Reconstruction":

The Bureau of Indian Affairs should be replaced by a new unit in the federal government which represents an equality of responsibility among and between the President, the Congress, and the Governments of the separate Indian Nations (or their respective people collectively), and equal standing in the control of relations between the Federal Government and Indian Nations...

16. Priorities and Purpose of the Proposed New Office:

17. Indian Commerce and Tax Immunities:

The Congress should enact a statute or Joint Resolution certifying that trade, commerce, and transportation of Indians remain wholly outside the authority, control, and regulation of the several States...

18. Protection of Indians' Religious Freedom and Cultural Integrity:

The Congress shall proclaim its insistence that the religious freedom and cultural integrity of Indian people shall be respected and protected throughout the United States, and provide that Indian religion and culture, even in regenerating or renaissance or developing stages, or when manifested in the personal character and treatment of one's own body, shall not be interfered with, disrespected, or denied...

19. National Referendums, Local Options, and Forms of Indian Organization:...

20. Health, Housing, Employment, Economic Development, and Education:

...The proposed $15,000,000,000 budget for the 1970s remainder could provide for completed construction of 100,000 now housing units; create more than 100,000 new permanent, income and tribal revenue-producing jobs on reservations and lay foundation for as many more in years following; meet all the economic and industrial development needs of numerous communities; and make education at all levels, and provide health services or medical care to all Indians as a matter of entitlement and fulfilled right. Yet, we now find most Indians unserved and programs not keeping pace with growing problems under a billion dollar plus budget annually - approximately a service cost of $10,000 per reservation Indian family per year, or $100,000 in this decade ... Death remains a standard cure for environmentally induced diseases afflicting many Indian children without adequate housing facilities, heating systems, and pure water sources ... Indian communities have been fragmented in governmental, social, and constitutional functions as they have become restructured or de-structured to accommodate the fragmentation in governmental programming and contradictions in federal policies...

Russell Means: On the Siege of Wounded Knee

In the following article, Russell Means (1939–), a prominent member of the AIM, writing over twenty years after the events, recalls the way in which the Indians involved fortified and defended their positions from the military superiority of the FBI. He outlines the political message of Wounded Knee and how it tied in with the broader social and political movements of 1970s America.

As Pedro Bissonette, vice president of the Oglala Sioux Civil Rights Organization, and I drove into the village of Wounded Knee on the Sioux Indian Pine Ridge Reservation in South Dakota on the night of February 27, 1973, we were at the end of a long line of almost two hundred automobiles ... During those moments, I could still hear the words of the traditional chiefs of my Oglala Lakota (Sioux) Nation, spoken earlier that fateful day.

Chief Fools Crow had told us, "Go to Wounded Knee. There you will be protected." I knew what he meant. In the frigid winter of 1890, the U.S. Army had brutally murdered Chief Big Foot and over three hundred of my people. Now that ground was consecrated, and the spirits of our ancestors would protect us as we made our stand against the U.S. government once again.

I remembered how the Oglala Chiefs had recently listened to their people's anguished pleas and descriptions of oppression, repression and suppression at the hands of the federal government's puppet tribal government. Women and girls had been raped. Men jailed. Money and valuables extorted. Homes firebombed, I now realized a critical mass had been achieved. The Lakotas were ready to die, if necessary, to end nearly one hundred years of deceit and abuse at the hands of the U.S. government. We were taking back our freedom one foot at a time, one community at a time, one reservation at a time, and it was going to start right now.

Arriving in darkness, the three hundred Lakotas and the two dozen veterans of the American Indian Movement (AIM) began to dig in around the Wounded Knee museum and general store. I started to direct the defense from the high point at the Catholic church, asking those who were Vietnam veterans to take charge of our defenses and establish roadblocks and patrols in the hills around us. All we had were a few hunting rifles and the integrity and moral force of a thousand generations of our ancestors. The cavalry would be arriving again momentarily, and we needed to be ready for them.

Our goals were threefold: enforcement of the 1868 Fort Laramie Treaty, which guaranteed our nation's territories and sovereignty; Senate investigations of corruption within the Bureau of Indian Affairs; and free, honest elections on the local Pine Ridge Reservation.

We were also hoping that our stand would inspire other American Indians and other Americans in general to continue their struggles for freedom. For the past decade, led by the black liberation struggle, a wide range of movements - the youth at UC-Berkeley, the peace movement, the women's liberation struggle, the environmentalists - were demonstrating for their respective causes. It had been an exhilarating time in America, but a time that had been totally misunderstood by the people who considered themselves the guardians of freedom, the conservatives on the right of the political spectrum.

I failed to sleep much that first night, knowing what awaited us. As dawn approached, the radio began to report what was happening. We had taken white people hostage, and one had escaped (in reality, one of the local merchants had abandoned his wife and small children when he realized the Indians were coming to repossess their community, so he invented the hostage story to conceal his cowardice). The radio also reported - accurately - that the Feds were mobilizing, and would soon surround Wounded Knee.

Our breath could be seen in the freezing dawn light while I stood with Severt Young Bear and Edgar Bear Runner and said, "We probably won't get out of this alive." Edgar agreed and Severt added, "Just like our ancestors."

At that moment, I realized we would be forced to defend Wounded Knee to the death. Judging by their past actions, we were convinced the U.S. government would not negotiate our demands...

Soon the FBI's agent in charge arrived at one of our roadblocks. Pedro Bissonette, Vern Long, president of the Oglala Sioux Civil Rights Organization, and I took our demands to him. As we walked back toward our forces at Wounded Knee, he yelled, "Who do you think you are? You're in a fishbowl. Don't you understand? We can wipe you out!" With that hard line response began the most protracted and intense confrontation between American Indians and the United States government since the end of the Indian Wars in 1890.

For seventy-one days, through three blizzards and more than five million rounds of ammunition expended by the Feds, we experienced a freedom we had not known for a century and have not known since. This wasn't the pseudo-freedom of America that gets bandied about every Fourth of July or during political campaign sloganeering. This was the real, no-holds-barred freedom my ancestors had known before we were corralled into the U.S.-run concentration camps known as Indian reservations.

The media came from all over the globe to report on this armed insurrection by a group of people the U.S. government would have the world believe were safely pacified and out of sight, out of mind. All three major broadcast networks arrived, at times with three entire crews each, to cover the events outside and inside Wounded Knee. The added impact of the print media inside the "Knee" and the intense media coverage in general were some of the major reasons we did not suffer the same fate as our ancestors.

During the Seventies, Wounded Knee proved to be the third most photographed event of that era, surpassed only by the Vietnam War and Watergate. In a poll taken among Americans during the siege, 93 percent were aware of the events at Wounded Knee while only 78 percent knew Spiro Agnew was the vice president of the country.

The siege lasted until May 8. Firefights and skirmishes abounded during that time. To make our limited firepower appear more impressive, we would take our one Kalashnikov Ak-47- with its distinctive and respected bark - and periodically run it from bunker to bunker, shooting off a quick burst at each spot. Then we would paint a length of stovepipe and allow the press to stumble across what appeared to be a rocket launcher or bazooka.

Heroes were made, and discoveries, too. Oscar Bear Runner, a World War II veteran in his mid-fifties, backpacked through the federal lines to bring in needed supplies. Two brave pilots - Bill Zimmerman and Rocky Madrid - flew planes with painted-over identification numbers, dodging sniper bullets to bring in medicine, food and ammunition...

We emerged from the siege at Wounded Knee with two American Indian patriots dead by sniper fire - Frank Clearwater and Buddy Lamont, a Vietnam vet - and fifteen wounded. More than six hundred were arrested in Wounded Knee- or en route to the siege - and faced multiple federal charges. In the end, not one person, black, brown, red, yellow or white, was convicted on any of the original charges.

At Wounded Knee, just as our ancestors had done, we decided to end the siege by putting our faith and trust in the words and documents of the United States government. And once again, the promises given to end the siege were never honoured. How could we have foreseen that those we demanded to negotiate with in the White House - Domestic Council Chief John Ehrlichman,

White House Chief of Staff H.R. Haldeman, Presidential Counsel John W. Dean III and Attorney General John Mitchell - would end up in prison and the hundreds of fighters at Wounded Knee would not? Now that is spiritual power!

During the siege at Wounded Knee the American Indians of North America began feeling a resurgence of dignity and pride - an immeasurable benefit that continues to this very day...

Our aim at Wounded Knee was to force the U.S. government to live up to its own laws. From that, one can draw the real lesson of our stand there: It is the duty of every responsible American to ensure that their government upholds the spirit and the laws of the United States Constitution.

FBI Memorandum on Wounded Knee: 'The Use of Special Agents of the FBI in a Paramilitary Law Enforcement Operation in Indian Country', 24 April 1974

In contrast to the Indian perspectives on the occupation of Wounded Knee, the US government memorandum describes events that occurred from the outside. It examines the 'paramilitary law enforcement situation' used by the federal agencies and the different types and amounts of military hardware deemed essential to deal with a few hundred Indians the FBI assumed to be violent criminals.

UNITED STATES GOVERNMENT Memorandum

TO: Mr. Gebhardt

FROM: J.E. O'Connell

SUBJECT: THE USE OF SPECIAL AGENTS OF THE FBI IN A PARAMILITARY LAW ENFORCEMENT OPERATION IN THE INDIAN COUNTRY.

PURPOSE: This position paper was prepared for use of the Director of the FBI to brief the Attorney General and the Deputy Attorney General (DAG) on the role of the FBI in the event of a major confrontation in Indian country (Federal jurisdiction) where (1) the President decides against the use of troops; and (2) the FBI is ordered by the President and/or the Attorney General to deploy FBI Special Agents in a paramilitary law enforcement situation, in lieu of the use of troops.

There is attached for ready reference a document captioned "Background Paper on the American Indian and the Takeover of Wounded Knee by the American Indian Movement (AIM)." This study outlines early history of the American Indian, jurisdiction of the FBI to investigate within the Indian country, background on AIM and their record for violence, history and background concerning the Pine Ridge Indian Reservation of the Oglala Sioux Tribe in South Dakota, a prelude to the occupation of Wounded Knee, the occupation of Wounded Knee by AIM and the use of FBI, U. S. Marshals and the Bureau of Indian Affairs (BIA) Police at Wounded Knee, South Dakota, during the period February 27 – May 8, 1973, in a paramilitary law enforcement situation...

FBI INVOLVEMENT: The FBI was instructed by the Department of Justice (DOJ) in the latter part of 1972 to conduct extremist and criminal investigations pertaining to AIM. During the afternoon of February 27, 1973, approximately 200 members and supporters of AIM, carrying weapons, left Calico Hall, Pine Ridge, South Dakota, in a car caravan and were under surveillance by a few FBI Special Agents. Under the leadership of Dennis James Banks and Russell Charles Means, the caravan moved into Wounded Knee, South Dakota, on the Pine Ridge Indian Reservation where they took eleven hostages and burglarised the Wounded Knee trading post in violation of Federal statutes involving crime on an Indian reservation. A decision was made by SAC Joseph H. Trimbach, Minneapolis Division, to set up roadblocks to contain the militants, which roadblocks were manned by FBI Agents, U. S. Marshals, and BIA Police. This is how the FBI first became involved in the Wounded Knee armed standoff against the U. S. Government.

ROLE OF THE WHITE HOUSE, JUSTICE DEPARTMENT AND OTHER AGENCIES: Decisions were made by the AG after regular and continuous consultation with responsible officials representing the White House, namely Mr. John D. Ehrlichman, Assistant to the President for Domestic Affairs, Mr. Leonard Garment, Special Consultant to the President, and his assistant, Bradley Patters: and officials in the U. S. Department of the Interior. On February 28, 1973, the situation at Wounded Knee was evaluated in a series of meetings between former AG Richard G. Kleindiens; former DAG Joseph T. Sneed, former Associate DAG Charles D. Ablard, and others. These three officials were responsible for the decision making of the DOJ. Department of the Interior officials and the BIA were involved as these agencies administer Indian reservations under Federal jurisdiction.

PROBLEMS CONFRONTING THE FBI: The various other Federal agencies involved in the Wounded Knee takeover were the U. S. Marshals Service (USMS), BIA Police, DOJ Attorneys, public information officers and Community Relations Service, the U. S. Attorneys (USAs), Department of Defence, and the U. S. Army. The DOJ sent Ralph Erickson, Special Assistant to the AG, to Wounded Knee as the senior U. S. Government representative on the scene. He was subsequently followed by 4 other DOJ and/or Department of the Interior officials who assumed this role during the 71-day siege from February 28 – May 8, 1973. Throughout the operation there was a definite lack of continuity as each senior representative replaced another ... The AG issued instructions there was to be no confrontation and negotiations with the militants by representatives of the DOJ were to be entered into to resolve the matter and have the hostages released.

There was a divided authority among the many agencies present at Wounded Knee, including church and social groups. The senior Government representative, Departmental Attorneys, and members of the USA's Staff issued conflicting instructions ... For example, on March 4, 1973, after consulting with Colonel Warner, Ralph Erickson issued orders that the use of deadly force by the law enforcement officers on the scene could only be used in self-defence to avoid death or serious bodily harm. In the application of force the officers, including FBI Agents, were to aim to wound rather than kill. This was in direct conflict with the policy of the Bureau that an Agent is not to shoot any person except when necessary in self-defence, that is, when he reasonably believes that he or another is in danger of death or grievous bodily harm. Special Agents are not trained to shoot to wound. Special Agents are trained to shoot in self-defence to neutralise the deadly force...

On a number of occasions the Acting Director and officials of the FBI requested the Administration and the Department to consider the use of troops at Wounded Knee. In Washington, D. C., DOJ officials in conjunction with other Governmental agencies explored the possibility of using troops. Colonel Warner on the scene recommended to the Chief of Staff of the Army against the use of troops. The Government concluded that such use would be undesirable because (1) it would substantially increase the risk of loss of life, (2) the full prestige of the U. S. Government would be committed to what was primarily a dispute between rival tribal factions and (3) the use of Army troops against these Indians might be misinterpreted by the press and some citizens.

The FBI encountered extreme problems, both in the field and at FBIHQ, in adapting to a paramilitary role. The FBI was not equipped logistically to operate in a paramilitary situation in open terrain which ultimately ended in a 71-day siege. The FBI and USMS had to be equipped with military equipment, including Armoured Personnel Carriers (APCs), M-16s, automatic infantry weapons, chemical weapons, steel helmets, gas masks, body armour, illuminating flares, military clothing and rations...

OPINIONS OF THE SACS WHO WERE ON THE SCENE: ... complete confusion existed as there were a number of DOJ representatives on the scene, each issuing conflicting orders. There was no coordination between the agencies other than that provided by the FBI, nor was there any advance planning done ... The military did not realise in many cases that they were there to assist and not direct the FBI...

OPINIONS OF FBIHQ PERSONNEL: ... As the FBI was utilizing approximately 3 SACs and 150 Agents per day at Wounded Knee in a defensive perimeter along with other Federal officers which were receiving hostile fire, it was necessary to insure that nothing was done in a decision making role at the White House or DOJ which might result in Federal law enforcement officers taking heavy casualties. It was reported in the initial phase of Wounded Knee that the militants were in possession of an M-60 machine gun and AK-47s (Communist automatic assault rifles), which could result in heavy casualties. It was necessary to convince the decision makers that APCs were necessary for the protection of the Special Agents and U. S. Marshals. When the APCs came under hostile fire they could not be moved to a more secure position without authority from the AG. It is the consensus of opinion among the headquarters supervisors that no Government official who is not trained law enforcement officer be permitted to direct a law enforcement operation the magnitude of Wounded Knee.

RECOMMENDATION: ... They should understand the FBI due to its long years of experience and training is able to make law enforcement decisions without over-reacting to protect the general public, its Special Agent personnel, and the violators of the law. The AG and DAG should be advised it is our broad policy in such instances as this to "get in and get out as quickly as possible" with complete regard for the safety of all concerned...

Kevin Barry McKiernan:'Notes from a Day at Wounded Knee', The Minnesota Leader, 1974

In the next article, Kevin Barry McKiernan, a free-lance photographer who spent seven weeks at the Wounded Knee occupation, describes from a page of his diary the bloodiness of the events, at times reminiscent of events in Vietnam, and the ferocity of the attacks on young and old Indians by the federal agencies that surrounded Wounded Knee in 1973.

April 17, 1973: Dawn

Food drop! I scramble awake from the floor of the trailer house and run outside. It seems incredible! Three single engine planes fly-in from the north, dipping low wing to wing over Wounded Knee. Seven silky parachutes float to earth. The aircraft fan out, disappearing over the pine-studded hills. They're gone as quickly as they came.

One parachute lands in a field across Manderson Road. Food! What a beautiful sight for sore eyes and hungry bellies. People are flocking from everywhere...

Then all hell breaks loose. There's sniper fire from "Vulture," the largest of the federal helicopters. It's raking Manderson Road where food's being carried to the Security Building for distribution. Bullets are dancing in the dirt around Florine Hollowhorn's kids. It's like a salt-shaker pouring around them. A miracle nobody's hit. I grab some food and run back to the trailer.

7:00 a.m.

Automatic gunfire from Armoured Personnel Carriers (APC's) on the hill behind the trailer. In minutes there are sounds of shooting all over town. AIM's are running for cover under trailers, behind cars, down in the trenches, from building to building behind the community center.

Mary Ellen leaves the new-born baby with Grandma to go for food to the trailer next door. A federal sniper's tracer bullet splatters the metal door frame inches from her arm. She dashes inside. The round lies imbedded near the knob, smoldering as the door bangs closed behind her. Bullets go through both trailers. Our bedroom window shatters. Trailers are so shabbily built they offer about as much protection as a Dixie Cup.

9:00 a.m.

Federal fire seems confined to north and west sides of Wounded Knee … Helicopters flying high around our perimeters. AIM's fire on them but they're out of range. Junior is shot through the left palm while reloading his own pistol.

Automatic fire coming in from the hills. Single shots from .22 rifles and 20 gauge shotguns going out from the village. Sounds dueling in the morning sunlight. CRACK-CRACK-CRACK! Plip! Boom! Plip! Boom! Grandma sits on the couch holding the week-old baby she delivered. She's calmly braiding the long black hair of her 35 year old son, a Philadelphia truckdriver after he left the reservation in Kansas … Grandma's got a .38 Special stuck in the bosom of her dress. She still refuses to be driven uptown from the trailer where she's made her home these past weeks.

Breakfast Some rice. I ask Mary Ellen if she'll take the baby to safer quarters over at the trading post, if I can get a vehicle to the trailer to pick them up. She says yes. But the only car with gas is the white Toyota---which ran up the hill behind us carrying men and guns an hour ago. There was a crazy face-off with an APC. Everybody got pinned down. They crawled down the hill backwards, abandoning the car. I can't get to it, but I'll see if anything else is running.

Grab the Minolta still camera and cautiously venture out, carrying three pop bottles full of drinking water for the guys in the closest bunker. Hop, crawl and scramble across the road. Flatten out under the bullets whizzing overhead I remember what Bobby said; if the rounds are only whizzing, they're at least a yard above you; if they're cracking, "They're right on you!" Sweating. Make my way a few hundred yards up to the swig of water and leave the pop bottles. Notice a green van parked outside by the sandbags. Yell to the people across the field in the houses: "Is the truck running?" A girl sticks her head out of the closest project home---"No, it's out of gas!" Fifty yard dash to her doorway. Clutching the Minolta. Running for my life.

Three people in the house, all in the kitchen lying down below the window lines. A pregnant Chippewa girl is on the floor, her back propped up against the sink pipes. There are a couple of guns on the table. I grab a walkie-talkie and try to call Pawnee Command Post to get a car down here for Mary Ellen. No response. Batteries are weak.

Two more people burst into the kitchen. Bad news. Someone's been shot! Up in the old Episcopal church on the hill near King Cobra bunker. Hurt bad, they say. That new nurse sprained her ankle trying to run through fire to get to him. Others trying to stretcher him out over the draws and through Big Foot's burial ground. But the fire's too heavy. They're trapped somewhere halfway to the field hospital.

11:00 a.m.

Up from the lower projects comes Mary Ellen hurrying, babe in arms. She's flanked by Ray and Gwen carrying guns. Two girls, Venona and Kamook, raising white flags behind them. As they weave from house to house, the APC fire is still loud but it doesn't seem to be hitting near them. I run down to meet them. We make our way back to the house. Mary Ellen and the baby ought to be safe in the basement.

11:30 a.m.

A tall young kid from Rosebud named Bo, that mouthy, shovy character who's always asking me why I'm taking pictures, decides to make a run for the trading post. He saddles up the white stallion I rode the other day. He mounts up, pushes his cowboy hat down tight over his straight black hair and digs in the spurs. Everybody's cheering for him as he gallops south through the ditches along Manderson Road. APC's on the hill open up with short, steady bursts. He crests the ridge in a cloud of dust. He's whipping that horse flank to flank. Bullets are popping in the dirt ahead of him. Underneath him. Behind him. Then the clip-clops grow fainter. And the gunfire subsides as he disappears toward the Big Foot Trail. How he made it I'll never know.

Ray is reading war comics and seems to be relaxing out on the back porch in the morning sun. Gwen paces back and forth through the yard among the junked cars, barking dogs and laundry on the line. Then they decide they'll try to make it uptown, too. It's crazy to go through the ditches where Bo went. The only way is the back gulches, then up to the church shack near King Cobra where that guy was hit. I grab my camera and follow. We go up the hills and down the canyons, out of sight from the APC's. Gwen's leading with her drawn .22 pistol. Ray's behind, with one of his two handguns out. I'm bringing up the rear with my 50mm Minolta.

The last two hundred yards are wide open up the west side of the hill to the church. We're zig-zagging but still a hell of a target. Final sprint to the door. Somebody throws it open. We burst out of breath into the darkened interior.

I see a guy with three days beard growth lying on a mattress by a blanket-shrouded window. He motions me to get down, pointing his carbine at the wet wooden floor underneath my boots---"There was a guy just got shot here! He was sitting in a chair where you're standing. Get the hell down!"

I sink to the floor. A white basin at my feet is full of blood. Somebody else says it's from the man they just carried out, a 47 year old Apache. Look around the room. Bullet holes in the sides of the walls. Guy with the carbine points to the hole which passaged the round that struck the man: "Frank Clearwater. He was just sitting there in that chair. Just woke up. Almost everybody else was still sleeping ... " He points to the half-dozen mattresses that line the floor around the pot-bellied stove in the middle of the shack. "...Bullet came through the wall, blew the back of his head off. He never knew what hit him. And he just came in yesterday with his wife. She was pregnant. They hitchhiked all the way from North Carolina. He never even picked up a gun…"

Now I remember Frank! He and his wife were the ones who showed up yesterday in the Security Building. Asked me for blankets I told them where to find some, then shot the shit with Frank for a few minutes. I had a little Bull Durham tobacco left. Asked him if he had any rolling papers. "No," he said, "but here's cigarette … take couple. I just got in and there's still a full pack." They were Pall Malls.

Noon

Ray and Gwen are lying on the floor. Ray's filling the chambers of his .38 with new rounds. The World War II Medal of Honor earned under General MacArthur in Asia as a 2nd Lieutenant in the U.S. Army lies pinned on his chest next to a red and white AIM button. An American flag is sewn upside down on the back of his jersey. Cree, Cheyenne, Apache and Seminole---what a mixture in this guy---who as a young kid almost 30 years ago enlisted in the Service to keep the world safe for democracy. Gwen's still panting form the run…

…Occasionally, I pop out by the trench where there's a telescope mount with heavy metal field glasses like those you'd find at the top of the Empire State or in Golden Gate Park by the San Francisco Bay. I can see really well as far west as that APC position on the hill behind the trailers. Magnification is powerful, but the focus is ripply from this distance. It's producing heat waves, but I can see two APC's, a jeep and five men up close enough to make out which men are carrying weapons. Wish I had a telephoto lens like this on my minolta.

Bobo, the crazy little guy who broke the spindle on my tape recorder at the wedding the other night, bursts into the bunker. His face is awash with sweat, a medicine bag is hanging on a rawhide cord form his neck. "Where's the nurse with the sprained ankle?" He's been sent out to guide her back to the hospital downtown, where three Indians now lie wounded. She's needed more than ever since the doctor's gone out with Frank up to RB#1, to get medovacked to the Pine Ridge Hospital.

He's got no gun, but he's planned a route to town. Ann, the California photographer, and I decide to go, too. We jump out of the bunker and into the trench (which leads to a halfway carved tunnel under the house). Plan is to try to run from ditch to ditch down the east side of the hill until we reach the Manderson Road. "I can't run!" The nurse yells to Bobo. "You gotta run! Do you want to stay alive?" he says. She's starting to get hysterical. Bobo's already up out of the trench and zig-zagging down the flare-burnt hillside. Then Ann, a Nikon camera and lens bouncing all over the front of her dungaree jacket. I grab the nurse's hand and we careen down the hill, diving in the first ditch. It's a shallow one, offering little or no protection from the Feds on the ridge to the east. She's crying out with pain from her injured leg. Bobo's yelling we got to get the hell out of here. I suggest we make a run for Big Foot's grave, then try to make it behind the tombstones and through the cemetery weeds to the Catholic Church. Bobo says the fire from the western ridges is too heavy. Nurse keeps calling to Bobo, "Brother, I can't Brother, it's too dangerous, Brother, my leg…"

Spurts of automatic fire as we reach Big Foot Trail and cross it. Drag, pull, cajole nurse into running with me. She's half-freaked out. Of course, I might be too, if I'd seen that guy's head half blown off.

12:30 p.m.

We make it. Hospital's in a low key frenzy. Three wounded (included Junior). Junior's in main dispensary unconscious, and i.v. into his right arm, his left hand bandaged from the bullet wound. Sara is doing dishes in a careful, almost hiding way in the kitchen. There's a guy named Daryl lying on a stretcher in the TV room with three bullets in his right arm and a bullet hole in his foot. Eva's got an i.v. going into him, Black Elk's got peyote trying to work the bullets to the surface in his arms. No luck. They're M-16 "tumblers," like they used in Vietnam. Who knows where they go after hitting you. The kid's half in shock. "I didn't have a gun. They pinned me down in gully. Didn't have a chance … Even in Vietnam they wouldn't have done this to me." Another Vietnam vet lies on a plywood bunk across the room. He's got a bullet in his heel, and they can't get his boot off.

People running in and out, dodging bullets from the street. Whole squad of guys pinned against trailer wall 40 feet across from hospital door. I sit with Grace Black Elk. We're all numb. Firing outside is constant. It doesn't seem real. Daryl calls for music. Portable record player begins playing Indian drum chants. Medics are given tourniquets and other supplies in little packs, then dispatched to the bunkers. (Daryl had lain in the gully across from the Catholic church for 45 minutes before any help could be gotten to him.) I tell people I'll make a dash across the street to the trading post basement for more still film, the movie camera and the recorder. Somebody yells out, "Don't go! They'll be dragging you in here in a minute!"…

CHAPTER ELEVEN
LEONARD PELTIER

The case of Leonard Peltier and the circumstances surrounding his conviction for the murder of two FBI agents in 1975 remains a contentious issue within Indian country and among law enforcement agencies throughout the United States. Soon after the momentous events at Wounded Knee in 1973, bloody battles broke out between factions of the Lakota Nation on the Pine Ridge reservation in South Dakota. On one side were traditional Oglala Lakota, supported by the American Indian Movement (AIM), who wanted a return to traditional customs, and those on the other, led by Tribal Chairman Richard Wilson, wanted the continued support of the federal government and the tacit support of the FBI.[1] In an attempt to diffuse the situation, the federal government sent out federal agencies. Many of the traditional Lakota were suspicious of federal personnel and believed they supported Richard Wilson and his enforcement gangs, known as the GOONs. In direct opposition to the violence that was perpetrated by Wilson and his henchmen, AIM, which included Leonard Peltier (1944–) as a committed member, became involved with protecting the traditional faction of Oglala Lakota people on the Pine Ridge reservation. In the end, tensions spilled over, and in June 1975, Pine Ridge reservation became the place where, once again, direct intense conflict occurred between a number of Indians, including AIM members, and the federal authorities including the FBI, US Marshals and S.W.A.T. teams. The confrontation led to a number of deaths in the reservation including an Indian named Joseph Stuntz and the deaths of two FBI agents, named Ronald Williams and Jack Coler. Leonard Peltier was sentenced as a result of the deaths of the FBI men, a crime he adamantly denies he committed. For over thirty years, Peltier and his lawyers have attempted to clear his name but after numerous appeals and public support from noted politicians and activists, he still remains in federal prison with, it seems, little chance of parole or a presidential pardon. A number of Indians and prominent supporters from all over the world consider Leonard Peltier to be a political prisoner. Many serving within law enforcement agencies and federal courts see him as a brutal killer who provoked outrage.

Fierce violence engulfed many Indian lives and families in 1975 at Pine Ridge, including Deborah White Plume, an Oglala-Lakota.[2] The events that led to the death of Stuntz, Williams and Coler began on 24 June 1975, when a warrant was issued for the arrest of James Theodore Eagle. FBI agents Williams and Coler were instructed to find him. On 25 June 1975, the agents entered part of the reservation referred to as the Jumping Bull property, but were told that Eagle had disappeared. Then on the morning of 26 June 1975, large numbers of armed FBI agents, BIA police and US Marshals assembled close to the reservation. Williams and Coler found themselves in pursuit of a red and white pick-up truck headed towards the Jumping Bull property.[3] Shortly after, a gunfight erupted between the agents who were situated close to the property protected by their car and the Indians who were inside the property and fighting for their lives. Details of the precise nature of the shootout are contradictory but the official and legally binding version is that AIM members, including Leonard Peltier, found the two incapacitated agents on the ground and shot them point-blank in the head. Other versions of events suggest that because federal personnel had surrounded the AIM members, it was their plan to take the agents hostage.[4] However, before the AIM members got within a reasonable distance of the two men, a red pick-up truck appeared and stopped at the position of the FBI agents. The AIM members heard shots of gunfire, and the driver of the truck drove away. After the FBI discovered the two bodies, they and other federal personnel invaded the Jumping Bull property and shot at everything in sight, tragically killing Joseph Stuntz.[5] A week after the shootings, William F. Muldrow, a senior member of US Civil Rights Commission, was invited to the reservation to establish what happened. His findings lambasted the aggressive reaction of the federal authorities and cast doubt on many points of critical information.[6]

Soon after the federal invasion of Pine Ridge reservation, the federal authorities began a large manhunt for four Indians including Leonard Peltier. Almost six months after the murder of Williams and Coler, Peltier became one of the most wanted men in America. Leonard Peltier was arrested on 6 February 1976, by the Royal Canadian Mounted Police in Alberta, Canada. The US government undertook extradition proceedings. The evidence that secured Peltier's extradition included the affidavits of Myrtle Poor Bear, an Indian woman with a history of mental illness.[7] Leonard Peltier was extradited from Canada and returned to the United States on 16 December 1976.[8]

On 14 March 1977, Leonard Peltier was being tried for the first-degree murder of FBI agents Williams and Coler in Fargo, North Dakota. Judge Edward McManus was supposed to preside over the Leonard Peltier trial but at the last hour, he was removed in favour of Judge Paul Benson.[9] From the outset, the early decisions made by the judge were considered by many Indians to be controversial. Some of the non-admissible factors that the court held back from the jury included allegedly illicit practices used by the FBI to obtain the affidavits given by Myrtle Poor Bear and the general environment of intimidation, violence and murder that surrounded Pine Ridge reservation from 1973 to 1975. Peltier was not allowed to rely on the self-defence argument.[10] The lawyers of the US government prosecution argued that Peltier was the person who discovered agent Coler and shot him in the head and who shot agent Williams in the head while he was unconscious and defenceless.[11]

In contrast, Peltier's lawyer spoke of how an uneasy co-existence on the Pine Ridge reservation between the disparate groups of Indians meant that any gunfire produced a reaction of self-defence or indeed, a reaction of fight or die. Moreover, without any form of distinguishable identification on them, Coler and Williams looked like any other people, and the AIM Indians believed that it was another gunfight with the GOONs of Richard Wilson. Ultimately, the defence admitted the physical evidence of the shooting but argued it was very difficult to prove that Peltier shot either of the agents.[12] Notwithstanding the lack of direct evidence that physically placed Leonard Peltier over the bodies of the two agents, on 18 April 1975, the jury found him guilty of the first-degree murder of agents Coler and Williams. Then on 26 June 1975, Peltier was convicted.[13] He was sentenced to imprisonment for life and during the sentencing, he spoke cogently and eloquently about the biased actions and rulings of the judge during the duration of the trial and of being set up by the FBI and the judicial process.[14]

Leonard Peltier was sent to the prison at Marion in Illinois and for over thirty years has served his sentence. However, his resolve remains strong and within the confines of his prison walls, he remains a person who inspires many Indian communities. To some, he is a modern-day hero whose resolve is even more remarkable for not asking the alleged perpetrator of the crimes to come forward and absolve him.[15]

Conflict continues to surround the issue of parole for Leonard Peltier and divides American society. Law enforcement bodies have called for Peltier to remain in prison until his dying day. Others, including many prominent politicians and judges from around the world, have advocated his release. Some even within law enforcement circles believe that Peltier was set-up, including congressman and former FBI agent Don Edwards (1915–). In contrast, Louis J. Freeh (1950–), former director of the FBI, has stated that he believes that Peltier should not be pardoned because it would betray the values of the legal system and the memories of the FBI agents who died.[16] The depth of feeling about Peltier has also produced a reaction from the judiciary and, in particular, from Senior Judge Gerald W. Heaney (1918–), who presided over one of Peltier's appeals.[17] Heaney supported the idea of parole because Peltier had served his time and sentence and therefore, from a legal standpoint, was entitled to be released from prison. In addition prominent international organisations, such as Amnesty International, have campaigned to free Leonard Peltier from prison.[18] Peltier has the right to a full parole hearing sometime in 2009. However, on 13 January 2009, he was transferred to a prison at Canaan, Pennsylvania, and was severely beaten by younger inmates, after which he was placed in solitary confinement.

Peltier's story highlights the continued uneasy relationship between certain Indians and the American system of government and its legal system.

SOURCES

Testimony of Deborah White Plume Given during
a Congressional Briefing, 17 May 2000

The violence that engulfed the lives of those on Pine Ridge reservation during 1975 was fierce. In the following document, Deborah White Plume, Oglala-Lakota, vividly recalls, over twenty-five years later in a transcript presented from the congressional briefing for Leonard Peltier, the reign of terror carried out by Dick Wilson and his GOON squad, and how her family and the traditional Oglala-Lakota people were tragically affected by violence on the reservation. White describes the distrust and resentment felt by her and her people towards the FBI and their failure to investigate heinous crimes then taking place on the reservation.

Welcome. Good afternoon. My thanks to the people who made this day possible for Leonard. My name is Deborah White Plume. I am an Oglala-Lakota mother and grandmother. I came here from the Pine Ridge Reservation in South Dakota. On Pine Ridge, while Dick Wilson was the Oglala-Sioux tribal chairman, our Traditional People suffered much violence. This time period is referred to as the Reign of Terror. Wilson and his GOONs targeted Traditional People, American Indian Movement people, and people who supported Lakota traditions and AIM. During that violent period, probably 90 percent of the violence was enacted by the GOONs. My family was directly impacted by such violence. I came here today to tell you about a tragedy that has befallen my family.

On November 17, 1974 the home of my mother was attacked by an off-duty Federal Bureau of Indian Affairs police officer who was known to be a Wilson supporter. He drove up to my mother's home and opened fire. My mother and I were preparing a meal. I heard a voice yell, "He has a gun!" Rapid-fire gunshots exploded all around me. I grabbed my three-year-old son and turned to protect him. I saw my mother fall, shot in the back, lay unmoving at my feet.

As I dove for the door holding my son, I saw his arm explode. I felt a burning in my own arm and a burning on my right temple. As we hit the floor, I felt another burning -- this time on my left temple. I saw the thumb of my son's left hand explode and disappear. I lay on my son, covering him with my body. From the floor, I saw my step-dad lay unconscious, blood pouring from a chest wound. I saw Lou, a family friend, laying across the doorway, blood spilling from his leg.

The firing lasted perhaps two minutes. I heard at least two different kinds of rounds going off. When the firing stopped, the house was filled with smoke and debris clouded the air. I stepped over the bodies and ran outside, carrying my son who lay very still in my arms, his eyes glazed and scaring me. I saw the car of the off-duty Federal Bureau of Indian Affairs police officer pulling away very very fast.

A neighbour drove me with my son to the emergency room. From the ER, we were flown to the Army Hospital in Denver. They said we would be sent there because no hospitals in the area could handle the type of gunshot wound my son had taken, and to save his arm, his only chance was a military hospital.

While we were being treated at the ER and waiting for the airplane to come after us, the federal officer who shot us was brought in with a gunshot wound to the head. While I did not know it until much later, he died that day. To this day, it is unknown who shot him.

While I was at the hospital in Denver, an individual in a nurse's uniform wheeled me to a room where a white man was sitting. He questioned me, but I didn't know anything. Later I learned he was probably FBI and people began to guard my hospital room.

On the day of the shooting, I saw another person in the back seat of the car [of the off-duty BIA police officer] shooting at us as the car drove away. I am unaware of any investigation identifying who that second person was.

The violence that was taken against my family is one example of many terrifying and sad things that happened on our reservation. During the years of Wilson's tenure as Oglala-Sioux tribal chairman, our people suffered violence on a daily basis. Most of the crimes were never solved. There was no justice shown to the victims of the crimes done against us. For those of us who lived there, it was common knowledge that Traditional People and AIM people were usually the victims of the beatings, shootings, car crashes, [and] destruction of property. Our people did not trust the tribal government, we did not trust the BIA police, we did not trust the FBI. Dick Wilson had the support of tribal government, tribal government had the support of the BIA, and the BIA had the support of the FBI.

From then until today, many of our people have maintained vigilant observation of what occurs around us every minute of every day. We do this because we do not know if and when the BIA and the FBI may lash out again against us. Living with such conditions creates much hardship for many of our people.

We are old, and we die before our time, and we want Leonard to be free. That is my statement.

Excerpt from Leonard Peltier's *Prison Writings:*
My Life Is My Sun Dance

In extracts taken from his prison writings, Leonard Peltier (1944–) describes his strength of character and sees himself as one Indian among many through the centuries who has suffered on behalf of his people. Peltier ends with his thoughts on parole and his undiminished hope of one day leaving prison as a free man.

The time has come for me to set forth in words my personal testament--not because I'm planning to die, but because I'm planning to live.

This is the twenty-third year of my imprisonment for a crime I didn't commit. I'm now fifty-four years old. I've been in here since I was thirty-one. I've been told I have to live out two lifetime sentences plus seven years before I get out of prison in the year Two Thousand and Forty One. By then I'll be ninety-seven. I don't think I'll make it. My life is an extended agony. I feel like I've lived a hundred lifetimes in prison already. But I'm prepared to live thousands more on behalf of my people. If my imprisonment does nothing more than educate an unknowing and uncaring public about the terrible conditions Indian people continue to endure, then my suffering has had--and continues to have--a purpose. My people's struggle to survive inspires my own struggle to survive. Each of us must be a survivor.

I acknowledge my inadequacies as a spokesman, my many imperfections as a human being. And yet, as the Elders taught me, speaking out is my first duty, my first obligation to myself and to my people. To speak your mind and heart is Indian Way. In Indian Way, the political and the spiritual are one and the same. You can't believe one thing and do another. What you believe and what you do are the same thing. In Indian Way, if you see your people suffering, helping them is an absolute necessity. It's not a social act of charity or welfare assistance; it's a spiritual act, a holy deed.

I know who and what I am. I am an Indian--an Indian who dared to stand up to defend his people. I am an innocent man who never murdered anyone nor wanted to. And, yes, I am a Sun Dancer. That, too, is my identity. If I am to suffer as a symbol of my people, then I suffer proudly. I will never yield.

If you, the loved ones of the agents who died at the Jumping Bull property that day, get some salve of satisfaction out of my being here, then at least I can give you that, even though innocent of their blood. I feel your loss as my own. Like you, I suffer that loss every day, every hour. And so does my family. We know that inconsolable grief. We Indians are born, live and die with inconsolable grief. We've shared our common grief for twenty-three years now, your families and mine, so how can we possibly be enemies anymore? Maybe it's with you and with us that the healing can start. You, the agents' families, certainly weren't at fault that day in 1975, any more than my family was, and yet you and they have suffered as much as, even more than, anyone there. It seems it's always the innocent who pay the highest price for injustice. It's seemed that way all my life. To the still-grieving Coler and Williams families I send my prayers if you will have them. I hope you will. They are the prayers of an entire people, not just my own. We have many dead of our own to pray for, and we join our prayers of sorrow to yours. Let our common grief be our bond. I state to you absolutely that, if I could possibly have prevented what happened that day, your menfolk would not have died. I would have died myself before knowingly permitting what happened to happen. And I certainly never pulled the trigger that did it. May the Creator strike me dead this moment if I lie. I cannot see how my being here, torn from my own grandchildren, can possibly mend your loss.

I swear to you, I am guilty only of being an Indian...

No doubt, my name will soon be among the list of our Indian dead. At least I'll have good company--for no finer, kinder, braver, wiser, worthier men and women have ever walked this Earth than those who have already died for being Indian. Our dead keep coming at us, a long, long line of dead, ever-growing, never-ending. To list all their names would be impossible, for the great majority died unknown, unacknowledged. Yes, the roll call of our Indian dead needs to be cried out, to be shouted from every hilltop in order to shatter the terrible silence that tries to erase the fact that we ever existed.

I would like to see a redstone wall like the blackstone wall of the Vietnam War Memorial. Yes, right there on the Mall in Washington, D.C. And on that redstone wall--pigmented with the living blood of our people (and I would happily be the first to donate that blood)--would be the names of all the Indians who ever died for being Indian. It would be dozens of times longer than the Vietnam Memorial, which celebrates the deaths of fewer than 60,000 brave lost souls. The number of our brave lost souls reaches into the many millions, and every one of them remains unquiet until this day.

Yes, the voices of Sitting Bull and Crazy Horse, of Buddy Lamont and Frank Clearwater, of Joe Stuntz and Dallas Thundershield, of Wesley Bad Heart Bull and Raymond Yellow Thunder, of Bobby Garcia and Anna Mae Aquash ... those and so, so many others. Their stilled voices cry out at us and demand to be heard.

People often ask me what my position is, or was, in AIM--the American Indian Movement. That requires an explanation. AIM is not an organization. AIM, as its name clearly says, is a movement ... No one person or special group of people runs AIM ... AIM is the People. AIM will be there when every one of us living today is gone. AIM will raise new leaders in every generation. Crazy Horse belonged to AIM. Sitting Bull belonged to AIM. They belong to us still, and we belong to them. They're with us now...

My legal appeals for a new trial will continue. We also continue to seek parole or Presidential clemency. In late 1993, and again in 1998, the U.S. Parole Commission rejected my appeal for parole, telling me to apply again in the year 2008. The simple act of changing my "consecutive" life-sentences to "concurrent" life-sentences--a change of one word--would give me my freedom and return to me at least a part of my life, if only my old age. I pray the Parole Commission will make that one-word change.

My appeals attorney, former U.S. Attorney General Ramsey Clark, submitted in November 1993 a formal application for executive clemency from President Clinton, meaning not a pardon but a Presidential order giving me simple release from prison for "time served." This, apparently, is my best hope of freedom. The request was turned over for review to the Department of Justice, which must make a formal recommendation to the President after reviewing my case. Nearly five imprisoned years later I still await that recommendation. I pray hard it will come soon. I pray an eagle will fly off the flagstaff in the President's Oval Office and at last deliver that long-delayed recommendation from the Attorney General's desk to the President's desk. And while the President sits there considering this innocent Indian man's appeal for clemency, I pray that that eagle will stand there on his desk, stare into his eyes, and join its cry to the cry of the millions of people around the world who have written to the President, appealing for my release. With all my heart I personally appeal to him for his consideration and for his compassion. I am an Indian man. My only desire is to live like one.

In the Spirit of Crazy Horse
LEONARD PELTIER

Affidavits of Myrtle Poor Bear, 1976

In the following text, the three affidavits signed by Myrtle Poor Bear are presented in full. Subtle changes are evident between each of the three documents about the alleged relationship between Poor Bear and Peltier, and the actions of Peltier on the fateful day of 26 June 1975.

Affidavit on February 19, 1976

Myrtle Poor Bear, being first duly sworn, deposes and states:

1. I am an American Indian, born February 20, 1952, and reside at Allen, South Dakota, one of the United States of America.

2. I first met Leonard Peltier in Bismarck, North Dakota, during 1971. During March, 1975, I again met Leonard Peltier at St. Francis, South Dakota, United States of America. During April, 1975, I went to North Dakota to see him as a girl friend of his. About the last week of May during 1975 I and Leonard Peltier went to the Jumping Bull Hall near Oglala, South Dakota, United States of America. There were several houses and about four or five tents. When Leonard arrived, he gave orders on what was to be done. I was his girl friend at this time. About a week after we arrived, about the second week of June, 1975, Leonard Peltier and several others began planning how to kill either Bureau of Indian Affairs Department, United States Government police or Federal Bureau of Investigation, United States Government, agents who might come into this area. Leonard Peltier was mostly in charge of the planning. All persons involved in the planning had special assignments. There was also a detailed escape route planned over the hills near the Jumping Bull Hall area. I was present during this planning. Leonard Peltier always had a rifle and usually had a pistol near him. The pistol was usually under a car seat. About one day before the Special Agents of the Federal Bureau of Investigation were killed, Leonard Peltier said he knew the Federal Bureau of Investigation or the Bureau of Indian Affairs were coming to serve an arrest warrant on Jimmy Eagle. Leonard Peltier told

people to get ready to kill them and he told me to get my car filled with gas to be ready for an escape. I left Jumping Bull Hall at this point and did not return. During August, 1975, I met Leonard Peltier again at Crow Dog's Paradise on the Rosebud Indian Reservation, South Dakota, United States of America. We talked about the killing of the two Federal Bureau of Investigation agents near Jumping Bull Hall. Leonard said it makes him sick when he thinks about it. He said that one of the agents surrendered, but he kept shooting. He said it was like a movie he was watching but it was real, he was just acting right in it. He said he lost his mind and just started shooting. He said he shot them and just kept pulling the trigger and couldn't stop.

Subscribed and sworn to before me this 19th day of February, 1976...

Affidavit on February 23, 1976

Myrtle Poor Bear, being first duly sworn, deposes and states:

1. I am an American Indian born February 20, 1952, and reside at Allen, South Dakota, one of the United States of America.

2. I first met Leonard Peltier in Bismarck, North Dakota, during 1971. During March, 1975, I again met Leonard Peltier at St. Francis, South Dakota, United States of America. During April, 1975, I went to North Dakota to see him as a girl friend of his. About the last week of May during 1975 I and Leonard Peltier went to the Jumping Bull Hall near Oglala, South Dakota, United States of America. There were several houses and about four or five tents. When Leonard arrived, he gave orders on what was to be done. I was his girl friend at this time. About a week after we arrived, about the second week of June, 1975, Leonard Peltier and several others began planning how to kill either Bureau of Indian Affairs Department, United States Government police or Federal Bureau of Investigation, United States Government, agents who might come into this area. Leonard Peltier was mostly in charge of the planning. All persons involved in the planning had special assignments. There was also a detailed escape route planned over the hills near the Jumping Bull Hall area. I was present during this planning. Leonard Peltier always had a rifle and usually had a pistol near him. The pistol was usually under a car seat. About one day before the Special Agents of the Federal Bureau of Investigation were killed, Leonard Peltier said he knew the Federal Bureau of Investigation or the Bureau of Indian Affairs were coming to serve an arrest warrant on Jimmy Eagle. Leonard Peltier told people to get ready to kill them and he told me to get my car filled with gas to be ready for an escape, which I did. I was present the day the Special Agents of the Federal Bureau of Investigation were killed. I saw Leonard Peltier shoot the FBI agents. During August, 1975, I met Leonard Peltier again at Crow Dog's Paradise on the Rosebud Indian Reservation, South Dakota, United States of America. We talked about the killing of the two Federal Bureau of Investigation agents near Jumping Bull Hall. Leonard said it makes him sick when he thinks about it. He

said that one of the agents surrendered, but he kept shooting. He said it was like a movie he was watching but it was real, he was acting right in it. He said he lost his mind and just started shooting. He said he shot them and just kept pulling the trigger and couldn't stop.

Subscribed and sworn to before me this 23rd day of February, 1976...

Affidavit on March 31, 1976

...Myrtle Poor Bear, being first duly sworn, deposes and states:

1. That I am the Myrtle Poor Bear, of Allen, South Dakota, United States of America, who was the deponent in an affidavit sworn the 23rd day of February, 1976. This affidavit is sworn by me to give further information.

2. Attached hereto and marked Exhibit "A" to this, my Affidavit, is a photograph marked February 12, 1976, and I testify and depose that the person show on the said photograph is a person known to me as Leonard Peltier and is the person I spoke of in my disposition of February 23, 1976, and the person referred to herein as Leonard Peltier.

3. I recall the events of June 26, 1975, which occurred at the area of Jumping Bull Hall near Oglala on the Pine Ridge Indian Reservation in the State of South Dakota, United States of America.

4. Sometime during the early part of that day, at approximately 12:00 Noon, Leonard Peltier came into the residence of Harry Jumping Bull which is located in the area of Jumping Bull Hall and said, "They're coming." I understood this to mean that police or agents of the Federal Bureau of Investigation were in the immediate area. A short time later, I saw a car which I recognized to be a government car near Harry Jumping Bull's house. I went down to the creek bottom a couple of hundred yards from the house. I heard shooting. I left the creek bottom area and walked approximately 50 yards to where I saw two cars, both of which I recognized to be government cars, because of the large radio antennaes mounted on the rear of these cars and I had previously seen many cars of a similar type driven by government agents in the same area. When I got to the car, Leonard Peltier was facing a man which I believed to be a special agent of the Federal Bureau of Investigation. This man was tall with dark hair. This man threw a handgun to the side and said something to the effect that he was surrendering. Leonard Peltier was pointing a rifle in the direction of this man. The man was holding his arm as if he was wounded and was leaning against the car previously mentioned. There was another man who I believed to be a special agent of the Federal Bureau of Investigation lying face down on the ground and there was blood underneath him. I started to leave and was grabbed by the hair by another person and could not get away. I turned again and saw Leonard Peltier shoot the man who was standing against the car. I heard a shot come from the rifle that Leonard Peltier was holding and I saw that rifle jump up still in his hands. I saw that man's body jump into the air and fall to the ground. The man fell face down on the ground. This happened in

an instant. I freed myself from the person that was holding me and ran up to Leonard Peltier just as he was aiming his rifle at the man who had just fallen to the ground. I pounded Leonard Peltier on the back. He yelled something at me which I cannot recall. I turned, ran and left the area. As I was running away, I heard several more shots from the area from which I had just fled.

Subscribed and sworn to before me this 31st day of March, 1976...

Leonard Peltier: One of the Most Wanted Criminals in America, 1975

The following document, a written memorandum from the director of the FBI, announces that Leonard Peltier has become one of the ten most wanted fugitives in the United States following the murder of two FBI agents on the Pine Ridge reservation.

SUBJECT: LEONARD PELTIER...

THE CRIME: On June 26, 1975, while on duty on the Oglala Sioux Indian Reservation, Pine Ridge, South Dakota, two FBI Agents were shot to death. It is alleged that Peltier and three others perpetrated these murders ... Peltier escaped capture at Portland, Oregon, after an exchange of gunfire with Oregon State Police officers on November 14, 1975.

THE CRIMINAL: A 31-year-old Indian male who was born in Grand Forks, North Dakota, Peltier has demonstrated a penchant for violence. Peltier has arrests for attempted murder and for carrying a concealed firearm, as well as numerous arrests for drunk and disorderly conduct. Peltier should be considered armed and extremely dangerous, as well as an escape risk.

PROCESS: On November 25, 1975, Federal warrants were issued at Rapid City, South Dakota, and Portland, Oregon, charging Peltier with killing two Federal officers and with possession of firearms. On August 9, 1974, a Federal warrant was issued at Milwaukee, Wisconsin, charging Peltier with unlawful interstate flight to avoid prosecution for attempted murder.

"TEN MOST WANTED FUGITIVES": Peltier replaces William Lewis Herron, Jr ... The list, as of Monday, p.m., December 22, 1975, will be:

Charles Lee Herron	IO#4163	Katherine Ann Power	IO#4402
Benjamin Hoskins Paddock	IO#4261	Billy Dean Anderson	IO#4649
Dwight Alan Armstrong	IO#4396	Robert Gerald Davis	IO#4657
David Sylvan Fine	IO#4398	Leonard Peltier	IO#4681
Leo Frederick Burt	IO#4399		

...THEY ARE ALL ARMED AND DANGEROUS...

Opening Speech by the Lawyer of Leonard Peltier
in *United States v. Leonard Peltier*, 1977

In the following key excerpts, the lawyer representing Leonard Peltier presents the violent history of the reservation up to the shootings and contends that it was difficult to prove that Peltier was the person who shot the FBI agents due to a lack of direct physical evidence.

MR. LOWE [Leonard Peltier's Attorney]: Ladies and gentlemen of the jury...

The one thing that is quite clear in this case is that what took place on June 26th, 1975, was an American tragedy by any standard of measure. What the government has said is two-thirds correct. In one regard the government said two young men are dead and we mourn for their families and that is true. But the other third of that is that one young Indian man is dead and we mourn for his family as well. All three lives are a loss to all of us and we all mourn for all of their families...

The first sentence is, theory one is the absolute innocence in fact of Mr. Peltier of any criminal charge on June 26, 1975.

The second theory of our case is that there is not one shred of believable evidence that will appear before you to convict Mr. Peltier of that criminal charge on June 26, 1975...

Factually in this case we will probably stipulate to virtually the vast majority of what Mr. Sikma [Government Lawyer] said. There is very little dispute about much of the physical evidence in this case. Cartridges, weapons, things of that nature. What is significant and what I trust caught your attention is that Mr. Sikma only spoke perhaps for a total of 30 seconds out of the time he was on his feet about Mr. Peltier and where Mr. Peltier was and what Mr. Peltier did.

We believe that the evidence you will want to be most alert for is evidence relating to Mr. Peltier and whether or not he was doing certain things or located in certain places or doing certain things.

I want to alert you to the importance of the time sequence. You have already heard Mr. Sikma describe radio transmissions that took place at about ten minutes to 12:00 and this time can be pinned down because there was certain electronic recordings of radio transmissions with a timer and me of death will be stipulated as being noon on June 26th, 1975. The shooting that you heard of the other agent coming in took place in the afternoon after that time and at some point later in the afternoon a group of people, including Mr. Peltier, left the tent area and ... that they went through, past, over, around about 100 FBI agents and actually there was no arrest of any of the people in that group.

...Another factor which is going to be very important is the state of mind. Now when I say state of mind, what I'm speaking of is what was going on subjectively inside of the minds of the people, particularly that were in what we call the Jumping Bull area. I will mention in passing that in truth this was not Harry Jumping Bull's, it was Cecilia Jumping Bull's. You will probably hear Cecilia Jumping Bull testify...

But the state of mind in the various people, Indians and others in the area here will be very important, will be important for several reasons. First of all, we believe there will be evidence that at a certain time shortly before noon there were people, I believe there may be testimony that Mr. Peltier was among them, in the tent area and that they heard shooting and that they heard something on the order of 20 shots that appeared to be coming from somewhere in the north; and that when they heard these shots their first reaction was that the camp was somehow under attack; that their first reaction was self-defence. They were being attacked, "We have got to protect ourselves, the women and children." There were women and children in the houses that are pointed out "residences"; and that the men, including some young teenagers, in the tent area reacted by grabbing weapons and running up to try to fend off whatever the attack was...

The state of minds of the ones you have, people around the residence shooting at these two white men, who we now identified as special agent Williams and special agent Coler, will be very important also. The testimony will be that neither of these two agents were wearing a uniform of any kind. They were in just what I would call country clothes, slacks and shirts or something like that, working pants and shirts, no uniforms or badges displayed or special hats. The cars had no markings on them or big red lights or anything of that nature. And one of the things that you will have to decide is with regard to the people shooting, whether they even knew or reasonably recognized that these were FBI agents...

Finally, if as the government has told you they will prove or expect to prove that one or more people shot and killed these two agents at very close range...

Finally, it is possible, and we don't know what the government will argue, that the government will try to show some responsibility in Mr. Peltier for the conduct of others there. On what basis I'm not quite sure.

The idea that he was one of the group that were doing something, and it will be important to you to know whether the people there were acting as a group or whether they were acting as individuals, whether they had a common design or just what was the situation, so that's the state of mind that is going to be very important there and the evidence we believe will show pretty clearly what that was.

The second state of mind which will be very important for you will be the state of mind of various witnesses for the defence and for the prosecution who come before you. The motivation, why the witnesses are testifying, and I think it will be fairly safe to say that all witnesses will be testifying pursuant to a Subpoena so in one sense they're here because they're required by law to be here, but it will be up to you to determine the credibility of each of the witnesses...

One of the most difficult things for you in this trial, I believe, will be to take yourselves mentally and emotionally on a trip from Fargo, North Dakota to the Pine Ridge Indian Reservation and assimilate the surroundings and the atmosphere that existed on June 26, 1975...

There was an atmosphere, we believe the evidence will show, in 1975 of violence and fear and oppression on the Pine Ridge Reservation which is likened to nothing that most of us have ever experienced in our lifetime, certainly nothing that any of us in the white community have experienced in my recorded lifetime or I believe any of yours.

We believe the evidence will show that beginning with, and I think an arbitrary point because in 1973 there was a general activity which erupted into the now famous Wounded Knee Occupation on the Pine Ridge Reservation and Wounded Knee is on the Pine Ridge Reservation not very far from Oglala where this all took place and part of the reason for the Wounded Knee Occupation and the events which took place surrounding this event in 1975 related to the oppressive atmosphere, the fear, the violence that was going on there and somehow through the evidence we are going to try to insert you there emotionally so you can sense and judge what took place and determine the mental state particularly of the actors in this drama on the basis of what took place there because if you judge them on what would happen in similar circumstances in Fargo the evidence will show, I believe, that it is not a valid determination.

Now what am I speaking of. I will tell you that some of the evidence that will indicate this to you is as follows:

In the three years surrounding 1975 on the Pine Ridge Reservation with a population of eight thousand people there were two hundred forty-three deaths by violence. Now that's a little hard to assimilate, to think about.

In order to get you to have a feel for that I will tell you that my investigation indicates that the Fargo-Moorhead complex, the metropolitan area here has about eighty thousand people in it, a little bit more than that but let's call it eighty thousand. This would be equivalent over the past three years of having twenty-four hundred thirty deaths by violence in Fargo-Moorhead. Twenty-four hundred and thirty deaths by violence.

The vast majority never resulted in arrests and there were very, very few prosecutions successful in convictions.

The result is that life is cheap on the reservations; everybody is armed for their self-defence; killings are only the tip of the iceberg; beatings were regular things.

We'll have evidence of a little girl who lost her eye when she was walking along the road and someone just shot at her...

The evidence will show that everybody on the reservation, and when I say everybody, obviously the Government may find one or two people or a handful that aren't all armed but for all intents and purposes everybody feels a need to be armed...

The evidence will show that one family in fifty on the reservation has a telephone and in fact within this entire Jumping Bull Compound as it is sometimes called there was no telephone so that if trouble starts you are on your own and there's not much of any way to get help even if you had a telephone there.

The nearest police were the Bureau of Indian Affairs police, twelve miles away from Pine Ridge … So people have to be self-reliant much as they were in the old west and the old six gunned justice, self-defence by weapons…

The evidence will show and we'll have testimony from residents of Pine Ridge that if anybody approaches, the reaction is not what you'd have, they'd grab the gun, turn out the lights and sort of peak out the windows…

In the area of tents you'll hear referred to as Tent City there were a lot of tents; there were teepees, there were huts, there were camper tents and there were a lot of weapons … and there's no question that the people there, that the evidence will show that they had armed themselves as everybody else on the reservation had.

There's no doubt that the evidence will show that the members who were in this encampment who were active in the American Indian Movement, some of them were certainly in low leadership positions, feared for their lives for one reason or another and carried weapons from time to time as they moved from place to place as a lot of people on the reservation did from time to time.

Prior to this incident there was a tribal chief who had been elected in what was a questionable election, that from the evidence will be named Dick Wilson.

Dick Wilson ran a ruthless, violent regime. The evidence will be that he had a series of henchmen who beat people, shot at people, carried out all sorts of violence in order to maintain him in power.

A term that is going to be used is goons. When I first heard it I found it offensive because I thought it was the kind of nickname that indicates a prejudice that most of us rebel against but I then found that everybody including the people themselves called the people I'm talking about goons, Dick Wilson and his goons and apparently on the reservation everybody including the goons called the people goons who worked for Dick Wilson.

In any event you will hear both sides referring to goons from time to time and these were the henchmen of Dick Wilson, a bunch of roughnecks.

The evidence will be extensive as to the terror that these people carried out and that these were people who were feared and one of the reasons that the people in this camp were armed was the rear of raids by goons.

We will bring out evidence in addition in support of the need for self-defence, self-arming, that the traditional Indians on the reservation and also the members of AIM who had had some experience in the area believed that they could not count on the FBI to give them equal protection of law and that this affected their mental state, again that if they became under attack, even if they could get a call for help to the BIA or the FBI, that it would, probably would not avail them...

We will also show that the American Indian Movement people, including people in this camp, believed that there were provocateurs enlisted by various people trying to cause violence and to try to draw AIM into various confrontations in order to discredit them, in order to get them and their leaders into all serving jail terms...

The facts will show that Mr. Peltier and a number of other people involved here had been in Farmington, New Mexico for an AIM conference, much as the American Legion has a conference or other groups have conferences, and they had come back to the Jumping Bulls' at the invitation of elder traditional Indians in the area in order to try to help the people there to overcome the problems of violence and oppression and help them to organize to help themselves.

Contrary to what Mr. Sikma indicated, I believe the evidence will be that Mr. Peltier had lived in this area for several months; that it was for all intents and purposes, in other words, his home at that time.

We will produce evidence that will show that the people there including Mr. Peltier were engaged in community projects to help uplift the Indian, particularly the traditional older Indians there who were having difficulty in coping with problems, trying to get many of the Indians in the area to stop drinking, to gain more self-respect and take care of themselves...

...there were FBI S.W.A.T. teams deployed in the Pine Ridge area. Members of these teams -- in fact Special Agent Coler was a member of a S.W.A.T. team...

We will show that the people there, including Mr. Peltier, were aware or believed that the FBI had certain counterintelligence programs which over the years had been attempting to disrupt the American Indian Movement by provocateurs or by confrontations or other things and in their mind the logical extension of that could include the FBI provoking trouble with them...

The Government will produce witnesses. I suggest that there will be witnesses and evidence given from this witness chair which you will find is unbelievable.

At least one Government witness will admit to having lied under oath in this case or in a proceeding...

We will introduce evidence to show, both in cross-examination of some of the Government witnesses, particularly the young Indians, that the Government has given inducements to some of these witnesses which will colour their testimony in your eyes to the point of disbelief...

That other Indian witnesses, we believe it will be shown, have been offered immunity or the opportunity to get out of some kind of trouble, not just Indian witnesses.

We believe that you will also find some Indian witnesses have in their mind, whether true or not, that their lives are in danger if they do not cooperate with the FBI and testify at this trial...

And finally, we believe that you will find a witness, at least one witness whose mental imbalance is so gross as to render her testimony unbelievable.

Turning to the day in question, there is no dispute that Leonard Peltier had been living in this area and was in the area off and on during that immediate period and probably on this day. It is certainly undisputed that late in the afternoon he left the tent area and went through the FBI lines undetected. The Government will introduce a whole lot of fingerprints. We are willing to stipulate to all of them. I don't know if the Government will accept the stipulation. There is no question he was in there. We don't need his fingerprints. We will tell you that right now, that's not disputed.

The evidence will be -- and I didn't hear Mr. Sikma say this, whether that's significant or not -- that the radio transmission from the agents said they were following a red pickup truck – that's going to be very important -- and I would alert you to that. Keep in mind the red pickup truck, and the reason for that is that there was no red pickup truck ever found nor any occupants of a red pickup truck ever found as far as the evidence discloses. The FBI agents and the two vehicles were chasing a red pickup truck. The testimony was: It looks like they are going to run for it – that's the radio transmission. I hope we have enough gas, it looks like they are going to shoot at us, and then shooting and then some comments, cries -- somebody has to get on the high ground or we are dead for sure, something to that effect. You will get it directly. The important thing I want to alert you to is it was a red pickup.

There is testimony -- there will be testimony, we believe that sometime after noon a red pickup truck ran a roadblock and got away and was never caught, and we suggest that that is very significant testimony in light of the testimony of the radio transmissions that they were engaged in a gunfight with somebody in a red pickup truck...

We do not believe that there will be any dispute over the pathology of death, that is, the way the death occurred on these two agents, or on the dead Indian man, We, I suspect -- I frankly don't know any of the pathology we would not stipulate to. There is little doubt about it. Mr. Sikma stated that both of these agents were shot and killed at a distance of, in one case, a contact shot, and in the other one, a four foot away shot. For purposes of discussion here -- and I think probably for purposes of the trial – that's undisputed ... certainly this is not a case in which somebody who was seen up at one of the houses got a lucky, long-range shot away and killed an agent. That simply is not the evidence, according to what the Government says, and certainly according to what I understand the evidence will be. That will limit severely the evidence as to what will be critical as to who shot and killed the agent and whether that was a justifiable killing, and if Mr. Peltier was one of them or was aiding and abetting the person or persons who did do it...

We believe that the evidence will show shocking Governmental misconduct. We believe that the evidence will be at a level that you will probably have difficulty believing, but we believe it will be so clear-cut when it is complete, that you will -- pursuant to what the Judge has told you in repeatedly ruling on this case -- based purely on what you hear in this courtroom, conclude that there was a Governmental misconduct of monumental proportions in this case.

You have told the Judge that you would try this case on the evidence, and that's all we ask. You have sworn to do what the Defendant, Mr. Peltier, believes the U.S. Government has never done, sworn to be impartial and unbiased toward him and sworn to give him a fair trial in the United States courtroom. That is all he could ask.

When the Government evidence is over, two things are going to be clear … First, that this is a real American tragedy, and second, that the Government has utterly failed to prove Leonard Peltier guilty beyond a reasonable doubt…

Opening Statement by the Lawyers of the United States Government in *United States v. Leonard Peltier*, 1977

In the following excerpts the position of the prosecution is set out in detail. They examine the facts about the warrant for the arrest of James Theodore Eagle and the pursuit of a red and white pick-up truck that finally led to a gunfight in the Jumping Bull property between agents Coler and Williams and a number of Indians. After the gunfight, the government argues, Peltier and other Indians walked down a hill and discovered Williams, where, it was alleged, Peltier shot Williams in the head and soon after, found Coler and shot him several times in the head while he was unconscious and incapacitated.

MR. SIKMA [Assistant United States Attorney]: May it please the Court, ladies and gentlemen of the jury. It's a difficult task which is going to confront you in the next couple of weeks. You are going to have to decide whether or not Leonard Peltier is guilty beyond a reasonable doubt of the charges which the judge just indicated to you. It's a serious charge so you have to be concerned … But it's also a very serious matter from the other point of view because there are two men whose lives were taken away while they were 27 and the other 28 years old, two young FBI agents. And as I say this to you, because it's important not only to make sure that you don't convict a defendant when you have a reasonable doubt as to his guilt but it is also important for you to keep in mind throughout the course of this trial that you make sure that justice is done. You cannot waiver from that point of view. You must see that justice is done…

The defendant is charged with a crime, with two offences: first degree murder, the murder of Ronald A. Williams, special agent of the FBI, while he was in the course of his duties as an agent. The other charge is first degree murder of Jack R. Coler while Jack R. Coler was in the official capacity as an FBI agent carrying out his sworn duty.

Let me tell you a couple things first about Ronald Williams. Ronald Williams is a native of Los Angeles. He was 27 years old at the time he died …

A couple months before he was killed he was assigned to the Pine Ridge Indian Reservation.

Jack Coler was also from Los Angeles, California. He was 28 years old at the time he died. He was also a special agent of the FBI...

Now the FBI has the responsibility of investigating major crimes on the reservation. Among them the crime of robbery, crimes of burglary, the various felony crimes.

On the 24th of June, 1975, Ronald Williams and Jack Coler were assigned the case of James Theodore Eagle. James Theodore Eagle was at that time on the reservation and he was charged with a crime of robbery. Since there was a Warrant outstanding, it was their duty to find James Theodore Eagle.

...The Pine Ridge Indian Reservation where this took place is located here in the south-western part of South Dakota...

The agents on the 25th were working in the town of Pine Ridge and another town of Oglala, South Dakota...

Highway 18 will be discussed a lot during the course of this trial. You will notice here that the Jumping Bull Hall, see this, "Jumping Bull Hall," this area on the map is generally known as the property of Harry Jumping Bull. Highway 18 runs past Harry Jumping Bull's property.

To the northwest Oglala, South Dakota is located, about 3.3 miles. Pine Ridge is located 12.2 miles to the southeast of the Jumping Bull Property.

Now on the date in question, or before the date in question, on the 24th to be exact, James Theodore Eagle and three companions were charged with a felony offence as I stated earlier.

At that time a Warrant went out for their arrest. Two of the other individuals were arrested and Agents Williams and Coler were assigned to look for James Theodore Eagle.

I believe the evidence will show that James Theodore Eagle had been seen in the area of the Jumping Bull property.

Now you'll notice that there are one, two, three, four houses here. The evidence I believe will also show that in the back area, there's an area back here to the southeast of the Jumping Bull's main residence which is a wooded, in a wooded area which had a number of tents and I believe the evidence will show that the defendant and his companions were staying in this area for a couple of weeks prior to the date of the 26th of June.

Now I believe the evidence will show that Jimmy Eagle was observed in this general area and consequently Special Agents Williams and Coler went to look for him on the 25th, the day before the date of the murders.

On the evening of the 25th they appeared there. I believe the evidence will show that they could not locate him but were advised at that time that he had been there but that he was gone.

I believe that the evidence will show that on the next day they once again set out to locate Jimmy Eagle and serve him the rest of it.

Now this is the time, I remind you, when the defendant and his companions, about twelve of them, were occupying the area in a tent and they were also in the area of these residents from time to time.

On the afternoon of the 26th of June at about 11:00 o'clock Special Agent Adams, while he was working, assigned to another case in that area, drove into Pine Ridge, South Dakota which I mentioned is about twelve miles to the southeast of the Jumping Bull residence.

…He observed Special Agent Williams talking with another agent and determined that Special Agent Williams was going out to look for James Theodore Eagle and that they were going in that direction.

Shortly before noon, since he was by himself, he left in the opposite direction to the south to go out to get some lunch. This was about quarter to 12:00 on the 26th of June.

While travelling in his car he heard a radio transmission and because he knew Special Agent Williams well he recognized his voice and he heard something to say to the effect that they were following a vehicle. It seems that it was a red and while vehicle of some kind; that he heard other communications which indicated that they were still following the vehicle and then he heard the communication, "It looks like they're going to shoot at us," and then immediately over the sound of the radio net he heard the sound of gunfire.

He immediately stopped his car and turned around and headed back toward the Pine Ridge, or toward the Oglala area.

When he turned around he made some contact during this time with Special Agent Williams. He heard him state that he had to get on the high ground. He heard him talk about Jumping Bull Hall.

He did not know precisely where Jumping Bull Hall was but he drove in that direction…

Meanwhile Special Agents Williams and Coler were following a vehicle.

Apparently and, I believe that during the course of the trial you will have to put evidence together. Sometimes circumstantial evidence is the best evidence that there is to show a certain thing…

I believe that this evidence will show that Special Agents Williams and Coler travelled down [a] road; that when they got down … they were communicating with Special Agent Adams to the fact that he'd better get on the high ground or they'd be dead men.

That at this time Special Agent Williams and Coler, while they were armed with their service revolvers, did not have on their person a long rifle.

Now I believe that the, this will show that the area from the housing to the bottom of the hill is approximately two hundred yards. Now with a pistol, I believe the agents will be able to testify that with a pistol that's a long ways to fire with any accuracy.

However, with a high-powered rifle that's a very short distance to fire.

Special Agents Williams and Coler, Special Agent Coler apparently got out of his car and went to the trunk where he had a 308 carbine rifle.

I believe that the, that he took the weapon out of his car and at this time I believe that Special Agent Coler's car was parked in a manner which was pointing it right towards this green house because that's where it was found. It was found in this area; the trunk was open.

I believe that Special Agent Williams' car was running parallel to this road that runs along an area which takes the bodies of Special Agents Williams and Coler.

I believe that the evidence will show that during this time while the gunfire was going on Special Agent Williams was trying to get Special Agent Adams to find the location.

That while, Special Agent Coler meanwhile went to the back of his car to get a gun out of the trunk, the 308 carbine, that a bullet went through the trunk and went into his arm and nearly tore his arm off.

It was in such a manner that I believe the evidence will show the injury would have been so great and cause such extreme pain that he would have been disabled from it. He may have eventually gone unconscious from it.

Sometime during this time Special Agent Coler, or Special Agent Williams was shot in the shoulder. The bullet went from the top of his shoulder out his underarm and into his side. He was shot with a 44 magnum carbine.

At this time or sometime after he was shot I believe that the evidence will show that he took off his shirt and made tourniquet for Special Agent Coler's right arm.

I believe that Special Agent Coler at that time was laying out alongside of his car.

I believe about this time while he was doing this the defendant Leonard Peltier and his companions came from this area of the, of these cars here. There are some junk cars that were parked along there. There are some houses in this area. I believe the evidence will show that they were being fired at from these two areas.

A number of individuals were firing at them with high powered weapons;

That when they stopped firing, that the defendant and his companions went to the bottom of the hill; when they got to the bottom of the hill, that Special Agent Coler had been, or Special Agent Williams had been shot two times.

He had been shot in the left shoulder and he was wounded in the side. He was shot in the right foot.

And at that time while ho had his hand extended in front of his face and the defendant and his companions at close range, the gun was placed up against his hand and the trigger was pulled, a high-powered weapon.

The bullet went through his hand and into his face and tore away the back of his head.

He was, I believe medical evidence will show, was killed instantly.

Special Agent Coler at this time was laying on the ground unconscious or unable to defend himself.

I believe from the photographs, from the reconstruction of the events you will see that while Special Agent Coler was laying on the ground the gun was held not more than four feet from his forehead. He was shot in the right side; that the bullet carried away the top front part of the skull. This would not in itself probably have been a fatal shot but immediately thereafter he was shot in the side of the jaw on the right side. The bullet went through his jaw, tore away the bottom of the jaw and killed him instantly.

Meanwhile Special Agent Adams and two Bureau of Indian Affairs police were coming, were travelling from Pine Ridge down toward this area.

…That in this particular, when he got to this point, that his car and the car of the Bureau of, BIA police was fired upon, both front tires shot out of the vehicles.

He began backing up into this area and he backed his car until he got to an area right along here parallel with Highway 18. There's an old road which is to the southwest of Highway 18 running parallel to it and his car got stuck there, while a front tire was shot out, he had a flat tire. He couldn't move and he remained pinned down and stayed in this area throughout the afternoon until 4:30 that afternoon.

Throughout the afternoon more agents came. I believe that the Government and the Defendant will agree that Special Agent Williams and Coler died approximately 12:00 o'clock noon; and so at this time, if you recall, if you look at the evidence, I believe that you will find that at this time the offence had already been committed. I believe that at that time the agents were already dead, had already been murdered; but other agents and other police, members of the Bureau of Indian Affairs, moved into the area in an attempt to capture the persons who had fired the shots.

…During the afternoon a couple of times there were attempts made to negotiate with the people in this area. I believe though that the evidence will be that all negotiations were unsuccessful. One of the assailants was killed during the course of the gunfight in which the agents were trying to get into the area; but I believe the evidence will show that during the time from 12:00 o'clock until 4:30, until the agents' well-being was known, that no one was certain as to whether or not Special Agents Williams, Special Agent Coler were hostages or what their condition was, so during this time I think you will find very little firing was done by the law enforcement agents going into the area.

Later in the afternoon the Defendant and his companions, about six or seven of them, or eight of them, met in the area by the tents. They waited there for a while. They loaded a red and white Chevy van with supplies and discussed whether or not they would attempt to run the roadblock. They decided to abandon this idea and decided to escape out the back way which they did, and they travelled for a couple of days into the hills around the -- toward the direction of Pine Ridge and in various areas, and eventually their trail was lost.

…On September 5th the FBI had warrants for a number of persons … They had warrants for a number of people living at the Al Running residence.

In serving these warrants they arrested a man by the name of Butler and others; but Dino Butler was a man, I believe the evidence will show, who was in the area of the tents, was living in the area with Leonard Peltier.

I believe that the evidence will show that around this area certain evidence was found, firearms, spent cartridge cases and so forth were found in the area of the Al Running residence where the Defendant had been and where Dino Butler was arrested.

But on of the things that was found in an automobile on that property was Special Agent Williams' service revolver.

...While they were driving there at this time their car caught fire. The muffler got hot, and the car caught fire. They ran from the vehicle, but it exploded. The vehicle exploded, and a number of items were found. One of the things that was found in this vehicle was a 308 carbine rifle. In this 308 carbine there was -- this was a gun that was assigned to Special Agent Coler.

Now, there was also a firearm found there that was connected to the crime scene.

Now, during the course of the trial we are going to use a variety of exhibits in order to help you ... This is Government Exhibit 34-b. It is a spent cartridge case...

Now, Government Exhibit 34-b, when it is offered into evidence ... [and] it was found in the trunk of Special Agent Coler's car...

Government Exhibit 34-a is a picture of an AR Fischer Rifle.

Now, if this is offered into evidence, the reason that we chose to number this cartridge casing 34-b is because, I believe the evidence will show, that Government Exhibit 34-b was fired from Government Exhibit 34-a...

...Leonard Peltier was a fugitive until February 6 when the Royal Canadian Mounted Police caught him in the area of the Jasper National Park, which is a small boy's camp in Alberta, Canada.

...Well, I have stated that I have by no means stated the evidence. I have given you an idea of how the defendant was traced ... and how the items which they had on their person or near to them connected directly-back to the area of the death of special agent Ronald Williams and Jack Coler.

Throughout the course of the trial I ask you to look for connection, pay close attention to it because there are a number of items that are involved that are rather complex. But throughout the course of the trial, as I said earlier, the defendant starts out and there is no evidence against him, but throughout the course of the trial you'll be seeing evidence placed in one at a time, pieces of evidence will come in. I believe they will show circumstantial and direct evidence of the defendant's guilt in this matter.

...I believe you will find that a paper bag was found in a recreational vehicle, a vehicle which Leonard Peltier was driving, and on this paper bag, for example, there was fingerprints of Leonard Peltier. Inside of the paper bag, special agent Coler's personal firearm along with some shell casings, empty shell casings which had been fired.

...I ask you to listen closely and it's our contention by the close of the trial the government will have proven its case against the defendant beyond a reasonable doubt.

Remember, only one person is on trial ... The defendant is on trial for two counts of first degree murder and I ask you to keep that in mind when you're considering the evidence...

Leonard Peltier Is Convicted of Two Counts of First-Degree Murder and Sentenced to Two Consecutive Life Sentences, 18 April 1977

In the following text, the jury find Leonard Peltier guilty of the first-degree murder of agents Jack Coler and Ronald Williams.

...THE COURT: The record may show that about 3:30 this afternoon the Court received a written note signed by Mr. Dallas Rossow, Foreman, which read as follows:

The jury has reached a verdict and is ready to deliver it.

Mr. Nelson, will you take the verdict?

THE CLERK: The jury will please listen to the verdict as I read it and as it shall be recorded.

As to Count 1, Ronald A. Williams, the jury finds the Defendant guilty of first degree murder.

As to the killing of Jack R. Coler, Count 2, the jury finds the Defendant guilty of first degree murder.

Dated this 18th day of April, 1977.

Signed, Dallas Rossow, Foreman.

...THE COURT: ... A pre-sentence report is ordered, and sentencing will be set on a date to be determined by the Court.

Members of the Jury, it is now a real pleasure for me to advise that you are discharged and you may return home.

I will just add this: That earlier this afternoon before I knew that you had reached a verdict, and of course, before I had any idea of what your verdict would be, I dictated a letter to each of you expressing the appreciation of the Court for the service that you have rendered. You will get that letter in the mail...

THE COURT: The Court is adjourned.

(Whereupon, at 4:45 o'clock, p.m., the trial of the above-entitled matter was closed.)

Leonard Peltier Is Sentenced, 1 June 1977

Provided here is the sentencing of Leonard Peltier (1944–) and an impassioned speech by Peltier about what he felt were the biased actions and rulings of the

judge from the start to the end of the trial as well as clear evidence of an FBI
set-up covered up by the judge himself.

BE IT REMEMBERED that heretofore on Wednesday, the 1st day of June, 1977,
the ... Defendant came before the Court for sentencing at the hour of 4:00
o'clock, p.m., before the Honourable PAUL BENSON, one of Judges of said
court at Fargo, North Dakota...

...THE COURT: Mr. Peltier, do you desire to make a statement in your own
behalf or present any information to the Court which the Court might
consider in mitigation of punishment in your case?

DEFENDANT PELTIER: Yes I do.

Judge Benson, there is no doubt in my mind or my people's you are going
to sentence me to two consecutive life terms. You are and have always been
prejudiced against me and any Native Americans who have stood before you.
You have openly favoured the Government all through this trial, and you are
happy to do whatever the FBI would want you to do in this case.

I did not always believe this to be so. When I first saw you in the
courtroom in Sioux Falls, your dignified appearance misled me into thinking
that you were a fair minded person who knew something of the law and who
would act in accordance with the law which meant that you would be
impartial and not favour one side or the other in this lawsuit.

That has not been the case, and I now firmly believe you will impose
consecutive life terms solely because that's what you think will waive the
displeasures of the FBI. Yet my people nor myself do not know why you would
be so concerned about an organization that has brought so much shame to
the American people, but you are. Your conduct during this trial leaves no
doubt, that you will do the bidding of the FBI without any hesitation.

You are about to perform an act which will close one more chapter in the
history of the failure of the United States Courts and the failure of the people
of the United States to do justice in the case of a native American. After
centuries of murder, of murder of millions of my people, brothers and sisters,
by the white race of America could I have been wise in thinking that you
would break that tradition and, commit an act of Justice? Obviously not,
because I should have realized that what I detected was only a very thin layer
of dignity and surely of not fine character.

If you think my accusations have been harsh and, unfounded, I will explain
why I have reached this conclusion and why I think my criticism has not been
harsh enough.

First, each time my defence team tried to expose FBI misconduct in their
investigation of this lawsuit and tried to prevent evidence of this, you claimed
it was irrelevant to this trial, but the prosecution was allowed to present their
case with evidence that was in no way relevant to this lawsuit.

...Second, you could not make a reasonable decision about my sentence
because you suffer from at least one of three defects that prevent a rational

275

conclusion. You plainly demonstrated this in your decision about the Jimmy Eagle, and Myrtle Poor Bear aspects of this case.

In Jimmy's case, for some unfounded reason that only a Judge who constantly and openly ignores the law, would call it irrelevant to my trial.

In the mental torture of Myrtle Poor Bear you said the testimony would shock the conscience of the jury and the American people if believed, but you decided what was to be believed and what was not to be believed, not the jury.

Your conduct shocks the conscience of what the American legal system stands for -- the search for the truth by a jury of citizens. What was it that made you afraid to let that testimony in -- your own guilt of being part of a corrupted pre-planned trial to get a conviction, no matter how your reputation would be tarnished?

For these reasons I strongly believe you will do the bidding of the FBI and give me two consecutive life terms.

Third, in my opinion anyone who failed to see the relationship between the undisputed facts of these events surrounding the investigation used by the FBI in their interrogation of the Navajo youths -- Wilfred Draper who was tied to a chair for three hours and denied access to his attorney or the outright threats to Norman Brown's life, the bodily harm threatened to Mike Anderson, and finally the murder of Anna Mae Aquash -- must be blind, stupid or without human feeling, so there is no doubt or little chance that you have the ability to avoid doing today what the FBI wants you to do which is to sentence me to two life terms running consecutively.

Fourth, you do not have the ability to see that the conviction of an AIM activist helps to cover up what the Government's own evidence showed, that large numbers of Indian people engaged in that fire fight on June 26th, 1975. You do not have the ability to see that the Government must suppress the fact that there is a growing anger amongst Indian people and that native Americans will resist any further encroachment by the military forces of the capitalist Americans which is evidenced by the large number of Pine Ridge residents who took up arms on June 26th, 1975, to defend themselves.

Therefore, you do not have the ability to carry out your responsibilities towards me in an impartial way and will run my two life terms consecutively.

Fifth, I stand before you as a proud man. I feel no guilt. I have done nothing to feel guilty about. I have no regrets of being a Native American activist. Thousands of people in the United States, Canada and around the world, have and will continue to support me to expose the injustice that occurred in this courtroom.

I do feel pity for your people that they must live under such a ugly system. Under your system you are taught greed, racism and corruption, and the most serious of all, the destruction of our mother earth. Under the Native American system we are taught all people are brothers and sisters, to share the wealth with the poor and needy; but the most important of all is to respect and preserve the earth, to me considered to be our mother. We feed from her breast. Our mother gives us life at birth; and when it is time to leave this world, she again takes us back into her womb; but the main thing we are taught is to preserve her for our children and grandchildren because they are next who will live upon her.

No, I am not the guilty one here and should be called a criminal. The white race of America is the criminal for the destruction of our lands and my people...

Sixth, there are less than four hundred Federal Judge for a population of over two hundred million Americans. Therefore, you have a very powerful and important responsibility which should be carried out impartially, but you never have been impartial where I was concerned. You have the responsibility of protecting constitutional rights and laws; but where I was concerned you neglected to even consider my or Native American's constitutional rights; but the most important of all you have neglected our human rights. If you were impartial, you would have had an open mind on all the factual disputes in this case; but you were unwilling to allow for even the slightest possibility that a law enforcement officer could lie on the stand...

Again, to cover up your part in this, you will call me a heartless, cold-blooded murderer who deserves two life sentences consecutively.

Seven, I cannot expect a Judge who has openly tolerated the conditions I have been jailed under to make an impartial decision on whether I should be sentenced to concurrent or consecutive life terms. You have been made aware of the following conditions which I had to endure at the Grand Forks county jail since the time of the verdict.

One, I was denied access to a phone to call my attorneys concerning my appeal.

Two, I was locked in solitary confinement without shower facilities, soap, towels, sheets or pillow.

Three, the food was uneatable, what little there was.

Four, my family, brothers, sisters, mother and father who travelled long distance from the reservation were denied visitations.

No human being should be subject to such treatment while you parade around and pretend to be a decent, impartial and law-abiding.

You knowingly allowed your fascist Chief Deputy Marshal to play storm trooper.

Again, the only conclusion that comes to my mind is you have, and always knew, you would sentence me to two consecutive life terms.

Finally, I honestly believe that you made up your mind long ago that I was guilty and that you were going to sentence me to the maximum sentence permitted under the law, but this does not surprise me because you are a high-ranking member of the white racist American establishment which has consistently said "In God we trust" while they went about the business of murdering my people and attempting to destroy our culture. The only thing I am guilty of and which I was convicted for was of being Chippewa and Sioux blood and for believing our sacred religion.

...THE COURT: Mr. Hultman, does the United States have any recommendations or comments to offer?

MR. HULTMAN: ... In this instance there was not one life which was taken, but two; and because of the prosecution that has taken place in the course of this trial, because that penalty does indicate that a life term is the minimum sentence in the case of a life being taken, it seems to me, your Honour, that is appropriate --

...MR. HULTMAN: In the course of the taking of this particular life, your Honour, not one life was taken as far as this particular trial is concerned, but the taking of two; and it seems to me that in light of that, that consecutive terms would be appropriate.

THE COURT: Mr. Peltier, you were convicted as charged --

DEFENDANT PELTIER: (Interrupting) I was railroaded.

THE COURT: (Continuing) -- as charged in the indictments of two counts of premeditated murder. You were convicted and found guilty on each of those counts. The evidence is clearly sufficient to support the verdict of the jury.

You profess an interest and a dedication to the native people of this country, but you have performed a great disservice to those native people.

VOICE FROM AUDIENCE: Same to you.

DEFENDANT PELTIER: What about the Gestapo tactics being used on the Pine Ridge residents? What do you call that? The cold-blooded murder of Anna Mae Aquash, what do you call that?

...THE COURT: On the verdict of the jury, it is adjudged that the Defendant, Leonard Peltier, has been convicted of the offence of first degree murder as charged in Count 1 and Count 2 of the indictment in violation of Title 18, United States Code, Section 2 -- Section 1111 and Section 1114.

It is further adjudged that the Defendant be committed to the custody of the Attorney General of the United States for imprisonment for life on Count 1.

It is further adjudged that the Defendant, Leonard Peltier, be committed to the custody of the Attorney General of the United states for imprisonment for life on Count 2, the sentence on Count 2 to run consecutively to the sentence on Count 1...

THE COURT: Is there anything more?

MR. TAIKEFF: Nothing at this time, your Honour.

THE COURT: Court is adjourned.

William Muldrow: Report by the US Civil Rights Commission on Law Enforcement Misconduct on Pine Ridge Reservation, 9 July 1975

Only two weeks after the bloody conflict in 1975, William F. Muldrow, a senior member of the US Civil Rights Commission, released a report, outlined below, about the overreaction and gung-ho attitude of the federal authorities inside the reservation in response to the shooting of the FBI agents. Muldrow contrasts this FBI reaction to the inaction and ignorance of the FBI over the hundreds of deaths and incessant violence that had plagued the reservation environment from 1973 to 1975. Muldrow casts doubt on some of the evidence and explanations used by the FBI to justify their manhunt and describes how he was invited to the funeral of Joseph Stuntz, the Indian man who died in FBI gunfire.

...At about 1:00p.m. on Thursday, June 26, two FBI Agents were shot to death on the Pine Ridge Reservation near the town of Oglala, South Dakota. The FBI immediately launched a large-scale search for the suspected slayers which has involved 100 to 200 combat-clad FBI Agents, BIA policeman, SWAT teams, armoured cars, helicopters, fixed-wing aircraft, and tracking dogs. An increasing volume of requests for information regarding the incident and numerous reports and complaints of threats, harassment, and search procedures conducted without due process of law by the FBI, prompted my visit to the reservation to gather firsthand information...

I was on the reservation from July 1-3...

This particular incident of violence must be seen in the context of ... frustration, and crime which has increasingly pervaded life on the reservation during the last three years. Unemployment approaches 70 percent and the crime rate is four times that of Chicago. There have been eighteen killings on the reservation so far this year and uncounted beatings, fights, and shootings. Many of these incidents have never been explained or, in the minds of many residents, even satisfactorily investigated. The tribal government has been charged by reservation residents with corruption, nepotism, and with maintaining control through a reign of terror.

Tribal officials, including the President of the Council [Richard Wilson], have been indicted in connection with such an incident (on a misdemeanour charge, although guns and knives were involved)...

During World War II ... the FBI was given jurisdiction to investigate felonies on the reservation and this has never been relinquished. The number of FBI agents assigned to the reservation was recently increased in an attempt to cope with the mounting crime rate. One of the agents who was killed last week was on special assignment from Colorado.

Many of the facts surrounding the shooting are either unknown by officials or have not been made public. Media representatives felt that the FBI was unnecessarily restrictive in the kind and amount of information it provided. It is patently clear that many of the statements that have been released regarding the incident are either false, unsubstantiated, or directly misleading. Some of these statements were highly inflammatory, alleging that the agents were "led into a trap" and "executed." As a result, feelings have run high.

The FBI had arrest warrants for four Native Americans who had allegedly assaulted, kidnapped, and robbed a white man and a boy. Residents of the reservation and an attorney from the Wounded Knee Legal Offense/Defense Committee with whom I talked felt that the warrants were issued merely on the word of the white people without adequate investigation. Such a thing, they point out, would never have happened had the Indians been the accusers and typifies unequal treatment often given to Indian people.

The two agents killed in the shooting had been to several houses on the reservation looking for the wanted men. The occupants of some of these houses claimed that the agents had been abusive and threatening. Some of the Native Americans that I talked with, who had been involved in the Wounded Knee incident, have a genuine fear that the FBI is "out to get" them. When the two agents were killed they had no warrants in their possession.

The bodies of the agents were found down in the valley several hundred yards from the houses where the shooting supposedly occurred. "Bunkers" described in newspaper accounts turned out to be aged root cellars. "Trench fortifications" were non-existent. Persons in the houses were in the process of preparing a meal when the shooting occurred. One of the houses, owned by Mr. and Mrs. Harry Jumping Bull, contained children and several women one of whom was pregnant...

The body of Joseph Stuntz, the young Native American killed in one of the houses during the shooting, was seen shortly after the shooting lying in a mud hole as though it had been dumped there on purpose. He was later given a traditional hero's burial attended by hundreds of people from the reservation.

Sixteen men were reportedly involved in the shooting though no one knows how this figure was determined. The FBI has never given any clear indication that it knows the identity of these men. Incredibly, all of them, though surrounded by State and BIA police and FBI agents, managed to escape in broad daylight during the middle of the afternoon.

In the days immediately following the incident there were numerous accounts of persons being arrested without cause for questioning, and of houses being searched without warrants...

...Individual FBI agents with whom I talked were deeply upset over the "execution" of their comrades.

Most of the Native Americans received me cordially and I was invited to attend the burial of Joseph Stuntz. Some expressed appreciation for my presence there as an observer and suggested that the Commission might be the only body capable of making an impartial investigation of the Pine Ridge situation. My interview with Dick Wilson was less satisfactory. He stated that he could give me no information and that he did not "feel like talking about civil rights at a time like this."

...The FBI was conducting a full-scale military operation ... Their presence there has created deep resentment on the part of many of the reservation residents who do not feel that such a procedure would be tolerated in any non-Indian community in the United States. They point out that little has been done to solve the numerous murders on the reservation, but when two white men are killed, "troops" are brought in from all over the country at a cost of hundreds of thousands of dollars.

...Many Native Americans feel that the present large-scale search operation is an over reaction which takes on aspects of a vendetta...

Amnesty International Appeal for the Release of Leonard Peltier, 1999

In the following extract, Amnesty International reviews the evidence of the original case, details the weaknesses that resulted in Peltier's conviction and concludes that the conviction remains weak at best.

...Amnesty International has investigated this case for many years. Although Amnesty International has not adopted Leonard Peltier as a prisoner of conscience, the organization remains concerned about the fairness of the proceedings leading to his conviction and believes that political factors may have influenced the way in which the case was prosecuted...

Background and Summary of Amnesty International's Concerns

...Peltier was a leading activist with the American Indian Movement (AIM) whose members were involved in a campaign to protect traditional Indian lands and resources and had come into conflict with both the Pine Ridge tribal government and the FBI. Two other AIM members, Darelle (Dino) Butler and Robert Robideau, were originally charged with the FBI agents' murder and were tried separately in 1976. They admitted being present during the gunfight but were acquitted on grounds of self-defence, after submitting evidence about the atmosphere of fear and terror which existed on the reservation prior to the shoot-out.

There is evidence that the government intensified its pursuit of Leonard Peltier after the acquittal of Butler and Robideau. Peltier was extradited from Canada partly on the testimony of Myrtle Poor Bear, an American Indian woman who signed a statement saying she had seen Peltier shoot the agents at close range. Poor Bear, who was a notoriously unreliable witness, later retracted this statement as having been obtained under duress and said she had never even met Peltier. The prosecution did not use Myrtle Poor Bear as a witness at Peltier's trial. However, they introduced ballistics evidence which purported to show that it was Peltier's gun which killed the agents at close range after they were already wounded and disabled. This evidence effectively prevented Peltier from being able to present the same self-defence argument which had resulted in the Butler/Robideau acquittals. However, serious questions have since been raised about the reliability of this ballistics evidence.

The government has continued to argue that, even if they can no longer prove that Peltier killed the agents, he is still guilty of "aiding and abetting" in the murders through being in the group involved in the exchange of gunfire from a distance. However, Amnesty International believes that the doubts which have been raised about Peltier's role in the actual killings of the agents undermine the whole case against him, as "proof" that he was the actual killer was a key element in the prosecution's case at the trial.

Amnesty International's concerns about various aspects of the case are outlined in a letter to the US Attorney General dated 23 June 1995 ... These concerns include the following:

- The FBI knowingly used perjured testimony to obtain Leonard Peltier's extradition from Canada to the USA. The FBI later admitted that it knew that the affidavits of Myrtle Poor Bear, an alleged eye-witness to the murders, were false. This in itself casts serious doubt on the *bona fides* of the prosecution, even though Poor Bear's affidavits were not used at Peltier's trial.

- Leonard Peltier's attorneys were not permitted to call Myrtle Poor Bear as a defence witness to describe to the trial jury how she had been coerced by the FBI into signing false affidavits implicating Peltier. The trial judge refused to allow her to appear on the grounds that her testimony could be "highly prejudicial" to the government.

- Evidence which might have assisted Leonard Peltier's defence was withheld by the prosecution. This included a 1975 telex from an FBI ballistics expert which stated that, based on ballistics tests, the rifle alleged to be Peltier's had a "different firing pin" from the gun used to kill the two agents. At a court hearing in 1984, an FBI witness testified that the telex had been merely a progress report and that another bullet casing tested later had been found to match "positively" with the rifle linked to Peltier. However, the reliability of the government's ballistics evidence remains in dispute.

- The ballistics evidence presented at Peltier's trial was crucial to the prosecution's case. It was presented as the main evidence linking Peltier as the actual point-blank killer of the two FBI agents. Without this evidence, the case against Peltier would have been no stronger than the case against Dino Butler and Robert Robideau, who were also charged with the Pine Ridge killings. Butler and Robideau were tried separately and permitted to argue that there was an atmosphere of such fear and terror on the reservation that their move to shoot back at the agents constituted legitimate self-defence. They were acquitted.

- The trial judge refused to allow the defence to introduce evidence of serious FBI misconduct relating to the intimidation of witnesses (the testimony of Myrtle Poor Bear). Had such evidence been presented, it may have cast doubt in the jury's mind about the reliability of the main prosecution witnesses, three young Indians (Anderson, Draper and Brown) whose testimony (that Peltier was in possession of an AR-15 rifle during the shoot-out) was the main evidence linking Peltier to the alleged murder weapon.

The United States Court of Appeal for the Eighth Circuit ruled in 1986 that the prosecution had indeed withheld evidence which would have been favourable to Leonard Peltier and would have allowed him to cross examine witnesses more effectively. However, it concluded that this had not materially affected the outcome of the trial, and it upheld Peltier's conviction. However, the judge who wrote this opinion, Judge Gerald Heaney, has since expressed his concern about the case...

Parole application

The parole Commission decided at Peltier's last full, formal parole hearing in 1993 that his case would not be formally reviewed again for a further 15 years - setting his next parole hearing for December 2008. Since then there have been several interim hearings at which the Commission has refused to reconsider the decision to deny parole on the grounds that Peltier did not accept criminal responsibility for the murders of the two FBI agents. This is despite the fact that, after one such hearing, the Commission acknowledged that, "the prosecution has conceded the lack of any direct evidence that you personally participated in the executions of the two FBI agents ... " Peltier has always denied that he was involved in killing the agents.

In June 1999 Peltier's lawyers filed a *habeas corpus* petition in a federal district court, claiming that the parole board's decision not to hear the case again for 15 years was arbitrary and unconstitutional, and a violation of guidelines which should be applied to the case. The petition also states that changes in the laws and procedures relating to parole since 1975 have been wrongly applied retroactively in Peltier's case, meaning that he has been required to serve far longer in prison than was the case at the time of his conviction.

Letter from FBI Director Louis J. Freeh to President Bill Clinton, December 2000

In the following letter, Louis J. Freeh (1950–), former director of the FBI, outlines the raw feelings that continue to haunt him and his agency over the death of the two FBI agents, calling on President Clinton to refuse the pardon of Leonard Peltier. In addition, Freeh echoes the feelings of the Williams and Coler families and describes the consideration of a pardon as the antithesis of a legal system that is supposed to protect those people who serve their country's legal system.

December 5, 2000

The Honourable Bill Clinton
President of the United States
Washington, D.C. 20500

Dear Mr. President,

I would like to share with you a letter I sent to Attorney General Janet Reno regarding Leonard Peltier and respectfully request that the consecutive life sentences Peltier is serving for the brutal murder of two FBI Agents not be commuted. I make this request on behalf of the Agents and employees of the FBI who have asked me to so on their behalf. It is they and the families of the two slain Agents who will most suffer the hurt and shaken confidence in policing under the rule of law that Peltier's release is certain to cause.

After a lengthy trial and despite repeated appeals, the facts have not changed. FBI Special Agents Ron A. Williams and Jack R. Coler were grievously wounded during an overwhelming ambush as they searched for a robbery suspect. While disabled they were executed at point blank range. Both were shot in the head, Agent Williams as he held up his hand in a desperate attempt to shield his face from the blast. Peltier was convicted by a jury for these murders, a brutal and cold-blooded episode in the middle of the other instances of total disregard for life and disrespect for the laws that govern us all. His conviction has stood the test of multiple appeals to multiple courts including the U.S. Supreme Court.

Mr. President, there is no issue more deeply felt within the FBI or more widely shared within the law enforcement community than the belief that this attack by Peltier was nothing less than a complete affront to out cherished system of government under the rule of law. The inevitable haziness brought on by the passage of time does not diminish the brutality of the crimes or the torment to the surviving families. But we in the law enforcement family respectfully ask that you look beyond the actual crimes to what these remorseless acts represent. To both the servants of the public charged with protecting their safety and to the protected, the premeditated execution of two young FBI Agents is the most vile disrespect for all that we cherish under our law and our God and for which moderation can only signal disrespect.

Finally, the families of Agents Coler and Williams have asked that I extend their plea to you as well. Theirs is the lifelong agony few can understand. For that reason and many others, some that we share, they respectfully plead to you that the vicious murderer of a son and a father not be heroically elevated above the cold and hardened criminal he chose to be and that brought him to this point.

Sincerely,

Louis J. Freeh
Director [FBI]

Rebuttal Statement from Congressman Don Edwards at the National Press Club, Washington, D.C., 14 December 2000

In the following document, congressman and former FBI agent Don Edwards (1915–) argues that the opposition to clemency for Peltier is incorrect because the evidence and actions of the FBI at the original trial were untrue and flawed and it follows that Peltier was wrongly convicted.

12/14/00

Hon. Don Edwards
P.O. Box 7151
Carmel, CA
93221

As a former Congressman from California for over thirty years, a former FBI agent and a citizen committed to justice, I wish to speak out strongly against the FBI's efforts in opposing the clemency appeal of Leonard Peltier. I served as Chairman of the Subcommittee on Civil and Constitutional Rights in the U.S. House of Representatives.

I took a personal interest in Mr. Peltier's case and became convinced that he never received a fair trial. Even the government now admits that the theory it presented against Mr. Peltier at trial was not true. After 24 years in prison, Leonard Peltier has served an inordinate amount of time and deserves the right to consideration of his clemency request on the facts and the merits.

The FBI continues to deny its improper conduct on Pine Ridge during the 1970's and in the trial of Leonard Peltier. The FBI used Mr. Peltier as a scapegoat and they continue to do so today. At every step of the way, FBI agents and leadership have opposed any admission of wrongdoing by the government, and they have sought to misrepresent and politicize the meaning of clemency for Leonard Peltier. The killing of FBI agents at Pine Ridge was reprehensible, but the government now admits that it cannot prove that Mr. Peltier killed the agents.

Granting clemency to Mr. Peltier should not be viewed as expressing any disrespect for the current agents or leadership of the FBI, nor would it represent any condoning of the killings that took place on Pine Ridge. Instead, clemency for Mr. Peltier would recognize past wrongdoing and the undermining of the government's case since trial. Finally, it would serve as a crucial step in the reconciliation and healing between the U.S. Government and Native Americans, on the Pine Ridge Reservation and throughout the country...

Letter from US Senior Circuit Judge Gerald W. Heaney to Senator Daniel K. Inouye about Leonard Peltier, 18 April 1991

In a letter to Senator Inouye, Judge Gerald W. Heaney (1918–), who presided over one of the number of Peltier appeals in federal court, points out that it is now time to think about releasing Leonard Peltier from prison because he has served his time.

Re: Leonard Peltier

Dear Senator Inouye:

Unfortunately I did not receive your letter of February 1, 1991 until April 13, 1991. When I did receive your letter, I was visiting your state. Thus, this is my first chance to reply.

As you know, I wrote the opinion in United States v. Peltier, 800 F. 2d 772 (8th Cir. 1986), and I sat as a member of the court in an earlier appeal, United States v. Peltier, 731 F. 2d 550 (8th Cir. 1984). In the case I authored, our court concluded:

There is a possibility that the jury would have acquitted Leonard Peltier had the records and data improperly withheld from the defense been available to him in order to better exploit and reinforce the inconsistencies casting strong doubts upon the government's case. Yet, we are bound by the Bagley test requiring that we be convinced, from a review of the entire record, that had the data and records withheld been made available, the jury probably would have reached a different result. We have not been so convinced.

United States v. Peltier, 731 F. 2d at 779-80. No new evidence has been called to my attention which would cause me to change the conclusion reached in that case.

There are, however, other aspects of the case that the President may see fit to consider in determining whether he should take action to commute or otherwise mitigate the sentence of Leonard Peltier. My thoughts on these other aspects result from a very careful study of the records of the Peltier trial and the post-trial evidence and from a study of the record in the Robideaux-Butler trial before Judge McManus in Iowa, a trial which resulted in the acquittal of Robideaux and Butler.

First, the United States government over-reacted at Wounded Knee. Instead of carefully considering the legitimate grievances of the Native Americans, the response was essentially a military one which culminated in a deadly firefight on June 26, 1975 between the Native Americans and the FBI agents and the United States marshals.

Second, the United States government must share the responsibility with the Native Americans for the June 26 firefight. It was an intense one in which both government agents and Native Americans were killed. While the government's role in escalating the conflict into a firefight cannot serve as a legal justification for the killing of the FBI agents at short range, it can properly be considered as a mitigating circumstance.

Third, the record persuades me that more than one person was involved in the shooting of the FBI agents. Again, this fact is not a legal justification for Peltier's actions, but it is a mitigating circumstance.

Fourth, the FBI used improper tactics in securing Peltier's extradition from Canada and in otherwise investigating and trying the <u>Peltier</u> case. Although our court decided that these actions were not grounds for reversal, they are, in my view, factors that merit consideration in any petition for leniency filed.

Fifth, Leonard Peltier was tried, found guilty, and sentenced. He has now served more than fourteen years in the federal penitentiary. At some point, a healing process must begin. We as a nation must treat Native Americans more fairly. To do so, we must recognise their unique culture and their great contributions to our nation. Favourable action by the President in the Leonard Peltier case would be an important step in this regard. I recognise that this decision lies solely within the President's discretion. I simply state my view based on the record presented to our court. I authorise you to show this letter to the President if you desire to do so...

CHAPTER TWELVE
CONTEMPORARY FEDERAL INDIAN LAW AND JURISDICTION

Today, one of the most contentious issues facing Indian nations is the erosion of Indian sovereignty and tribal jurisdiction over non-Indians within reservations by the US Supreme Court.[1] From the early days of the American republic, there have been conflicts between Indian sovereignty, federal law and state law. These seemingly irreconcilable differences are ongoing and continue to dominate contemporary federal Indian law. Although the first Supreme Court case to rule on Indian issues was *Fletcher v. Peck* (1810), the origins of what has become known as federal Indian law, that is, cases that involve Indian jurisdictional issues before the US Supreme Court, began with the Marshall trilogy; *Johnson v. McIntosh* (1823), *Cherokee Nation v. Georgia* (1831) and *Worcester v. Georgia* (1832). Since 1959, there has been a significant increase in the numbers of Indian law cases reaching the Supreme Court and particularly from 1973 the court has delivered opinions that have significantly eroded key areas of Indian civil, criminal and taxation jurisdiction on reservations. However, this does not mean that the court has consistently ruled against the tribes from 1973 to the present day. Notably, the Supreme Court has upheld tribal taxation law on a number of occasions and upheld tribal civil jurisdiction in certain circumstances. In reaction to contradictory case law and unprecedented numbers of opinions against the Indian nations, in 2003, the US Senate Committee on Indian Affairs conducted a hearing into the actions of the Supreme Court. This hearing almost resulted in the Senate passing congressional bill S.578, also known as the 'Hicks-fix', which would have overturned a number of Supreme Court decisions.[2] However, despite the goodwill of Congress, this bill failed and today the Supreme Court continues to erode inherent tribal sovereignty.

In 1959, with the case of *Williams v. Lee*, the modern era of federal Indian law began.[3] This was the first case since the Marshall trilogy that raised direct questions about inherent tribal sovereignty and the authority and jurisdiction of Indian nations over their lands and people within those lands. Although the *Williams* opinion resulted in a dramatic win for tribal authority over non-Indians it also contained the seeds of future erosion of tribal jurisdiction over non-Indians and certain lands within reservations. The erosion of inherent tribal sovereignty over non-Indians by the US Supreme Court has been a gradual process from 1959 through cases such as *Kake v. Egan* (1962), *Metlakatla Indians v. Egan* (1962), *Warren Trading Post Co. v. Arizona Tax Commission* (1965), *Kennerly v. District Court of Montana* (1971), *McClanahan v. Arizona State Tax Comm'n* (1973), *Mescalero Apache Tribe v. Jones* (1973) and *United States v. Mazurie* (1975).[4] However, some of these cases, as well as many others throughout the period, resulted in Indian victories and opinions in favour of tribal sovereignty and jurisdiction over non-Indians.[5] A change in the mindset of the US Supreme Court Justices over inherent tribal sovereignty was revealed in 1978, when the court dramatically and categorically ruled against the inherent sovereignty of the Indian nations for the first time in the modern era.

The decision handed down by the majority of Supreme Court justices in the case of *Oliphant v. Suquamish Tribe* (1978) was a bombshell that fundamentally damaged Indian rights over non-Indians and took away the right of Indians to prosecute non-Indians in tribal courts.[6] It left all Indian nations powerless to try non-Indians for crimes committed on reservations and revealed a Supreme Court that did not have the patience for tribal sovereignty in a modern-day America. In the opinion, written by Justice William H. Rehnquist, the majority of seven justices believed that because Indian nations had been incorporated into the territory of the United States many centuries ago, Indians had lost some attributes of their own sovereignty and therefore, some jurisdictional powers over non-Indians.[7] Indeed, the court concluded that in order for the Indians to have the relevant powers, it was up to Congress to pass separate legislation.[8]

Despite this loss of one of the key elements of tribal sovereignty, the Supreme Court was a lot more benevolent in Indian taxation cases up until 2001, when a unanimous Supreme Court radically limited tribal taxation authority over non-Indians in certain parts of the reservation.[9] During the early 1980s, the Supreme Court had only just decided the controversial case of *Oliphant*, but rather than apply the same principles in taxation case law, the Supreme Court in *Washington v. Confederated Tribes* (1980), also known as *Colville*, ruled that tribes had jurisdiction to tax non-Indians inside the reservation.[10] Despite this strong ruling in favour of tribal jurisdiction, the Supreme Court also allowed the states to have taxation authority over non-Indians inside the reservation. This reduced tribal profits.[11] The inherent right of the tribes to tax non-Indians was further entrenched in 1982 when the Supreme Court decided *Merrion v. Jicarilla Apache Tribe*, ruling that the inherent taxation authority of the tribes extended over non-Indians and non-Indian companies inside the reservation.[12] These modern-day precedents continued to be the legal standard until *Atkinson Trading Co., v. Shirley* (2001), when the Supreme Court justices dramatically changed course and ruled that the tribes did not have inherent sovereignty to tax non-Indians on non-Indian lands of the reservation.[13] This radical change in the principles of taxation case law was based on the governing principles of civil case law, which had generally ruled that tribes did not have jurisdiction over non-Indians in certain parts of the reservation.

One of the most significant Supreme Court decisions in the modern era of federal Indian law was *Montana v. United States* (1981).[14] The facts of the case involved whether the Crow tribe had the right to regulate non-Indian fishing and hunting rights inside the Crow reservation, based on the belief that they still owned the river bed inside the reservation. The Supreme Court declared that the tribe did not have civil jurisdiction over non-Indians inside non-Indian parts of the reservation unless the tribe could prove one of the two exceptions to the general rule, which later became known as the *Montana* exceptions. However, despite the incontrovertible damage caused by the *Montana* opinion, there were some protections offered to tribal jurisdiction when the Supreme Court upheld the findings of the Court of Appeals and the principle that the tribes had inherent sovereignty over non-Indians on tribal lands.[15] Between 1981 and 2001, the Supreme Court justices further eroded tribal civil jurisdiction over non-Indians in the reservation, and then in 2001, in the case of *Nevada v. Hicks*, the Supreme Court justices denied the application of tribal sovereignty over non-Indians on tribal and non-Indian lands inside the reservation.[16] The majority of Supreme Court justices controversially ruled that the states had inherent sovereignty over non-Indians, which usurped Indian sovereignty and jurisdiction inside their own homelands. In the future this decision has the potential to severely damage the cultures and traditions of many Indian nations.

Soon after the *Hicks* opinion, the National Congress of the American Indian (NCAI) issued a draft declaration called the Tribal Sovereignty Protection Initiative, also known as the Hicks-Fix, to combat the divisive and negative effects of Supreme Court case law.[17] The NCAI declared that all Indian nations had to work together to limit, and eventually end the destructive nature of the opinions of the Supreme Court and protect their lands and cultural identities.

In 2002, less than a year after the *Hicks* opinion, the US Senate Committee on Indian Affairs held an oversight hearing on the impact of the Supreme Court decisions, and a number of prominent Indians presented testimony about the negative impact of the Supreme Court decisions on the everyday lives of Indian peoples.[18] Senators Ben Nighthorse Campbell (1933–) and Daniel K. Inouye (1924–), both Indians, introduced the hearing and Inouye, as chairman of the committee, offered opening remarks that examined the importance of inherent tribal sovereignty throughout the centuries. He pointed out that the Supreme Court was the only branch of the federal government that was eroding the long recognised concept of tribal sovereignty. Vice-Chairman Campbell echoed the views of Inouye. The powerful remarks of the chairman and vice-chairman were followed by direct evidence from reservation Indians, such as Robert Yazzie (1947–), Chief Justice of the Navajo Nation, and John St. Clair, Chief Judge of the Shoshone and Arapahoe Tribal Court on the Wind River Indian Reservation in Wyoming, who linked the decisions of the Supreme Court to the damaging actions that were being played out on many Indian reservations. The opinions of the Supreme Court have affected the day-to-day lives of the Navajo, with non-Indians refusing to obey civil laws and pay tribal taxes and also the lives of the Arapahoe and Shoshone, with many non-Indian crimes going unpunished and non-Indians refusing to pay tribal taxes or obey tribal law.[19]

On 7 March 2003, the US Senate introduced S.578, a bill that was designed to amend the original Homeland Security Act of 2002, and allow the tribes to have the appropriate jurisdiction and authority inside the reservations to respond to acts of terrorism in light of the attacks on New York, Washington and Pennsylvania on 11 September 2001. The bill, also known as the 'Hicks-fix', reaffirmed the principles of inherent tribal sovereignty and conflicted directly with over thirty years of Supreme Court precedent that had previously eroded inherent tribal sovereignty.[20] The key points of S.578 recognised the historic government-to-government relationship between the United States and hundreds of Indian tribes. It identified contemporary tribal powers and how they could be used to defeat terrorism. However, section thirteen of the bill was the most controversial because it supported the extension of tribal sovereignty over reservation lands and all of the people within those lands, subject only to federal law. Therefore, the reaffirmation of tribal sovereignty contained in section thirteen was antithetical to the principles of the Judiciary, and the Legislature was doctrinally at odds with the Judiciary regarding the relevant tribal powers over reservation lands and over non-Indians in the reservation. However, this conflict of principles ended when S.578 and its controversial section thirteen was not passed into law. Instead, in 2005, Congress introduced a similar bill, S.477, without the controversial section thirteen and the provisions to reverse the case law of the US Supreme Court, which had protected non-Indians from tribal sovereignty and allowed state law to operate inside the reservation.[21]

The erosion of Indian sovereignty and jurisdiction over non-Indians on reservation lands and over reservation lands in general serves to limit the real and day-to-day powers of all Indian nations and unquestionably affects tribal cultures and identities, tribal economies and tribal societies within reservation homelands. The consistent erosion of Indian criminal, civil and taxation jurisdiction over non-Indians inside the reservation by the Supreme Court, particularly from 1973, continues to this day and may one day end with the nullification of all Indian power over everyone except their own tribal members on tribal land. With little protection of inherent tribal sovereignty from the Supreme Court or indeed Congress, Indian nations face an uncertain future.

SOURCES

Senator Ben Nighthorse Campbell: Statement to the US Senate Committee on Indian Affairs Hearing on the Rulings of the US Supreme Court as They Affect the Powers and Authorities of the Indian Tribal Governments, 27 February 2002

In this document, Senator Ben Nighthorse Campbell (1933–) discusses the importance of Federal–Indian relations and forcefully argues that the continued erosion of tribal sovereignty will ultimately result in the dismantling of all tribal powers.

...At yesterday's hearing on Indian trust management reform, we heard from distinguished legal scholars about the legal and political foundation of the Federal-tribal relationship. We heard about Chief Justice John Marshall, who we credit with firmly establishing the role of the U.S. Supreme Court in the Federal system and the role he played in Indian jurisprudence...

The pendulum of Federal Indian policy has been swinging back and forth right from the beginning of our Republic: Treaties, relocation, reservations, allotment, assimilation, termination, and to the current policy of self-determination. But Indian self-determination is more than a slogan to be carelessly thrown around. Chief Justice Marshall's decisions are grounded in it, and President Nixon knew what it meant in 1970, when he issued his famous Special Message to Congress on Indian Affairs.

Local decision-making is important. It is an important part of Federal Indian policy, but it's an important fact to many of us here in Congress, too, and that's why we believe in states' rights and local jurisdiction and the ability of people to make their own decisions at the local level. It is really the core of the principles of American freedoms to me and many of us that are here.

It is also a key concept because it works. Local governments know best what works for their citizens, and Indian tribes are no different in this respect than any other local government. As important as the legal tenets of Federal Indian law and policy are, I'm just as concerned with the practical results that the recent decisions of the U.S. Supreme Court will have on that policy and on the future of Indian tribal governments in America.

An Indian tribal government that can't legally defend its territory isn't a sovereign government at all. An Indian tribal government that is unable to levy a tax on a hotel or things of that nature that enjoy the benefits and the amenities of the tribe with the things that the tribe provides certainly cannot survive very long.

In short, I feel, if left unchecked, the philosophy and reasoning of the Supreme Court cases will mean that in fairly short order Indian tribes will be left with very little, if any, powers at all. If this trend continues, the current vigour of Indian tribal governments will be a distant memory, and the tribes themselves will become little more than social clubs or mechanisms for funding Federal dollars to Indian people.

The advances of rehabilitating tribal economies will be reversed if tribes lack fundamental authority over people and events that are located on their lands. Massive refederalization on Indian issues will take place, which is not healthy for the tribes, for tribal members, or local citizens, or the taxpayer. This result is not, in my view, what the U.S. Constitution sets out envisioned, and does not represent the views of, I believe, the majority on this committee or in Congress generally.

With that, Mr. Chairman, I'd ask unanimous consent that my formal statement be included in the record...

Robert Yazzie: Testimony to the US Senate Committee on Indian Affairs Hearing on the Rulings of the US Supreme Court as They Affect the Powers and Authorities of the Indian Tribal Governments, 27 February 2002

In this document, Robert Yazzie (1947–), chief justice of the Navajo Nation, outlines the social and economic impact of the court opinions on the everyday lives of the Indians, and in particular, how non-Indians have refused to obey tribal civil laws and pay tribal taxes, even though the Navajo have a fully functional and recognised legal system.

The rulings [of the United States Supreme Court] have caused many problems. Neither Indians or non-Indians have a clear understanding of what happens when someone commits an act or causes harm in Indian country, and victims of crime are helpless because of the failure of Federal prosecutors to prosecute. One of the problems from the rulings is that the docket of the Navajo Nation Supreme Court is crowded with jurisdictional challenges.

Another, businesses with right-of-ways or leases of Navajo Nation land, such as utilities and pipeline, are now claiming that the Navajo Nation has no authority to regulate or sue them. Navajos are being denied the right to access to our courts when they are involved in motor vehicle accidents or incidents on highway rights of-way across Navajo Nation land...

State police officers are entering the Navajo Nation and engaging in misconduct or violations of the Treaty of 1868. One situation involved a high-speed chase that resulted in a death. County deputies are entering the Navajo Nation to siege license plates without a hearing, and they are attempting to arrest Navajos for crimes committed outside the Navajo Nation without following Navajo extradition laws.

Navajo trial courts are being sidetracked from the nuts-and-bolts of deciding cases because of the large number of jurisdictional challenges. Creditors are now saying, "We do not need to follow Navajo Nation consumer protection laws."

In sum, recent U.S. Supreme Court decisions have made it impossible to maintain a functioning civil government in the Navajo Nation to safeguard the public.

We are all concerned of the way things have changed after September 11, 2001, but you may not be aware of the consequence for Indian country. The U.S. Department of Justice has released reports on the fact that crimes in Indian country are far higher than other parts of the United States, and domestic violence in Indian country is out of control.

Given decisions of the Federal Bureau of Investigations and the U.S. Department of Justice to make the war on terrorism and homeland defence priorities, I am concerned about our power to punish and our power to prevent crime. The ability of Indian nations to effectively exercise jurisdiction and to address crime and social problems must be maintained.

There are also fears expressed by the U.S. Supreme Court about whether tribal courts can and will protect individual civil rights. Mr. Chairman, Mr. Vice Chairman, I give you my assurance that the courts of the Navajo Nation can and do provide individuals these protections.

One controversial issue is that tribal courts do not appoint counsel for indigents. This is not true. We have a law for appointing counsel that fully complies with the Federal constitutional standard that an indigent must have counsel if there is a likelihood of a jail sentence.

Non-Indians challenge the fairness of Indian customary law. Non-Indians assume that traditional Indian law is some kind of mystery, something to be feared. In our legal system decisions are written in English, in plain words, the commonsense nature of Navajo common-law. The Navajo Nation Bar Association has 400 members. They are required to learn Navajo common law. Many non-Indian lawyers appear before the Navajo Nation courts and administrative hearing officers, making arguments in Navajo, using Navajo common-law.

The lack of jurisdiction to regulate activities and to hear a case because one or both of the parties are non-Navajo or the activity or event took place on lands that may or may not be Indian country is a nightmare. The Navajo Nation legal system is open, visible, and easy to understand. Under the Navajo Nation Bill of Rights that predates the Indian Civil Rights Act, all protections of the U.S. Constitution are available.

Recent rulings of the Supreme Court are not grounded in the Constitution. In fact, the U.S. Supreme Court has openly invited Congress to clarify these jurisdiction complexities. It is time for Congress to act.

The Navajo Nation asks this committee today to commit itself and the Congress to work with Indian nations to resolve these jurisdictional problems by legislatively recognizing and affirming the inherent authority of Indian nations to regulate the activities of all individuals within their territorial jurisdiction...

John St. Clair: Testimony to the US Senate Committee on Indian Affairs Hearing on the Rulings of the US Supreme Court as They Affect the Powers and Authorities of the Indian Tribal Governments, 27 February 2002

In the following document, John St. Clair, chief judge of the Shoshone and Arapahoe Tribal Court Wind River Indian Reservation, Wyoming, presents a succinct account of the cases that have eroded the powers of his tribe. He explains how the lack of tribal criminal powers means that many non-Indians go unpunished for criminal actions against Indians, and many have refused to pay taxes or be regulated by tribal laws within the reservation.

The Wind River Indian Reservation is approximately 3,500 square miles in area, and it's inhabited by approximately 12,000 members of both tribes, plus other Indians living within the exterior boundaries. In addition, there are about 25,000 non-Indians.

The Shoshone and Arapahoe Tribal Court, through a comprehensive law and order code, extends jurisdiction over all persons who have significant contacts with the reservation and over all Indians who commit offences that are prohibited in the law and order code. It consists of a chief Judge who must be a professional attorney and three Associate Judges. There is an appeals court that consists of remaining judges who did not sit as trial judges...

The recent U.S. Supreme Court decisions have become a major concern for the tribes due to their intensified passion to limit the sovereignty of tribal governments. As stated before by the other witnesses, tribes have lost, between 1990 and 2000, 23 out of 28 cases argued by the U.S. Supreme Court.

Beginning with *Oliphant* v. *Suquamish Tribe* in 1978, the tribes held by implication for the first time, the Court held that tribes are without inherent jurisdiction to try non-Indians for crimes. From this case, a new doctrine has emerged that tribes lack certain powers that are inconsistent with their dependent status, even when Congress has not acted to terminate those powers.

This new doctrine has been extended to the civil area, the regulatory area in *Montana* v. *United States* and the adjudicatory area in *Strate* v. *A–1 Contractors;* recently, in *Atkinson Trading Post* v. *Shirley* to a hotel occupancy tax imposed by the Navajo Nation. The most recent extension was mentioned before, *United States* v. *Hicks,* where was held that tribes lacked jurisdiction over civil suits against State officials for violating the rights of Indians on Indian land within a reservation.

The impact of Oliphant and its progeny on the powers and authorities of Indian tribal governments is that it severely restricts the ability to exercise basic regulatory and adjudicatory functions when dealing with everyday activities on reservations. When both Indians and non-Indians are involved in domestic violence, alcohol and/or drug-related disturbances, or other criminal activity, the tribes can only adjudicate the Indians while non-Indians, even when detained and turned over to State officials, go unpunished. This double standard of justice creates resentment and projects the image that non-Indians are above the law in the area where they choose to live or choose to enter into.

The effect on tribes of not being able to regulate taxing, hunting and fishing, the environment, zoning, and even traffic places limitations on economic development and self-sufficiency. Without the ability to generate revenues to fund basic governmental functions, tribes become more and more dependent upon Federal grants, contracts, and compacts as a sole source of funding. This results in increased economic burden that ultimately falls on the Federal Government.

Now tribal courts constitute one of the front-line institutions that are involved in issues involving sovereignty. While charged with providing reliable and equitable adjudication of increased numbers of criminal cases by both Indians and non-Indians and complex civil litigation, tribes are increasingly underfunded.

Tribes and their courts also agonize over the same issues that Federal and State courts do, such as violence against women, sexual abuse of children, alcohol and substance abuse, gang violence, child neglect, pollution of the air, the water, and the earth. These are just some of the common, yet complicated, problems that arise on Indian reservations…

This recent trend of the U.S. Supreme Court toward judicial termination poses the greatest threat to tribes since the allotment era of the 19th century and congressional termination of the mid-20th century, and it runs counter to the proclaimed Federal policy of self-determination that has repudiated the allotment and the termination policies.

The third sovereign, America's third sovereign, the Indian tribes occupying Indian country, have come before you today to ask that you utilize the plenary power of Congress found in the Indian commerce clause, Article I, Section 8, Clause 3, of the U.S. Constitution and request that you restore and reaffirm the inherent and regulatory adjudicatory authority of tribes over all persons and all land within Indian country as defined in 18 U.S.C. section 1151. This approach would place the exercise of jurisdiction in the hands of the tribes and the extent of it within their organic and case law, making it a question of tribal law.

I want to also add that recent Supreme Court Justices have invited Congress to rectify these decisions that diminish tribal sovereignty through legislation. Just the other day, Justice Breyer in a speech invited Congress to act…

Senator Daniel K. Inouye: Statement to the US Senate Committee on Indian Affairs Hearing on the Rulings of the US Supreme Court as They Affect the Powers and Authorities of the Indian Tribal Governments, 27 February 2002

In this document, Daniel K. Inouye (1924–), as chairman of the committee, offers opening remarks that examine the importance of inherent tribal sovereignty which pre-dates the American Constitution.

…Well before this country was founded, Indian nations exercised dominion and control over approximately 550 million acres of land. Their governments pre-existed the formation of the U.S. Government, and, indeed, were so sophisticated that the framers of the U.S. Constitution modelled what was to become America's governmental structure after the Government of the Iroquois Confederacy.

The recognition of the Indian tribes as sovereign governments has its origins in the Constitution of the United States, which in Article III, Section 8, Clause 3, provides that, "The Congress shall have the power to regulate commerce with foreign nations and among the several States and with the Indian tribes."

From that time forward, this status of Indian tribal governments as separate sovereigns has informed the laws enacted by the Congress and signed into law by the President for over 200 years, and until relatively recently, has served as the foundation for the rulings of the U.S. Supreme Court.

In the early 1830's the U.S. Supreme Court's Chief Justice John Marshall articulated the fundamental principles upon which the body of Federal Indian law would be constructed in a series of cases that are now referred to as the *Cherokee* cases. Yesterday this committee received testimony from Professor Reid Chambers, who observed that at the time of Chief Justice Marshall's rulings, the Cherokee Nation had a written constitution, an elected bicameral legislature, a tribal judicial system, schools, an established military, a written language, and a much higher adult literacy rate than any State of the Union at that time.

Today tribal governments have not only discarded the mantle of "ward" to the United States "guardian" of Chief Justice Marshall's day, but have assumed a wide range of government responsibilities that were formally the exclusive province of the National Government.

Although Federal policies have vacillated and congressional acts have reflected those changes in policy, beginning in 1934 with the enactment of the Indian Reorganization Act, and reinforced in 1970 with the establishment of the Federal Policy of Native Self-Determination and Tribal Self-Governance, two of the three branches of the U.S. Government have consistently acted in concert to reaffirm the legal status of Indian tribal governments as sovereign governments.

We are here today because there is a third branch of the U.S. Government, the Judicial Branch, that appears to be headed in a decidedly different direction than the other two branches of the National Government. If there were a few aberrations from the Supreme Court precedent and Federal statutory law, one might not have cause for concern, but those that study the law and the rulings of the U.S. Supreme Court instruct us that the Court is on a steady march to divest native governments of their governmental powers and authorities.

Principles long and well-established, such as the fact that tribal governments retain all of their inherent sovereign powers and authorities not relinquished by them in treaties or abrogated by an express act of the Congress, appear to have been cast aside. The fundamental principle that tribal governments have authority to exercise jurisdiction over their territory, just as other governments do, is being steadily eroded by the Court's rulings.

Notwithstanding the provisions of the U.S. Constitution proscribing discrimination on the basis of race, the Court seems to be consistently imposing limitations on the exercise of tribal government jurisdiction based upon the race and ethnicity of those over whom jurisdiction is exercised.

The historical foundations of the relationship between sovereign governments, the Federal, State, and tribal governments, appear to no longer have any legal import in the Court's rulings.

Last, but certainly not least, from the perspective of the branch of the government that the U.S. Constitution charges with conducting relations with foreign governments, the several states, and Indian tribes, the Congress—one is hard-pressed to find reference in the Court's opinions to the context in which the rest of America is operating; namely, Federal laws and the policies they reflect…

National Congress of American Indians (NCAI): Tribal Sovereignty Protection Initiative (The 'Hicks-Fix'), 2001

In the following document, the NCAI declaration describes the cases that have limited inherent tribal sovereignty and the ways in which Indian peoples need to be proactive in order to defend their legal rights and more importantly their cultural identities.

The United States Supreme Court issued five decisions affecting the rights of Indian tribes in its recent term that ended on Jun 28, 2001. The Court decided against the tribes in four out of five instances. In particular, the decisions in Nevada v. Hicks and Atkinson Trading Co. v. Shirley raise strong concerns that the Supreme Court is on an accelerating trend toward removing tribal jurisdiction over the conduct of non-Indians within tribal territory.

Even as tribal governments have made significant strides in reasserting their rights to govern, over the last twenty years Supreme Court decisions, such as Montana v. U.S., Brendale v. Yakima Nation, Oliphant vs. Suquamish Indian Tribe, and Strate v. A-1 Contractors have significantly limited the civil and criminal jurisdiction of tribal governments over events that occur within their territorial boundaries. The most recent Supreme Court cases make it clear that tribal governments are in an increasingly defensive posture in the federal courts, and it is likely that the upcoming years will prove to be even more damaging if this defensive posture is maintained. In the long term, this erosion of jurisdiction threatens to make tribal governments ineffective in protecting the cultural identities of their communities.

On September 11, 2001, tribal leaders from across the country met in Washington, DC, to discuss these recent court decisions. They reached consensus to mount an organized effort to halt and reverse the Supreme Court's erosion of tribal sovereignty. The Sovereignty Protection Initiative will:

- Develop federal legislation to reaffirm tribal jurisdiction
- Form a Supreme Court project to support and coordinate tribal advocacy before the Supreme Court
- Promote strategies for tribal governance that will Protect tribal jurisdiction
- Increase tribal participation in the selection of the federal judiciary
- Develop a media and advocacy strategy to inform Congress, the public, and tribal leadership about tribal governance and that will promote the overall initiative
- Implement a fundraising campaign to support NCAI and NARF and their related expenses in promoting the initiative

Oliphant v. Suquamish Indian Tribe, 1978

In the following document, the key facts and observations made in the opinion of Justice William H. Rehnquist are outlined. Since, in the view of the Supreme Court, Indian peoples had never in their history had the right to prosecute non-Indians they did not allow them to do so in 1978.

...The Suquamish Indians are governed by a tribal government which in 1973 adopted a Law and Order Code. The Code, which covers a variety of offences from theft to rape, purports to extend the Tribe's criminal jurisdiction over both Indians and non-Indians...

...non-Indian residents of the Port Madison Reservation...Mark David Oliphant was arrested by tribal authorities during the Suquamish's annual Chief Seattle Days celebration and charged with assaulting a tribal officer and resisting arrest...Daniel B. Belgrade was arrested by tribal authorities after an alleged high-speed race along the Reservation highways that only ended when Belgrade collided with a tribal police vehicle...

Respondents do not contend that their exercise of criminal jurisdiction over non-Indians stems from affirmative congressional authorization or treaty provision. Instead, respondents urge that such jurisdiction flows automatically from the "Tribe's retained inherent powers of government over the Port Madison Indian Reservation." Seizing on language in our opinions describing Indian tribes as "quasi-sovereign entities"...the Court of Appeals agreed and held that Indian tribes, "though conquered and dependent, retain those powers of autonomous states that are neither inconsistent with their status nor expressly terminated by Congress." According to the Court of Appeals, criminal jurisdiction over anyone committing an offence on the reservation is a "sine qua non" of such powers.

The Suquamish Indian Tribe does not stand alone today in its assumption of criminal jurisdiction over non-Indians. Of the 127 reservation court systems that currently exercise criminal jurisdiction in the United States, 33 purport to extend that jurisdiction to non-Indians. Twelve other Indian tribes have enacted ordinances which would permit the assumption of criminal jurisdiction over non-Indians. Like the Suquamish these tribes claim authority to try non-Indians not on the basis of congressional statute or treaty provision but by reason of their retained national sovereignty.

The effort by Indian tribal courts to exercise criminal jurisdiction over non-Indians, however, is a relatively new phenomenon. And where the effort has been made in the past, it has been held that the jurisdiction did not exist. Until the middle of this century, few Indian tribes maintained any semblance of a formal court system...

But the problem did not lie entirely dormant for two centuries. A few tribes during the 19th century did have formal criminal systems. From the earliest treaties with these tribes, it was apparently assumed that the tribes did not have criminal jurisdiction over non-Indians absent a congressional statute or treaty provision to that effect...

...While Congress never expressly forbade Indian tribes to impose criminal penalties on non-Indians, we now make express our implicit conclusion of nearly a century ago that Congress consistently believed this to be the necessary result of its repeated legislative actions.

...While not conclusive on the issue before us, the commonly shared presumption of Congress, the Executive Branch, and lower federal courts that tribal courts do not have the power to try non-Indians carries considerable weight...

...But an examination of our earlier precedents satisfies us that, even ignoring treaty provisions and congressional policy, Indians do not have criminal jurisdiction over non-Indians absent affirmative delegation of such power by Congress. Indian tribes do retain elements of "quasi-sovereign" authority after ceding their lands to the United States and announcing their dependence on the Federal Government...But the tribes' retained powers are not such that they are limited only by specific restrictions in treaties or congressional enactments. As the Court of Appeals recognized, Indian tribes are prohibited from exercising both those powers of autonomous states that are expressly terminated by Congress and those powers "inconsistent with their status"...

...Upon incorporation into the territory of the United States, the Indian tribes thereby come under the territorial sovereignty of the United States and their exercise of separate power is constrained so as not to conflict with the interests of this overriding sovereignty...

We have already described some of the inherent limitations on tribal powers that stem from their incorporation into the United States. In Johnson v. M'Intosh, we noted that the Indian tribes' "power to dispose of the soil at their own will, to whomsoever they pleased," was inherently lost to the overriding sovereignty of the United States. And in Cherokee Nation v. Georgia, the Chief

Justice observed that since Indian tribes are "completely under the sovereignty and dominion of the United States, ... any attempt [by foreign nations] to acquire their lands, or to form a political connexion with them, would be considered by all as an invasion of our territory, and an act of hostility."

...In the first case to reach this Court dealing with the status of Indian tribes, Mr. Justice Johnson in a separate concurrence summarized the nature of the limitations inherently flowing from the overriding sovereignty of the United States as follows: "[T]he restrictions upon the right of soil in the Indians, amount ... to an exclusion of all competitors [to the United States] from their markets; and the limitation upon their sovereignty amounts to the right of governing every person within their limits except themselves." Fletcher v. Peck (1810)...By submitting to the overriding sovereignty of the United States, Indian tribes therefore necessarily give up their power to try non-Indian citizens of the United States except in a manner acceptable to Congress. This principle would have been obvious a century ago when most Indian tribes were characterized by a "want of fixed laws [and] of competent tribunals of justice"...It should be no less obvious today, even though present-day Indian tribal courts embody dramatic advances over their historical antecedents.

We recognize that some Indian tribal court systems have become increasingly sophisticated and resemble in many respects their state counterparts...Finally, we are not unaware of the prevalence of non-Indian crime on today's reservations which the tribes forcefully argue requires the ability to try non-Indians. But these are considerations for Congress to weigh in deciding whether Indian tribes should finally be authorized to try non-Indians. They have little relevance to the principles which lead us to conclude that Indian tribes do not have inherent jurisdiction to try and to punish non-Indians...

Montana v. United States, 1981

Provided here are key sections from the Supreme Court opinion which ruled that Indian nations did not have civil jurisdiction over non-Indians in non-Indian lands within reservations, unless they could prove one of two exceptions to this general rule.

...This case concerns the sources and scope of the power of an Indian tribe to regulate hunting and fishing by non-Indians on lands within its reservation owned in fee simple by non-Indians. Relying on its purported ownership of the bed of the Big Horn River, on the treaties which created its reservation, and on its inherent power as a sovereign, the Crow Tribe of Montana claims the authority to prohibit all hunting and fishing by nonmembers of the Tribe on non-Indian property within reservation boundaries...

...Today, roughly 52 percent of the reservation is allotted to members of the Tribe and held by the United States in trust for them, 17 percent is held in trust for the Tribe itself, and approximately 28 percent is held in fee by non-Indians. The State of Montana owns in fee simple 2 percent of the reservation, the United States less than 1 percent.

...Since the 1950's, the Crow Tribal Council has passed several resolutions respecting hunting and fishing on the reservation, including Resolution No. 74–05, the occasion for this lawsuit. That resolution prohibits hunting and fishing within the reservation by anyone who is not a member of the Tribe. The State of Montana, however, has continued to assert its authority to regulate hunting and fishing by non-Indians within the reservation.

Though the parties in this case have raised broad questions about the power of the Tribe to regulate hunting and fishing by non-Indians on the reservation, the regulatory issue before us is a narrow one. The Court of Appeals held that the Tribe may prohibit nonmembers from hunting or fishing on land belonging to the Tribe or held by the United States in trust for the Tribe, and with this holding we can readily agree...What remains is the question of the power of the Tribe to regulate non-Indian fishing and hunting on reservation land owned in fee by nonmembers of the Tribe...

...as [a] source [of] the Tribe's power to regulate non-Indian hunting and fishing on non-Indian lands within the reservation, the Court of Appeals also identified...the inherent sovereignty of the Tribe over the entire Crow Reservation...

This Court most recently reviewed the principles of inherent sovereignty in United States v. Wheeler. In that case, noting that Indian tribes are "unique aggregations possessing attributes of sovereignty over both their members and their territory," the Court upheld the power of a tribe to punish tribal members who violate tribal criminal laws. But the Court was careful to note that, through their original incorporation into the United States as well as through specific treaties and statutes, the Indian tribes have lost many of the attributes of sovereignty. The Court distinguished between those inherent powers retained by the tribes and those divested:

"The areas in which such implicit divestiture of sovereignty has been held to have occurred are those involving the relations between an Indian tribe and nonmembers of the tribe...

These limitations rest on the fact that the dependent status of Indian tribes within our territorial jurisdiction is necessarily inconsistent with their freedom independently to determine their external relations. But the powers of self-government, including the power to prescribe and enforce internal criminal laws, are of a different type. They involve only the relations among members of a tribe. Thus, they are not such powers as would necessarily be lost by virtue of a tribe's dependent status"...

Thus, in addition to the power to punish tribal offenders, the Indian tribes retain their inherent power to determine tribal membership, to regulate domestic relations among members, and to prescribe rules of inheritance for members. But exercise of tribal power beyond what is necessary to protect tribal self-government or to control internal relations is inconsistent with the dependent status of the tribes, and so cannot survive without express congressional delegation ... Since regulation of hunting and fishing by nonmembers of a tribe on lands no longer owned by the tribe bears no clear relationship to tribal self-government or internal relations, the general principles of retained inherent sovereignty did not authorize the Crow Tribe to adopt Resolution No. 74–05.

The Court recently applied these general principles in Oliphant v. Suquamish Indian Tribe, rejecting a tribal claim of inherent sovereign authority to exercise criminal jurisdiction over non-Indians. Stressing that Indian tribes cannot exercise power inconsistent with their diminished status as sovereigns, the Court quoted Justice Johnson's words in his concurrence in Fletcher v. Peck - the first Indian case to reach this Court - that the Indian tribes have lost any "right of governing every person within their limits except themselves." Though Oliphant only determined inherent tribal authority in criminal matters, the principles on which it relied support the general proposition that the inherent sovereign powers of an Indian tribe do not extend to the activities of nonmembers of the tribe. To be sure, Indian tribes retain inherent sovereign power to exercise some forms of civil jurisdiction over non-Indians on their reservations, even on non-Indian fee lands. A tribe may regulate, through taxation, licensing, or other means, the activities of nonmembers who enter consensual relationships with the tribe or its members, through commercial dealing, contracts, leases, or other arrangements ... A tribe may also retain inherent power to exercise civil authority over the conduct of non-Indians on fee lands within its reservation when that conduct threatens or has some direct effect on the political integrity, the economic security, or the health or welfare of the tribe...

No such circumstances, however, are involved in this case. Non-Indian hunters and fishermen on non-Indian fee land do not enter any agreements or dealings with the Crow Tribe so as to subject themselves to tribal civil jurisdiction. And nothing in this case suggests that such non-Indian hunting and fishing so threaten the Tribe's political or economic security as to justify tribal regulation...

Nevada v. Hicks, 2001

In the following text, key extracts from the case highlight the limitations placed on the civil jurisdiction of Indian nations over non-Indians within their own reservations, and the potency of state law inside the reservations.

...This case presents the question whether a tribal court may assert jurisdiction over civil claims against state officials who entered tribal land to execute a search warrant against a tribe member suspected of having violated state law outside the reservation.

[Floyd] Hicks is one of about 900 members of the Fallon Paiute-Shoshone Tribes of western Nevada. He resides on the Tribes' reservation of approximately 8000 acres established by federal statute in 1908. In 1990 Hicks came under suspicion of having killed, off the reservation, a California bighorn sheep, a gross misdemeanour under Nevada law...

Approximately one year later, a tribal police officer reported to the warden that he had observed two mounted bighorn sheep heads in respondent's home...and respondent's home was again (unsuccessfully) searched by three wardens and additional tribal officers.

Respondent, claiming that his sheep-heads had been damaged, and that the second search exceeded the bounds of the warrant, brought suit against the Tribal Judge, the tribal officers, the state wardens in their individual and official capacities, and the State of Nevada in the Tribal Court in and for the Fallon Paiute-Shoshone Tribes...

We first inquire, therefore, whether the Fallon Paiute-Shoshone Tribes-- either as an exercise of their inherent sovereignty, or under grant of federal authority--can regulate state wardens executing a search warrant for evidence of an off-reservation crime.

Indian tribes' regulatory authority over non-members is governed by the principles set forth in *Montana* v. *United States* (1981), which we have called the "pathmarking case" on the subject ... In deciding whether the Crow Tribe could regulate hunting and fishing by non-members on land held in fee simple by non-members, *Montana* observed that, under our decision in *Oliphant* v. *Suquamish Tribe* (1978), tribes lack criminal jurisdiction over non-members. Although, it continued, "*Oliphant* only determined inherent tribal authority in criminal matters, the principles on which it relied support the general proposition that the inherent sovereign powers of an Indian tribe do not extend to the activities of non-members of the tribe." ... Where non-members are concerned, the "exercise of tribal power *beyond what is necessary to protect tribal self-government or to control internal relations* is inconsistent with the dependent status of the tribes, and so cannot survive without express congressional delegation."...

Both *Montana* and *Strate* rejected tribal authority to regulate non-members' activities on land over which the tribe could not "assert a landowner's right to occupy and exclude,"...Respondents and the United States argue that since Hicks's home and yard *are* on tribe-owned land within the reservation, the Tribe may make its exercise of regulatory authority over non-members a condition of non-members' entry. Not necessarily. While it is certainly true that the non-Indian ownership status of the land was central to the analysis in both *Montana* and *Strate*, the reason that was so was *not* that Indian ownership suspends the "general proposition" derived from *Oliphant* that "the inherent sovereign powers of an Indian tribe do not extend to the activities of non-members of the tribe" except to the extent "necessary to protect tribal self-government or to control internal relations." *Oliphant* itself drew no distinctions based on the status of land. And *Montana*, after announcing the general rule of no jurisdiction over non-members, cautioned that "[t]o be sure, Indian tribes retain inherent sovereign power to exercise some forms of civil jurisdiction over non-Indians on their reservations, even on non-Indian fee lands,"--clearly implying that the general rule of *Montana* applies to both Indian and non-Indian land. The ownership status of land, in other words, is only one factor to consider in determining whether regulation of the activities of non-members is "necessary to protect tribal self-government or to control internal relations." It may sometimes be a dispositive factor. Hitherto, the absence of tribal ownership has been virtually conclusive of the absence of tribal civil jurisdiction; with one minor exception, we have never upheld under *Montana* the extension of tribal civil authority over non-members on non-Indian land…But the existence of tribal ownership is not alone enough to support regulatory jurisdiction over non-members…

In *Strate*, we explained that what is necessary to protect tribal self-government and control internal relations can be understood by looking at the examples of tribal power to which *Montana* referred: tribes have authority "[to punish tribal offenders,] to determine tribal membership, to regulate domestic relations among members, and to prescribe rules of inheritance for members"…Tribal assertion of regulatory authority over non-members must be connected to that right of the Indians to make their own laws and be governed by them…

Our cases make clear that the Indians' right to make their own laws and be governed by them does not exclude all state regulatory authority on the reservation. State sovereignty does not end at a reservation's border. Though tribes are often referred to as "sovereign" entities, it was "long ago" that "the Court departed from Chief Justice Marshall's view that 'the laws of [a State] can have no force' within reservation boundaries. "Ordinarily," it is now clear, "an Indian reservation is considered part of the territory of the State."…

While it is not entirely clear from our precedent whether [state] authority entails the corollary right to enter a reservation (including Indian-fee lands) for enforcement purposes, several of our opinions point in that direction…

We conclude today, in accordance with these prior statements, that tribal authority to regulate state officers in executing process related to the violation, off reservation, of state laws is not essential to tribal self-government or internal relations--to "the right to make laws and be ruled by them." The State's interest in execution of process is considerable, and even when it relates to Indian-fee lands it no more impairs the tribe's self-government than federal enforcement of federal law impairs state government…

The States' inherent jurisdiction on reservations can of course be stripped by Congress…But with regard to the jurisdiction at issue here that has not occurred…

Because the Fallon Paiute-Shoshone Tribes lacked legislative authority to restrict, condition, or otherwise regulate the ability of state officials to investigate off-reservation violations of state law, they also lacked adjudicative authority to hear respondent's claim that those officials violated tribal law in the performance of their duties...State officials operating on a reservation to investigate off-reservation violations of state law are properly held accountable for tortuous conduct and civil rights violations in either state or federal court, but not in tribal court.

Washington v. Confederated Tribes (Colville), 1980

Provided here are some of the key parts of a long opinion that discuss the inherent sovereignty of the tribes to tax non-Indians inside the reservations.

In recent Terms we have more than once addressed the intricate problem of state taxation of matters involving Indian tribes and their members ... We return to that vexing area in the present cases. Although a variety of questions are presented, perhaps the most significant is whether an Indian tribe ousts a State from any power to tax on-reservation purchases by non-members of the tribe by imposing its own tax on the transaction or by otherwise earning revenues from the tribal business.

...At the outset, the State argues that the Colville, Makah, and Lummi Tribes have no power to impose their cigarette taxes on nontribal purchasers. We disagree. The power to tax transactions occurring on trust lands and significantly involving a tribe or its members is a fundamental attribute of sovereignty which the tribes retain unless divested of it by federal law or necessary implication of their dependent status...

The widely held understanding within the Federal Government has always been that federal law to date has not worked a divestiture of Indian taxing power. Executive Branch officials have consistently recognized that Indian tribes possess a broad measure of civil jurisdiction over the activities of non-Indians on Indian reservation lands in which the tribes have a significant interest...According to the Solicitor of the Department of the Interior:

"Chief among the powers of sovereignty recognized as pertaining to an Indian tribe is the power of taxation. Except where Congress has provided otherwise, this power may be exercised over members of the tribe and over non-members, so far as such non-members may accept privileges of trade, residence, etc., to which taxes may be attached as conditions."

Federal courts also have acknowledged tribal power to tax non-Indians entering the reservation to engage in economic activity...No federal statute cited to us shows any congressional departure from this view. To the contrary, authority to tax the activities or property of non-Indians taking place or situated on Indian lands, in cases where the tribe has a significant interest in the subject matter ... In these respects the present cases differ sharply from Oliphant v. Suquamish Indian Tribe (1978), in which we stressed the shared assumptions of the Executive, Judicial, and Legislative Departments that Indian tribes could not exercise criminal jurisdiction over non-Indians.

Tribal powers are not implicitly divested by virtue of the tribes' dependent status. This Court has found such a divestiture in cases where the exercise of tribal sovereignty would be inconsistent with the overriding interests of the National Government, as when the tribes seek to engage in foreign relations, alienate their lands to non-Indians without federal consent, or prosecute non-Indians in tribal courts which do not accord the full protections of the Bill of Rights...In the present cases, we can see no overriding federal interest that would necessarily be frustrated by tribal taxation. And even if the State's interests were implicated by the tribal taxes, a question we need not decide, it must be remembered that tribal sovereignty is dependent on, and subordinate to, only the Federal Government, not the States.

The Tribes contend that their involvement in the operation and taxation of cigarette marketing on the reservation ousts the State from any power to exact its sales and cigarette taxes from non-members purchasing cigarettes at tribal smokeshops...

It is painfully apparent that the value marketed by the smokeshops to persons coming from outside is not generated on the reservations by activities in which the Tribes have a significant interest...What the smokeshops offer these customers, and what is not available elsewhere, is solely an exemption from state taxation. The Tribes assert the power to create such exemptions by imposing their own taxes or otherwise earning revenues by participating in the reservation enterprises. If this assertion were accepted, the Tribes could impose a nominal tax and open chains of discount stores at reservation borders, selling goods of all descriptions at deep discounts and drawing custom from surrounding areas. We do not believe that principles of federal Indian law, whether stated in terms of pre-emption, tribal self-government, or otherwise, authorize Indian tribes thus to market an exemption from state taxation to persons who would normally do their business elsewhere.

...Washington does not infringe the right of reservation Indians to "make their own laws and be ruled by them," Williams v. Lee (1959), merely because the result of imposing its taxes will be to deprive the Tribes of revenues which they currently are receiving. The principle of tribal self-government, grounded in notions of inherent sovereignty and in congressional policies, seeks an accommodation between the interests of the Tribes and the Federal Government, on the one hand, and those of the State, on the other...While the Tribes do have an interest in raising revenues for essential governmental programs, that interest is strongest when the revenues are derived from value generated on the reservation by activities involving the Tribes and when the taxpayer is the recipient of tribal services. The State also has a legitimate governmental interest in raising revenues, and that interest is likewise strongest when the tax is directed at off-reservation value and when the taxpayer is the recipient of state services...

A second asserted ground for the invalidity of the state taxes is that they somehow conflict with the Tribes' cigarette ordinances and thereby are subject to pre-emption or contravene the principle of tribal self-government. This argument need not detain us. There is no direct conflict between the state and tribal schemes, since each government is free to impose its taxes without ousting the other...

Merrion v. Jicarilla Apache Tribe, 1982

The following excerpts are taken from the opinion that ruled in favour of Indian nations, declaring that they have the right to tax non-Indians and non-Indian companies inside the reservation.

Pursuant to long-term leases with the Jicarilla Apache Tribe, petitioners, 21 lessees, extract and produce oil and gas from the Tribe's reservation lands...petitioners challenge an ordinance enacted by the Tribe imposing a severance tax on "any oil and natural gas severed, saved and removed from Tribal lands."

...Petitioners argue, and the dissent agrees, that an Indian tribe's authority to tax non-Indians who do business on the reservation stems exclusively from its power to exclude such persons from tribal lands...We disagree with the premise that the power to tax derives only from the power to exclude...

In Washington v. Confederated Tribes of Colville Indian Reservation (1980), we addressed the Indian tribes' authority to impose taxes on non-Indians doing business on the reservation. We held that "[t]he power to tax transactions occurring on trust lands and significantly involving a tribe or its members is a fundamental attribute of sovereignty which the tribes retain unless divested of it by federal law or necessary implication of their dependent status."...The power to tax is an essential attribute of Indian sovereignty because it is a necessary instrument of self-government and territorial management. This power enables a tribal government to raise revenues for its essential services. The power does not derive solely from the Indian tribe's power to exclude non-Indians from tribal lands. Instead, it derives from the tribe's general authority, as sovereign, to control economic activity within its jurisdiction, and to defray the cost of providing governmental services by requiring contributions from persons or enterprises engaged in economic activities within that jurisdiction...

The petitioners avail themselves of the "substantial privilege of carrying on business" on the reservation ... They benefit from the provision of police protection and other governmental services, as well as from "'the advantages of a civilized society'" that are assured by the existence of tribal government ... Numerous other governmental entities levy a general revenue tax similar to that imposed by the Jicarilla Tribe when they provide comparable services. Under these circumstances, there is nothing exceptional in requiring petitioners to contribute through taxes to the general cost of tribal government...

Viewing the taxing power of Indian tribes as an essential instrument of self-government and territorial management has been a shared assumption of all three branches of the Federal Government ... In Colville, the Court relied in part on a 1934 opinion of the Solicitor for the Department of the Interior. In this opinion, the Solicitor recognized that, in the absence of congressional action to the contrary, the tribes' sovereign power to tax "'may be exercised over members of the tribe and over non-members, so far as such non-members may accept privileges of trade, residence, etc., to which taxes may be attached as conditions.'" ... Colville further noted that official executive pronouncements have repeatedly recognized that "Indian tribes possess a broad measure of civil jurisdiction over the activities of non-Indians on Indian reservation lands in which the tribes have a significant interest ... , including jurisdiction to tax."...

Similarly, Congress has acknowledged that the tribal power to tax is one of the tools necessary to self-government and territorial control...

Thus, the views of the three federal branches of government, as well as general principles of taxation, confirm that Indian tribes enjoy authority to finance their governmental services through taxation of non-Indians who benefit from those services. Indeed, the conception of Indian sovereignty that this Court has consistently reaffirmed permits no other conclusion. As we observed in United States v. Mazurie ... "Indian tribes within 'Indian country' are a good deal more than 'private, voluntary organizations.'" They "are unique aggregations possessing attributes of sovereignty over both their members and their territory." ... Adhering to this understanding, we conclude that the Tribe's authority to tax non-Indians who conduct business on the reservation does not simply derive from the Tribe's power to exclude such persons, but is an inherent power necessary to tribal self-government and territorial management...

We are not persuaded by the dissent's attempt to limit an Indian tribe's authority to tax non-Indians by asserting that its only source is the tribe's power to exclude such persons from tribal lands. Limiting the tribes' authority to tax in this manner contradicts the conception that Indian tribes are domestic, dependent nations, as well as the common understanding that the sovereign taxing power is a tool for raising revenue necessary to cover the costs of government.

...Most important, petitioners and the dissent confuse the Tribe's role as commercial partner with its role as sovereign. This confusion relegates the powers of sovereignty to the bargaining process undertaken in each of the sovereign's commercial agreements. It is one thing to find that the Tribe has agreed to sell the right to use the land and take from it valuable minerals; it is quite another to find that the Tribe has abandoned its sovereign powers simply because it has not expressly reserved them through a contract.

Confusing these two results denigrates Indian sovereignty. Indeed, the dissent apparently views the tribal power to exclude, as well as the derivative authority to tax, as merely the power possessed by any individual landowner or any social group to attach conditions, including a "tax" or fee, to the entry by a stranger onto private land or into the social group, and not as a sovereign power. The dissent does pay lipservice to the established views that Indian tribes retain those fundamental attributes of sovereignty, including the power to tax transactions that occur on tribal lands, which have not been divested by Congress or by necessary implication of the tribe's dependent status ... and that tribes "are a good deal more than 'private, voluntary organizations.'" United States v. Mazurie. However, in arguing that the Tribe somehow "lost" its power to tax petitioners by not including a taxing provision in the original leases or otherwise notifying petitioners that the Tribe retained and might later exercise its sovereign right to tax them, the dissent attaches little significance to the sovereign nature of the tribal authority to tax, and it obviously views tribal authority as little more than a landowner's contractual right...

Moreover, the dissent implies that the power to tax depends on the consent of the taxed as well as on the Tribe's power to exclude non-Indians. Whatever place consent may have in contractual matters and in the creation of democratic governments, it has little if any role in measuring the validity of an exercise of legitimate sovereign authority. Requiring the consent of the entrant deposits in the hands of the excludable non-Indian the source of the tribe's power, when the power instead derives from sovereignty itself. Only the Federal Government may limit a tribe's exercise of its sovereign authority ... Indian sovereignty is not conditioned on the assent of a non-member; to the contrary, the non-member's presence and conduct on Indian lands are conditioned by the limitations the tribe may choose to impose.

...Without regard to its source, sovereign power, even when unexercised, is an enduring presence that governs all contracts subject to the sovereign's jurisdiction, and will remain intact unless surrendered in unmistakable terms.

No claim is asserted in this litigation, nor could one be, that petitioners' leases contain the clear and unmistakable surrender of taxing power required for its extinction. We could find a waiver of the Tribe's taxing power only if we inferred it from silence in the leases. To presume that a sovereign forever waives the right to exercise one of its sovereign powers unless it expressly reserves the right to exercise that power in a commercial agreement turns the concept of sovereignty on its head, and we do not adopt this analysis.

...In Worcester v. Georgia, Chief Justice Marshall observed that Indian tribes had "always been considered as distinct, independent political communities, retaining their original natural rights." Although the tribes are subject to the authority of the Federal Government, the "weaker power does not surrender its independence - its right to self-government, by associating with a stronger, and taking its protection." Adhering to this understanding, we conclude that the Tribe did not surrender its authority to tax the mining activities of petitioners, whether this authority is deemed to arise from the Tribe's inherent power of self-government or from its inherent power to exclude non-members. Therefore, the Tribe may enforce its severance tax unless and until Congress divests this power, an action that Congress has not taken to date...

Atkinson Trading Co. v. Shirley, 2001

Provided here are important extracts from the opinion that ruled against previous taxation cases issued by the Supreme Court and declared that tribes had lost the right to tax non-Indians on non-Indian lands of the reservation.

...In *Montana* v. *United States* (1981), we held that, with limited exceptions, Indian tribes lack civil authority over the conduct of non-members on non-Indian fee land within a reservation. The question with which we are presented is whether this general rule applies to tribal attempts to tax non-member activity occurring on non-Indian fee land. We hold that it does...

In 1916, Hubert Richardson, lured by the possibility of trading with wealthy Gray Mountain Navajo cattlemen, built the Cameron Trading Post just south of the Little Colorado River near Cameron, Arizona. G. Richardson ... purchased the land directly from the United States, but the Navajo Nation Reservation, which had been established in 1868, was later extended eight miles south so that the Cameron Trading Post fell within its exterior boundaries ... This 1934 enlargement of the Navajo Reservation--which today stretches across northeast Arizona, northwest New Mexico, and southeast Utah--did not alter the status of the property: It is, like millions of acres throughout the United States, non-Indian fee land within a tribal reservation.

Richardson's "drafty, wooden store building and four small, one-room-shack cabins overlooking the bare river canyon," ... have since evolved into a business complex consisting of a hotel, restaurant, cafeteria, gallery, curio shop, retail store, and recreational vehicle facility. The current owner, petitioner Atkinson Trading Company, Inc., benefits from the Cameron Trading Post's location near the intersection of Arizona Highway 64 (which leads west to the Grand Canyon) and United States Highway 89 (which connects Flagstaff on the south with Glen Canyon Dam to the north). A significant portion of petitioner's hotel business stems from tourists on their way to or from the Grand Canyon National Park.

In 1992, the Navajo Nation enacted a hotel occupancy tax, which imposes an 8 percent tax upon any hotel room located within the exterior boundaries of the Navajo Nation Reservation ... The non-member guests at the Cameron Trading Post pay approximately $84,000 in taxes to respondents annually...

Tribal jurisdiction is limited: For powers not expressly conferred them by federal statute or treaty, Indian tribes must rely upon their retained or inherent sovereignty. In *Montana*, the most exhaustively reasoned of our modern cases addressing this latter authority, we observed that Indian tribe power over non-members on non-Indian fee land is sharply circumscribed ... Surveying our cases in this area dating back to 1810, see *Fletcher* v. *Peck* (1810) (Johnson, J., concurring) (stating that Indian tribes have lost any "right of governing every person within their limits except themselves"), we noted that "through their original incorporation into the United States as well as through specific treaties and statutes, Indian tribes have lost many of the attributes of sovereignty." ... We concluded that the inherent sovereignty of Indian tribes was limited to "their members and their territory": "[E]xercise of tribal power beyond what is necessary to protect tribal self-government or to control internal relations is inconsistent with the dependent status of the tribes."...

Although we extracted from our precedents "the general proposition that the inherent sovereign powers of an Indian tribe do not extend to the activities of non-members of the tribe," ... we nonetheless noted in *Montana* two possible bases for tribal jurisdiction over non-Indian fee land. First, "[a] tribe may regulate, through taxation, licensing, or other means, the activities of non-members who enter consensual relationships with the tribe or its members, through commercial dealings, contracts, leases, or other arrangements." ... Second, "[a] tribe may ... exercise civil authority over the conduct of non-Indians on fee lands within its reservation when that conduct threatens or has some direct effect on the political integrity, the economic security, or the health or welfare of the tribe."...

The framework set forth in *Montana* "broadly addressed the concept of 'inherent sovereignty.'" *Strate* v. *A-1 Contractors* (1997) ... In *Strate*, we dealt with the Three Affiliated Tribes' assertion of judicial jurisdiction over an automobile accident involving two non-members travelling on a state highway within the reservation ... Recognizing that *Montana* "immediately involved regulatory authority," we nonetheless concluded that its reasoning had "delineated--in a main rule and exceptions--the bounds of the power tribes retain to exercise 'forms of civil jurisdiction over non-Indians.'" ... "Subject to controlling provisions in treaties and statutes, and the two exceptions identified in *Montana*, the *civil authority* of Indian tribes and their courts with respect to non-Indian fee lands generally 'do[es] not extend to the activities of non-members of the tribe.'"...

Citing our decision in *Merrion*, respondents submit that *Montana* and *Strate* do not restrict an Indian tribe's power to impose revenue-raising taxes. In *Merrion*, just one year after our decision in *Montana*, we upheld a severance tax imposed by the Jicarilla Apache Tribe upon non-Indian lessees authorized to extract oil and gas from tribal land. In so doing, we noted that the power to tax derives not solely from an Indian tribe's power to exclude non-Indians from tribal land, but also from an Indian tribe's "general authority, as sovereign, to control economic activity within its jurisdiction."...

Merrion, however, was careful to note that an Indian tribe's inherent power to tax only extended to "'transactions occurring on *trust lands* and significantly involving a tribe or its members.'" ... There are undoubtedly parts of the *Merrion* opinion that suggest a broader scope for tribal taxing authority than the quoted language above. But *Merrion* involved a tax that only applied to activity occurring on the reservation, and its holding is therefore easily reconcilable with the *Montana-Strate* line of authority, which we deem to be controlling ... An Indian tribe's sovereign power to tax--whatever its derivation--reaches no further than tribal land.

We therefore do not read *Merrion* to exempt taxation from *Montana's* general rule that Indian tribes lack civil authority over non-members on non-Indian fee land. Accordingly, as in *Strate*, we apply *Montana* straight up. Because Congress has not authorized the Navajo Nation's hotel occupancy tax through treaty or statute...

Indian tribes are "unique aggregations possessing attributes of sovereignty over both their members and their territory," but their dependent status generally precludes extension of tribal civil authority beyond these limits ... The Navajo Nation's imposition of a tax upon non-members on non-Indian fee land within the reservation is, therefore, presumptively invalid...

Extracts from Senate Bill S.578, 7 March 2003

Provided here are key excerpts from S.578, introduced in the 1st Session of the 108th Congress in the United States Senate, 7 March 2003, which show the recognition of the government-to-government relationship between the Indian nations and the United States. Section thirteen reaffirms inherent tribal sovereignty, directly conflicting with many of the opinions issued by the Supreme Court from 1978.

To amend the Homeland Security Act of 2002 to include Indian tribes among the entities consulted with respect to activities carried out by the Secretary of Homeland Security, and for other purposes.

IN THE SENATE OF THE UNITED STATES

MARCH 7, 2003

Mr. INOUYE (for himself, Mr. CAMPBELL, Mr. AKAKA, and Ms. CANTWELL) introduced the following bill; which was read twice and referred to the Committee on Governmental Affairs.

A BILL

To amend the Homeland Security Act of 2002 to include Indian tribes among the entities consulted with respect to activities carried out by the Secretary of Homeland Security, and for other purposes.

Be it enacted by the Senate and House of Representatives of the United States of America in Congress assembled,

SECTION I. SHORT TITLE.

This Act may be cited as the "Tribal Government Amendments to the Homeland Security Act of 2002."

SEC. 2. FINDINGS AND PURPOSES.

(a) FINDINGS.—Congress finds that—

(1) there is a government-to-government relationship between the United States and each Indian tribal government;

(2) through statutes and treaties, Congress has recognized the inherent sovereignty of Indian tribal governments and the rights of Native people to self determination and self-governance;

(3) each Indian tribal government possesses the inherent sovereign authority—
    (A) (i) to establish its own form of government;
     (ii) to adopt a constitution or other organic governing documents; and
     (iii) to establish a tribal judicial system;
and
    (B) to provide for the health and safety of those who reside on tribal lands, including the provision of law enforcement services on lands under the jurisdiction of the tribal government;

(4) tribal emergency response providers, such as tribal emergency public safety officers, law enforcement officers, emergency response personnel, emergency medical personnel and facilities (including tribal and Indian Health Service emergency facilities), and related personnel, agencies, and authorities—
    (A) play a crucial role in providing for the health and safety of those who reside on tribal lands; and
    (B) are necessary components of a comprehensive system to secure the homeland of the United States;

(5) there are more than 25 Indian tribes that have primary jurisdiction over—
    (A) lands within the United States that are adjacent to the Canadian or Mexican border; or
    (B) waters of the United States that provide direct access by boat to lands within the United States;

(6) the border lands under the jurisdiction of Indian tribal governments comprise more than 260 miles of the approximately 7,400 miles of international border of the United States;

(7) numerous Indian tribal governments exercise criminal, civil, and regulatory jurisdiction over lands on which dams, oil and gas deposits, nuclear or electrical power plants, water and sanitation systems, or timber or other natural resources are located; and

(8) the involvement of tribal governments in the protection of the homeland of the United States is essential to the comprehensive maintenance of the homeland security of the United States.

(b) PURPOSES.—The purposes of this Act are to ensure that—

(1) the Department of Homeland Security consults with, involves, coordinates with, and includes Indian tribal governments in carrying out the mission of the Department under the Homeland Security Act of 2002 (Public Law 107–296); and

(2) Indian tribal governments participate fully in the protection of the homeland of the United States…

SEC. 13. CONGRESSIONAL AFFIRMATION AND DECLARATION OF TRIBAL GOVERNMENT AUTHORITIES.

(a) IN GENERAL.—For the purpose of this Act, Congress affirms and declares that the inherent sovereign authority of an Indian tribal government includes the authority to enforce and adjudicate violations of applicable criminal, civil, and regulatory laws committed by any person on land under the jurisdiction of the Indian tribal government, except as expressly and clearly limited by—
    (1) a treaty between the United States and an Indian tribe; or
    (2) an Act of Congress.

(b) SCOPE.—The authority of an Indian tribal government described in subsection (a) shall—
    (1) be concurrent with the authority of the United States; and
    (2) extend to—
        (A) all places and persons within the Indian country (as defined in section 1151 of title 18, United States Code) under the concurrent jurisdiction of the United States and the Indian tribal government; and
        (B) any person, activity, or event having sufficient contacts with that land, or with a member of the Indian tribal government, to ensure protection of due process rights.

CHAPTER THIRTEEN
INDIAN GAMING

The origins of the Indian gaming revolution began in the 1970s. More than three decades on it has become a multi-billion dollar industry and one of the most controversial and publicised issues in modern-day America. Although this is a recent Indian economic phenomenon, gambling has been a central part of some Indian cultures and has lived, such as those of the Pawnee and Arikara, for hundreds of years.[1] The US Supreme Court has considered important Indian gaming cases such as *California v. Cabazon Band of Mission Indians* (1987), and Congress has legislated the Indian Gaming Regulatory Act (IGRA) of 1988.[2] Despite the well-publicised success of the gaming operations of the Mashantucket Pequot in Connecticut, the Oneida of New York and the Mille Lacs Band of Minnesota, as well as the billions of dollars being made annually by 'Indians', gaming has caused considerable problems for a number of other Indian nations. Gaming has sometimes resulted in inter-tribal divisions between those who see it as positive economic development and those who believe it cannot be reconciled with tribal culture. For some Indian communities, gaming has caused significant financial loss and brought crippling social problems.[3] In addition, the rise of Indian gaming throughout the United States has resulted in power struggles between Indian nations and States of the Union. Gaming has also caused problems for non-Indian society.[4] However, in other instances Indian gaming has resulted in significant benefits for the States of the Union and non-Indian societies that surround Indian gaming facilities.[5]

The Indian gaming revolution began in earnest in 1979 when the Seminole Indians of Florida opened a bingo hall and offered prizes of thousands of dollars in direct contravention to a Florida state law. In response, the State of Florida attempted to impose its regulatory statutes, arguing that the federal government had transferred regulatory jurisdiction over the Indians to the state. It attempted to close down the Seminole operation. The Seminole counteracted by suing.[6] Eventually, the issue was resolved when a federal court in *Seminole Tribe of Florida v. Butterworth* (1981) sided with the Seminole, declaring that they had the right as sovereigns to establish gaming operations on reservation lands.[7] Soon after the landmark success of the Seminole, the United States saw a gradual increase in the number of Indian gaming operations.

However, the foundations and origins of the large-scale Indian casino gambling industry were not established until after the US Supreme Court decision in *California v. Cabazon Band of Indians* (1987). In this legal precedent, the Supreme Court ruled that the State of California did not have authority to apply its regulatory laws to an Indian gaming operation inside an Indian reservation. The Supreme Court reasoned that Congress, pursuant to Public Law 280, did not sanction California with the authority to regulate this kind of issue and because California had gaming operations, it was contradictory to attempt to prevent Indian gaming ventures.[8] Furthermore, the Supreme Court reasoned that because federal law did not prohibit Indian gaming and federal government actively supported tribal economic development, the Indians had the right to conduct gaming operations.[9] In effect, the Supreme Court ruled that all Indian nations had the inherent sovereign right to pursue gaming inside reservation boundaries without undue interference from the States of the Union.

A year later in a direct response to the opinion of the Supreme Court, the US Congress passed the IGRA, 1988, to provide a regulatory framework for Indian gaming throughout the United States. It is important to remember that Indian gaming was started by tribal governments as a tool to address socio-economic needs and not in response to the introduction of this IGRA. The introduction of the IGRA was a direct response to state complaints about the loss of jurisdiction over gaming within state borders and was intended to balance the interests of tribal and state governments. The Act divides the regulation of Indian gaming into three separate classes, with Indians having direct authority over Class I and II gaming, and Class III gaming subject to compacts or agreements made between the relevant tribe or tribes and the State of the Union in question.[10] Such compacts have become a central part of the relationship between Indian nations and the States in Indian gaming matters. They allow a tribe to operate Class III gaming, which, in theory, brings in substantial revenue and in addition, allows the state to gain a fixed amount of money or a percentage of the annual profits made by the Indian gaming operation. Overall, more than two hundred Indian nations have signed and operate compacts with twenty-three States of the Union. One of these compacts includes the Seneca and the State of New York.[11]

Indian gaming has divided opinion among many Indian communities. Some support the social and cultural opportunities that it makes possible while others argue that gaming is contrary to Indian values and heritage. In Arizona, elders of the Quechan Nation are continuing their battle to end the construction and opening of a $200 million casino facility which they argue is too close to sacred sites and contrary to the land use deemed appropriate by their ancestors.[12] In contrast, for the Kickapoo Indian Nation of Kansas, gaming has brought unprecedented economic and social benefits to the reservation and as a direct result, many Kickapoo have returned to their homelands.[13] Gaming has also allowed the United South and Eastern Tribes to reclaim their heritage and strengthen their cultures and reservation infrastructures.[14] However, in contrast, the Navajo Nation has struggled to reconcile the often lucrative rewards of gaming with its attendant social and cultural costs.[15] Despite gambling being a part of Navajo culture, the decision to allow large gaming operations into the reservation has proved a problematic choice for the

people and government of the Navajo Nation over the last ten years.
Despite concerns that gaming will introduce social problems, such
as gambling addiction, alcoholism and increased violence within the
reservation, in 2004 the Navajo voted to start construction of a casino.
Indeed, the first Navajo casino in Church Rock opened its doors at the
end of 2008 and in early 2009, reports suggest that business is booming.[16]

Not every Indian community has benefited from the gaming economic
revolution in Indian country. In 2006, there were 225 Indian nations
engaged in Class II or III gaming in 28 States of the Union and there
were, in total, 423 tribal governmental gaming operations in existence.
In 2006, the total tribal governmental revenues from Indian gaming were
$25.7 billion, with a relatively small number of Indian nations making
large profits and a significant number of Indian nations generating
reasonable revenues.[17] To a large number of Indian nations, including the
Menominee of Wisconsin, Mescalero Apache Tribe of New Mexico,
Choctaw Nation of Oklahoma and Rosebud Sioux Tribe, gaming has
allowed investment in reservation services which has decreased
unemployment rates and reduced levels of poverty.[18] In 1999, the
Menominee reported that gaming revenues had lifted them out of a
'Third World' standard of living, and allowed them to invest in
reservation infrastructure and services as well as help them protect their
homelands and culture.[19] Indian gaming, in the opinion of Indians such
as Ernest L. Stevens, Jr., a member of the Oneida of Wisconsin and
former Chairman of the National Indian Gaming Association, and
non-Indians such as Joseph P. Kalt, Professor of International Political
Economy and head of the Harvard Project on American Indian
Economic Development at Harvard University, has been successful in
generating much needed revenue, given Indians Nations the opportunity
to strive for self-sufficiency, and offers an important tool for the economic
survival of many Indian nations throughout the United States.[20]
However, there are many Indian groups who cannot profit from gaming
or have suffered hardship as a direct result. The Yakima Indian Nation in
1991 had to file for bankruptcy due in part to an embezzlement scandal
surrounding a bingo hall.[21] Other Indian nations have not been able to
generate gaming revenues because their reservations are located too far
away from densely populated urban centres.[22]

Whilst there is a perception in American society that the vast majority
of Indians and Indian nations benefit from and are involved in gaming
this is not the case. Generally, since the 1980s, the foundations of
economic development in Indian country have not been exclusively
reliant on gaming opportunities. Instead, many Indian nations have relied
on diverse strategies including the sale of natural resources, the setting up
of tourist industries and leisure parks and the development of local
businesses. For example the Mississippi Choctaws have virtually

eliminated unemployment on their lands with the creation of thousands of jobs in Choctaw-owned factories, enterprises, schools and government agencies. Other examples include the Salish & Kootenai Tribes, which regenerated its Flathead reservation through a private sector economy that includes tribally owned retail and service industries, and the Winnebago of Nebraska who diversified away from gaming and set up Winnebago Ho-Chunk Inc. enterprises, which cut tribal unemployment from approximately 70% in 1994 to 13% in 2000.[23] There is plenty of evidence to suggest that non-gaming Indian nations have, in the economic sense, outperformed the Indian nations that have established gaming operations within reservations.[24]

Moreover, the entire Indian gaming industry was founded on the inherent sovereignty of Indian Nations and this independent authority has allowed them to grasp an unprecedented economic opportunity and open casinos on their lands. The issue of tribal sovereignty and the continuation of a government-to-government relationship between the US and all Indian nations remains paramount to the continued success of Indian gaming operations.[25] The re-affirmation of Indian self-determination by successive US Presidents from Presidents Lyndon B. Johnson and Richard M. Nixon to William Clinton and George W. Bush Jr. (1946–) has strengthened the Executive's commitment to this government-to-government relationship.[26] However, sovereignty has also given rise to problems including tensions over what constitutes an 'Indian' legally and over the erosion of tribal sovereignty connected with the wealth generated by Indian gaming.[27] In addition, there has been ill feeling between long established Indian nations and those who have recently been given federal status by the US government and opened successful and profitable casinos.[28]

The overall economic benefits associated with Indian gaming have led many tribes to open or attempt to open Indian casinos off-reservation based in more densely populated areas. Off-reservation gaming has become one of the most contentious issues in Indian country and the United States as the issue affects Indian and non-Indian communities alike. A contemporary dispute involves the Warm Springs Tribe of Oregon who wish to build a casino over 38 miles from the boundary of their reservation but within the boundary of their historic lands before it was ceded by treaty to the United States. Support and opposition to this specific project has transcended Indian and non-Indian communities. Indian opposition has come from another local tribe called the Confederated Tribes of the Grand Ronde Community of Oregon, who believe the Warm Springs casino would harm their reservation economy and affect the provision of tribal government services inside their reservation.[29] Likewise, some non-Indians oppose the casino. A pressure group called Friends of the Columbia Gorge in Oregon are concerned that the casino would destroy the surrounding environment and impact on the wildlife and the natural resources of the area.[30] However, despite the opposition groups, there is also strong and resolute support for the casino from many non-Indians, including Carol York, an elected county Commissioner in Hood River County, Oregon who has argued that strong local support has developed in favour of the Warm Springs development because it has been moved away from the original location of an area of beauty.[31] In addition, the gaming venture is intensely supported by the Warm Springs Tribe who believe that the casino would bring economic regeneration to the reservation and benefit the future of all tribal members.[32] The problem of off-reservation gaming is not exclusive to Oregon it continues to be a contentious issue for many Indian nations including the Seneca Nation in Buffalo, St. Regis Mohawk Tribe in New York and the Menominee in Wisconsin.

Indian gaming over the last thirty years has without question created an economic revolution for many Indian nations in Indian country, and despite the global economic problems encountered in 2008 and 2009, the gaming industry continues to remain strong and vibrant. Although the late 1970s saw the beginning of the Indian gaming industry that exists today, the genesis of the industry in the minds of Indians and non-Indians began with the infamous Supreme Court case of *California v. Cabazon Band of Indians* in 1987, which declared that the inherent sovereignty of all Indian nations allowed them to operate gaming enterprises within reservations. Despite the limitations placed on inherent tribal sovereignty by the introduction of the IGRA by Congress in 1988, many hundreds of Indian nations have attempted to gain a foothold in gaming, sometimes procuring lands to open casinos off-reservation, in order to benefit Indian reservations, governmental services and the cultures and heritage of their respective nations. Gaming is often put forward as an endorsement of Indian sovereignty and of the government-to-government relationship between the Indian nations and the American state. However, not all Indian nations have been successful in their pursuit of addressing economic and social ills through opening casinos in reservations. Many Indian nations have rejected it as an economic tool. It is important to note that Indian nations have opened and pursued many other business interests within their reservations, and that this economic diversity is important for the future economic and social successes of all Indian nations.

SOURCES

Testimony of the Menominee Tribe of Wisconsin: The National Gambling Impact Study Commission Subcommittee on Indian Gaming, Seattle Hearing, 7 January 1999

In the following excerpt, the Menominee Tribe of Wisconsin explain that gaming revenue has allowed them to spend money on tribal education, health provision, and services to protect the community such as fire and police services. Furthermore, gaming revenue has allowed the Menominee to invest money in the protection of their homelands, their culture and future survival.

Gaming revenues support almost 8,000 Menominee Tribal members and help protect a land base of approximately 235,000 acres of heavily forested areas, traversed by numerous waterways. The Tribe has never had enough funding to meet the needs of these concerns. Without gaming revenues, the Tribe would be unable to maintain its present level of support for both its people or its natural resources. We can cite statistics, but they only tell part of the story.

Numbers translate into people; people who are personally affected if gaming revenues stop. Tribal people will suffer from:

• Inadequate health protection, the ravages of diabetes which result in blindness and limb amputation, high blood pressure and an early mortality rate for all ages of tribal society;

• Lack of educational opportunities and preparation for a computer age for children;

• Lack of family support and child care for those parents who are the working poor;

• Lack of facilities for elder care which means many elders are abandoned in their last days;

• Lack of adequate police and fire protection which results in fear for safety in the tribal community;

• Lack of the ability for Tribal Government to raise its members out of poverty and from a living standard that is near Third World proportions.

These are some of the effects on tribal people. In addition, the Tribe is a government that is responsible for protection of the lands we have left. The land, the air, the water, every aspect of tribal environment comes under the mantle of tribal government. Gaming revenues enable the Tribe to attract other funds to increase the meager funds available to assist the Tribe in saving its natural resources.

Tribes do not pay income taxes on gaming revenues. The Indian Gaming Regulatory Act prohibits states from taxing tribal gaming revenues. Non-Indian gaming employees do pay income tax to the state.

Tribal Gaming is closely regulated by the National Indian Gaming Commission, State compact and Tribal regulations. The Menominee Tribe is in full compliance with all regulations, and has been since the beginning of Indian Gaming.

...The Tribe offers counselling and support for compulsive gamblers. Gamblers Anonymous is an on-going activity on the Reservation; however, compulsive gambling is not a significant problem in our area.

The Tribe devotes gaming revenues to a Department of Historic Preservation which is entirely devoted to cultural events. Of tremendous importance to the Tribe is the establishment of a Language and Culture Commission which trains teachers in the Menominee language and provides language classes for all levels of tribal society. The result of these activities has been a revitalization of Menominee language and an increase in fluency in Menominee language made possible through gaming revenues.

The importance of continued gaming revenues for the Tribe cannot be overestimated. Without those revenues, the Tribe would sink back into an economic depression that would condemn tribal members to unrelieved poverty and degradation of the natural resources which remain under tribal control.

Indian Gaming has helped the Menominee Tribe to get nearer to a level playing field as compared with the majority of society in this country. Nearer, yes, but far from level as yet. Indian gaming gives us a chance to help ourselves. We can and we will help ourselves out of poverty with Indian gaming revenues...

Testimony of Brian Patterson: Oversight Hearing on the National Indian Gaming Commission before the Senate Committee on Indian Affairs, 17 April 2008

Provided here is the testimony of Brian Patterson, president of the United South and Eastern Tribes, Inc. (USET) and enrolled member of the Oneida Indian Nation, to the Senate Committee on Indian Affairs in 2008. Patterson describes the economic and social benefits that gaming has brought to the United South and Eastern Tribes, which include the Eastern Band of Cherokee, Mississippi Band of Choctaw, Miccosukee Tribe, Seminole Tribe of Florida, the Chitimacha Tribe of Louisiana, the Seneca Nation of Indians, the Coushatta Tribe of Louisiana, the St. Regis Band of Mohawk Indians, the Penobscot Indian Nation, the Passamaquoddy Tribe Indian Township, the Passamaquoddy Pleasant Point, the Houlton Band of Maliseet Indians, the Tunica-Biloxi Indians of Louisiana, the Poarch Band of Creek Indians, the Narragansett Indian Tribe, the Mashantucket Pequot Tribe, the Wampanoag Tribe of Gay Head (Aquinnah), the Alabama-Coushatta Tribe of Texas, the Oneida Indian Nation, the Aroostook Band of Micmac Indians, the Catawba Indian Nation, the Jena Band of Choctaw Indians, the Mohegan Tribe of Connecticut, the Cayuga Nation and the Mashpee Wampanoag Tribe.

...United South and Eastern Tribes, Inc. is a non-profit, inter-tribal organization that collectively represents its member tribes at the regional and national levels. USET represents twenty-five federally recognized tribes.

Included among the members of USET are some of the largest gaming tribes in the United States. We also represent tribes with more modest gaming facilities, as well as tribes that currently do not engage in gaming.

...Indian gaming has been described as "the only federal Indian economic initiative that ever worked." That is absolutely correct. Indian gaming has served as a critical economic tool to enable Indian nations to once again provide essential governmental services to their members, re-assert their sovereignty, and promote the goals of self-determination and self-sufficiency.

Prior to the advent of Indian gaming, many Indian nations, while legally recognized as sovereign governments, were not able to provide basic, governmental services to their people. They had all of the legal attributes of sovereign nations, but many did not have the practical ability to be an effective government for their members. Consequently, despite a strong and proud tradition, Indian nations languished in a two hundred year cycle of poverty.

Today, the resources of Indian gaming operations are used to provide essential governmental services to tribal members. Indian nations across the country are using gaming revenues to invest in dozens of tribal member programs, including home ownership initiatives, tuition assistance for everything from elementary schools to post-doctorate work, health insurance for all tribal members, and access to top-notch health clinics.

We cannot calculate the intangible benefits of the impact such economic development has created, including the impact on the most important matter for an Indian nation – its human resources. Suffice it to say that in many situations, Indian governments have seen their members move from unemployment rolls to being gainfully employed.

Reclaiming a past heritage also has been a priority for all USET members, and gaming proceeds have enabled Indian nations to make tremendous gains in this area. In many respects, these individual efforts culminated collectively in the dedication of the National Museum of the American Indian in September 2004. I am proud to note that the three largest contributions to the building of this tremendous institution came from Indian nations that are Members of USET...

Testimony of Steve Cadue: The National Gambling Impact Study Commission, 9 November 1998

In the following document, Steve Cadue, tribal official for the Kickapoo Indian Nation of Kansas, points out the phenomenal social and economic benefits gaming has brought the Kickapoo Nation and the way that these factors have allowed many Kickapoo to return to the reservation and strengthen their culture.

...During my tribal political career I have participated in many efforts to achieve economic self-sufficiency for our Kickapoo Nation. Probably our best success in economic development was our tribal Farm and Ranch program and the Kickapoo Trading post which sells gasoline and diesel fuel. These economic development ventures were greatly supported by federal agency grants coupled with our own investments. We have continually searched for other economic development, but our rural isolation, lack of infrastructure and lack of financial resources prevented us from attaining any sound economic development. Please keep in mind that federal Indian reservation were established in the most isolated rural areas of the United States and were never designed to support industry. Now, we are beginning to see economic opportunities due to the financial assets we have achieved via Indian Gaming.

We own and operate our Golden Eagle Casino, a Class III Indian gaming facility regulated in a compact agreement with the State of Kansas. We employ approximately 400 Indians and non-Indians in our gaming and restaurant facility. We were the first Class III Indian gaming operation in Kansas and have been in operation since May 1996...When we examine the economic multiplier-effect, the greatest beneficiary is our neighbouring non-reservation businesses due to the fact that we do not have shopping, banking, or manufacturing plants on our Kickapoo reservation; thus, a miniscule percentage of the casino employees wages currently is being spent on the reservation.

...The economic success and resultant professional, skilled and semi-skilled ability required in Indian gaming has attracted Kickapoo tribal members to return to their homeland, where family and friendship ties are once again renewed and Kickapoo customs and traditions will experience a renaissance. Old Kickapoo songs sung in our Kickapoo language will be sung again and our beautiful history will be recaptured. And a diversified economy springing forth from reinvested casino revenues will resort in even greater return of our talented Kickapoo people.

We have allocated our casino revenue for: adult Kickapoo education, Headstart, Kickapoo language learning programs, health care, senior citizen programs, housing, recreational programs, cultural programs, i.e., Kickapoo Pow Wow, land acquisition, road programs, tribal court services, water resource planning and tribal police service and facilities.

It is clear that our Indian casinos are a driving force in the economic growth of north-eastern Kansas. The economic impact of Indian gaming has created jobs, generated income, increased the sales of goods and services and most important of all, made our Indian people equal business partners in the marketplace. Pride in our Indian entrepreneurship is the most valuable commodity of all. This has all been accomplished without public funding agency assistance.

...genuine [Indian] Self-Determination cannot be achieved without financial resources. Only now with the financial ability of Indian Gaming can our Indian people fully utilize the self-governing powers of the Indian Reorganization Act

[1934] and the Indian Self-Determination and Education Assistance Act [1975]. As we now reach the year 2000, we can finally join the rest of the great capital freedom marketplace of America via the benefits of Indian Gaming.

...Indian Gaming revenue has given us a chance, and opportunity to realize some dreams. Our task to overcome poverty is a formidable challenge and will require the wisest of decisions and faith in ourselves and in prayer but our Kickapoo people are strong and determined to achieve true Self-Determination. So, as you continue your deliberations, recall the old Indian adage of "walking a mile in our moccasins" to understand the self-governing rights, values and benefits that Indian Gaming has brought to our Indian people.

Our reports cannot tell the real story of Indian gaming...

Testimony of J.R. Mathews: Oversight Hearing on the National Indian Gaming Commission before the Senate Committee on Indian Affairs, 17 April 2008

In the following extract, J.R. Mathews, vice-chairman of the Quapaw Tribe of Oklahoma and member of the Executive Committee of the National Indian Gaming Association, explains the specific contributions that Indian gaming has made to individual Indian nations and how the revenues have also helped surrounding communities.

I am speaking today on behalf of the National Indian Gaming Association and its 184 Member Tribes. NIGA is a tribal government association dedicated to supporting Indian gaming and defending Indian sovereignty...

Indian Gaming: The Native American Success Story

...Tribes are using revenues to build or rebuild their communities, while putting tribal members to work and providing basic and essential tribal government services. Tribes are also generating significant taxes to Federal, state and local governments through Indian gaming and making significant charitable contributions to their communities and other Indian tribes. Last year, Indian gaming generated $26.5 billion in gross revenues (before capital costs, salaries, expenses and depreciation, etc.) for tribal governments. That means tribal governments created more than 700,000 jobs through Indian gaming nationwide and generated almost $12 billion in Federal, state and local revenue.

Here are some examples of the tribal community infrastructure and the essential government services that Indian gaming revenues provide:

- The Mescalero Apache Tribe of New Mexico built a new high school;
- The Choctaw Nation of Oklahoma built a new hospital;
- Gila River established a new police and emergency medical unit;
- The Pechanga Band established a new fire department;
- The Mohegan Tribe is building a water system for the Tribe and seven of its surrounding communities;

- The Rosebud Sioux Tribe established child care and provides new school clothes for impoverished students;
  - The Fort Berthold Tribes established a new Headstart center;
  - The Tohono O'odham Nation is funding the Tohono O'odham Community College and used $30 million to fund a student scholarship program; and
  - Several tribal governments provided major funding for the new Smithsonian Museum of the American Indian.

...The development of Indian lands is a benefit to surrounding communities. For example, Gila River EMTs serve as first responders to accidents in their stretch of I-10. The Pechanga Band's Fire Department responded to the California wildfires, working hard to save homes and lives in neighboring communities.

Indian gaming benefits neighboring Indian tribes as well. The Shakopee Mdewakanton Sioux Tribe, for example, has generously assisted many Indian tribes in Minnesota, the Dakotas, and Nebraska, including refinancing the Oglala Sioux Tribe's debt, providing a grant to help build a new nursing home for the Cheyenne River Sioux Tribe and an economic development grant for the Santee Sioux Tribe...

President George W. Bush: Memorandum for the Heads of Executive Departments and Agencies, Government-to-Government Relationship with Tribal Governments, 23 September 2004

In the following document, George W. Bush (1946–), forty-third president of the United States, reaffirms his government's commitment to tribal sovereignty and the government-to-government relationship between the United States and Indian nations.

The United States has a unique legal and political relationship with Indian tribes and a special relationship with Alaska Native entities as provided in the Constitution of the United States, treaties, and Federal statutes. Presidents for decades have recognized this relationship. President Nixon announced a national policy of self-determination for Indian tribes in 1970. More recently, Executive Order 13175, entitled Consultation and Coordination with Indian Tribal Governments, was issued in 2000. I reiterated my

Administration's adherence to a government-to-government relationship and support for tribal sovereignty and self-determination earlier this year in Executive Order 13336, entitled American Indian and Alaska Native Education.

My Administration is committed to continuing to work with federally recognized tribal governments on a government-to-government basis and strongly supports and respects tribal sovereignty and self-determination for tribal governments in the United States. I take pride in acknowledging and reaffirming the existence and durability of our unique government-to-government relationship and these abiding principles.

This commitment begins at the White House, where my Director of Intergovernmental Affairs serves as my White House liaison with all Indian nations and works with federally recognized tribal governments on an intergovernmental basis. Moreover, it is critical that all departments and agencies adhere to these principles and work with tribal governments in a manner that cultivates mutual respect and fosters greater understanding to reinforce these principles.

Accordingly, the head of each executive department and agency (agency) shall continue to ensure to the greatest extent practicable and as permitted by United States law that the agency's working relationship with federally recognized tribal governments fully respects the rights of self-government and self-determination due tribal governments. Department or agency inquiries regarding this memorandum, specifically those related to regulatory, legislative, or budgetary issues, should be directed to the Office of Management and Budget.

This memorandum is intended only to improve the internal management of the executive branch and is not intended to, and does not, create any right, benefit, or trust responsibility, substantive or procedural, enforceable at law or in equity, by a party against the United States, its agencies, entities, or instrumentalities, its officers or employees, or any other person.

GEORGE W. BUSH

Statement from Ernest L. Stevens, Jr.: Chairman of the Native American Indian Gaming Association, 2006

The following extracts are taken from the statement of Ernest L. Stevens, Jr., of the Oneida of Wisconsin and former chairman of the National Indian Gaming Association from 2001, before the Committee on Resources US House of Representatives, 11 May 2006, in which he discusses the overall success of gaming in Indian country. He argues that gaming has helped generate unprecedented levels of revenue, allowed Indians to become more self-sufficient and to take pride in Indian sovereignty.

...My name is Ernest Stevens, Jr. and I serve as Chairman of the National Indian Gaming Association ... NIGA is an association of 184 tribal governments that use Indian gaming to generate essential government revenue.

Indian gaming is our Native American success story. After decades of poverty and economic devastation, about 60% of Indian tribes in the lower 48 states use gaming revenues to rebuild community infrastructure, provide basic health, education, and social programs for their citizens, and provide hope and opportunity for an entire generation of Indian youth.

Does Indian gaming solve all of Indian country's problems? No. Many tribes cannot use gaming because of their remote locations, and we call upon Congress to fulfil its trust responsibility to provide funding for education, health care, essential government services and basic community infrastructure, like water systems and police and fire protection. For many others in rural areas with high unemployment, Indian gaming provides its greatest benefit through jobs. Indeed, in many rural areas, Indian gaming provides the catalyst for regional job growth for both Indians and non-Indians.

Even with these challenges, Indian gaming has proven to be the best tool for economic development in Indian country and our best opportunity for tribal self-sufficiency and self-determination.

For NIGA and its Member Tribes, our primary mission is to preserve tribal sovereignty and to protect Indian gaming as a means of generating essential tribal government revenue. Tribes are committed to effective regulation of Indian gaming. Experience demonstrates that the highest standard of regulation can be achieved while promoting tribal sovereignty and self-determination.

…No one has a greater interest in maintaining the integrity of Indian gaming than tribal governments. For the past 30 years, Tribes have been dedicated to building and maintaining strong regulatory systems, realizing the need to protect government revenue. Under IGRA [Indian Gaming Regulatory Act], Congress envisioned that tribal governments would be the primary day-to-day regulators of Indian gaming. This vision is a reality, as Tribes today regulate Indian gaming through tribal gaming commissions…

In closing, Indian Tribes are committed to both the highest standards of regulation for Indian gaming and respect for Indian sovereignty…

Cheryl Kennedy, February 2006

Provided here are the viewpoints of Cheryl A. Kennedy, Tribal Council Chairwoman of the Confederated Tribes of the Grand Ronde Community of Oregon, who opposes Warm Springs casino because of its potential to take away much-needed revenue for tribal government and subsequently affect the provision of services to the reservation.

Since 1996, Grand Ronde has opposed efforts by tribes to have land taken into trust for gaming outside original reservation boundaries or not adjacent to a current reservation. Grand Ronde's opposition to off-reservation gaming stems from our concern that off-reservation casinos (1) weaken public and government support for Indian gaming (2) undermine the purpose of IGRA - to promote development of strong reservation economies through on-reservation casinos, and (3) invite disputes among tribes when located in areas where more than one tribe has a significant historical connection.

Our concerns are not speculative. Public opinion polls in Oregon1 show that Oregonians currently support Indian gaming on reservation lands.

However, the polls also show that Oregonians are concerned about the expansion of gaming and fear, as does Grand Ronde, that approval of an off-reservation casino…will lead to a proliferation of casinos near urban areas. A gaming initiative was, in fact, recently filed in Oregon by private developers seeking to operate a casino in Troutdale, a city near Portland.

These developers were no doubt encouraged by the Governor's recent approval of Oregon's first off-reservation casino at Cascade Locks, the Cowlitz Tribe's efforts to build a casino sixteen miles north of Portland, and the Yakama Nation's statements about locating a casino near Portland…

Until last year, the State of Oregon had an Indian gaming policy limiting each Oregon tribe to one on-reservation casino. The compact between the State of Oregon and Grand Ronde, as well as the gaming compacts with other Oregon tribes, reflects this policy. This policy changed last May when Oregon's Governor signed a new gaming compact with the Confederated Tribes of Warm Springs, authorizing the State's first off-reservation casino in the Columbia River Gorge town of Cascade Locks…

In building and investing in Spirit Mountain Casino, Grand Ronde based significant economic decisions on the State's long-standing policy against off-reservation casinos. An off-reservation casino in Cascade Locks would have significant adverse impacts on Grand Ronde's reservation economy. Cascade Locks is forty miles from the Portland, Oregon metropolitan area – the market from which Spirit Mountain Casino draws most of its customers. Our analysis indicates that an off-reservation casino in Cascade Locks would result in a loss of revenue at Spirit Mountain of at least twenty-two percent, if not more. The loss of Spirit Mountain Casino's customers and revenue to an off-reservation casino in Cascade Locks would have a devastating impact on the Tribe's ability to provide critical services and meaningful employment opportunities to Tribal members, particularly if the Tribe is foreclosed from pursuing an off-reservation casino of its own in order to protect its investment.

Warm Springs has the largest reservation in Oregon2 at more than 640,000 acres. It has a diverse economic base that includes forest products, hydroelectric power, ranching, recreation, and tourism. In contrast, Grand Ronde is a restored tribe with a small reservation of approximately 11,000 acres. Our on-reservation casino is the only significant source of revenue for the Tribe. It would be unfair to permit Warm Springs, with their large reservation, to pursue an off-reservation casino that would so severely impact Grand Ronde's investment in on-reservation gaming.

As a final point, we believe off-reservation casinos invite disputes between tribes when more than one tribe has a historical connection to a proposed gaming site. Grand Ronde has a long historical and cultural connection to the Cascade Locks area. The ancestors of Grand Ronde tribal members lived along the Columbia River since time immemorial. In the Treaty of January 22, 1855, antecedent bands and tribes of Grand Ronde ceded lands along the Columbia River, from Oak Point east to Cascade Falls. Chief Tamolth signed this treaty on behalf of the Watlala Tribe ("of Tumawaters") of the Gorge. His descendants are well represented among the Grand Ronde people today.

Grand Ronde understands and supports Warm Springs' desire to meet the needs of its membership, but meeting the needs of its membership should not come at the expense of the on-reservation economy of another Oregon tribe. This is particularly true when Warm Springs could pursue a viable on-reservation alternative to meet its needs. We believe a casino on the Warm Springs Reservation, near the town of Warm Springs, is an economically viable alternative to an off-reservation casino in Cascade Locks, and one the Confederated Tribes of Grand Ronde could support. Such a casino would draw a significant number of patrons from and around the City of Bend. Bend is located in Deschutes County, the fastest growing county in the State of Oregon for the past ten years. Bend is the largest city in Central Oregon with an adult population expected to exceed 123,000 by 2009...

Grand Ronde appreciates your efforts to consult with Indian Country regarding gaming issues as they are critical to the economy and welfare of our Tribe, our Reservation and our members...

Testimony of Miriam Jorgensen: Oversight Hearing on Economic Development, 10 May 2006

In the text below, Miriam Jorgensen, Research Director for the Harvard Project on American Indian Economic Development and Associate Director for Research Native Nations Institute at the University of Arizona, argues that non-gaming tribal economies and incomes have outstripped those of tribes that have followed the gaming path. Indeed, she believes that Indian self-determination has been the foundation for unprecedented recent levels of economic growth in Indian country which are allowing Indian tribes to slowly catch up with the overall economic standards of American society.

Since the passage of the Indian Self-Determination and Education Assistance Act of 1975 (P.L. 93-638), the Planner's Approach to economic development gradually has been giving way to policies of self-determination in the economic sphere. Under these policies, Native nations' officials, rather than outside decision makers, have been more able to set the agendas, design the programs and policies, reap the benefits of development, and – importantly – be held accountable for failure in development. The result is a little-noticed boom in economic development in Indian Country. Since the early 1990s, both gaming tribes *and non-gaming* tribes have been experiencing rates of economic growth about three times the rate of the US as a whole...

Mainstream media portrayals of the casino enterprises that many tribal governments have built since the late 1980s conjure an image of easy money and previously unseen riches for Native nations. But the long history of poverty and low incomes in Indian Country has not been wiped away by gaming...although approximately 200 tribes operate gaming enterprises, low incomes (as well as the underemployment and unemployment that low incomes signal) are much more the rule than the exception for gaming and non-gaming tribes alike. Native nations such as the Crow Creek Sioux Tribe (reservation in SD), San Carlos Apache Tribe (reservation in AZ), and numerous others have pursued gaming, but by 2000 still had household incomes that were less than 60 percent of the median household income in the rest of the United States...

In fact, during the first full decade of Indian gaming, real household incomes on reservations without gaming actually grew more rapidly (33%) than on reservations with gaming (24%) – and both far outstripped the meager 4% growth in the median American household's income during the entire decade of 1990-2000. And therein lies the other side of the economic story in Indian Country: Native America is in the midst of an economic boom, with rates of income growth sustained over the 1990s and into the new millennium that match those of virtually any international case of rapid development...

Just as I am careful to note that this boom is not attributable to gaming *per se*, it also is not attributable to some large influx of federal dollars: the improvement in average incomes in Indian Country since the late 1980s has occurred even though overall federal funding to Indians was not increased. Instead...the truly important change appears to be a practical commitment (by both the US federal government and Native nations) to self-determination...

A final note in this review of the evidence of economic growth in Indian Country is that the progress is tenuous. Policies of self-determination are poorly understood and under constant pressure for repeal. Even at the high rates of income growth seen in recent years, it would take decades for incomes in Indian Country to catch up to US average income levels. And, in some sense, that is not the goal of Native communities. Income and material well-being are hardly the be all and end all for America's Native nations. The citizens of Native nations may count political perpetuation, matters of cultural identity, and quality of life and quality of community (which cannot easily be measured in dollars) as more important shared goals. But as long as poverty, unemployment, and under-employment are a Native nation's prevailing economic reality, its citizenry will struggle to hold everything else together. Families will be forced to undertake extraordinary steps to access even the bare necessities, individuals will tend to face the unwanted choice of looking off-reservation for even modest economic opportunity, and because of these necessary focuses, other progress may be difficult to achieve. As a result, persistent economic underdevelopment and attendant poverty are pressing concerns across Indian Country...

California v. Cabazon Band of Mission Indians, 1987

The following are key extracts from the Supreme Court opinion that declared the State of California had no regulatory authority over an Indian nation inside reservation boundaries.

The Cabazon and Morongo Bands of Mission Indians, federally recognized Indian Tribes, occupy reservations in Riverside County, California. Each Band...conducts bingo games on its reservation. The Cabazon Band has also opened a card club at which draw poker and other card games are played. The games are open to the public and are played predominantly by non-Indians coming onto the reservations. The games are a major source of employment for tribal members, and the profits are the Tribes' sole source of income. The State of California seeks to apply to the two Tribes [a statute]...That statute does not entirely prohibit the playing of bingo but permits it when the games are operated and staffed by members of designated charitable organizations who may not be paid for their services...Asserting that the bingo games on the two reservations violated each of these restrictions, California insisted that the Tribes comply with state law...

The Court has consistently recognized that Indian tribes retain "attributes of sovereignty over both their members and their territory," United States v. Mazurie (1975), and that "tribal sovereignty is dependent on, and subordinate to, only the Federal Government, not the States," Washington v. Confederated Tribes of Colville Indian Reservation (1980). It is clear, however, that state laws may be applied to tribal Indians on their reservations if Congress has expressly so provided...

In Public Law 280, Congress expressly granted six States, including California, jurisdiction over specified areas of Indian country within the States and provided for the assumption of jurisdiction by other States...California was granted broad criminal jurisdiction over offenses committed by or against Indians within all Indian country within the State. Section 4's grant of civil jurisdiction was more limited. In Bryan v. Itasca County (1976), we interpreted 4 to grant States jurisdiction over private civil litigation involving reservation Indians in state court, but not to grant general civil regulatory authority. We held, therefore, that Minnesota could not apply its personal property tax within the reservation. Congress' primary concern in enacting Pub. L. 280 was combating lawlessness on reservations. The Act plainly was not intended to effect total assimilation of Indian tribes into mainstream American society. We recognized that a grant to States of general civil regulatory power over Indian reservations would result in the destruction of tribal institutions and values...

...if the intent of a state law is generally to prohibit certain conduct, it falls within Pub. L. 280's grant of criminal jurisdiction, but if the state law generally permits the conduct at issue, subject to regulation, it must be classified as civil/regulatory and Pub. L. 280 does not authorize its enforcement on an Indian reservation...

...California does not prohibit all forms of gambling. California itself operates a state lottery...and daily encourages its citizens to participate in this state-run gambling. California also permits parimutuel horse-race betting...The Tribes assert that more than 400 card rooms similar to the Cabazon card club flourish in California, and the State does not dispute this fact...There is no effort to forbid the playing of bingo by any member of the public over the age of 18. Indeed, the permitted bingo games must be open to the general public...In light of the fact that California permits a substantial amount of gambling activity, including bingo, and actually promotes gambling through its state lottery, we must conclude that California regulates rather than prohibits gambling in general and bingo in particular.

...But that an otherwise regulatory law is enforceable by criminal as well as civil means does not necessarily convert it into a criminal law within the meaning of Pub. L. 280...

Because the state and county laws at issue here are imposed directly on the Tribes that operate the games, and are not expressly permitted by Congress, the Tribes argue that the judgment below should be affirmed without more...Our cases, however, have not established an inflexible per se rule precluding state jurisdiction over tribes and tribal members in the absence of express congressional consent...

This case also involves a state burden on tribal Indians in the context of their dealings with non-Indians since the question is whether the State may prevent the Tribes from making available high stakes bingo games to non-Indians coming from outside the reservations. Decision in this case turns on whether state authority is pre-empted by the operation of federal law; and "[s]tate jurisdiction is pre-empted . . . if it interferes or is incompatible with federal and tribal interests reflected in federal law, unless the state interests at stake are sufficient to justify the assertion of state authority..." The inquiry is to proceed in light of traditional notions of Indian sovereignty and the congressional goal of Indian self-government, including its "overriding goal" of encouraging tribal self-sufficiency and economic development...

These are important federal interests. They were reaffirmed by the President's 1983 Statement on Indian Policy. More specifically, the Department of the Interior, which has the primary responsibility for carrying out the Federal Government's trust obligations to Indian tribes, has sought to implement these policies by promoting tribal bingo enterprises...The Department of Housing and Urban Development and the Department of Health and Human Services have also provided financial assistance to develop tribal gaming enterprises...Here, the Secretary of the Interior has approved tribal ordinances establishing and regulating the gaming activities involved...

These policies and actions, which demonstrate the Government's approval and active promotion of tribal bingo enterprises, are of particular relevance in this case. The Cabazon and Morongo Reservations contain no natural resources which can be exploited. The tribal games at present provide the sole source of revenues for the operation of the tribal governments and the provision of tribal services. They are also the major sources of employment on the reservations. Self-determination and economic development are not within reach if the Tribes cannot raise revenues and provide employment for their members. The Tribes' interests obviously parallel the federal interests.

California seeks to diminish the weight of these seemingly important tribal interests by asserting that the Tribes are merely marketing an exemption from state gambling laws…Here, however, the Tribes are not merely importing a product onto the reservations for immediate resale to non-Indians. They have built modern facilities which provide recreational opportunities and ancillary services to their patrons, who do not simply drive onto the reservations, make purchases and depart, but spend extended periods of time there enjoying the services the Tribes provide. The Tribes have a strong incentive to provide comfortable, clean, and attractive facilities and well-run games in order to increase attendance at the games… the Cabazon and Morongo Bands are generating value on the reservations through activities in which they have a substantial interest…

The sole interest asserted by the State to justify the imposition of its bingo laws on the Tribes is in preventing the infiltration of the tribal games by organized crime. To the extent that the State seeks to prevent any and all bingo games from being played on tribal lands while permitting regulated, off-reservation games, this asserted interest is irrelevant and the state and county laws are pre-empted. Even to the extent that the State and county seek to regulate short of prohibition, the laws are pre-empted. The State insists that the high stakes offered at tribal games are attractive to organized crime, whereas the controlled games authorized under California law are not. This is surely a legitimate concern, but we are unconvinced that it is sufficient to escape the pre-emptive force of federal and tribal interests apparent in this case…

We conclude that the State's interest in preventing the infiltration of the tribal bingo enterprises by organized crime does not justify state regulation of the tribal bingo enterprises in light of the compelling federal and tribal interests supporting them. State regulation would impermissibly infringe on tribal government, and this conclusion applies equally to the county's attempted regulation of the Cabazon card club…

Indian Gaming Regulatory Act, 1988

Provided here are important extracts from the 1988 Act that divided Indian gaming operations into three separate classes, Class I, II, and III, and ensured that the States of the Union and the federal government had a voice in Indian gaming matters.

…Sec. 2701 Findings

The Congress finds that -

(1) numerous Indian tribes have become engaged in or have licensed gaming activities on Indian lands as a means of generating tribal governmental revenue;

(2) Federal courts have held that section 81 of this title requires Secretarial review of management contracts dealing with Indian gaming, but does not provide standards for approval of such contracts;

(3) existing Federal law does not provide clear standards or regulations for the conduct of gaming on Indian lands;

(4) a principal goal of Federal Indian policy is to promote tribal economic development, tribal self-sufficiency, and strong tribal government; and

(5) Indian tribes have the exclusive right to regulate gaming activity on Indian lands if the gaming activity is not specifically prohibited by Federal law and is conducted within a State which does not, as a matter of criminal law and public policy, prohibit such gaming activity.

Sec. 2702. Declaration of policy

The purpose of this chapter is -

(1) to provide a statutory basis for the operation of gaming by Indian tribes as a means of promoting tribal economic development, self-sufficiency, and strong tribal governments;

(2) to provide a statutory basis for the regulation of gaming by an Indian tribe adequate to shield it from organized crime and other corrupting influences, to ensure that the Indian tribe is the primary beneficiary of the gaming operation, and to assure that gaming is conducted fairly and honestly by both the operator and players; and

(3) to declare that the establishment of independent Federal regulatory authority for gaming on Indian lands, the establishment of Federal standards for gaming on Indian lands, and the establishment of a National Indian Gaming Commission are necessary to meet congressional concerns regarding gaming and to protect such gaming as a means of generating tribal revenue.

Sec. 2703. Definitions

For purposes of this chapter...

(4) The term "Indian lands" means -
    (A) all lands within the limits of any Indian reservation; and
    (B) any lands title to which is either held in trust by the United States for the benefit of any Indian tribe or individual or held by any Indian tribe or individual subject to restriction by the United States against alienation and over which an Indian tribe exercises governmental power.

(5) The term "Indian tribe" means any Indian tribe, band, nation, or other organized group or community of Indians which -
    (A) is recognized as eligible by the Secretary for the special programs and services provided by the United States to Indians because of their status as Indians, and
    (B) is recognized as possessing powers of self-government.

(6) The term "class I gaming" means social games solely for prizes of minimal value or traditional forms of Indian gaming engaged in by individuals as a part of, or in connection with, tribal ceremonies or celebrations.

(7) (A) The term "class II gaming" means -

(i) the game of chance commonly known as bingo (whether or not electronic, computer, or other technologic aids are used in connection therewith)…

(III)…including (if played in the same location) pull-tabs, lotto, punch boards, tip jars, instant bingo, and other games similar to bingo…

(B) The term "class II gaming" does not include

(i) any banking card games, including baccarat, chemin de fer, or blackjack (21), or

(ii) electronic or electromechanical facsimiles of any game of chance or slot machines of any kind…

(8) The term "class III gaming" means all forms of gaming that are not class I gaming or class II gaming…

Sec. 2704. National Indian Gaming Commission

(a) There is established within the Department of the Interior a Commission to be known as the National Indian Gaming Commission…

Sec. 2710. Tribal gaming ordinances

(a) Jurisdiction over class I and class II gaming activity.

(1) Class I gaming on Indian lands is within the exclusive jurisdiction of the Indian tribes and shall not be subject to the provisions of this Act.

(2) Any class II gaming on Indian lands shall continue to be within the jurisdiction of the Indian tribes, but shall be subject to the provisions of this Act…

(3) (A) Any Indian tribe having jurisdiction over the Indian lands upon which a class III gaming activity is being conducted, or is to be conducted, shall request the State in which such lands are located to enter into negotiations for the purpose of entering into a Tribal-State compact governing the conduct of gaming activities. Upon receiving such a request, the State shall negotiate with the Indian tribe in good faith to enter into such a compact.

(B) Any State and any Indian tribe may enter into a Tribal-State compact governing gaming activities on the Indian lands of the Indian tribe, but such compact shall take effect only when notice of approval by the Secretary of such compact has been published by the Secretary in the Federal Register…

Sec. 2719. Gaming on lands acquired after October 17, 1988

(a) Prohibition on lands acquired in trust by Secretary. Except as provided in subsection (b), gaming regulated by this Act shall not be conducted on lands acquired by the Secretary in trust for the benefit of an Indian tribe after the date of enactment of this Act [enacted Oct. 17, 1988] unless--

(1) such lands are located within or contiguous to the boundaries of the reservation of the Indian tribe on the date of enactment of this Act [enacted Oct. 17, 1988]; or

(2) the Indian tribe has no reservation on the date of enactment of this Act [enacted Oct. 17, 1988] and--

(A) such lands are located in Oklahoma and--

(i) are within the boundaries of the Indian tribe's former reservation, as defined by the Secretary, or

(ii) are contiguous to other land held in trust or restricted status by the United States for the Indian tribe in Oklahoma; or

(B) such lands are located in a State other than Oklahoma and are within the Indian tribe's last recognized reservation within the State or States within which such Indian tribe is presently located.

(b) Exceptions.

(1) Subsection (a) will not apply when--

(A) the Secretary, after consultation with the Indian tribe and appropriate State and local officials, including officials of other nearby Indian tribes, determines that a gaming establishment on newly acquired lands would be in the best interest of the Indian tribe and its members, and would not be detrimental to the surrounding community, but only if the Governor of the State in which the gaming activity is to be conducted concurs in the Secretary's determination; or

(B) lands are taken into trust as part of--

(i) a settlement of a land claim,

(ii) the initial reservation of an Indian tribe acknowledged by the Secretary under the Federal acknowledgment process, or

(iii) the restoration of lands for an Indian tribe that is restored to Federal recognition...

Statement of Joseph P. Kalt: National Gambling Impact Study Commission, March 1998

In the following excerpts, Joseph P. Kalt, Professor of International Political Economy and head of the Harvard Project on American Indian Economic Development at Harvard University, in testimony to the National Gambling Impact Study Commission on 16 March 1998, argues that gaming has been very important to Indian economic survival.

...Our primary objectives have been to try to get a handle on what is working in Indian Country when it comes to sustained economic development and socially successful reservations. Our work has put us in the field for many hundreds of man-days, and we have worked with dozens of gaming and non-gaming tribes. Through our research and advising, we have seen clear patterns emerge when it comes to the impacts of gaming and other economic development strategies…

It is perhaps useful to begin with a discussion of perceptions versus reality. I am continually struck by the extent to which public perception of the impact of gaming in Indian Country is coloured by the phenomenal financial success of a tiny handful of tribes—led, of course, by the Mashantucket Pequot Tribe in Connecticut. In 1996, more than half of all Indian gaming revenues were generated by only 8 tribes' operations—out of a total 112 Class III facilities. The media's attention to these cases obscures the facts that only about one-third of the nation's 550+ tribes have any gaming operations at all, and that for every highly visible, well-run, well-capitalized casino there are many more tribal operations that are modest enterprises providing employment and income in low-volume, rural markets.

Whether it is the tiny operation operating out of a pre-fab building on the Pine Ridge reservation in South Dakota, serving travellers moving between Rapid City and northern Nebraska; the development of the Hon-Dah facility at a vacation crossroads in the White Mountains of Arizona; or the development of a destination resort at Fond du Lac in rural Minnesota, our research repeatedly finds that tribal gaming enterprises yield positive economic and social benefits to those tribes that exercise their sovereignty and choose to enter the game.

The contributions that gaming is making to the affected tribes come in two primary forms: the first is *economic*. The jobs, personal income, and governmental revenues that gaming enterprises generate *are* making dents in the long-standing problems of poverty and associated social ills in Indian Country. The second kind of contribution is *institutional*. The success of tribal gaming enterprises is enabling tribes to break decades of institutional dependence in which tribal governments have been compelled to operate as *de facto* appendages to federal programs and bureaucracies. If there is one thing that our research on gaming and non-gaming tribes alike demonstrates it is that economic, social, and political success in Indian Country does not occur unless tribes have the sovereignty to govern themselves on their own terms with their own institutions…

Tribal gaming operations are the epitome of self-determination and self-government. If and when they are undertaken, they represent acts of political will, expressed through tribal members' own governments. Tribal gaming enterprises are not private for-profit businesses. Rather, they are publicly owned enterprises that provide employment and income. If successful, they generate revenues available to meet the needs of reservation citizens and to fund investments by tribal governments in the social and physical infrastructure that is so needed at so many reservations.

The contributions of tribes' investments in the gaming industry can only be assessed against the backdrop of long-standing deficits of income, infrastructure, employment, education, and social health that plague Indian Country. That is, measurements of employment gains, income improvements, and the like must be gauged against how far America's reservation citizens have to go. The deficits of economic and social deprivation in Indian Country are simply staggering.

...As of the 1990 U.S. Census, just as Class III gaming was entering the picture for tribes, Indians on reservations were America's poorest population. Per capita income in Indian Country was only $4,478, compared to $14,420 for the average American. More than half of all Indian persons on reservations were living below the poverty line, as opposed to 13% for the U.S. as a whole. Educational attainment lagged sharply behind the nation overall. Reflecting the virtual absence of a productive private sector on many reservations, almost one-half of American Indians on reservations worked in government jobs (compared to 15% in the total U.S. population). Unemployment on reservations pushed over 40% at a time when the national economy showed 6%. In fact, in the late 1990s, unemployment on reservations commonly exceeds 50%, and in some places real joblessness pushes above 90%. On reservations such as Northern Cheyenne in Montana or Rosebud Sioux in South Dakota, the economy subsists overwhelmingly on governmental transfer payments. Along with these economic factors, indicators of social ill-being, from suicide to tuberculosis and from the quality of roads to the age of school buildings, are discouraging in their seriousness.

It is in this environment of extreme deprivation that successful gaming ventures can make their contributions. For, it is important to reiterate that, unlike the net income earned by private owners—shareholders—of private gaming operations, tribal gaming enterprises yield public revenues. These revenues are employed by tribal governments to meet the needs of their citizens in much the same way that state government lotteries support states' legitimate governmental functions and obligations. The use of tribes' gaming revenues is in accord with the Indian Gaming Regulatory Act of 1988 (IGRA) ... Typical uses of tribal governments' gaming revenues...span the range from health and education to community infrastructure and job training.

...Through tribal-state gaming compacts, contributions are made directly to non- Indian governments' and local communities' programs—from state universities and law enforcement to chambers of commerce and off-reservation elementary schools.

Tribal gaming operations are not only enhancing the ability of tribal governments to meet the needs of their citizens. They are also making direct and indirect contributions to reservation and off-reservation economies through the commerce they create. Apart from the generation of governmental revenues, Indian gaming operations create income and jobs, as well as tax revenues and savings on unemployment and income assistance. For the longer term, they provide critical workplace experience to otherwise unemployed individuals, and such experience is repeatedly shown to be the key to increases in standards of living and workplace advancement.

Perhaps the most widely studied impacts of Indian gaming are those in Wisconsin. There it is estimated that Indian gaming is contributing a net addition to employment of approximately 18,000 workers and on the order of $1 billion per year to the state's gross domestic product. In study after study, tribal unemployment is reduced with the introduction of gaming, and ancillary employment is created both on and off reservation as patrons travel, feed, and lodge themselves during their visits. Improvements in employment are accompanied by net increases in income and sales taxes for state and local governments, and AFDC and unemployment insurance costs are reduced. Finally, multiple studies consistently find that crime is reduced with the advent of tribal gaming—apparently correlated with the improvements in employment and income.

The impacts that tribes are having, and that they are bringing to surrounding communities, when they decide to undertake and succeed in developing gaming operations have led many outside Indian Country to view the rights of tribes to enter the industry as some sort of welfare program for tribes. This perspective fails to recognize that the decisions of a tribe to enter gaming—or to forgo gaming—are acts of self-governance that do not differ in character from those taken by a state or a national government. Importantly, research indicates that tribes with long cultural histories of receptivity to and social control over gambling have been more likely to enter into gaming than tribes with long-standing cultures that are more resistant to gambling. In other words, the tribes that have been most willing to undertake gaming have been those for whom it is most culturally appropriate, and numerous tribes have voted down gaming as self-determined acts of self-governance.

Herein lies the most important impact of tribes' rights to embark on gaming. Just as with economic progress in sectors other than gaming, tribes' powers of self-government are repeatedly found to be the prerequisite of success. Both the economics and the morality of the issue argue against reining in the rights of tribal citizens to govern themselves. To do so not only violates basic rights, but also portends a return to policies of dependence and subjugation. Policies that have made Native Americans and their governments dependents of the federal or state governments have been the most destructive of tribal members' well-being. For many tribes, gaming has provided the opportunity and the resources for breaking the cycles of dependence.

Nation–State Gaming Compact between the Seneca Nation of Indians and the State of New York, April 2002

In the following document, key parts of the gaming compact between the Seneca and the State of New York highlight tribal and state jurisdictions and responsibilities, the land involved in this specific Indian gaming operation and the percentage of profits earned by the state of New York from Seneca gaming.

This Compact is made and entered into between the Seneca Nation of Indians, a sovereign Indian nation ("Nation") and the State of New York ("State") pursuant to the provisions of the Indian Gaming Regulatory Act, 25 U.S.C. §§ 2701 et seq. ("IGRA").

WHEREAS, the Nation is a sovereign Indian nation recognized by the United States of America, possessing all sovereign fights and powers pertaining thereto; and

WHEREAS, the State is a state of the United States of America, possessing all sovereign rights and powers pertaining thereto.

NOW, THEREFORE, the NATION and the STATE, consistent with the Memorandum of Understanding between the State Governor and the President of the Seneca Nation of Indians executed on January 20th 2001, and in consideration of the undertakings and agreements hereinafter set forth, hereby enter into this Class III Gaming Compact...

4. TERM OF COMPACT.

...(b) Termination Date. This Compact shall terminate on the fourteenth (14th) anniversary of the Effective Date, unless renewed...

(c) Renewals.

(1) Unless either Party objects in writing delivered to the other Party no later than one hundred twenty (120) days prior to the expiration of the fourteen (14)-year term established pursuant to Paragraph 4(b) the term of this Compact shall be renewed automatically for an additional period of seven (7) years.

(2) In the event either Party does timely object to the automatic renewal of the term of this Compact, the Parties shall meet promptly following the receipt of such written objection and use their best efforts to address the objecting Party's concerns through frequent and regular good faith negotiations...

(d) Early Termination.

(1) Either Party may terminate this Compact at any time if any of the following occurs:

a. The IGRA is repealed;

b. The Nation adopts a referendum revoking the Nation's authority to conduct Class III Gaming; or,

c. The other Party commits a Material Breach...

5. NATION REGULATORY AUTHORITY.

(a) General Responsibility. The SGA [Seneca Gaming Authority] shall have responsibility for the on-site regulation of Class III Gaming undertaken by the Nation pursuant to this Compact...

(b) Specific Elements of SGA's Regulatory Responsibilities. The Nation shall ensure that the SGA regulates the Class III Gaming undertaken by the Nation pursuant to this Compact...

(e) Investigations. SGA inspectors shall have authority to investigate any matter relating to the regulation of the Nation's Class III Gaming operations pursuant to this Compact.

(f) Provision of Reports; Process and Resolution of Disputes. The SGA shall cooperate with the SGO [State Gaming Officials] and shall make immediately available to the SGO all patron complaints, incident reports, gaming violations, surveillance logs, and security reports…

(g) Fines. The SGA shall be empowered by the Nation regulation to impose fines and other appropriate sanctions on the Nation Gaming Operation and its employees, licensees and vendors within the jurisdiction of the Nation for violations of this Compact…

6. STATE RESPONSIBILITY.

(a) Generally. The SGO shall have responsibility to ensure Nation compliance with the terms of this Compact…

(c) Access. For purposes of fulfilling its responsibilities…SGO shall be afforded immediate, unfettered access to all areas of the Gaming Facilities during all hours of operation without notice. SGO shall be afforded full access to areas of the Gaming Facilities in which money is counted or kept only when accompanied by SGA personnel, or when SGA otherwise provides permission…

(e) Conduct of State personnel. SGO shall take all reasonable measures to avoid interfering with the conduct of Class III Gaming and related activities and operations of the Nation Gaming Operation.

(g) Investigations. The SGO shall have the authority to investigate any alleged violations of this Compact. The SGA and the Nation Gaming Operation shall cooperate with the SGO in such investigations…

(j) Cultural Exchange. The State agrees and understands that the Nation possesses its own unique social customs, traditions, laws, and history. In order to make SGO and State personnel working at, or in conjunction with, a Gaming Facility more aware of the Nation's culture, traditions, laws and history and for purposes of fostering an environment that is consistent therewith, the Nation may conduct periodic cultural seminars in a mariner of its choosing for all such personnel. It shall be the policy of the Nation and the State that such employees attend such seminars…

7. LAW ENFORCEMENT MATTERS.

(a) Jurisdiction. Nothing in this Compact shall affect the law enforcement jurisdiction of the Nation or the State over the Nation's lands as provided by applicable law…

8. ACCOUNTING STANDARDS AND AUDITING REQUIREMENTS.

(a) Books and records. The Nation Gaming Operation shall make and keep books and records that accurately and fairly reflect each day's transactions, including but not limited to receipt of funds, expenses, prize claims, prize disbursements or prizes liable to be paid, and other financial transactions of or related to the Nation's Gaming Facilities, so as to permit preparation of monthly and annual financial statements in conformity with Generally Accepted Accounting Principles as applied to the gaming industry and to maintain daily accountability…

11. SITES FOR GAMING FACILITIES.

(a) Subject to the provisions of this Paragraph 11, the Nation may establish Gaming Facilities:

(1) in Niagara County, at the location in the City of Niagara Falls…or at such other site as may be determined by the Nation in the event the foregoing site is unavailable to the Nation for any reason; and

(2) in Erie County, at a location in the City of Buffalo to be determined by the Nation, or at such other site as may be determined by the Nation in the event a site in the City of Buffalo is rejected by the Nation for any reason; and

(3) on current Nation reservation territory, at such time and at such location as may be determined by the Nation.

(b) With respect to the sites referenced m subparagraphs 11(a)(1) and 11(a)(2):

(1) The sites shall be utilized for gaming and commercial activities traditionally associated with the operation or conduct of a casino facility;

(2) The State agrees to assist the Nation in acquiring the site…within the limits of the Seneca Settlement Act funds that the Nation has committed to the acquisition of such site;a. No later than thirty (30) days after the execution of this Compact by both Parties, the State, through the Empire State Development Corporation ("ESDC") or otherwise, shall transfer fee title to the Niagara Falls Convention Centre and such other property as the State may own within the boundaries of the parcel…in fee simple to the Nation in consideration of a payment from the Nation of one dollar ($1.00) in funds appropriated by the Seneca Settlement Act;

b. The Nation shall lease back to the State the Niagara Fails Convention Centre building for a period of twenty-one (21) years for an annual lease payment of one dollar ($1.00);

c. The State, in turn, shall lease to the Nation the Niagara Falls Convention Centre building for a period of twenty one (21) years for an annual lease payment of one dollar ($1.00) until such time as the Nation constructs and begins operation of a permanent Gaming Facility in the Niagara Falls, at which time the Nation shall pay to the State the balance, as of July 1, 2002, of the general obligation bonds pledged in connection with the Niagara Falls Convention Centre; and,

d. The State shall assist the Nation in whatever manner appropriate including the exercise of the power of eminent domain, to obtain the remaining lands…on the best economic terms possible. In the event the State does obtain all or part of the lands...through exercise of the power of eminent domain, it shall promptly convey such lands to the Nation at a price equal to the cost of acquisition...

(4) The Nation agrees that it will use all but five million dollars ($5,000,000) of the funds remaining from amounts appropriated by the Seneca Settlement Act to acquire the parcels in the City of Niagara Fails and the City of Buffalo.

(c) The Nation agrees that it will dedicate Seneca Settlement Act funds remaining after the acquisition of the sites referenced in Paragraph 11(a)(1) and 11(a)(2) to the acquisition of parcels to meet the housing needs of the Nation's members...

12. EXCLUSIVITY AND STATE CONTRIBUTION.

(a) Exclusivity.

(1)...the Nation shall have total exclusivity with respect to the installation and operation of, and no person, or entity other than the Nation shall be permitted to install or operate, Gaming Devices, including slot machines, within the geographic area defined by: (i) to the east, State Route 14 from Sodus Point to the Pennsylvania border with New York; (ii) to the north, the border between New York and Canada; (iii) to the south, the Pennsylvania border with New York; and (iv) to the west, the border between New York and Canada and the border between Pennsylvania and New York.

(2) In the event the Tuscarora Indian Nation or the Tonawanda Band of Seneca Indians initiate negotiations with the State to establish a Class III Gaming compact, the State may agree to include Gaming Devices in any such compact that permits gaming facilities within the geographical area of exclusivity set forth in Paragraph 12(a)(1) without causing a breach of this Paragraph 12; (i) provided however, that in no event shall the State permit another Indian nation to establish a Class III Gaming facility within a twenty five (25) mile radius of any Gaming Facility site authorized under this Compact unless such facility is to be established on federally recognized Indian lands existing as of the Effective Date of this Compact.

(3) The exclusivity granted under Paragraph 12(a)(1) shall cease to apply with respect to any one of the sites authorized under this Compact: (i) if the Nation fails to commence construction on such site with thirty six (36) months of the Effective Date; or (ii) if the Nation fails to commence Class III Gaming operations on such site within sixty (60) months of the Effective Date...

(b) State Contribution.

(1) In consideration of the exclusivity granted by the State pursuant to Paragraph 12(a), the Nation agrees to contribute to the State a portion of the proceeds from the operation and conduct of each category of Gaming Device for which exclusivity exists, based on the net drop of such machines (money dropped into machines, after payout but before expense) and totaled on a cumulative quarterly basis to be adjusted annually at the end

of the relevant fiscal year, in accordance with the sliding scale set forth below ("State Contribution"):

Years 1-4

18%, with "Year 1" commencing on the date on which the first Gaming Facility established pursuant to this Compact begins operation, and with Payments during this initial period are to be made on an annual basis.

Years 5-7

22%, with payments during this period to be made on a semi-annual basis.

Years 8-14

25%, with payments during this period to be made on a quarterly basis.

(2) In the event the States reaches a compact with another Indian tribe regarding Gaming Devices of a like kind that has State contribution provisions that are more favourable to the Indian tribe than those set forth herein, the terms of such other compact shall be automatically applicable to this Compact at the Nation's option...

14. PARTY DISPUTE RESOLUTION.

(a) Purpose. The Nation and the State intend to resolve disputes in a manner that will foster a spirit of cooperation and efficiency in the administration of and compliance by each Party with the provisions of this Compact...

16. AMENDMENT AND MODIFICATION.

(a) Amendment and modification. The provisions of this Paragraph 16 shall govern the amendment and modification of this Compact. The Compact and its Appendices may be amended or modified by written agreement of the Nation and the State...

IN WITNESS WHEREOF, the Parties have executed this Agreement as of the date indicated below.

DATE: _____   _____

PRESIDENT
SENECA NATION OF INDIANS

_____

GOVERNOR
STATE OF NEW YORK

Carol York, 2006

In this extract, Carol York, an elected county commissioner in Hood River County, Oregon, explains that the Warm Springs development proposed by the Warm Springs tribe has much local support not least because the tribe agreed to move the location of the casino from an area of beauty to another area in need of redevelopment.

...Hood River County is located east of the Portland, Oregon metropolitan area. It is bordered by the Columbia River on the north, the Mount Hood National Forest on the South and Wasco County on the east...

For the last 8 years – since 1998 -- Hood River County has been actively involved in a local debate about Class III gaming in our County. The Confederated Tribes of the Warm Springs own trust property located immediately east of the City of Hood River – the largest city in our County. While the Warm Springs own and operate a casino in a temporary location on their reservation located approximately 38 miles south of Hood River, since 1998, they have explored the possibility of moving their casino from its existing location to their trust property in Hood River.

However, in *response* to local community opposition to the citing of a casino on their trust property in Hood River – property which happens to be located on beautiful and prominent headlands overlooking the Columbia River Gorge National Scenic Area - the Warm Springs have chosen instead, to pursue the acquisition of vacant industrial zoned land in the economically disadvantaged City of Cascade Locks...While the City of Cascade Locks, like the City of Hood River is located within the Columbia Gorge National Scenic Area, the Act creating the National Scenic Area recognized the need for continued economic development in the Gorge and specifically carved out Urban Growth Boundaries within the National Scenic Area where new economic development activity is both permissible and encouraged...

Despite the significant hurdles faced by the Warm Springs...to move their casino to an area in the Gorge that has been designated for economic development, out of respect for the scenic integrity of the Gorge, respect of the local community desire to preserve the natural characteristics of the Tribe's trust land in Hood River, and in response to an *invitation* from the City of Cascade Locks and the Port of Cascade Locks, to locate their casino in Cascade Locks, the Warm Springs have pursued this option.

I am here today to testify that the Hood River County Commission *unanimously* supports efforts to locate the Warm Springs Class III gaming facility in Cascade Locks, as does the Wasco County Commission to our east, and the Skamania and Klickitat County Commissions, which are located across the Columbia River from Cascade Locks in Washington State. The Cascade Locks City Council is also strongly supportive, and the City of North Bonneville, Washington (located across the river from Cascade Locks) is also on record in support of the proposal. *None* of these local units of government has come to support this casino proposal on a whim or without deliberate, open public debate which has taken place over many years. In our County alone, the issue was discussed at countless meetings -- all open to the public – before our County Commission came to its unanimous decision to support the casino in Cascade Locks. And in the City of Cascade Locks, despite that City's limited budget and dwindling tax base, the City Councillors spent significant financial resources to conduct a professionally managed and tightly controlled public survey on the sense of the community about the development of a casino within the city limits. Survey results show that 68% of survey respondents either strongly or somewhat strongly support development of a casino in Cascade Locks.

Is there opposition to this proposal? Yes, of course there is - what significant public works or economic development project doesn't have some level of opposition? Is it overwhelming? No, it is not. Is a majority of the opposition coming from within our County or from within the community of Cascade Locks? Absolutely not. Opposition to this project is largely coming from outside the community and is being funded and fanned by interests that have direct financial interests in limiting additional gaming in Oregon or, in the name of protecting the environment, oppose even the smallest forms of economic development in the Gorge. Today these groups oppose this proposed development of the Cascade Locks Industrial Park. A few months ago, this same friends group opposed reopening a historic roadside inn in the Gorge as a bed and breakfast because it, in their minds, was incompatible with the National interest of protecting the Gorge as a national scenic area. Where does it end?

The Columbia River Gorge *is* a national treasure. But not every square inch of the Gorge is suitable to be protected as if it were wilderness – Congress recognized that when it passed the Scenic Act in 1986. The images at the conclusion of this testimony provide for the Committee a perspective on the "scenic quality" of the industrial park where this proposed project will be located, and where in compliance with the National Scenic Act, economic development activities are targeted.

As a local public official, I talk on a frequent basis to the constituents who elect me. I see them in the grocery store, I buy gas from them for my car. I know them, they know me. I believe I am representing their interests and their desires. If they disagree, I hear about it in person, not in a letter or email.

Furthermore, this casino proposal has been debated for a long enough period that numerous local elections have taken place since it was first proposed. In the last Port election, the pro-casino candidate won 79% of the vote. The voters support candidates supportive of the Warm Springs, of a casino in Cascade Locks, and the jobs that it would bring to this depressed community. I submit that local elections are the ultimate public process. Opponents claim they haven't been heard -- maybe they just aren't voters eligible to vote in our own local elections?

…The proposed project in Cascade Locks would also meet qualitative thresholds associated with being located within the same state where the proposing tribe's reservation is now located. Further, the Warm Springs proposal also seeks to locate the facility on exclusive aboriginal land as well as Treaty ceded territory...

I suggest that our County's experiences to date should be viewed as the "model" for how the process is supposed to work when conducting a thorough investigation and vigorous community debate about off-reservation gaming. Opponents to this proposal argue that they have not had adequate time or opportunity to be heard. Is it the outcome they are objecting to or the process? I submit that it is the outcome. They are not pleased that every unit of local government directly involved has endorsed the project. They are not pleased that the Governor has endorsed the proposed project and signed a Compact to allow it to move forward. And they are not pleased that even nearby local governmental units located across state boundary lines have also endorsed the project.

...to prevent model projects, such as this one, from moving forward to build on ceded aboriginal territory in a community where they are welcomed, would ultimately force the Warm Springs - for their own economic welfare and viability - to revisit building a casino on their Trust land in Hood River. Such an outcome would be a tragedy for all parties – the Confederated Tribes of the Warm Springs, the Cities of Cascade Locks and Hood River, Hood River County, the region including Oregon and Washington, and the Columbia River Gorge National Scenic Area...

Michael Lang, 2006

In the following document, Michael Lang, conservation director of Friends of the Columbia Gorge, highlights why he and the Friends of the Columbia Gorge oppose the Warm Springs casino. He argues that it would be a detriment to the environment and the natural resources of the area.

...Friends of the Columbia Gorge (Friends) supports reform to the Indian Gaming Regulatory Act (IGRA) by requiring greater community consultation and approval and placing restrictions on what is commonly referred to as "off-reservation gaming"...

Friends of the Columbia Gorge (Friends) is a non-profit organization with 4,200 members dedicated to protecting and enhancing the scenic, natural, cultural, and recreational resources of the Columbia River Gorge...

The Columbia River Gorge is truly a national scenic treasure. Stretching 85 miles in length, it is the only sea level passage through the Cascade Mountains. Its dramatic cliffs, plunging waterfalls and diversity of climates and ecosystems have captivated people for thousands of years. The Columbia River Gorge National Scenic Area Act (Scenic Area Act), passed by Congress in 1986, protects and enhances the aesthetic, biological, ecological, economic, historic, and recreational values of the Columbia River Gorge...

The Columbia River Gorge National Scenic Area in Oregon, as well as Washington, would be significantly and adversely impacted by the Tribe's proposed casino complex, intended to consist of a 600,000-square-foot facility that would include a casino, hotel, spa, restaurants, and several meeting and entertainment venues. The proposed casino and its immense parking areas would be visible from the Pacific Crest National Scenic Trail, the Historic Columbia River Highway, Interstate 84 and the Columbia River. These are all designated as "key viewing areas" within the National Scenic Area. The proposed casino would be visible for miles along the Columbia River Gorge and would adversely affect the scenic beauty of the Columbia River Gorge. The casino would significantly increase the level of noise and light pollution in the Gorge. The Scenic Area and the Columbia River would receive the wastewater discharge caused by this casino resort. A substantial containment system for parking lot run-off would have to be built. Fish and wildlife habitat, including existing bald eagle sites, osprey nests, blue heron rookeries, and salmon habitat would likely be harmed by the casino development.

The casino is projected to attract three million visitors each year, increasing automobile traffic and causing air pollution in an area that is already suffering from this problem. According to "IMPROVE" visibility monitoring sites within the Columbia River Gorge, visibility is impaired 95% of the time within the National Scenic Area due to air pollution. The recently released "Fog Water Deposition Study," carried out by the U.S. Forest Service, reports that acid rain and fog levels within the National Scenic Area are ten to thirty times more acidic than normal rainfall. Introducing millions more cars into the Columbia River Gorge every year would only exacerbate this existing problem. Perhaps most damaging would be the spin-off development and cumulative effects associated with such a large-scale casino. These impacts would disrupt the carefully balanced land use plan that has been achieved under the National Scenic Area Act.

For these reasons, Friends of the Columbia Gorge and its allies are opposed to the Warm Springs Tribe's effort to relocate an established and successful casino from its existing reservation to an off-reservation location within the heart of a National Scenic Area. We have joined with the Oregon Restaurant Association, the Oregon Family Council, the Confederated Tribes of the Grand Ronde and many other citizen groups, both within the Gorge and across the state, to oppose a mega-casino within our national scenic treasure, the Columbia River Gorge.

...We have long been opposed to the Warm Springs Tribe's efforts to relocate its existing, successful, on-reservation casino from its 640,000-acre reservation to an off-reservation site in the Columbia River Gorge. Although many area tribes have a historical relationship with the Gorge and a desire to establish off-reservation casinos, Warm Springs is the only Tribe to have pressured the State to allow it to exploit the natural values of the Columbia River Gorge to advance its economic self-interest by siting a casino resort as close as possible to the Portland metropolitan area, the state's largest population center.

...Former Governor Kitzhaber opposed both the Cascade Locks and Hood River [gaming] sites on a number of grounds, including the State's longstanding policy of limiting Indian gaming to one casino per Tribe located on an established reservation. This policy has worked well for the State and the Tribes, preventing the undesirable and environmentally harmful practice of "casino-shopping," while at the same time allowing the Tribes to advance their economic goals through on-reservation development in a manner fair to all Tribes. With nine in-state Tribes, eight of which have existing on-reservation casinos, the implementation of Oregon's longstanding policy has been a model of fairness and certainty, promoting economic growth balanced with sound environmental and land use management principles.

However, since the election of our current Governor in 2002, we feel that the political, legislative and statutory processes have failed to protect the people of Oregon and the Columbia River Gorge. We, including our diverse group of allies, have been shut out of the political process by a Governor, who as a candidate promised to oppose the Warm Springs Gorge Casino proposal, but as Oregon's Governor, turned his back on his supporters and negotiated a compact with the Tribe with no process for input from the public. Never were the residents of the Gorge, citizens of Oregon or members of other tribes in Oregon consulted about a proposal that would throw out Oregon's current policy barring off-reservation casinos, place the state's largest casino resort in the middle of a National Scenic Area and set a precedent for a dramatic increase in gambling in the state...

The very reason why the Warm Springs Tribe is seeking the establishment of an off-reservation casino in Cascade Locks is to exploit the gaming market in the Portland metro area. Cascade Locks is at the very edge of the Tribe's aboriginal range and is as close as the Tribe can get to the metro area ... .the concerns of Portland, Gresham, Vancouver, Troutdale and many other surrounding communities won't matter to the BIA even though these communities and their citizens will be adversely impacted by added traffic, congestion, and the social impacts that are associated with increased gambling.

Oregonians are opposed to off-reservation casinos in general and to an off-reservation casino in the Columbia Gorge, in particular. In recent poll of registered voters in Oregon 63% of respondents were opposed to an off-reservation casino in the Columbia Gorge and 68% would vote against it if it were put before Oregon voters in the form of a referendum...

It is no surprise that Oregon residents are opposed to an off-reservation casino within one of the crown jewels of our state. The Columbia River Gorge National Scenic Area is precisely the kind of location that should be protected from development of this nature.

Our lives, our land and a jewel in America's crown are being sold and paid for with reservation shopping and trust land roulette...

The Warm Springs Tribe has long been recognized as an extraordinarily successful tribe in a number of sources, including Charles Wilkinson's book "*Blood Struggle,*"-, which features Warm Springs as a prime example of a self-sufficient tribe. Please consider that the Warm Springs Tribe has a vast reservation with U.S. Highway 26 running through it and an intersection with U.S. Highway 97 only 10 miles from the eastern boundary of the reservation. This area is the fastest growing region in the State of Oregon. However, the Tribe's existing casino is located miles away from U.S. Highway 26 in an isolated part of the Warm Springs' reservation.

If the Warm Springs Tribe were to locate a new *on-reservation* casino along U.S. Highway 26, that casino would generate much more revenue for this already successful Tribe, provide many more jobs for tribal members closer to their homes, maintain Oregon's policy barring off-reservation casinos and would protect the Columbia River Gorge, one of America's natural scenic treasures, from the ill-effects of a Las Vegas-sized casino.

In addition, we respectfully propose that the committee consider the prohibition of casinos within our national parks, wilderness areas, national scenic areas and national recreation areas due to the inherent conflicts between large-scale casino gaming and the preservation of natural, scenic and natural resource-based recreational values. The Congress of the United States has made a determination that these are special places. The Columbia Gorge National Scenic Area was established by Congress to protect and provide for the enhancement of the scenic, cultural, recreational and natural resources of the Columbia River Gorge...

We are waging a titanic battle to save the very resource this Congress acted so wisely to protect. Please do not ignore our pleas for help...

CHAPTER FOURTEEN

INDIAN REPRESENTATION, MUSEUMS AND THE REPATRIATION OF INDIAN BONES

After centuries of cultural misrepresentation and oppression, Indian communities in today's America are reclaiming control over their cultural heritages. Since the 1970s many have found new ways to voice their concerns over the protection of their cultural images and cultural artefacts, and over how best to celebrate and preserve tribal cultures for future generations. Conflict has focused around the question of who has the right to represent and speak for Indians in cultural, legal and economic issues, who has the right to ownership of Indian bones and artefacts and whether such items should be displayed for public consumption in museums. There has been ongoing conflict and protest over the derogatory use of Indian images by American sports teams and universities.

The rise of Indian economic power and Indian sovereignty within the boundaries of the United States of America during the last few decades has led debates over what and who is an 'Indian'. With the rise in Indian gaming profits, increases in the numbers of Indian groups claiming federal recognition and an overall increase in the Indian population, the question has become even more contested. Since the 1970s Indian ethnicity has had its own wider cultural kudos but it is an identity many feel should be limited only to those who are enrolled members of a specific tribe.[1] Today, Indian country is composed of over 550 federally recognised tribes, and according to a US Census Bureau press release in May 2008, the Indian population in 2007, which includes American Indian and Alaska Natives, had risen to 4,536,857, an increase of over 300,000 people from 2000.[2] The dramatic increase in the Indian population over the last few decades is connected to the cultural and political resurgence Indian nations have undergone since the 1970s. The change in how Indian identity is generally perceived has encouraged many to take pride in their Indian ancestry often in conjunction with another ethnic background on new forms of elective census. Since Indian identity may carry with it both benefits in the form of legal rights and responsibilities in the form of taxes and kinship, this change has not always been smooth. Established tribal groups have on occasion taken exception to the federal recognition of other Indian groups. For example, the Tuscarora of North Carolina bitterly oppose the Lumbee federal recognition process currently being conducted by Congress and have argued that the Lumbee have attempted to steal their heritage and culture.[3] The Lumbee contend that the Tuscarora are a splinter-group of the Lumbee and despite the controversy, Congress seems to be heading towards passing the Lumbee Recognition Act into law. In addition, the Eastern Band of Cherokee, who also reside in North Carolina, have argued against the federal recognition of the Lumbee and believe that large amounts of intermarriage with other races has nullified their claims to become an Indian tribe. Some Indian nations guard their own definitions of what it is to be an Indian very closely. The White Mountain Apache require substantial tribal ancestry to become a tribal member, while other tribes such as the Cherokee and the Pequot do not require any particular degree of tribal ancestry from people wanting to become members. Similarly the Oglala on Pine Ridge Reservation do not require tribal members to have a certain amount of Indian blood to qualify as members, only that they commit to the Oglala culture and lifestyle.[4]

We are currently in the heart of a sustained period of protest by Indian Nations over the return or repatriation of religious artefacts and the skeletal remains of their ancestors. Over centuries many non-Indians such as federal army and States of the Union troops, collectors and scientists have plundered Indian country of cultural materials and human remains.[5] Exhibits of human bones and historical and cultural artefacts, such as pottery, blankets and objects of spiritual significance were readily displayed in museums and held by federal institutions and private collectors without the consent of the Indian nations concerned. Non-Indian archaeologists and anthropologists argued that it was essential for American institutions to acquire and continue to examine indigenous human bones so as to discover more about the people and the surrounding environments in which they lived. In contrast, Indian communities felt that their ancestors did not have dignity in death and that their remains should be returned to their nations and buried on their homelands. Indian remains were returned in 1989, when New York State Museum gave back twelve wampum belts to the Onondaga and in 1990, when Zuni war gods displayed in museums around the United States were returned to their homelands in New Mexico.[6] After strong protests by Indian Nations and national and local Indian organisations in 1990 the US Congress passed the Native American Graves Protection and Repatriation Act (NAGPRA), also known as Public Law 101–601. The act set-up a mechanism that allowed for the protection of Native American burial sites and for the repatriation of Indian remains to federally recognised Indian nations. The act declared that any museum and institution that received federal funds had to provide an inventory of all Indian remains and allow it to be made available to the relevant Indian nation. The act has prompted an unprecedented era of co-operation between federal agencies, museums and universities and Indian nations and, importantly, began to reverse centuries of cultural theft. NAGPRA remains an ongoing process rather than an event since compliance with its mandates has been uneven. Many battles over appropriate restitution of Indian bones and objects remain to be fought but NAGPRA is a key federal building block in what is inevitably a long-term process of humanizing Indian peoples in terms of how they are thought of by mainstream America.

On 21 September 2004, the National Museum of the American Indian opened its doors for the first time. The museum project began in 1989 when President George Bush signed the National Museum of the American Indian Act (NMAI), also known as Public Law 101–185 into law, the idea being to rectify the injustice that up until that point there had been no national museum devoted exclusively to the history and future of all Indian peoples. The Act was to establish a museum and 'living memorial' on the National Mall in Washington, D.C. dedicated to the study and research of Native America cultures, and exhibiting rare and important artefacts and historic objects from the Native American collections at the Heye Museum in New York and the Smithsonian Institution in Washington, D.C. After fifteen years of debate and in-fighting between Indian interested parties and negotiations and controversy between Indians and non-Indians over the design, construction and funding of the Museum, the grand opening of the museum took place. The day was marked by a number of eloquent and emotional speeches made by individuals including Senator Ben Nighthorse Campbell (1933–), Senator Daniel K. Inouye, Richard West, Jr. (1943–), Lawrence Small and President Alejandro Toledo of Peru. The event spoke to the cultural prominence of all Indians in twenty-first century America. Although the ceremony put forward a positive image of indigenous America, some, including Marc Fisher from the Washington Post, were critical. He openly questioned the sparse content of the museum, the lack of information about modern-day relationships between Indians and society and the lack of data on Indian Nations in twenty-first century America.[7]

During the early 1990s Indian activists began to take on the corporate and multi-million dollar sports teams over their derogatory use of Indian names and mascots.[8] Indian organisations such as the National Coalition on Racism in Sports and Media and the Inter-tribal Council of the Five Civilised Tribes have argued that the use of Indian mascots in teams such as the Cleveland Indians and Washington Redskins is racist and overtly oppressive. They argue that it demeans all Indians in the minds of Americans and peoples around the world.[9] It is felt that the use of 'Indian' sports images sends out a message that perpetuates the racial, cultural and spiritual stereotyping of indigenous people as 'inferior red-skinned savages', a message that can be traced from the time of Christopher Columbus, through the colonial period and within the Western and other media into the present day. The constant bombardment of negative images of Indians on television, in the newspapers and in sports stadiums is held to negatively impact upon the self-image of the young and old in Native America.

Much of the conflict over the appropriation of Indian names by sports teams takes the form of direct protest, battles in courtrooms and corporate boardrooms, in the media and in Congress. In 1998, on the opening day of the baseball season, five protestors, Vernon Bellecourt, Juan Reyna, James Watson, Charlene Teters, and Zizwe Tchiquka protested at Jacobs Field, the home of the Cleveland Indians baseball team, over the derogatory and racist use of the team mascot, Chief Wahoo. They burned an effigy of Chief Wahoo and were arrested by Cleveland police. In protest at their arrest, the group sued the Cleveland Police and other local agencies. After years of legal proceedings, in 2004 their arguments that the police violated their constitutional rights were dismissed when the Ohio Supreme Court ruled in favour of the police.[10] There have been a number of other protests over the use of Indian images against teams such as the Washington Redskins and the Atlanta Braves. In some instances University sports teams have changed their names and even banned the use of negative Indian imagery. Non-Indian organisations such as the United States Commission on Civil Rights have also long supported the push to banish the use of pejorative images of Indians in American society.[11] It is worth noting the disparity – racist and pejorative depictions of Black and Hispanic peoples have long been removed from sports insignia, memorabilia and from the uniforms of sports teams.

Over the last four decades Indian activism has done a great deal to redress the negative images of Indians that pervade American society. Indian individuals and groups have battled for the repatriation of Indian remains and religious artefacts from American museums and private collectors and have voiced their concerns over a negative stereotype being promulgated to global audiences by American sports teams through their mascots and team uniforms. The opening of the National Museum of the American Indian in 2004 goes some way towards a national recognition that the 'Indians' did not disappear at Wounded Knee in 1890 and the close of the frontier. On the contrary, the museum testifies to the power and resilience of Indian peoples in the twenty-first century and to their cultural, economic and political potential in generations to come.

SOURCES

Grand Opening Speech by W. Richard West, Jr.:
National Museum of the American Indian, 21 September 2004

*In the following text, W. Richard West, Jr. (1943–), director of the National
Museum of the American, Smithsonian Institution, at the opening ceremony
of the National Museum of the American Indian in Washington, D.C.,
describes the cultural importance of the opening of the museum and places the
significance of the day within the long history of the divergent lives of all
Indian Nations within the Americas.*

For a decade and a half I have thought about what I would say in the next
seven minutes. I realize that no reflections of mine can possibly match in
significance what we celebrate today on America's National Mall. But once
in a great while, something so important and so powerful occurs that, just for
a moment, history seems to stand still – and silent - in honor. I sense that
this place and this time in the fall equinox season of 2004 is one of those
moments. As a small part of that moment, I now offer these words to you
with humility and great respect.

I have thought so often, as the Director and as a Southern Cheyenne, about
the true meaning of the National Museum of the American Indian. Like all of
you, I have a deep pride in creating this cultural and spiritual marker for the
ages on America's National Mall – this beautiful Native place. As a museum, it
celebrates, which often have not been known or understood, the truly great
cultural accomplishments of the Native peoples of the Americas long before
others came. It also insists that Native communities and cultures are very
much alive, if often challenged by hard circumstances, throughout the
hemisphere. It uses the voices of Native peoples themselves in telling the
histories and stories of Native America, past and present.

I always have believed, however, that the National Museum of the American
Indian is really a symbol for something bigger and more important than even
that beautiful Native place just across the street. And that is this: it is a symbol
for the hope, centuries in the making, that the hearts and minds of all
Americans, beyond this museum and throughout the Americas, will open and
welcome the presence of the first peoples in their history and in their
contemporary lives.

We have lived in these lands and sacred places for thousands of years. We
thus are the original part of the cultural heritage of every person hearing
these words today, whether you are Native or non-Native. We have felt the
cruel and destructive edge of the colonialism that followed contact and lasted
for hundreds of years. But, in our minds and in history, we are not its victims.
As the Mohawks have counseled us, "It is hard to see the future with tears in
your eyes." We have survived and, from a cultural standpoint, triumphed

against great odds. We are here now - 40,000,000 indigenous people throughout the Americas and in hundreds of different cultural communities. And we will insist, as we must, that we remain a part of the cultural future of the Americas, just as we were a part of its past and fought so hard to be a part of its present.

But the National Museum of the American Indian is even more significant as a symbol for this: that, at long last, the culturally different histories, cultures, and peoples of the Americas can come together in new mutual understanding and respect. That understanding and respect make possible the true cultural reconciliation that until now has eluded American history.

This prayerful hope has been stated before with far more eloquence than mine, and I want you to hear those words now. Exactly a century ago, on September 21, 1904, Native America lost one of its most legendary patriot chiefs. He was known in English as Chief Joseph, but to his own people he was Hinmatoowyalahtqit. He made his plea in 1879, just after he had barely failed in his legendary march to seek freedom in Canada from the United States Seventh Cavalry:

If the white man wants to live in peace with the Indian, there need be no trouble. Treat all men alike. ... Give them all an even chance to live and grow. All men were made by the same Great Spirit. They are brothers.

So in the spirit of Hinmatoowyalahtqit and at the opening of the National Museum of the American Indian, I say, on this September 21st, to those of you within sight and sound of this occasion who descend from those who came, "Welcome to Native America." And I say to those of you who descend from the Native ancestors who were here, "Welcome home."...

Senator Ben Nighthorse Campbell: National Museum of the American Indian, 21 September 2004

Provided here are extracts from the speech made by Senator Ben Nighthorse Campbell (1933–) at the opening ceremony of the National Museum of the American Indian. Campbell describes the importance of the museum within the context of changing federal policy of the American government. He describes the museum as a dedication and monument in celebration of all past and future Indian generations.

Senator Dan Inouye, my friend and colleague, to whom we owe so much, often says that Washington is a city of monuments and yet, there is not one monument to the Native people of this land. This magnificent structure is that monument in which we will tell our story.

Indeed it is a monument to the Mimbres, the Anasazi, the Toltecs and Hopewell, the Chacoans, the Mayans and hundreds of other cultures now long gone, who lived in communities called Tikal, Tenochtitlan, Cahokia and a multitude of other enlightened communities while European cities were in their infancy.

They were communities inhabited by farmers and doctors, teachers and craftsmen, housewives and soldiers, priests and astronomers, who with all their collective wisdom could not have known that earth mother would someday be called real estate. They knew not alcohol or drug abuse, Tuberculosis or Cholera, Smallpox or Aids or even the common cold. How much we can learn from them.

It is a monument to the millions of Native people who died of sickness, slavery, starvation and war until they were reduced from an estimated 50 million people in North and Central America to just over 200,000 souls in the United States by 1900. Only 400 years after the old world collided with their world, the Native people of this land became America's first endangered species.

In spite of this sad truth, this beautiful structure is also a monument to the 190 thousand American Indian Veterans who served with honor and courage in our armed forces, defending a nation that was founded on religious freedom while practicing their own was often against the law. They faithfully carried out the orders of the Commander in Chief, even though before 1924, they could not legally vote for him because they were not considered citizens.

It is a monument to our elders, who as children, were taken from their loved ones and placed in boarding schools that often had the adage: "kill the Indian to save the child."

All too often they were beaten for speaking their Native language or praying to their God. All too many chose suicide as their only alternative, but those who endured through shorn of their hair and stripped of their dignity were never shorn of their spiritualism or stripped of their pride. They are our mothers and fathers.

It is a monument to a people who were here before the birth of a boy king in Egypt called Tutankhamen and before the Greek poet Homer wrote the Iliad and before Caesar watched Roman chariots race in the Circus Maximus and before Christ walked the hills near the Sea of Galilee.

And last, it is a monument to all the dreamers who helped make this day come true.

As I leave public office in a few short months, I am reminded of a stanza from the Navaho chant of The Beauty Way. The Navaho people sing:

In the House of Long Life,
    There I wander,
In the House of Happiness,
    There I Wander,
Beauty is before me and behind me,
Beauty is above me and below me,
Beauty is all around me,
    With it I wander,
In old age traveling,
    With it I wander,
On the beautiful trail Am I,
    With it I wander

Thanks to the efforts of all those assembled today and to so many more, we celebrate the opening of this house of happiness, this house of long life and walk the trail of beauty.

To all our friends here today I say: the sacred hoop has been restored. The circle is complete.

Inter-Tribal Council of the Five Civilised Tribes: Mascot Resolution, No. 2001–08, 14 July 2001

The following document is a resolution passed by the Inter-tribal Council of the Five Civilized Tribes declaring that the use of Indian mascots and symbols in sports is derogatory and propagates an inaccurate historical stereotype. It argues that these images affect the self-confidence of all Indians and supports the position of the US Commission on Civil Rights calling for a ban on all pejorative uses of Indian images.

WHEREAS, the Intertribal Council of the Five Civilized Tribes is an organization that united the tribal governments of the Chickasaw, Choctaw, Cherokee, Muscogee (Creek), and Seminole Nations, representing over 400,000 Indian people throughout the United States; and

WHEREAS, the Intertribal Council of the Five Civilized Tribes Education Committee is dedicated to promoting quality education for American Indian students that includes cultural awareness and a sense of diversity among America's student population; and

WHEREAS, the Five Civilized Tribes believe the use of derogatory American Indian images such as mascots by public schools perpetuate a stereotypical image of American Indians that is likely to have a negative impact on the self-esteem of American Indian children; and

WHEREAS, negative images and stereotypes about American Indians as mascots contributes to a hostile learning environment that affirms the negative images and stereotypes that persist in America about American Indians; and

WHEREAS, American Indians as mascots is a negative means of appropriating and denigrating our cultural identity that involves the display and depiction of ceremonial symbols and practices that may have religious significance to American Indians; and

WHEREAS, to continue the negative use of American Indian's tribal names and images is an offensive and disgusting practice that would be considered intolerable were other ethnic groups or minorities depicted in a similar manner; and

WHEREAS, on April 13, 2001, the United States Commission on Civil Rights issued a Statement on the Use of Native American Images and Nicknames as Sports Symbols that called for an end to the use of American Indian images and team names by non-Indian schools; that stereotyping of any racial, ethnic, religious or other groups when promoted by public education institutions, teach all students that stereotyping of minority groups is acceptable, a dangerous lesson in a diverse society; that schools have a responsibility to educate their students; they should not use influence to perpetuate misrepresentations of any culture or people; and

NOW THEREFORE, BE IT RESOLVED, that the Intertribal Council of the Five Civilized Tribes joins the United States Commission on Civil Rights call to eliminate the stereotypical use of American Indian names and images as mascots in sports and other events and to provide meaningful education about real American Indian people, current American Indian issues, and, the rich variety of American Indian cultures in the U.S...

Public Law 101–185: The National Indian Museum of the American Indian Act, 1989

Provided here are key extracts from the National Indian Museum of the American Indian Act passed in 1989. The act highlights how there has been no museum exclusively dedicated to the research and celebration of the divergent Indian cultures within the United States. The new museum is to be housed on the National Mall in Washington, D.C.

SECTION I. SHORT TITLE.

This Act may be cited as the 'National Museum of the American Indian Act.'

SEC. 2. FINDINGS.

The Congress finds that--

(1) there is no national museum devoted exclusively to the history and art of cultures indigenous to the Americas;

(2) although the Smithsonian Institution sponsors extensive Native American programs, none of its 19 museums, galleries, and major research facilities is devoted exclusively to Native American history and art;

(3) the Heye Museum in New York, New York, one of the largest Native American collections in the world, has more than 1,000,000 art objects and artefacts and a library of 40,000 volumes relating to the archaeology, ethnology, and history of Native American peoples;

(4) the Heye Museum is housed in facilities with a total area of 90,000 square feet, but requires a minimum of 400,000 square feet for exhibition, storage, and scholarly research;

(5) the bringing together of the Heye Museum collection and the Native American collection of the Smithsonian Institution would--

(A) create a national institution with unrivaled capability for exhibition and research;

(B) give all Americans the opportunity to learn of the cultural legacy, historic grandeur, and contemporary culture of Native Americans;

(C) provide facilities for scholarly meetings and the performing arts;

(D) make available curatorial and other learning opportunities for Indians; and

(E) make possible traveling exhibitions to communities throughout the Nation;

(6) by order of the Surgeon General of the Army, approximately 4,000 Indian human remains from battlefields and burial sites were sent to the Army Medical Museum and were later transferred to the Smithsonian Institution;

(7) through archaeological excavations, individual donations, and museum donations, the Smithsonian Institution has acquired approximately 14,000 additional Indian human remains;

(8) the human remains referred to in paragraphs (6) and (7) have long been a matter of concern for many Indian tribes, including Alaska Native Villages, and Native Hawaiian communities which are determined to provide an appropriate resting place for their ancestors;

(9) identification of the origins of such human remains is essential to addressing that concern; and

(10) an extraordinary site on the National Mall in the District of Columbia (U.S. Government Reservation No. 6) is reserved for the use of the Smithsonian Institution and is available for construction of the National Museum of the American Indian.

SEC. 3. NATIONAL MUSEUM OF THE AMERICAN INDIAN.

(a) ESTABLISHMENT- There is established, within the Smithsonian Institution, a living memorial to Native Americans and their traditions which shall be known as the 'National Museum of the American Indian.'

(b) PURPOSES- The purposes of the National Museum are to--

(1) advance the study of Native Americans, including the study of language, literature, history, art, anthropology, and life;

(2) collect, preserve, and exhibit Native American objects of artistic, historical, literary, anthropological, and scientific interest;

(3) provide for Native American research and study programs...

SEC. 4. AUTHORITY OF THE BOARD OF REGENTS TO ENTER INTO AN AGREEMENT PROVIDING FOR TRANSFER OF HEYE FOUNDATION ASSETS TO THE SMITHSONIAN INSTITUTION.

The Board of Regents is authorized to enter into an agreement with the Heye Foundation, to provide for the transfer to the Smithsonian Institution of title to the Heye Foundation assets...

SEC. 7. MUSEUM FACILITIES.

(a) NATIONAL MUSEUM MALL FACILITY- The Board of Regents shall plan, design, and construct a facility on the area bounded by Third Street, Maryland Avenue, Independence Avenue, Fourth Street, and Jefferson Drive, Southwest, in the District of Columbia to house the portion of the National Museum to be located in the District of Columbia. The Board of Regents shall pay not more than 2/3 of the total cost of planning, designing, and constructing the facility from funds appropriated to the Board of Regents. The remainder of the osts shall be paid from non-Federal sources...

United States Commission on Civil Rights: Use of Native American Images and Nicknames as Sports Symbols, 13 April 2001

The following text is a document released by the US Commission on Civil Rights calling for all American sports teams to end the use of derogatory and stereotypical images of Indians which humiliate, trivialise and offend Indian cultures and religions.

The U.S. Commission on Civil Rights calls for an end to the use of Native American images and team names by non-Native schools. The Commission deeply respects the right of all Americans to freedom of expression under the First Amendment and in no way would attempt to prescribe how people can express themselves. However, the Commission believes that the use of Native American images and nicknames in schools is insensitive and should be avoided. In addition, some Native American and civil rights advocates maintain that these mascots may violate anti-discrimination laws. These references, whether mascots and their performances, logos, or names, are disrespectful and offensive to American Indians and others who are offended by such stereotyping. They are particularly inappropriate and insensitive in light of the long history of forced assimilation that American Indian people have endured in this country.

Since the civil rights movement of the 1960s many overtly derogatory symbols and images offensive to African-Americans have been eliminated. However, many secondary schools, post-secondary institutions, and a number of professional sports teams continue to use Native American nicknames and imagery. Since the 1970s, American Indians leaders and organizations have vigorously voiced their opposition to these mascots and team names because they mock and trivialize Native American religion and culture.

It is particularly disturbing that Native American references are still to be found in educational institutions, whether elementary, secondary or post-secondary. Schools are places where diverse groups of people come together to learn not only the "Three Rs," but also how to interact respectfully with people from different cultures. The use of stereotypical images of Native

Americans by educational institutions has the potential to create a racially hostile educational environment that may be intimidating to Indian students. American Indians have the lowest high school graduation rates in the nation and even lower college attendance and graduation rates. The perpetuation of harmful stereotypes may exacerbate these problems.

The stereotyping of any racial, ethnic, religious or other groups when promoted by our public educational institutions, teach all students that stereotyping of minority groups is acceptable, a dangerous lesson in a diverse society. Schools have a responsibility to educate their students; they should not use their influence to perpetuate misrepresentations of any culture or people. Children at the elementary and secondary levels usually have no choice about which school they attend. Further, the assumption that a college student may freely choose another educational institution if she feels uncomfortable around Indian-based imagery is a false one. Many factors, from educational programs to financial aid to proximity to home, limit a college student's choices. It is particularly onerous if the student must also consider whether or not the institution is maintaining a racially hostile environment for Indian students.

Schools that continue the use of Indian imagery and references claim that their use stimulates interest in Native American culture and honors Native Americans. These institutions have simply failed to listen to the Native groups, religious leaders, and civil rights organizations that oppose these symbols. These Indian-based symbols and team names are not accurate representations of Native Americans. Even those that purport to be positive are romantic stereotypes that give a distorted view of the past. These false portrayals prevent non-Native Americans from understanding the true historical and cultural experiences of American Indians. Sadly, they also encourage biases and prejudices that have a negative effect on contemporary Indian people. These references may encourage interest in mythical "Indians" created by the dominant culture, but they block genuine understanding of contemporary Native people as fellow Americans.

The Commission assumes that when Indian imagery was first adopted for sports mascots it was not to offend Native Americans. However, the use of the imagery and traditions, no matter how popular, should end when they are offensive. We applaud those who have been leading the fight to educate the public and the institutions that have voluntarily discontinued the use of insulting mascots. Dialogue and education are the roads to understanding. The use of American Indian mascots is not a trivial matter. The Commission has a firm understanding of the problems of poverty, education, housing, and health care that face many Native Americans. The fight to eliminate Indian nicknames and images in sports is only one front of the larger battle to eliminate obstacles that confront American Indians. The elimination of Native American nicknames and images as sports mascots will benefit not only Native Americans, but all Americans. The elimination of stereotypes will make room for education about real Indian people, current Native American issues, and the rich variety of American Indians in our country.

Bellecourt v. City of Cleveland, 2004

The following document is a transcript of the opinion issued by the Ohio Supreme Court in Bellecourt v. City of Cleveland (2004). In the decision authored by Judge O'Connor, the court examines whether the arrest of protestors by the Cleveland police after they burned the Cleveland Indians baseball team mascot, Chief Wahoo, violated the protestors' constitutional rights to free speech.

April 10, 1998, opening day for the Cleveland Indians baseball team, was a blustery day in downtown Cleveland. Among the onlookers near Jacobs Field, the Indians' ballpark, were throngs of cheering fans as well as groups of spirited protestors. The protestors, including appellees Vernon Bellecourt, Juan Reyna, James Watson, Charlene Teters, and Zizwe Tchiquka, perceived the team's moniker and Chief Wahoo logo as disparaging to Native American culture. "[The Chief Wahoo logo is a red-faced, hooked-nosed, grinning caricature of a Native American.]"

Following animated yet peaceful speeches and marches, the protestors entered a cordoned area near Jacobs Field. In the presence of several safety personnel, the protestors doused a newspaper-stuffed effigy of Chief Wahoo with lighter fluid and set it afire. As the fire struggled to spread, Bellecourt sprayed additional lighter fluid on the effigy. The fire then quickly accelerated, and within seconds the effigy disintegrated, sending burning remnants to the sidewalk. Cleveland police extinguished what remained of the fire and arrested Bellecourt, Tchiquka, and Reyna. Shortly thereafter, Watson and Teters ignited an accelerant-soaked effigy of Little Black Sambo – apparently as an emblematic condemnation of the use of racially offensive symbols. Police then arrested Watson and Teters. Though appellant, the city of Cleveland, booked appellees on charges of aggravated arson and detained appellees overnight, the city did not prosecute appellees for violating any law.

...appellees sued the city, the arresting officers and their commander, David Regetz, and Chief of Police Rocco Pollutro for civil-rights violations stemming from their allegedly baseless arrest and detention...

Our ultimate inquiry is whether Cleveland is liable to appellees...for violating their constitutional right to free speech. Such liability will attach to a municipality only if the municipality itself has inflicted a constitutionally significant injury by executing a policy or custom...

Without question, the effigy burnings were constitutionally protected speech ... Moreover, appellees concede, and we agree, that extinguishment of the waning flames after the effigies had disintegrated does not raise an issue of constitutional significance because by that time, the protected speech had concluded. Appellees urge, however, that the right to free speech is hollow if it is exercised at the expense of arrest. Though we generally agree with this proposition, we find it inapplicable here because any suppression of speech was incidental to Cleveland's important interest in preventing harm caused by fire...

...the record demonstrates that Cleveland arrested appellees not because they burned effigies, but because of a perceived public safety threat in the manner in which they burned the effigies. Under the facts before us, we determine that the arrests were narrowly tailored to Cleveland's asserted interest in preserving public safety. Accordingly, Cleveland is not liable to appellees...

Native American Graves Protection and Repatriation Act (NAGPRA), 1990

Provided here are key parts of the NAGPRA, also known as Public Law 101-601, passed by Congress on 16 November 1990. The Act states that museums and institutions given federal funds were required to compile an inventory of all Indian objects within a given time frame and allow the repatriation of these items to the Indian nations that requested them. The Act protects Indian graves and any future discovery of Indian remains on American soil.

...To provide for the protection of Native American graves, and for other purposes.

Be it enacted by the Senate and House of Representatives of the United States of America in Congress assembled,

SECTION 1. SHORT TITLE.

This Act may be cited as the "Native American Graves Protection and Repatriation Act."...

SEC 3. OWNERSHIP.

(a) NATIVE AMERICAN HUMAN REMAINS AND OBJECTS.

The ownership or control of Native American cultural items which are excavated or discovered on Federal or tribal lands after the date of enactment of this Act shall be (with priority given in the order listed)-

(1) in the case of Native American human remains and associated funerary objects, in the lineal descendants of the Native American; or

(2) in any case in which such lineal descendants cannot be ascertained, and in the case of unassociated funerary objects, sacred objects, and objects of cultural patrimony--

(A) in the Indian tribe or Native Hawaiian organization on whose tribal land such objects or remains were discovered;

(B) in the Indian tribe or Native Hawaiian organization which has the closest cultural affiliation with such remains or objects and which, upon notice, states a claim for such remains or objects; or

(C) if the cultural affiliation of the objects cannot be reasonably ascertained and if the objects were discovered on Federal land that is recognized by a final judgment of the Indian Claims Commission or the United States Court of Claims as the aboriginal land of some Indian tribe--

(1) in the Indian tribe that is recognized as aboriginally occupying the area in which the objects were discovered, if upon notice, such tribe states a claim for such remains or objects, or

(2) if it can be shown by a preponderance of the evidence that a different tribe has a stronger cultural relationship with the remains or objects than the tribe or organization specified in paragraph

(1), in the Indian tribe that has the strongest demonstrated relationship, if upon notice, such tribe states a claim for such remains or objects...

(c) INTENTIONAL EXCAVATION AND REMOVAL OF NATIVE AMERICAN HUMAN REMAINS AND OBJECTS.

The intentional removal from or excavation of Native American cultural items from Federal or tribal lands for purposes of discovery, study, or removal of such items is permitted only if--

(1) such items are excavated or removed pursuant to a permit issued under section 4 of the Archaeological Resources Protection Act of 1979...

(2) such items are excavated or removed after consultation with or, in the case of tribal lands, consent of the appropriate (if any) Indian tribe or Native Hawaiian organization...

(d) INADVERTENT DISCOVERY OF NATIVE AMERICAN REMAINS AND OBJECTS.

(1) Any person who knows, or has reason to know, that such person has discovered Native American cultural items on Federal or tribal lands-after the date of enactment of this Act shall notify, in writing, the Secretary of the Department ... the appropriate Indian tribe or Native Hawaiian organization with respect to tribal lands ... If the discovery occurred in connection with an activity, including (but not limited to) construction, mining, logging, and agriculture, the person shall cease the activity in the area of the discovery, make a reasonable effort to protect the items discovered before resuming such activity, and provide notice under this subsection...

SEC. 5. INVENTORY FOR HUMAN REMAINS AND ASSOCIATED

FUNERARY OBJECTS.

(a) IN GENERAL.--Each Federal agency and each museum which has possession or control over holdings or collections of Native American human remains and associated funerary objects shall compile an inventory of such items and, to the extent possible based on information possessed by such museum or Federal agency, identify the geographical and cultural affiliation of such item...

SEC. 7. REPATRIATION.

(a) REPATRIATION OF NATIVE AMERICAN HUMAN REMAINS AND OBJECTS POSSESSED OR CONTROLLED BY FEDERAL AGENCIES AND MUSEUMS.--

(1) If, pursuant to section 5, the cultural affiliation of Native American human remains and associated funerary objects with a particular Indian tribe or Native Hawaiian organization is established, then the Federal agency or museum, upon the request of a known lineal descendant of the Native American or of the tribe or organization and pursuant to subsections (b) and (e) of this section, shall expeditiously return such remains and associated funerary objects...

(3) The return of cultural items covered by this Act shall be in consultation with the requesting lineal descendant or tribe or organization to determine the place and manner of delivery of such items...

(5) Upon request and pursuant to subsections ... sacred objects and objects of cultural patrimony shall be expeditiously returned...

SEC. 9. PENALTY.

(a) PENALTY.--Any museum that fails to comply with the requirements of this Act may be assessed a civil penalty by the Secretary of the Interior pursuant to procedures established by the Secretary through regulation...

SEC. 10. GRANTS.

(a) INDIAN TRIBES AND NATIVE HAWAIIAN ORGANIZATIONS.--The Secretary is authorized to make grants to Indian tribes and Native Hawaiian organizations for the purpose of assisting such tribes and organizations in the repatriation of Native American cultural items...

SEC. 12. SPECIAL RELATIONSHIP BETWEEN FEDERAL GOVERNMENT AND INDIAN TRIBES.

This Act reflects the unique relationship between the Federal Government and Indian tribes and Native Hawaiian organizations and should not be construed to establish a precedent with respect to any other individual, organization or foreign government...

ENDMATTER

NATIVE AMERICA TIMELINE

No date (since time immemorial) Continued presence of Indian ancestors in what is today known as the Americas

200,000 BC–28,000 BC Scientific evidence of human presence in the Americas

12,000 BC–16,000 BC Humans enter the Great Plains

3400–3000 BC Mound complex built at Watson Brake, Louisiana

AD 700 Cahokia established

c.900 Chaco Canyon established

Pre-1400 Iroquois Great League of Peace formed

1492 Christopher Columbus 'discovers' and 'invades' the Americas

c.1450–1500 Apache begin to enter the Southern Plains

1535 Jacques Cartier claims eastern Canada for France

1550 The great debate between Bartolomé de Las Casas and Juan Ginés de Sepúlveda

1565 Spanish found St. Augustine, Florida

1598 Juan de Oñate establishes a Spanish colony in New Mexico

1603 Samuel de Champlain voyages in the northeast

1607 English settle at Jamestown, Virginia

1622 Powhatan Indians go to war with the English in Virginia

1644 Second Powhatan war against the English

1675–1676 King Philip's War

1680 Pueblo Revolt began and the Pueblo villages successfully united to overthrow the Spanish for a number of years

1700–1701 Iroquois establish peace with Britain and France

c.1735 Comanche displace the Apache from the Southern Plains

1746 Wichita and Comanche form an alliance

1754–1763 The Seven Years' War or the 'French and Indian War'

1763 Pontiac's War (also termed Pontiac's Rebellion)

1763 Suspected use of Smallpox blankets by the British during Pontiac's Rebellion

1776–1783 American Revolution

1778 Treaty with the Delaware, the first treaty between an Indian nation and the United States

1787 The US Constitution is formed and Congress assumes authority to regulate commerce with Indian tribes

1791 Little Turtle and Blue Jacket lead the north-western Indian confederacy and defeat an army of the United States under the control of General Arthur St. Clair

1795 Treaty of Grenville where north-western tribes ceded most of Ohio

1800 Comanche and Kiowa form an alliance

1805–1811 Tecumseh attempts to unite the tribes of the east

1810 Cherokee begin to migrate into Arkansas

1813 The death of Tecumseh in the Battle of Thames

1817–1818 First Seminole War in Florida

1823 *Johnson v. McIntosh*

1824 Bureau of Indian Affairs is established within the War Department

1828 Cherokee Phoenix newspaper established

1830 Indian Removal Act authorises the removal of Indians from the east to the west of the Mississippi River

1831 *Cherokee Nation v. Georgia*

1832 *Worcester v. Georgia*

1835 Treaty of New Echota, where the treaty party cede Cherokee lands in the east for lands to the west of the Mississippi

1835–1842 Second Seminole War

1838–1839 Cherokee Trail of Tears

1849 Bureau of Indian Affairs (BIA) is transferred from the War Department to the Department of the Interior

1851 United States signs the Fort Laramie peace treaty

1864 Massacre of Sand Creek

1864 Navajo Long Walk

1868 Fort Laramie Treaty signed which assigns the Teton Sioux, Northern Arapaho and Northern Cheyenne to reservations

1869 Ely S. Parker becomes the first Indian to head the Bureau of Indian Affairs (BIA)

1871 Congress ends formal treaty-making with Native American nations

1876 The Battle of Little Big Horn

1881 Sitting Bull surrenders to the US army

1883 Ex parte Crow Dog establishes that the US government has no criminal authority to arrest and try tribal members for crimes committed in tribal reservations

1885 Major Crimes Act gives the American government control over certain crimes in tribal reservations and reverses Ex parte Crow Dog

1887 Dawes Act (General Allotment Act)

1889 The Ghost Dance emerges on Plains reservations

1890 Massacre of Wounded Knee

1900 Indian population: 237,000

1903 *Lone Wolf v. Hitchcock* establishes that the American government has plenary control over tribal affairs and can unilaterally abrogate treaties

1924 Indian Citizenship Act

1928 Meriam Report, 'The Problem of Indian Administration' criticised American policy towards the Indians

1934 Indian Re-organisation Act

1942 Iroquois declare war on Germany

1944 National Congress of the American Indian is formed

1953 House Concurrent resolution 108 and Public Law 180 are passed by Congress

1959 *Navajo Times* established

1959 *Williams v. Lee* establishes the inherent sovereignty of the tribes within the reservation

1961 American Indian Chicago Conference and the National Indian Youth Council are formed

1968 N. Scott Momaday, House Made of Dawn (awarded the Pulitzer Prize)

1968 American Indian Movement (AIM) established

1969 Seizure of Alcatraz Island

1970 Blue Lake returned to the Taos Pueblo

1972 Trail of Broken Treaties march reaches Washington, DC and occupies the Bureau of Indian Affairs (BIA) building

1973 Wounded Knee, South Dakota occupied by American Indian Movement (AIM) members and supporters

1977 Leonard Peltier is convicted of the murder of two FBI agents

1978 *Oliphant v. Suquamish Indian Tribe* establishes that tribes do not have inherent criminal authority to arrest and prosecute non-members in tribal court

1978 Longest Walk from Alcatraz to Washington, DC

1979 The first Indian gaming establishment is opened in Florida

1980 Teton Sioux are awarded $122.5 million for the illegal taking of the Black Hills but the Sioux insist on the return of the lands

1980 Maine Indian Land Claims Settlement Act

1981 *Montana v. United States* establishes that tribes do not have inherent sovereignty over non-member hunting and fishing on non-member lands of the reservation

1982 *Merrion v. Jicarilla Apache Tribe* establishes that Native American tribes have inherent sovereignty to tax non-members and non-member businesses within the reservation

1985 Wilma Mankiller becomes principal chief of the Cherokee Nation

1989 Public Law 101–185, The National Museum of the American Indian Act (NMAIA) is passed by Congress

1990 Native American population almost reaches two million

1992 Mashantucket Pequot opens Foxwoods Casino in Connecticut

2000 Native American population reaches 4.1 million (2.5 million classed as 'Indian' and 1.6 million classed as mixed heritage)

2001 *Nevada v. Hicks* and *Atkinson Trading Co., Inc v. Shirley*

2001 The Supreme Court Project is established by the Native American Rights Fund (NARF) and the National Congress of the American Indian (NCAI) to prevent cases getting to the Supreme Court

2004 The National Museum of the American Indian is opened in Washington, DC

2004 Cecilia Five Thunder elected as the first woman leader of the Oglala Lakota

2006 Bureau of the Census publication entitled, *American Indian- and Alaska Native-Owned Firms: 2002*, showed that in 2002 there were 201,837 Native American businesses which generated $26.873 billion

2009 Leonard Peltier has the right to a full parole hearing

SOURCES AND COPYRIGHT HOLDERS

Chapter One: Origins of the World and 'Discovery'

Origin Myth of Acoma. Excerpt from Matthew Stirling, 'The Origin Myth of Acoma and Other Records' (Washington: Smithsonian Institution Bureau of American Ethnology, Bulletin 135, 1942).
Iroquois Creation Myth. Excerpt from 'Iroquois Creation Myth' as described within The Journal of Major John Norton, 1816, Carl F. Kinck and James J. Talman (eds). (Toronto: Champlain Society, 1970). Reprinted with permission.

Chapter Two: Spirituality and Faith, 1550–1805

Juan Ginés de Sepúlveda: Justified Spanish Conquest and Indian Enslavement, 1550. Excerpt from Juan Ginés de Sepúlveda (who justified Spanish conquest and Indian enslavement), 1550 from Lewis Hanke, All Mankind is One, 74–76, 85–86. (De Kalb: Northern Illinois University Press, 1974). Used with permission of Northern Illinois University Press.
David Brainerd: The Life and Diary of the Rev. David Brainerd, 1744–1746. Excerpt from David Brainerd, Journal and letter extracts of a missionary, 1743–1746. Source: An Account of the Life of the Late Reverend Mr. David Brainerd, published by Jonathan Edwards, 1749. Materials available on http://www.wholesomewords.org/ biography/biorpbrainerd.html.

Chapter Five: Removal Era, 1800s–1840s

Chief John Ross: Cherokee Letter Protesting the Treaty of New Echota, 1836. Excerpt from Ross, John, The Papers of Chief John Ross: Volume 1, 1807–1839, Gary E. Moulton (ed.). (Norman: University of Oklahoma Press, 1985). © 1985 by University of Oklahoma Press. Reprinted with permission.
Protest of George W. Harkins over Removal: 'We Must Go Forth as Wanderers in a Strange Land!' 1831. Excerpt from Protest of George W. Harkins over Removal, originally published in the Niles' Register, 1800s. Reprinted in Muriel H. Wright, 'We must go forth as wanderers in a strange land!' American Indian, December, 1926 (New York: Da Capo Press, 1926).

Chapter Six: Three Key Events in Western Expansion: Sand Creek (1864), Little Big Horn (1876) and Wounded Knee (1890).

George Bent: Firsthand Account of the Sand Creek Massacre, 1864. Excerpt from Grinnell, George Bird, The Fighting Cheyennes (Norman: University of Oklahoma Press, 1956). © 1956 by University of Oklahoma Press. Reprinted with permission.

Chapter Fourteen: Indian Representation, Museums and the Repatriation of Indian Bones

Inter-Tribal Council of the Five Civilised Tribes: Mascot Resolution, No. 2001–08, 14 July 2001. Excerpt from: Inter-tribal Council of the Five Civilized Tribes Mascot Resolution No. 2001–08, 14 July 2001. Source: Inter-tribal Council of the Five Civilized Tribes (Oklahoma).

NOTES

Introduction

1. Calloway, *First Peoples*.
2. Ibid; and Daniel Richter, *Facing East from Indian Country: A Native History of Early America* (Cambridge, MA: Harvard University Press, 2001).
3. Joane Nagel, *American Indian Ethnic Renewal: Red Power and the Resurgence of Identity and Culture* (New York: Oxford University Press, 1995).

Chapter One

1. Colin G. Calloway, *First Peoples: A Documentary Survey of American Indian History* (Boston: Bedford/St. Martin's, 1999).
2. James Axtell, *The European and the Indian: Essays in the Ethnohistory of Colonial North America* (New York: Oxford University Press, 1981); Gretchen D. Starr-Lebeau, *American Eras: Early American Civilisations and Exploration to 1600* (Detroit: Gale, 1998); Harold Driver, *Indians of North America*, 2nd ed. (Chicago: The University of Chicago Press, 1969); William T. Hagan, *American Indians* (Chicago: University of Chicago Press, 1961); Sharon O'Brien, *American Indian Tribal Governments* (Norman: University of Oklahoma Press, 1989).
3. James A. Brown, 'America before Columbus', Chapter 1 in *Indians in American History: An Introduction*, 2nd ed. Edited by Frederick E. Hoxie and Peter Iverson (Wheeling, IL: Harlan Davidson, Inc., 1998); Jeanne Kay, 'The Fur Trade and Native American Population Growth', *Ethnohistory* 31 (1984), 266; Daniel Richter, *Facing East from Indian Country: A Native History of Early America* (Cambridge, MA: Harvard University Press, 2001); Linda Barrington, ed., *The Other Side of the Frontier: Economic Explorations into Native American History* (Colorado: Westview Press, 1999); Neal Salisbury, 'The Indians' Old World: Native Americans and the Coming of Europeans', *William and Mary Quarterly* 53 (1996), 435–458; and Stephen Cornell, *The Return of the Native: American Indian Political Resurgence* (New York: Oxford University Press, 1988).
4. Stuart J. Fiedel, *Prehistory of the Americas* (Cambridge: University of Cambridge Press, 1987); Philip Kopper, *The Smithsonian Book of North American Indians: Before the Coming of the Europeans* (Washington, DC: Smithsonian, 1986); and Calloway, *First Peoples*.
5. Steven W. Hackel, 'The Staff of Leadership: Indian Authority in the Missions of Alta California', *The William and Mary Quarterly* 54 (1997), 347–376.
6. Calloway, *First Peoples*.
7. Charles C. Mann, *1491: New Revelations of the Americas Before Columbus* (New York: Alfred A. Knopf, 2005); Vine Deloria, Jr., *Red Earth, White Lies: Native Americans and the Myth of Scientific Fact* (New York: Scribner, 1995); and R. David Edmunds, Frederick E. Hoxie and Neal Salisbury, *The People: A History of Native America* (Boston: Houghton Mifflin Company, 2007).
8. David Stannard, *American Holocaust* (Oxford: Oxford University Press, 1992); and Calloway, *First Peoples*.
9. Brown, 'America before Columbus'; and Richter, *Facing East from Indian Country*.
10. Lenore A. Stiffarm and Phil Lane, Jr., 'The Demography of Native North America: A Question of American Indian Survival', chapter. 1 in *The State of Native America: Genocide, Colonization, and Resistance*, ed. M. Annette Jaimes (Boston, MA: South End Press, 1992), 23–53; Russell Thornton, *American Indian Holocaust and Survival: A Population History since 1492* (Norman: University of Oklahoma Press, 1987); and William M. Denevan, 'The Pristine Myth: The Landscape of the Americas in 1492', *Annals of the Association of American Geographers* 82 (1992), 369–385.

11. Susan Castillo and Ivy Schweitzer, eds, *The Literatures of Colonial America: An Anthology* (Massachusetts: Blackwell Publishing Company, 2001).

12. Carl F. Klinck and James J. Talman, eds, *The Journal of Major John Norton, 1816* (Toronto: Champlain Society, 1970); Matthew W. Stirling, Origin Myth of Acoma and Other Records (Washington, DC: United States Government Printing Office, 1942); Castillo and Schweitzer, *The Literatures of Colonial America*; and Paul G. Zolbrod, *Diné Bahane: The Navajo Creation Story* (Albuquerque: University of New Mexico Press, 1984).

13. Christopher Columbus, *The Journal of Christopher Columbus*, trans. Cecil Jane (London: Anthony Blond & The Orion Press, 1960); Cornell, *The Return of the Native*; Alfred Taiaiake, *Peace, Power, Righteousness: An Indigenous Manifesto* (Toronto: Oxford University Press, 1999); and David Hurst Thomas, *Skull Wars: Kennewick Man, Archaeology, and the Battle for Native American Identity* (New York: Basic Books, 2000).

14. S. James Anaya, *Indigenous Peoples in International Law* (New York: Oxford University Press, 2000); James E. Falkowski, *Indian Law/Race Law* (Praeger: New York, 1992); and Robert A. Williams, Jr., *The American Indian in Western Legal Thought: The Discourse of Conquest* (New York: Oxford University Press, 1990).

15. Denevan, 'The Pristine Myth'; and Williams, Jr., *The American Indian in Western Legal Thought*.

16. Frances Gardiner Davenport, ed., *European Treaties Bearing on the History of the United States and its Dependencies to 1648* (Washington, DC: Carnegie Institution of Washington, 1917); and Williams, Jr., *The American Indian in Western Legal Thought*.

Chapter Two

1. Wendell H. Oswallt and Sharlotte Neely, *This Land Was Theirs*, 5th ed. (Mountain View, CA: Mayfield Publishing Company, 1996).

2. G. Torrence, 'Art of the Mesquakie', Chapter 1 in Art of the Red Earth People: The Mesquakie of Iowa, eds, G. Torrence and R. Hobbs (Seattle: University of Washington Press, 1989).

3. Oswallt and Neely, *This Land*.

4. Ibid.

5. Ibid.

6. Such books and articles on this topic include, Paul A. Delcourt and Hazel R. Delcourt, *Prehistoric Native Americans and Ecological Change: Human Ecosystems in Eastern North America since the Pleistocene* (New York: Cambridge University Press, 2004); and Robert J. Smith, 'Resolving the Tragedy of the Commons by Creating Private Property Rights in Wildlife', *The Cato Journal* 1 (1981), 439–468.

7. Lewis Hanke, *All Mankind is One: A Study of the Disputation of between Bartolomé de Las Casas and Juan Ginés de Sepúlveda in 1550 on the Intellectual and Religious Capacity of the American Indians* (Dekalb: Northern Illinois University Press, 1974).

8. Colin G. Calloway, *First Peoples: A Documentary Survey of American Indian History* (Boston: Bedford/St. Martin's, 1999); and Colin G. Calloway, *The World Turned Upside Down: Indian Voices From Early America* (Boston: Bedford/St. Martin's, 1994).

9. Ibid.

10. George P. Hammond and Agapito Rey, eds, *Don Juan de Oñate: Colonizer of New Mexico, 1595–1628* (Albuquerque: University of New Mexico, 1953), vol 1, 480–485; Susan Castillo and Ivy Schweitzer, *The Literatures of Colonial America* (Massachusetts: Blackwell Publishers, Ltd., 2001), 181–194.

11. Jonathan Edwards, *The Life and Diary of David Brainerd*. Norman Pettit, ed. (New Haven: Yale University Press, 1985); and for a detailed history of Brainerd look at, *Christian Biography Resources*, http://www.wholesomewords.org/biography/biorpbrainerd.html (accessed 5 January 2008).

12. Some of the unpublished works of Samson Occum, such as 'A Short Narrative of My Life', 1768, can be found in the Papers of Eleazar Wheelock, Collection 126, Reel 14, at Dartmouth College, Hanover in New Hampshire.

13. Daniel Drake, *Lives of Celebrated American Indians* (Boston: Bradbury, Soden & Co., 1843), 283–287.

Chapter Three

1. Wendell H. Oswallt and Sharlotte Neely, *This Land Was Theirs*, 5th ed. (Mountain View, CA: Mayfield Publishing Company, 1996).

2. Colin G. Calloway, *The World Turned Upside Down: Indian Voices from Early America* (Boston: Bedford/St. Martin's Press, 1994).

3. Robert A. Williams, Jr., *The American Indian in Western Legal Thought: The Discourse of Conquest* (New York: Oxford University Press, 1990).

4. Patricia Seed, *Ceremonies of Possession: Europe's Conquest of the New World, 1492–1640* (New York: Cambridge University Press, 1995).

5. James E. Falkowski, *Indian Law/Race Law: A Five-Hundred-Year-History* (New York: Praeger, 1992); S. James Anaya, *Indigenous Peoples in International Law* (New York: Oxford University Press, 1996); and Williams, Jr., *The American Indian in Western Legal Thought*.

6. George Peckham, A True Report of the Late Discoveries and Possession, Taken in the Right of the Crown of England, of the Newfound Lands: by that Valiant and Worthy Gentleman, Sir Humphrey Gilbert Knight, 1583; Extracts from this work are found on, Norton Anthology of English Literature, http://www.wwnorton.com/college/english/nael/16century/topic_2/peckham.htm (accessed 21 May 2008).

7. William Apes, *Eulogy on King Philip* (Boston: Published by the Author, 1836).

8. Colin G. Calloway, *First Peoples: A Documentary Survey of American Indian History* (Boston: Bedford/St. Martin's, 1999).

9. Ibid.

10. Susan Castillo and Ivy Schweitzer, *The Literatures of Colonial America: An Anthology* (Malden, MA: Blackwell Publishers, 2001).

11. Calloway, *The World Turned Upside Down*.

12. William F. Ganong, trans. and ed., *New Relation of Gaspesia, with the Customs and Religion of the Gaspesian Indians*, by Chrestien Le Clerq (Toronto: Champlain Society, 1910).

13. W.L. Grant, *Voyages of Samuel de Champlain* (New York: Charles Scribners' Sons, 1907).

14. Calloway, *First Peoples*.

15. Angie Debo, *A History of the Indians of the United States* (Norman: University of Oklahoma Press, 1970); and Calloway, *First Peoples*.

16. Ronald Wright, *Stolen Continents: The Indian Story* (London: Pimlico, 1992); and Anthony F.C. Wallace, *The Death and Rebirth of the Seneca* (New York: Alfred A. Knopf, 1970).

17. Gregory Evans Dowd, *A Spirited Resistance: The North American Indian Struggle for Unity, 1745–1815* (Baltimore, MD: Johns Hopkins University Press, 1992); Colin G. Calloway, *First Peoples: A Documentary Survey of American Indian History* (Boston: Bedford/St. Martin's, 1999); and John Sugden, *Tecumseh: A Life* (New York: Henry Holt, 1998).

Chapter Four

1. Colin G. Calloway, *First Peoples: A Documentary Survey of American Indian History* (Boston: Bedford/St. Martin's, 1999).

2. Ibid.

3. Andrew L. Knaut, *The Pueblo Revolt of 1680: Conquest and Resistance in Seventeenth-Century New Mexico* (Norman: University of Oklahoma Press, 1995).

4. Richard White, *The Middle Ground: Indians, Empires and Republics in the Great Lakes Region, 1650–1815* (Cambridge: Cambridge University Press, 1991).

5. Calloway, *First Peoples*.

6. Russell Bourne, *The Red King's Rebellion: Racial Politics in New England, 1675–1678* (New York: Oxford University Press, 1990); Jill Lepore, *The Name of War: King Philip's War and the Origins of American Identity* (New York: Knopf, 1998); and Armstrong Starkey, *European and Native American Warfare, 1675–1815* (London: UCL Press, 1998).

7. Albert B. Hart, ed., *American History Told by Contemporaries* (New York: The Macmillan Co., 1897).

8. Colin G. Calloway, *The World Turned Upside Down: Indian Voices from Early America* (Boston: Bedford/St. Martin's, 1994).

9. Colin G. Calloway, *The American Revolution in the Indian Country: Crisis and Diversity in Native American Communities* (Cambridge: Cambridge University Press, 1995); and Gregory Evans Dowd, *A Spirited Resistance: The North American Indian Struggle for Unity, 1745–1815* (Baltimore: Johns Hopkins University Press, 1992).

10. John W., Harpster, ed., *Pen Pictures of Early Western Pennsylvania* (Pittsburgh: University of Pittsburgh Press, 1938).

11. Lester K. Born, *British manuscripts project; a checklist of the microfilms prepared in England and Wales for the American Council of Learned Societies, 1941–1945* (Reprint, New York: Greenwood Press, 1968); Elizabeth A. Fenn, 'Biological Warfare in Eighteenth-Century North America: Beyond Jeffrey Amherst', *Journal of American History*, vol 86, no. 4 (March, 2000), 1552–1580; Elizabeth A. Fenn, *Pox Americana: The Great Smallpox Epidemic of 1775–82* (New York: Hill and Wang, 2001); and E. Wagner Stearn and Allen E. Stearn, *The Effect of Smallpox on the Destiny of the Amerindian* (Boston: Bruce Humphries, 1945).

12. Charles J. Kappler, ed., *Indian Affairs: Laws and Treaties*, vol 2, *Treaties* (Washington, DC: Government Printing Office, 1904).

13. Calloway, *First Peoples*.

14. Charles J. Kappler, ed., *Indian Affairs: Laws and Treaties*, vol 4, *Laws* (Washington, DC: Government Printing Office, 1929).

15. Calloway, *The World Turned Upside Down*.

16. E.A. Cruickshank, ed., *The Correspondence of Lieut. Governor John Graves Simcoe*, vol 5 (Toronto: Ontario Historical Society, 1923–1931).

17. W.C. Vanderwerth, *Indian Oratory: Famous Speeches by Noted Indian Chieftains* (Norman: University of Oklahoma Press, 1971); and Calloway, *First Peoples*.

18. Dowd, *A Spirited Resistance*; and R. David Edmunds, *The Shawnee Prophet* (Lincoln: University of Nebraska Press, 1983).

19. Benjamin B. Thatcher, *Indian Biographies* (New York: J&J Harper, 1832).

20. H.B. Cushman, *History of the Choctaw, Chickasaw and Natchez Indians* (Greenville, Texas: 1899); and Angie Debo, *A History of the Indians of the United States* (Norman: University of Oklahoma Press, 1970).

21. R. David Edmunds, Frederick E. Hoxie and Neal Salisbury, *The People: A History of Native America* (Boston: Houghton Mifflin Company, 2007); and Starkey, *European and Native American Warfare*.

Chapter Five

1. Stephen E. Ambrose, *Undaunted Courage: Meriwether Lewis, Thomas Jefferson, and the Opening of the American West* (New York: Simon & Schuster, 1996); and Stacey Bredhoff, *American Originals* (Seattle: The University of Washington Press, 2001).

2. John R. Wunder, *'Retained by the People' A History of American Indians and the Bill of Rights* (New York: Oxford University Press, 1994); and Colin G. Calloway, *First Peoples: A Documentary Survey of American Indian History* (Boston: Bedford/St. Martin's, 1999).

3. Calloway, *First Peoples*.

4. *Johnson v. McIntosh*, 21 U.S. 543 (1823); and Lindsay G. Robertson, *Conquest by Law: How the Discovery of America Dispossessed Indigenous Peoples of Their Lands* (New York: Oxford University Press, 2005).

5. James D. Richardson, ed., *A Compilation of the Messages and Papers of the Presidents*, Vol. 3 (New York: Bureau of National Literature, Inc., 1897); and Robert V. Remini, *The Legacy of Andrew Jackson: Essays on Democracy, Indian Removal and Slavery* (Baton Rouge: Louisiana State University Press, 1990).

6. William Marder and Paul Tice, eds, *Indians in the Americas: The Untold Story* (San Diego, CA: Book Tress Press, 2005); and Albert L. Hurtado and Peter Iverson, eds, *Major Problems in American Indian History* (Lexington, MA: D.C. Heath and Company, 1994).

7. Numerous volumes and editions of the Cherokee Phoenix (1828–1834) can be found in at the Hunter Library at Western Carolina University, Cullowhee, NC and at The Cherokee Phoenix, http://library.wcu.edu/CherokeePhoenix/ (accessed 21 May 2008).

8. Calloway, *First Peoples*; R. David Edmunds, Frederick E. Hoxie and Neal Salisbury, *The People: A History of Native America* (Boston: Houghton Mifflin Company, 2007); and Michael D. Green, *The Politics of Indian Removal: Creek Government and Society in Crisis* (Lincoln: University of Nebraska Press, 1982).

9. Jeremiah Evarts, ed., *Speeches on the Passage of the Bill for the Removal of the Indians Delivered in the Congress of the United States* (Boston: Perkins and Marvin, 1830); and Francis Paul Prucha, *American Indian Treaties: The History of a Political Anomaly* (Berkeley: University of California Press, 1997).

10. Joseph C. Burke, 'The Cherokee Cases: A Study in Law, Politics, and Morality', *Stanford Law Review* 21 (1969), 500–531; and Anthony F.C. Wallace, *The Long, Bitter Trail: Andrew Jackson and the Indians* (New York: Hill and Wang, 1993).

11. *Cherokee Nation v. Georgia*, 30 U.S. 1 (1831); Jill Norgren, *The Cherokee Cases: The Confrontation of Law and Politics* (New York: McGraw-Hill. Inc., 1996); Petra T. Shattuck and Jill Norgren, *Partial Justice: Federal Indian Law in a Liberal Constitutional System* (Providence, London: Berg Publishers, Inc., 1993); and Burke, 'The Cherokee Cases'.

12. *Worcester v. Georgia*, 31 U.S. 515 (1832); Norgren, *The Cherokee Cases*; and Burke, 'The Cherokee Cases'.

13. The words of William Wirt can be found in, William Eubanks, 'Destruction of the Cherokee People in 1901', *Cherokee Advocate*, 20 April 1901.

14. James Taylor Carson, *Searching for the Bright Path: The Mississippi Choctaws from Prehistory to Removal* (Lincoln: University of Nebraska Press, 1999); and Edmunds, Hoxie and Salisbury, *The People*.

15. Wayne Moquin and Charles Van Doren, eds, *Great Documents in American Indian History* (New York: DaCapo Press, 1995).

16. M.B. Pierce, Address on the Present Condition and Prospects of the Aboriginal Inhabitants of North America with Particular Reference to the Seneca Nation (Philadelphia: J. Richards, 1839); also available at Seneca Removal Texts, http://anpa.ualr.edu/digital_library/Seneca%20Removal%20Texts.htm (accessed 1 July 2008).

17. Thomas Loraine McKenney, *Memoirs, Official and Personal: with Sketches of Travels Among the Northern and Southern Indians; Embracing a War Excursion, and Descriptions of Scenes Along the Western Borders*, vol 2 (New York: Paine and Burgess, 1846); and Thomas McKenney, *Sketches of a Tour of the Lakes* (Philadelphia: American Philosophical Society, 2002).

18. *Exec. Doc. No. 286, 24th Cong.*, 1st session, 1–2, Washington, DC.

19. Gary E. Moulton, ed., *The Papers of Chief John Ross: Volume I: 1807–1839; Volume II: 1840–1866* (Norman: University of Oklahoma Press, 1985).

20. Thomas Bryan Underwood, *Cherokee Legends and The Trail of Tears* (Knoxville, Tennessee: McLemore, 1956); Ronald N. Satz, *American Indian Policy in the Jacksonian Era* (Lincoln: University of Nebraska Press, 1975); Theda Perdue, *Cherokee Women: Gender and Culture Change, 1700–1835* (Lincoln: University of Nebraska Press, 1998); William G. McLoughlin, *Cherokee Renascence in the New Republic.* Princeton (New Jersey: Princeton University Press, 1996); and John Ehle, *The Trail of Tears: The Rise and Fall of the Cherokee Nation* (New York: Doubleday, 1988).

21. A number of newspaper articles about the removal of the Cherokee, Chickasaw, Choctaw, Creek, Seminole and Seneca are available from the Arkansas Gazette, Arkansas Advocate, Batesville News and Helena Constitutional Journal, 1830–1849, http://anpa.ualr.edu/trail_of_tears/indian_removal_project/a_chronicle/a_chronicle. htm (accessed 21 May 2008).

22. Sharon O'Brien, *American Indian Tribal Governments* (Norman: University of Oklahoma Press, 1989).

23. Remini, *The Legacy of Andrew Jackson.*

24. Edmunds, Hoxie and Salisbury, *The People.*

Chapter Six

1. R. David Edmunds, Frederick E. Hoxie and Neal Salisbury, *The People: A History of Native America* (Boston: Houghton Mifflin Company, 2007); Jerome A. Greene and Douglas D. Scott, *Finding Sand Creek: History, Archaeology, and the 1864 Massacre Site* (Norman: University of Oklahoma Press, 2004); Stan Hoig, *The Sand Creek Massacre* (Norman: University of Oklahoma Press, 1961); Patrick M. Mendoza, *Song of Sorrow: Massacre at Sand Creek* (Denver, Colorado: Willow Wind Pub. Co., 1993); and David Svaldi, *Sand Creek and the Rhetoric of Extermination: A Case Study in Indian-White Relations* (Lanham, MD: University Press of America, 1989).

2. George Bird Grinnell, *The Fighting Cheyennes* (Norman: University of Oklahoma, 1956); David Fridtjof Halaas and Andrew E. Masich, *Halfbreed: The Remarkable True Story of George Bent-Caught Between the Worlds of the Indian and the White Man* (Cambridge, MA: Da Capo Press, 2004); and George E. Hyde, *Life of George Bent, Written from His Letters*, ed. Savoie Lottinville (Norman: University of Oklahoma Press, 1968).

3. Joint Committee on the Conduct of the War, Massacre of Cheyenne Indians, 38th Congress, 2nd session (Washington, DC, 1865); and Reginald S. Craig, *The Fighting Parson: The Biography of Colonel John M. Chivington* (Los Angeles: Westernlore Press, 1959).

4. Two Editorials from the Rocky Mountain News in 1864 depicted Chivington as a hero. See, Documents on the Sand Creek Massacre, http://www.pbs.org/weta/thewest/resources/archives/four/sandcrk.htm (accessed 21 May 2008).

5. Edmunds, Hoxie and Salisbury, *The People.*

6. Ibid.; Brian W. Dippie, *Custer's Last Stand: The Anatomy of an American Myth* (Reprint, Lincoln: University of Nebraska Press, 1996); Richard Allan Fox, Jr., *Archaeology, History, and Custer's Last Battle* (Norman: University of Oklahoma Press, 1993); Robert M. Utley, *Cavalier in Buckskin: George Armstrong Custer and the Western Military Frontier* (Norman: University of Oklahoma Press, 1988); Robert M. Utley and Wilcomb E. Washburn, *The History of the Indian Wars* (London: Mitchell Beazley, 1978); and Robert M. Utley, *The Indian Frontier of the American West, 1846–1890* (Albuquerque: University of New Mexico Press, 1984).

7. New York Herald (July 1876); and Utley, *Cavalier in Buckskin.*

8. Garrick Mallery, *Picture Writing of the American Indians*, Tenth Annual Report of the Bureau of Ethnology, 1888–1889, Smithsonian Institution, Bureau of American Ethnology, 1893; Wayne Moquin and Charles Dore, eds, *Great Documents in American*

Indian History (New York: Praeger, 1973); Joseph Kossuth Dixon, *The Vanishing Race, The Last Great Indian Council: A Record in Picture & Story of the Last Great Indian Council, Participated in by Eminent Indian Chiefs from Nearly Every Indian Reservation in the United States. Together with the Story of Their Lives as Told by Themselves – Their Speeches and Folklore Tales – Their Solemn Farewell and the Indians' Story of the Custer Fight* (Garden City, NY: Doubleday, Page and Co., 1913); and Richard G. Hardorff, ed., *Indian Views of the Custer Fight: A Source Book* (Norman: University of Oklahoma Press, 2005).

9. James Mooney, *The Ghost-Dance Religion and the Sioux Outbreak of 1890*, Fourteenth Annual Report (Part 2) of the Bureau of Ethnology to the Smithsonian Institution, 1892–1893 (Washington, DC: Government Printing Office, 1896).

10. Colin G. Calloway, *First Peoples: A Documentary Survey of American Indian History* (Boston: Bedford/St. Martin's, 1999).

11. Annual Report of the Secretary of War for 1891, vol I (Washington, DC: Government Printing Office, 1891); and Virginia W. Johnson, *The Unregimented General. A Biography of Nelson A. Miles* (Boston, MA: Houghton Mifflin, 1962).

12. Mooney, *The Ghost-Dance Religion and the Sioux Outbreak of 1890*; Edmunds, Hoxie and Salisbury, *The People*.

Chapter Seven

1. James D. Richardson, ed., *A Compilation of the Messages and Papers of the Presidents, Volume 8, part 2: Chester A. Arthur* (New York: Bureau of National Literature, 1897).

2. R. David Edmunds, Frederick E. Hoxie and Neal Salisbury, *The People: A History of Native America* (Boston: Houghton Mifflin Company, 2007).

3. Theodore H. Haas, 'The Legal Aspects of Indian Affairs from 1887 to 1957', *The Annals of the American Academy of Political and Social Science* 311 (1957), 12–22; Janet A. McDonnell, *The Dispossession of the American Indian* (Bloomington: Indiana University Press, 1991).

4. William Eubanks, 'Destruction of the Cherokee People in 1901', *Cherokee Advocate*, 20 April 1901.

5. First Annual Message, 3 December 1901, 57th Cong., 1st session, in *Compilation of the Messages and Papers of the Presidents, 1789–1902*, ed. J.D. Richardson (Washington, DC: Government Printing Office, 1904); and Virgil J. Vogel, *This Country Was Ours: A Documentary History of the American Indian* (New York: Harper & Row, 1972).

6. *Official Report of the Nineteenth Annual Conference of Charities and Correction* (1892), Reprinted in Richard H. Pratt, 'The Advantages of Mingling Indians with Whites', *Americanizing the American Indians: Writings by the 'Friends of the Indian' 1880–1900* (Cambridge, MA: Harvard University Press, 1973); and David Wallace Adams, *Education for Extinction: American Indians and the Boarding School Experience, 1875–1928* (Lawrence: University of Press of Kansas, 1995).

7. David Murray, *Modern Indians: Native Americans in the Twentieth Century* (England: British Association for American Studies, 1982).

8. *Ex parte Kan-gi-Shun-ca*, (Crow Dog), 109 U.S. 556 (1883); and Sidney L. Harring, *Crow Dog's Case: American Indian Sovereignty, Tribal Law, and United States Law in the Nineteenth Century* (New York: Cambridge University Press, 1994).

9. *House Executive Document*, no. 1, 51st Cong., 2nd session, serial 2841, clxvii; and Francis Paul Prucha, ed., *Documents of United States Indian Policy*, 2nd ed. (Lincoln: University of Nebraska Press, 1990).

10. Leo W. Simmons, ed., *Sun Chief: Autobiography of a Hopi Indian* (New Haven, CT: Yale University Press, 1942); and Zitkala-Ša (Gertrude Bonnin), *American Indian Stories* (Washington: Hayworth Publishing House, 1921).

11. Luther Standing Bear, *My People, the Sioux* (Boston: Houghton, Mifflin, 1928); Luther Standing Bear, *Land of the Spotted Eagle* (Lincoln: University of Nebraska Press, 1978); Charles Alexander Eastman, *Indian Boyhood* (New York: McClure, Phillips, 1902); and Charles A. Eastman, *From the Deep Woods to Civilisation: Chapters in the Autobiography of an Indian*. 1916. (Reprint, Lincoln: University of Nebraska Press, 1977).

Chapter Eight

1. Sharon O'Brien, *American Indian Tribal Governments* (Norman: University of Oklahoma Press, 1989).
2. D.S. Otis, *The Dawes Act and the Allotment of Indian Lands* (Norman: University of Oklahoma Press, 1973).
3. Lewis Meriam, *The Problem of Indian Administration* (Baltimore: Johns Hopkins, 1928); and Colin G. Calloway, *First Peoples: A Documentary Survey of American Indian History* (Boston: Bedford/St. Martin's, 1999).
4. Vine Deloria, Jr., and Clifford M. Lytle, *The Nations Within: The Past and Future of American Sovereignty* (Austin, University of Texas Press, 1984).
5. R. David Edmunds, Frederick E. Hoxie and Neal Salisbury, *The People: A History of Native America* (Boston: Houghton Mifflin Company, 2007).
6. Rupert Costo, 'Federal Indian Policy, 1933–1945', in Kenneth R. Philp, ed., *Indian Self-Rule: First Hand Accounts of Indian-White Relations from Roosevelt to Reagan* (Salt Lake City: Howe Brothers Publishers, 1988).
7. Edmunds, Hoxie and Salisbury, *The People*.
8. Ibid.
9. Donald Parman, *The Navajo Indian and the New Deal* (New Haven: Yale University Press, 1976); Deloria, Jr., and Lytle, *The Nations Within*; Vine Deloria, Jr., and Clifford M. Lytle, *American Indians, American Justice* (Austin: University of Texas Press, 1983); and Thomas Biolsi, *Organising the Lakota: The Political Economy of the New Deal on the Pine Ridge and Rosebud Reservations* (Tucson: University of Arizona Press, 1992).
10. Edmunds, Hoxie and Salisbury, *The People*.
11. *Annual Report of the Secretary of the Interior, 1934* (Washington, DC: U.S. Government Printing Office, 1934).
12. James S. Olson and Raymond Wilson, *Native Americans in the Twentieth Century* (Urbana and Chicago: University of Illinois Press, 1984); and Laurence M. Hauptman, *The Iroquois and the New Deal* (Syracuse: Syracuse University Press, 1981).
13. Theodore H. Haas, 'The Legal Aspects of Indian Affairs from 1887 to 1957', *The Annals of the American Academy of Political and Social Science* 311 (1957), 12-22.
14. Deloria, Jr., and Lytle, *The Nations Within*.
15. James F. Downs, *The Two Worlds of the Washo: An Indian Tribe of California and Nevada* (New York: Holt, Reinhart and Winston, 1966).
16. Peter, Iverson, *'We Are Still Here' American Indians in the Twentieth Century* (Wheeling, IL: Harlan Davidson, Inc, 1998); *Annual Report of the Secretary of the Interior, 1934* (Washington, DC: U.S. Government Printing Office, 1934); and Charles F. Wilkinson, *Blood Struggle: The Rise of Modern Indian Nations* (New York: W. W. Norton & Company, 2005).
17. John R. Wunder, *'Retained by the People' A History of American Indians and the Bill of Rights* (New York: Oxford University Press, 1994).

Chapter Nine

1. Kenneth R. Philp, *Termination Revisited: American Indians on the Trail to Self-Determination, 1933–1953* (Lincoln: University of Nebraska Press, 1999).

2. Arthur V. Watkins, 'Termination of Federal Supervision: The Removal of Restrictions over Indian Property and Person', *The Annals of the American Academy of Political and Social Science* 311 (1957), 47–55.

3. Donald L. Fixico, *Termination and Relocation: Federal Indian Policy, 1945–1960* (Albuquerque: New Mexico Press, 1986); and Carole E. Goldberg, 'Public Law 280: The Limits of State Jurisdiction over Reservation Indians', *UCLA Law Review* 22 (1975), 535–594.

4. Sharon O'Brien, *American Indian Tribal Governments* (Norman: University of Oklahoma Press, 1989); and Kenneth R. Philp, 'Stride Toward Freedom: The Relocation of Indians to Cities, 1952-1960', *Western Quarterly* 16 (1985), 175–190.

5. R. David Edmunds, Frederick E. Hoxie and Neal Salisbury, *The People: A History of Native America* (Boston: Houghton Mifflin Company, 2007); and Fixico, *Termination and Relocation*.

6. Charles F. Wilkinson, *Blood Struggle: The Rise of Modern Indian Nations* (New York: W. W. Norton & Company, 2005); James S. Olson and Raymond Wilson, *Native Americans in the Twentieth Century* (Urbana and Chicago: University of Illinois Press, 1984); and Vine Deloria, Jr., *Custer Died For Your Sins: An Indian Manifesto* (Reprint, Norman: University of Oklahoma Press, 1988).

7. Arthur V. Watkins, 'Termination of Federal Supervision: The Removal of Restrictions over Indian Property and Person', *The Annals of the American Academy of Political and Social Science* 311 (1957), 47–55; Joint Hearings Before the Committees on Interior and Insular Affairs, Subcommittees, 'Termination of Federal Supervision over Certain Tribes of Indians: On S.2749 and H.R.7322', 83rd Congress, 2nd session (Washington, DC: United States Government Printing Office, 1954); and Wilkinson, *Blood Struggle*.

8. Albert L. Hurtado and Peter Iverson, eds, *Major Problems in American Indian History* (Lexington, MA: D.C. Heath and Company, 1994).

9. Wilkinson, *Blood Struggle*; Olson and Wilson, *Native Americans*; Arrell Morgan Gibson, *The American Indian: Prehistory to the Present* (Lexington, MA: D.C. Heath and Company, 1980); Stephen H. Herzberg, 'The Menominee Indians: From Treaty to Termination', *Wisconsin Magazine of History* 60 (1977), 266–329; Patricia K. Ourada, *The Menominee Indians: A History* (Norman: University of Oklahoma Press, 1978); Nicholas C. Peroff, *Menominee Drums: Tribal Termination and Restoration, 1954–1974* (Norman: University of Oklahoma Press, 1982); Theodore Stern, *The Klamath Tribe: A People and Their Reservation* (Seattle: University of Washington Press, 1965); and Susan Hood, 'Termination of the Klamath Tribe of Oregon', *Ethnohistory* 19 (1972), 379–392.

10. Wilkinson, *Blood Struggle*.

11. Joint Hearings, 'Termination of Federal Supervision over Certain Tribes of Indians'.

12. Colin G. Calloway, *First Peoples: A Documentary Survey of American Indian History* (Boston: Bedford/St. Martin's, 1999).

13. Ada Deer, 'Explains How Her People Overturned Termination, 1974', Chapter 14 in *Major Problems in American Indian History*, 2nd ed., eds, Albert L. Hurtado and Peter Iverson (Boston: Houghton Mifflin Company, 2001); and Ada Deer, 'Menominee Restoration: How the Good Guys Won', *Journal of Intergroup Relations* 3 (1974), 41–50.

14. *Williams v. Lee*, 358 U.S. 217 (1959); and Dewi Ioan Ball, 'The Silent Revolution: How the Key Attributes of Tribal Power have been Fundamentally Eroded by the United States Supreme Court from 1973'. PhD diss., University of Wales, Swansea, 2007.

15. *Menominee Tribe v. United States*, 391 U.S. 404 (1968).

16. Lyndon B. Johnson, *Public Papers of the Presidents of the United States: Lyndon B. Johnson, 1968–69*. Vol. 1 (Washington, DC: Government Printing Office, 1968).

17. Richard Nixon, *Public Papers of the Presidents of the United States: Richard Nixon, 1970* (Washington, DC: Government Printing Office, 1971); and Jack D. Forbes, *Native Americans and Nixon, Presidential Politics and Minority Self-Determination, 1969–1972* (Los Angeles: American Indian Studies Centre, UCLA, 1981).

18. Fixico, *Termination and Relocation*.

Chapter Ten

1. Vine Deloria, Jr., *Custer Died For Your Sins: An Indian Manifesto* (1969; reprint, Norman: University of Oklahoma Press, 1988); and Vine Deloria, Jr., and Clifford M. Lytle, *The Nations Within: The Past and Future of American Indian Sovereignty* (Austin: University of Texas Press, 1984).

2. Troy Johnson, Joane Nagel and Duane Champagne, eds, *American Indian Activism: Alcatraz to the Longest Walk* (Urbana: University of Illinois Press, 1997); Troy Johnson, *The Occupation of Alcatraz Island: Indian Self-Determination and the Rise of Indian Activism* (Urbana: University of Illinois Press, 1996); Adam Fortunate Eagle, *Alcatraz! Alcatraz! The Indian Occupation of 1969–71* (San Francisco: Heyday Books, 1992); and Peter Blue Cloud, ed., *Alcatraz Is Not an Island* (Berkeley, CA: Wingbow Press, 1972).

3. Roger Daniels and Spencer C. Olin, Jr., *Racism in California: A Reader in the History of Oppression* (New York: Macmillan, 1972); and Fortunate Eagle, *Alcatraz!*.

4. Charles Wilkinson, *Blood Struggle: The Rise of Modern Indian Nations* (New York: W. W. Norton & Company, 2005); and Wilma Mankiller, *Mankiller: A Chief and Her People* (New York: St. Martin's Press, 1993).

5. R. David Edmunds, Frederick E. Hoxie and Neal Salisbury, *The People: A History of Native America* (Boston: Houghton Mifflin Company, 2007).

6. Vine Deloria, Jr., *Behind the Trail of Broken Treaties: An Indian Declaration of Independence* (Austin: University of Texas Press, 1985); Duane Champagne, ed., *Chronology of North Native American History: From Pre-Columbian Times to the Present* (Detroit: Gale Research Inc., 1994); and Wilkinson, *Blood Struggle*.

7. Edmunds, Hoxie and Salisbury, *The People*; and Paul Chaat Smith and Robert Allen Warrior, *Like a Hurricane: The Indian Movement from Alcatraz to Wounded Knee* (New York: The New Press, 1996).

8. John Katz, 'Damage to BIA Third Heaviest Ever in U.S.', *The Washington Post*, Saturday, 11 November 1972.

9. Edmunds, Hoxie and Salisbury, *The People*; and Smith and Warrior, *Like a Hurricane*.

10. Peter Matthiessen, *In the Spirit of Crazy Horse* (New York: Viking, 1983); Robert Burnette and John Koster, *The Road to Wounded Knee* (New York: Bantam Books, 1974); and *Voices from Wounded Knee, 1973: In the Words of the Participants* (Rooseveltown, NY: Akwesasne Notes, Mohawk Nation, 1974).

11. Ibid.

12. An article by Russell Means on the events of Wounded Knee appears in; Ashley Kahn, Holly George-Warren, Shawn Dahl, eds, *Rolling Stone the '70s* (Little, Brown and Company, 1998).

13. United States Government Memorandum, 'The Use of Special Agents of the FBI in a Paramilitary Law Enforcement Operation in the Indian Country', 24 April 1975. This six page document can be viewed on, FOIA Documents FBI War Against AIM, http://www.freepeltiernow.org/LEGAL/WAR.htm (accessed 2 April 2008).

14. Kevin Barry McKiernan, 'Notes from a Day at Wounded Knee', *Minnesota Leader*, 30 December 1974.

15. Jim Vander Wall, 'A Warrior Caged: The Continuing Struggle of Leonard Peltier', Chapter 10 in *The State of Native America: Genocide, Colonization, and Resistance*, ed., M. Annette Jaimes, (Boston, MA: South End Press, 1992).

Chapter Eleven

1. Colin G. Calloway, *First Peoples: A Documentary Survey of American Indian History* (Boston: Bedford/St. Martin's, 1999).

2. On 17 May 2000, Deborah White Plume spoke at the Congressional Briefing for Leonard Peltier, Washington, DC, and the transcript can be found at, U.S. vs. Leonard

Peltier Trial Transcript Excerpts, http://ishgooda.org/peltier/00-05whiteplume.htm (accessed 31 March 2008).

3. Jim Vander Wall, 'A Warrior Caged: The Continuing Struggle of Leonard Peltier', Chapter 10 in *The State of Native America: Genocide, Colonization, and Resistance*, ed. M. Annette Jaimes (Boston, MA: South End Press, 1992).

4. Ibid.

5. Ibid.

6. William F. Muldrow, U.S. Civil Rights Commission Report on Official Misconduct on the Pine Ridge Reservation, 9 July 1975. This four page document can be viewed at, FOIA Documents, RESMURS Investigation, http://www.freepeltiernow.org/LEGAL/RESMURS.htm (accessed 31 March 2007).

7. The three official Myrtle Bear affidavits can be found at, FOIA Documents Extradition, http://www.freepeltiernow.org/LEGAL/EXTRADITION.htm (accessed 31 March 2007); and Wall, 'A Warrior Caged'.

8. Peter Matthiessen, *In the Spirit of Crazy Horse* (New York: Viking, 1983).

9. Jim Messerschmidt, The Trial of Leonard Peltier (Boston: South End Press, 1983); and The Peltier Trial, http://www.freepeltiernow.org/trial.htm (accessed 15 September 2007).

10. Wall, 'A Warrior Caged'.

11. *United States v. Leonard Peltier* (No. C77-3003) (1977) (Volume I, Pp. 1–54).

12. Ibid.

13. *United States v. Leonard Peltier* (No. C77-3003-01) (1977) (Volume XXV, Pp. 5266–5285).

14. *United States v. Leonard Peltier* (No. C77-3003-01) (1977) (Volume XXVI, Pp. 1–14).

15. Leonard Peltier, *Prison Writings: My Life is My Sun Dance* (New York: St. Martin's Press, 1999).

16. Don Edwards, Statement at the National Press Club, Washington, DC, 14 December 2000. This statement can be found at, Statement by former FBI agent condemning FBI anti-Peltier demo, http://www.iacenter.org/polprisoners/lp_fbi3.htm (accessed 15 September 2007).

17. Letter from Senior Circuit Judge Gerald W. Heaney to Senator Daniel K. Inouye, 'Re: Leonard Peltier', 18 April 1991. This two page letter can be found at, FOIA Documents Post-Conviction, http://www.freepeltiernow.org/LEGAL/POST_CONVICTION.htm (accessed 14 December 2007).

18. Amnesty International, 'USA: Appeal for the release of Leonard Peltier', July 1999 [Index number: AMR 51/160/1999]. This document can be found at, USA: Appeal for the Release of Leonard Peltier, http://www.amnesty.org/en/library/asset/AMR51/160/1999/en/dom-AMR51601999en.html (accessed 21 May 2008).

Chapter Twelve

1. The use of the term non-Indians in this chapter refers to non-Native Americans.

2. *A bill to amend the Homeland Security Act of 2002 to include Indian tribes among the entities consulted with respect to activities carried out by the Secretary of Homeland Security, and for other purposes*, 108th Cong., 1st session, S.578. The equivalent bill, H.R. 2242, was introduced in the House of Representatives on 22 May 2003.

3. Charles F. Wilkinson, *American Indians, Time, and the Law* (New Haven: Yale University Press, 1987).

4. Dewi Ioan Ball, 'The Silent Revolution: How the Key Attributes of Tribal Power have been Fundamentally Eroded by the United States Supreme Court from 1973', PhD. diss., University of Wales, Swansea, 2007.

5. See *Arizona v. California*, 373 U.S. 546 (1963); *Menominee Tribe of Indians v. United States*, 391 U.S. 404 (1968); *Choctaw Nation v. Oklahoma*, 397 U.S. 620 (1970); *Mattz v. Arnett*, 412 U.S. 481 (1973); and William C. Canby, *American Indian Law: in a Nutshell* (St. Paul, MN: West Group, 1998).

6. *Oliphant v. Suquamish Indian Tribe*, 435 U.S. 191 (1978). For discussions on *Oliphant* see, Ball, 'The Silent Revolution'; David E. Wilkins, *American Indian Sovereignty and the U.S. Supreme Court: The Masking of Justice* (Austin: University of Texas Press, 1997); Christopher B. Chaney, 'The Effect of the United States Supreme Court's Decisions During the Last Quarter of the Nineteenth Century on Tribal Criminal Jurisdiction', *Brigham Young University Journal of Public Law* 14 (2000): 173–189; Geoffrey C. Heisey, 'Oliphant and Tribal Criminal Jurisdiction over Non-Indians: Asserting Congress's Plenary Power to Restore Territorial Jurisdiction', *Indiana Law Journal* 73 (1998), 1051–1078; and Peter C. Maxfield, 'Oliphant v. Suquamish Tribe: The Whole is Greater than the Sum of the Parts', *Journal of Contemporary Law* 19 (1993), 391–443.

7. Ibid.

8. Ibid.

9. *Atkinson Trading Co., v. Shirley*, 532 U.S. 645 (2001).

10. *Washington v. Confederated Tribes*, 447 U.S. 134 (1980). See, Stephen L. Pevar, *The Rights of Indians and Tribes: The authoritative ACLU guide to Indian and tribal rights*. 3rd ed. (Carbondale and Edwardsville: Southern Illinois University Press, 2002); Ball, 'The Silent Revolution'; Blake A. Watson, 'The Thrust and Parry of Federal Indian Law', *University of Dayton Law Review* 23 (1998), 437–514; and L. Scott Gould, 'The Consent Paradigm: Tribal Sovereignty at the Millennium', *Columbia Law Review* 96 (1996), 809–902.

11. Ibid.

12. *Merrion v. Jicarilla Apache Tribe*, 455 U.S. 130 (1982). See, N. Bruce Duthu, 'The Thurgood Marshall Papers and the Quest for a Principled Theory of Tribal Sovereignty: Fuelling the Fires of Tribal/State Conflict', *Vermont Law Review* 21 (1996), 47-110; Robert J. Nordhaus, G. Emlen Hall, and Anne Alise Rudio, 'Revisiting Merrion v. Jicarilla Apache Tribe: Robert Nordhaus and Sovereign Indian Control Over Natural Resources on Reservations', *Natural Resources Journal* 43 (2003), 223–284; and Ball, 'The Silent Revolution'.

13. *Atkinson Trading Co. v. Shirley*, 532 U.S. 645 (2001); and Ball, 'The Silent Revolution'.

14. *Montana v. United States*, 450 U.S. 544 (1981). See, Ball, 'The Silent Revolution'; Russell Lawrence Barsh and James Youngblood Henderson, 'Contrary Jurisprudence: Tribal Interests in Navigable Waterways before and After Montana v. United States', *Washington Law Review* 56 (1981), 627–685; Alex Tallchief Skibine, 'The Court's Use of the Implicit Divestiture Doctrine to Implement Its Imperfect Notion of Federalism in Indian Country', *Tulsa Law Journal* 36 (2000), 267–304; and Canby, Jr., *American Indian Law*.

15. *Montana v. United States*, 450 U.S. 544 (1981); and Ball, 'The Silent Revolution'.

16. *Nevada v. Hicks*, 533 U.S. 353 (2001). See, Joseph William Singer, 'Canons Of Conquest: The Supreme Court's Attack on Tribal Sovereignty', *New England Law Review* 37 (2003), 641–668; Melanie Reed, 'Native American Sovereignty Meets a Bend in the Road: Difficulties in Nevada v. Hicks', *Brigham Young University Law Review* 2002 (2002), 137–174; Amy Crafts, 'Nevada v. Hicks and its implication on American Indian Sovereignty', *Connecticut Law Review* 34 (2002), 1249–1280; Catherine Struve, 'How Bad Law Made a Hard Case Easy: Nevada v. Hicks and the Subject Matter Jurisdiction of Tribal Courts', *University of Pennsylvania Journal of Constitutional Law* 5 (2003), 288–317; Robert N. Clinton, 'There Is No Federal Supremacy Clause for Indian Tribes', *Arizona State Law Journal* 34 (2002), 113–260; and Ball, 'The Silent Revolution'.

17. National Congress of the American Indian, *Concept paper, 2003 Legislative Proposal on Tribal Governance and Economic Enhancement 25 July 2002* (Washington, DC: National Congress of the American Indian, 2002).

18. Senate Committee on Indian Affairs, *Rulings of the U.S. Supreme Court as They Affect the Powers and Authorities of the Indian Tribal Governments: Hearing on the Concerns of Recent Decisions of the U.S. Supreme Court and the Future of Indian Tribal Governments in America*, 107th Cong., 2nd session, 27 February 2002.

19. Ibid.

20. U.S. Library of Congress, Congressional Research Service, *Indian Tribal Government Amendments to the Homeland Security Act: S. 578 and Indian Tribal Sovereignty*, by M. Maureen Murphy (Washington, DC: Government Printing Office, 2003); U.S. Library of Congress, Congressional Research Service, *Indian Tribal Government Amendments to the Homeland Security Act: S. 578 and Indian Tribal Sovereignty*, by M. Maureen Murphy (Washington, DC: Government Printing Office, 2005); and Ball, 'The Silent Revolution'.

21. Ibid.

Chapter Thirteen

1. John R. Wunder, *'Retained by the People': A History of American Indians and the Bill of Rights* (New York: Oxford University Press, 1994).

2. *California v. Cabazon Band of Mission Indians*, 480 U.S. 202 (1987).

3. Wunder, *'Retained by the People'*.

4. Akim D. Reinhardt and John R. Wunder, 'Tribal Government Authority Versus Federal Jurisdiction', in *Treaties with American Indians: Volume I*, ed. Donald L. Fixico (Santa Barbara, CA: ABC-CLIO, 2008); and Kathryn R.L. Rand, 'Caught in the Middle: How State Politics, State Law, and State Courts Constrain Tribal Influence Over Indian Gaming', *Marquette Law Review* 90 (2007), 971–1008.

5. Stephen Cornell and Joseph P. Kalt, 'Sovereignty and Nation-Building: The Development Challenge in Indian Country Today', *American Indian Culture and Research Journal* 22 (1998), 187–214; and Don Cossetto, 'The Economic and Social Implications of Indian Gaming: The Case of Minnesota', *American Indian Culture and Research Journal* (Winter 1995), 119–132.

6. Colin G. Calloway, *First Peoples: A Documentary Survey of American Indian History* (Boston: Bedford/St. Martin's, 1999).

7. *Seminole Tribe of Florida v. Butterworth*, 658 F.2d 310 (1981).

8. *California v. Cabazon Band of Mission Indians*, 480 U.S. 202 (1987).

9. Ibid.

10. W. Dale Mason, *Indian Gaming: Tribal Sovereignty and American Politics* (Norman: University of Oklahoma Press, 2000); and Jonathan B. Taylor and Joseph P. Kalt, 'Cabazon, the Indian Gaming Regulatory Act, and The Socioeconomic Consequences of American Indian Governmental Gaming a Ten-Year Review, American Indians on Reservations: A Databook of Socioeconomic Change between the 1990 and 2000 Censuses', Harvard Project on American Indian Economic Development, January 2005.

11. J.R. Mathews, 'Oversight Hearing on the National Indian Gaming Commission', Senate Committee on Indian Affairs, 17 April 2008, 110th Congress, 2nd session, 17 April 2008 (Washington, DC: U.S. Government Printing Office, 2008); Kenneth W. Grant II, Katherine A. Spilde, Jonathan B. Taylor, 'Social and Economic Consequences of Indian Gaming in Oklahoma', Joint Occasional Papers on Native Affairs No. 2003–04, Harvard Project on American Indian Economic Development, 2003. Numerous Indian Nations have signed gaming compacts with States of the Union and one example of a gaming compact was signed between the Seneca and the

State of New York on 12 April 2002 and the document can be found at the website of the Seneca Nation of Indians, Nation-State Gaming Compact between the Seneca Nation of Indians and the State of New York, http://www.sni.org/gaming.pdf (accessed 15 September 2007).

12. A report on this ongoing battle within the Quechan Nation can be found at, Quechan elders take fight against casino resort to Washington, http://www.indiancountry.com/content.cfm?id=1096417941 (accessed 15 August 2008).

13. On 9 November 1998, the Kickapoo Indian Nation of Kansas presented a thirty-seven page report to the National Gambling Impact Study Commission about the benefits of gaming for the Nation and its reservation. This report can be found at, Testimony Golden Eagle Kickapoo Tribe in Kansas, presented to: National Gambling Impact Study Commission, http://www.indiangaming.org/library/studies/1058-Kickapoo-Tribe.pdf (accessed 21 May 2007).

14. Brian Patterson, 'Oversight Hearing on the National Indian Gaming Commission', Senate Committee on Indian Affairs, 17 April 2008, 110th Congress, 2nd session, 17 April 2008 (Washington, DC: U.S. Government Printing Office, 2008).

15. For a detailed explanation of the ambivalence of the Navajo Nation to gaming, see the testimony presented by Ferdinand Notah, Division Director for the Division of Economic Development, Navajo Nation, to the National Gambling Impact Study Commission in 1998. This document is found at, National Gambling Impact Study Commission: Contents, http://govinfo.library.unt.edu/ngisc/meetings/jul3098/jul30con.html (accessed 2 April 2007).

16. The decision of the Navajo to open a casino at Church Rock can be found in a press release on the Navajo website at, After three-and-a-half year wait, Navajo President Joe Shirley, Jr., signs documents to make Navajo gaming a reality at Church Rock, http://www.navajo.org/News%20Releases/George%20Hardeen/Apr08/Loan_documents_signed_to_build_first_Navajo_casino,_for_April_11.pdf (accessed 21 May 2008). The success of the casino can be found at, 'News from Indian Country, Navajo Nation's Fire Rock casino expands slot machines', http://indiancountrynews.net/index.php?option=com_content&task=view&id=6087&Itemid=99999999 (accessed 21 May 2009).

17. National Indian Gaming Association, Indian Gaming Facts, http://www.indiangaming.org/library/indian-gaming-facts/index.shtml (accessed 31 March 2008).

18. Mathews, 'Oversight Hearing on the National Indian Gaming Commission'.

19. The Menominee of Wisconsin presented evidence to the National Gambling Impact Study Commission on 7 January 1999 in support of the economic benefits of gaming. This document can be found at, Testimony Presented before the NGISC Sub-Committee on Indian Gaming, Seattle Hearing, http://indiangaming.org/library/studies/1062-Menominee_Apsanahkwat.pdf (accessed 31 March 2007).

20. Joseph P. Kalt, 'Statement of Professor Joseph P. Kalt Before the National Gambling Impact Study Commission', Harvard Project on American Indian Economic Development, 1998. This document can be found at, Research and Publications, http://www.hks.harvard.edu/hpaied/pubs/pub_145.htm (accessed 14 December 2007); and Ernest L. Stevens, 'Minimum Internal Control Standards' (MICS) for Indian Gaming, Oversight Hearing before the Committee on Resources, U.S. House of Representatives, 109th Congress, 2nd session, 11 May 2006 (Washington, DC: U.S. Government Printing Office, 2006).

21. Wunder, 'Retained by the People'.

22. Generally, see the statement made by Jacob Coin about Indian gaming in 1998 at, National Gambling Impact Study Commission: Contents, http://govinfo.library.unt.edu/ngisc/meetings/jul3098/jul30con.html (accessed

15 September 2007); and Gary C. Anders, 'Indian Gaming: Financial and Regulatory Issues.' Chapter 6 in Contemporary Native American Political Issues, edited by Troy R. Johnson (Walnut Creek, California: AltaMira Press, 1999).

23. Stephen Cornell and Joseph P. Kalt, 'Reloading the Dice: Improving the Chances for Economic Development on American Indian Reservations', Chapter 1 in *What Can Tribes Do? Strategies and Institutions in American Economic Development*, edited by Stephen Cornell and Joseph P. Kalt, American Indian Studies Centre (Los Angeles: University of California Press, 1992); Stephen Cornell and Joseph P. Kalt, 'Two approaches to economic development in American Indian Nations: One works, the other doesn't', Harvard Project on American Indian Economic Development and the Native Nations Institute for Leadership, Management, and Policy Joint Occasional Papers on Native Affairs No. 2005–02, 2005; and Mike McBride III, 'Your Place or Mine? Commercial Transactions between Indian Tribes and Non-Indians in Oklahoma - New Rules for Tribal Sovereign Immunity', *Oklahoma Bar Journal* 67 (1996), 3183–3256.

24. Miriam Jorgensen, 'Oversight Hearing on Economic Development', United States Senate Committee on Indian Affairs, 109th Congress, 2nd session, 10 May 2006 (Washington, DC: U.S. Government Printing Office, 2006). However, contrast the position of Jorgensen to the overall conclusion of, Taylor and Kalt, 'Cabazon, the Indian Gaming Regulatory Act'.

25. Taylor and Kalt, 'Cabazon, the Indian Gaming Regulatory Act'; and William Thompson and Diana R. Dever, 'Indian Gaming Promotes Native American Sovereignty', Chapter 2 in *Native American Rights*, ed. Tamara L. Roleff (San Diego: Greenhaven Press, 1998).

26. The commitment of George W. Bush to the government-to-government relationship was declared on 23 September 2004 by a White House memorandum. This document can be found at, 'Memorandum for the Heads of Executive Departments and Agencies Government-to-Government Relationship with Tribal Governments', http://www.whitehouse.gov/news/releases/2004/09/20040923-4.html (accessed 21 May 2007).

27. Clay Akiwenzie, 'Indian Gaming Could Destroy Native American Culture', Chapter 2 in *Native American Rights*, ed. Tamara L. Roleff (San Diego: Greenhaven Press, 1998).

28. Anders, 'Indian Gaming'.

29. Cheryle A. Kennedy, 'Oversight Hearing on Indian Gaming', Testimony Before the United States Senate Committee on Indian Affairs, 109th Congress, 2nd session, 28 February 2006 (Washington, DC: U.S. Government Printing Office, 2006).

30. Michael Lang, 'Oversight Hearing on Indian Gaming', Testimony Before the United States Senate Committee on Indian Affairs, 109th Congress, 2nd session, 28 February 2006 (Washington, DC: U.S. Government Printing Office, 2006).

31. Carol York, 'Oversight Hearing on Indian Gaming', Testimony Before the United States Senate Committee on Indian Affairs, 109th Congress, 2nd session, 28 February 2006 (Washington, DC: U.S. Government Printing Office, 2006).

32. Ron Suppah, 'Oversight Hearing on Indian Gaming', Testimony Before the United States Senate Committee on Indian Affairs, 109th Congress, 2nd session, 28 February 2006 (Washington, DC: U.S. Government Printing Office, 2006).

Chapter Fourteen

1. For a detailed examination of Federal recognition and the processes and criteria used by the Bureau of Indian Affairs (BIA) and Congress to define, what they think, is an Indian tribe see, Mark Edwin Miller, *Forgotten Tribes: Unrecognized Indians and the Federal Acknowledgement Process* (Lincoln: University of Nebraska Press, 2004).

2. The U.S. Bureau of the Census press release and accompanying population data tables can be found at, Table 1: Estimates of the Population by Race Alone or in Combination and Hispanic Origin for the United States and States: 1 July 2007, http://www.census.gov/Press-Release/www/2008/cb08-67table1.xls (accessed 21 May 2008).

3. R. David Edmunds, Frederick E. Hoxie and Neal Salisbury, *The People: A History of Native America* (Boston: Houghton Mifflin Company, 2007).

4. Colin G. Calloway, *First Peoples: A Documentary Survey of American Indian History* (Boston: Bedford/St. Martin's, 1999); M. Annette Jaimes, 'Federal Indian Identification Policy: A Usurpation of Indigenous Sovereignty in North America', Chapter 4 in *The State of Native America: Genocide, Colonization, and Resistance*, ed. M. Annette Jaimes (Boston, MA: South End Press, 1992); and Edmunds, Hoxie and Salisbury, *The People*.

5. Calloway, *First Peoples*.

6. Troy R. Johnson , 'Part V: Repatriation', in *Contemporary Native American Political Issues*, ed. Troy R. Johnson (Walnut Creek, CA: AltaMira Press, 1999).

7. Marc Fisher, 'Indian Museum's Appeal, Sadly, Only Skin-Deep', *The Washington Post*, 21 September 2004.

8. Ward Churchill, 'Using Indian Names for Sports Teams Harms Native Americans', Chapter 1 in *Native American Rights*, ed. Tamara L. Roleff (San Diego: Greenhaven Press, 1998).

9. For a discussion of some of the issues, see National Coalition on Racism in Sports and Media, http://www.aimovement.org/ncrsm/ (accessed 21 May 2007).

10. *Bellecourt v. Cleveland*, 104 Ohio St.3d 439, 2004-Ohio-6551 (2001).

11. In 2001, the United States Commission on Civil Rights released a statement about the use of Native American images by sports teams. This document can be found at, Statement of the U.S. Commission on Civil Rights on the Use of Native American Images and Nicknames as Sports Symbols, http://www.usccr.gov/press/archives/2001/041601st.htm (accessed 15 September 2007).

BIBLIOGRAPHY

Chapter One

Alfred, Taiaiake. 1999. *Peace, Power, Righteousness: An Indigenous Manifesto.* Toronto: Oxford University Press.

Axtell, James. 1988. *After Columbus: Essays in the Ethnohistory of Colonial North America.* New York: Oxford University Press.

———. 1992. *Beyond 1492: Encounters in Colonial North America.* New York: Oxford University Press.

———. 1981. *The European and the Indian: Essays in the Ethnohistory of Colonial North America.* New York: Oxford University Press.

Barrington, Linda (ed.). 1999. *The Other Side of the Frontier: Economic Explorations into Native American History.* Colorado: Westview Press.

Berkhofer, Robert F., Jr. 1979. *The White Man's Indian: Images of the American Indian from Columbus to the Present.* New York: Vintage Books.

Brown, James A. 1998. 'America before Columbus'. Chapter 1 in *Indians in American History: An Introduction.* 2nd ed. Edited by Frederick E. Hoxie and Peter Iverson. Wheeling, IL: Harlan Davidson, Inc.

Calloway, Colin G. 1999. *First Peoples: A Documentary History Survey of American Indian History.* Boston: Bedford/St. Martin's.

———. 1994. *The World Turned Upside Down: Indian Voices from Early America.* Boston: Bedford/St. Martin's.

Champagne, Duane (ed.). 1994. *Chronology of North Native American History: From Pre-Columbian Times to the Present.* Detroit: Gale Research Inc.

Claassen, Cheryl and Rosemary A. Joyce (eds). 1997. *Women in Prehistory: North American and Mesoamerica.* Philadelphia: University of Pennsylvania Press.

Clifton, James A. (ed.). 1996. *The Invented Indian: Cultural Fictions and Government Politics.* New Brunswick, NJ: Transaction Publishers.

Colson, Elizabeth. 1986. 'Political Organization in Tribal Societies: A Cross-Cultural Comparison'. *The American Indian Quarterly* 1: 5–19.

Columbus, Christopher. 1960. *The Journal of Christopher Columbus.* Translated by Cecil Jane. London: Anthony Blond & The Orion Press.

Cook, Maurice A. 1943. 'Virginia Ethnology from an Early Relation'. *William & Mary Quarterly Historical Magazine* 23: 101–129.

Debo, Angie. 1970. *A History of the Indians of the United States.* Norman: University of Oklahoma Press.

Deloria, Philip J. and Neal Salisbury (eds). 2002. *A Companion to American Indian History.* Oxford: Blackwell Publishers.

Deloria, Vine, Jr. 1995. *Red Earth, White Lies: Native Americans and the Myth of Scientific Fact.* New York: Scribner.

Driver, Harold. 1969. *Indians of North America,* 2nd ed. Chicago: The University of Chicago Press.

Echo-Hawk, Roger C. 2000. 'Ancient History in the New World: Integrating Oral Traditions and the Archaeological Record in Deep Time'. *American Antiquity* 65: 267–290.

Edmunds, David R., Frederick E. Hoxie and Neal Salisbury. 2007. *The People: A History of Native America.* Boston: Houghton Mifflin Company.

Fowler, Loretta. 2003. *The Columbia Guide to American Indians of the Great Plains.* New York: Columbia University Press.

Fried, Morton H. 1975. *The Notion of Tribe.* Menlo Park, CA: Cummings Publishing Company.

Gibson, Arrell Morgan. 1980. *The American Indian: Prehistory to Present*. Lexington, MA: D.C. Heath and Company.

Hoxie, Frederick E. and Peter Iverson (eds). 1998. *Indians in American History: An Introduction*. 2nd ed. Wheeling, IL: Harlan Davidson, Inc.

Hurtado, Albert L. and Peter Iverson (eds). 1994. *Major Problems in American Indian History*. Lexington, MA: D.C. Heath and Company.

Iverson, Peter. 1998. *'We Are Still Here' American Indians in the Twentieth Century*. Wheeling, IL: Harlan Davidson, Inc.

Jaimes, Annette M. (ed.). 1992. *The State of Native America: Genocide, Colonization, and Resistance*. Boston: South End Press.

Josephy, Alvin M. (ed.). 1991. *America in 1492: The World of the Indian before the Arrival of Columbus*. New York: Knopf.

———. 1994. *500 Nations: An Illustrated History of North American Indians*. New York: Alfred A. Knopf.

Kehoe, Alice Beck. 2002. *American Before the European Invasions*. New York: Longman.

Krech, Shepard III. 1999. *The Ecological Indian: Myth and History*. New York: W.W. Norton.

Mann, Charles C. 2005. *1491: New Revelations of the Americas Before Columbus*. New York: Alfred A Knopf.

Merrell, James H. 1984. The Indians' New World: The Catawba Experience'. *The William and Mary Quarterly* 41: 537–565.

Miller, Bruce G. and Daniel B. Boxberger. 1994. 'Creating Chiefdoms: The Puget Sound Case'. *Ethnohistory* 41: 267–293.

Nabokov, Peter. 2002. *A Forest of Time: American Indian Ways of History*. Cambridge: Cambridge University Press.

Oswallt, Wendell H. and Sharlotte Neely. 1996. *This Land was Theirs: A Study of North American Indians*. 5th ed. Mountain View, CA: Mayfield Publishing Company.

Porter, Joy and Kenneth M. Roemer (eds). 2005. *The Cambridge Companion to Native American Literature*. Cambridge: Cambridge University Press.

Richter, Daniel. 2001. *Facing East from Indian Country: A Native History of Early America*. Cambridge, MA: Harvard University Press.

Salisbury, Neal. 1996. 'The Indians' Old World: Native Americans and the Coming of Europeans'. *William and Mary Quarterly* 53: 435–458.

Shaffer, Lynda Norene. 1992. *Native Americans before 1492: The Moundbuilding Centres of the Eastern Woodlands*. Armonk, NY: M.E. Sharpe.

Silko, Leslie Marmon. 1996. *Yellow Women and a Beauty of the Spirit: Essays on Native American Life Today*. New York: Simon and Schuster.

Stannard, David E. 1992. *American Holocaust: The Conquest of the New World*. New York: Oxford University Press.

Starr-Lebeau, Gretchen D. 1998. *American Eras: Early American Civilisations and Exploration to 1600*. Detroit: Gale.

Sullivan, Lawrence E. (ed.). 1989. *Native American Religions: North America*. New York: Macmillan.

Swanton, John R. 1952. *The Indian Tribes of North America*. Washington, DC: US Government Printing Office.

Thomas, David Hurst. 2000. *Skull Wars: Kennewick Man, Archaeology, and the Battle for Native American Identity*. New York: Basic Books.

Thornton, Russell. 1987. *American Indian Holocaust and Survival: A Population History since 1492*. Norman: University of Oklahoma Press.

Vogel, Virgil J. 1972. *This Country Was Ours: A Documentary History of the American Indian*. New York: Harper & Row.

Washburn, Wilcomb. 1975. *The Indian in America*. New York: Harper & Row Publishers.

Wearne, Philip. 1996. *Return of the Indian: Conquest and Revival in the Americas*. London: Cassell.

Weeks, Philip (ed.). 1988. *The American Indian Experience a Profile: 1524 to the Present*. Wheeling, IL: Forum Press, Inc.

Williams, Robert A., Jr. 1990. *The American Indian in Western Legal Thought: The Discourse of Conquest*. New York: Oxford University Press.

Wunder, John R. 1994. *'Retained by the People' A History of American Indians and the Bill of Rights*. New York: Oxford University Press.

Zolbrod, Paul G. 1984. *Din? Bahane': The Navajo Creation Story*. Albuquerque: University of New Mexico Press.

Chapter Two

Alfred, Taiaiake. 1999. *Peace, Power, Righteousness: An Indigenous Manifesto*. Toronto: Oxford University Press.

Axtell, James. 1988. *After Columbus: Essays in the Ethnohistory of Colonial North America*. New York: Oxford University Press.

———. 1992. *Beyond 1492: Encounters in Colonial North America*. New York: Oxford University Press.

———. 1981. *The European and the Indian: Essays in the Ethnohistory of Colonial North America*. New York: Oxford University Press.

———. 1990. *The Invasion Within: The Contest of Cultures in Colonial North America*. New York: Oxford University Press.

Berkhofer, Robert F., Jr. 1979. *The White Man's Indian: Images of the American Indian from Columbus to the Present*. New York: Vintage Books.

Blodget, Harold. 1935. *Samsom Occum*. Hanover: Dartmouth College Publications.

Bowden, Henry Warner. 1981. *American Indians and Christian Missions: Studies in Cultural Conflict*. Chicago: University of Chicago Press.

Calloway, Colin G. 1999. *First Peoples: A Documentary Survey of American Indian History*. Boston: Bedford/St. Martin's.

———. 1997. *New World for All: Indians, Europeans and the Remaking of Early America*. Baltimore, MD: Johns Hopkins University Press.

Conforti, Joseph. 1985. 'Jonathan Edwards's Most Popular Work: The Life of David Brainerd and Nineteenth-Century Evangelical Culture'. *Church History* 54: 188–201.

———. 1985. 'David Brainerd and the Nineteenth Century Missionary Movement'. *Journal of the Early Republic* 5: 309–329.

Delacourt, Paul A. and Hazel R. Delcourt. 2004. *Prehistoric Native Americans and Ecological Change: Human Ecosystems in Eastern North America since the Pleistocene*. New York: Cambridge University Press.

Deloria, Philip J. and Neal Salisbury eds 2002. *A Companion to American Indian History*. Oxford: Blackwell Publishers.

Deloria, Vine., Jr. 1994. *God is Red: A Native View of Religion*. Golden: Fulcrum Publishing.

———. 1999. *For This Land: Writings on Religion in America*. New York: Routledge.

Densmore, Christopher. 1999. *Red Jacket: Iroquois Diplomat and Orator*. Syracuse: Syracuse University Press.

Dickason, Olive Patricia. 1984. *The Myth of the Savage and the Beginnings of French Colonialism in the Americas*. Calgary: University of Alberta Press.

Dowd, Gregory Evans. 1992. *A Spirited Resistance: The North American Indian Struggle for Unity, 1745–1815*. Baltimore, MD: Johns Hopkins University Press.

Drake, Daniel. 1843. *Lives of Celebrated American Indians*. Boston: Bradbury, Soden & Co.

Edwards, Jonathan. 1985. *The Life and Diary of David Brainerd*. Norman Pettit (ed.). New Haven: Yale University Press.

Fowler, Loretta. 2003. *The Columbia Guide to American Indians of the Great Plains*. New York: Columbia University Press.

Gibson, Arrell Morgan. 1980. *The American Indian: Prehistory to the Present*. Lexington, MA: D.C. Heath and Company.

Hagan, William T. 1961. *American Indians*. Chicago: The University of Chicago Press.

Hahn, Steven C. 2004. *The Invention of the Creek Nation, 1670–1763*. Lincoln: University of Nebraska Press.

Hanke, Lewis. 1974. *All Mankind is One: A Study of the Disputation of between Bartolomé de Las Casas and Juan Ginés de Sepúlveda in 1550 on the Intellectual and Religious Capacity of the American Indians*. Dekalb: Northern Illinois University Press.

Hu-DeHart, Evelyn. 1981. *Missionaries, Miners and Indians: Spanish Contact with the Yaqui Nation of Northwestern New Spain, 1533–1820*. Tucson: The University of Arizona Press.

Jaenen, Cornelius J. 1976. *Friend and Foe: Aspects of French-Amerindian Cultural Contact in the Sixteenth and Seventeenth Centuries*. New York: Columbia University Press.

Jennings, Francis. 1984. *The Ambiguous Iroquois Empire: The Covenant Chain Confederation of Indian tribes with English Colonies from its beginnings to the Lancaster Treaty of 1744*. New York: W.W. Norton & Company.

———. 1975. *The Invasion of America: Indians, Colonialism and the Cant of Conquest*. Chapel Hill: University of North Carolina Press.

John, Elizabeth A.H. 1996. *Storms Brewed in Other Men's Worlds: The Confrontation of Indians, Spanish, and French in the Southwest, 1540–1795*. 2nd ed. Norman: University of Oklahoma Press.

Las Casas, Bartolomé. 1971. *History of the Indies*. New York: Harper and Row.

Merrell, James H. 1984. 'The Indians' New World: The Catawba Experience'. *The William and Mary Quarterly* 41: 537–565.

———. 1989. *The Indians' New World: Catawbas and Their Neighbours from European Contact through the Era of Removal*. Chapel Hill: University of North Carolina Press.

Milanich, Jerald T. 1995. *Florida Indians and the Invasion from Europe*. Gainesville: University Press of Florida.

Oswallt, Wendell H. and Sharlotte Neely. 1996. *This Land Was Theirs*. 5th ed. Mountain View, CA: Mayfield Publishing Company.

Parker, Arthur C. 1998. *Red Jacket: Seneca Chief*. Lincoln: University of Nebraska Press.

Parkman, Francis. 1997. *The Jesuits in North America in the Seventeenth Century*. Lincoln: University of Nebraska Press.

Perdue, Theda. 1979. 'Letters from Brainerd'. *Journal of Cherokee Studies* 4: 6–9.

Pointer, Richard W. 1994. '"Poor Indians" and the "Poor in Spirit": The Indian Impact on David Brainerd'. *The New England Quarterly* 67: 403–426.

Poole, Stafford. 1974. Translated, edited and annotated. *In Defence of the Indians: The Defence of the Most Reverend Lord, Don Fray Bartolomé de Las Casas, of the Order of Preachers, Late Bishop of Chiapa, Against the Persecutors and Slanderers of the Peoples of the New World Discovered Across the Seas*. DeKalb: University of Northern Illinois University Press.

Porter, Joy and Kenneth M. Roemer (eds). 2005. *The Cambridge Companion to Native American Literature*. Cambridge: Cambridge University Press.

Richter, Daniel. 2001. *Facing East from Indian Country: A Native History of Early America*. Cambridge, MA: Harvard University Press.

———. 1992. *The Ordeal of the Longhouse: The Peoples of the Iroquois League in the Era of Colonization*. Chapel Hill, NC: University of North Carolina Press.

Ronda, James P. 1977. 'We Are Well as We Are': An Indian Critique of Seventeenth-Century Christian Missions'. *William and Mary Quarterly* 34: 66–82. Rowda, James P. 1981. 'Generations of Faith: The Christian Indians in Martha's Vineyard', *William and Mary Quarterly* 3: 369–394.

Salisbury, Neal. 1982. *Manitou and Providence: Indians, Europeans and the Making of New England, 1500–1643*. New York: Oxford University Press.

Sheehan, Bernard W. 1980. *Savagism and Civility: Indians and Englishmen in Colonial Virginia*. Cambridge: Cambridge University Press.

Smith, Robert J. 1981. 'Resolving the Tragedy of the Commons by Creating Private Property Rights in Wildlife'. *Cato Journal* 1: 439–468.

Thwaites, Reuben G. (ed.). 1896–1901. *The Jesuit Relations and Allied Documents: Travels and Explorations of the Jesuit Missionaries in New France, 1610–1791*, vol. 71. Cleveland: Burrows Brothers.

Washburn, Wilcomb E. 1975. *The Indian in America*. New York: Harper & Row, Publishers.

Weber, David J. 1992. *The Spanish Frontier in North America*. New Haven: Yale University Press.

White, Richard. 1991. *The Middle Ground: Indians, Empires and Republics in the Great Lakes Region, 1650–1815*. Cambridge: Cambridge University Press.

Williams, Robert A., Jr. 1990. *The American Indian in Western Legal Thought: The Discourse of Conquest*. New York: Oxford University Press.

Chapter Three

Alfred, Taiaiake. 1999. *Peace, Power, Righteousness: An Indigenous Manifesto*. Toronto: Oxford University Press.

Anaya, James S. 2000. *Indigenous Peoples in International Law*. New York: Oxford University Press.

Axtell, James. 1992. *Beyond 1492: Encounters in Colonial North America*. New York: Oxford University Press.

———. 1981. *The European and the Indian: Essays in the Ethnohistory of Colonial North America*. New York: Oxford University Press.

———. 1985. *The Invasion Within: The Contest of Cultures in Colonial North America*. New York: Oxford University Press.

———. 1995. *The Rise and fall of the Powhatan Empire: Indians in Seventeenth-Century Virginia*. Williamsburg, VA: The Colonial Williamsburg Foundation.

Bear, Luther Standing. 1933. *Land of the Spotted Eagle*. Boston: Houghton Mifflin.

Berkhofer, Robert F., Jr. 1979. *The White Man's Indian: Images of the American Indian from Columbus to the Present*. New York: Random House.

Calloway, Colin G. 1997. *New Worlds for All: Indians, Europeans, and the Remaking of Early America*. Baltimore: John Hopkins University Press.

———. 1995. *The American Revolution in Indian Country: Crisis and Diversity in Native American Communities*. Cambridge: Cambridge University Press.

Cave, Alfred. 1996. *The Pequot War*. Amherst: University of Massachusetts Press.

Cronon, William. 1983. *Changes in the Land: Indians, Colonists, and the Ecology of New England*. New York: Hill and Wang.

Crosby, Alfred. 1972. *The Columbian Exchange: Biological and Cultural Consequences of 1492*. Westport, CT: Greenwood Press.

Debo, Angie. 1970. *A History of the Indians of the United States*. Norman: University of Oklahoma Press.

Deloria, Philip J. and Neal Salisbury (eds). 2004. *A Companion to American Indian History*. Malden, MA: Blackwell Publishing.

Deloria, Vine, Jr. 1985. *Behind the Trail of Broken Treaties: An Indian Declaration of Independence*. Austin: University of Texas Press.

Dowd, Gregory Evans. 1992. *A Spirited Resistance: The North American Indian Struggle for Unity, 1745–1815*. Baltimore, MD: Johns Hopkins University Press.

Downes, Randolph C. 1940. *Council Fires on the Upper Ohio: A Narrative of Indian Affairs in the Upper Ohio Valley until 1795*. Pittsburgh: University of Pennsylvania Press.

Edmunds, David R. 1983. *The Shawnee Prophet*. Lincoln: University of Nebraska Press.

———. 1984. *Tecumseh and the Quest for Indian Leadership*. Boston: Little, Brown and Company.

Fowler, Loretta. 2003. *The Columbia Guide to American Indians of the Great Plains*. New York: Columbia University Press.

Ganong, William F. 1910. Translated. and edited. *New Relation of Gaspesia, with the Customs and Religion of the Gaspesian Indians, by Chrestien LeClerq*. Toronto: Champlain Society.

Gibson, Arrell Morgan. 1980. *The American Indian: Prehistory to the Present*. Lexington, MA: D.C. Heath and Company.

Gleach, Frederic W. 1997. *Powhatan's World and Colonial Virginia: A Conflict of Cultures*. Lincoln: University of Nebraska Press.

Hahn, Steven C. 2004. *The Invention of the Creek Nation, 1670–1763*. Lincoln: University of Nebraska Press.

Hanke, Lewis. 1974. *All Mankind is One: A Study of the Disputation of between Bartolomé de Las Casas and Juan Ginés de Sepúlveda in 1550 on the Intellectual and Religious Capacity of the American Indians*. Dekalb: Northern Illinois University Press.

———. 1935. *The First Social Experiments in America: A Study in the Development of Spanish Indian Policy in the Sixteenth Century*. Cambridge: Harvard University Press.

———. 1949. *The Spanish Struggle for Justice in the Conquest of America*. Philadelphia: University of Pennsylvania Press.

Helps, Arthur. 1855–1861. *The Spanish Conquest in America and Its Relation to the History of Slavery and to the Government of the Colonies*. London: J.W. Parker & Sons.

Hennepin, Louis. 1938. *Father Louis Hennepin's Description of Louisiana Newly Discovered to the Southwest of New France By Order of the King*. Translated by Marion E. Cross. Minneapolis: University of Minnesota Press.

Horsman, Reginald. 1991. *Expansion and American Indian Policy, 1783–1812*. Reprint, Norman: University of Oklahoma Press.

Jennings, Francis. 1984. *The Ambiguous Iroquois Empire: The Covenant Chain Confederation of Indian tribes with English Colonies from its beginnings to the Lancaster Treaty of 1744*. New York: W.W. Norton & Company.

———. 1975. *The Invasion of America: Indians, Colonialism and the Cant of Conquest*. Chapel Hill: University of North Carolina Press.

Kehoe, Alice B. 1992. *North American Indians: A Comprehensive Account*. 2nd ed. New Jersey: Prentice-Hall, Inc.

Marks, Greg C. 1992. 'Indigenous Peoples in International Law: The Significance of Francisco de Vitoria and Bartolomé de Las Casas', *Australian Year Book of International Law* 13: 1–51.

Martin, Joel. 1991. *Sacred Revolt: The Muskogee's Struggle for a New World*. Boston: Beacon Press.

O'Brien, Jean. 1997. *Dispossession by Degrees: Indian Land and Identity in Natick, Massachusetts, 1650–1790*. Cambridge: Cambridge University Press.

O'Brien, Sharon. 1989. *American Indian Tribal Governments*. Norman: University of Oklahoma Press.

Oswallt, Wendell H. and Sharlotte Neely. 1996. *This Land Was Theirs*. 5th ed. Mountain View, CA: Mayfield Publishing Company.

Pommersheim, Frank. 1995. *Braid of Feathers: American Indian Law and Contemporary Tribal Life*. Berkeley: University of California Press.

Porter, Joy and Kenneth M. Roemer (eds). 2005. *The Cambridge Companion to Native American Literature*. Cambridge: Cambridge University Press.

Richter, Daniel. 1992. *The Ordeal of the Longhouse: The Peoples of the Iroquois League in the Era of Colonization*. Chapel Hill, NC: University of North Carolina Press.

Rountree, Helen C. 1990. *Pocahontas's People: The Powhatan Indians of Virginia Through Four Centuries*. Norman: University of Oklahoma Press.

———. 1988. *The Powhatan Indians of Virginia*. Norman: University of Oklahoma Press.

Seed, Patricia. 1995. *Ceremonies of Possession in Europe's Conquest of the New World, 1492–1640*. Cambridge: Cambridge University Press.

Sugden, John. 1998. *Tecumseh: A Life*. New York: Henry Holt.

Taylor, John. 1980. *Spanish Law Concerning Discoveries, Pacifications and Settlements among the Indians*. Salt Lake City: University of Utah Press.

Thwaites, Reuben G. (ed.) 1896–1901. *The Jesuit Relations and Allied Documents: Travels and Explorations of the Jesuit Missionaries in New France, 1610–1791*, vol. 71. Cleveland: Burrows Brothers.

Washburn, Wilcomb E. 1975. *The Indian in America*. New York: Harper Colophon Books.

White, Richard. 1991. *The Middle Ground: Indians, Empires and Republics in the Great Lakes Region, 1650–1815*. Cambridge: Cambridge University Press.

Wilkins, David E. and K. Tsianina Lomawaima. 2001. *Uneven Ground: American Indian Sovereignty and Federal Law*. Norman: University of Oklahoma Press.

Williams, Robert A., Jr. 1990. *The American Indian in Western Legal Thought: The Discourse of Conquest*. New York: Oxford University Press.

Wright, Ronald. 1992. *Stolen Continents: The Indian Story*. London: Pimlico.

Chapter Four

Anderson, Gary Clayton. 1999. *The Indian Southwest, 1580–1830: Ethnogenesis and Reinvention*. Norman: University of Oklahoma Press.

Axtell, James. 1988. *After Columbus: Essays in the Ethnohistory of Colonial North America*. New York: Oxford University Press.

———. 1992. *Beyond 1492: Encounters in Colonial North America*. New York: Oxford University Press.

———. 1981. *The European and the Indian: Essays in the Ethnohistory of Colonial North America*. New York: Oxford University Press.

———. 1990. *The Invasion Within: The Contest of Cultures in Colonial North America*. New York: Oxford University Press.

Berkhofer, Robert F., Jr. 1979. *The White Man's Indian: Images of the American Indian from Columbus to the Present*. New York: Vintage Books.

Born, Lester K. 1968. *British manuscripts project; a checklist of the microfilms prepared in England and Wales for the American Council of Learned Societies, 1941–1945*. Reprint, New York: Greenwood Press.

Calloway, Colin G. 1995. *The American Revolution in the Indian Country: Crisis and Diversity in Native American Communities*. Cambridge: Cambridge University Press.

———. 1990. *The Western Abenakis of Vermont, 1600–1800: War, Migration, and the Survival of an Indian People*. Norman: University of Oklahoma Press.

———. 1994. *The World Turned Upside Down: Indian Voices from Early America*. Boston: Bedford/St. Martin's.

Cave, Alfred. 1996. *The Pequot War*. Amherst: University of Massachusetts Press.

Clayton, Andrew R.L. and Frederika J. Teute (eds). 1998. *Contact Points: American Frontiers from the Mohawk Valley to the Mississippi, 1750–1830*. Chapel Hill: University of North Carolina Press.

Cronon, William. 1983. *Changes in the Land: Indians, Colonists, and the Ecology of New England*. New York: Hill and Wang.

Cruickshank, E.A. (ed.). 1923–1931. *The Correspondence of Lieut. Governor John Graves Simcoe*, vol. 5. Toronto: Ontario Historical Society.

Debo, Angie. 1970. *A History of the Indians of the United States*. Norman: University of Oklahoma Press.

Downes, Randolph C. 1940. *Council Fires on the Upper Ohio: A Narrative of Indian Affairs on the Upper Ohio until 1795*. Pittsburgh: University of Pittsburgh Press.

Dowd, Gregory Evans. 1992. *A Spirited Resistance: The North American Indian Struggle for Unity, 1745–1815*. Baltimore: Johns Hopkins University Press.

Drake, Samuel Gardner. 1837. *Biography and History of the Indians of North America*. Boston: Antiquarian Institute.

Edmunds, David R. 1983. *The Shawnee Prophet*. Lincoln: University of Nebraska Press.

———. 1984. *Tecumseh and the Quest for Indian Leadership*. Boston: Little, Brown and Company.

Edmunds, David R., Frederick E. Hoxie and Neal Salisbury. 2007. *The People: A History of Native America*. Boston: Houghton Mifflin Company.

Fenn, Elizabeth A. 2000. 'Biological Warfare in Eighteenth-Century North America: Beyond Jeffrey Amherst'. *Journal of American History*, vol. 86. (March 4): 1552–1580.

———. 2001. *Pox Americana: The Great Smallpox Epidemic of 1775–82*. New York: Hill and Wang.

Gibson, Arrell Morgan. 1980. *The American Indian: Prehistory to the Present*. Lexington, MA: Heath.

Gleach, Frederic W. 1997. *Powhatan's World and Colonial Virginia: A Conflict of Cultures*. Lincoln: University of Nebraska Press.

Grinde, Donald A., Jr. 1977. *The Iroquois and the Founding of the American Nation*. San Francisco: Indian Historian Press.

Hagan, William T. 1979. *American Indians*. Revised edition. Chicago: University of Chicago Press.

Hahn, Steven C. 2004. *The Invention of the Creek Nation, 1670–1763*. Lincoln: University of Nebraska Press.

Harpster, John W. (ed.). 1938. *Pen Pictures of Early Western Pennsylvania*. Pittsburgh: University of Pittsburgh Press.

Hinderaker, Eric. 1997. *Elusive Empires: Constructing Colonialism in the Ohio Valley, 1673–1800*. Cambridge: Cambridge University Press.

Horsman, Reginald. 1991. *Expansion and American Indian Policy, 1783–1812*. Reprint, Norman: University of Oklahoma Press.

Jennings, Francis. 1984. *The Ambiguous Iroquois Empire: The Covenant Chain Confederation of Indian tribes with English Colonies from its beginnings to the Lancaster Treaty of 1744*. New York: W.W. Norton and Company.

———. 1975. *The Invasion of America: Indians, Colonialism and the Cant of Conquest*. Chapel Hill: University of North Carolina Press.

Knaut, Andrew. 1995. *The Pueblo Revolt: Conquest and Resistance in Seventeenth-Century New Mexico*. Norman: University of Oklahoma Press.

Lepore, Jill. 1998. *The Name of War: King Philip's War and the Origins of American Identity*. New York: Knopf.

Merrell, James H. 1984. 'The Indians' New World: The Catawba Experience'. *The William and Mary Quarterly* 41: 537–565.

O'Brien, Jean. 1997. *Dispossession by Degrees: Indian Land and Identity in Natick, Massachusetts, 1650–1790*. Cambridge: Cambridge University Press.

O'Connell, Barry (ed.). 1992. *On Our Own Ground: The Complete Writings of William Apes, a Pequot*. Amherst: University of Massachusetts Press.

Parkman, Francis. 1886. *The Conspiracy of Pontiac and the Indian War after the Conquest of Canada*. Boston: Little, Brown.

Perdue, Theda. 1998. *Cherokee Women: Gender and Culture Change, 1700–1835*. Lincoln: University of Nebraska.

Prucha, Francis Paul. 1984. *The Great Father: The United States Government and the American Indians*, vol. 2. Lincoln: University of Nebraska Press.

Reff, Daniel T. 1991. *Disease, Depopulation, and Culture Change in Northwestern New Spain, 1518–1764*. Salt Lake City: University of Utah Press.

Rountree, Helen C. 1990. *Pocahontas's People: The Powhatan Indians of Virginia Through Four Centuries*. Norman: University of Oklahoma Press.

Sando, Joe S. 1992. *Pueblo Nations: Eight Centuries of Pueblo Indian History*. Santa Fe: Clear Light Publishers.

Sheehan, Bernard. 1973. *Seeds of Destruction: Jeffersonian Philanthropy and the American Indian*. New York: W.W. Norton and Company.

Slotkin, Richard and James K. Folsom (eds). 1978. *So Dreadful a Judgement: Puritan Responses to King Philip's War, 1676–1677*. Middletown, CT: Wesleyan University Press.

Starkey, Armstrong. 1998. *European and Native American Warfare, 1675–1815*. London: UCL Press.

Stearn, Wagner E. and Allen E. Stearn. 1945. *The Effect of Smallpox on the Destiny of the Amerindian*. Boston: Bruce Humphries.

Sugden, John. 1998. *Tecumseh: A Life*. New York: Henry Holt.

Sword, Wiley. 1987. *President Washington's Indian War*. Norman: University of Oklahoma Press.

Thorpe, Francis N. (ed.). 1909. *Federal and State Constitutions: Colonial Charters and Other Organic Laws of the States, Territories, and Colonies, Now or Heretofore Forming the United States of America*, vol. 2. Washington, DC: U.S. Government Printing Office.

Vanderwerth, W.C. 1971. *Indian Oratory: Famous Speeches by Noted Indian Chieftains*. Norman: University of Oklahoma Press.

Washburn, Wilcomb E. 1975. *The Indian in America*. New York: Harper Colophon Books.

White, Richard. 1991. *The Middle Ground: Indians, Empires and Republics in the Great Lakes Region, 1650–1815*. Cambridge: Cambridge University Press.

Chapter Five

Andrew, John A., III. 1992. *From Revivals to Removal; Jeremiah Evarts, The Cherokee Nation, and the Search for the Soul of America*. Athens, GA: University of Georgia Press.

Ball, Dewi Ioan. 2007. 'The Silent Revolution: How the Key Attributes of Tribal Power have been Fundamentally Eroded by the United States Supreme Court from 1973'. PhD diss., University of Wales, Swansea.

Beck, David. 2002. *Siege and Survival: A History of the Menominee Indians, 1634–1856*. Lincoln: University of Nebraska Press.

Burke, Joseph C. 1969. 'The Cherokee Cases: A Study in Law, Politics, and Morality'. *Stanford Law Review* 21: 500–531.

Carson, James Taylor. 1999. *Searching for the Bright Path: The Mississippi Choctaws from Prehistory to Removal*. Lincoln: University of Nebraska Press.

Cherokee Nation v. Georgia, 30 U.S. 1 (1831).

Cohen, Felix S. 1941. *Handbook of Federal Indian Law*. Washington, DC: US Government Printing Office.

Cotterill, R.S. 1954. *The Southern Indians: The Story of the Civilized Tribes Before Removal*. Norman: University of Oklahoma Press.

DeRosier, Arthur H., Jr. 1970. *The Removal of the Choctaw Indians*. Knoxville: University of Tennessee Press.

Dowd, Gregory Evans. 1992. *A Spirited Resistance: The North American Indian Struggle for Unity, 1745–1815*. Baltimore, MD: Johns Hopkins University Press.

Edmunds, David. R. 1978. *The Potawatomis: Keepers of the Fire*. Norman: University of Oklahoma Press.

Ehle, John. 1988. *The Trail of Tears: The Rise and Fall of the Cherokee Nation*. New York: Doubleday.

Evarts, Jeremiah. 1981. *Cherokee Removal: The 'William Penn' Essays & Other Writings by Jeremiah Evarts*. Edited, with an introduction by Francis Paul Prucha. Knoxville: University of Tennessee Press, Knoxville.

Every, Dale Van. 1966. *Disinherited: The Lost Birthright of the American Indian*. New York: William Morrow & Company.

Gibson, Arrell Morgan. 1980. *The American Indian: Prehistory to the Present*. Lexington, MA: D.C. Heath and Company.

Foreman, Grant. 1932. *Indian Removal: The Emigration of the Five Civilized Tribes of Indians.* Norman: University of Oklahoma Press.

Green, Michael D. 1979. *The Creeks: A Critical Bibliography.* Bloomington, IN: Indiana University Press for the Newberry Library, Centre for the History of the American Indian.

———. 1982. *The Politics of Indian Removal: Creek Government and Society in Crisis.* Lincoln: University of Nebraska Press.

Hagan, William T. 1961. *American Indians.* Chicago: The University of Chicago Press.

Hauptman, Laurence M. and L. Gordon McLester III (eds). 1999. *The Oneida Indian Journey: From New York to Wisconsin, 1784–1860.* Madison: University of Wisconsin Press.

Hawk, Black. 1834. *Life of Black Hawk.* Boston: Russell, Odiorne & Metcalf.

Horsman, Reginald. 1967. *Expansion and American Indian Policy, 1783–1812.* Norman: University of Oklahoma Press.

———. 1970. *The Origin of Indian Removal, 1815–1824.* East Lansing, MI: Michigan State University Press for Historical Society of Michigan.

———. 1981. *Race and Manifest Destiny: the Origins of American Racial Anglo-Saxonism.* Massachusetts: Harvard University Press.

Johnson v. M'Intosh, 21 U.S. 543 (1823).

Johnston, Carolyn Ross. 2003. *Cherokee Women in Crisis: Trail of Tears, Civil War, and Allotment 1838–1907.* Tuscaloosa: University of Alabama Press.

McLoughlin, William G. 1996. *Cherokee Renascence in the New Republic.* Princeton, NJ: Princeton University Press.

———. 1975. 'Thomas Jefferson and the Beginnings of Cherokee Nationalism'. *William and Mary Quarterly* 32: 547–580.

Maddox, Lucy. 1991. *Removals: Nineteenth-Century American Literature and the Politics of Indian Affairs.* New York: Oxford University Press.

Mahon, John K. 1967. *History of the Second Seminole War, 1835–1842.* Gainesville: University of Florida Press.

Moulton, Gary. 1978. *John Ross: Cherokee Chief.* Athens: University of Georgia Press.

Norgren, Jill. 1996. *The Cherokee Cases: The Confrontation of Law and Politics.* New York: McGraw-Hill. Inc.

Prucha, Francis Paul. 1962. *American Indian Policy in the Formative Years: The Indian Trade and Intercourse Acts, 1790–1834.* Cambridge, MA: Harvard University Press.

———. 1969. 'Andrew Jackson's Indian Policy: A Reassessment'. *Journal of American History* 56: 527–539.

———. 1984. *The Great Father: The United States Government and the American Indians,* vol. 2. Lincoln: University of Nebraska Press.

Perdue, Theda. 1998. *Cherokee Women: Gender and Culture Change, 1700–1835.* Lincoln: University of Nebraska Press.

Robertson, Lindsay G. 2005. *Conquest by Law: How the Discovery of America Dispossessed Indigenous Peoples of Their Lands.* New York: Oxford University Press.

Rogin, Michael Paul. 1975. *Fathers and Children: Andrew Jackson and the Subjugation of the American Indian.* New York: Knopf.

Satz, Ronald N. 1975. *American Indian Policy in the Jacksonian Era.* Lincoln: University of Nebraska Press.

———. 1979. *Tennessee's Indian People: From White Contact to Removal, 1540–1840.* Knoxville, TN: University of Tennessee Press and Tennessee Historical Commission.

Shattuck, Petra T. and Jill Norgren. 1993. *Partial Justice: Federal Indian Law in a Liberal Constitutional System.* Providence, London: Berg Publishers, Inc.

Sheehan, Bernard W. 1974. *Seeds of Extinction: Jeffersonian Philanthropy and the American Indian.* Chapel Hill: University of North Carolina Press.

Spence, Mark David. 1999. *Dispossessing the Wilderness: Indian Removal and the Making of the National Parks.* New York: Oxford University Press.

Spores, Ronald. 1993. 'Too Small a Place: The Removal of the Willamette Valley Indians, 1850–1856'. *American Indian Quarterly* 17:171–191.

Sturgis, Amy. 2006. *The Trail of Tears and Indian Removal*. Connecticut: Greenwood Press.

Swindler, William F. 1975. 'Politics as Law: The Cherokee Cases'. *American Indian Law Review* 3: 7–20.

Thornton, Russell. 1987. *American Indian Holocaust and Survival: A Population History since 1492*. Norman: University of Oklahoma Press.

Underwood, Thomas Bryan. 1956. *Cherokee Legends and the Trail of Tears*. Knoxville: McLemore.

Wallace, Anthony F.C. 1993. *The Long Bitter Trail: Andrew Jackson and the Indians*. New York: Hill and Wang.

Washburn, Wilcomb E. 1975. *The Indian in America*. New York: Harper & Row, Publishers.

Wilkins, Thurman. 1970. *Cherokee Tragedy: The Story of the Ridge Family and the Decimation of a People*. New York: McMillan Co.

Wirt, William. 1830. *Opinion on the Right of the State Georgia to Extend Her Laws Over the Cherokee Nation*. Baltimore, MD: F. Lucas, Jr.

Worcester v. Georgia, 31 U.S. 515 (1832).

Wunder, John R. 1985. 'No More Treaties: The Resolution of 1871 and the Alteration of Indian Rights to their Homelands', in *Working the Range: Essays on the History of Western Land Management and the Environment*, edited by John R. Wunder. Westport, CT: Greenwood Press.

Young, Mary E. 1958. 'Indian Removal and Land Allotment: The Civilised Tribes and Jacksonian Justice'. *American Historical Review* 64: 31–45.

————. 1961. *Red Skins, Ruffle Shirts, and Red Necks: Indian Allotments in Alabama and Mississippi, 1830–1860*. Norman, OK: University of Oklahoma Press.

Chapter Six

Ambrose, Stephen E. 1986. *Crazy Horse and Custer*. New York: New American Library.

Brown, Dee. 1970. *Bury My Heart at Wounded Knee: An Indian History of the American West*. New York: Holt, Rinehart and Winston Publishers.

Carey, Raymond G. 1964. 'The Puzzle of Sand Creek'. *Colorado Magazine* 41 (Fall): 279–298.

Craig, Reginald S. 1959. *The Fighting Parson: The Biography of Colonel John M. Chivington*. Los Angeles: Westernlore Press.

Custer, George A. 1966. *My Life on the Plains*. Lincoln: University of Nebraska Press.

Cutler, Bruce. 1995. *The Massacre at Sand Creek: Narrative Voices*. Norman: University of Oklahoma Press.

Debo, Angie. 1995. *A History of the Indians of the United States*. London: Pimlico.

DeMallie, Raymond J. 1982. 'The Lakota Ghost Dance: An Ethnohistorical Account'. *Pacific Historical Review* 51 (November): 385–405.

Dippie, Brian W. 1996. *Custer's Last Stand: The Anatomy of an American Myth*. 1976. Reprint, Lincoln: University of Nebraska Press.

Dixon, Joseph Kossuth. 1913. *The Vanishing Race: The Last Great Indian Council: A Record in Picture & Story of the Last Great Indian Council, Participated in by Eminent Indian Chiefs from Nearly Every Indian Reservation in the United States. Together with the Story of Their Lives as Told by Themselves – Their Speeches and Folklore Tales – Their Solemn Farewell and the Indians' Story of the Custer Fight*. Garden City, NY: Doubleday, Page and Co.

Dugan, Bill. 1994. *Sitting Bull*. San Francisco: HarperCollins.

Fowler, Loretta. 1982. *Arapahoe Politics, 1851–1978*. Lincoln: University of Nebraska Press.

Fox, Richard Allan, Jr. 1993. *Archaeology, History, and Custer's Last Battle*. Norman: University of Oklahoma Press.

Gibson, Arrell M. 1980. *The American Indian in: Prehistory to the Present.* Lexington, MA: D.C. Heath.

Greene, Jerome A. and Douglas D. Scott. 2004. *Finding Sand Creek: History, Archaeology, and the 1864 Massacre Site.* Norman: University of Oklahoma Press.

Halaas, David Fridtjof and Andrew E. Masich. 2004. *Halfbreed: The Remarkable True Story of George Bent-Caught Between the Worlds of the Indian and the White Man.* Cambridge, MA: Da Capo Press.

Hardorff, Richard G. (ed.). 2005. *Indian Views of the Custer Fight: A Source Book.* Norman: University of Oklahoma Press.

Hatch, Thom. 2004. *Black Kettle: The Cheyenne Chief Who Sought Peace But Found War.* Hoboken, NJ: John Wiley & Sons.

Hittman, Michael. 1997. *Wovoka and the Ghost Dance,* edited by Don Lynch. Lincoln: University of Nebraska Press,

Hoig, Stan. 1961. *The Sand Creek Massacre.* Norman: University of Oklahoma Press.

Hyde, George E. 1968. *Life of George Bent, Written from His Letters,* edited by Savoie Lottinville. Norman: University of Oklahoma Press.

Jaimes, M. Annette. 1992. 'Sand Creek: The Morning After'. Introduction in *The State of Native America: Genocide, Colonization, and Resistance,* edited by M. Annette Jaimes. Boston, MA: South End Press.

Jensen, Richard E., R. Eli Paul and John E. Carter. 1991. *Eyewitness at Wounded Knee.* Lincoln: University of Nebraska Press.

Johnson, Virginia W. 1962. *The Unregimented General. A Biography of Nelson A. Miles.* Boston, MA: Houghton Mifflin.

Kehoe, Alice B. 1989. *The Ghost Dance: Ethnohistory and Revitalisation.* New York: Holt, Rinehart and Winston.

Mendoza, Patrick M. 1993. *Song of Sorrow: Massacre at Sand Creek.* Denver, CO: Willow Wind Pub. Co.

Miles, Nelson A. 1890. *Personal Recollections and Observations of General Nelson A. Miles.* Chicago, IL: Werner Co.

———. 1911. *Serving the Republic. Memoirs of the Civil and Military Life of Nelson A. Miles, Lieutenant-General, United States Army.* New York: Harper and Bros.

Mooney, James. 1896. *The Ghost-Dance Religion and the Sioux Outbreak of 1890.* Fourteenth Annual Report (Part 2) of the Bureau of Ethnology to the Smithsonian Institution, 1892–1893. Washington, DC: US Government Printing Office.

Moore, John H. 1996. *The Cheyenne.* Cambridge, MA: Blackwell.

Moses, L.G. 1985. 'The Father Tells Me So! Wovoka: The Ghost Dance Prophet'. *American Indian Quarterly* 9: 335–351.

Nichols, David A. 1978. *Lincoln and the Indians, Civil War Policy and Politics.* Columbia, MO: University of Missouri Press.

O'Brien, Sharon. 1989. *American Indian Tribal Governments.* Norman: University of Oklahoma Press.

Olson, James C. 1965. *Red Cloud and the Sioux Problem.* Lincoln: University of Nebraska Press.

Ortiz, Simon J. 1981. *From Sand Creek.* New York: Thunder's Mouth Press.

Ostler, Jeffrey. 2004. *The Plains Sioux and U.S. Colonialism from Lewis and Clark to Wounded Knee.* New York: Cambridge University Press.

Rankin, Charles E. (ed.). 1996. *Legacy: New Perspectives on the Battle of the Little Big Horn.* Helena: Montana Historical Society.

Scott, Douglas D., Richard A. Fox Jr., Melissa A. Connor and Dick Harmon. 1989. *Archaeological Perspectives on the Battle of the Little Bighorn.* Norman: University of Oklahoma Press.

Standing Bear, Luther. 1975. *My People the Sioux.* Lincoln: University of Nebraska Press.

Svaldi, David. 1989. *Sand Creek and the Rhetoric of Extermination: A Case Study in Indian-White Relations.* Lanham, MD: University Press of America.

Thornton, Russell. 1987. *American Indian Holocaust and Survival: A Population History since 1492*. Norman: University of Oklahoma Press.

U.S. Senate. *Hearings before the Committee on the Judiciary*. 'To liquidate the liability of the United States for the Massacre of the Sioux Indian men, women and children at Wounded Knee on December 29, 1890'. 94th Congress, 2nd. session, 1976.

Utley, Robert M. 1988. *Cavalier in Buckskin: George Armstrong Custer and the Western Military Frontier*. Norman, OK: University of Oklahoma Press.

———. 1984. *The Indian Frontier of the American West, 1846–1890*. Albuquerque: University of New Mexico Press.

———. 1993. *The Lance and the Shield: The Life and Times of Sitting Bull*. New York: Henry Holt.

———. 1963. *The Last Days of the Sioux Nation*. New Haven: Yale University Press.

Utley, Robert M. and Wilcomb E. Washburn. 1978. *The History of the Indian Wars*. London: Mitchell Beazley.

Weeks, Philip. 1990. *Farewell, My Nation: The American Indian and the United States, 1820–1890*. Arlington Heights, IL: Harlan Davidson.

White, Lonnie J. 1967. 'From Bloodless to Bloody: The Third Colorado Cavalry and the Sand Creek Massacre'. *Journal of the West* 6 (October): 535–581.

White, Richard. 1978. 'The Winning of the West: The Expansion of the Western Sioux in the Eighteenth and Nineteenth Centuries'. *Journal of American History* 65: 319–343.

Chapter Seven

Adams, David Wallace. 1995. *Education for Extinction: American Indians and the Boarding School Experience, 1875–1928*. Lawrence: University Press of Kansas.

Ahern, Wilbert H. 1997. 'An Experiment Aborted: Returned Indian Students in the Indian School Service, 1881–1908'. *Ethnohistory* 44: 263–304.

Archuleta, Margaret L., Brenda J. Child and K. Tsianina Lomawaima (eds). 2000. *Away from Home: American Indian Boarding School Experiences, 1879–2000*. Phoenix: Heard Museum.

Bannan, Helen M. 1978. 'The Idea of Civilization and American Indian Policy Reformers in the 1880s'. *Journal of American Culture* I (Winter): 787–799.

Bear, Luther Standing. 1978. *Land of the Spotted Eagle*. Lincoln: University of Nebraska Press.

———. 1928. *My People, the Sioux*. Boston: Houghton Mifflin.

Berthrong, Donald J. 1976. *The Cheyenne and Arapaho Ordeal: Reservation and Agency Life in the Indian Territory, 1875–1907*. Norman: University of Oklahoma Press.

———. 1979. 'Legacies of the Dawes Act: Bureaucrats and Land Thieves at the Cheyenne-Arapaho Agencies of Oklahoma'. *Arizona and the West* 21 (Winter): 335–354.

Cadwalader, Sandra L. and Vine Deloria, Jr. (ed.) 1984. *The Aggressions of Civilisation: Federal Indian Policy Since the 1880s*. Philadelphia: Temple University Press.

Carlson, Leonard A. 1981. *Indians, Bureaucrats, and Land, The Dawes Act and the Decline of Indian Farming*. Westport, CT: Greenwood Press.

Child, Brenda. 1998. *Boarding School Seasons: American Indian Families, 1900–1940*. Lincoln, University of Nebraska Press.

Cobb, Amanda J. 2000. *Listening to our Grandmothers' Stories: The Bloomfield Academy for Chickasaw Females, 1852–1949*. Lincoln: University of Nebraska Press.

Coleman, Michael. 1993. *American Indian Children at School, 1850–1930*. Jackson: University Press of Mississippi.

Deloria, Vine, Jr. and Clifford M. Lytle. 1984. *The Nations Within: The Past and Future of American Sovereignty*. Austin: University of Texas Press.

Eastman, Charles A. 1977. *From the Deep Woods to Civilisation: Chapters in the Autobiography of an Indian*. 1916. Reprint, Lincoln: University of Nebraska Press.

————. 1902. *Indian Boyhood*. New York: McClure, Phillips and Co.

Ellis, Clyde. 1996. *To Change Them Forever: Indian Education at the Rainy Mountain Boarding School, 1893–1920*. Norman: University of Oklahoma Press.

Ex parte Kan-gi-Shun-ca (Crow Dog), 109 U.S. 556 (1883).

Fritz, Henry E. 1963. *The Movement for Indian Assimilation, 1860–1890*. Philadelphia, PA: University of Pennsylvania Press.

Gibson, Arrell Morgan. 1980. *The American Indian: Prehistory to Present*. Lexington, MA: D.C. Heath and Company.

Haas, Theodore H. 1957. 'The Legal Aspects of Indian Affairs from 1887 to 1957'. *The Annals of the American Academy of Political and Social Science* 311: 12–22.

Hagan, William T. 1956. 'Private Property: The Indian's Door to Civilisation'. *Ethnohistory* 3 (Spring): 126–137.

Harring, Sidney L. 1994. *Crow Dog's Case: American Indian Sovereignty, Tribal Law, and United States Law in the Nineteenth Century*. New York: Cambridge University Press.

Hendrick, Irving G. 1981. 'The Federal Campaign for the Admission of Indian Children into Public Schools, 1890–1934'. *American Indian Culture and Research Journal* 5: 13–32.

Horne, Esther Burnett and Sally McBeth. 1998. *Essie's Story: The Life and Legacy of a Shoshone Teacher*. Lincoln: University of Nebraska Press.

Hoxie, Frederick E. 1984. *A Final Promise: The Campaign to Assimilate the Indians, 1880–1920*. Lincoln: University of Nebraska Press.

Hyer, Sally. 1990. *One House, One Voice, One Heart: Native American Education at the Santa Fe Indian School*. Santa Fe: Museum of New Mexico Press.

Johnston, Mary Antonio. 1948. *Federal Relations with the Great Sioux Indians of South Dakota, 1887–1933, With Particular Reference to Land Policy under the Dawes Act*. Washington, DC: Catholic University of America Press.

Lindsey, Donal F. 1995. *Indians at Hampton Institute 1877–1923*. Urbana: University of Illinois Press.

Lomawaima, Tsianina. 1994. *They called It Prairie Light: The Story of Chilocco Indian School*. Lincoln: University of Nebraska Press.

McDonnell, Janet A. 1991. *The Dispossession of the American Indian, 1887–1934*. Bloomington: Indiana University Press.

Mardock, Robert Winston. 1971. *The Reformers and the American Indian*. Columbia: University of Missouri Press.

Meyer, Melissa L. 1994. *The White Earth Tragedy: Ethnicity and Dispossession at a Minnesota Anishinaabe Reservation, 1889–1920*. Lincoln: University of Nebraska Press.

Mihesuah, Devon A. 1993. *Cultivating the Rosebuds: The Education of Women at the Cherokee Female Seminary, 1851–1909*. Urbana: University of Illinois Press.

Otis, D. S. (ed.). 1973. *The Dawes Act and the Allotment of Indian Lands*. Norman: University of Oklahoma Press.

Pratt, Richard Henry. 1964. *Battlefield and Classroom: Four Decades with the American Indian, 1867–1904*, edited by Robert M. Utley. New Haven: Yale University Press.

Priest, Loring Benson. 1942. *Uncle Sam's Stepchildren: The Reformation of United States Indian Policy, 1865–1887*. New Brunswick: Rutgers University Press.

Prucha, Francis Paul. 1976. *American Indian Policy in Crisis: Christian Reformers and the Indians, 1865–1900*. Norman: University of Oklahoma Press.

Prucha, Francis Paul. (ed.). 1978. *Americanizing the American Indians: Writings by the 'Friends of the Indian', 1880–1990*. Lincoln: University of Nebraska Press.

————. 1984. *The Great Father: The United States Government and the American Indians*, vol. 2. Lincoln: University of Nebraska Press.

Riney, Scott D. 1999. *The Rapid City Indian School, 1989–1933*. Norman: University of Oklahoma Press.

Royster, Judith V. 1995. 'The Legacy of Allotment'. *Arizona State Law Journal* 27: 1–78.

Simmons, Leo W. (ed.). 1942. *Sun Chief: The Autobiography of a Hopi Indian, by Don C. Talayesva*. New Haven: Yale University Press.

Stockel, Henrietta H. 1993. *Survival of the Spirit: Chiricahua Apaches in Captivity*. Reno: University of Nevada Press.

Trennert, Robert A. 1988. *The Phoenix Indian School: Forced Assimilation in Arizona, 1900–1935*. Norman: University of Oklahoma Press.

Utley, Robert M. 1984. *The Indian Frontier of the American West, 1846–1890*. Albuquerque: University of New Mexico Press.

Vogel, Virgil (ed.). 1972. *This Country was Ours: A Documentary History of the American Indian*. New York: Harper & Row.

Washburn, Wilcomb E. 1975. *The Assault on Indian Tribalism: The General Allotment Law (Dawns Act of 1887)*. Philadelphia: Lippincott.

———. 1971. *Red Man's Land, White Man's Law: A Study of the Past and Present Status of the American Indian*. New York: Charles Scribner's Sons.

Wilkinson, Charles F. 1987. *American Indians, Time, and the Law*. New Haven: Yale University Press.

Wilson, Raymond. 1983. *Ohiyesa: Charles Eastman, Santee Sioux*. Urbana: University of Illinois Press.

Zitkal-Ša. 1921. *American Indian Stories*. Washington: Hayworth Publishing House.

Chapter Eight

Beck, David R. M. 2005. *The Struggle for Self-Determination: History of the Menominee Indians Since 1854*. Lincoln: University of Nebraska Press.

Berkey, Curtis. 1976. 'The Legislative History of the Indian Reorganization Act'. *American Indian Journal* 2 (July): 15–22.

Bernstein, Alison. 1984. 'A Mixed Record: The Political Enfranchisement of American Indian Women During the Indian New Deal'. *Journal of the West* 23: 13–20.

Biolsi, Thomas. 1992. *Organising the Lakota: The Political Economy of the New Deal on the Pine Ridge and Rosebud Reservations*. Tucson: University of Arizona Press.

Cadwalader, Sandra L. and Vine Deloria, Jr. (ed.). 1984. *The Aggressions of Civilisation: Federal Indian Policy Since the 1880s*. Philadelphia: Temple University Press.

Cohen, Felix S. 1941. *Handbook of Federal Indian Law*. Washington, DC: US Government Printing Office.

Cohen, Lucy Kramer, Charlotte Lloyd Walkup and Benjamin Reifel. 1986. 'Felix Cohen and the Adoption of the IRA', in *Indian Self-Rule: First-Hand Accounts of Indian-White Relations from Roosevelt to Reagan*. Kenneth R. Philp. (ed.). Salt Lake City: Howe Brothers.

Collier, John. 1963. *From Every Zenith: A Memoir and Some Essays on Life and Thought*. Denver: Sage Books.

Critchlow, Donald T. 1981. 'Lewis Meriam, Expertise, and Indian Reform'. *Historian* 43 (May): 325–344.

Deloria, Vine, Jr. (ed.). 1985. *American Indian Policy in the Twentieth Century*. Norman: University of Oklahoma Press.

———. 2002. *The Indian Reorganization Act: Congresses and Bills*. Norman: University of Oklahoma Press.

Deloria, Vine, Jr. and Clifford M. Lytle. 1984. *The Nations Within: The Past and Future of American Sovereignty*. Austin: University of Texas Press.

Downs, James F. 1966. *The Two Worlds of the Washo: An Indian Tribe of California and Nevada*. New York: Holt, Reinhart and Winston.

Ducheneaux, Frank. 1976. 'The Indian Reorganization Act and the Cheyenne River Sioux'. *American Indian Journal* 2 (August): 8–14.

Edmunds, R. David, Frederick E. Hoxie and Neal Salisbury. 2007. *The People: A History of Native America*. Boston: Houghton Mifflin Company.

Fouberg, Erin Hogan. 2000. *Tribal Territory, Sovereignty, and Governance: A Study of the Cheyenne River and Lake Traverse Indian Reservations*. New York: Garland Publishing, Inc.

Fowler, Loretta. 2002. *Tribal Sovereignty and the Historical Imagination: Cheyenne-Arapaho Politics*. Lincoln: University of Nebraska Press.

Haas, Theodore. 1947. *Ten Years of Tribal Government under the I.R.A.* Washington, DC: Government Printing Office.

Hauptman, Laurence M. 1981. *The Iroquois and the New Deal*. Syracuse: Syracuse University Press.

Hertzberg, Hazel W. 1971. *The Search for an American Indian Identity: Modern Pan-Indian Movements*. Syracuse: Syracuse University Press.

Hoxie, Frederick E., Peter C. Mancall and James H. Merrell (eds). 2001. *American Nations: Encounters in Indian Country, 1850 to the Present*. New York: Routledge.

Iverson, Peter. 1998. '*We Are Still Here' American Indians in the Twentieth Century*. Wheeling, IL: Harlan Davidson, Inc.

Kelly, Lawrence C. 1983. *The Assault on Assimilation: John Collier and the Origins of Indian Policy Reform*. Albuquerque: University of New Mexico Press.

———. 1975. 'The Indian Reorganization Act: The Dream and the Reality'. *Pacific Historical Review* 44: 291–312.

Kelly, William H. (ed.). 1954. *Indian Affairs and the Indian Reorganization Act: The Twenty Year Record*. Tucson: University of Arizona Press.

Kersey, Harry A., Jr. 1989. *The Florida Seminoles and the New Deal, 1933–1942*. Boca Raton: Florida Atlantic University Press.

Kickingbird, Lynn. 1976. 'Attitudes Toward the Indian Reorganisation Bill'. *American Indian Journal* 2 (July): 8–14.

Koppes, Clayton. 1977. 'From New Deal to Termination: Liberalism and Indian Policy, 1933–1953'. *Pacific Historical Review* 46 (November): 543–566.

Kunitz, Stephen J. 1971. 'The Social Philosophy of John Collier'. *Ethnohistory* 78 (Summer): 213–229.

Leupp, Francis E. 1910. *The Indian and his Problem*. New York: Scribner's Sons.

McNickle, D'Arcy. 1973. *Native American Tribalism, Indian Survivals and Renewals*. New York: Oxford University Press.

Mekeel, Scudder. 1944. 'An Appraisal of the Indian Reorganisation Act'. *American Anthropology* 46: 209–217.

Meriam, Lewis, et al. 1928. *The Problem of Indian Administration*. Baltimore: John Hopkins Press for the Institute for Government Research, Brookings Institution.

Mitchell, Dalia Tsuk. 2007. *Architect of Justice: Felix S. Cohen and the Founding of American Legal Pluralism*. Ithaca: Cornell University Press.

Nash, Jay B. (ed.). 1938. *The New Day for the Indians: A Survey of the Working of the Indian Reorganization Act of 1934*. New York: Academy Press.

Olson, James S. and Raymond Wilson. 1984. *Native Americans in the Twentieth Century*. Urbana and Chicago: University of Illinois Press.

Parker, Dorothy R. 1992. *Singing an Indian Song: A Biography of D'Arcy McNickle*. Lincoln: University of Nebraska Press.

Parman, Donald. 1976. *The Navajo Indian and the New Deal*. New Haven: Yale University Press.

Philp, Kenneth R. 1977. *John Collier's Crusade for Indian Reform, 1920–1954*. Tucson: University of Arizona Press.

Prucha, Francis Paul. 1984. *The Great Father: The United States Government and the American Indians*, vol. 2. Lincoln: University of Nebraska Press.

Rosier, Paul C. 2001. *Rebirth of the Blackfeet Nation, 1912–1954*. Lincoln: University of Nebraska Press.

Rusco, Elmer R. 2000. *A Fateful Time: The Background and Legislative History of the Indian Reorganization Act*. Reno: University of Nevada Press.

Schrader, Robert Fay. 1983. *The Indian Arts and Crafts Board: An Aspect of Indian New Deal Policy*. Albuquerque: University of New Mexico Press.

Smith, Jane F. and Robert M. Kvasnicka (eds). 1976. *Indian-White Relations: A Persistent Paradox*. Washington, DC: Howard University Press.

Smith, Michael T. 1971. 'The Wheeler-Howard Act of 1934: The Indian New Deal'. *Journal of the West* 10: 521–534.

Szasz, Margaret. 1974. *Education and the American Indian: The Road to Self-Determination, 1928–1973*. Albuquerque: University of New Mexico Press.

Taylor, Graham D. 1980. *The New Deal and American Indian Tribalism: The Administration of the Indian Reorganization Act, 1934–1945*. Lincoln: University of Nebraska Press.

Washburn, Wilcomb. 1984. 'Fifty-Year Perspective on the Indian Reorganization Act'. *American Anthropologist* 86 (June): 279–289.

White, Graham and John Maze. 1985. *Harold Ickes of the New Deal: His Private Life and Public Career*. Cambridge: Harvard University Press.

Wunder, John R. 1994. *'Retained by the People' A History of American Indians and the Bill of Rights*. New York: Oxford University Press.

Zimmerman, William. Jr. 1957. 'The Role of the Bureau of Indian Affairs since 1935'. *The Annals of the American Academy of Political and Social Science* 311: 31–40.

Chapter Nine

Ablon, Joan. 1964. 'Relocated American Indians in the San Francisco Bay Area: Social Interaction and Indian Identity'. *Human Organization* 23 (Winter): 296–304.

Ball, Dewi Ioan. 2007. 'The Silent Revolution: How the Key Attributes of Tribal Power have been Fundamentally Eroded by the United States Supreme Court from 1973'. PhD diss., University of Wales, Swansea.

Bernstein, Alison. 1991. *American Indians and World War II: Toward a New Era in Indian Affairs*. Norman: University of Oklahoma Press.

Boender, Debra R. 1979. 'Termination and the Administration of Glenn L. Emmons as Commissioner of Indian Affairs, 1953–1961'. *New Mexico Historical Review* 54 (October): 287–304.

Burt, Larry W. 1982. *Tribalism in Crisis: Federal Indian Policy, 1953–1961*. Albuquerque: University of New Mexico Press.

Castile, George Pierre. 1998. *To Show Heart: Native American Self-Determination and Federal Indian Policy, 1960–1975*. Tucson: University of Arizona Press.

Danforth, Sandra C. 1973. 'Repaying Historical Debts: The Indian Claims Commission'. *North Dakota Law Review* 49 (Winter): 359–403.

Debo, Angie. 1955. 'Termination of the Oklahoma Indians'. *American Indian* 7 (Spring): 17–23.

Deer, Ada. 1974. 'Menominee Restoration: How the Good Guys Won'. *Journal of Intergroup Relations* 3: 41–50.

Deloria, Vine, Jr. (ed.). 1985. *American Indian Policy in the Twentieth Century*. Norman: University of Oklahoma Press.

———. 1983. *American Indians, American Justice*. Austin: University of Texas Press.

———. 1988. *Custer Died For Your Sins: An Indian Manifesto*. 1969. Reprint, Norman: University of Oklahoma Press.

Drinnon, Richard. 1987. *Keeper of Concentration Camps: Dillon S. Myer and American Racism*. Berkeley: University of California Press.

Edmunds, David. R., Frederick E. Hoxie and Neal Salisbury. 2007. *The People: A History of Native America*. Boston: Houghton Mifflin Company.

Fixico, Donald L. 1986. *Termination and Relocation: Federal Indian Policy, 1945–1960*. Albuquerque: New Mexico Press.

Forbes, Jack D. 1981. *Native Americans and Nixon, Presidential Politics and Minority Self-Determination, 1969–1972*. Los Angeles: American Indian Studies Centre, UCLA.

Fouberg, Erin Hogan. 2000. *Tribal Territory, Sovereignty, and Governance: A Study of the Cheyenne River and Lake Traverse Indian Reservations*. New York: Garland Publishing, Inc.

Gibson, Arrell Morgan. 1980. *The American Indian: Prehistory to Present*. Lexington, MA: D.C. Heath and Company.

Gundlach, James. 1978. 'Native American Migration and Relocation: Success or Failure'. *Pacific Sociological Review* 21 (January): 117–127.

Goldberg, Carole E. 1975. 'Public Law 280: The Limits of State Jurisdiction over Reservation Indians'. *UCLA Law Review* 22: 535–594.

Graves, Theodore and Minor Van Arsdale. 1966. 'Values, Expectations and Relocation: The Navajo Migrant to Denver'. *Human Organization* 25 (Winter): 300–307.

Hagan, William T. 1981. 'Tribalism Rejuvenated: The Native American since the era of Termination'. *Western History Quarterly* 12: 4–16.

Hauptman, Laurence M. 1986. *The Iroquois Struggle for Survival: World War II to Red Power*. Syracuse: Syracuse University Press.

Herzberg, Stephen H. 1977. 'The Menominee Indians: From Treaty to Termination'. *Wisconsin Magazine of History* 60: 266–329.

———. 1978. 'The Menominee Indians: Termination to Restoration'. *American Indian Law Review* 6: 143–204.

Hood, Susan. 1972. 'Termination of the Klamath Tribe of Oregon'. *Ethnohistory* 19: 379–392.

Iverson, Peter. 1998. '*We Are Still Here' American Indians in the Twentieth Century*. Wheeling, IL: Harlan Davidson, Inc.

Johnson, Lyndon B. 1968. *Public Papers of the Presidents of the United States: Lyndon B. Johnson, 1968–69*. vol. 1. Washington, DC: US Government Printing Office.

LaFarge, Oliver. 1957. 'Termination of Federal Supervision: Disintegration and the American Indian'. *Annals of the American Academy of Political and Social Science* 311 (May): 41–46.

LeDuc, Thomas. 1957. 'The Work of the Indian Claims Commission under the Act of 1946'. *Pacific Historical Review* 26 (February): 1–16.

Lurie, Nancy Oestreich. 1972. 'Menominee Termination: From Reservation to Colony'. *Human Organization* 31: 257–270.

Menominee Tribe v. United States, 391 U.S. 404 (1968).

Neils, Elaine M. 1971. *Reservation to City: Indian Migration and Federal Relocation*. Chicago: University of Chicago Press.

Nixon, Richard. 1971. *Public Papers of the Presidents of the United States: Richard Nixon, 1970*. Washington, DC: US Government Printing Office.

Olson, James S. and Raymond Wilson. 1984. *Native Americans in the Twentieth Century*. Urbana and Chicago: University of Illinois Press.

Orfield, Gary. 1965. *A Study of the Termination Policy*. Denver: National Congress of American Indians.

Ourada, Patricia K. 1978. *The Menominee Indians: A History*. Norman: University of Oklahoma Press.

Peroff, Nicholas C. 1982. *Menominee Drums: Tribal Termination and Restoration, 1954–1974*. Norman: University of Oklahoma Press.

Philp, Kenneth R. 1985. 'Stride Toward Freedom: The Relocation of Indians to Cities, 1952–1960'. *Western Quarterly* 16: 175–190.

———. 1999. *Termination Revisited: American Indians on the Trail to Self-Determination, 1933–1953*. Lincoln: University of Nebraska Press.

Quinn, William W., Jr. 1990. 'Federal Acknowledgement of American Indian Tribes: The Historical Development of a Legal Concept'. *American Journal of Legal History* 34 (October): 331–364.

Ritter, Beth R. 1992. 'The Ponca Tribe of Nebraska: The Process of Restoration of a Federally-Terminated Tribe'. *Human Organization* 51: 1–16.

Rosenthal, Harvey D. 1990. *Their Day in Court: A History of the Indian Claims Commission.* New York: Garland.

Shames, Deborah (ed.). 1972. *Freedom with Reservation: The Menominee Struggle to Save their Land and People.* Madison: University of Wisconsin Press.

Stefon, Frederick J. 1978. 'The Irony of Termination, 1943–1958'. *Indian Historian* 11 (September): 3–14.

Stern, Theodore. 1965. *The Klamath Tribe: A People and Their Reservation.* Seattle: University of Washington Press.

Szasz, Margaret. 1974. *Education and the American Indian: The Road to Self-Determination, 1928–1973.* Albuquerque: University of New Mexico Press.

Thornton, Russell, Gary D. Sandefur and Harold G. Grasmick. 1982. *The Urbanization of American Indians: A Critical Bibliography.* Bloomington: Indiana University Press for the Newberry Library.

Walch, Michael C. 1983. 'Terminating the Indian Termination Policy'. *Stanford Law Review* 35 (July): 1181–1215.

Watkins, Arthur V. 1957. 'Termination of Federal Supervision: The Removal of Restrictions over Indian Property and Person'. *The Annals of the American Academy of Political and Social Science* 311: 47–55.

Wilkinson, Charles F. 2005. *Blood Struggle: The Rise of Modern Indian Nations.* New York: W.W. Norton & Company.

Wilkinson, Charles F. and Eric R. Biggs. 1977. 'Evolution of the Termination Policy'. *American Indian Law Review* 5: 139–184.

Williams v. Lee, 358 U.S. 217 (1959).

Wunder, John R. 1994. '*Retained by the People' A History of American Indians and the Bill of Rights.* New York: Oxford University Press.

Chapter Ten

Ball, Dewi Ioan. 2007. 'The Silent Revolution: How the Key Attributes of Tribal Power have been Fundamentally Eroded by the United States Supreme Court from 1973'. PhD diss., University of Wales, Swansea.

Baringer, Sandra K. 1997. 'Indian Activism and the American Indian Movement: A Bibliographical Essay'. *American Indian Culture and Research Journal* 21: 217–250.

BIA I'm Not Your Indian Anymore. Rooseveltown, NY: Akwesasne Notes, 1973.

Blue Cloud, Peter (ed.). 1972. *Alcatraz Is Not an Island.* Berkeley, CA: Wingbow Press.

Burnette, Robert and John Koster. 1974. *The Road to Wounded Knee.* New York: Bantam Books.

Castile, George Pierre. 1990. *To Show Heart: Native American Self-Determination and Federal Indian Policy, 1960–1975.* Tucson: University of Arizona Press.

Champagne, Duane (ed.). 1994. *Chronology of North Native American History: From Pre-Columbian Times to the Present.* Detroit: Gale Research Inc.

Churchill, Ward and James Vander Wall. 1988. *Agents of Repression: The FBI's Secret War against the Black Panther Party and the American Indian Movement.* Boston: South End Press.

Cobb, Daniel M. 2002. 'Us Indians Understand the Basics': Oklahoma Indians and the Politics of Community Action, 1964–1970'. *Western Historical Quarterly* 33 (1, Spring): 41–66.

Cornell, Stephen. 1984. 'Crises and Response in Indian-White Relations: 1960–84'. *Social Problems* 32 (October): 44–59.

———. 1988. *The Return of the Native: American Indian Political Resurgence*. New York: Oxford University Press.

Clarkin, Thomas. 2001. *Federal Indian Policy in the Kennedy and Johnson Administrations, 1961–1969*. Albuquerque: University of New Mexico Press.

Crow Dog, Mary and Richard Erdoes. 1990. *Lakota Women*. New York: Grove Weidenfeld.

Deloria, Vine, Jr. (ed.). 1985. *American Indian Policy in the Twentieth Century*. Norman: University of Oklahoma Press.

———. 1983. *American Indians, American Justice*. Austin: University of Texas Press.

———. 1985. *Behind the Trail of Broken Treaties: An Indian Declaration of Independence*. Austin: University of Texas Press.

———. 1988. *Custer Died For Your Sins: An Indian Manifesto*. 1969. Reprint, Norman: University of Oklahoma Press.

Dewing, Rolland. 1985. *Wounded Knee: The Meaning and Significance of the Second Incident*. New York: Irvington Publishers.

———. 1995. *Wounded Knee II*. Chadron, NE: Great Plains Network.

Fortunate Eagle, Adam. 1992. *Alcatraz! Alcatraz! The Indian Occupation of 1969–71*. San Francisco: Heyday Books.

Gibson, Arrell Morgan. 1980. *The American Indian: Prehistory to Present*. Lexington, MA: D.C. Heath and Company.

Gonzalez, Mario and Elizabeth Cook-Lynn. 1998. *The Politics of Hallowed Ground: Wounded Knee and the Struggle for Indian Sovereignty*. Urbana: University of Illinois Press.

Gross, Emma R. 1989. *Contemporary Federal Policy Toward Indians*. Westport, CT: Greenwood Press.

Hecht, Robert A. 1981. *The Occupation of Wounded Knee*. Charlotteville, NY: SamHar Press.

Hertzberg, Hazel. 1971. *The Search for an American Indian Identity, Modern Pan-Indian Movements*. Syracuse, NY: Syracuse University Press.

Iverson, Peter. 1998. *'We Are Still Here' American Indians in the Twentieth Century*. Wheeling, IL: Harlan Davidson, Inc.

Johnson, Lyndon B. 1970. *Public Papers of the Presidents of the United States: Lyndon B. Johnson, 1968–69*. vol. 2. Washington, DC: US Government Printing Office.

Johnson, Troy. 1996. *The Occupation of Alcatraz Island: Indian Self-Determination and the Rise of Indian Activism*. Urbana: University of Illinois Press.

Johnson, Troy, Joane Nagel and Duane Champagne (eds). 1997. *American Indian Activism: Alcatraz to the Longest Walk*. Urbana: University of Illinois Press.

Josephy, Alvin M., Jr. 1984. *Now That the Buffalo's Gone: A Study of Today's American Indians*. Norman: University of Oklahoma Press.

———. 1972. *Red Power: The American Indians' Fight for Freedom*. New York: McGraw-Hill.

Kipp, Woody. 2004. *Viet Cong at Wounded Knee: The Trail of a Blackfeet Activist*. Lincoln: University of Nebraska Press.

Kotlowski, Dean J. 2003. 'Alcatraz, Wounded Knee, and Beyond: The Nixon and Ford Administrations Respond to Native American Protest'. *Pacific Historical Review* 72 (May 2): 201–227.

LaGrand, James B. 2002. *Indian Metropolis: Native Americans in Chicago, 1945–1975*. Urbana and Chicago: University of Illinois Press.

Lyman, Stanley D. 1991. *Wounded Knee 1973: A Personal Account*. Lincoln: University of Nebraska Press.

Mankiller, Wilma. 1993. *Mankiller: A Chief and Her People*. New York: St. Martin's Press.

Matthiessen, Peter. 1983. *In the Spirit of Crazy Horse*. New York: Viking.

Means, Russell and Marvin J. Wolf. 1995. *Where White Man Fear to Tread: The Autobiography of Russell Means*. New York: St. Martin's Press.

Mihesuah, Devon Abbott. 2003. *Indigenous American Women: Decolonization, Empowerment, Activism*. Lincoln: University of Nebraska Press.

Nagel, Joane. 1995. *American Indian Ethnic Renewal: Red Power and the Resurgence of Identity and Culture*. New York: Oxford University Press.

Nixon, Richard. 1971. *Public Papers of the Presidents of the United States: Richard Nixon, 1970*. Washington, DC: US Government Printing Office.

Oakley, Christopher Arris. 2005. *Keeping the Circle: American Indian Identity In Eastern North Carolina, 1885–2004*. Lincoln and London: University of Nebraska Press.

Olson, James S. and Raymond Wilson. 1984. *Native Americans: In the Twentieth Century*. Urbana and Chicago: University of Illinois Press.

Ortiz, Roxanne D. 1980. 'Wounded Knee 1890 to Wounded Knee 1973: A Study in United States Colonialism'. *Journal of Ethnic Studies* 8 (Summer): 1–15.

Philp, Kenneth R. (ed.). 1986. *Indian Self-Rule: First Hand Accounts of Indian-White Relations from Roosevelt to Reagan*. Salt Lake City, UT: Howe Brothers.

Sayer, John William. 1997. *Ghost Dancing the Law: The Wounded Knee Trials*. Cambridge, MA: Harvard University Press.

Smith, Paul Chaat and Robert Allen Warrior. 1996. *Like a Hurricane: The Indian Movement from Alcatraz to Wounded Knee*. New York: The New Press.

Stern, Kenneth S. 1994. *Loud Hawk: The U.S. versus the American Indian Movement*. Norman: University of Oklahoma Press.

United States Congress Senate. *Committee on Interior and Insular Affairs. Subcommittee on Indian Affairs. Occupation of Wounded Knee: Hearings before the Subcommittee on Indian Affairs of the Committee on Interior and Insular Affairs, United States Senate, Ninety-third Congress, first session on the causes and aftermath of the Wounded Knee takeover June 16, 1973, Pine Ridge, South Dakota, June 17, 1973, Kyle, South Dakota*. Washington: U.S. Government Printing Office, 1974.

Voices from Wounded Knee, 1973: In the Words of the Participants. Rooseveltown, NY: Akwesasne Notes, Mohawk Nation, 1974.

Wilkinson, Charles. 2005. *Blood Struggle: The Rise of Modern Indian Nations*. New York: W.W. Norton & Company.

Zimmerman, Bill. 1976. *Airlift to Wounded Knee*. Chicago: Swallow Press.

Chapter Eleven

Arden, Harvey and George Blitch. 2004. *Have You Thought Of Leonard Peltier Lately?* Houston: HYT Publishing.

Banks, Dennis and Richard Erdoes. 2005. *Ojibwa Warrior: Dennis Banks and The Rise Of The American Indian Movement*. Norman: University of Oklahoma Press.

Baringer, Sandra K. 1997. 'Indian Activism and the American Indian Movement: A Bibliographical Essay'. *American Indian Culture and Research Journal* 21: 217–250.

BIA I'm Not Your Indian Anymore. Rooseveltown, NY: Akwesasne Notes, 1973.

Burnette, Robert and John Koster. 1974. *The Road to Wounded Knee*. New York: Bantam Books.

Castile, George Pierre. 1990. *To Show Heart: Native American Self-Determination and Federal Indian Policy, 1960–1975*. Tucson: University of Arizona Press.

Champagne, Duane (ed.). 1994. *Chronology of North Native American History: From Pre-Columbian Times to the Present*. Detroit: Gale Research Inc.

Churchill, Ward and James Vander Wall. 1988. *Agents of Repression: The FBI's Secret War against the Black Panther Party and the American Indian Movement*. Boston: South End Press.

Cobb, Daniel M. 2002. '"Us Indians Understand the Basics": Oklahoma Indians and the Politics of Community Action, 1964–1970'. *Western Historical Quarterly* 33 (1, Spring): 41–66.

Cornell, Stephen. 1984. 'Crises and Response in Indian-White Relations: 1960–84'. *Social Problems* 32(October): 44–59.

———. 1988. *The Return of the Native: American Indian Political Resurgence*. New York: Oxford University Press.

Crow Dog, Mary and Richard Erdoes. 1990. *Lakota Women*. New York: Grove Weidenfeld.

Deloria, Vine, Jr. (ed.). 1985. *American Indian Policy in the Twentieth Century*. Norman: University of Oklahoma Press.

———. 1983. *American Indians, American Justice*. Austin: University of Texas Press.

———. 1985. *Behind the Trail of Broken Treaties: An Indian Declaration of Independence*. Austin: University of Texas Press.

———. 1988. *Custer Died For Your Sins: An Indian Manifesto*. 1969. Reprint, Norman: University of Oklahoma Press.

Dewing, Rolland. 1985. *Wounded Knee: The Meaning and Significance of the Second Incident*. New York: Irvington Publishers.

———. 1995. *Wounded Knee II*. Chadron, NE: Great Plains Network.

Gibson, Arrell Morgan. 1980. *The American Indian: Prehistory to Present*. Lexington, MA: D.C. Heath and Company.

Gonzalez, Mario and Elizabeth Cook-Lynn. 1998. *The Politics of Hallowed Ground: Wounded Knee and the Struggle for Indian Sovereignty*. Urbana: University of Illinois Press.

Gross, Emma R. 1989. *Contemporary Federal Policy Toward Indians*. Westport, CT: Greenwood Press.

Hecht, Robert A. 1981. *The Occupation of Wounded Knee*. Charlotteville, NY: SamHar Press.

Iverson, Peter. 1998. *'We Are Still Here' American Indians in the Twentieth Century*. Wheeling, IL: Harlan Davidson, Inc.

Johnson, Troy. 1997. *American Indian Activism: Alcatraz to the Longest Walk*. Urbana and Chicago: University of Illinois Press.

———. 1996. *The Occupation of Alcatraz Island: Indian Self-Determination and the Rise of Indian Activism*. Urbana: University of Illinois Press.

Johnson, Troy, Joane Nagel and Duane Champagne (eds). 1997. *American Indian Activism: Alcatraz to the Longest Walk*. Urbana: University of Illinois Press.

Josephy, Alvin M., Jr. 1972. *Red Power: The American Indians' Fight for Freedom*. New York: McGraw-Hill.

Kotlowski, Dean J. 2003. 'Alcatraz, Wounded Knee, and Beyond: The Nixon and Ford Administrations Respond to Native American Protest'. *Pacific Historical Review* 72 (May 2): 201–227.

LaGrand, James B. 2002. *Indian Metropolis: Native Americans in Chicago, 1945–1975*. Urbana and Chicago: University of Illinois Press.

Lyman, Stanley D. 1991. *Wounded Knee 1973: A Personal Account*. Lincoln: University of Nebraska Press.

Mankiller, Wilma. 1993. *Mankiller: A Chief and Her People*. New York: St. Martin's Press.

Matthiessen, Peter. 1983. *In the Spirit of Crazy Horse*. New York: Viking.

Means, Russell and Marvin J. Wolf. 1995. *Where White Man Fear to Tread: The Autobiography of Russell Means*. New York: St. Martin's Press.

Messerschmidt, Jim. 1983. *The Trial of Leonard Peltier*. Boston: South End Press.

Mihesuah, Devon Abbott. 2003. *Indigenous American Women: Decolonization, Empowerment, Activism*. Lincoln: University of Nebraska Press.

Nagel, Joane. 1995. *American Indian Ethnic Renewal: Red Power and the Resurgence of Identity and Culture*. New York: Oxford University Press.

Olson, James S. and Raymond Wilson. 1984. *Native Americans: In the Twentieth Century*. Urbana and Chicago: University of Illinois Press.

Ortiz, Roxanne D. 1980. 'Wounded Knee 1890 to Wounded Knee 1973: A Study in United States Colonialism'. *Journal of Ethnic Studies* 8 (Summer): 1–15.

Peltier, Leonard. 1999. *Prison Writings: My Life is my Sun Dance*. New York: St. Martin's Press.

Peterson, John M. 1994. *Aim on Target: The FBI's War on Leonard Peltier and the American Indian movement*. Leonard Peltier Defence Committee.

Philp, Kenneth R. (ed.). 1986. *Indian Self-Rule: First Hand Accounts of Indian-White Relations from Roosevelt to Reagan*. Salt Lake City, UT: Howe Brothers.

Sayer, John William. 1997. *Ghost Dancing the Law: The Wounded Knee Trials*. Cambridge, MA: Harvard University Press.

Smith, Paul Chaat and Robert Allen Warrior. 1996. *Like a Hurricane: The Indian Movement from Alcatraz to Wounded Knee*. New York: The New Press.

Stern, Kenneth S. 1994. *Loud Hawk: The U.S. versus the American Indian Movement*. Norman: University of Oklahoma Press.

Trimbach, Joseph H. and John M. Trimbach. 2007. *American Indian Mafia: An FBI Agent's True Story about Wounded Knee, Leonard Peltier, and the American Indian Movement (AIM)*. Colorado: Outskirts Press.

United States Congress. Senate *Committee on Interior and Insular Affairs. Subcommittee on Indian Affairs. Occupation of Wounded Knee: Hearings before the Subcommittee on Indian Affairs of the Committee on Interior and Insular Affairs, United States Senate, Ninety-third Congress, first session on the causes and aftermath of the Wounded Knee takeover June 16, 1973, Pine Ridge, South Dakota, June 17, 1973, Kyle, South Dakota*. Washington: U.S. Government Printing Office, 1974.

Voices from Wounded Knee, 1973: In the Words of the Participants. Rooseveltown, NY: Akwesasne Notes, Mohawk Nation, 1974.

Wall, Jim Vander. 1992. 'A Warrior Caged: The Continuing Struggle of Leonard Peltier'. Chapter 10 in *The State of Native America: Genocide, Colonization, and Resistance*, edited by M. Annette Jaimes. Boston, MA: South End Press.

Weyler, Rex. 1984. *Blood of the Land: The Government and Corporate War Against the American Indian Movement*. New York: Vintage Books.

Wilkinson, Charles. 2005. *Blood Struggle: The Rise of Modern Indian Nations*. New York: W.W. Norton & Company.

Zimmerman, Bill. 1976. *Airlift to Wounded Knee*. Chicago: Swallow Press.

Chapter Twelve

Ball, Dewi Ioan. 2007. 'The Silent Revolution: How the Key Attributes of Tribal Power have been Fundamentally Eroded by the United States Supreme Court from 1973'. PhD diss., University of Wales, Swansea.

Bloch, David J. 2004. 'Colonizing the Last Frontier'. *American Indian Law Review* 29: 1–41.

Burch, Jordan. 1994. 'How Much Diversity Is The United States Really Willing to Accept?' *Ohio Northern University Law Review* 20: 957–979.

Canby, William C., Jr. 1998. *American Indian Law: in a Nutshell*. St. Paul, MN: West Group.

Chaney, Christopher B. 2000. 'The Effect of the United States Supreme Court's Decisions During the Last Quarter of the Nineteenth Century on Tribal Criminal Jurisdiction'. *Brigham Young University Journal of Public Law* 14: 173–189.

Clinton, Robert N. 1981. 'State Power over Indian Reservations: A Critical Comment on Burger Court Decisions'. *South Dakota Law Review* 26: 434–446.

———.1995. 'The Dormant Indian Commerce Clause'. *Connecticut Law Review* 27: 1055–1249.

Coffey, Wallace and Rebecca Tsosie. 2001. 'Rethinking the Tribal Sovereignty Doctrine: Cultural Sovereignty and the Collective Future of Indian Nations'. *Stanford Law and Policy Review* 12: 191–210.

Cohen, Felix S. 1941. *Handbook of Federal Indian Law*. Washington, DC: US Government Printing Office.

Deloria, Vine, Jr. and Clifford M. Lytle. 1983. *American Indians, American Justice*. Austin: University of Texas Press.

———. 1984. *The Nations Within: The Past and Future of American Indian Sovereignty*. Austin: University of Texas Press.

Dussias, Allison M. 1993. 'Geographically-Based and Membership-Based Views of Indian Tribal Sovereignty: The Supreme Court's Changing Vision'. *University of Pittsburgh Law Review* 55: 1–97.

Duthu, N. Bruce. 1996. 'The Thurgood Marshall Papers and the Quest for a Principled Theory of Tribal Sovereignty: Fuelling the Fires of Tribal/State Conflict'. *Vermont Law Review* 21: 47–110.

Falkowski, James E. 1992. *Indian Law/Race Law*. Praeger: New York.

Fouberg, Erin Hogan. 2000. *Tribal Territory, Sovereignty, and Governance: A Study of the Cheyenne River and Lake Traverse Indian Reservations*. New York: Garland Publishing, Inc.

Fredericks III, John. 1999. 'America's First Nations: The Origins, History and Future of American Indian Sovereignty'. *Journal of Law and Policy* 7: 347–410.

Frickey, Philip P. 1999. 'A Common Law for Our Age of Colonialism: The Judicial Divestiture of Indian Tribal Authority over Nonmembers'. *Yale Law Journal* 109: 1–85.

———. 1997. 'Adjudication and Its Discontents: Coherence and Conciliation in Federal Indian Law'. *Harvard Law Review* 110: 1754–1784.

———. 1990. 'Congressional Intent, Practical Reasoning, and the Dynamic Nature of Federal Indian Law'. *California Law Review* 78: 1137–1240.

Getches, David H. 2001. 'Beyond Indian Law: The Rehnquist Court's Pursuit of States' Rights, Colour Blind Justice and Mainstream Values'. *Minnesota Law Review* 86: 267–362.

———. 1996. 'Conquering the Cultural Frontier: The New Subjectivism of the Supreme Court in Indian Law'. *California Law Review* 84: 1573–1655.

Gould, L. Scott. 1996. 'The Consent Paradigm: Tribal Sovereignty at the Millennium'. *Columbia Law Review* 96: 809–902.

Heisey, Geoffrey C. 1998. 'Oliphant and Tribal Criminal Jurisdiction over Non-Indians: Asserting Congress's Plenary Power to Restore Territorial Jurisdiction'. *Indiana Law Journal* 73: 1051–1078.

Johnson, Ralph W. and Berrie Martinis. 1995. 'Chief Justice Rehnquist and the Indian Cases'. *Public Land Law Review* 16: 1–25.

Krakoff, Sarah. 2001. 'Undoing Indian Law One Case at a Time: Judicial Minimalism and Tribal Sovereignty'. *American University Law Review* 50: 1177–1268.

Laurence, Robert. 2000. 'Symmetry and Asymmetry in Federal Indian Law'. *Arizona Law Review* 42: 861–934.

Lopach, James J., Margery Hunter Brown and Richmond L. Clow. 1998. *Tribal Government Today: Politics on Montana Indian Reservations*. Revised edition. Colorado: University Press of Colorado.

McSloy, Steven Paul. 1993. 'Back To The Future: Native American Sovereignty In The 21st Century'. *New York University Review of Law and Social Change* 20: 217–302.

Maxfield, Peter C. 1993. 'Oliphant v. Suquamish Tribe: The Whole is Greater than the Sum of the Parts'. *Journal of Contemporary Law* 19: 391–443.

Miller, Todd. 2001. 'Easements on Tribal Sovereignty'. *American Indian Law Review* 26: 105–131.

Minnis, Michael. 1991. 'Judicially-Suggested Harassment of Indian Tribes: The Potawatomis Revisit Moe and Colville'. *American Indian Law Review* 16: 289–318.

Mitchell, John Arai. 1994. 'A World without Tribes? Tribal Rights of Self-Government and the Enforcement of State Court Orders in Indian Country'. *University of Chicago Law Review* 61: 707–732.

National Congress of the American Indian. *Concept paper, 2003 Legislative Proposal on Tribal Governance and Economic Enhancement 25 July 2002*. Washington, DC: National Congress of the American Indian, 2002.

Newton, Nell Jessup. 1984. 'Federal Power over Indians: Its Sources, Scope, and Limitations'. *University of Pennsylvania Law Review* 132: 195–288.

Nordhaus, Robert J., G. Emlen Hall and Anne Alise Rudio. 2003. 'Revisiting Merrion v. Jicarilla Apache Tribe: Robert Nordhaus and Sovereign Indian Control over Natural Resources on Reservations'. *Natural Resources Journal* 43: 223–284.

Pevar, Stephen L. 2002. *The Rights of Indians and Tribes: The authoritative ACLU guide to Indian and tribal rights*. 3rd ed. Carbondale and Edwardsville: Southern Illinois University Press.

Pommersheim, Frank. 1995. *Braid of Feathers: American Indian Law and Contemporary Tribal Life*. Berkeley: University of California Press.

———. 1999. 'Coyote Paradox: Some Indian Law Reflections from the Edge of the Prairie'. *Arizona State Law Journal* 31: 439–481.

Rey-Bear, Daniel I.S.J. 1996. 'The Flathead Water Quality Standards Dispute: Legal Bases for Tribal Regulatory Authority Over Non-Indian Reservation Lands'. *American Indian Law Review* 20: 151–224.

Royster, Judith V. 1995. 'The Legacy of Allotment'. *Arizona State Law Journal* 27: 1–78.

Senate Committee on Indian Affairs. *Rulings of the U.S. Supreme Court as They Affect the Powers and Authorities of the Indian Tribal Governments: Hearing on the Concerns of Recent Decisions of the U.S Supreme Court and the Future of Indian Tribal Governments in America*. 107th Cong., 2nd session, 27 February 2002.

Shattuck, Petra T. and Jill Norgren. 1993. *Partial Justice: Federal Indian Law in a Liberal Constitutional System*. Providence: Berg Publishers, Inc.

Singer, Joseph William. 2003. 'Canons Of Conquest: The Supreme Court's Attack on Tribal Sovereignty'. *New England Law Review* 37: 641–668.

———. 1991. 'Sovereignty and Property'. *Northwestern University Law Review* 86: 1–56.

Skibine, Alex Tallchief. 1995. 'Reconciling Federal and State Power inside Indian Reservations with the Right of Tribal Self-Government and the Process of Self-Determination'. *Utah Law Review* 1995: 1105–1156.

Struve, Catherine. 2003. 'How Bad Law Made a Hard Case Easy: Nevada v. Hicks and the Subject Matter Jurisdiction of Tribal Courts'. *University of Pennsylvania Journal of Constitutional Law* 5: 288–317.

Watson, Blake A. 1998. 'The Thrust and Parry of Federal Indian Law'. *University of Dayton Law Review* 23: 437–514.

Wilkins, David E. 1997. *American Indian Sovereignty and the U.S. Supreme Court: The Masking of Justice*. Austin: University of Texas Press.

Wilkins, David E. and K. Tsianina Lomawaima. 2001. *Uneven Ground: American Indian Sovereignty and Federal Law*. Norman: University of Oklahoma Press.

Wilkinson, Charles F. 1987. *American Indians, Time, and the Law*. New Haven: Yale University Press.

Williams, Robert A., Jr. 1986. 'The Algebra of Federal Indian Law: The Hard Trail of Decolonizing and Americanizing the White Man's Indian Jurisprudence'. *Wisconsin Law Review* 1986: 219–299.

———. 2005. *Like a Loaded Weapon: The Rehnquist Court, Indian Rights, and the Legal History of Racism in America*. Minneapolis: University of Minnesota Press.

Yazzie, Robert. 1999. '"Watch Your Six": An Indian Nation Judge's View of 25 Years of Indian Law, Where We Are and Where We Are Going'. *American Indian Law Review* 23: 497–503.

Chapter Thirteen

Anders, Gary C. 1999. 'Indian Gaming: Financial and Regulatory Issues'. Chapter 6 in *Contemporary Native American Political Issues*, edited by Troy R. Johnson. Walnut Creek, CA: AltaMira Press.

Ansson, Richard J. and Ladine Oravetz. 2002. 'Tribal Economic Development: What Challenges Lie Ahead for Tribal Nations as They Continue to Strive for Economic Diversity?' *Kansas Journal of Law and Public Policy* 11: 441–484.

Ball, Dewi Ioan. 2007. 'The Silent Revolution: How the Key Attributes of Tribal Power have been Fundamentally Eroded by the United States Supreme Court from 1973'. PhD diss., University of Wales, Swansea.

Benedict, Jeff. 2000. *Without Reservation: How a Controversial Indian Tribe Rose to Power and Built the World's Largest Casino*. New York: HarperCollins Publishers.

Bodinger de Uriarte, John J. 2007. *Casino and Museum: Representing Mashantucket Pequot Identity*. Tucson: University of Arizona Press.

Bordewich, Fergus M. 1996. *Killing the White Man's Indian: Reinventing Native Americans at the End of the Twentieth Century*. New York: Doubleday.

California v. Cabazon Band of Mission Indians, 480 U.S. 202 (1987).

Canby, William C., Jr. 1998. *American Indian Law: In a Nutshell*. St. Paul, MN: West Group.

Cornell, Stephen and Joseph P. Kalt. 1992. 'Reloading the Dice: Improving the Chances for Economic Development on American Indian Reservations'. Chapter 1 in *What Can Tribes Do? Strategies and Institutions in American Economic Development*, edited by Stephen Cornell and Joseph P. Kalt. American Indian Studies Centre, Los Angeles: University of California Press,

———. 2005. 'Two approaches to economic development in American Indian nations: One works, the other doesn't'. Harvard Project on American Indian Economic Development and the Native Nations Institute for Leadership, Management, and Policy Joint Occasional Papers on Native Affairs No. 2005–2002.

Cornell, Stephen, Miriam Jorgenson, Joseph P. Kalt and Katherine A. Spilde. 2005. 'Seizing the Future: Why Some Native Nations Do and Others Don't'. Harvard Project on American Indian Economic Development Joint Occasional Papers on Native Affairs 2005–01.

Cornell, Stephen and Joseph P. Kalt. 1998. 'Sovereignty and Nation-Building: The Development Challenge in Indian Country Today'. *American Indian Culture and Research Journal* 22: 187–214.

Cozzetto, Don A. and Brent W. LaRocque. 1996. 'Compulsive Gambling in the Indian Community: A North Dakota Case Study'. *American Indian Culture and Research Journal* 20: 73–86.

Cramer, Renée Ann. 2005. *Cash, Colour, and Colonialism: The Politics of Tribal Acknowledgment*. Norman: University of Oklahoma Press.

Darian-Smith, Eve. 2004. *New Capitalists: Law, Politics, and Identity Surrounding Casino Gaming on Native American Land*. Belmont, CA: Thomson/Wadsworth.

Eadington, W.R. 1990. *Native American Gaming and the Law*. Reno, NV: University of Nevada, Institute for the Study of Gambling and Commercial Gaming.

Fletcher, Matthew L.M. 2004. 'Commentary: In Pursuit of Tribal Economic Development as a Substitute for Reservation Tax Revenue'. *North Dakota Law Review* 80: 809–826.

Fromson, Brett. 2003. *Hitting the Jackpot: The Inside Story of the Richest Indian Tribe in History*. New York: Atlantic Monthly Press.

Goldin, Nicholas S. 1999. 'Casting a New Light on Tribal Casino Gaming: Why Congress Should Curtail the Scope of High Stakes Indian Gaming'. *Cornell Law Review* 84: 798–854.

Harvard Project on American Indian Economic Development. *The State of the Native Nations: Conditions Under U.S. Policies of Self-Determination*. New York: Oxford University Press., 2007.

Hosmer, Brian, and Colleen O'Neill (eds). 2004. *Native Pathways: American Indian Culture and Economic Development in the Twentieth Century*. Boulder: University Press of Colorado.

Hoxie, Frederick E., Peter C. Mancall, and James H. Merrell, (eds) *American Nations: Encounters in Indian Country, 1850 to the Present*. New York: Routledge, 2001.

Kalt, Joseph P. and Joseph William Singer. 2004. 'Myths and Realities of Tribal Sovereignty: The Law and Economics of Indian Self-Rule'. Harvard Project on American Indian Economic Development Joint Occasional Papers on Native Affairs 2004–2003.

Lane, Ambrose I., Sr. 1995. *Return of the Buffalo The Story Behind America's Indian Gaming Explosion*. Connecticut: Greenwood Publishing Group.

Light, Steven Andrew and Kathryn R.L. Rand. 2005. *Indian Gaming and Tribal Sovereignty: The Casino Compromise*. Lawrence: University Press of Kansas.

Light, Steven Andrew, Kathryn R.L. Rand and Alan Meister. 2004. 'Spreading the Wealth: Indian Gaming and Revenue Sharing Agreements'. *North Dakota Law Review* 80: 657–669.

Mason, W. Dale. 2000. *Indian Gaming: Tribal Sovereignty and American Politics*. Norman: University of Oklahoma Press.

———. 1998. 'Tribes and States: A New Era in Intergovernmental Affairs', *Publius* 28: 111–130.

Pasquaretta, Paul. 2003. *Gambling and Survival in Native North America*. Tucson: University of Arizona Press.

Rand, Kathryn R.L. 2007. 'Caught in the Middle: How State Politics, State Law, and State Courts Constrain Tribal Influence Over Indian Gaming'. *Marquette Law Review* 90: 971–1008.

———. 2002. 'There Are No Pequots on the Plains: Assessing the Success of Indian Gaming'. *Chapman Law Review* 5: 47–86.

Rand, Kathryn R.L. and Steven Andrew Light. 2008. *Indian Gaming Law: Cases and Materials*. North Carolina: Carolina Academic Press.

———. 2006. *Indian Gaming Law and Policy*. North Carolina: Carolina Academic Press.

Santoni, Roland J. 1993. 'The Indian Gaming Regulatory Act: How Did We Get Here? Where Are We Going?' *Creighton Law Review* 26: 387–437.

Staudenmaier, Heidi McNeil. 2004. 'Off-Reservation Native American Gaming: An Examination of the Legal and Political Hurdles'. *Nevada Law Journal* 4: 301–319.

Taylor, Jonathan B. and Joseph P. Kalt. 2005. 'Cabazon, the Indian Gaming Regulatory Act, and The Socioeconomic Consequences of American Indian Governmental Gaming a Ten-Year Review, American Indians on Reservations: A Databook of Socioeconomic Change between the 1990 and 2000 Censuses'. Harvard Project on American Indian Economic Development (January).

Tsosie, Rebecca. 1997. 'Negotiating Economic Survival: The Consent Principle and Tribal-State Compacts Under the Indian Gaming Regulatory Act'. *Arizona State Law Journal* 29: 25–96.

Turner, Allen C. 1987. 'Evolution, Assimilation, and State Control of Gambling in Indian Country: Is *Cabazon v. California* an Assimilationist Wolf in Preemption Clothing?' *Idaho Law Review* 24: 318–326.

Valley, David J. 2003. *Jackpot Trail: Indian Gaming in Southern California*. San Diego, CA: Sunbelt Publications.

Wilkins, David E. 2002. *American Indian Politics and the American Political System*. New York: Rowman and Littlefield Publishers.

Wilkinson, Charles. 2005. *Blood Struggle: The Rise of Modern Indian Nations*. New York: W.W. Norton & Company.

Chapter Fourteen

Ackerman, Douglas W. 1997. 'Kennewick Man: The Meaning of "Cultural Affiliation" and "Major Scientific Benefit" in the Native American Graves Protection and Repatriation Act'. *Tulsa Law Journal* 33: 359–384.

Alfred, Taiaiake. 1999. *Peace, Power, Righteousness: An Indigenous Manifesto*. Toronto: Oxford University Press.

Amato, Christopher A. 2002. 'Digging Sacred Ground: Burial Site Disturbances and the Loss of New York's Native American Heritage'. *Columbia Journal of Environmental Law* 27: 1–44.

Berkhofer, Robert F., Jr. 1979. *The White Man's Indian: Images of the American Indian from Columbus to the Present*. New York: Vintage Books.

Blair, Bowen. 1979. 'Indian Rights: Native Americans Versus American Museums – A Battle for Artifacts'. *American Indian Law Review* 7: 125–154.

Bluemel, Erik B. 2005. 'Accommodating Native American Cultural Activities on Federal Public Lands'. *Idaho Law Review* 41: 475–563.

Bordewich, Fergus M. 1996. *Killing the White Man's Indian: Reinventing Native Americans at the End of the Twentieth Century*. New York: Doubleday.

Clifton, James A. (ed.). 1996. *The Invented Indian: Cultural Fictions and Government Politics*. New Brunswick, NJ: Transaction Publishers.

Cornell, Stephen. 1988. *The Return of the Native: American Indian Political Resurgence*. New York: Oxford University Press.

Deloria, Philip J. 1998. *Playing Indian*. New Haven: Yale University Press.

Deloria, Philip J. and Neal Salisbury (ed.). 2002. *A Companion to American Indian History*. Oxford: Blackwell Publishers.

Deloria, Vine, Jr. 1988. *Custer Died For Your Sins: An Indian Manifesto*. 1969. Reprint, Norman: University of Oklahoma Press.

———. 1995. *Red Earth, White Lies: Native Americans and the Myth of Scientific Fact*. New York: Scribner.

Durham, Jimmie. 1992. 'Cowboys and ... Notes on Art, Literature, and American Indians in the Modern American Mind'. Chapter 15 in *The State of Native America: Genocide, Colonization, and Resistance*, edited by M. Annette Jaimes. Boston, MA: South End Press.

Dussias, Allison M. 2005. 'Kennewick Man, Kinship, and the "Dying Race": The Ninth Circuit's Assimilationist Assault on the Native American Graves Protection and Repatriation Act'. *Nebraska Law Review* 84: 55–161.

Edmunds, R. David, Frederick E. Hoxie and Neal Salisbury. 2007. *The People: A History of Native America*. Boston: Houghton Mifflin Company.

Goldberg, Carole. 1999. 'Acknowledging the Repatriation Claims of Unacknowledged California Tribes'. Chapter 10 in *Contemporary Native American Political Issues*, edited by Troy R. Johnson. Walnut Creek, CA: AltaMira Press.

Hauptman, Laurence M. 1995. *Tribes and Tribulations: Misconceptions about American Indians and Their Histories*. Albuquerque: University of New Mexico Press.

Hauptman, Laurence M. and Jack Campisi. 2001. 'Eastern Indian Communities Strive for Recognition'. Chapter 14 in *Major Problems in American Indian History*. 2nd ed., edited by Albert L. Hurtado and Peter Iverson. Boston: Houghton Mifflin Company.

Hibbert, Michelle. 1998/1999. 'Galileos or Grave Robbers? Science, the Native American Graves Protection and Repatriation Act, and the First Amendment'. *American Indian Law Review* 23: 425–458.

Hubert, Jane. 1989. 'A Proper Place for the Dead: A Critical Review of the 'Reburial' Issue'. *Journal of Indigenous Studies* 1: 28–62.

Hurtado, Daniel J. 1993. 'Native American Graves Protection and Repatriation Act: Does It Subject Museums to an Unconstitutional "Taking"?' *Hofstra Property Law Journal* 6: 1–83.

Hutt, Sherry. 2004. 'If Geronimo Was Jewish: Equal Protection and the Cultural Property Rights of Native Americans'. *Northern Illinois University Law Review* 24: 527–562.

Kelly, Michael J. 1999. 'A Skeleton in the Closet: The Discovery of "Kennewick Man" Crystalizes the Debate Over Federal Law Governing Disposal of Ancient Human Remains'. *University of Hawaii Law Review* 21: 41–68.

Lannan, Robert W. 1998. Anthropology and Restless Spirits: The Native American Graves Protection and Repatriation Act, and the Unresolved Issues of Prehistoric Human Remains. *Harvard Environmental Law Review* 22: 369–384.

McLaughlin, Robert H. 1996. 'The Native American Graves Protection and Repatriation Act: Unresolved Issues Between Material Culture and Legal Definitions'. *University of Chicago Law School Roundtable* 3: 767–790.

Mihesuah, Devon A. 2000. *Repatriation Reader: Who Owns American Indian Remains?* Lincoln: University of Nebraska Press.

Miller, Mark Edwin. 2004. *Forgotten Tribes: Unrecognized Indians and the Federal Acknowledgement Process*. Lincoln: University of Nebraska Press.

Nagel, Joanne. 1997. *American Indian Ethnic Renewal: Red Power and the Resurgence of Identity and Culture*. New York: Oxford University Press.

Pavlik, Steve. 1992. 'The U.S. Supreme Court Decision on Peyote in Employment Division v. Smith: A Case Study in the Suppression of Native American Religious Freedom'. *Wicazo Sa Review* 8: 30–39.

Peregoy, Robert M. 1999. 'Nebraska's Landmark Repatriation Law: A Study of Cross-Cultural Conflict and Resolution'. Chapter 9 in *Contemporary Native American Political Issues*, edited by Troy R. Johnson. Walnut Creek, CA: AltaMira Press.

Porter, Joy and Kenneth M. Roemer (eds). 2005. *The Cambridge Companion to Native American Literature*. Cambridge: Cambridge University Press.

Riley, Angela R. 2005. '"Straight Stealing": Towards an Indigenous System of Cultural Property Protection'. *Washington Law Review* 80: 69–164.

Ritchie, Lucas. 2005. 'Indian Burial Sites Unearthed: The Misapplication of the Native American Graves Protections and Repatriation Act'. *Public Land and Resources Law Review* 26: 71–96.

Robidoux, Michael A. 2006. 'The Nonsense of Native American Sport Imagery: Reclaiming a Past that Never Was'. *International Review for the Sociology of Sport* 41: 201–219.

Shoemaker, Nancy. 1999. *American Indian Population Recovery in the Twentieth Century*. Albuquerque: University of New Mexico Press.

Thomas, David Hurst. 2000. *Skull Wars: Kennewick Man, Archaeology, and the Battle for Native American Identity*. New York: Basic Books.

Trainor, Daniel J. 1995. 'Native American Mascots, Schools, and the Title VI Hostile Environment Analysis'. *University of Illinois Law Review* 1995: 971–1001.

Tsosie, Rebecca. 2005. 'The New Challenge of Native Identity: An Essay on "Indigeneity" and "Whiteness."' *Washington University Journal of Law and Policy* 18: 55–98.

———. 1999. 'Privileging Claims to the Past: Ancient Human Remains and Contemporary Cultural Values'. *Arizona State Law Journal* 31: 583–677.

Weston, Mary Ann. 1996. *Native Americans in the News: Images of Indians in the Twentieth Century Press*. Westport, CT: Greenwood Press.

Wilkins, David E. 2002. *American Indian Politics and the American Political System*. New York: Rowman and Littlefield Publishers.

———. 1997. *American Indian Sovereignty and the U.S. Supreme Court: The Masking of Justice*. Austin: University of Texas Press.

Wilkinson, Charles F. 2005. *Blood Struggle: The Rise of Modern Indian Nations*. New York: W.W. Norton & Company.

INDEX

FIGHTING WORDS

Fighting Words is an innovative and accessible new military history series, each title juxtaposing the voices of opposing combatants in a major historical conflict. Presented side by side are the testimonies of fighting men and women, the reportage of nations at war, and the immediate public responses of belligerent war leaders. Together, they offer strikingly different perspectives on the same events.

The extracts are short and snappy, complemented by brief introductions which set the scene. They vividly recreate the conflicts as they were experienced. At the same time, they open up new perspectives and challenge accepted assumptions. Readers will question the nature of primary sources, the motivations of the authors, the agendas that influence media reports and the omissions inherent in all of the sources. Ultimately, readers will be left to ponder the question: whose history is this?

Competing Voices from the Crusades
Andrew Holt and James Muldoon

Competing Voices from the Pacific War
Chris Dixon, Sean Brawley and Beatrice Trefalt

Competing Voices from Native America
Dewi Ioan Ball and Joy Porter

Competing Voices from the Russian Revolution
Michael C. Hickey

Competing Voices from World War II in Europe
Harold J. Goldberg

Competing Voices from the Mexican Revolution
Chris Frazer

Competing Voices from Revolutionary Cuba
John M. Kirk and Peter McKenna